The Instrument Pilot Handbook

The Instrument Pilot Handbook

A Reference Manual and Exam Guide

Courtney L. Flatau

Jerome F. Mitchell

VAN NOSTRAND REINHOLD COMPANY
New York Cincinnati Toronto London Melbourne

Copyright © 1980 by Litton Educational Publishing, Inc.
Library of Congress Catalog Card Number 79-93
ISBN 0-442-22411-7 (cloth)
ISBN 0-442-22412-5 (paper)

All rights reserved. No part of this work covered by the copyright
hereon may be reproduced or used in any form or by any
means—graphic, electronic, or mechanical, including photo-
copying, recording, taping, or information storage and retrieval
systems—without written permission of the publisher.

Printed in the United States of America
Designed by Loudan Enterprises

Published by Van Nostrand Reinhold Company
A division of Litton Educational Publishing, Inc.
135 West 50th Street, New York, NY 10020, U.S.A.

Van Nostrand Reinhold Limited
1410 Birchmount Road
Scarborough, Ontario, M1P 2E7, Canada

Van Nostrand Reinhold Australia Pty. Ltd.
17 Queen Street
Mitcham, Victoria 3132, Australia

Van Nostrand Reinhold Company Limited
Molly Millars Lane
Wokingham, Berkshire, England

16 15 14 13 12 11 10 9 8 7 6 5 4 3 2 1

Library of Congress Cataloging in Publication Data

Flatau, Courtney L
The Instrument Pilot Handbook: A
Reference Manual and Exam Guide
Includes index.
1. Instrument flying. I. Mitchell, Jerome F.,
joint author. II. Title.
TL711.B6F53   629.132'52   79-93
ISBN 0-442-22411-7 hardcover
     0-442-22412-5 paperback

CREDITS

Advisory Circular 90-62, Courtesy of the Federal Aviation Administration: Figures 4-27, 4-28; *Aerodynamics for Naval
Aviators, NAVAIR 00-80T-80*, Courtesy of H. H. Hurt, Jr.,
author, Naval Operations Aviation Training Division: Figure
1-3; *Airmans Information Manual*, Courtesy of the Federal Aviation Administration: Figures 3-11, 3-15, 4-2, 4-14, 4-31, 4-39,
4-40, 4-46, 4-47, 4-48, 4-49, 7-17, 9-23; *Airport/Facility
Directory*, Courtesy of the National Ocean Survey: Figures 7-1
A-F, 7-2, 7-3, 7-4, Questions 7-11, 7-15, 7-26, 7-46; *Aviation
Weather, AC-00-6A*, Courtesy of the Federal Aviation Administration: Figures 3-2, 3-3, 3-13, 3-14; *Aviation Weather
Services, AC 00-45A*, Courtesy of the Federal Aviation Administration: Figures 3-10, 3-22, 3-24, 3-25, 3-26, 3-27, 3-29,
3-30, 3-31, 3-35, 3-36, 3-37, 3-39, 3-40, 3-45, 3-46;
Beechcraft Pilot's Operating Handbook, Courtesy of Beech Air-
craft Corporation: Figures 1-21 A-E, 5-22, 5-24, 5-26, 5-28,
5-29, Questions 5-11, 5-12, 5-15, 5-16, 5-17, 5-18; *Cessna
Pilot's Owners Manual*, Courtesy of Cessna Aircraft Company:
Figure 1-22; Courtesy of Aero Products Research, Inc.: Figures
5-1 A-B, 5-5, 5-6, 5-7, 5-8, 5-9, 5-10, 5-11, 5-12, 5-14, 5-15,
5-16, 5-17, 5-18A, 5-18B, 5-18C, 5-18D; Courtesy of the Ben-
dix Corporation-Avionics Division: Figure 4-25; Courtesy of
Bonzer, Inc.: Figure 4-29; Courtesy of the Jeppeson-Sanderson
Company: Figure 5-19; Courtesy of the King Radio Corporation:
Figures 4-3, 4-13, 4-23, 4-36, 4-38, 4-41; Courtesy of Narco
Scientific Industries-Avionics Division: Figure 4-35; Courtesy of
Rockwell International-Collins Radio Group: Figure 4-32;
Enroute Low Altitude Chart, Courtesy of the National Ocean
Survey: Figures 7-8, 7-13, 7-14, Questions 7-3, 7-4, 7-5, 7-6,
7-7, 7-8, 7-9, 7-16, 7-17, 7-18, 7-19, 7-20, 7-21, 7-33, 7-34,
7-35, 7-36, 7-39, 7-40, 7-54, 7-57, 7-59, 8-7, 8-8, Appendix
G-3; *Enroute Low Altitude Chart Legend*, Courtesy of the Na-
tional Ocean Survey: Appendix G-2; *Federal Aviation Ad-
ministration Flight Plan*, Courtesy of the Federal Aviation Ad-
ministration: Figure 7-18; *IFR & VFR Exam-o-Grams*, Courtesy
of the Federal Aviation Administration: Figures 4-44, 4-45; *IFR
Wall Planning Chart*, Courtesy of the National Ocean Survey:
Figure 7-7; *Legend Instrument Approach Procedures Charts*,
Courtesy of the National Ocean Survey: Figures 9-4, 9-5, 9-6,
9-8, 9-9, 9-10, 9-11, 9-13, 9-14, Question 9-42; *Instrument
Approach Procedures Charts*, Courtesy of the Federal Aviation
Administration: Figures 9-7, 9-15, 9-16, 9-18, 9-19, 9-20, 9-21,
9-22, Questions 9-3, 9-4, 9-5, 9-6, 9-8, 9-9, 9-10, 9-15, 9-16,
9-17, 9-25, 9-26, 9-27, 9-28, 9-34, 9-35, 9-36, 9-37, 9-38,
9-45, 9-46, 9-47, 9-55, 9-56, 9-57, 9-58, 9-62; *Instrument Flying Handbook AC 61-27B*, Courtesy of the Federal Aviation Administration: Figures 2-17, 4-8, 4-11, 4-12, 4-15, 4-16, 4-17,
4-18, 4-19, 4-20, 4-21, 4-22; *Instrument Pilot Examination
Guide, AC 61-8A*, Courtesy of the Federal Aviation Administration: Question 5-10; *Instrument Rating Written Test Guide, AC
61-8C*, Courtesy of the Federal Aviation Administration: Figures
5-21, 5-23, 5-25, Question 5-14; *Notices to Airman*, Courtesy
of the Federal Aviation Administration: Figures 7-5, 7-6, Question 7-13; *Profile Descent Procedures Chart*, Courtesy of the National Ocean Survey: Figure 9-2; *Standard Instrument Departure
Charts*, Courtesy of the National Ocean Survey: Figure 8-1,
Questions 8-34, 8-35, 8-36, 8-37; *Standard Terminal Arrival
Routes Charts*, Courtesy of the National Ocean Survey: Figure
9-1, Questions 9-43, 9-61; *United States Standard for Terminal
Instrument Procedures*, Courtesy of the Federal Aviation Administration: Figure 4-43.

Contents

Acknowledgments   6

Introduction   7

1. **Aerodynamic Factors Relating to Instrument Flight**   8
2. **Flight Instruments**   25
3. **Weather**   48
4. **Aids to Navigation**   105
5. **Flight Computer and Performance Charts**   161
6. **Preflight Regulations**   190
7. **Flight Planning**   212
8. **Departure and En Route Procedures**   252
9. **Terminal Procedures**   279
10. **Emergency Procedures and Good Operating Practices for Instrument Pilots**   324
11. **Physiological Considerations of Flight**   330

Bibliography   333

Appendix A: Clearance Shorthand   334

Appendix B: International-ICAO Morse Code and Phonetic Alphabet   335

Appendix C: Conversion Charts   336

Appendix D: Check Lists   340

Appendix E: Answers to Chapter Questions and Exercises   341

Appendix F: Glossary   354

Appendix G: Reference Illustrations   361

Index   366

Acknowledgments

Rarely is a book of this type the result of the work of a single person. There have been literally hundreds of people who helped in some way during the preparation of this book, and while it is not possible to name each in this space, the authors gratefully acknowledge all assistance and cooperation.

In particular, thank you to the following companies from which we have reproduced printed materials, charts, photographs, drawings or other items: Aero Products Research, Inc.; Beech Aircraft Corporation; Bendix Corporation–Avionics Division; Bonzer, Inc.; Cessna Aircraft Company; Jeppesen-Sanderson Company; King Radio Corporation; Narco Scientific Industries–Avionics Division; Rockwell International–Collins Radio Group.

For information and advice we are indebted to the personnel of the Rapid City, South Dakota General Aviation District Office, Flight Service Station, National Weather Service, and Control Tower.

Special thanks to Robert Kusserow for the cover artwork, and to the staff members and friends who were instrumental in the completion of this text: proofreading and editorial assistance, Joan Vance, Elizabeth A. Raabe, and Marshall Damgaard; drafting, Edward Becker, Jim Helman, Robert J. Moore, Gregg Poe, Roy Pulfrey, Wally Widboom, and Todd Wilkinson; photography, Thomas Forchtner and John E. Hillard; typing and manuscript preparation Deborah Burcham, Ruth Jaros, Janet Noble, Mary Pond, and Joan Vance; and Thomas Cheney and Arthur M. Olsen for their astute suggestions.

Last, but not least, thank you to an old friend Mr. Victor Frier, Jr. without whose encouragement this book would not have become a reality.

Introduction

Some years ago, when we were instrument pilot applicants, we found ourselves in the common position of wondering what was the best way to prepare for the written examination. We certainly wish somebody could have suggested an exact method of studying for this exam without reading every book relating to instrument flight. There were a seemingly endless number of publications that could be studied, none of which could even come close to satisfying the total requirements for aeronautical information necessary to pass the instrument written examination.

After we became instructors, we again felt the need for a complete reference manual which could be used to "brush up" on some of the fine points that most pilots have forgotten at one time or another.

After much coaxing from our fellow pilots and other friends, we decided to do something about our frustrations. We have gathered notes, ideas, and rules of thumb based upon years of reviewing countless publications written to assist the instrument pilot. The result is a book designed to meet the needs of the average private or commercial pilot seeking the instrument rating.

The Instrument Pilot Handbook: A Reference Manual and Exam Guide was written primarily for the general aviation pilot flying the average subsonic fixed-wing aircraft at altitudes generally below 18,000 feet MSL within the 48 contiguous States.

This book is a unique blend of information which satisfies the level of aeronautical knowledge necessary to pass the FAA Instrument Rating—Airplane Written Examination. This text concisely presents a combination of study tips, logical comparisons, rules of thumb, stumbling-block notes, easy-to-understand explanations of pertinent regulations, and some intelligent statements of pilot wisdom. Naturally, the aeronautical charts contained in this book should not be used for navigation purposes.

Typical FAA-type questions and answers regularly found on the Instrument Rating—Airplane Written Examination are included at the end of each chapter. This book employs a paragraph numbering system. As you will note by referring to Appendix E in this book, all chapter questions are answered and the corresponding appropriate reference paragraph and figure numbers are provided for easy, accurate and rapid reference. In many instances, where a question may be particularly challenging, remarks are provided in Appendix E to further aid the reader in understanding and answering the question correctly.

We hope you will find that many of the hassles of studying have been eliminated. Additionally, you may find it helpful after studying the entire book to just review the questions at the end of each chapter and if necessary review the reference material by the use of this book's unique referencing system.

Good luck in your studies!

1.

Aerodynamic Factors Relating to Instrument Flight

1.1 Many private and commercial pilots are relatively skilled aviators without possessing a thorough background of basic aerodynamics. The instrument pilot, however, must be endowed with a more complete understanding of aerodynamics since flight during instrument conditions requires precise control deflections only after correct instrument interpretation and analysis. This chapter reviews several major topics of aerodynamics that should be of concern to every pilot.

ANGLE OF ATTACK AND RELATIVE WIND

1.2 Two commonly misunderstood subject areas pertain to the angle of attack and the relative wind. Unfortunately, relative wind is frequently misunderstood to be parallel to the earth's surface. Actually the relative wind, motion of the air relative to the aircraft, is parallel and opposite in direction to the flight path of the aircraft. (Figure 1-1)

1.3 The acute angle measured between the chord line of the aircraft wing (a straight line connecting the leading edge of an airfoil with the trailing edge) and the relative wind is called the angle of attack. (Figure 1-2) Lift is not only a function of air density, wing area, true airspeed, and type of airfoil, but is also a function of angle of attack up to the stalling angle, at which point lift decreases rapidly with any further increase in angle of attack. Naturally a change in angle of attack during flight can compensate for many factors affecting lift during flight. An example of this relationship: a greater angle of attack may be required at lower airspeeds, high density altitudes, and increased gross weights.

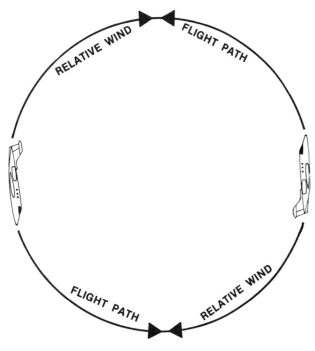

Figure 1-1. The Relationship of Relative Wind to an Aircraft's Flight Path

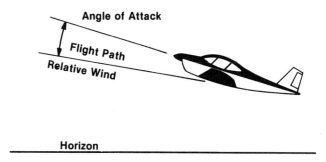

Figure 1-2. Angle of Attack

DRAG

1.4 The total drag can be defined as the sum of induced drag and parasitic drag. The drag which is created by aircraft components producing lift is called induced drag. Unlike induced drag, parasitic drag is defined as drag created by those aircraft parts not contributing to lift. The relationship of induced drag and parasitic drag at various airspeeds is depicted in Figure 1-3. Note that induced drag decreases with speed, but parasitic drag increases with speed.

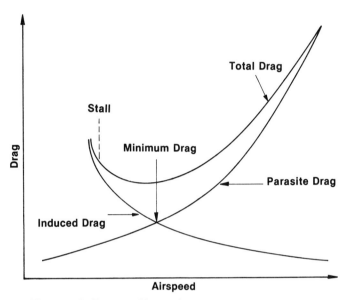

Figure 1-3. Drag vs. Airspeed

THE RELATIONSHIP OF LIFT AND WEIGHT

1.5 Lift and weight are balanced forces in level unaccelerated flight at a constant airspeed. (Figure 1-4) The force of lift acts perpendicular to the relative wind and the force of weight is directed towards the center of the earth. When lift and weight are in equilibrium, the aircraft will maintain a constant altitude. If the magnitude of lift is greater than the effect of weight, the aircraft will climb. Conversely, if the magnitude of lift is less than the effect of weight, the aircraft will descend.

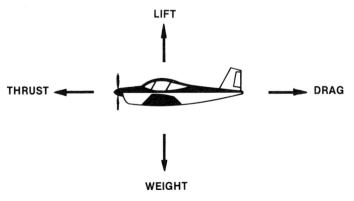

Figure 1-4. The Four Forces

1.6 At a constant angle of attack, any change in airspeed will change the magnitude of lift. Since a higher airspeed increases lift, in order to maintain a constant altitude a lower angle of attack is required, and naturally the opposite is true for a slower airspeed. If more power is applied than is required for level flight, the aircraft will accelerate if held level or climb if the airspeed is held constant.

THE EFFECT OF AIR DENSITY ON LIFT

1.7 When air density changes, lift is influenced. Air density is affected by temperature, pressure, and humidity. An increase in temperature or humidity, or a decrease in pressure would decrease air density. Since a reduction in air density decreases lift, if an aircraft is to maintain its lift, the airspeed must be increased or the angle of attack must be increased.

1.8 Naturally at a given airspeed and angle of attack when air density decreases, lift generated by the wings also decreases. This is not the only adverse effect of decreased air density. The propeller is nothing more than a miniature airfoil and consequently does not produce as much lift when there is a decrease in air density. The engine also produces less horsepower which also results in less than optimum performance.

THE RELATIONSHIP OF THRUST AND DRAG

1.9 Thrust and drag are balanced forces in level flight at a constant airspeed. (Figure 1-3) Thrust can be defined as a force parallel to the longitudinal axis of the aircraft. Drag is a force that is parallel to the relative wind. When thrust is either increased or decreased during level unaccelerated flight, there will also be a corresponding change in airspeed. This higher or lower airspeed will stabilize when the forces of thrust and drag balance. It is important to note that as the speed of an airfoil doubles, the lift and drag will quadruple, assuming the angle of attack remains constant.

THE RELATIONSHIP OF WEIGHT AND ANGLE OF ATTACK

1.10 A specific angle of attack is required to maintain level flight at a constant airspeed at a given weight. If the weight is increased, a greater angle of attack is needed in order to maintain level flight. An increase in thrust is also required to maintain the same airspeed.

LIFT IN A CLIMB OR DESCENT

1.11 Upon entering a climb or descent from straight and level flight, without any change of power, a change in the balanced forces occurs. In a climb, as the angle of attack changes, a component of the weight acts in the same direction and parallel to the total drag of the aircraft, thereby increasing the total drag and decreasing the airspeed. When an aircraft is in a descent, a component of the weight acts forward along the flight path parallel to the thrust, causing a gradual increase in airspeed as well as an increase in drag.

1.12 To maintain a constant airspeed when entering a climb or descent from straight and level flight, thrust (power) must be changed. The amount of power change depends on the change in angle of attack.

LIFT IN A TURN

1.13 Lift acts in a direction perpendicular to the relative wind and to the lateral axis of the aircraft. The lifting force is separated into two components while the airfoil is in a bank. One component of the lifting force acts in a vertical plane while the other acts in a horizontal plane. (Figure 1-5) Weight is opposed by the vertical component of lift while the horizontal component of lift acts in the opposite direction of centrifugal force.

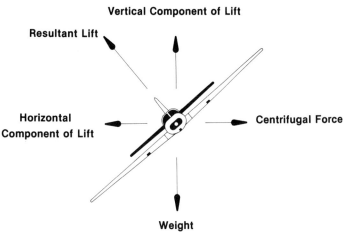

Figure 1–5. The Components of Lift

1.14 When an aircraft initiates a turn without increasing the total lift (without increasing elevator deflection), there is a decrease of lift in the vertical plane. This reduction of lift in the vertical plane is a result of the separation of lift into the two components. Since there is a loss of lift in the vertical plane, it is not possible for the aircraft to sustain a constant altitude if the airspeed and pitch remain constant. It is possible, however, to maintain a constant altitude after a turn has been initiated only if a change in airspeed or angle of attack, or a change in the combination of airspeed and angle of attack is implemented. The resultant increase in lift must be sufficient to increase the vertical component of lift to the magnitude necessary to sustain flight in a level attitude. (Figure 1-6)

1.15 The horizontal lift component provides the necessary force to cause an aircraft to turn. This component of lift is equal in magnitude but opposite in direction to centrifugal force.

Figure 1–6. The Division of Lift Components

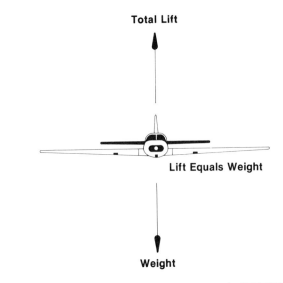

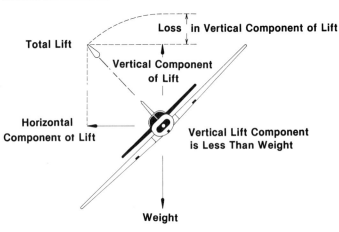

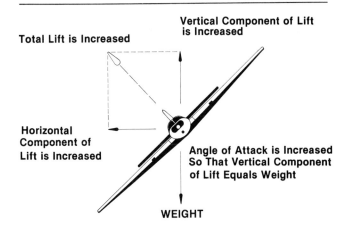

LOAD FACTOR

1.16 Load factor is the ratio of the total air load on the structure of an aircraft to the gross weight of that aircraft. In level flight an aircraft's load factor is one; in other words, the wings are supporting a load equal to the weight of the aircraft. (Figure 1-7)

1.17 When an airplane is in a coordinated level turn, the airplane's wings are supporting the airplane's weight and the added centrifugal force. As the angle of bank increases, the centrifugal force increases and, consequently, the resultant load factor increases. At a 60° angle of bank, the load factor is two; therefore, the airplane's wings are supporting a load equal to twice the weight of the airplane. At a 90° angle of bank, the load factor becomes infinite.

1.18 *Special Note: Stalling speed increases directly with the square root of the load factor. For this reason pilots should avoid steep turns at low airspeeds. Structural ice accumulation and vertical gusts in turbulent air can also increase the load factor to a critical level.*

THE RELATIONSHIP OF AIRSPEED, ANGLE OF BANK, RATE OF TURN, AND RADIUS OF TURN

1.19 Perhaps the best method of analyzing the airspeed, angle of bank, rate of turn, and the radius of turn relationship is to study the ground tracks of two airplanes flying at different airspeeds. (Figure 1-8) Assume that there are two airplanes (A and B) turning at a standard rate of 3° per second. Assume that airplane A is traveling at a ground speed of 100 knots and that airplane B is traveling at a ground speed of 200 knots. Airplane A will cover a distance of 3.33. . . nautical miles in a period of two minutes and airplane B will cover a distance of 6.66. . . nautical miles in a two-minute period. If both aircraft initiate their turns at point C at the same time, in two minutes both aircraft will return to the same point. It can be further deduced that if airspeed is increased during a turn while the angle of bank remains constant, the radius and area of the turn will also increase.

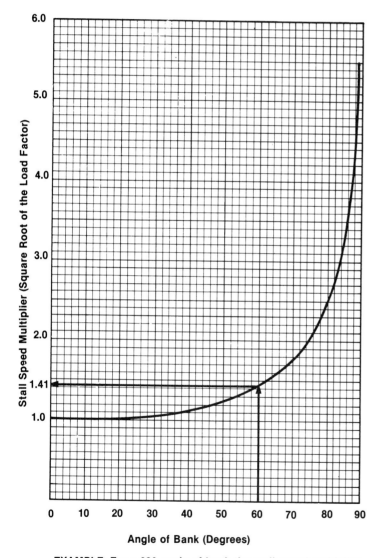

EXAMPLE: For a 60° angle of bank the stall speed multiplier is 1.41. If the stalling speed in level flight is 70 knots, the stalling speed in a 60° angle of bank is 1.41 x 70, or 98.7 knots.

Figure 1-7. Stall Speed Multiplier vs. Angle of Bank

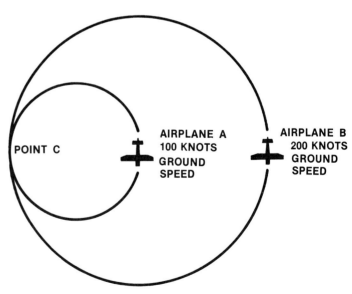

Figure 1-8. Relationship Between Airspeed and Radius of Turn

1.20 Rate of turn is determined by angle of bank and airspeed. If the airspeed of an aircraft is increased and if the rate of turn is to remain constant, the angle of bank must also be increased. (Figure 1-9)

1.21 *Rule of Thumb: If a pilot chooses to maintain a constant rate of turn but alters the airspeed or angle of bank, the following rules apply:*

Increase Bank—Increase Airspeed
Increase Airspeed—Increase Bank
Decrease Bank—Decrease Airspeed
Decrease Airspeed—Decrease Bank

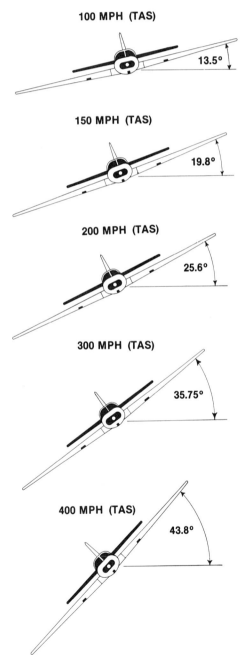

100 MPH (TAS)
13.5°

150 MPH (TAS)
19.8°

200 MPH (TAS)
25.6°

300 MPH (TAS)
35.75°

400 MPH (TAS)
43.8°

Figure 1-9. Angle of Bank vs. Airspeed at a Constant Rate of Turn

SLIPS AND SKIDS

1.22 During unaccelerated, straight and level flight, an airplane's longitudinal axis points in line with its flight path, except when the airplane is slipping or skidding. An airplane can be yawed toward either side of its flight path through rudder or rudder trim deflection. This same yawing effect can be created through the inaccurate rigging of the ailerons. If one aileron is properly aligned and the other aileron is deflected slightly downward, the airplane will yaw in the direction of the depressed aileron. If an airplane is trimmed properly and the forces are in equilibrium about the airplane's three axes, stabilizing forces will act to maintain equilibrium.

1.23 While in a controlled slip, an airplane is banked and the banking normally results in a turn. (Forward slips are possible, however.) Through application of rudder deflection opposite to the direction of bank, an airplane is prevented from turning. This banking produces a sideways movement of the airplane with respect to the direction influenced by rudder deflection.

1.24 While an airplane is in a slipping turn, the bank is excessive for the rate of turn. Consequently, the airplane is yawed toward the outside of the flight path. Since the airplane is banked excessively for the rate of turn, the centrifugal force is less than the horizontal lift component. (Remember, in a coordinated turn the magnitude of centrifugal force is equal to the magnitude of the horizontal lift component.) (Figure 1-10) The balance between the horizontal lift component and centrifugal force can be reestablished by increasing the rate of turn, decreasing the bank, or a combination of the two changes.

1.25 A skid results when an airplane yaws to the left or right of the desired flight path. Centrifugal force in excess of the magnitude of the horizontal lift component causes a skidding turn. Since the rate of turn is too great for the angle of bank, a reduction in the rate of turn (rudder), an increase in bank, or a combination of the two changes is necessary to recoordinate the turn.

1.26 *Special Note: Slips are generally the product of the cross-controlling of ailerons and rudders.*

Example: Left aileron control deflection and right rudder control deflection.

Skids result when an excessive amount of rudder control is deflected in the same direction as the aileron control.

Example: Left aileron control deflection, excessive left rudder control deflection.

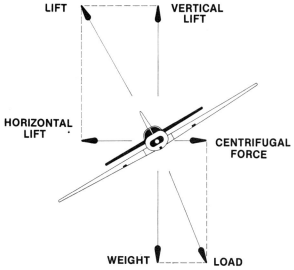

A. SLIPPING TURN
Horizontal Lift Component More Than Centrifugal Force

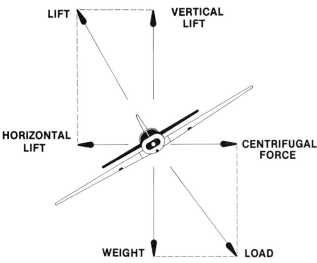

B. SKIDDING TURN
Horizontal Lift Component Less Than Centrifugal Force

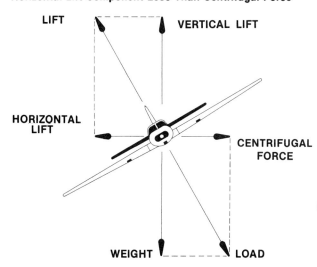

C. NORMAL TURN
Horizontal Lift Component Equals Centrifugal Force

Figure 1–10. Forces During Slipping, Skidding, and Normal Turns

UNUSUAL ATTITUDES

1.27 Many instrument pilot applicants have difficulty determining proper test responses pertaining to unusual attitudes. This area deserves careful analysis. The pitch of the unusual attitude generally dictates the proper course of action.

1.28 If an aircraft is in a nose-high unusual attitude, recovery should be initiated by *first* increasing power (if necessary) then applying forward *elevator* pressure to lower the nose of the aircraft to prevent a stall. Bank correction should be applied to level the aircraft only after the pitch correction has been implemented.

1.29 When an aircraft is in a nose-low unusual attitude, the corrective sequence should *begin* with a reduction of power (if necessary) followed by *bank* corrections and the reestablishment of the pitch attitude. In many instances a nose-low unusual attitude may be or could become a spiral; therefore, bank recovery should be initiated before a pitch change since an initial pitch change would only tighten a possible spiral. The corrective control application sequence for unusual attitudes should be almost simultaneously applied, but the pilot should take care to insure that the initial sequence for recovery is correct.

1.30 *Rule of Thumb: Unusual attitude recovery procedures.*

Nose high—Power, Pitch then Bank.
Nose low—Power, Bank then Pitch.

WAKE TURBULENCE

1.31 Trailing vortices from all aircraft have certain characteristics which allow pilots to predict with reasonable accuracy the position and intensity of the wake turbulence. All airplane wings will produce trailing vortices that rotate in opposite directions toward the airplane. Wake turbulence starts after an airplane rotates for departure and terminates upon aircraft touchdown. (Figure 1-11)

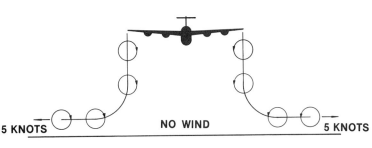

Figure 1–11. Wake Turbulence Movement in Ground Effect

1.32 Vortices, during a no-wind condition, will sink to within 200 feet of the ground and then move laterally outward at a speed of approximately five knots. A large aircraft flying at a constant altitude will generate vortices that will descend at a rate of 400 to 500 feet per minute. These vortices generally level off approximately 900 feet below the flight altitude. (Figure 1-12)

1.33 The greatest vortex turbulence is generated by heavy, *clean* (flaps and gear retracted), and slow-moving aircraft. Why a clean aircraft? A clean aircraft does not employ the use of flaps as a dirty aircraft does, so a clean aircraft will require a greater angle of attack for any given situation. Remember, wake turbulence is a function of angle of attack.

Vortex Avoidance Procedures

1.34 The following rules should be appropriately applied upon encountering vortex turbulence:

1. Pilots should avoid flying directly behind or below heavy aircraft.

2. When landing behind a heavy aircraft, a plane should remain above the heavier aircraft's flight path and land beyond the heavier aircraft's touchdown point. (Figure 1-13)

3. When landing behind a heavy aircraft that is departing, touchdown should be planned to occur prior to the departing aircraft's point of rotation. (Figure 1-14)

4. When departing behind a heavy aircraft, lift-off should be accomplished prior to the heavy aircraft's rotation point. A climb should then be continued above the flight path of the heavier aircraft until a turn can be executed to clear any wake turbulence. (Figure 1-15)

5. When landing behind a heavy aircraft on a parallel runway that is closer than 2,500 feet, caution should be exercised. To preclude any possibilities of encountering wake turbulence on parallel runways, pilots should remain above the preceding aircraft's flight path and land beyond the heavier aircraft's point of touchdown. (Figure 1-16)

6. When landing on intersecting runways, if the touchdown point of a large aircraft is past the intersection, the touchdown point of a light aircraft should be located prior to the runway intersection. (Figure 1-17)

7. Light crosswinds or quartering tailwinds can result in upwind vortices remaining in the touchdown zone for prolonged periods. (Figure 1-18)

8. Flight behind large aircraft should be upwind of the larger aircraft's flight path whenever possible.

1.35 *Rule of Thumb: To avoid wake turbulence an interval of at least 2 minutes should be observed before landing or departing behind a heavy aircraft.*

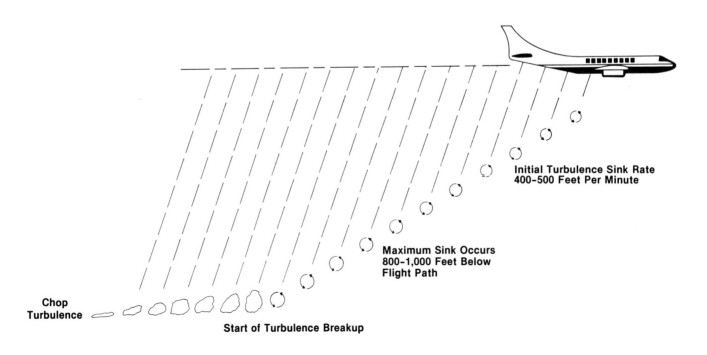

Initial Turbulence Sink Rate 400–500 Feet Per Minute

Maximum Sink Occurs 800–1,000 Feet Below Flight Path

Chop Turbulence

Start of Turbulence Breakup

Figure 1–12. Wake Turbulence Sink Characteristics

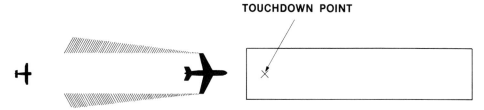

Figure 1-13. Landing Procedure Behind a Landing Heavy Aircraft

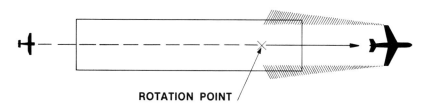

ROTATION POINT

Figure 1-14. Landing Procedure Behind a Departing Heavy Aircraft

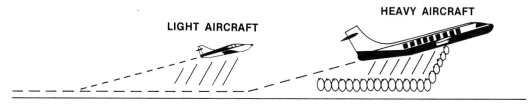

LIGHT AIRCRAFT

HEAVY AIRCRAFT

Figure 1-15. Departure Procedure Behind a Departing Heavy Aircraft (Departing from Same Runway)

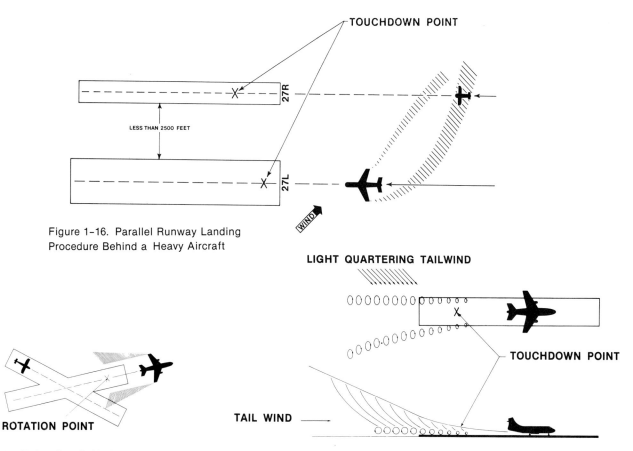

TOUCHDOWN POINT

27R

LESS THAN 2500 FEET

27L

WIND

Figure 1-16. Parallel Runway Landing Procedure Behind a Heavy Aircraft

LIGHT QUARTERING TAILWIND

TOUCHDOWN POINT

ROTATION POINT

Figure 1-17. Landing Behind a Departing Heavy Aircraft—Intersecting Runways

TAIL WIND

Figure 1-18. Quartering Tailwind Effects on Wake Turbulence

15

WEIGHT AND BALANCE

1.36 Prior to *all* flights all pilots are required (by Federal Aviation Regulations) to insure that the weight and balance limitations of their aircraft are not exceeded. An increase in an aircraft's gross weight almost always has an adverse effect on stability, irrespective of the center of gravity location. Since all aircraft are designed for specific load limits and balance conditions, flight when an aircraft is not within these designated limitations can prove to be disastrous.

1.37 The following definitions are of relevance during the course of the discussion of weight and balance:

Empty weight—The weight of the basic aircraft, fixed ballast, fixed equipment, hydraulic fluid, *unusable fuel* and *undrainable oil.*

Useful load—The weight of the pilot, co-pilot, passengers, *usable fuel, drainable oil,* and baggage. Useful load can be calculated by subtracting the empty weight from the maximum allowable takeoff weight.

Gross weight—The empty weight plus the crew, passengers, usable fuel, drainable oil, ballast, baggage, and cargo.

Maximum landing weight—The maximum weight at which an aircraft may normally be landed.

Maximum gross weight—The maximum that a loaded aircraft can weigh during any configuration of flight.

Datum reference plane—An arbitrary reference plane (designated by the manufacturer) used in weight and balance computations from which horizontal distances of specific loads are measured. The datum reference plane is generally located at the nose of the aircraft or at the firewall; however, in some of the older aircraft, the datum reference plane is located at the leading edge of the wing.

Arm—The horizontal distance in inches from the center of gravity of a load to the datum reference plane. The algebraic sign is positive if any load is aft of the datum and negative if any load or force is forward of the datum reference plane.

Center of Gravity (C.G.)—The location at which a body would balance if it were possible to support that body at that location. The aircraft C.G. can be assumed to be the mass center of the aircraft.

Moment—A force applied at the end of an arm. The weight (in pounds) multiplied by the length of the arm (in inches) equals the moment (in pound-inches). The total moment of an aircraft is the product of the total weight of the aircraft multiplied by the distance between the C.G. and the datum reference plane.

C.G. range—Allowable C.G. travel within prescribed manufacturer limits. Almost every aircraft's C.G. will vary in position from flight to flight, due to different loading conditions.

Reduction factor—A moment which, when divided by a constant, results in a moment index. Reduction factors are employed to simplify weight and balance computations. Some common reduction factors are 100, 1,000, and 10,000.

Forward and Rearward C.G.s

1.38 There is much to be considered when dealing with forward and rearward (or aft) centers of gravity. The following will serve as a review for C.G. considerations.

1.39 If two airplanes of the same model and weight are maintaining the same power, the airplane with the most rearward C.G. will have a higher airspeed. Surprised? Review Figure 1-19 and note the C.G. location of airplanes A and B. Both aircraft have a tail-down force at cruise airspeed. The magnitude of this tail-down moment is dependent upon the location of the center of gravity, since both aircraft must be in equilibrium about the center of lift. From the drawings it can easily be deduced that even though both aircraft may have the same weight, the amount of lift required is also dependent upon the location of the center of gravity. (Note that a forward C.G. requires more lift.) It can be further deduced that the aircraft with a C.G. farthest forward will require more power to fly at a constant altitude. Hence, the aircraft with the C.G. more rearward will require less power to maintain a constant altitude and, consequently, will maintain a higher airspeed.

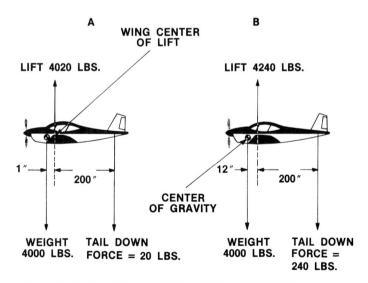

Figure 1-19. The Effects of C.G. Position on Required Lift During Cruise Flight

1.40 With an aft C.G., "nose-down" trim is necessary, and, as a result in some cases an aircraft's tail surface may actually carry some of the aircraft's weight, thereby relieving the wings of some of the aircraft's weight. This, however, can become a dangerous situation when the rearward center of gravity limit is exceeded.

1.41 With a forward C.G., "nose-up" trim is necessary for most aircraft to maintain a level cruising flight. Nose-up trim produces a tail-down force which, as previously discussed, increases the total lift requirements if a constant altitude is to be maintained. This situation requires an increase in angle of attack, which results in increased drag and a higher stalling speed. More control pressure in many instances also may be necessary.

1.42 Although a slight increase in airspeed can be realized by an aft C.G., caution should be exercised so the rearward center of gravity limits are not exceeded. An aircraft's static and dynamic longitudinal stability will generally decrease, especially at slow airspeeds, as the center of gravity is moved further aft. Under some conditions an aircraft may even have violent stall characteristics. Some of the undesirable characteristics of forward and aft C.G.s are:

1. Forward C.G.—Decreased performance; higher stalling speed; increased control pressures required at low airspeed; increased drag; increased wing loading.
2. Rearward (aft) C.G.—Violent stall characteristics, decreased stability.

1.43 *Rule of Thumb: Stability increases with forward loading. Stability decreases with aft loading.*

1.44 Most pilots will agree that the more statically stable an aircraft becomes (as the C.G. is moved forward) the better its flight characteristics will become. This is true, but only up to a certain point. If an aircraft were to become too statically stable, an extreme amount of control pressure would become necessary to displace the aircraft from its attitude. The result of this extreme static stability is control problems.

1.45 As the center of gravity moves rearward, aircraft stability can change from positive to neutral to negative. These types of situations (neutral and negative static stability) promote accidents. As the C.G. moves rearward, an aircraft becomes less statically stable and loses its ability to return to its trimmed attitude. With a further fuel burn-off, it is possible for some neutrally statically stable aircraft to become negatively statically stable. The final result would be an airplane that could become impossible to control.

Airplane Flight Manual/Operations Limitations

1.46 General weight and balance data parameters can be found in an Airplane Flight Manual or an Owner's Handbook.

1.47 Some general weight and balance parameters are: maximum weight; location of the aircraft datum; allowable center of gravity range; and baggage compartment structural limits and C.G. considerations.

1.48 Pilots should be cautioned *not* to use any aircraft weight and moment information that may have been used in example problems for a specific airplane in an Airplane Flight Manual or Owner's Handbook. When working a weight and balance problem, a pilot should obtain the information concerning that particular aircraft's actual weight and balance from the airplane weight and balance records. These records are part of the Airplane Flight Manual but are generally not part of the Owner's Handbook. Normally these records consist of a specific form, specially printed, giving such specific information as: original airplane empty weight; center of gravity (empty aircraft); useful load; and original equipment list.

1.49 From time to time many aircraft have a change in equipment which, consequently, changes the actual aircraft empty weight and/or empty C.G. Any significant change must be recorded in the aircraft airframe logbook as well as on the weight and balance form.

1.50 All aircraft have specific loading limitations according to the category of aircraft. (Figure 1-20) Caution should be exercised in distributing the load. An aircraft may be within gross weight limits and within C.G. limits but still not safe to fly! Why? Consider the baggage compartment. Generally baggage compartments are equipped with a weight placard indicating the baggage compartment structural limits. Consider the following example: An aircraft is in the utility category; the baggage compartment is placarded for a maximum weight of 220 pounds.

AIRPLANE CATEGORY	POSITIVE G's	NEGATIVE G's
Normal	2.5 to 3.8	−1.0 to 1.52
Utility	4.4	−1.76
Acrobatic	6.0	−3.0

Figure 1-20. Load Factor Requirements for Aircraft with Gross Weights Below 12,500 Pounds

1.51 From the chart in Figure 1-20 it can be determined that utility category aircraft are certified for a maximum positive load factor of 4.4 Gs. The floor of the baggage compartment of the airplane must then be able to support a total load of 968 pounds (4.4 x 220 = 968). It is easy to see that just a 100-pound overload imposes a potential structural overload of 440 pounds! Baggage compartment weights in excess of 220 pounds, therefore, could contribute to structural failure.

Computation of Aircraft Weight and Balance

1.52 Every weight and balance problem involves adding the weight of such items as usable fuel, baggage, occupants, and oil to the airplane's empty weight. The sum of these weights must not exceed the maximum allowable gross weight. The second part of weight and balance computation involves the computation of the moments of the items that were added to the aircraft empty weight. The moments of these items are then added to the airplane's empty weight moment. The gross weight and the total moment must then fall within the design limits. Pilots should be aware that any change in aircraft empty weight, useful load, and empty weight moment will result from the addition or removal of equipment. It follows that a pilot should refer to the most recently dated FAA ACA–337 form. This form (if any) will indicate the current empty weight and empty weight moment.

1.53 *Special Note: Since the aircraft empty weight includes the weight of any unusable fuel and undrainable oil, when computing weight and balance problems a pilot should add a maximum amount of fuel weight only equal to the maximum usable fuel weight if full fuel is required. Unusable fuel may vary from approximately 1/2 gallon to about 5 gallons per tank for most General Aviation Aircraft.*

1.54 The following examples of the three most commonly used methods (the table method, the graph method, and the computation method) of calculating weight and balance problems for light aircraft should be studied in great detail since they are an integral part of the *Instrument Rating—Airplane Written Examination.*

The Table Method

1.55 The table method of computing weight and balance does not require the actual calculation of moments. Tables are provided to allow pilots to determine moments for a variety of items at various weights. The example in Figure 1-21 is similar to a table actually used by an aircraft currently in production.

1.56 As with most light airplanes, the weights for the baggage compartment and all seats are represented in 10-pound increments. The weight and moments for the fuel supply are depicted in 5-gallon increments. The moments shown on the table are all divided by 100 (moment/100) for ease in reading.

1.57 The procedure for computing a weight and balance problem using the table method is generally quite simple. The weight of such items as pilot, passengers, fuel, oil, and baggage (useful load items) is added to the airplane's empty weight. The moments of the useful load are then added to the moment of the empty airplane. The last step of the problem occurs when the total moment and the total weight are compared to the center of gravity table. (Figure 1-21) Note that the aircraft weights are listed in 10-pound increments. Minimum and maximum allowable moments are shown for each increment. If the total moment lies within the minimum and maximum moment limits for the corresponding weight, the airplane C.G. is within allowable limits. A sample table method loading problem follows:

Given:

Maximum certificated gross weights 3,300 lbs. (from weight and balance data)

Empty weight	2,036 lbs.
Empty moment (lb.-ins./100)	1,579 lb.-ins./100
Useful load	1,264 lbs.
Maximum allowable baggage compartment weight	270 lbs.
Oil	12 qts.
Usable fuel 2 wing tanks	40 gals. each tank
Unusable fuel each tank	.5 gal.

Assume the following conditions:

Maximum permissible fuel to be carried in this flight situation	
Baggage compartment	60 lbs.
Pilot	200 lbs.
Front seat passenger	200 lbs.
Rear seat passenger (forward position)	155 lbs.
Rear seat passenger (forward position)	200 lbs.

Solution:

	Weight (lbs.)	Moment (lb.-ins./100)
A. Empty airplane	2,036	1,579
B. Pilot	200	170
C. Front seat passenger	200	170
D. Rear seat passenger	155	188
E. Rear seat passenger	200	242
F. Oil, 12 qts. (3 gals.)	23*	6
G. Fuel, 71 gals.	426*	320
H. Baggage	60	90
I. Total	3,300	2,765

1.58* *Special Note: Assume oil weighs 7.5 pounds per gallon. Fuel weighs 6.0 pounds per gallon.*

1.59 Steps B, C, D, E, G, and H of the solution can be easily found from the excerpt of Figure 1-21. The moment/100 for the 155-pound passenger can be easily interpolated. Since the 155-pound moment is exactly halfway between the moments 182 and 194, the moment/100 for the 155-pound passenger is 188 lb.-ins.

Figure 1–21. Weight and Balance Tables

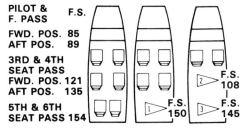

DIMENSIONAL AND LOADING DATA

LEVELING POINTS

FRONT JACK POINTS F.S. 83.1   REAR JACK POINT F.S. 271.0

SEATING, BAGGAGE AND EQUIPMENT ARRANGEMENTS

	F.S.
PILOT & F. PASS	
FWD. POS.	85
AFT POS.	89
3RD & 4TH SEAT PASS	
FWD. POS.	121
AFT POS.	135
5TH & 6TH SEAT PASS	154

2 > F.S. 108
1 > F.S. 150
3 > F.S. 145

1 ▷ MAXIMUM WEIGHT 270 POUNDS INCLUDING EQUIPMENT AND BAGGAGE WITH 5th and 6th SEATS REMOVED OR STOWED.

2 ▷ MAXIMUM WEIGHT 200 POUNDS FORWARD OF REAR SPAR INCLUDING EQUIPMENT AND CARGO WITH 3rd and 4th SEATS REMOVED.

3 ▷ MAXIMUM WEIGHT 270 POUNDS AFT OF REAR SPAR INCLUDING EQUIPMENT AND CARGO WITH 3rd, 4th, 5th and 6th SEATS REMOVED.

USEFUL LOAD WEIGHTS AND MOMENTS
OCCUPANTS

	Front Seats		Rear Seats (3rd and 4th)		Fifth and Sixth Seats	
	Fwd Position	Aft Position	Fwd Position	Aft Position		
	ARM 85	ARM 89	ARM 121	ARM 135	ARM 154	
WEIGHT	MOM/100	MOM/100	MOM/100	MOM/100	WEIGHT	MOM/100
120	102	107	145	162	30	46
130	110	116	157	176	40	62
140	119	123	169	189	50	77
150	128	134	182	202	60	92
160	136	142	194	216	70	108
170	144	151	206	230	80	123
180	153	160	218	243	90	139
190	162	169	230	256	100	154
200	170	178	242	270	110	169
					120	185
					130	200
					140	216
					150	231
					160	246
					170	262

NOTE: OCCUPANT POSITIONS SHOWN ARE FOR THE SEATS ADJUSTED THE MAXIMUM RANGE. INTERMEDIATE POSITIONS WILL REQUIRE INTERPOLATION OF THE MOMENT/100 VALUES.

BAGGAGE		CARGO
ARM 150	Fwd of Spar (3rd and 4th Seats Removed)	Aft of Spar 3rd, 4th 5th and 6th Seats Removed
	ARM 108	ARM 145
Weight / Mom/100	Mom/100	Mom/100
10 / 15	11	15
20 / 30	22	29
30 / 45	32	44
40 / 60	43	58
50 / 75	54	73
60 / 90	65	87
70 / 105	76	102
80 / 120	86	116
90 / 135	97	131
100 / 150	108	145
110 / 165	119	160
120 / 180	130	174
130 / 195	140	189
140 / 210	151	203
150 / 225	162	218
160 / 240	173	232
170 / 255	184	247
180 / 270	194	261
190 / 285	205	276
200 / 300	216	290
210 / 315		305
220 / 330		319
230 / 345		334
240 / 360		348
250 / 375		363
260 / 390		377
270 / 405		392

USEFUL LOAD WEIGHTS AND MOMENTS

USABLE FUEL

LEADING EDGE TANKS ARM 75		
Gallons	Weight	Moment 100
5	30	23
10	60	45
15	90	68
20	120	90
25	150	113
30	180	135
35	210	158
40	240	180
44	264	198
50	300	225
55	330	248
60	360	270
65	390	293
70	420	315
74	444	333

OIL

Quarts	Weight	Moment 100
12	23	6

MOMENT LIMITS vs WEIGHT (Continued)

Weight	Minimum Moment 100	Maximum Moment 100
3200	2595	2721
3210	2606	2729
3220	2617	2736
3230	2629	2743
3240	2640	2751
3250	2652	2758
3260	2663	2766
3270	2675	2773
3280	2686	2780
3290	2698	2788
3300	2709	2795

1.60 To determine maximum permissible fuel for Step G, it is necessary to first determine the total weight of Steps A, B, C, D, E, F, and H and then subtract this total from the maximum allowable gross weight.

Empty weight	2,036	Maximum allowable	
Pilot	200	gross weight	3,300 lbs.
Front seat passenger	200	Aircraft weight (as	
Rear seat passenger	155	loaded)	-2,864 lbs.
Rear seat passenger	200		426 lbs.
Baggage	60		
Oil	23		
Total	2,864		

1.61 By referring to the fuel moment chart, the fuel moment can be determined to be 6/24 of the way between the moments/100 of 315 and 333 lb.-ins.

1.62 The final step to this solution (Step I) indicates the total weight and total moment. By simply referring to the gross weight moment limits chart, it can be deduced that the moment of the aircraft (as loaded) falls within the allowable minimum and maximum moment limits.

1.63 If the load would have been distributed differently (that is, rear seats from the forward to the aft position, less fuel/more baggage, and so forth), the airplane most likely would have been outside acceptable C.G. limits. This is an excellent example of the importance of proper load distribution.

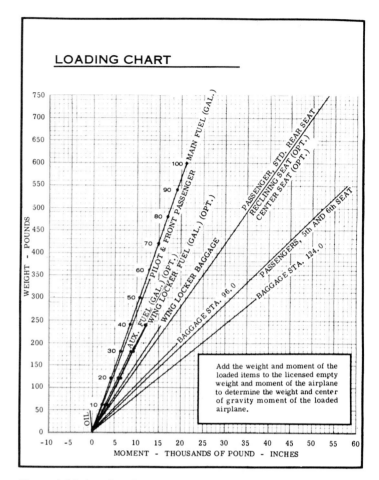

Figure 1-22. Loading Chart

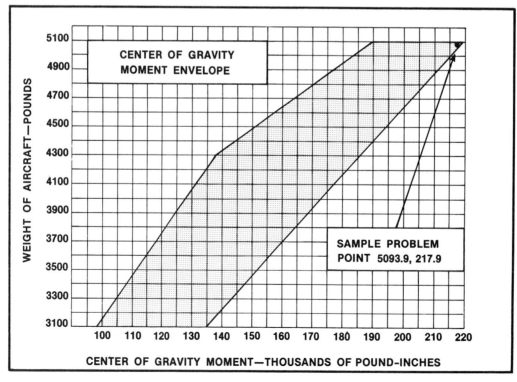

Figure 1-23. Center of Gravity Moment Envelope

The Graph Method

1.64 The graph method is perhaps the easiest method of computing weight and balance for an airplane. Unlike the table method of computing weight and balance, it is never necessary to interpolate moments. Moments for each weight are easily determined by simply reading the loading chart. (Figure 1-22) The airplane total weight must be first computed to insure that the maximum gross weight is not exceeded. The total aircraft moment is then computed by adding the moments of all items to be loaded to the airplane empty weight moment. After the total weight and total moment have been computed, the last step of this problem is to determine if the C.G. falls within the center of gravity moment envelope. (Figure 1-23) A sample graph method loading problem follows:

Given:

Maximum certificated gross weight	5,100 lbs.
Empty weight	3,375.1 lbs.
Empty moment (lb.-ins./1000)	123.3 lb.-ins./1000
Useful load	1,724.9 lbs.
Maximum baggage compartment weight	600 lbs.
Oil capacity	26 qts.
Oil moment	0.2 lb.-ins./1000
Maximum usable fuel (main tanks)	100 gals.
Unusable fuel (main tanks)	2 gals.
Maximum usable fuel (auxiliary tanks)	30 gals.
Unusable fuel (auxiliary tanks)	1 gal.

Assume the following conditions:

Pilot	170 lbs.
Front seat passenger	200 lbs.
Middle seat passenger	180 lbs.
Middle seat passenger	160 lbs.
Rear seat passenger	160 lbs.
Rear seat passenger	Empty
Baggage	200 lbs.
Fuel	Full main tanks

Solution:

	Weight (lbs.)	Moment (lb.-ins./1000)
A. Empty airplane	3,375.1	123.3
B. Pilot	170	6.5
C. Front seat passenger	200	7.5
D. Middle seat passenger	180	12.7
E. Middle seat passenger	160	11.2
F. Rear seat passenger	160	16.7
G. Oil, 26 qts. (6.5 gals.)	48.75	-0.2
H. Fuel, 100 gals.	600	21.0
I. Baggage	200	19.2
J. Total	5,093.85	217.9

The moments/1000 for items B through F can be readily determined from the loading chart. (Simply locate each weight on the loading chart on the vertical column, advance horizontally to the right to the appropriate diagonal line, and then proceed below to the bottom of the chart to determine the applicable moment index.) Item G, however, is generally given in the actual weight and balance data and Owner's Manual. With this particular airplane, the oil is forward of the datum plane; therefore, the moment is expressed in negative terms. Consequently, the moment for the oil must be subtracted from the other moments.

1.65 Since the intersection of the vertical line denoting the moment index of 217.9 lb.-ins. and the horizontal line denoting the aircraft gross weight of 5,093.85 pounds falls within the center of gravity moment envelope, the airplane is within weight and center of gravity limitations.

The Computation Method

1.66 The computation method is the basis for all of the other methods of weight and balance analysis. Since this method provides the basic steps in determining C.G. location, it is imperative that all pilots be familiar with this method.

1.67 The load adjuster method, graph method, and table method are derivations of the computation method. The other methods of computing weight and balance were devised to save time in determining the location of the center of gravity.

1.68 The steps involved in the computation method of weight and balance are often misunderstood but really are not very difficult.

1. The first step in the computation method is that of listing weights and arms of such items as the empty aircraft, pilot and passengers, cargo, baggage, and other loose equipment.
2. The total aircraft weight should then be computed and compared to the approved gross weight of the airplane. (If the total gross weight is in excess of the approved gross weight, the load must be reduced until the airplane's gross weight is within approved gross weight limits.)
3. The weight of each item must be multiplied by its arm to determine the moment of the item.
4. The moments of each item should be added together to determine the total aircraft moment.
5. After the total aircraft weight and total aircraft moment have been computed, the center of gravity of the loaded airplane can then be calculated by dividing the total moment by the total airplane weight.

A sample computation method loading problem follows:

Given:

Airplane empty weight	1,700 lbs; arm 36 ins.
Oil capacity	8 qts; arm *minus* 14 ins.
Maximum usable fuel	45 gals; arm 50 ins.
Pilot and front seat passenger	arm 38 ins.
Rear seat passengers	arm 72 ins.
Baggage area	arm 97 ins.
Maximum baggage compartment weight	170 lbs.
Approved C.G. limits	38.5 ins. to 44.9 ins.
Maximum allowable gross weight	2,750 lbs.

Assume:

Pilot weight	175 lbs.
Front seat passenger weight	160 lbs.
Rear seat passengers weight	300 lbs.
Fuel	25 gals.
Baggage	60 lbs.

Solution:

	Weight (lbs.)	Arm (ins.)	Moment (lb.-ins.)
Empty airplane	1,700	+36	+ 61,200
Oil	15	-14	- 210
Fuel	150	+50	+ 7,500
Pilot	175	+38	+ 6,650
Front seat passenger	160	+38	+ 6,080
Rear seat passengers	300	+72	+ 21,600
Baggage	60	+97	+ 5,820
Total	2,560		+ 108,640

Center of gravity = 42.44 inches.

Changing Loads and the Resulting C.G.

1.69 Whenever a load is moved in an airplane or even when fuel is burned in flight, the C.G. changes its location. The magnitude of the change of the C.G. depends upon the weight of the aircraft, the weight of the load that is moved, and the distance that the load is moved. The following problem and solution exemplify how changing loads affect the C.G.

Given:

Prior to takeoff an airplane is loaded to a gross weight of 3,000 pounds with the C.G. located at station 110.2. After landing at the destination airport assume: 120 pounds of baggage is added at station 117, 70 pounds is removed from station 125.1, and 20 gallons of fuel has been burned from station 120.5. Find the new C.G.

Solution:

	Weight (lbs.)		Arm (ins.)		Moment (lb.-ins.)
A. Airplane	+ 3,000	x	+ 110.2 =		+ 330,600
B. Baggage (added)	+ 120	x	+ 117.0 =		+ 14,040
C.	3,120	x			344,640
D. Baggage (removed)	- 70	x	+ 125.1 =		- 8,757
E.	3,050				335,883
F. Fuel (burned) 20 gal. x 6 lb/gal.	- 120	x	+ 120.5 =		- 14,460
G.	2,930				321,423

H. C.G. = $\dfrac{\text{Total moment}}{\text{Total weight}}$ C.G. = $\dfrac{321,423}{2,930}$ = 109.70

1.70 As seen in the solution of this problem, the basic formula of "weight multiplied by the arm equals moment" plays a very important role in the solution. Steps A, B, D, and F calculate the new aircraft moment. Steps C, E, and G consist of the addition or subtraction of weights and moments.

1.71 When recalculating the C.G., if an item is removed from the rear of the datum reference plane, the weight and the moment of the item should be subtracted from the total weight and total moment. (Refer to Steps D and F.) If an item is added to the rear of the datum reference plane, the weight and the moment of the item should be added to the total weight and total moment. (Refer to Step B.)

1.72 If an item is removed forward of the datum reference plane, the absolute value of the moment should be added to the total moment, but the weight of that item should be subtracted from the total aircraft weight. If an item is added forward of the datum reference plane, the resulting moment should be subtracted from the total aircraft moment, and the weight should be added to the total aircraft weight.

1.73 *Special Note: Remember, a shifting of a load is nothing more than removing a load from one station and adding another load of equal weight at another station.*

CHAPTER 1: QUESTIONS

For answers see Appendix E

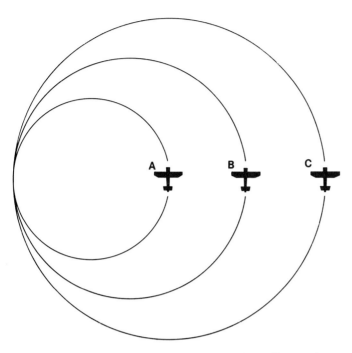

1. Assume the three aircraft in the illustration above are making coordinated turns. Which of the following statements is correct?

Aircraft A	Aircraft B	Aircraft C
Bank 25°	Bank 25°	Bank 25°
TAS 100 mph	TAS 150 mph	TAS 200 mph

1. Airplane A will have one-half the rate of turn and one-half the radius of turn of airplane C.
2. Airplane C will have a greater radius of turn and a lesser rate of turn than airplane B.
3. Airplanes A, B, and C will have equal rates of turn but airplane C will have the greatest radius of turn.
4. Airplane C will have a greater radius of turn and a greater rate of turn than airplane B.

2. Assume an airplane is turning at a rate of 3° per second, and the airspeed is increased by 100 knots. If the rate of turn is to remain at 3° per second:

1. The angle of bank will remain the same, but the radius will increase.
2. The angle of bank will remain the same, but the radius will decrease.
3. The angle of bank should be increased, and the radius will decrease.
4. The angle of bank should be increased, and the radius will increase.

3. What is the determinant force that causes an aircraft to turn when a wing is lowered?

1. A horizontal component of lift.
2. A vertical component of lift.
3. Centrifugal force.
4. A combination of resultant forces produced by the deflection of the elevator and ailerons.

4. What is the proper procedure and order for using the controls to recover from a diving spiral?

1. Raise the nose, level the wings, and reduce power.
2. Level the wings, reduce power, and raise the nose.
3. Raise the nose, implement rudder correction, and reduce power.
4. Reduce power, level the wings, and raise the nose to the horizon.

5. Assume an airplane is landing on Runway 12 with a reported wind of 080° at five knots. Which of the following statements is true pertaining to wake turbulence of an airplane departing on the same runway ahead of the landing airplane?

1. The upwind vortex will tend to remain over the takeoff area.
2. The downwind vortex will tend to remain over the takeoff area.
3. Both wingtip vortices will dissipate rapidly.
4. Both vortices will move downwind at a rapid rate.

6. Assume a large aircraft has landed on Runway 25R. The reported wind is calm. To avoid wake turbulence, a light aircraft landing on Runway 25L:

1. Should make a normal approach, because the wake turbulence will remain over Runway 25R.
2. Should make an approach above the glide path of the large aircraft and land beyond its touchdown point.
3. Should abort the landing.
4. Should make an approach below the glide path of the large aircraft and land prior to its touchdown point.

7. Which of the following are correct statements pertaining to load factor?

A. Load factor is the ratio of the total air load on the structure of an aircraft to the gross weight of that aircraft.
B. As an airplane's angle of bank increases, the resultant load factor increases.
C. Stalling speed increases directly with the square root of load factor.
D. When an aircraft is in level flight, the load factor is one.

1. A, B, and D.
2. A and D.
3. B and C.
4. A, B, C, and D.

8. Which of the following are correct statements pertaining to drag?

A. Total drag can be defined as the sum of induced and parasitic drag.
B. Induced drag increases with speed.
C. Parasitic drag increases with speed.
D. Induced drag is created by aircraft components producing lift.

   1. A, B, and D.
   2. A, C, and D.
   3. B and C
   4. B and D.

9. Assume an aircraft is in a left, skidding turn. If the pilot is to coordinate the turn while *maintaining* the same rate of turn, the correct pilot action would be:

   1. Increase left aileron.
   2. Decrease left rudder.
   3. Increase right rudder.
   4. Increase left aileron and increase right rudder.

10. The gross weight of a loaded airplane was determined to be 4,000 pounds with the C.G. located at station 70.7. If 146 pounds are moved from station 155.0 to station 72.2, the location of the new C.G. will be:

   1. 69.80 inches aft of the datum.
   2. 67.91 inches aft of the datum.
   3. 67.68 inches aft of the datum.
   4. 67.58 inches aft of the datum.

11. An airplane is loaded to a gross weight of 2,519.2 pounds with the C.G. at station 119.9. If 147 pounds of baggage are added at station 103, what will be the new location of the C.G. after 25 gallons of fuel have been expended from station 46?

   1. 120.14 inches aft of the datum.
   2. 122.23 inches aft of the datum.
   3. 123.23 inches aft of the datum.
   4. 123.32 inches aft of the datum.

12. A weight placard located in the baggage compartment generally indicates the:

   1. Structural limits of the baggage compartment.
   2. Maximum baggage compartment tiedown strength.
   3. Maximum allowable baggage volume.
   4. Maximum airplane C.G. with no baggage.

13. During a refueling stop it is determined that an airplane weighs 3,150 pounds with the C.G. located 60.1 inches aft of the datum. Thirty gallons of fuel are taken on and 60 pounds of baggage are removed. What is the new weight and C.G.? (The fuel cells are located 70 inches aft of the datum, and the baggage compartment is located 95 inches aft of the datum.)

   1. 3,280 pounds and 60.00 inches aft of the datum.
   2. 3,270 pounds and 60.00 inches aft of the datum.
   3. 3,170 pounds and 59.72 inches aft of the datum.
   4. 3,270 pounds and 59.72 inches aft of the datum.

2.

Flight Instruments

2.1 This chapter reviews those instruments basic to attitude instrument flying. Rather than discuss in detail the ''how to's'' of instrument flying, the individual instruments are discussed in detail as to how they function during different flight situations.

GYRO INSTRUMENTS

2.2 The attitude indicator, heading indicator, and turn and slip indicator are the three gyro instruments found in most aircraft. These three instruments contain a gyro rotor driven by suction or electricity, and employ the principles of a gyro.

2.3 The principles that govern a rotating gyro are rigidity in space and gyroscopic precession. Rigidity in space simply means the rotor inside a gyro instrument maintains a constant attitude in space unless the gyro is acted upon by an outside force. The two factors which primarily determine the quality of the gyroscope are rotor mass and rotor speed.

2.4 The attitude indicator and heading indicator employ the principle of rigidity in space. The spinning gyro in each of these instruments will maintain constant position with respect to the horizon or direction. The aircraft heading and attitude then can be compared to these references. (Refer to Figure 2-1.) Essentially, the rotors of these instruments will remain in a constant plane of rotation, and the aircraft will rotate about these gyros.

2.5 Any movement of the gyro spin axis from its alignment in space is called precession. Precession (as related to gyro instruments) is caused by the movement of the rotor spin axis from its original alignment in space by an applied force. Precession can be caused by an unintentional force such as rotor imbalance, bearing friction, or air friction.

Some precession forces are intentionally applied by erection mechanisms or torque motors to align the gyro spin axis in relation to the earth's surface.

2.6 Moving the entire gyroscope in straight and level unaccelerated flight will not cause precession because there is no force causing the gyro axis to tilt or turn. When an aircraft is turned, however, gyroscopic precession causes the gyro rotor to tilt, thereby influencing the gyro instrument indications. (The principles that influence a gyroscope are further reviewed in Figure 2-2.)

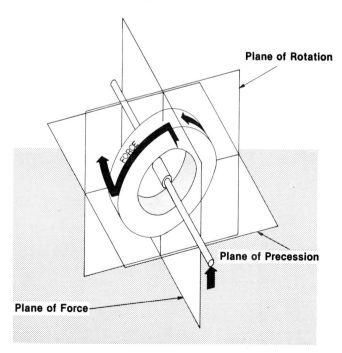

Figure 2-1. A Gyro Maintaining a Constant Plane of Rotation

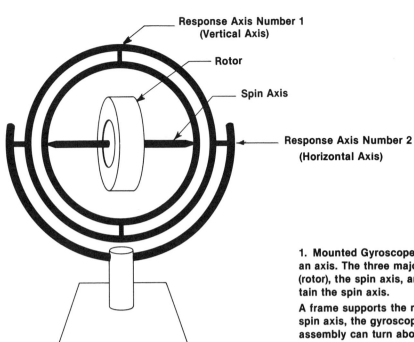

Response Axis Number 1
(Vertical Axis)

Rotor

Spin Axis

Response Axis Number 2
(Horizontal Axis)

1. Mounted Gyroscope—A gyroscope is a mass rotating on an axis. The three major components are the spinning mass (rotor), the spin axis, and the gimbals which are used to contain the spin axis.

A frame supports the rotor and gimbals. Disregarding the spin axis, the gyroscope has two degrees of freedom; the assembly can turn about a vertical axis (response axis Number 1) and also about a horizontal axis (response axis Number 2).

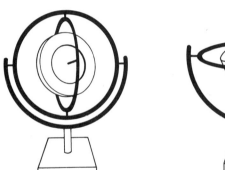  

2. A gyro is a wheel, universally mounted, so that only one point—its center of gravity—is in a fixed position, the wheel being free to turn in any direction around this point.

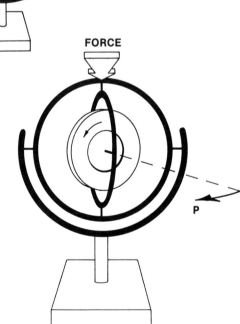

FORCE

P

3. A spinning rotor of a gyroscope exhibits a high degree of rigidity and the gyro's spin axis will maintain the same direction in space when the base mount is moved.

4. Gyroscopic precession, simply stated, is an intrinsic quality of all rotating bodies; specifically, the application of a force perpendicular to the plane of rotation will effect a maximum displacement of the rotating body about 90° later in the rotation cycle from the point at which the force was applied.

FOR EXAMPLE: If a force is applied about the horizontal axis, as illustrated, the gyro will turn or "precess" about the vertical axis in the direction indicated by arrow P.

Figure 2-2. Principles of the Gyroscope

Turn and Slip Indicator

2.7 The turn and slip indicator essentially consists of a combination of two instruments: a gyro-operated turn indicator and an inclinometer which reacts to gravity and/or centrifugal force. This indicator is sometimes called a turn and bank indicator. The turn indicator portion of this instrument employs the principle of gyroscopic precession and uses a restricted mounting which allows only the spin axis to tilt. (Figure 2-3) As the aircraft turns, the gyro is caused to precess in the opposite direction. A reversing mechanism causes the turn needle to indicate the direction of turn. The needle will then indicate the direction and rate of turn, and the inclinometer ball will show the quality of the turn.

2.8 A spring is attached between the gyro assembly and the instrument case to hold the gyro upright when no precession is applied. Tension on the spring may be adjusted to calibrate the instrument for a given rate of turn. Mechanical stops prevent the gyro assembly from tilting more than 45° to either side. A damping mechanism is used to prevent excessive oscillation of the turn needle.

2.9 The gyro that drives the turn needle derives its energy from either electricity or suction. The main reason for having electricity as the most common source of energy is safety. Normally in light aircraft the attitude and heading indicators are vacuum driven. In the event of a vacuum system and generator failure, the turn and slip indicator

would continue to supply the pilot with rate of turn information from current supplied by the aircraft battery.

2.10 The rate of turn instrument (the needle) may be calibrated into a two-minute turn indicator. A full deflection (Figure 2-4) on a two-minute turn needle indicates the aircraft is turning 3° per second. A half standard rate of turn of 1.5° per second is called a four-minute turn. The half standard rate turn is generally used by jet aircraft since at higher speeds the angle of bank would be quite steep to maintain a 3° per second turn.

2.11 The inclinometer consists of a curved glass tube filled with a clear fluid and containing a ball. This instrument indicates the relationship between the angle of bank and the rate of turn. During a coordinated turn, the horizontal component of lift and centrifugal force are in balance, and the ball will remain centered.

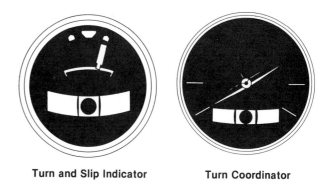

Turn and Slip Indicator   **Turn Coordinator**

Figure 2-4. Standard-Rate (Two-Minute) Turn Indicators

Figure 2-3. The Interior View of a Turn and Slip Indicator

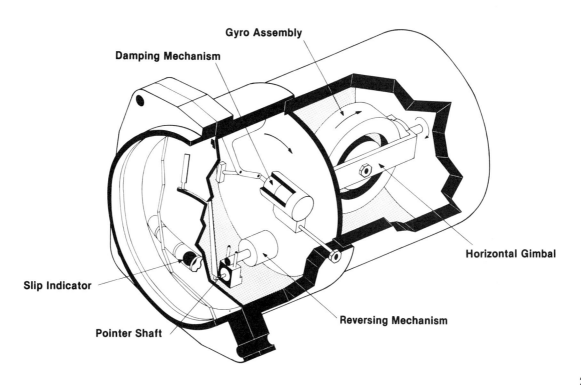

Gyro Assembly

Damping Mechanism

Horizontal Gimbal

Slip Indicator

Reversing Mechanism

Pointer Shaft

2.12 A slip or a skid will result when the horizontal component of lift and centrifugal force are not in balance. To balance these forces, a pilot should apply right rudder or decrease right aileron deflection if the ball is on the right side of the instrument. If the ball is on the left side of the instrument, the pilot should, naturally, apply left rudder or decrease the amount of left aileron deflection. Remember the old pilot cliché, "Step on the ball."

2.13 In a standard rate of turn, the nose of the aircraft is turning at 3° per second, *regardless* if the turn is a slipping, skidding, or coordinated turn. *Only* the quality of the turn is indicated by the position of the ball in the inclinometer. (Figure 2-5)

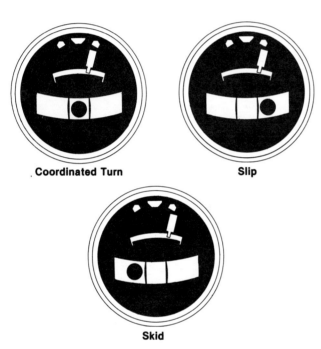

Coordinated Turn Slip

Skid

Figure 2-5. A Standard Rate Two-Minute Turn

2.14 Pilots should check the turn indicator prior to departure. When a turn is being executed while taxiing, the turn indicator will indicate a skid since the centrifugal force forces the ball toward the outside of the turn. (Figure 2-6)

Figure 2-6. A Typical Indication While Taxiing for Departure

The Attitude Indicator

2.15 The attitude indicator, also referred to as the artificial horizon, provides the pilot with a substitute for the natural horizon. This instrument allows the pilot to maintain the desired attitude while flying during instrument conditions.

2.16 The attitude indicator derives its energy either from a vacuum system or from electricity. Attitude indicators in single-engine and light multiengine aircraft normally employ the vacuum system. (Figure 2-7) The electric attitude indicator, used primarily in the larger aircraft, provides the pilot with an improved presentation through all flight attitudes and altitudes. (Figure 2-8)

Figure 2-7. A Vacuum-Driven Attitude Indicator

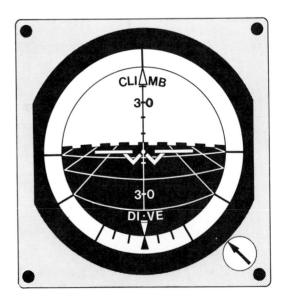

Figure 2-8. Electric-Powered Attitude Indicator

2.17 The attitude indicator makes use of the principle of rigidity in space. The instrument housing which is attached to the aircraft revolves about the gyro which remains in its relative plane of rotation. A white horizontal line divides the instrument face and represents the actual horizon. A miniature aircraft attached to the case will give the perspective of the aircraft relative to the earth's horizon. The miniature aircraft can be adjusted vertically to align with the horizontal line and will not tilt since it is fixed to the case of the attitude indicator.

2.18 The electric attitude indicator will have an "off" flag during power interruptions. The vacuum system may have low vacuum, clogged filters, or partially blocked lines which would cause a delayed indication. The vacuum system is generally not used at high altitudes due to the low atmospheric pressure. The older types of vacuum-driven attitude indicators have bank limits of approximately 100° or 110° and pitch limits of 60° to 70°.

2.19 All instruments and equipment should have a thorough preflight inspection, especially before a flight in instrument conditions. The attitude indicator is the only instrument that gives the pilot a continuous exact picture presentation of the aircraft attitude; therefore, this instrument in particular must have a careful preflight inspection. A certain amount of warm-up time is required for gyro instruments. The time required for electric gyro instruments to reach operational efficiency is a minimum of three minutes and for a vacuum-driven instrument, a minimum of five minutes is necessary to reach the desired gyro speed.

2.20 While taxiing, the horizon bar of the attitude indicator should indicate a level attitude, and the bank indication should not exceed 5°. The vibration of the horizon bar should stop after a sufficient warm-up period. If any of these conditions are not present after the gyro has had adequate time to reach normal operating speed, instrument flight should *not* be attempted.

2.21 If a gyro rotor has been tumbled by exceeding either the pitch or bank limits, it will erect at a rate of 8° per minute. Excessive wear on the gimbals will occur if the gyro is often forced to its limits. (A gimbal is a device that permits a body to incline freely in any direction or suspends it so that it will remain level when its support is tipped.)

2.22 Errors in both pitch and bank indications are usually at a maximum after 180° of turn. When an aircraft rolls out after a 180° turn, the attitude indicator will momentarily indicate a slight climbing turn to the right. A 360° turn, however, will reflect a level attitude because the induced precession error created during the first 180° of turn will be cancelled during the second 180° of turn. Attitude in-

dication errors may also be caused by acceleration and deceleration. An induced indication of a climb will be reflected on the attitude indicator during aircraft acceleration. The converse is true for deceleration.

The Heading Indicator (Directional Gyro)

2.23 The primary advantages of having a gyro for heading reference are stability in turbulence and freedom of the magnetic compass turning errors. There are two types of gyroscopic heading indicators, and both employ the principle of rigidity in space. The primary type of heading indicator is a basic gyro that must be set to the magnetic heading. A gyroscopic heading indicator may have a circular compass card (older type) (Figure 2-9), or an azimuth compass card (newer type) (Figure 2-10).

Figure 2-9. Circular Compass Card Heading Indicator

Figure 2-10. Azimuth Compass Card Heading Indicator

2.24 The above heading indicators should be checked about every fifteen minutes against the compass for precession error. The maximum acceptable error is 3° during a fifteen-minute period. Perhaps the main causes for these instrument errors are bearing friction, worn bearings, precession, and simply missetting the gyro.

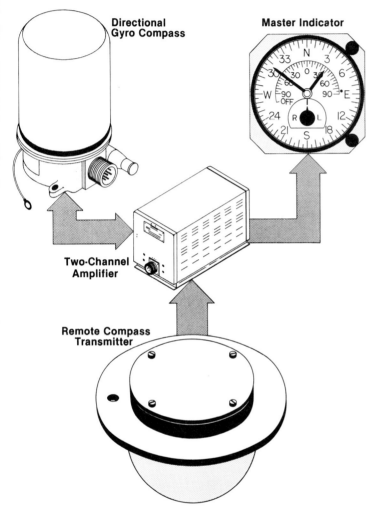

Figure 2–11. A Remote Indicating Compass

2.25 The gyroscopic heading indicator may be powered either by vacuum or by electricity; however, light aircraft generally use vacuum to power the heading indicator in conjunction with the attitude indicator.

2.26 Generally, the level of suction for the heading indicators must register within the limits of 3.5 to 5.0 inches of mercury, with four inches of mercury being the preferred level. The operational pitch and bank limits are generally 55°. Beyond these limits the compass card will spin rapidly. This condition can be rectified by caging, resetting, and uncaging the instrument.

2.27 The second type of gyroscopic heading indicator is a gyro slaved to a magnetic compass called a remote indicating compass. The slaved gyro system is to be found in virtually all large and high performance aircraft, and in increasingly large numbers of light aircraft flown in serious IFR operations, due to its greater accuracy. (Figure 2-11)

The Magnetic Compass

2.28 All aircraft are required, as prescribed by Federal Aviation Regulations (FAR) Part 91, to have a magnetic compass. The magnetic compass functions basically as a magnet that is being influenced by an electromagnetic field of energy. (Figure 2-12) The magnets mounted inside the compass are, essentially, influenced by the flux lines of the earth's electromagnetic fields.

2.29 The earth acts as a magnetic bar with the magnetic north pole being approximately 1,000 statute miles from the geographic north pole. The electromagnetic lines of force flowing between the poles form the earth's electromagnetic field. These lines of force are parallel to the surface at the equator, and the inclination increases to a maximum at the earth's magnetic poles. The magnetic bar of the compass aligns itself with these lines of force.

Figure 2-12. The Earth's Magnetic Field

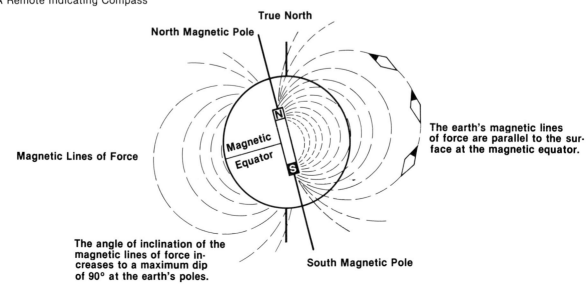

Variation

2.30 Magnetic variation is the angular difference between true north and magnetic north. A line connecting 0° points of variation is termed the agonic line. Other lines of equal magnetic variation are called isogonic lines. (Figure 2-15) Both agonic and isogonic lines are curved because the earth's composition and irregular features influence the electromagnetic field surrounding the earth. The variation is easterly if the compass points to the east of true north, and the variation is westerly if the compass points to the west of true north. (Figure 2-16) Pilots must be aware of the amounts of variation to determine true and magnetic courses.

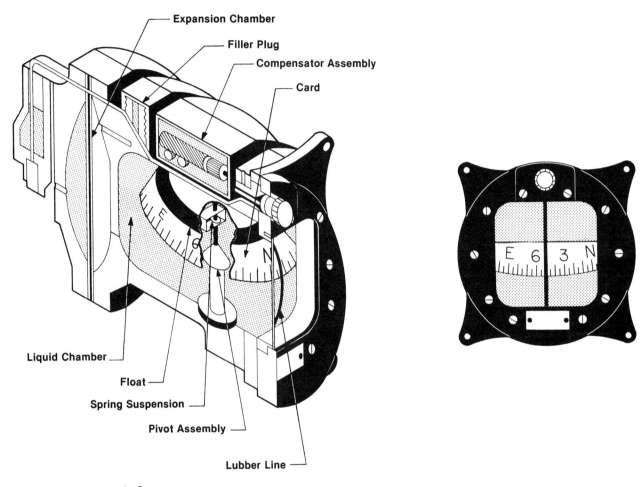

Figure 2-13. The Magnetic Compass

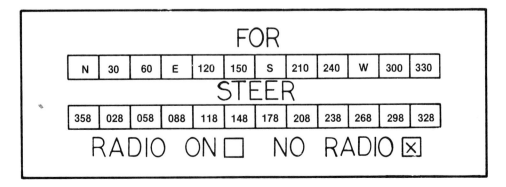

Figure 2-14. Compass Correction Card

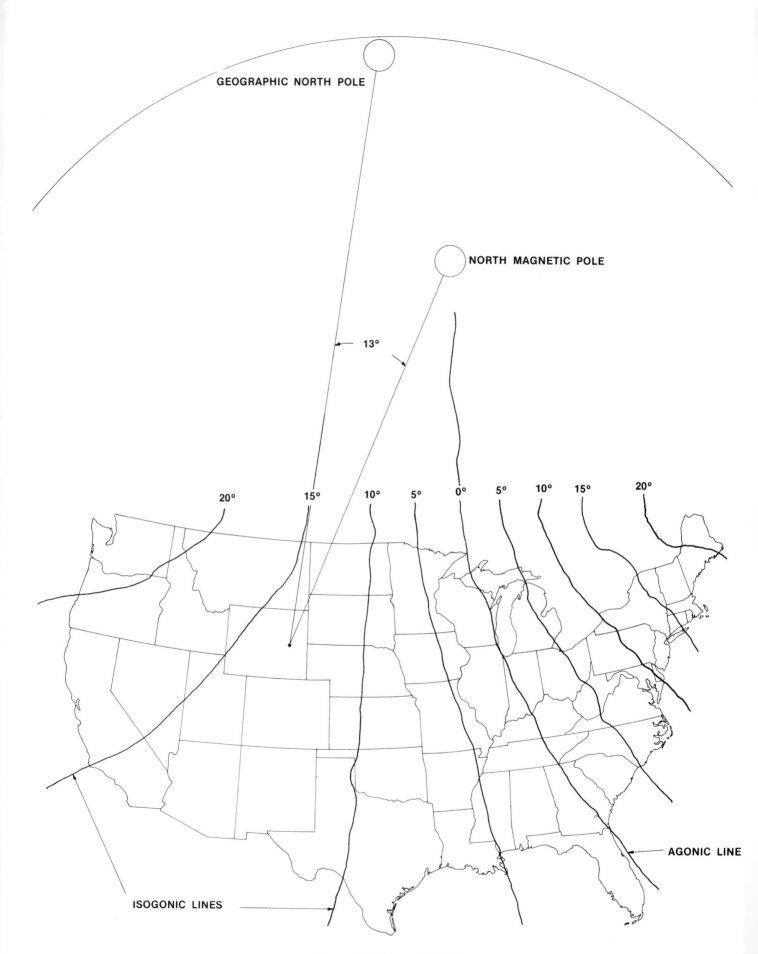

GEOGRAPHIC NORTH POLE

NORTH MAGNETIC POLE

13°

20° 15° 10° 5° 0° 5° 10° 15° 20°

AGONIC LINE

ISOGONIC LINES

Figure 2-15. Lines of Variation

Compass Construction

2.31 The magnetic compass is constructed with two magnetic bars mounted on a compass card. The compass card and the magnetized bars are attached to a float and balanced on a pivot point. (Figure 2-13) A compass case containing the whole float assembly is filled with a clear fluid which lubricates the pivot, relieves the weight on the bearings through buoyancy on the compass card, and dampens the oscillations. The compass card rotates on the pivot point and is free to tilt up to an angle of 18°. At the rear of the compass bowl, a diaphragm is installed to allow for any expansion or contraction of the liquid, thus preventing the formation of bubbles or possible bursting of the case. Compensation magnets are located on the top of the compass case to counteract deviations. These magnets can be adjustd by two sets of screws.

Reading the Compass

2.32 The compass card generally has letters indicating cardinal headings, and each 30° interval is labelled numerically. The compass card is further graduated into 5° and 10° increments.

Magnetic Compass Deviation Error

2.33 Magnetic disturbances within the aircraft cause deviation error. This accounts for the fact that compasses are calibrated with most of the electrical equipment operating, since this condition would promote maximum compass deviation. Deviation errors remaining after the compass has been calibrated are recorded on a compass correction card which is required to be inside all airplanes. (Figure 2-14) The addition or deletion of electrical equipment or the routine on/off operation can significantly influence compass deviation. Just for reference, on a smooth and level flight, a pilot should turn the pitot heat on and notice the heading change of the magnetic compass. The pitot heat and landing lights generally change the compass indication a minimum of 5°

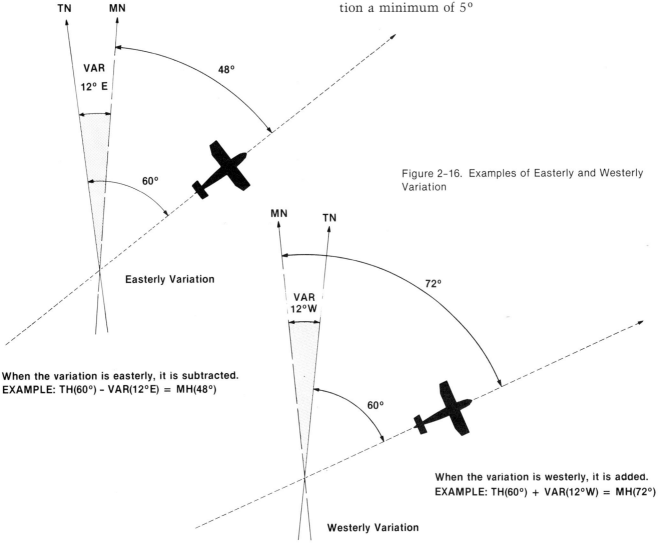

Figure 2-16. Examples of Easterly and Westerly Variation

When the variation is easterly, it is subtracted.
EXAMPLE: TH(60°) - VAR(12°E) = MH(48°)

When the variation is westerly, it is added.
EXAMPLE: TH(60°) + VAR(12°W) = MH(72°)

Magnetic Dip

2.34 Dip error results from the tendency of the magnetic compass to point down as well as north at any northern latitude. Magnetic dip error is the cause of acceleration and deceleration errors as well as northerly and southerly turning errors. This downward component of the earth's magnetic field (which produces magnetic dip) is the greatest at the magnetic north pole and is not prevalent at the equator. The amount of magnetic dip will increase with the degrees of latitude. (Figure 2-17) The compass card does not tilt or follow the vertical component of the earth's magnetic lines of force during straight and level, unaccelerated flight. Consequently, the compass portrays an accurate indication because the center of gravity is below the pivot point and the card is balanced in the fluid.

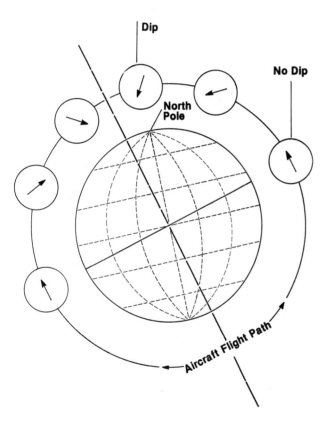

Figure 2-17. Magnetic Dip Increases with the Degrees of Latitude

Northerly Turn Error

2.35 The compass card banks with the aircraft as a result of centrifugal force. An erroneous turn is indicated by the compass when the compass card is in a banked attitude because the vertical component of the earth's magnetic field causes the north-seeking ends of the compass to dip to the low side of the turn. This error, called northerly turn error, is most prevalent on headings of south or north.

2.36 When instituting a turn (in the Northern Hemisphere) from the heading of north, the compass will initially indicate a turn in the opposite direction of the actual turn then lag behind the true rate of turn. Upon reaching a heading of east or west (assuming an aircraft is not accelerating or decelerating), the compass will register the correct heading. While continuing a turn toward a southerly heading, the compass indication will lead the actual magnetic heading of the aircraft. (Figure 2-18) The amount of the lead or the lag is approximately equal to the degrees of latitude at which the turn is being executed.

Compass Turns

2.37 A pilot will generally use a gyroscopic heading indicator for determining aircraft heading while executing a turn. Since this is not always possible, the magnetic compass becomes the alternate course of action. In order to initiate roll-out on the proper heading using the compass, a pilot must know how to apply the principles of northerly turn error. The following are examples of how northerly turn error can be applied as a factor in turning to an exact heading: (For the purpose of this discussion, it is assumed all turns are completed at bank angles of less than 18° to assure free rotation of the compass card, and that the necessary lead for roll-out for most aircraft is 5°.)

Example 1: For a left turn from south to north at 30° north latitude; with 15° angle of bank, roll-out should be initiated on a heading of 035°. (360° + 30° N latitude + 5° roll-out lead = 035°.) (Figure 2-19)

Example 2: For a left turn from north to south, at 45° north latitude; with a 15° angle of bank, roll-out should be initiated on a heading of 140°. (180° - 45° N latitude + 5° roll-out lead = 140°.)

2.38 *Rule of Thumb: North lags—South leads.*

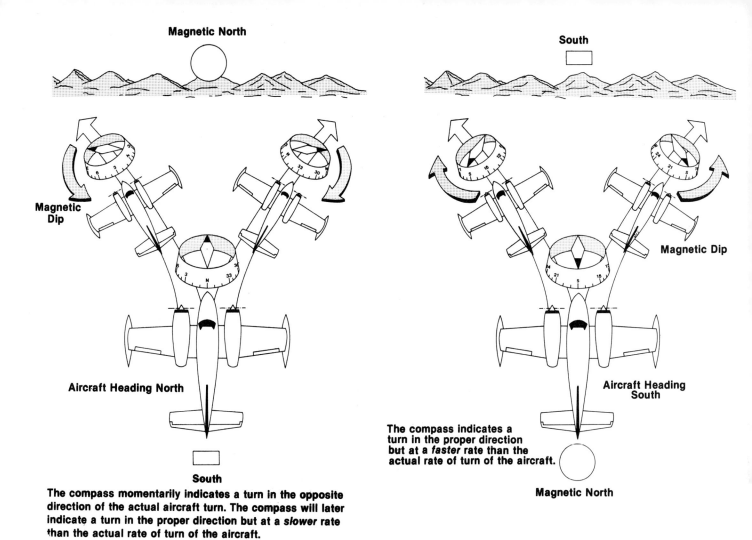

Magnetic North

South

Magnetic Dip

Magnetic Dip

Aircraft Heading North

Aircraft Heading South

The compass indicates a
turn in the proper direction
but at a *faster* rate than the
actual rate of turn of the aircraft.

Magnetic North

South

The compass momentarily indicates a turn in the opposite
direction of the actual aircraft turn. The compass will later
indicate a turn in the proper direction but at a *slower* rate
than the actual rate of turn of the aircraft.

Figure 2-18. Northerly Turning Error

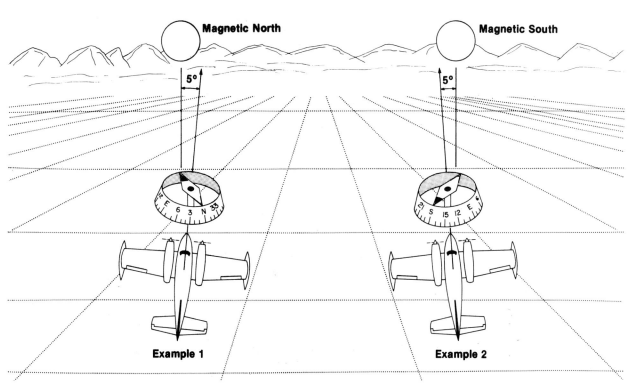

Magnetic North

Magnetic South

5°

5°

Example 1

Example 2

Figure 2-19. Roll-Out Lead—North Latitude

Acceleration Error

2.39 Acceleration error is the result of inertia, the vertical component of the earth's magnetic field, and the compass card's pendulous type mountings that tilt during speed changes. This error is most apparent on an easterly or westerly heading. When accelerating or climbing at a constant indicated airspeed on a heading of east or west, the indication that a compass will yield is a turn toward the north. When decelerating or descending at a constant indicated airspeed on an easterly or westerly heading, the compass will indicate a turn toward the south.

2.40 *Special Note: When climbing or descending at a constant airspeed, acceleration error is constantly present because the true airspeed is constantly changing.*

2.41 The word *ANDS* is a special memory aid that has assisted many pilots in remembering the relationship between direction of error and change in airspeed.

ANDS: Accelerate-North/Decelerate-South

Oscillation Error

2.42 Oscillation error (erratic oscillation of the compass card) is the result of turbulence and/or poor pilot technique. All of the previously mentioned errors also effect the magnetic compass during periods of oscillation error.

2.43 *Special Note: Reliable heading information from the compass can be taken only during smooth, straight, and level flight when the aircraft is not accelerating or decelerating.*

THE PITOT-STATIC SYSTEM

2.44 Every instrument pilot should have a thorough understanding of the instruments that function in response to pressure supplied by the pitot-static system. These instruments provide a lifeline through varied weather conditions and a safe return to the runway of the pilot's choice.

2.45 There are two instruments that derive their indications solely from static pressure: the vertical velocity indicator (also called vertical speed indicator) and the altimeter. The static system also supplies static pressure to the airspeed indicator. (Figure 2-20)

2.46 Static pressure is usually *sensed* through small holes known as static ports. These openings are often located flush with the fuselage in areas of minimum airstream disturbance. Static ports are generally connected by a "Y" assembly to prevent large pressure errors. (Figure 2-21)

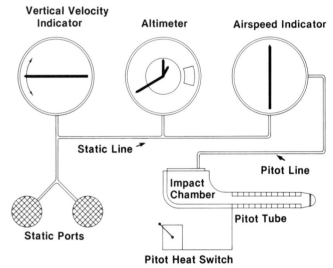

Figure 2-21. The "Y" Assembly Pitot-Static System

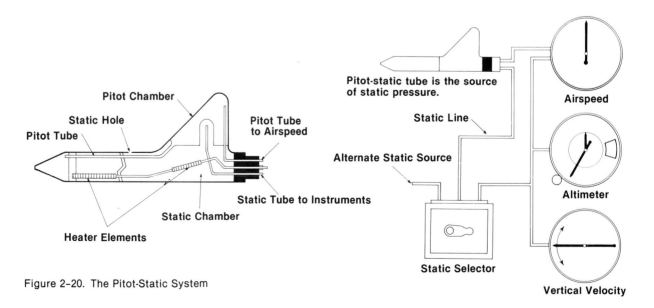

Figure 2-20. The Pitot-Static System

36

2.47 While some aircraft are equipped with a single static port, other aircraft may be equipped with dual static ports or even a combination static port-pitot tube. The one major drawback of having just one static port located on an aircraft is the fact that, whenever an aircraft is in uncoordinated flight, erroneous airspeed indications result.

2.48 Structural icing, under normal circumstances, will not block the static ports because of the static port locations. They may become blocked, however, by wax, water in the line, or ice splash during take-off roll. Many pilots have had the combination pitot-static system ice over as a result of structural icing. From this experience it can be learned that the small expense of an alternate static source is indeed worthwhile.

2.49 Should the static system become obstructed, many aircraft are equipped with an alternate static source normally located under the dash within reach of the pilot. If the alternate static source is switched to the "on" position, it will sense a lower ambient pressure, causing the altimeter and airspeed indicators to reflect slightly higher indications and the vertical velocity indicator to register a momentary climb. A lower cabin pressure in a nonpressurized aircraft is the result of the venturi effect of the aircraft cabin passing through the air.

2.50 *Special Note: Pilots of pressurized aircraft should become familiar with the location of the alternate static source. If the alternate static source is located in the pressurized cabin, the aircraft should be depressurized prior to activation of the alternate static source.*

2.51 Should an aircraft not equipped with an alternate static source experience an emergency where another static source is needed, the following procedure is recommended: Select the least important instrument (generally the vertical velocity indicator), then carefully break the glass trying to preserve the use of the instrument. Since the instrument case is connected to the static line, the three instruments that are connected to the static system will once again function. As mentioned previously, the airspeed indicator and altimeter will indicate higher readings. If the vertical velocity indicator is used as an alternate static source, the air entering the vertical velocity indicator case will pass through the calibrated leak into the static lines. This calibrated leak in the vertical velocity indicator will cause the airspeed indicator and the altimeter to lag and the vertical velocity indicator to register reverse indications.

2.52 The airspeed indicator is the only instrument that derives impact air pressure from the pitot tube. The pitot tube is usually located in an area of minimum air disturbance and parallel to the longitudinal axis of the aircraft. An electric heat element is located in most pitot heads to prevent the formation of ice. The pitot heat should be activated *prior to* flying into icing conditions or through visible moisture. All preflight checks should include a check of the pitot heat by turning the pitot heat switch to the "on" position and feeling the pitot tube.

2.53 If the pitot tube should become blocked, the result would be an inaccurate airspeed indicator. To overcome this potential problem, every pilot's checkout of an instrument aircraft should include special emphasis on power settings and pitch indications.

Airspeed Indicator

2.54 The airspeed indicator displays the differential in pressures of the impact (ram pressure from the pitot tube) and static pressures (atmospheric pressure from the static ports). (Refer to Figure 2-22.) The indicator case is sealed and connected to the static line. A diaphragm inside the case is connected to an impact pitot pressure line. During flight the aircraft accelerates or decelerates causing an expansion or contraction of the diaphragm. Through a mechanical linkage the expansion or contraction of the diaphragm is reflected as an airspeed change.

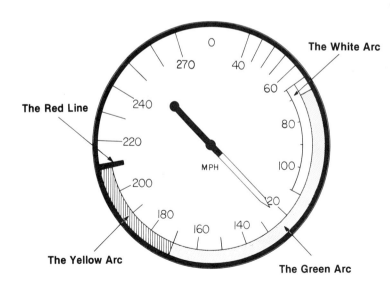

Figure 2-22. The Airspeed Indicator

Airspeed Indicator Error

2.55 Position error is essentially the difference between actual static pressure and "sensed" static pressure. The flow of the slipstream agitates the air at the static ports, thereby preventing actual pressure measurement. Each aircraft manufacturer must design the static error to be at a minimum when the aircraft is operated through a wide range of angles of attack. This is sometimes accomplished by equipping the aircraft with more than one static source.

2.56 Compressibility errors are caused by the compression of air into the pitot tube at high airspeeds which produces higher than typical readings. This error is negligible at airspeeds below 200 miles per hour and at pressure altitudes less than 10,000 feet.

2.57 Density error is promoted by variances in temperature for which the instrument is unable to compensate. (The standard airspeed indicator's design is based on standard sea level atmospheric conditions.)

Airspeed Definitions

2.58 The following symbols are used to designate some of the operating speeds:

V	=	Velocity.
V_{ne}	=	Never exceed speed (red line).
V_{so}	=	Power-off stalling speed with gear and flaps in landing position (lower limit of the white arc).
V_{s1}	=	Power-off stalling speed with gear and flaps retracted (lower limit of the green arc).
V_{mo}	=	Maximum operating limit speed (upper limit of the green arc).
V_{FE}	=	Maximum flaps extended speed (upper limit of the white arc).
V_y	=	Best rate of climb speed with one engine inoperative. Multiengine aircraft only. (Blue line)
V_{mc}	=	Minimum controllable airspeed with the critical engine inoperative. Multiengine aircraft only. (Lower red line)

2.59 Additional V speeds that are not marked on the airspeed indicator include:

V_a	=	Maneuvering speed.
V_x	=	Best angle of climb.
V_{le}	=	Maximum landing gear extension speed.
V_y	=	Best rate of climb. Single-engine aircraft only.
V_{lo}	=	Maximum landing gear operating speed.

2.60 The principle types of airspeeds that most general aviation pilots are concerned with are defined as follows:

Indicated airspeed (IAS)—Airspeed displayed by the airspeed indicator. Uncorrected for airspeed system errors.

Calibrated airspeed (CAS)—Indicated airspeed corrected for instrument error and installation error in the pitot-static system. (Calibrated airspeed is equal to true airspeed in standard atmosphere at sea level.)

True airspeed (TAS)—Airspeed of an aircraft relative to undisturbed air, determined by calibrated airspeed corrected for density error.

2.61 *Rule of Thumb: An approximate TAS can be calculated without the use of the flight computer by adding 2 percent of the IAS to the IAS for each 1,000 feet of altitude above sea level.*

Example: Assume a pilot is flying at an altitude of 10,000 feet MSL at an indicated airspeed of 120 knots. 10 (thousands of feet) x .02 x 120 (units of airspeed) = 24 (units of airspeed).

120 knots + 24 knots = 144 knots (TAS).

The Airspeed Indicator Operating Ranges

2.62 All airspeed indicators depict color-coded operating ranges and limits in *calibrated airspeed.* (Figure G-1 in the Appendix.) When reading the airspeed indicator, note that the pointer denotes indicated airspeed.

White arc—Displays the flap operating range. The lower limit of the white arc indicates the power-off stalling speed at maximum gross weight with flaps and gear fully extended and the cowl flaps closed. The upper limits of the white arc indicate the maximum calibrated airspeed that the aircraft can be flown with flaps fully extended.

Green arc—Represents the normal operating range. The lower limits of the green arc indicate the power-off stalling speed at maximum gross weight with gear and flaps retracted.

Yellow arc—Depicts the caution range. Flight in this range of airspeed should be avoided except in smooth air.

2.63 Maneuvering speed (V_a) is the maximum speed at which full abrupt deflection of the aircraft controls can be exerted without exceeding the structural limits of the aircraft. This speed is listed in the owner's handbook, or it can be roughly computed by multiplying the power-off stall speed with the flap and gear retracted (V_{s1}) by 1.7.

Changes in Indicated Airspeed

2.64 The standard airspeed indicator is not always an accurate instrument for measuring airspeed. The primary limitations of the instrument are due to the fact that the design and operation are premised upon atmospheric conditions that seldom exist. Humidity and temperature are two constantly changing factors that influence air density. Humid air is less dense than dry air since the water vapor molecule is less dense than the normal air molecule. Cold air has more molecules per cubic inch than warm air; therefore, cold air is more dense. During flight into dry, cold air, there are more air molecules per cubic inch forced into the pitot tube than in a warmer, moist environment. This results in a greater pressure differential between ram air in the pitot tube and outside air pressure in the static port; thus, a higher indicated airspeed results.

The Vertical Velocity Indicator

2.65 The vertical velocity indicator, also called the vertical speed indicator or rate of climb indicator, is used to reflect the rate of change in aircraft altitude. (Figure 2-23) This valuable information is most often used for maintaining specific rates of climb or descent during the course of normal instrument flight.

2.66 The vertical velocity indicator is enclosed within a sealed case and connected to the static source through a calibrated leak. A diaphragm within the case is connected directly to the static source. Changing pressures contract or expand the diaphragm which is connected to an indicating needle through the use of gears and levers. When the pressure in the vertical velocity indicator case is equal to the pressure in the diaphragm (during level flight), the vertical velocity needle will indicate zero. During an entry into a climb or descent, the static pressure in the diaphragm changes and the needle immediately reflects a change of vertical direction. However, it is possible to encounter situations that could promote a delay of as much as nine seconds before a reliable rate of climb or descent is indicated; this is due to a lag of air pressure stabilizing in the instrument case through the calibrated leak. The vertical velocity indicator, unlike the altimeter, measures the rate of change of pressure rather than the pressure itself. The magnitude of deflection is proportionate to the magnitude of rate of change of pressure. The vertical velocity indicator is somewhat limited in use due to the calibrated leak. Erroneous indicator indications sometimes evolve from abrupt changes in aircraft attitude since air over the static ports becomes unstable. This instrument is subject to reversal error during these abrupt pitch changes.

The Pressure Altimeter

2.67 The altimeter measures the height of an aircraft above a given reference plane. The earth's atmosphere exerts a pressure due to the weight of the atmosphere and, naturally, atmospheric pressure decreases at a predictable rate with an increase in altitude. (Figure 2-24) The altimeter case is connected to a static source. Inside the case a series of aneroid wafers are connected mechanically to the altimeter pointer which displays changes in altitude as the static pressure changes.

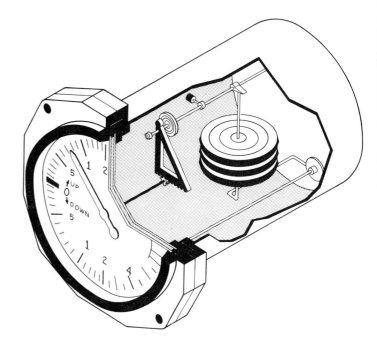

Figure 2-23. The Vertical Velocity Indicator

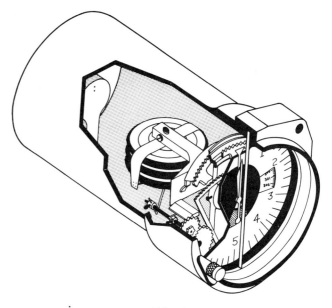

Figure 2-24. The Pressure Altimeter

Reading the Altimeter

2.68 In the example shown (Figure 2-25), a pilot should first read the innermost triangular tipped pointer (Hand A) which indicates increments of 10,000 feet. In this example the altitude can be determined by the 10,000-foot pointer to be midway between 10,000 and 20,000 feet or approximately 15,000 feet. Hand B is commonly called the 1,000-foot hand. In this example the 1,000-foot hand reads midway between 4,000 and 5,000 feet. It can now be deduced that the indicated altitude is between 14,000 and 15,000 feet. The final step in determining the exact altitude is the determination of the altitude by the hand commonly called the 100-foot hand (Hand C). Hand C indicates 560 feet. The summation of the three hands yields 14,560 feet.

Figure 2-25. An Altimeter Reading 14,560 Feet Indicated Altitude

2.69 *Special Note: A surprising number of instrument test applicants incorrectly respond to test questions relating to altimeter indications. The reason? The average applicant has no set procedure for reading the altimeter. Review the previous example closely. Over 90 percent of the applicants that incorrectly answer this type of question "thought" that they could correctly read an altimeter.*

Altimeter Accuracy

2.70 The altimeter must be checked for accuracy before each flight. To determine if the altimeter is accurate, a pilot should set the currently reported local altimeter setting in the Kollsman window. The variance in feet between field elevation and the altimeter reading should then be noted. A second method of determining altimeter accuracy is setting the field elevation under the altimeter pointers, then comparing the difference between the currently reported altimeter pressure setting and the actual altimeter pressure setting. The altimeter should be checked and recalibrated before flying by reference to instruments, if the error is greater than 75 feet.

2.71 Although the altimeter is manufactured within closely prescribed tolerances, the following errors will affect its indications:

Mechanical error—The result of misalignment or slippage of gears and levers which transmit aneroid expansion and contractions to the pointers.

Scale error—Caused by the aneroid wafers not conforming to design specifications for a particular differential in pressure. This error is inconsistent throughout the instrument range. For example, an instrument could read 30 feet low at 1,000 feet, yet it could read 30 feet high at 3,000 feet.

Reversal error—Occurs during abrupt pitch changes which create disturbed airflow around the static ports. This nonuniform airflow around the static ports causes erratic movement of the altimeter pointers.

Hysteresis error—The lag in altitude indications caused by the elastic properties of the materials used in the aneroid wafers. (Whenever a substantially rapid altitude change is initiated, it takes a short time for the aneroid wafers to adjust to the new pressure level.)

2.72 Since the reporting station pressure readings are constantly changing, a pilot should reset the altimeter often. This is accomplished with the altimeter setting dial, commonly known as the Kollsman window.

2.73 *Rules of Thumb:*

1. *The pressure level will change approximately one inch of mercury for every 1,000 feet of altitude change.*

2. *When the altimeter setting is increased, the altimeter pointers will reflect a proportionate increase in altitude.*

Example: With a 29.92 altimeter setting at sea level, the altitude pointer will indicate 0 feet on a standard day. If the setting is increased to 30.22, the pointer will indicate 300 feet.

Types of Altitudes

2.74 Pilots should be familiar with the following types of altitudes:

Altitude—Elevation with respect to any assumed reference level.

Absolute altitude—The actual altitude between the terrain and the aircraft. (Figure 2-26)

Pressure altitude—The indicated altitude when 29.92 inches of mercury is set in the Kollsman window of the altimeter. (Figure 2-26)

Indicated altitude—The altitude registered on the altimeter scale.

Calibrated altitude—Indicated altitude corrected for installation error.

True altitude—The true height above sea level; it is the calibrated altitude adjusted for nonstandard atmospheric conditions. (Figure 2-26)

Flight level—A level of constant atmospheric pressure related to a reference datum of 29.92 inches of mercury expressed in 100s of feet. In other words, a calibrated altitude referenced with 29.92 inches of mercury in the Kollsman window of the altimeter. Flight levels begin at 18,000 feet in the United States. (*Example:* 18,000 feet equals Flight Level [FL] 180.)

Density altitude—The altitude in the standard atmosphere at which the air has the same density as the air at the location in question. Density altitude is not considered a height reference; rather it is used as an index to aircraft performance. High density altitude reduces aircraft performance while low density altitude contributes to aircraft performance. (*Example:* At an airport at 3,000 feet MSL with a density altitude of 6,000 feet, an aircraft will perform as though it is at an altitude of 6,000 feet in the standard atmosphere.) Density altitude is determined by adjusting pressure altitude for nonstandard temperature variation (as discussed in paragraph 5.27).

2.75 Even if a pilot maintains the closest reported station altimeter setting, this does not necessarily compensate for nonstandard conditions aloft. The temperature difference when flying from a warm air mass to a cold air mass contributes to altimeter error, thereby decreasing the true altitude.

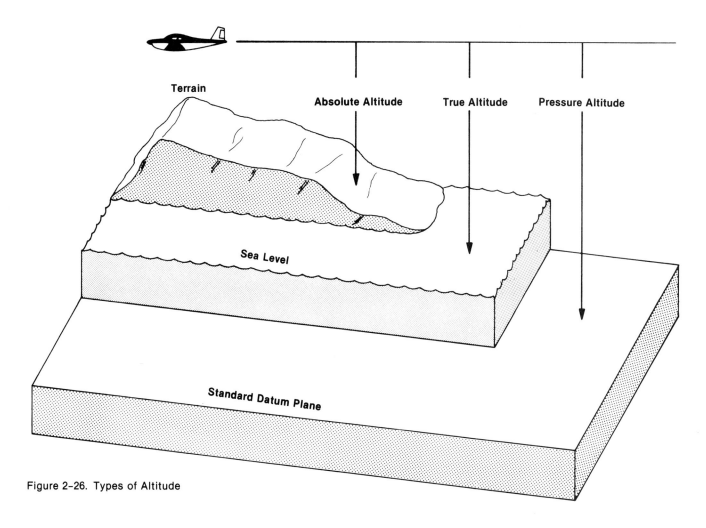

Figure 2-26. Types of Altitude

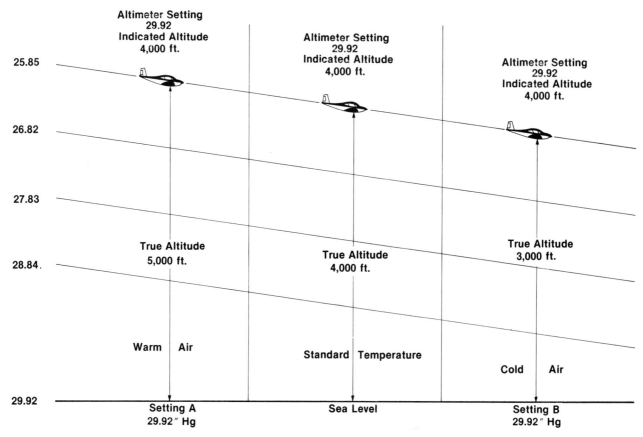

Figure 2-27. When Flying Into Cold Air True Altitude Decreases

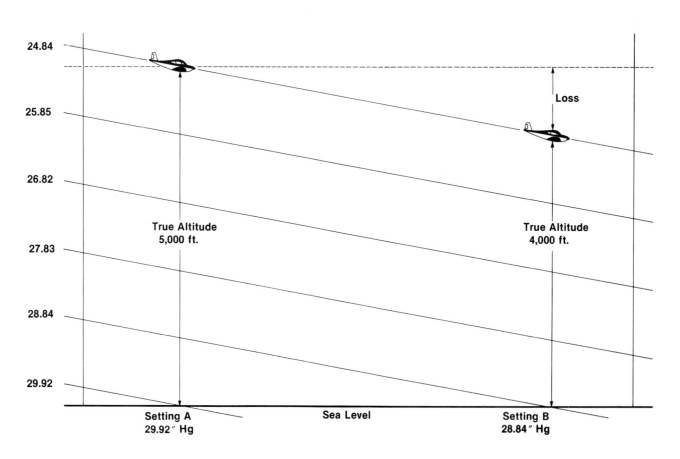

Figure 2-28. When Flying Into Low Pressure True Altitude Decreases

(Figure 2-27) Cold air is heavier in weight than warm air of the same volume. Since air contracts when the temperature decreases, the pressure level where the altimeter would indicate 4,000 feet is lower than it would be under standard conditions. The aircraft in Figure 2-27 is flying from the setting A area to the setting B area. It has an altimeter setting of 29.92 inches of mercury with a constant *indicated altitude* of 4,000 feet. The true altitude has decreased, however. It is easy to conclude that when flying from a warm air mass to a cold air mass with a constant altimeter setting, the true altitude will decrease. The converse is also true. When flying from cold to warm, the true altitude increases.

2.76 True altitude also decreases when flying a constant indicated altitude from an area of high pressure to an area of low pressure. (Figure 2-28) Essentially, an aircraft is following sloping constant pressure lines and, consequently, the aircraft will be lower than its altimeter indicates. The converse is true when flying from a low pressure area to a high pressure area.

2.77 *Rule of Thumb: "When flying from hot to cold or high to low, look out below."* (When flying from a high pressure area to a low pressure area or a warm air mass to a cold air mass, an aircraft's actual *altitude will be lower than the indicated altitude. The converse is also true when flying from cold to hot or low to high.)*

PRIMARY AND SUPPORTING INSTRUMENTS

2.78 Attitude instrument flying is achieved through the control of aircraft spatial position by the use of aircraft instruments. These instruments may be grouped as they relate to control function and aircraft performance, as follows:

Power Instruments—Manifold pressure gauge (MP); tachometer (RPM); airspeed indicator.

Bank Instruments—Attitude indicator; turn and slip indicator; heading indicator.

Pitch Instruments—Altimeter; airspeed indicator; attitude indicator; vertical speed indicator.

2.79 The power, bank, and pitch control requirements for any instrument flight maneuver are most clearly indicated by specific instruments. The instruments which provide the most essential and pertinent information are called *primary instruments*. The other instruments which supplement the information registered on the primary instruments are called *supporting instruments*. The idea of primary and supporting instruments does not lessen the value of any particular flight instru-

Flight Situation	Primary Pitch Instrument	Primary Bank Instrument	Primary Power Instrument
Straight and Level	Altimeter	Heading Indicator	Airspeed Indicator
Climb/Descent Entry (Constant Airspeed and Constant Heading)	1 Attitude Indicator (To Establish Initial Climb/Descent Attitude)* 2 Airspeed Indicator (After Airspeed Stabilizes on a Constant Value)**	Heading Indicator	Manifold Pressure Gauge or Tachometer - If Propeller is Fixed Pitch
Level-off From Climb/Descent (Constant Airspeed and Constant Heading)	Altimeter (As Level-off is Started)	Heading Indicator	Airspeed Indicator
Level Turn	Altimeter	1 Attitude Indicator (As Turn is Established)* 2 Turn Indicator (After Desired Angle of Bank is Attained)**	Airspeed Indicator
Climbing/Descending Turns	Airspeed Indicator (After Climbing/Descending Airspeed is Attained)	Turn Indicator (After Desired Angle of Bank is Attained)	Manifold Pressure Gauge or Tachometer - If Propeller is Fixed Pitch
Climbs/Descents (Constant Rate and Constant Heading)	1 Airspeed Indicator (Until Vertical Speed Indicator Reaches Desired Rate of Climb* 2 Vertical Speed Indicator (After Desired Rate of Climb is Reached)**	Heading Indicator	Airspeed Indicator

* *Initial Primary Instrument* as *Maneuver is Initiated*
** *Primary Instrument* After *Maneuver is Initiated*
NOTE: This Table is based on general instrument use of sub-sonic fixed-wing aircraft.

Figure 2-29. Some Examples of Primary Instruments During Different Flight Situations

ment, however. For example, the attitude indicator is the basic attitude reference and should always be used, when available, to establish and maintain pitch and bank attitudes. The table in Figure 2-29 exemplifies the use of primary instruments.

UNUSUAL ATTITUDES

2.80 A pilot can normally reestablish an aircraft to straight and level flight through the use of the attitude indicator. Yet, in an extreme unusual attitude, the attitude indicator may not indicate the true pitch attitude because the gyro limits may have been exceeded and, consequently, the gyro may have tumbled. An attitude indicator is also difficult to interpret while an aircraft is in an extreme attitude. For these reasons, the airspeed indicator and altimeter should be used to detect a nose-low or nose-high situation. The turn and slip indicator should be used as a primary instrument to return the aircraft to level flight, and the vertical velocity indicator should be used to note the magnitude of the rate of ascent or descent.

2.81 After initiating recovery from an unusual attitude, level pitch attitude is reached when the vertical velocity needle reverses its trend and the hands of the airspeed indicator and altimeter stop moving. Since the vertical velocity indicator registers the greatest change in indication in comparison to the other instruments influenced by static pressure, the vertical velocity indicator should be used to determine when an aircraft is in a level attitude.

CHAPTER 2: QUESTIONS

For answers see Appendix E

1. If a pilot should find his aircraft in an extreme nose-low unusual attitude, which of the following procedures should be employed to recover?

  1. Level the wings with the aid of the attitude indicator, then increase the pitch using the vertical velocity indicator.
  2. Level the wings with the aid of the turn and slip indicator, then increase the pitch until a level pitch attitude has been attained using the airspeed indicator, vertical velocity indicator, and the altimeter.
  3. Reduce the pitch attitude and level the wings with the aid of the attitude indicator.
  4. Increase the pitch attitude to level with the aid of the vertical velocity indicator, and level the wings with the aid of the turn and slip indicator.

2. When recovering from unusual attitudes without an operational attitude indicator, level flight is reached when:

  1. The hand of the vertical velocity indicator passes zero.
  2. The hands of the vertical velocity indicator and altimeter stop moving.
  3. The vertical velocity indicator, airspeed indicator, and altimeter needles reverse their trend.
  4. The hands of the altimeter and airspeed indicator stop moving, and the vertical velocity indicator needle reverses its trend.

3. The lower limit of the white arc on the airspeed indicator denotes the airplane's:

  1. Power-off stalling speed with flaps extended.
  2. Stalling speed at full power with flaps retracted.
  3. Power-off stalling speed with flaps retracted.
  4. Power-off stalling speed in a 60° bank.

4. Which of the following statements are *generally* true for light aircraft?

  1. A two-minute turn indicator is electric.
  2. A two-minute turn indicator and heading indicator are electric.
  3. The attitude indicator and two-minute turn indicator are vacuum-driven instruments.
  4. Heading indicator and attitude indicator are electric instruments.

5. Which turn coordinator(s) (below) indicates (indicate) a 3° per second turn?

  1. B only.
  2. B, C, and D.
  3. A and C.
  4. A, B, C, and D.

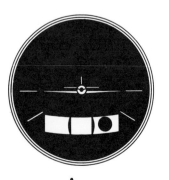
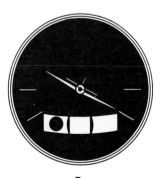

A   B   C   D

6. From the indication of the turn coordinator (above) it can be determined that the aircraft is:

1. Slipping to the right.
2. In straight and level flight.
3. Skidding with wings level.
4. Not turning but has the left wing down.

7. How would low vacuum pressure or clogged filters affect the visual indication of an attitude indicator?

1. The horizontal bar would tilt either to the left or right.
2. There would be no effect.
3. There would be a sluggish or delayed indication.
4. The miniature aircraft would not be lined up with the horizontal bar.

8. Pressure altitude can be determined while in flight by:

1. Adding 2 percent per thousand feet of altitude to the indicated altitude.
2. Setting 29.92 in the Kollsman window of the altimeter and reading pressure altitude directly from the altimeter.
3. Setting 29.92 in the Kollsman window and correcting for temperature.
4. Using the altitude correction card.

9. Airspeed indicator density error can be compensated for during flight:

1. By using the airspeed correction card.
2. By using the rule of thumb of adding 2 percent per thousand feet of altitude to the indicated altitude or by using the navigation computer to obtain TAS.
3. By adding ten knots for every 5° of temperature above standard temperature.
4. By readjusting the pitot tube.

10. What indication will a turn and slip indicator exhibit when an airplane is turning while taxiing?

1. The ball will move in the opposite direction of turn, and the needle will indicate a turn in the same direction as the turn.
2. The ball will move in the same direction of the turn, and the needle will indicate a turn in the same direction as the turn.
3. The ball will remain centered, but the needle will indicate a turn in the same direction as the turn.
4. The needle will remain centered, but the ball will move in the same direction as the turn.

11. Which instrument or instruments would be affected if an airplane were to take off with the pitot cover on the pitot tube? (Assume the airplane is equipped with side mounted static ports.)

1. The vertical velocity indicator, altimeter, and airspeed indicator.
2. The altimeter only.
3. The airspeed indicator only.
4. The altimeter and the vertical velocity indicator.

12. If a northbound airplane were to make a 360° turn at a constant altitude, airspeed and 15° bank, the magnetic compass would be most accurate at:

1. 0° and 180°.
2. 045°, 135°, 225°, and 315°.
3. 035°, 145°, 215°, and 325°.
4. 090° and 270°.

13. Which of the following indications, prior to an instrument departure, would indicate that the attitude indicator is unreliable?

A. The miniature aircraft is not lined up with the horizontal bar.
B. The horizontal bar does not maintain the horizontal position.
C. The horizontal bar tilts more than 5°.
D. The miniature aircraft remains fixed during a turn.
E. The horizontal bar continues to vibrate after a five-minute warm-up period.

1. B, C, and E.
2. A, B, and C.
3. A, C, and D.
4. B, D, and E.

14. Assume an airplane is making a normal, level turn in the Northern Hemisphere from a southerly heading. Which of the following statements is correct?

1. The compass card will turn at the same rate as the aircraft.
2. The compass card's rate of turn will lag behind the aircraft's rate of turn.
3. The compass card will turn in the same direction, but will lead the actual magnetic heading of the aircraft.
4. The compass card will turn in the same direction, but will lag the aircraft's heading.

15. If an airplane flies into an area of higher temperature and pressure than that of the area from which the airplane came, the true altitude will: (Assume that the pilot is attempting to fly at a constant altitude without resetting the altimeter setting.)

1. Increase.
2. Remain the same, but density altitude will decrease.
3. Decrease.
4. Remain the same, but the pressure altitude will decrease.

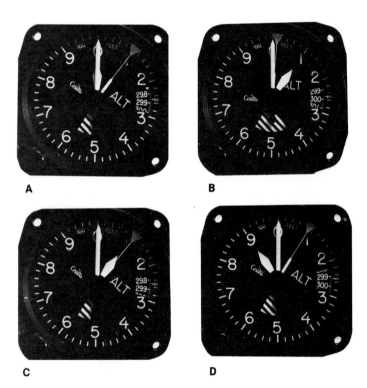

A   B

C   D

16. Which altimeter (above) indicates 10,000 feet?

1. A.
2. B.
3. C.
4. D.

17. Assume an airplane is accelerating and turning from a northerly heading at the equator. What errors are present when using the magnetic compass?

1. No error.
2. Northerly turn error.
3. Acceleration error.
4. Northerly turn error and acceleration error.

18. What compass error(s) is(are) present when an airplane is climbing at a *constant* airspeed on a magnetic heading of 90° at 45° of latitude?

1. No error.
2. Acceleration error.
3. Northerly turn error.
4. Acceleration error and northerly turn error.

19. A pilot operating an airplane at 30° north latitude, turning from a magnetic heading of 270° to a magnetic heading of south, should initiate roll-out on a magnetic heading of:

1. 155°.
2. 145°.
3. 215°.
4. 205°.

20. A pilot flying a magnetic heading of 090° at 40° north latitude decreases the aircraft's indicated airspeed 20 knots. What magnetic compass indication could the pilot expect?

1. The compass will indicate a turn to the north.
2. The compass will remain on a heading of 090°.
3. The compass will indicate a turn to the south.
4. The compass heading will indicate 095°.

21. Which instruments should be used to determine pitch attitude information before initiating recovery from an unusual flight attitude? (Assume the attitude indicator has exceeded its limits.)

1. Airspeed indicator and rate of climb indicator to detect approaching V_{mo}.
2. Airspeed indicator and altimeter to detect a nose-low or nose-high situation.
3. Turn and slip indicator to detect a turning situation.
4. Rate of climb indicator and turn indicator to determine a level flight attitude.

22. The hand of the airspeed indicator registers:

1. Indicated airspeed.
2. True airspeed.
3. Calibrated airspeed.
4. Equivalent airspeed.

23. An altimeter should not be used for IFR flight if the ground-check error is greater than:

1. 75 feet.
2. 100 feet.
3. 50 feet.
4. 0 feet.

24. What type of air mass would contribute to the highest *indicated* airspeed when an aircraft is cruising at a constant true airspeed?

1. Warm and moist.
2. Cold and moist.
3. Warm and dry.
4. Cold and dry.

ICARUS I

POWER OFF STALLING SPEED (5000 LBS.)			
ANGLE OF BANK			
0°	30°	45°	60°
GEAR AND FLAPS DOWN			
81 KTS 93 MPH	90 KTS 104 MPH	100 KTS 115 MPH	120 KTS 138 MPH
GEAR AND FLAPS UP			
93 KTS 107 MPH	101 KTS 116 MPH	112 KTS 129 MPH	134 KTS 154 MPH

25. It can be determined from the power-off stall speed chart (above) that:

A. The green arc begins at 93 knots (CAS).
B. The white arc begins at 81 knots (CAS).
C. The yellow arc begins at 112 knots (CAS).
D. The green arc begins at 112 knots (IAS).
E. The white arc begins at 100 knots (IAS).

  1. A, B, and C.
  2. A and B.
  3. C.
  4. A, D, and E.

26. Which of the following is true when switching to an alternate static pressure system?

A. The vertical velocity indicator will indicate a momentary climb.
B. The vertical velocity indicator will indicate a momentary descent.
C. The airspeed indicator will register an increase in airspeed.
D. The airspeed indicator will register a decrease in airspeed.
E. The altimeter will reflect an increase in altitude.
F. The altimeter will reflect a decrease in altitude.

  1. B, C, and E.
  2. A, D, and F.
  3. B, C, and E.
  4. A, C, and E.

27. The altimeter setting for a pilot's destination airport is 30.15'' Hg. If the pilot's altimeter is set to 29.95'' Hg, what altitude will the altimeter indicate upon touchdown? (Assume that the field elevation of the destination airport is 1,200 feet MSL.)

  1. 1,200 feet.
  2. 1,400 feet.
  3. 1,180 feet.
  4. 1,000 feet.

28. Which of the following statements about the attitude indicator are correct?

A. Errors in both pitch and bank indications are usually at a maximum after 180° of turn.
B. When an aircraft rolls out after a 180° turn, the attitude indicator will reflect a slight climbing turn to the left.
C. An induced indication of a climb will be indicated on the attitude indicator during aircraft acceleration.
D. An induced indication of a climb will be indicated on the attitude indicator during aircraft deceleration.

  1. A, B, and C.
  2. A and C.
  3. A and D.
  4. B and D.

29. Which instruments are considered pitch instruments?

  1. Attitude indicator, altimeter, airspeed indicator, and vertical speed indicator.
  2. Attitude indicator, heading indicator, and turn and slip indicator.
  3. Airspeed indicator, altimeter, and manifold pressure gauge or tachometer.
  4. Attitude indicator, manifold pressure gauge, and vertical speed indicator.

30. Which instrument shows the most pertinent information for bank control in straight and level flight?

  1. Turn and slip indicator.
  2. Attitude indicator.
  3. Heading indicator.
  4. Magnetic compass.

3.

Weather

3.1 Thunderstorms, snow, rain, hail, and fog affect the lives of every person, but to the pilot weather is a major consideration. All pilots should be equipped with a practical understanding of those meteorological concepts pertinent to aviation. This chapter reviews, in two major sections, those weather considerations essential to the instrument pilot. The first section concerns meteorology, and the second section contains information on interpretation of National Weather Service observations and forecasts. Familiarity with the following definitions will be necessary during the course of the discussion of this chapter.

Adiabatic—The process by which fixed relationships are maintained during changes in temperature, volume, and pressure in a body of air without heat being added or removed from the body.

Condensation level—The height at which a rising parcel or layer of air would become saturated if lifted adiabatically.

Coriolis force—A deflective force resulting from the earth's rotation. It acts to the right of wind direction in the Northern Hemisphere and to the left of wind direction in the Southern Hemisphere.

Dew point (Dew point temperature)—The temperature to which air must be cooled, at a constant moisture content and constant pressure, in order for saturation to occur.

Frontogenesis—The initial formation of a front or frontal zone.

Frontolysis—The dissipation of a front.

Isobar—A line of equal or constant barometric pressure.

Isotherm—A line of equal or constant temperature.

Jet streams—A quasi-horizontal stream of winds, 50 knots or more, concentrated within a narrow band embedded in the westerlies in the high troposphere.

Lapse rate—The rate of decrease, with height, of an atmospheric variable; commonly refers to decrease of temperature with height.

Orographic—Of, pertaining to, or caused by mountains, as in orographic clouds, orographic lift, or orographic thunderstorms.

Precipitation—Denotes drizzle, rain, snow, ice pellets (sleet), hail, or ice crystals.

Sounding—In meteorology, an upper-air observation; a radiosonde equipment observation.

Stability—A state of the atmosphere in which the vertical distribution of temperature is such that a parcel of air will resist displacement from its initial level.

Sublimation—The process involving change of state directly from a solid to a vapor (or from a vapor to a solid) without transformation through a liquid state.

Temperature inversion—An increase in temperature with height; a reversal of the normal decrease with height in the troposphere.

Tropopause—A very thin layer of atmosphere located at the top of the troposphere.

Troposphere—The layer of atmosphere extending from the earth's surface to the base of the tropopause. The troposphere extends to an altitude of 10 to 20 kilometers.

Upslope wind—Air mass flowing upwards over the contour of rising terrain.

METEOROLOGY

3.2 Volumes of books have been written on seemingly countless subjects dealing with meteorology. This section, however, emphasizes the most important meteorological concerns relating to instrument flight operations.

Standard Atmospheric Conditions

3.3 Air pressure and temperature during a standard day at sea level are designated as 1,013.2 millibars (29.92 inches of mercury and 101.32 kilopascals) and 15°C (59°F). The formulas used to describe the relationship between Fahrenheit and Centigrade are: $C = 5/9 \times (F - 32°)$ and $F = (9/5 \times C) + 32°$. Standard temperature and pressure at sea level should be committed to memory, not only for examinations, but also for use in everyday flying.

3.4 The average temperature lapse rate (up to an altitude of approximately 35,000 feet) used by pilots to approximate standard temperatures at cruising altitude is 2°C (3.5°F) per 1,000 feet of altitude change. This relationship can be expressed by the formula:

$$[(2)(N)-15][-1] = T$$

N = Number of thousands of feet MSL.
T = Temperature in degrees Centigrade.
This relationship can be additionally expressed as follows:

1. Double the number of thousands of feet in altitude.
2. Subtract 15 from the product of Step 1.
3. Change the value of the sign in Step 2 to the opposite of the result. For example, if Step 2 result has a positive sign (+) change this to a negative sign (-); and if the Step 2 result is (-) change to (+).
4. The result is the approximate temperature in degrees Centigrade.

Example: Find the approximate standard temperature for 12,000 feet.

1. 12 x 2 = 24
2. 24 - 15 = +9
3. +9 is changed to a -9

The approximate standard temperature at 12,000 feet is -9°C.

3.5 As briefly discussed in paragraph 2.73, the approximate pressure lapse rate often used to approximate pressure levels is one inch of mercury per 1,000 feet of altitude change. This relationship is generally used only up to altitudes of approximately 14,000 feet, since the atmospheric pressure tendencies may, at upper altitudes, vary greatly with seasons of the year, geographic location, and weather systems.

Stability

3.6 The air stability of the earth's atmosphere is a vital indicator used by the weather forecaster to predict general weather conditions. Forecasters understand that a stable atmosphere resists any upward or downward air displacement. But an unstable atmosphere permits an upward or downward air disturbance to grow. Usually, air stability is not critical to an aviator, but it does help the pilot understand certain weather phenomena.

3.7 Weather forecasters compare the relative values of the dry adiabatic and the moist adiabatic lapse rates of a parcel of air to measure stability of air. If a parcel of air is lifted (for example, moved up a mountain slope), it will expand because pressure decreases with an increase in altitude. This parcel of air will also cool as it rises if no heat is added or removed from the air parcel (adiabatic conditions). The dry adiabatic lapse rate (for a parcel of dry air) is approximately 3°C (5.4°F) per 1,000 feet. The moist adiabatic lapse rate (for a parcel of moist air) can vary from 1.2°C to 2.8°C per 1,000 feet, depending primarily on the temperature and, to a lesser extent, atmospheric pressure. Air stability can range from stable to conditionally unstable to unstable, depending on the actual adiabatic lapse rate of the air.

3.8 Air stability is reflected by the vertical motion of air masses. Vertical motion of the atmosphere can be induced by:

1. Convergence (inflow of air mass into an area).
2. Mechanical convection (orographic or frontal lifting).
3. Thermal convection (heat added by the earth's surface).

When this vertical motion is used to lift a parcel of air, and if the parcel of air cools at a slower rate than the surrounding air, the parcel becomes warmer and lighter in comparison to the surrounding air. Because of this, the parcel of air is considered to be unstable since it will continue to rise.

3.9 Occasionally, a sounding slope (the actual lapse rate of the atmosphere) lies between the dry and saturated adiabat. This air is called conditionally unstable air because, if conditionally unstable air is lifted, it will be stable until it reaches the condensation level; then it will become unstable. If this parcel of conditionally unstable air is lifted above the condensation level a small distance, it will ascend freely. Conditionally unstable air can be forced aloft above the condensation level by upslope winds (orographic lifting), convective currents, or the lifting action of a front.

3.10 The atmosphere's stability can be a guide to the type of cloud that will form and the resulting turbulence. Generally, if warm, moist stable air were forced aloft (this lifting action could be an upslope wind, for example), layered or stratiform clouds with very little turbulence would result. However, if warm moist *unstable* air were forced aloft, the formation of vertical or cumuliform clouds with turbulence and good visibility would be promoted.

3.11 Stability of an air mass can be modified by the surface over which the air mass flows. For example, a cold air mass flowing over a warm surface would tend to become more unstable. Conversely, some specific situations that are conducive to air mass *stability* are:

1. A warm air mass flowing over a cold air mass, which results in a temperature inversion. (Consequently, temperature inversions can only occur in a stable air mass.)

2. Sinking air, in which the heat of compression frequently causes a temperature inversion.

3. Removal of water vapor from lower atmospheric levels.

Because the cold air becomes stable, there will be very little mixing between the layers, and any pollutants generated will remain in the lower colder level, causing poor visibility due to haze and smog.

Air Mass Circulation

3.12 Differences in temperature of the earth's atmosphere and surface promote areas of unequal pressure. The general circulation of an air mass, in turn, is determined from the pressure patterns which are identified by isobars. (Figure 3-1) These pressure patterns, then, outline areas of high pressure and low pressure. The movement of the air mass is caused by pressure differentials existing between different locations. Air tends to flow from areas of high pressure to areas of lower pressure. The greater the difference in pressure between the two areas (the greater the pressure gradient), the faster the air mass will move.

3.13 An indication of the pressure gradient force is the spacing of the isobars. The closer the isobars, the greater the pressure gradient force. Pressure gradient force is perpendicular to the isobars. Pilots should realize that wind velocity is greatest in areas where the isobars are closely spaced.

3.14 The wind does not, however, flow directly from a high to a low pressure area but, instead, the wind flows parallel to the isobars at altitudes above 2,000 feet AGL. This is due to Coriolis force deflect-

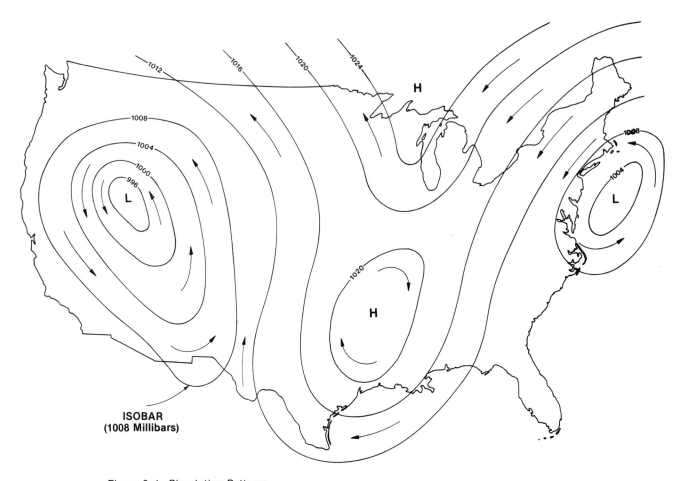

Figure 3-1. Circulation Patterns

ing air 90° to the right of the pressure gradient direction in the Northern Hemisphere and 90° to the left of the pressure gradient direction in the Southern Hemisphere. Coriolis force is also directly proportional to the wind speed. Therefore, as wind speed decreases, Coriolis force decreases. Figure 3-2 illustrates the relationship between Coriolis force, pressure gradient force, and resultant wind. Note that Coriolis force and pressure gradient force are in balance above 2,000 feet AGL.

3.15 In the Northern Hemisphere, the resultant wind flows clockwise around anticyclones (high pressure areas) and counterclockwise around cyclones (low pressure areas). (Figure 3-1) These cyclones and anticyclones tend to travel from west to east with the prevailing westerly winds.

3.16 Surface friction normally reduces the velocity of the resultant wind. (Figure 3-3) As a result, the Coriolis force, which is directly proportional to wind speed, decreases. But surface friction does not affect the pressure gradient force. The result is a pressure gradient force that is greater than Coriolis. Since the pressure gradient and Coriolis forces are no longer in balance, the greater pressure gradient force turns the wind toward the low pressure area. Once the wind flows across the isobars, the three forces will again be in balance. This left deflection of the wind crossing isobars varies from 10° over the ocean to 45° over rugged terrain. Surface friction force decreases rapidly with altitude and can be considered to be negligible at 2,000 feet AGL.

3.17 *Rule of Thumb: Due to surface friction, the velocity of the wind at the surface is usually less and deflected approximately 30° to the left of the wind aloft.*

Air Mass Characteristics

3.18 Air masses are classified according to their source regions. These regions are polar, tropic, maritime (moist air formed over water), and continental (dry air formed over land). These combinations of letters indicate source region, temperature, and moisture characteristics of each particular air mass:

Continental Polar (CP)—cold dry air
Continental Tropic (CT)—warm dry air
Maritime Polar (MP)—cold moist air
Maritime Tropic (MT)—warm moist air

Clouds

3.19 Clouds are divided into four categories. These categories are:

1. High clouds.
2. Middle clouds.
3. Low clouds.
4. Clouds with extensive vertical development.

The first three categories of clouds are further classified according to the way they are formed. Clouds formed by vertical currents in unstable air are cumulus, meaning accumulation or heap. These clouds are characterized by a lumpy, billowy appearance. Clouds formed by cooling a stable air mass are called stratus, meaning stratified or layered. These clouds are characterized by a uniform sheet-like appearance.

3.20 The prefix "nimbo-" and the suffix "-nimbus" mean raincloud. Accordingly, a stratified cloud from which rain is falling is called a nimbostratus cloud. Also, a heavy, swelling cumulus cloud which produces precipitation is called a cumulonimbus cloud. Streamers of precipitation

Figure 3-2. Pressure Gradient—Coriolis Force—Resultant Wind Relationship

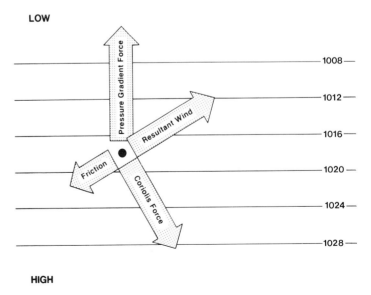

Figure 3-3. Pressure Gradient— Coriolis Force — Surface Friction — Resultant Wind Relationship

CLOUD TYPE	DESCRIPTION	AVERAGE CLOUD BASE HEIGHT	ASSOCIATED VISIBILITY: TURBULENCE AND ICING CONDITIONS	ASSOCIATED TYPE OF PRECIPITATION
STRATUS	A GRAY, UNIFORM, SHEET-LIKE CLOUD.	SURFACE TO 6,500 FEET.	SURFACE VISIBILITY - POOR. NO TURBULENCE. MODERATE ICING CAN EXIST AT TEMPERATURES NEAR OR BELOW FREEZING.	INTERMITTENT LIGHT DRIZZLE OR RAIN.
ALTOSTRATUS	A BLUISH VEIL OR LAYERED CLOUDS.	6,500 FEET TO 23,000 FEET.	SURFACE VISIBILITY - POOR. NO TURBULENCE. MODERATE ICING CAN EXIST.	CONTINUOUS LIGHT DRIZZLE OR SNOW.
NIMBOSTRATUS	A GRAY OR DARK MASSIVE CLOUD LAYER.	6,500 FEET TO 23,000 FEET.	RESTRICTED VISIBILITY DUE TO PRECIPITATION. NO TURBULENCE. MODERATE ICING CAN EXIST AT TEMPERATURES NEAR OR BELOW FREEZING.	CONTINUOUS DRIZZLE OR SNOW.
CUMULUS	A BRILLIANT WHITE CAULIFLOWER-SHAPED CLOUD.	1,000 FEET TO 10,000 FEET.	SURFACE VISIBILITY - GOOD. SOME TURBULENCE. NO SIGNIFICANT ICING.	SCATTERED SHOWERS - RAIN OR SNOW.
ALTOCUMULUS	COMPOSED OF WHITE OR GRAY COLORED LAYERS OR PATCHES OF SOLID CLOUDS.	6,500 FEET TO 23,000 FEET.	SURFACE VISIBILITY - GOOD. SOME TURBULENCE. SOME ICING (SMALL AMOUNTS).	SCATTERED SHOWERS - RAIN OR SNOW.
STRATOCUMULUS	CONSISTS OF NUMEROUS INDIVIDUALLY ROUNDED CLOUDLETS OR ROLLS.	SURFACE TO 6,500 FEET.	SURFACE VISIBILITY - GOOD. SOME TURBULENCE. POSSIBLE ICING AT SUBFREEZING TEMPERATURES.	LIGHT SHOWERS - RAIN OR SNOW.
CUMULONIMBUS	A MASSIVE VERTICAL CLOUD, WITH DOMES OR TOWERS, VERY DARK BLUE OR GRAY.	1,000 FEET TO 10,000 FEET.	SURFACE VISIBILITY - GOOD. VERY TURBULENT. POSSIBLE EXTREME ICING.	HEAVY SHOWERS - USUALLY RAIN.
CIRRUS	THIN, FEATHER-LIKE, ICE CRYSTAL CLOUDS IN PATCHES OR NARROW BANDS.	16,500 FEET TO 45,000 FEET.	NO TURBULENCE. NO ICING.	NONE.
CIRROSTRATUS	A THIN WHITISH CLOUD LAYER APPEARING LIKE A SHEET OR VEIL.	16,500 FEET TO 45,000 FEET.	NO TURBULANCE. LITTLE ICING.	NONE.
CIRROCUMULUS	THIN CLOUDS APPEARING AS SMALL WHITE FLAKES OR PATCHES OF COTTON.	16,500 FEET TO 45,000 FEET.	SOME TURBULENCE. SOME ICING.	NONE.

Figure 3-4. Table of Basic Cloud Types

trailing beneath clouds but evaporating before reaching the ground are called "virga." Figure 3-4 is a table of cloud descriptions, cloud bases, and associated weather.

3.21 A pilot can estimate the height of a cumuliform cloud base by first determining the surface temperature dew point spread. This cloud-base height can then be determined easily since the unsaturated air in a convective current cools at about 5.4°F (3.0°C) per 1,000 feet. However, the dew point temperature decreases at approximately 1°F (5/9°C) per 1,000 feet. Therefore, the convective current temperature and dew point temperature converge at approximately 4.4°F (2.5°C) per 1,000 feet.

3.22 To estimate the convective cloud-base layer in thousands of feet, the following formula can be used:

$$CB\ (MSL) = \frac{(ST - DP)}{CF} \times 1,000 + FE$$

CB = Cloud Base
ST = Surface Temperature
DP = Surface Dew Point Temperature
CF = Temperature Convergence Factor
FE = Field Elevation

The solution to cloud base height in thousands of feet can be additionally expressed as follows:

1. Divide 4.4 (for temperatures in F°) or 2.5 (for temperatures in C°), which are temperature convergence factors, into the surface temperature dew point spread.
2. Multiply the quotient by 1,000.
3. Add the product to the field elevation to obtain the altitude of the convective cloud base above sea level (MSL).

Example:

Field elevation	*1,200 feet MSL*
Dew point temperature	*36° F*
Surface temperature	*80° F*

1. $\dfrac{80 - 36}{4.4} \times 1,000 + 1,200 = CB$

2. $CB = 11,200$ *feet MSL*

Fronts

3.23 A front is a transition zone, or boundary, of discontinuity between two different air masses. The air mass properties meteorologists use to classify and locate a front are:
1. Temperature.
2. Dew point (moisture).
3. Wind.
4. Pressure.

3.24 *Rule of Thumb: Although wind direction and/or speed always changes across a front, a pilot, while flying, can generally most readily detect frontal passage by observing the air temperature and noting any temperature changes. When passing through any type of front in either direction, a pilot should always apply right wind drift correction to compensate for the change in direction of the wind.*

Cold Front

3.25 When advancing cold air replaces warm air at ground level, this line of discontinuity is known as a cold front. A typical cold front has a steep frontal slope due to surface friction. (Figure 3-5) Cold fronts move at approximately the speed of the wind component that is perpendicular to the front just above the frictional layer.

3.26 Clearing weather conditions are prevalent behind the narrow band of weather of the fast-moving cold front. Pilots should penetrate a cold front at right angles to minimize the time spent in crossing adverse weather.

3.27 A summary of flight conditions and weather conditions associated with the approach and passage of a normal cold front is tabulated below:
1. Flight conditions are usually turbulent in the frontal area.
2. Weather conditions include:
A. A narrow band of cumuliform clouds along the front.
B. Showery precipitation.
C. Generally high ceilings with good visibility.
D. Winds that are usually southerly, shifting to northwesterly with the passing of the front.
E. A decrease in temperature with frontal passage.
F. Falling pressure as the front approaches, followed by an abrupt rise in pressure after frontal passage.

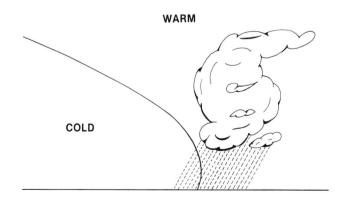

Figure 3-5. Cross Section of a Typical Cold Front

Warm Front

3.28 A warm front is the edge of an advancing warm air mass which is replacing a mass of cold air. Most warm fronts have a gentle frontal slope and a forward velocity that is about half the speed of a cold front, assuming the general wind flow is the same. (Figure 3-6) Generally, warm fronts cover an extensive area, and the associated weather will be long-lasting but not as intense as weather associated with a cold front.

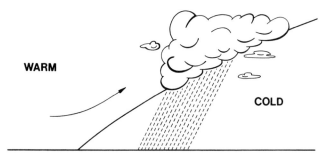

Figure 3-6. Cross Section of a Typical Warm Front

3.29 A summary of the flight conditions and weather conditions associated with the approach and passage of a normal warm front is tabulated below:

1. Flight conditions are usually smooth (except when cumuliform clouds are present).
2. Weather conditions include:
   A. An extensive area of stratiform clouds (occasionally cumuliform).
   B. A continuous band of precipitation along the front.
   C. Generally poor ceilings and visibilities due to low clouds and fog.
   D. Northeasterly movement.
   E. Winds from the southeast, usually shifting to the west, southwest.
   F. Increase in temperature after frontal passage.
   G. Falling pressure as the front approaches, followed by a pressure rise after frontal passage.

Stationary Front

3.30 A stationary front will usually have the same characteristics as a warm front. (Figure 3-7) When a front becomes stationary, the weather conditions occurring with it are usually less intense, but persist longer than those found with a cold or warm front.

Occluded Front

3.31 Occasionally, an air mass will overtake another air mass of different characteristics. When this occurs, an occluded front will be formed. Occluded fronts can be either cold front occlusions or

warm front occlusions. Figure 3-8 illustrates a cross section of an idealized cold front occlusion. In this example, the air in advance of the slow moving warm front was warmer than the air behind the faster moving cold front. Consequently, as the cold front overtook the warm front, the *cold* air moved under the *cool* air and lifted the warm front aloft, thereby forming a cold front occlusion. With a warm front occlusion, however, the air temperature conditions are reversed and the air in front of the warm front is colder than the air behind the cold front. Remembering the cold air is heavier than warm air, when the cold front (with the *cool* air behind it) overtakes the warm front (with the *colder* air in front of it), the warmer air (relative to the colder air ahead of the warm front) of the cold front actually slides over the top of the *colder* air ahead of the warm front. Subsequently, the cold front is forced aloft thus forming a warm front occlusion.

3.32 Pilots should realize that an occluded front is a combination of a cold front and a warm front. Hence, the weather encountered during flight through an occluded front may have the same adverse weather characteristics of BOTH the cold front and the warm front.

Thunderstorms

3.33 Thunderstorms should be regarded with caution and respect because they contain the most severe weather hazards. Pilots can expect heavy rain, strong gusts of wind, severe turbulence, hail, and lightning in the vicinity of thunderstorms.

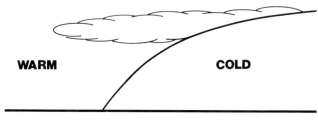

CROSS SECTION OF A TYPICAL STATIONARY FRONT
Figure 3-7.

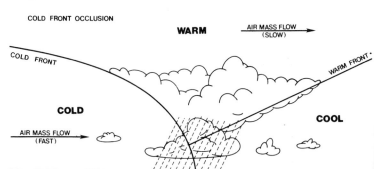

CROSS SECTION OF A TYPICAL OCCLUDED FRONT
Figure 3-8.

3.34 In order for a thunderstorm to form, these three basic conditions must be present in the atmosphere:

1. An unstable lapse rate (unstable air).
2. Some type of lifting action.
3. High moisture content.

When all three elements are present, the life cycle of a thunderstorm may begin. The three stages of a thunderstorm life cycle are the cumulus stage, mature stage, and dissipating stage. (Figure 3-9)

3.35 The cumulus stage is the initial, or growth, stage of a thunderstorm. Not all cumulus clouds will become thunderstorms, but the first phase of a thunderstorm is always a cumulus cloud. The main feature of the cumulus stage is the vertical building of the cumulus cloud into a cumulonimbus cloud. During this cumulus stage, the precipitation in the cloud is suspended by strong updrafts.

3.36 A thunderstorm is described as being in the mature stage when precipitation reaches the earth's surface. By this time, the precipitation particles have grown in size and increased in number, and can no longer be supported by the updrafts. As the precipitation falls, downdrafts are created from the friction produced by the falling particles. These downdrafts produce a strong horizontal outflow near the surface of the earth, accompanied by strong surface wind gusts and a sharp drop in temperature. All of the hazards associated with thunderstorms are of greatest intensity during the mature stage.

3.37 Downdrafts created by the falling precipitation characterize the dissipating stage. The dissipating stage of a thunderstorm is evident when precipitation decreases and the top of the storm cell develops the characteristic anvil shape. The anvil shape itself, however, *is not* an indication that the thunderstorm is dissipating, because a number of other individual thunderstorm cells may be growing. Pilots should be aware of the fact that a line of thunderstorms can consist of clusters of cells in all three stages of a life cycle.

3.38 Individual thunderstorms may range in size from less than 5 miles to more than 30 miles in diameter. Bases may vary from a few hundred feet above the ground in very moist climates to 10,000 feet or higher in drier climates. The cloud top height generally varies from 25,000 to 45,000 feet; however, tops can occasionally extend to heights above 65,000 feet.

3.39 Pilots can expect a rapid drop in pressure as a thunderstorm approaches. The pressure will rise abruptly upon the first wind gusts and initial rain showers. As a storm moves on, a gradual return to normal pressure can be expected.

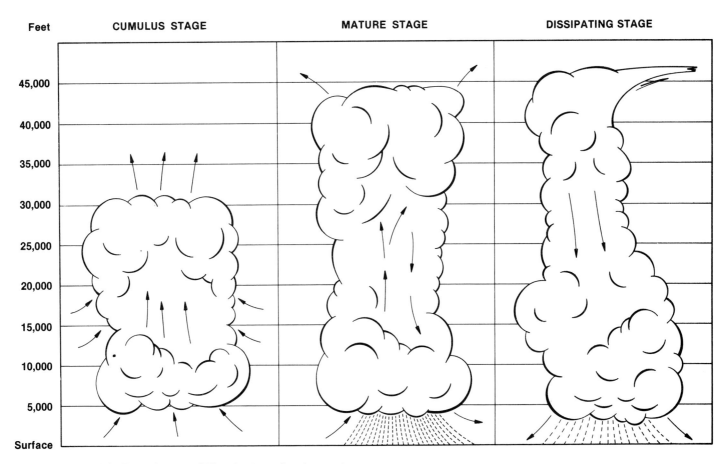

Figure 3-9. Three Stages of Thunderstorm Development

Lightning and Precipitation Static (Thunderstorm)

3.40 Lightning is a thunderstorm phenomenon that creates apprehension in many pilots. Lightning strikes on aircraft, however, are uncommon occurrences. A lightning strike on an aircraft can damage the communication and navigational equipment, but normally the occupants are protected in a metal aircraft fuselage. The probability of lightning striking an aircraft is greatest when the aircraft is operating at altitudes where temperatures are between -5°C and +5°C. Aircraft flying in clear weather in the vicinity of a thunderstorm can also be struck by lightning.

3.41 *Special Notes:*
1. Thunderstorms are always accompanied by lightning discharges.
2. A severe thunderstorm has more frequent lightning discharges.
3. A growing thunderstorm is indicated by an increased frequency of lightning discharges, and, conversely, a dissipating thunderstorm is indicated by a decreased frequency of lightning discharges.
4. The greatest lightning activity in a thunderstorm is followed by the greatest rainfall at the surface.
5. The most common hazard of lightning strikes on an airplane is the temporary blindness of the pilot.

3.42 Precipitation static is a high level of continuous noise in the aircraft radio receivers. This static is caused by intense constant corona discharges (static electricity) from sharp metallic edges of a flying aircraft. These corona discharges occur when an aircraft is flying in the vicinity of a thunderstorm or flying through ice, snow, rain, or dust particles. At night, this corona discharge is visible and is called "St. Elmo's Fire."

Types of Thunderstorms

3.43 One method by which thunderstorms are classified is according to their source of lift, which can be any of the following:
  1. Any type of front.
  2. Mountainous terrain.
  3. Convective currents.
  4. Convergence.
These latter three sources of lift may individually or collectively contribute to the formation of an air mass thunderstorm. Consequently, thunderstorms are generally identified as *frontal* or *air mass* thunderstorms.

Frontal Thunderstorms

3.44 Frontal thunderstorms are formed when an air mass is forced aloft by the upslope of a front. With its steep frontal slope, the cold front can produce some severe thunderstorms. A warm front, with its more gentle slope, will produce thunderstorms, but these storms are normally less intense. The most severe thunderstorms are usually associated with the occluded front because air, trapped between the two fronts, is being forced aloft. Pilots should be aware that thunderstorms associated with a warm front or occluded front may be embedded in stratiform clouds and may not be visible to the pilot.

Squall Line Thunderstorms

3.45 Squall line thunderstorms are similar to cold front thunderstorms, but are usually more severe. A squall line is any nonfrontal (generally continuous) line or narrow band of active thunderstorms. Usually, it develops from 50 to 300 miles ahead of and nearly parallel to a fast-moving cold front. Severe, steady state (continuous) thunderstorms are often contained in a squall line, which presents the single most intense weather hazard to aircraft. Some weather hazards associated with squall lines are hail, strong winds, severe turbulence, and tornadoes.

Air Mass Thunderstorms

3.46 Air mass thunderstorms are associated with a warm, moist air mass. These thunderstorms are generally isolated or scattered and may be classified as convective, orographic, or nocturnal. Since air mass thunderstorms are often scattered, they can usually be circumnavigated.

Convective Air Mass Thunderstorms

3.47 Convective air mass thunderstorms form over any type of land mass or water, almost anywhere. Solar heating warms areas of land which in turn radiate heat to the lower layers of the air. The warmed lower layers of air result in rising (convective) currents of air.

3.48 If cool, moist, unstable air passes over an area of land where heating from the surface promotes the formation of convective currents, it is quite likely that towering cumulus clouds will form and develop into a thunderstorm. The magnitude of thunderstorm intensity is dependent upon such factors as air mass moisture content and temperature variation between the air mass and land area. The land-type convective thunderstorms normally develop during afternoon hours and usually dissipate during the night or early morning hours after much of the heat received from the afternoon sun has been radiated into the atmosphere.

Orographic Air Mass Thunderstorms

3.49 Orographic thunderstorms are formed in mountainous regions where moist, unstable air flows up sloping terrain. It is common for the upslope motion to contribute to extensive areas of thunderstorm activity on the windward side of any mountainous area. These thunderstorms often form a long line similar to those associated with a cold front. Orographic thunderstorms persist until the upslope motion declines or the moisture level decreases.

Nocturnal Air Mass Thunderstorms

3.50 Nocturnal thunderstorms, as the name suggests, form during the evening and early morning hours. This type of thunderstorm is native to the Central Plains area during late spring and summer. Essentially these thunderstorms are activated when an unusually moist layer of air aloft is cooled (through radiation) to temperatures which cause the air to settle. The settling of the cooled air forces unstable surface air aloft, which triggers thunderstorm activity.

Piloting Procedures for Operations In and Near Thunderstorms

3.51 The following rules should be observed if flight through a thunderstorm is imminent:

1. Plan and maintain a course that will direct the aircraft through the storm in a minimum time.
2. Maintain a constant attitude. Maneuvering an aircraft in an attempt to maintain a constant altitude increases stresses on the aircraft.
3. Establish power settings which will produce the reduced turbulence penetration airspeed recommended in the aircraft flight manual. Reduced airspeed lessens the possibility of structural stresses on the aircraft.
4. Disengage the automatic pilot if it is being used. An operating automatic pilot will increase aircraft maneuvers, thus increasing the possibility of structural stresses.
5. To avoid the most critical icing, establish a penetration altitude below the freezing level or above the -15°C temperature level.
6. Activate both the pitot heat and carburetor heat. Icing can occur rapidly at any altitude and cause almost instantaneous power failure or loss of airspeed indication.
7. Cockpit lights should be turned up to the highest intensity to lessen the danger of temporary blindness from lightning.
8. Pilots should not attempt to reverse course after a thunderstorm has been entered. A straight course through the storm will most likely be the fastest way out of the hazards.

3.52 The following rules should be considered when flying in the *vicinity* of a thunderstorm:

1. A pilot's best choice of action is to land if a storm appears to be quite threatening, since the duration of a thunderstorm is generally not longer than a few hours.
2. Do not land or depart ahead of an approaching thunderstorm. The storm's first gust may be a 180° change from the existing wind direction. Changing wind velocities and directions, as well as the updrafts and downdrafts, can contribute to a loss of aircraft control.
3. Flying under a thunderstorm should not be attempted, even though the pilot may be able to see through to the other side of the storm. Turbulence under the storm could prove to be severe.
4. Circumnavigation of a thunderstorm should not be attempted if the storm covers 6/10 of an area or more (either by visual or airborne radar indication).
5. Flight into a cloud mass containing scattered embedded thunderstorms should not be attempted without the aid of airborne radar equipment.
6. Any thunderstorm identified as severe should be avoided by at least 20 miles since turbulence has been encountered at distances up to 20 miles from a severe thunderstorm. This is especially true regarding flight under the anvil of a large cumulonimbus cloud. (Roll clouds are also a visible sign of extreme turbulence in thunderstorms.)
7. If an aircraft possesses the capability to overfly a thunderstorm, the aircraft should clear the top of a known or suspected severe thunderstorm by at least 1,000 feet of altitude for each 10 knots of wind speed at the cloud top. (Turbulence has been encountered several thousand feet above a severe storm.)
8. Pilots must regard as severe any thunderstorm with tops of 35,000 feet or higher, whether the top is visually sighted or determined by radar.

Causes of Turbulence

3.53 Turbulence is normally associated with many different weather phenomena. The primary causes of turbulence can generally be divided into three classes:

1. Convective currents.
2. Obstructions to wind flow.
3. Wind shear.

The table in Figure 3-10 identifies the locations of probable turbulence with respect to intensity levels. The table in Figure 3-11 reviews the turbulence reporting criteria by classifying turbulence intensities according to aircraft reaction and the reactions inside the aircraft.

LIGHT TURBULENCE	MODERATE TURBULENCE	SEVERE TURBULENCE	EXTREME TURBULENCE
1. In hilly and mountainous areas even with light winds.	1. In mountainous areas with a wind component of 25 to 50 knots perpendicular to and near the level of the ridge:	1. In mountainous areas with a wind component exceeding 50 knots perpendicular to and near the level of the ridge:	1. In mountain wave situations, in and below the level of well-developed rotor clouds. Sometimes it extends to the ground.
2. In and near small cumulus clouds.	a. At all levels from the surface to 5,000 feet above the tropopause with preference for altitudes:	a. In 5,000-foot layers:	2. In growing severe thunderstorms (most frequently in organized squall lines) indicated by:
3. In clear-air convective currents over heated surfaces.	(1) Within 5,000 feet of the ridge level.	(1) At and below the ridge level in rotor clouds or rotor action.	a. Large hailstones (3/4 inch or more in diameter).
4. With weak wind shears in the vicinity of:	(2) At the base of relatively stable layers below the base of the tropopause.	(2) At the tropopause.	b. Strong radar echoes, or
a. Troughs aloft.	(3) Within the tropopause layer.	(3) Sometimes at the base of other stable layers below the tropopause.	c. Almost continuous lightning.
b. Lows aloft.	b. Extending outward on the lee of the ridge for 150 to 300 miles.	b. Extending outward on the lee of the ridge for 50 to 150 miles.	
c. Jet streams.			
d. The tropopause.	2. In and near thunderstorms in the dissipating stage.	2. In and near growing and mature thunderstorms.	
5. In the lower 5,000 feet of the atmosphere:	3. In and near other towering cumuliform clouds.	3. Occasionally in other towering cumuliform clouds.	
a. When winds are near 15 knots.	4. In the lower 5,000 feet of the troposphere:	4. 50 to 100 miles on the cold side of the center of the jet stream, in troughs aloft, and in lows aloft, where:	
b. Where the air is colder than the underlying surfaces.	a. When surface winds exceed 25 knots.	a. Vertical wind shears exceed 6 knots per 1,000 feet, and	
	b. Where heating of the underlying surface is unusually strong.	b. Horizontal wind shears exceed 40 knots per 150 miles.	
	c. Where there is an invasion of very cold air.		
	5. In fronts aloft.		
	6. Where:		
	a. Vertical wind shears exceed 6 knots per 1000 feet, and/or		
	b. Horizontal wind shears exceed 18 knots per 150 miles.		

Figure 3-10. Locations of Probable Turbulence

INTENSITY	AIRCRAFT REACTION	REACTION INSIDE AIRCRAFT	REPORTING TERM—DEFINITION
L I G H T	Turbulence that momentarily causes slight, erratic changes in altitude and/or attitude (pitch, roll, yaw). Report as *Light Turbulence;* or Turbulence that causes slight, rapid and somewhat rhythmic bumpiness without appreciable changes in altitude or attitude. Report as *Light Chop*	Occupants may feel a slight strain against seat belts or shoulder straps. Unsecured objects may be displaced slightly. Food service may be conducted and little or no difficulty is encountered in walking.	Occasional—Less than 1/3 of the time. Intermittent—1/3 to 2/3. Continuous—More than 2/3.
M O D E R A T E	Turbulence that is similar to Light Turbulence but of greater intensity. Changes in altitude and/or attitude occur but the aircraft remains in positive control at all times. It usually causes variations in indicated airspeed. Report as *Moderate Turbulence;* or Turbulence that is similar to Light Chop but of greater intensity. It causes rapid bumps or jolts without appreciable changes in aircraft altitude or attitude. Report as *Moderate Chop.*	Occupants feel definite strains against seat belts or shoulder straps. Unsecured objects are dislodged. Food service and walking are difficult.	Note—Pilots should report location(s), time (GMT), intensity, whether in or near clouds, altitude, type of aircraft and, when applicable, duration of turbulence. Duration may be based on time between two locations or over a single location. All locations should be readily identifiable. Example:
S E V E R E	Turbulence that causes large, abrupt changes in altitude and/or attitude. It usually causes large variations in indicated airspeed. Airspeed may be momentarily out of control. Report as *Severe Turbulence.*	Occupants are forced violently against seat belts or shoulder straps. Unsecured objects are tossed about. Food service and walking are impossible.	a. Over Omaha, 1232Z, Moderate Turbulence, in cloud, Flight Level 310, B707. b. From 50 miles south of Albuquerque to 30 miles north of Phoenix, 1210Z to 1250Z, occasional Moderate Chop, Flight Level 330, DC8.
E X T R E M E	Turbulence in which the aircraft is violently tossed about and is practically impossible to control. It may cause structural damage. Report as *Extreme Turbulence.*		

Figure 3-11. Turbulence Reporting Criteria Table

Convective Currents

3.54 Convective currents are created by the heating of the earth, which causes the heated air to rise, resulting in vertical turbulence or eddies. Cumulus cloud tops are usually a good indication of the upper limit of the convective currents. The cumulonimbus (thunderstorm) cloud is an excellent visual warning of extreme convective turbulence.

3.55 Thunderstorms are accompanied by virtually every type of turbulence. These strong updrafts, downdrafts, and outflows of air (first gust) with rapid changes in direction and velocity can cause turbulence in the extreme category.

3.56 Airborne or ground-based weather radar normally reflects areas of moderate to heavy precipitation and severe storms, but radar *does not* detect turbulence. The frequency and severity of turbulence usually increases with the highest moisture content area of a thunderstorm as detected by radar.

3.57 *Special Note: Flight between an area of strong or very strong radar echoes separated by 40 miles or less is not recommended due to the possibility of severe turbulence.*

Obstructions to Wind Flow

3.58 High mountain ranges can cause extreme turbulence extending 100 miles or more downwind. (Figure 3-12) Pilots flying through narrow mountain valleys and passes should use extreme caution, because the wind is usually much stronger and more turbulent than the general flow. Wind blowing over large mountain ridges is usually relatively smooth on the windward side. However, air spilling (rotor action) over the lee side of the mountains can produce strong updrafts and downdrafts.

3.59 Standing waves, sometimes referred to as mountain waves, are produced by winds over 50 knots blowing nearly perpendicular to a high mountain range. (Figure 3-13) Again, the magnitude of the turbulence, updrafts, and downdrafts can range from moderate to severe. Occasionally, the areas of violent air are marked by lens-shaped clouds. However, lens-shaped (*lenticular*) clouds may not be present, even though the turbulence is present.

3.60 *Special Note: If strong winds are present or forecast, pilots should anticipate turbulence and avoid flying on the lee side of mountains or mountain ranges.*

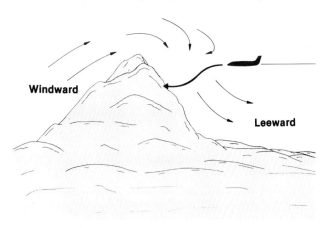

Windward

Leeward

Figure 3-12. Mountainous Terrain Turbulence

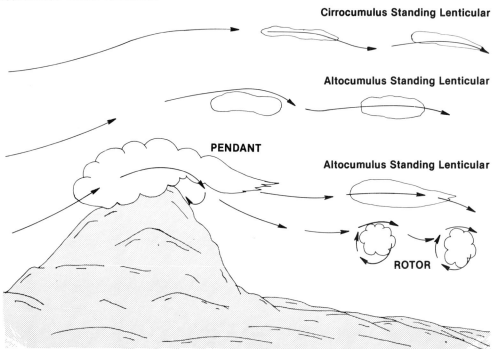

Cirrocumulus Standing Lenticular

Altocumulus Standing Lenticular

PENDANT

Altocumulus Standing Lenticular

ROTOR

Figure 3-13. Characteristic Cloud Formations of a Mountain Wave

Wind Shear

3.61 Wind shear is caused by a change in wind velocity or direction, horizontally or vertically, over a short distance. Types of weather phenomena which can produce shear turbulence are strong temperature inversions, fronts, thunderstorms, and jet streams.

3.62 A temperature inversion forms a layer of cold, dense air near the surface that has little movement. (Figure 3-14) However, in the warm air layer above a cold air layer, the wind may be quite strong. These strong winds in the warm layer cause eddy currents and turbulence. An aircraft climbing or descending through a turbulent zone very close to the surface may encounter a momentary loss of airspeed. Pilots should be especially on guard for a temperature inversion since very few clues are usually available.

3.63 Fronts and jet streams are examples of a large change in wind velocity or direction within small distances. This horizontal wind shear from fronts and jet streams often will not present a warning of impending turbulence. Therefore, a good weather briefing is important in order to anticipate areas of turbulence and the necessary direction to take to elude possible turbulence.

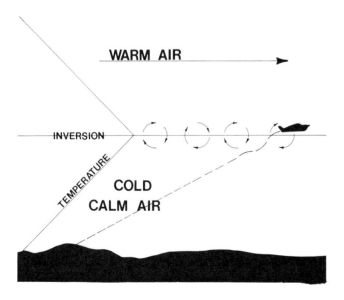

Figure 3–14. Low Level Temperature Inversion Wind Shear

Icing

3.64 Aircraft icing is a hazard that requires immediate decisions by alert pilots. Even with current icing reports, areas of icing often change rapidly, making accurate forecasting of icing impossible. Consequently, the most experienced aviators should, due to the unpredictability of ice, plan an alternate course of action during the pre-flight planning stage.

3.65 The formation of ice on an aircraft reduces its aerodynamic efficiency. Accumulation of ice on the airfoil not only adds weight but also disrupts the smooth flow of air, thereby increasing drag and decreasing lift. The propeller loses efficiency with the addition of ice, resulting in a decrease of thrust. Normally, the weight of the ice is not a major factor, unless the airplane is near critical load limits. The reduced airspeed from the formation of ice results in increased flying time in icing conditions, compounding the initial icing problem. Not only is general aircraft performance reduced, but the stalling speed is also increased.

3.66 Aircraft icing is often classified as structural, induction system, or instrument icing. (Instrument icing was previously discussed in chapter 2.) All three forms of icing occur in temperatures ranging from 0°C to -55°C. However, the most severe icing and the most rapid accumulations occur at temperatures between 0°C to -15°C.

Structural Icing

3.67 Types of structural icing are *rime*, *clear*, and *frost*. All structural icing, except frost, can only occur in visible moisture such as clouds or falling precipitation.

3.68 There are a number of factors that influence an aircraft's structural icing accretion rate. These factors are:

1. Larger drops of water tend to collect and form structural ice more rapidly than small drops of water.
2. The ice accretion rate is directly proportional to the amount of supercooled water in the atmosphere.
3. The rate of ice formation increases as the speed of an aircraft increases up to a speed of approximately 400 knots.
4. A large, blunt airfoil presents a larger collecting surface and accelerates the ice accumulation rate. After a layer of ice has once collected on an exposed airfoil, it presents a larger area for more ice to collect at a faster rate.

The table in Figure 3-15 reviews the reporting criteria for airframe icing intensities and accumulation rates.

TRACE	Ice becomes perceptible. Rate of accumulation slightly greater than rate of sublimation. It is not hazardous even though deicing/anti-icing equipment is not utilized, unless encountered for an extended period of time (over 1 hour).
LIGHT	The rate of accumulation may create a problem if flight is prolonged in this environment (over 1 hour). Occasional use of deicing/anti-icing equipment removes/prevents accumulation. It does not present a problem if the deicing/anti-icing equipment is used.
MODERATE	The rate of accumulation is such that even short encounters become potentially hazardous and use of deicing/anti-icing equipment or diversion is necessary.
SEVERE	The rate of accumulation is such that deicing/anti-icing equipment fails to reduce or control the hazard. Immediate diversion is necessary.

Pilot Report: Aircraft Identification, Location, Time (GMT), Intensity of Type, Altitude/FL, Aircraft Type, IAS.

Figure 3-15. Icing Intensity and Airframe Ice Accumulation Table

3.69 *Rime ice* is generally encountered when aircraft fly into stratiform clouds. This type of ice is milky in appearance and granular in form. The instantaneous freezing of *small* supercooled water droplets upon an aircraft's surface results in rime ice. This freezing process traps a large amount of air, causing the rime ice to have brittle characteristics. Since rime ice forms only upon the leading edges of aircraft and is brittle, it is comparatively easy to remove through the use of deicing equipment. This type of ice can accumulate in the temperature range between 0°C and -40°C, with the greatest amount of icing generally occurring at temperatures from -10°C to -20°C. (Figure 3-16)

3.70 *Clear (or glaze) ice* is considered to be the most hazardous type of structural icing. Clear ice is formed when *large* supercooled water droplets, usually from cumuliform clouds, adhere to aircraft. These water droplets do not freeze instantaneously upon contact, but flow back over the wing a short distance, spreading out and forming a smooth, transparent surface. This type of ice adheres so firmly to the aircraft that it is often *very difficult* to dislodge. The temperature range where clear ice is most frequently found is from 0°C to -10°C. Very seldom is aircraft structural icing all rime or all clear ice; rather it usually is a mixture of the two types. (Figure 3-17)

Figure 3-16. Rime Icing

Figure 3-17. Clear (Glaze) Icing

3.71 *Special Note: Freezing rain accumulates on aircraft surfaces rapidly and is the most dangerous of the clear icing conditions. This condition also presents the most difficult type of icing to dislodge from aircraft surfaces. As freezing rain falls to lower altitudes, ice pellets form. Pilots should understand that warm air temperatures exist at higher altitudes along with the possibility of severe icing conditions (freezing rain).*

3.72 *Frost* is too often underestimated by many pilots. Frost forms when the temperature of the collecting surface is at or below the dew point of the adjacent air and the dew point is below freezing. Remember, frost can also form on clear days or nights. *All* frost should be removed or polished smooth prior to departure since it spoils the smooth flow of air over the airfoil, resulting in an increased stalling speed. In flight, frost can form (by sublimation) when an aircraft is descending or climbing from a zone of subzero temperatures into a zone of warmer temperatures and high humidity.

Induction System Icing

3.73 One form of icing that affects the engine power output is impact ice that collects on the scoop inlets and carburetor-inlet screen. This impact ice can block the inlets to the carburetor, which will result in a power loss. Most aircraft have either a carburetor heating system or an alternate air system to compensate for impact ice.

3.74 Perhaps the most common type of induction system icing pilots encounter is carburetor ice. (Figure 3-18) Carburetor ice generally occurs in a temperature range between 14°F and 77°F (-10°C and 25°C). Aircraft engines are most susceptible to carburetor ice during humid, rainy days. Visible moisture is not a necessary condition of carburetor icing, however.

3.75 Carburetor ice is formed when the evaporating fuel cools the air as it enters the venturi in the carburetor. This cooling effect from the evaporating fuel causes the water vapor in the air entering the carburetor to freeze. A pressure decrease in the

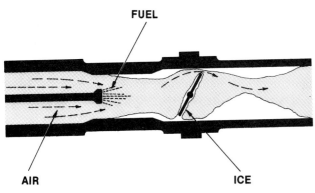

FUEL

AIR   ICE

Figure 3–18. Carburetor Icing

venturi-shaped carburetor throat also contributes to the cooling of the water vapor, although to a lesser degree.

3.76 The first indication of carburetor icing for aircraft equipped with fixed-pitch propellers is a loss of engine RPM. Airplanes equipped with constant speed propellers will experience a drop in manifold pressure. The RPM for airplanes equipped with constant speed propellers, however, will not decrease since the propeller pitch is varied automatically to offset any loss in power, thereby sustaining a steady RPM. As the carburetor icing increases, a roughness in engine operation may result for both the fixed-pitch and constant speed propeller equipped aircraft.

3.77 Whenever weather conditions are conducive to carburetor icing, the appropriate check should be initiated routinely to determine if a carburetor icing condition does exist.

3.78 When a pilot suspects carburetor ice, *full* carburetor heat should be promptly applied. The heat control should remain in the "full on" position until there is no doubt that the throat of the carburetor is completely clear of ice.

3.79 The application of full carburetor heat will result in an initial power loss since the hot air provided by the carburetor heat richens the fuel air mixture. Upon the initial power loss, airplanes equipped with fixed-pitch propellers will experience a drop in RPM, while a drop in manifold pressure can be expected for airplanes equipped with constant speed propellers.

3.80 If carburetor ice is present, the RPM or manifold pressure will increase as the ice is melted. If no carburetor icing is present after the carburetor heat is initially applied, the RPM or manifold pressure will not reflect any further change, after the initial drop in indication, until the carburetor heat control is repositioned to the "off" position. Once the carburetor heat control is repositioned in the "off" position, if carburetor ice *was* present, the RPM or manifold pressure will increase to a setting higher than the initial RPM or manifold pressure setting prior to the application of carburetor heat. If carburetor icing *was not* present, after the control is repositioned in the "off" position, the RPM or manifold pressure gauge will register the same reading as was indicated before the heat was applied.

3.81 *Special Note: The application of partial carburetor heat, or the application of carburetor heat for an insufficient amount of time, may complicate a potentially serious carburetor icing situation.*

Anti-icing and Deicing Aids

3.82 Anti-icing aids are used to *prevent* the formation of ice. Examples of anti-icing aids are anti-ice fluid and electric heat (often used on the propellers and windshields).

3.83 Anti-icing devices should be activated prior to or immediately upon entering a zone of icing conditions. Anti-icing fluids should be used sparingly to insure continued use of the fluid throughout the period of flight while in the icing zone.

3.84 Deicing aids are used to eliminate ice *after* it has formed. The most common type of deicing aid is the deicing boot, most often used on wings and tail assemblies. Deicing boots should be employed periodically only *after* a sufficient amount of ice (approximately 1/8-inch thickness) has accumulated on the boot surface. The deicing boots are inflated intermittently, and this swelling causes the ice accumulation to fracture. The fractured ice is then removed by the air stream.

3.85 Deicing boots should not be in operation during periods of takeoff or landing because an aircraft's airfoil can be sufficiently altered to adversely affect the aircraft's stall characteristics. Generally, deicing boots should not be continually operated in flight, since a pocket of air can develop beneath newly formed ice. (Figure 3-19)

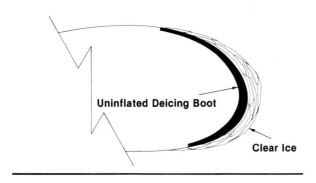

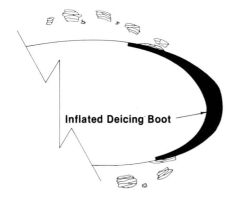

Figure 3-19. Deicing Boot Application

Relative Humidity and Dew Point

3.86 Relative humidity is the ratio (usually expressed as a percentage) of the actual amount of water vapor in the air at a given temperature, to the maximum amount of water vapor that the air could hold at that given temperature. For example, air that contains the maximum water vapor possible for a given temperature has a relative humidity of 100 percent. The amount of water vapor that can exist in a parcel of air is largely determined by the temperature. (This is why warm air can hold more water vapor than cold air.)

3.87 The dew point temperature is often used to determine how close the air is to being saturated (100 percent relative humidity). This is done by comparing the dew point temperature to the outside air temperature. As the temperature dew point spread decreases, the relative humidity increases. When the relative humidity reaches 100 percent, the outside air temperature and dew point temperature are the same.

Fog

3.88 The instrument pilot must be knowledgeable of the types and causes of fog since it is generally the most common cause of restrictions to visibilities near or below IFR departure and landing minimums. Fog is essentially a ground-based cloud which is composed of either ice crystals or water droplets, depending on the surface temperature. The table in Figure 3-20 reviews the types of fogs, how the specific types of fog form, and the general geographical area where each fog type is found.

3.89 Some atmospheric conditions ideal for the formation of fog are:

1. A close temperature dew point spread. (High relative humidity.)
2. A concentration of condensation nuclei. (Industrial areas often have fog due to the high concentration of condensation nuclei that are generated as products of combustion.)
3. Light surface winds.
4. A cooling process to initiate vapor condensation.
5. The addition of moisture to the air near the earth's surface.

WEATHER REPORTS AND FORECASTS

3.90 Since weather plays such a major role in flight operations, this section reviews those particular reports and forecasts that an instrument pilot should consider when determining a flight plan.

Surface Aviation Weather Reports (Sequence Reports)

3.91 When an observation is recorded and transmitted, it is considered to be a weather report. The two types of weather reports are:

1. The hourly weather observation.
2. The special weather observation.

FOG CLASSIFICATION TABLE

Type of Fog	Formation	Geographical Areas	Characteristics
ADVECTION	Forms where a moist air mass is moving over a colder surface. (Requires wind in order to form.)	Usually found in coastal areas.	Covers an extensive area for a long period of time.
RADIATION	Forms when a moist air mass is cooled to its dew point by the earth's surface. (Requires little or no wind in order to form.)	Generally restricted to land.	Generally clears after sunrise.
UPSLOPE	Forms when a moist air mass is forced to a higher elevation, which cools the air mass adiabatically. (Requires wind in order to form.)	Usually found along mountain slopes.	Moderately dense fog.
PRECIPITATION INDUCED	Forms when warm rain falls through cool air. Evaporation from the precipitation saturates the cool air, forming fog.	All areas.	Covers an extensive area.
ICE	Forms when the ambient temperature is much below freezing, and water vapor sublimates directly into ice crystals. (Requires little or no wind in order to form.)	All areas below -25°F.	Covers a small area and usually forms during evening hours.
STEAM	Forms when cold, dry air flows from land areas to open areas of warm water.	Found over open bodies of water.	Low-level turbulence and aircraft icing may be associated with this type of fog.

Figure 3-20.

The most common type is the hourly weather observation, which is sent out with the collective hourly reports. The second type is the special weather observation, recorded as frequently as necessary to report significant changes in weather.

3.92 Surface Aviation Weather Reports contain some or all of the following elements:

1. Station designator.
2. Type and time of report.
3. Sky condition and ceiling.
4. Visibility.
5. Weather and obstructions to vision.
6. Sea level pressure.
7. Temperature and dew point.
8. Wind direction, speed, and character.
9. Altimeter setting.
10. Remarks.

3.93 Five weather reports have been selected as examples for discussing the ten elements of a Surface Aviation Weather Report. (Figure 3-21) Each reporting station is identified by its three-letter location identifier. The five selected reporting stations are: Denver, Colorado (DEN); Miami, Florida (MIA); Salt Lake City, Utah (SLC); Kansas City, Missouri (MKC); and Sacramento, California (SAC).

3.94 *Special Note: Those elements not occurring at observation time or not pertinent to the observation are omitted from the report. When an element should be included but is unavailable, the letter* "M" *is transmitted in lieu of the missing element. Those elements that are included in the weather report are transmitted in the order of sequence that they are listed in paragraph 3.92.*

Location Identifier and Type of Report

3.95 A heading begins the record hourly collective on the local circuit, identifying the type of message, the circuit number, and the date and time of observations making up the collective reports. An example heading is: SA20 281800. The heading is decoded as follows: SA identifies the report as a Surface Aviation Weather Report; 20 is the circuit number; 28 is the day of the month; and the observations have been sent out over teletype at 1800 GMT. Since all weather reports and charts are issued according to Greenwich Mean Time (GMT or Zulu Time), instrument pilots should be able to readily convert local time to Greenwich Mean Time. A table and discussion pertaining to GMT is located in Appendix C-5.

3.96 A slightly different heading precedes each collective report (relay). It identifies the location of reporting stations, either:

1. By states, *or*
2. In relation to the local area report circuit.

Headings also indicate the time the relay began. *Example:* SA NEAR EAST201904. To the pilot, SA means Surface Aviation Weather Reports; area

SAMPLE SURFACE AVIATION WEATHER REPORT

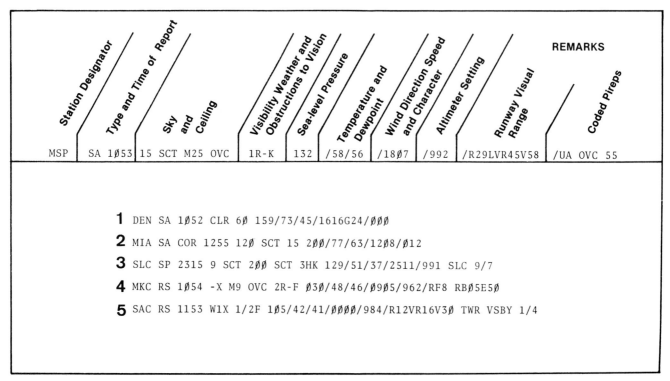

Figure 3-21.

covered by the relay is just east of the local circuit area (NEAR EAST); day of the month is the 20th (2Ø); and the time the observations were sent out over teletype was 1904 GMT (1904).

3.97 Relay designators other than states are INTERMEDIATE EAST, FAR EAST, NEAR NORTH, and other similar designators. The relay collectives are assembled by a centralized computer and are unique to each circuit.

3.98 Individual reports must each convey the time and report type designator. These reports include Special Reports (SP), Corrected Reports (COR), Record Reports (SA), and Record Special Reports (RS). Each reporting station is identified by a three-letter location identifier. Examples of different types of reports follow (Figure 3-21):

Example 1:

DEN SA 1Ø52 . . . .

This indicates a relayed report from Denver, Colorado (DEN) for 1100 GMT. All times transmitted in teletypewriter reports are GMT. The SA signifies a record hourly identification.

Example 2:

MIA SA COR 1255 . . . .

This signifies a correction to the 1300 GMT. Record hourly report as originally transmitted. The correction may transmit the complete Corrected Report, or it may contain only the corrected element or elements.

Example 3:

SLC SP 2315 . . . .

This heading indicates a Special Report of an observation taken at 2315 GMT to report a significant change in weather. This report is not relayed with the other reports relayed on the hour, but is relayed shortly after the observation time.

Example 4:

MKC RS 1Ø54 . . . .

This heading indicates a Record Special Report by the contraction RS. A Record Special Report is similar to an SP since it reports a significant change in weather. The RS differs, however, from the SP in that it is only relayed with the hourly reports. This particular report was from Kansas City, Missouri and the observation time was 1054 GMT.

Sky Condition and Ceiling

3.99 Sky conditions are reported by one of the sky cover designators as a clear sky, layer of clouds, or obscuring phenomena. (Figure 3-22) When the sky conditions are reported as a layer of clouds or obscuring phenomena, the height of the layer precedes the sky cover designator. The height of the reported layer or obscuration is reported in hundreds of feet *above ground level*.

SUMMARY OF SKY COVER DESIGNATORS

DESIGNATOR	MEANING
CLR	CLEAR. (Less than 0.1 sky cover.)
SCT	SCATTERED LAYER ALOFT. (0.1 through 0.5 sky cover.)
BKN*	BROKEN LAYER ALOFT. (0.6 through 0.9 sky cover.)
OVC*	OVERCAST LAYER ALOFT. (More than 0.9, or 1.0 sky cover.)
−SCT	THIN SCATTERED.
−BKN	THIN BROKEN. At least 1/2 of the sky cover aloft is transparent at and below the level of the layer aloft.
−OVC	THIN OVERCAST.
X*	SURFACE BASED OBSTRUCTION. (All of the sky is hidden by surface based phenomena.)
−X	SURFACE BASED PARTIAL OBSCURATION. (0.1 or more, but not all, of sky is hidden by surface based phenomena.)

*Sky condition represented by this designator may constitute a ceiling layer.

Figure 3-22.

3.100 In the first of the five sample reports (Figure 3-21) DEN is reporting clear skies, and the cloud height is omitted due to the absence of a sky cover. In the second report, MIA reports a scattered cloud layer at 12,000 feet above the reporting station.

3.101 SLC is reporting two scattered cloud layers. The first scattered layer is at 900 feet AGL and the second layer at 20,000 feet AGL. Pilots should note that cloud layers must be reported in ascending order of height. For each cloud layer above a lower layer or layers, the sky cover designator for that cloud layer represents the *total sky covered* by that layer and all lower cloud layers. Consequently, a Surface Aviation Weather Report could indicate a broken or overcast sky condition at an airport, when in fact two or more scattered cloud layers collectively could produce the effect of a broken or overcast sky condition. (Figure 3-23) Each layer in the SLC report is classified as scattered because the total sky cover from both layers is less than 5/10 coverage.

3.102 When a scattered, broken, overcast, or obscured sky cover is transparent so an observer can see blue sky or a higher cloud layer, the layer or obscuration is classified as "thin." To be classified as thin, a cloud layer must be half or more transparent.

3.103 Any phenomenon based at the surface and hiding all or part of the sky is reported as "sky obscured" or "sky partially obscured." (Figure 3-22) No height value will precede the designator for a *partial* obscuration since *vertical* visibility is not restricted by precipitation, fog, dust, blowing snow, or any other factors. However, a height value will precede a designator for an obscuration, and this height value denotes vertical visibility into the phenomena.

3.104 A ceiling is defined as:

1. The height (above the surface) of the base of the lowest layer of clouds or obscuring phenomena aloft that hides more than half of the sky (not classified as thin); or

2. The vertical visibility into an obscuration.

The table in Figure 3-24 lists and explains the ceiling designators which precede the height of a ceiling layer. The MKC and SAC (Figure 3-21) reports exemplify ceiling and obscuration sky cover designations. MKC is reporting a partial obscuration and a measured 900-foot overcast. SAC is reporting a total obscuration or indefinite 100 feet of vertical visibility, sky obscured.

3.105 The sky cover and ceiling, as determined from the ground, represent as nearly as possible what the pilot should experience in flight. For example, a pilot flying above a scattered cloud forma-

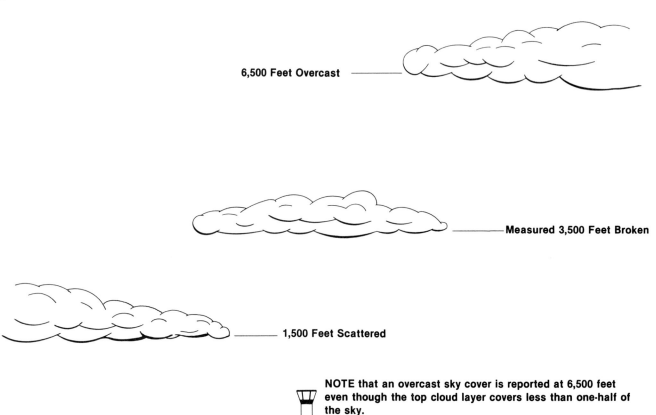

6,500 Feet Overcast

Measured 3,500 Feet Broken

1,500 Feet Scattered

NOTE that an overcast sky cover is reported at 6,500 feet even though the top cloud layer covers less than one-half of the sky.

Figure 3-23. Summation of Multiple Cloud Cover Layers

tion should see at least one-half of the surface below the aircraft. When a pilot is descending through a surface-based total obscuration, the ground should first become visible below from an altitude reported as vertical visibility into the obscuration. However, because of the differing viewing points of the pilot and the observer, these surface-reported values do not always exactly agree with what the pilot sees.

3.106 A variable ceiling height is indicated by the letter *V* following the ceiling height. Variable ceiling is reported only when it is critical to terminal operations. Following is an example of a variable report:

M3V OVC and, in the remarks section of a Surface Aviation Weather Report, CIG3V5. This report means "measured ceiling 300 feet variable overcast," and the remarks read "ceilings variable between 300 feet and 500 feet."

3.107 The following sky and ceiling conditions (extracted from the five selected reports) are decoded as follows:

DEN SA 1052 CLR	Denver, clear.
MIA SA COR 1255 120SCT	Miami, 12,000 scattered.
SLC SP 2315 9SCT 200SCT	Salt Lake City, 900 scattered, 20,000 scattered.
MKC RS 1054 -X M90VC	Kansas City, sky partially obscured, measured ceiling 900 overcast.
SAC RS 1153 W1X	Sacramento, indefinite ceiling 100 sky obscured.

Visibility

3.108 The next element of a Surface Aviation Weather Report, following the sky and ceiling section, is prevailing visibility. Prevailing visibility is defined as the greatest horizontal visibility which is equaled or exceeded throughout half of the horizontal circle surrounding an airport. It need not be a continuous half circle, however. The prevailing visibility is reported in statute miles and fractions thereof.

3.109 Again, referring to the five sample weather reports (Figure 3-21), the prevailing visibility in each report is:

DEN SA 1052 CLR 60	Visibility 60.
MIA SA COR 1255 120SCT 15	Visibility 15.
SLC SP 2315 9SCT 200SCT 3HK	Visibility 3, with haze and smoke.
MKC RS 1054 -X M90VC 2R-F	Visibility 2, with light rain and fog.
SAC RS 1153 W1X 1/2F	Visibility 1/2, with fog.

3.110 The prevailing visibility, at an airport with both a weather observing station and a control tower, is usually reported by the weather observing station. At times, however, when the visibility decreases below a certain defined value, the control tower reports the visibility. If the other observation is operationally significant, it will be reported in the remarks. Surface Aviation Weather Report number 5 in Figure 3-21 has a visibility reported in the remarks, TWR VSBY 1/4; meaning the control tower is reporting the visibility at ¼ statute mile.

Figure 3-24.

CEILING DESIGNATORS

CODED	MEANING
M	MEASURED. Heights determined by ceilometer, ceiling light, cloud detection radar, or by the unobscured portion of a landmark protruding into ceiling layer.
E	ESTIMATED. Heights determined from pilot reports, balloons, or other measurements not meeting criteria for measured ceiling.
W	INDEFINITE. Vertical visibility into a surface based obstruction. Regardless of method of determination, vertical visibility is classified as an indefinite ceiling.

Weather and Obstructions to Vision

3.111 Weather and obstructions to vision, when occurring at the station at observation time, are reported immediately following visibility. If observed at a distance from the station, they will be reported in the remarks. Terms used to report the weather include symbols for all forms of precipitation, as well as such terms as thunderstorm, tornado, funnel cloud, and waterspout. (Figure 3-25) Following the precipitation symbol, one of the following intensity symbols is reported:

Very light ——
Light   —
Moderate (no sign)
Heavy   +

WEATHER SYMBOLS AND MEANINGS

CODED	SPOKEN
TORNADO	TORNADO
FUNNEL CLOUD	FUNNEL CLOUD
WATERSPOUT	WATERSPOUT
T	THUNDERSTORM
T+	SEVERE THUNDERSTORM
R	RAIN
RW	RAINSHOWER
L	DRIZZLE
ZR	FREEZING RAIN
ZL	FREEZING DRIZZLE
A	HAIL
IP	ICE PELLETS
IPW	ICE PELLETS SHOWER
S	SNOW
SW	SNOW SHOWERS
SP	SNOW PELLETS
SG	SNOW GRAINS
IC	ICE CRYSTALS

Figure 3-25.

3.112 No intensity symbol is reported for hail (A) or ice crystals (IC). The letter T+, as reported on a Surface Aviation Weather Report, indicates a severe thunderstorm. A thunderstorm is defined as severe when surface winds are 50 knots or greater and/or hail is 3/4 inch or more in diameter.

OBSTRUCTIONS TO VISION SYMBOLS AND MEANINGS

CODED	SPOKEN
BD	BLOWING DUST
BN	BLOWING SAND
BS	BLOWING SNOW
BY	BLOWING SPRAY
D	DUST
F	FOG
GF	GROUND FOG
H	HAZE
IF	ICE FOG
K	SMOKE

Figure 3-26.

3.113 The table in Figure 3-26 includes the obstructions to vision. Intensities *are not* reported for obstructions to vision. An obscuring phenomenon on the surface or aloft will be printed in the remarks section of the report. When the phenomenon is surface-based and partially obscures the sky, the remarks will report the tenths of sky hidden and the obscuring phenomena. For example, MKC reports RF 8 in the remarks, which means 8/10 of the sky is hidden by rain and fog.

3.114 A layer of obscuring phenomena aloft will be reported in the sky and ceiling portion of the Surface Aviation Weather Report in the same position as a layer of cloud cover. But the remarks will identify the layer as an obscuring phenomenon. For example, a report may read 3Ø-BKN, and the remarks may read H3Ø-BKN. These indicate that the station is reporting a broken layer of haze with a 3,000-foot (AGL) base, but the haze is not concealing the sky since the haze is reported as being a thin layer.

Sea Level Pressure (Millibars)

3.115 Sea level pressure reported in millibars follows the weather and obstructions to vision section of the report. This sea level pressure is transmitted in a three-digit code to the nearest tenth of a millibar, with the decimal point omitted. To decode the pressure, add the prefix 9 or 10, because the sea level pressure rarely is greater than 960.0 millibars and is less than 1050.0 millibars. Sea level pressure in millibars is only transmitted in the hourly reports. Decoding the five Surface Aviation Weather Reports (Figure 3-21) will reveal sea level pressures as follows:

DEN SA 1Ø52 CLR 6Ø 159	1015.9 millibars
MIA SA COR 1255 12ØSCT 15 2ØØ	1020.0 millibars
SLC SP 2315 9SCT 2ØØSCT 3HK 129	1012.9 millibars
MKC RS 1Ø54 -X M9ØVC 2R-F Ø3Ø	1003.0 millibars
SAC RS 1153 W1X 1/2F 1Ø5	1010.5 millibars

Temperature and Dew Point

3.116 Following the sea level pressure on the report are the temperature and dew point. The temperature and dew point are reported to the nearest degree Fahrenheit. Sea level pressure, temperature, and dew point are all separated by a slash (/). The temperature is separated from the preceding element by a space if sea level pressure is not transmitted. When the temperature or dew point is below zero, a minus sign will precede them.

3.117 The temperatures and dew points from the five reports would read as follows:

DEN   73/45   Temperature 73°F, dew point 45°F.
MIA   77/63   Temperature 77°F, dew point 63°F.
SLC   51/37   Temperature 51°F, dew point 37°F.
MKC   48/46   Temperature 48°F, dew point 46°F.
SAC   42/41   Temperature 42°F, dew point 41°F.

Wind Direction and Speed

3.118 The wind reading is normally reported in four digits and is separated from the dew point by a slash. The first two digits are tens of degrees referenced to a direction of *true* north from which the wind is blowing. The second two digits represent speed in knots. A calm wind would be reported as 0000. When the windspeed is 100 knots or greater, 50 is added to the direction code and the hundred digit of the speed is omitted. For example, a reported wind of 8203 would be decoded to mean 320° at 103 knots. A pilot decoding the wind direction and speed will know that any encoded windspeeds 100 knots or greater have 50 added to the direction code and 100 subtracted from the speed. Therefore, in order to decode correctly, the pilot must reverse the encoding process. It is easy to recognize when coded direction has been increased by 50. Coded direction (in tens of degrees) ranges from 01 (010°) to 36 (360°). Thus, any coded direction of more than "36" indicates winds over 100 knots. (Coded direction for winds over 100 knots will range from 51 [01 + 50] through 86 [36 + 50].)

3.119 If the variation in windspeed is at least 10 knots between peaks and lulls, the windspeed is reported as a gust with the letter *G* separating the two speeds. For example, 3212G27 decodes to: Wind 320° at 12 knots with gusts to 27 knots.

3.120 If the wind speed suddenly increases by at least 15 knots to a sustained speed of 20 knots or more lasting for at least one minute, it is reported as a "squall." Squalls are reported by the letter *Q* between an average one-minute speed and the peak speed in knots. For example, a reported wind of 3530Q45 indicates a wind from 350° at 30 knots with peak speeds in the squalls to 45 knots.

3.121 A letter *E* will precede the wind group when any part of the wind report is "estimated," such as direction, speed, peak speed in gusts or squalls. Decoded wind reports from the five sample reports are:

DEN /1616G24/   Wind 160° at 16 knots with peak gusts to 24 knots.
MIA /1208/   Wind 120° at 8 knots.
SLC /2511/   Wind 250° at 11 knots.
MKC /0905/   Wind 090° at 5 knots.
SAC /0000/   Calm wind.

Altimeter Setting

3.122 A slash separates the wind report from the altimeter setting. Only the last three digits of altimeter settings are transmitted, without the decimal point. The normal altimeter setting ranges from 28.00 inches to 31.00 inches. Therefore, either a 2 or 3 prefix must be added to the coded setting. Since 29.92 inches of mercury is the standard sea level pressure, it can generally be assumed that the pressure will be reasonably close to that setting when determining whether to add a 2 or a 3 to the three-digit altimeter grouping. When an estimated altimeter is reported it will be prefixed with an *E*.

3.123 The five decoded altimeter settings are:

DEN /000   Altimeter 30.00″ Hg.
MIA /012   Altimeter 30.12″ Hg.
SLC /991   Altimeter 29.91″ Hg.
MKC /962   Altimeter 29.62″ Hg.
SAC /984   Altimeter 29.84″ Hg.

Remarks

3.124 The remarks, when given, will follow the altimeter setting separated by a slash. These remarks may include runway visibility, Runway Visual Range, heights of bases, tops of overcast, NOTAMs, and freezing level data.

Runway Visual Range and Runway Visibility

3.125 The general definition of visibility is the greatest distance an observer with normal eyes can see a prominent object. These visibilities are reported in statute miles and/or hundreds of feet. Pilots are concerned with different types of visibilities, in addition to prevailing visibility as previously discussed. The other visibilities pilots are concerned with are defined below:

Flight Visibility—The average forward horizontal distance, from the cockpit of an aircraft in flight, at which prominent unlighted objects may be seen and identified by day and prominent lighted objects may be seen and identified by night.

Ground Visibility—Prevailing horizontal visibility near the earth's surface as reported by an accredited observer.

Runway Visibility (RVV or VV)—The distance down the runway the pilot can see unlighted objects or unfocused lights of moderate intensity. This runway visibility may be determined by a transmissometer or by an observer and is reported in miles and fractions.

Runway Visual Range (RVR or VR)—An instrumentally derived horizontal distance a pilot should see down the runway from the approach end; it is based on either the sighting of high intensity runway lights or on the visual contrast of other objects, whichever yields the greatest visual range. The visibility is always reported in hundreds of feet. RVR, in contrast to prevailing or runway visibility, is based on what a pilot in a moving aircraft should see when looking down the runway. RVR is horizontal visual range, *not* slant visual range and is based on the measurement of a transmissometer made near the touchdown point of the instrument runway. The following terms are often used when discussing RVR:

A. **Touchdown RVR**—The RVR visibility readout values obtained from RVR equipment serving the runway touchdown zone.

B. **Mid-field RVR**—The RVR readout values obtained from RVR equipment located mid-field of the runway.

C. **Rollout RVR**—The RVR readout values obtained from RVR equipment located nearest the rollout end of the runway.

The table in Figure 3-27 is used for converting RVR to meteorological visibility when RVR information is not available.

RVR—VISIBILITY CONVERSION TABLE

RVR (FEET)	VISIBILITY (STATUTE MILES)
1600	1/4
2400	1/2
3200	5/8
4000	3/4
4500	7/8
5000	1
6000	1-1/4

Figure 3-27.

3.126 A runway visibility or Runway Visual Range Report consists of a runway designator and the contraction *VV* or *VR*, followed by the appropriate visibility or visual range. Both VV and VR reports were conducted during the 10-minute period preceding the observation time and the extremes in the visual reference during the preceding 10 minutes are separated by the letter *V*. When a single value is recorded this indicates that the visibility value remained constant during the preceding 10-minute period.

3.127 The following four examples explain how the runway visibility and Runway Visual Range readings are coded:

R25VV21/2	Runway 25, visibility 2½. (During the 10-minute period the visibility remained constant.)
R35RVV3/4V1	Runway 35 right, visibility between ¾ and 1 mile.
R14LVR 30V45	Runway 14 left, visual range variable between 3,000 feet and 4,500 feet.
R09VR18	Runway 9, visual range 1,800 feet. (During the 10-minute period the visibility remained constant.)

3.128 When the Runway Visual Range is greater than 6,000 feet, it will be denoted 60 + . If the VR is less than the minimum value that the transmissometer can observe, the minimum value will be followed by a minus sign. For example, R18VR12-V18 means Runway 18, visual range variable from less than 1,200 feet to 1,800 feet.

Heights of Bases and Tops of Sky Cover Layers

3.129 Pilot-reported tops of cloud layers or obscuring phenomena may be reported in the remarks section in hundreds of feet MSL. This report is preceded by the letters *UA* to identify the message as a pilot report. For example, /UA 40 OVC 70 means pilot report, base of the overcast 4000 feet MSL with the top of the overcast at 7000 feet MSL.

Notice to Airmen (NOTAM)

3.130 The NOTAM system is designed to inform pilots, as well as other users, of rapid changes in the National Airspace System when the time factor would normally preclude issuance of a chart or other appropriate publications. A NOTAM summary (NOSUM) is transmitted hourly for a specific geographical area. Following is a brief explanation of how NOTAM information can be interpreted and applied.

ADP—Automatic Data Processing Code
Indicates that NOTAM information follows. Can be either textual data, or reference, to a previous NOTAM.

NTF—NOTAM to follow code
When two or more new NOTAMs or cancellations or a combination of new NOTAMs and cancellations are transmitted in series, they will be separated without spacing, by an NTF arrow.

C *Cancelled NOTAM*

CNI—Current NOTAM Indicator Code
When there are current, *previously* transmitted, NOTAMs a CNI arrow will be appended to the report, followed by the current NOTAM serial numbers.

9/7 *Accountability Number*
Each NOTAM for a particular station is assigned its own accountability number. For example, the 9 indicates the ninth month and the 7 indicates the seventh NOTAM issued during the ninth month.

Sample Decoded NOTAM:
LGA2/11LGA VOR OTS ╱ C2/8 ╲ 2/9 2/10
La Guardia NOTAM 2/11 La Guardia VOR out of service ╱ NOTAM 2/8 cancelled ╲ NOTAMs 2/9 and 2/10 current.

Freezing Level Data

3.131 An upper air observation that determines the freezing level data would be decoded in the remarks sections as indicated by the example in the table in Figure 3-28. Note: If the sounding crossed the 0°C isotherm more than three times, the levels coded are the very lowest level and the top two levels.

Examples:

RADAT ZERO	The entire sounding was below 0°C.
RADAT MISG	The sounding terminated below the first crossing of the 0°C isotherm—temperatures were all above freezing.
RADAT 68052	Relative humidity 68 percent; only crossing of the 0° C isotherm was 5,200 feet MSL.
RADAT 68L032115	Relative humidity 68 percent, at the lowest (L) crossing. Crossings occurred at 3,200 and 11,500 feet MSL.

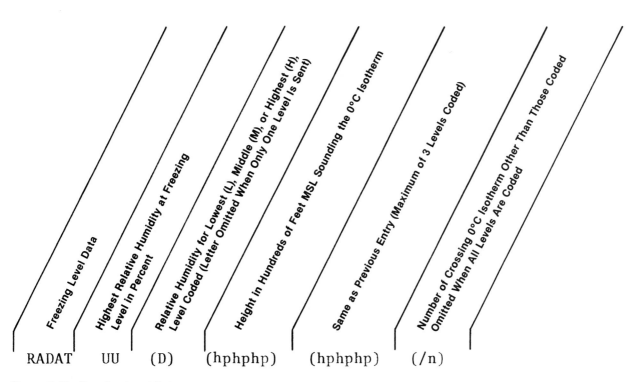

RADAT   UU   (D)   (hphphp)   (hphphp)   (/n)

Figure 3-28. Freezing Level Data

Pilot Weather Reports (PIREPs)

3.132 All ATC facilities are required to solicit and collect PIREPs when the reported ceilings are at or below 5,000 feet AGL, visibilities are at or below 5 miles, or thunderstorms are reported or forecast. Pilots are urged to cooperate by volunteering reports of cloud tops, upper cloud layers, thunderstorm locations, icing conditions, turbulence, and areas of strong winds. PIREP information should be reported in this order:

1. Location.
2. Time.
3. Phenomena encountered.
4. Altitude.
5. Type of aircraft (if report concerns turbulence or icing).

These PIREPs are transmitted over the teletypewriter in a group format or as a remark appended to a Surface Aviation Weather Report. The letters *UA*, as previously discussed, identify the message as a pilot report.

3.133 The PIREP excerpt below is decoded to assist pilots in reading coded PIREPs:

UA/OV MRB-PIT 1600 FL080/TP BE18/SK 004 BKN 012/022 BKN-OVC/TA 01/WV 280050/TB MDT/IC LGT RIME 035-060/RM R TURBC INCRS WWD.

Pilot Report/ Location from MRB to PIT *Time* 1600Z *Flight Level* 8,000 feet/ *Type Aircraft* BE 18/ *Sky Cover* 400 feet broken, tops 1,200 feet; second layer base 2,200 feet broken variable overcast/ *Temperature* 1°C/ *Wind* 280° at 50 knots/ *Turbulence* moderate/ *Icing* light rime from 3,500 feet to 6,000 feet/ *Remarks* moderate rain; turbulence increasing westward.

Radar Weather Reports (SD) (RAREP)

3.134 Radar Weather Reports are routinely transmitted on teletype circuits. These reports describe areas of general precipitation, thunderstorms, and severe storms as observed by radar. Radar stations report the location of precipitation along with its type, intensity, and trend. (In addition, this type of report includes a special "digital" section which is intended primarily for the use of the National Weather Service for computer compilation. However, the digital section will not be explored since it is of minimal value to the pilot.) The table in Figure 3-29 explains symbols denoting intensity and trend, and the table in Figure 3-30 explains the contractions used to report the operational status of radar. A sample report decoded in Figure 3-31 reviews the order and content of a Radar Weather Report.

PRECIPITATION INTENSITY AND INTENSITY TREND TABLE

INTENSITY		INTENSITY TREND	
SYMBOL	INTENSITY	SYMBOL	TREND
—	LIGHT	+	INCREASING
(NONE)	MODERATE		
+	HEAVY	—	DECREASING
++	VERY HEAVY		
X	INTENSE	NC	NO CHANGE
XX	EXTREME		
U	UNKNOWN	NEW	NEW ECHO

Figure 3-29.

TABLE OF CONTRACTIONS REPORTING OPERATIONAL STATUS OF RADAR

CONTRACTION	OPERATIONAL STATUS
PPINE	Equipment normal and operating in PPI (Plan Position Indicator) mode; no echoes observed.
PPIOM	Radar inoperative or out of service for preventative maintenance.
PPINA	Observations omitted or not available for reasons other than PPINE or PPIOM.
ROBEPS	Radar operating below performance standards.
ARNO	"A" scope or azimuth/range indicator inoperative.
RHINO	Radar cannot be operated in RHI (Range-height indicator) mode. Height data not available.

Figure 3-30.

SAMPLE RADAR WEATHER REPORT

OKC 1934 LN 8TRW++/+ 86/40 164/60/ 199/115 15W 2425
MT 570 AT 159/65 2 INCH HAIL RPRTD THIS ECHO

OKC 1934	LN	8	TRW++/+	86/40 164/60 199/115	15W	2425
A.	B.	C.	D.	E.	F.	G.

MT 570 AT 159/65	2 INCH HAIL RPRTD THIS ECHO
H.	I.

A. LOCATION IDENTIFIER AND TIME OF RADAR OBSERVATION (GMT)

B. ECHO PATTERN[1] (LINE IN THIS EXAMPLE)

C. COVERAGE IN TENTHS (8/10 OF THIS EXAMPLE)

D. TYPE, INTENSITY, AND TREND OF WEATHER[2] [THUNDERSTORM (T), VERY HEAVY RAINSHOWERS (RW++), INCREASING IN INTENSITY (/+)]

E. AZIMUTH (REFERENCE TRUE N) AND RANGE IN NAUTICAL MILES (NM) OF POINTS DEFINING THE ECHO PATTERN

F. DIMENSION OF ECHO PATTERN[3] (15 NM WIDE)

G. PATTERN MOVEMENT (LINE MOVING FROM 240° AT 25 KNOTS); MAY ALSO SHOW MOVEMENT OF INDIVIDUAL STORMS OR "CELLS"

H. MAXIMUM TOPS AND LOCATION (57,000 FEET)

I. REMARKS; SELF-EXPLANATORY IN PLAIN LANGUAGE CONTRACTIONS.

---

[1] ECHO PATTERN MAY BE A LINE (LN), FINE LINE (FINE LN), AREA (AREA), SPIRAL BAND AREA (SPIRAL BAND), OR SINGLE CELL (CELL).

[2] TELETYPEWRITER WEATHER SYMBOLS ARE USED. SEE TABLE 3-29 FOR INTENSITY AND INTENSITY TREND SYMBOLS.

[3] DIMENSION OF AN ECHO PATTERN IS GIVEN WHEN AZIMUTH AND RANGE DEFINE ONLY THE CENTER OR CENTER LINE OF THE PATTERN.

Figure 3-31.

Terminal Forecast (FT)

3.135 A U.S. Terminal Forecast is a forecast for an area within a 5-mile radius of the center of a runway complex for a specific airdrome. Terminal Forecasts are issued three times daily by the Weather Service Forecast Office (WSFO). The Terminal Forecast is valid for 18 hours with an additional 6-hour categorical outlook.

3.136 The content of a Terminal Forecast is similar to a Surface Aviation Weather Report. The following Terminal Forecast (Figure 3-32) is divided into elements which are decoded as explained.

MSP—The station identifier for Minneapolis, Minnesota.

262222—The forecast is valid beginning the 26th day of the month at 2200Z until 2200Z the following day.

C7X—The forecast ceiling layer is at 700 feet AGL and the sky is expected to be obscured.

2—Two miles visibility. The visibility is forecast in statute miles and fractions. An absence of a visibility entry specifically implies a visibility of more than six miles. When the visibility is six miles or less, the visibility restriction (such as snow) will also be described.

S-F—Light snow and fog. This section describes the weather and obstructions to vision with the same symbols used in Surface Aviation Weather Reports.

3420G30—The wind is forecast to be from 340° at 20 knots gusting to 30 knots. The omission of a wind entry specifically implies wind less than 10 knots.

OCNL C2X1/2 SF.—Remarks. This indicates a strong possibility of an occasional obscured ceiling at 200 feet AGL, visibility one-half mile with moderate snow and fog.

Ø7Z C2Ø OVC 5BS 3420G30.—An expected change in the weather conditions is expected at 0700 Zulu. The changes in conditions are anticipated to be a ceiling of 2,000 feet overcast, visibility of 5 miles with blowing snow, and a wind from 340° at a speed of 20 knots gusting to 30 knots.

16Z MVFR CIG WIND.—This is a 6-hour categorical outlook which follows the 18-hour forecast period and indicates that the ceiling is expected to be between 1,000 and 3,000 feet, the visibility is expected to be greater than 5 statute miles, and the wind is expected to be 25 knots or greater. The marginal VFR condition is due to a ceiling. The following is a complete listing of categorical groupings that are used to describe weather conditions beyond the initial 18-hour forecast period:

LIFR (Low IFR)—Ceiling less than 500 feet AGL and/or visibility less than 1 statute mile.

IFR—Ceiling 500 to less than 1,000 feet AGL and/or visibility 1 to less than 3 statute miles.

MVFR-(Marginal VFR)—Ceiling 1,000 to 3,000 feet AGL and/or visibility 3 to 5 statute miles inclusive.

VFR—Ceiling greater than 3,000 feet AGL and visibility greater than 5 statute miles; includes sky clear.

Figure 3-32. Sample Terminal Forecast

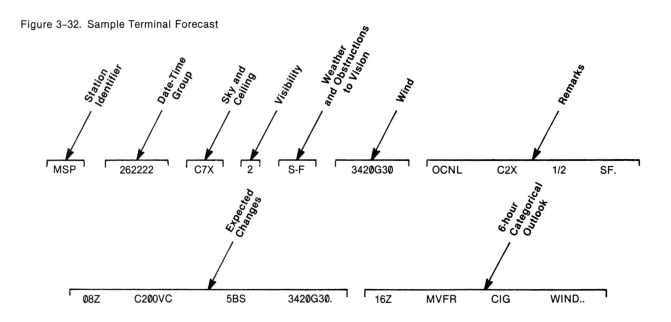

The cause of LIFR, IFR, or MVFR is also given by either ceiling or visibility restrictions or both. The contraction *CIG* and/or weather and obstruction to vision symbols are used to designate the forecast weather conditions for that category. If wind or gusts of 25 knots or greater are forecast for the outlook period, the word *WIND* is also included for all categories, including VFR.

Examples:

Ø4Z LIFR CIG—Instrument flying weather conditions due to ceiling forecast to below 500 feet.

Ø9Z IFR F—Instrument weather conditions due to visibilities restricted by fog.

16Z MVFR CIG H K—Marginal VFR flying conditions due to both ceiling and to visibility restricted by haze and smoke.

Ø4Z VFR WIND—VFR flying conditions; wind is expected to be 25 knots or greater.

Area Forecast (FA)

3.137 An Area Forecast is an 18-hour forecast of general weather conditions and also includes a 12-hour categorical outlook over an area the size of several states. (Figure 3-33) These Area Forecasts are prepared every 12 hours and all times arc GMT in whole hours. All wind directions are expressed in true direction and the speed in knots. Visibility is expressed in statute miles with all other distances expressed in nautical miles.

3.138 Area Forecasts are divided into the following sections:
1. Heading.
2. Forecast area.
3. Height statement.
4. Synopsis.
5. Significant clouds and weather, and outlook.
6. Icing and freezing level.

Figure 3-33 is an example of an Area Forecast.

Figure 3-33. Sample Area Forecast

```
MKC FA 211240.
13Z THU-Ø7Z FRI.
OTLK Ø7Z-19Z FRI.

WY CO KS NE SD ND...

HGTS ASL UNLESS NOTED...

SYNS... SFC HIGH OVR NRN RCKY AND WRN DAKS MOVG SLOLY SEWD.

SIGCLD AND WX...
WY...
NO SIGCLDS EXCP PSBL BRF CIG BLO 1Ø AND VSBYB BLO 3F VCNTY
CASPER TIL 15Z and CIG 4Ø BKN V SCT NERN SLPS BIGHORN  MTNS
TIL 18Z. OTLK... VFR.

CO...
NO SIGCLDS EXCP PSBL BRF CIG BLO 1Ø AND VSBYS 3FERN SLPS
IN SERN CO TIL 15Z AND 12Ø BKN CNTRL MTNS 17Z-Ø2Z. OTLK...
VFR.

KS...
NWRN PATCHY GNDFG WITH VSBYS LCLLY 3-5MI TIL 14Z WITH CIG
4Ø BKN DVLPG BY 16Z THEN CLRG AT ØØZ. SWRN CIG 1Ø-2Ø BKN
V SCT TIL 16Z THEN CIG 4Ø BKN CLRG AT ØØZ. CNTRL AND ERN
CIG BLO 1Ø AND VSBYS 3L-F IPVG TO CIG 25-3Ø BKN BY 17Z BCMG
CIG 8Ø BKN AFT Ø1Z THE CHC RW- EXTRM SERN. CLD TOPS TO 2ØØ.
OTLK... VFR.

NE...
PNHDL AND CNTRL NO SIGCLDS BUT PATCHY -X VSBYS BLO 3GF
PLATTE RVR VLY VCNTY NORTH PLATTE TIL 15Z. ERN CIG BLO 1Ø
VSBYS BRFLY 3R-L-F IPVG TO CIG 18 BRN V SCT AFT 18Z. CLD TOPS
TO 8Ø. OTLK... VFR.

SD...
WRN AND CNTRL NO SIGCLDS. ERN MOSTLY SCT CLDS WITH OCNL VSBYS
BLO 3GF WITH BRFLY CIG BLO 1Ø TIL 15Z THEN 2Ø-3Ø BKN V SCT
DVLPG AFT 17Z BUT CLRG AT SS. CLD TOPS 8Ø. OTLK... VFR.

ND...
CIG 1Ø-25 BKN OCNL CIG BLO 1Ø AND VSBYS BLO 3F TIL 15Z THEN
CIG 2Ø-4Ø BKN V SCT CLRG AT SS. ERN CLR EXCP OCNL VSBYS BLO
3GF SE TIL 15Z AND 4Ø SCT AFT 18Z. TOPS TO 9Ø. OTLK... VFR.

ICG...
LGT OCNL MDT MXD ICGICIP ABV FRZLVL. FRZLVL SFC WRN DAKS WY
WRN NE AND NRN CO SLPG TO 8Ø-11Ø SERN KS.
```

Heading

3.139 The heading identifies the forecast as an Area Forecast, and identifies the WSFO, the date and time of issue, and the valid periods of the forecast and outlook.

Area

3.140 The area of forecast area coverage is stated in contracted form.

Height Statement

3.141 All Area Forecasts contain the statement *HGTS ASL UNLESS NOTED*, which means all heights are above sea level unless noted. If these heights are above ground level it will be denoted in one of two ways:

1. The term *CIG* will be used to indicate above ground level, or

2. The term *AGL* which means above ground level.

Synopsis

3.142 The location and movement of. fronts, pressure systems, and circulation patterns is summarized in the Synopsis section. Moisture and stability conditions may be reported when appropriate.

Significant Clouds and Weather

3.143 The Significant Clouds and Weather (SIGCLD AND WX) section forecasts the cloudiness and weather significant to flight operations. This section of the forecast is put into paragraph form by states, well known geographical areas, or in reference to location and movement of a pressure system or front. Contained in the forecast is the obstruction to vision when the forecast visibility is expected to be 6 miles or less. Expected precipitation and thunderstorms are also always included. A categorical outlook for each breakdown area follows the *OTLK* which is the last statement in the paragraph.

Icing

3.144 The Icing section is identified by the contraction *ICG*. This section specifies the location, type, and extent of expected icing. The freezing level in hundreds of feet ASL is also included in the Icing section.

Forecast Winds and Temperatures Aloft (FD)

3.145 Winds and Temperatures Aloft Forecasts are produced twice a day for specific locations in the contiguous U.S. The heading contains the date and time the forecast was transmitted. (Figure 3-34)

3.146 The valid time period for each forecast is included in the FD heading, for example, FOR USE 1800-0300Z. The forecast temperatures in degrees Centigrade are preceded by a plus (+) or a minus (-) sign up through the 24,000-foot level. Since the temperatures above 24,000 feet are always negative, the negative sign is omitted from the printed FD for temperatures at altitudes above 24,000 feet.

3.147 The FD wind table has nine standard forecast wind levels on the line labeled FT. Depending upon station elevation, the 3,000, 6,000, 9,000, and 12,000-foot level winds are forecast for true altitude, and 18,000 feet and above are forecast for pressure altitude. No winds are forecast within 1,500 feet of the station elevation. Forecast temperatures are not included for the 3,000-foot level or for a level within 2,500 feet of station elevation.

3.148 To decode the four-digit wind group, the wind direction is referenced to true direction, and the speed is given in knots. For example, in Figure 3-34, the ABR forecast wind at the 3,000-foot level would be decoded as being from a true direction of 350° at 7 knots. When the coded wind group has six digits, the forecast temperature in degrees Centigrade is included. For example, the ABR forecast wind at the 6,000-foot level is from 330° at 13 knots and the temperature is forecast to be +1°C. A forecast windspeed less than 5 knots is coded as 9900 and is described as a ''light and variable'' wind. To decode the wind direction and speed when the speed is greater than 100 knots, 50 must be subtracted from the direction code and 100 must be added to the speed. For example, the DSM 30,000-foot forecast wind would be decoded as being from a true direction of 250° at 105 knots. The forecast temperature is -42°C.

Figure 3-34. Sample Winds and Temperatures Aloft Forecast

```
FD WBC 210544
BASED ON 210000Z DATA
VALID 212800Z FOR USE 1500-2100Z.  TEMPS NEG ABV 24000
```

FT	3000	6000	9000	12000	18000	24000	30000	34000	39000
ABR	3507	3313+01	3121-05	3030-10	2839-23	2742-33	255147	245655	245357
BFF		2507	2808-01	3013-07	3121-20	3222-32	322448	302858	293164
BIL		2213	2520-02	2728-08	2843-21	2847-33	285249	285758	285363
CZI			2517+00	2726-07	2834-20	2937-33	294149	294859	284965
DEN			3408+00	3612-06	3517-20	3521-32	352748	342958	322964
DIK		2706+01	2816-06	2728-12	2848-24	2957-35	296549	286657	275257
DLN			2317+01	2530-06	2736-20	2741-32	284648	285157	295164
DSM	3525	3516+07	3235+02	2845-04	2365-16	2385-28	750542	801551	800762

In-flight Weather Advisories (WST, WS, WA)

3.149 The primary purpose of the In-flight Weather Advisory Service is to notify en route pilots of developing potentially hazardous weather. Whether or not the particular condition described is potentially hazardous to a particular flight is for the pilot to evaluate on the basis of previous piloting experience and the operational limits of the aircraft. All heights are ASL unless noted and ceiling heights are always AGL. The advisories are of three types: Convective SIGMET (WST), Nonconvective SIGMET (WS), and AIRMET (WA). The format of the advisories consists of (1) a message identifier, (2) a flight precautions statement, and (3) further details if necessary.

3.150 Flight Service Stations (FSS) having voice facilities on VOR or radio beacons broadcast SIGMETs and AIRMETs during their valid period (when they pertain to the area within 150 nautical miles of the FSS) as follows:

1. SIGMETs at 15-minute intervals (Hr. + 00, Hr. + 15, Hr. + 30, Hr. + 45); and AIRMETs at 30-minute intervals (Hr. + 15* and Hr. + 45) during the first hour after issuance. (* Included in the scheduled weather broadcast.)

2. Thereafter, an alert notice will be broadcast at Hr. + 15** and Hr. + 45 during the valid period of the advisories. (** Included in the scheduled weather broadcast.) This notice simply alerts pilots of the fact that a certain AIRMET and/or SIGMET are still in effect. Pilots, after receiving the alert notice broadcast, should contact the nearest FSS to determine if the advisory is relative to their flight if they have not previously received the advisory.

Convective SIGMET (WST)

3.151 A SIGMET is issued concerning weather phenomena potentially hazardous to all categories of aircraft. Thunderstorms are the reason for the issuance of Convective SIGMETs. Such phenomena included in Convective SIGMETs are:

1. Tornadoes.
2. Lines of thunderstorms.
3. Embedded thunderstorms.
4. Areas of thunderstorms with areal coverages of 40 percent or more that appear to be of very strong, intense, or extreme levels of echo intensity as observed by weather radar.
5. Hail of ¾ inch or greater in diameter.

Any Convective SIGMET implies severe or greater turbulence, severe icing, and low-level wind shear and therefore is not specified in the advisory.

Nonconvective SIGMETs (WS)

3.152 Any nonconvective weather activity that is hazardous to all aircraft is listed in Nonconvective SIGMETs. Such phenomena include:

1. Severe or extreme turbulence.
2. Severe icing.
3. Widespread sandstorms/duststorms, lowering visibilities to less than 3 miles.

AIRMET (WA)

3.153 An AIRMET is issued concerning weather phenomena that may be potentially hazardous to single engine and light aircraft, and in some cases to other aircraft. Such phenomena include:

1. Moderate icing.
2. Moderate turbulence.
3. Sustained winds of 30 knots or greater at the surface.
4. Onset of extensive areas of visibility below 3 miles and/or ceilings less than 1,000 feet, including mountain ridges and passes.

Convective Outlook (AC)

3.154 A Convective Outlook (Figure 3-35) describes possible areas where both general and severe thunderstorms could occur during a 24-hour period. This outlook is transmitted by National Severe Storms Forecast Center (NSSFC) about three times daily and is primarily used as a tool for planning flights later in the day.

3.155 The expected conditions requiring a severe weather watch are:

1. Severe thunderstorms with either/or both:
   A. Damaging surface wind with gusts of 50 knots or more.
   B. Hail ¾ inch or greater in diameter.
2. Tornado activity.

3.156 In the text of the outlook, the notation *ABV SELS LIMITS* means the thunderstorm activity will meet the criteria for a severe weather watch.

```
AC MKC 020840

MKC AC 020840
VALID 021200-031200Z
SQLN CRNTLY IN ECNTRL TEX PNHDL EXTNDS NWD INTO NRN TEX PNHDL AND SW KANS
AS LN OF OVRRNG TSTMS.  THIS LN MOVG EWD 30 KT WILL GRDLY INTSFY DURG THE
FRNN WITH SVR TSTM ACTVTY WELL ABV SELS LIMITS EXPCD BGN BY LATE FRNN
CNTRL OKLA TO N CNTRL TEX MOVG EWD DURG AFTN THRU ERN OKLA SE KANS AND
NE TEX INTO MOST OF ARK SW AND SRN MO DURG AFTN AND EVE BFR DMNSHG.
INTSFY LATE EVE NE ARK SE MO W KY AND W TENN.

TSTMS DURG PRD EXPCD TO RT OF LN DRT INK HOB GCK STJ BRL DAY HTS LOZ BNA
LFK SAT DRT. FEW TSHWRS CRNTLY IN NEW ENG WILL KMNSH DURG FRNN HWVR
ISOLD TSHWRS ALSO EXPCD DURG THE PRD TO RT OF LN DOV IPT MSS.

FORECASTER (NAME)
```

Figure 3-35. Sample Convective Outlook

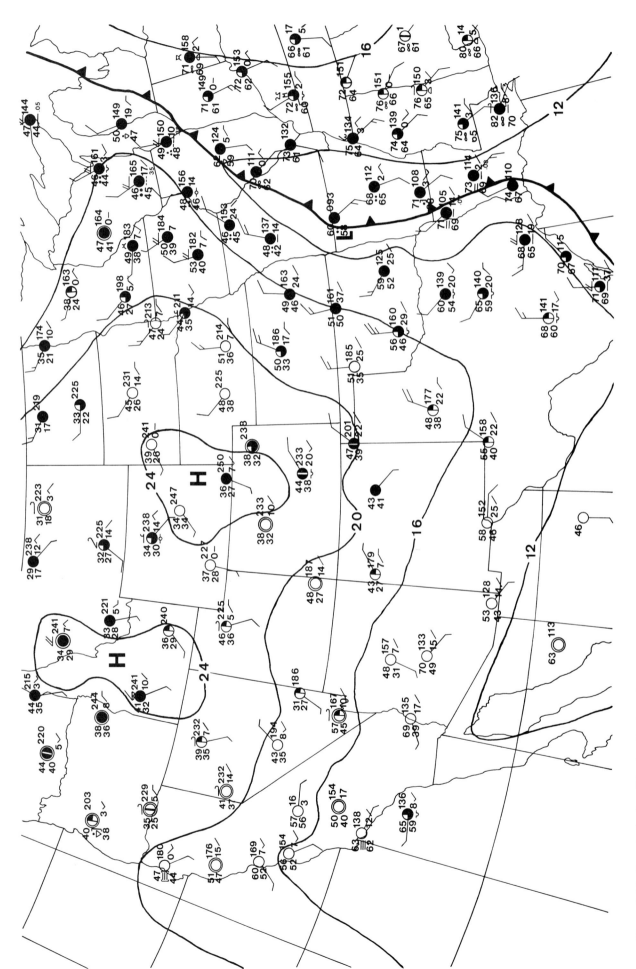

Figure 3–36. Sample Surface Weather Analysis Chart Excerpt

Surface Analysis Chart

3.157 The Surface Analysis Weather Chart presents a graphic view of the weather systems influencing the United States. These charts are issued at 3-hour intervals but pilots should be alerted to the fact that the data presented on the chart are already over one hour old at the time of issuance. Figure 3-36 illustrates a Surface Analysis Chart.

3.158 Since the Surface Analysis Weather Chart is essentially a report and not a forecast, this chart should be used in conjunction with other appropriate forecasts and reports. Remember, weather systems can move rapidly and conditions can sometimes change unexpectedly.

3.159 There are a number of symbols that are used to construct a station model on the Surface Analysis Chart. Some of the most common symbols are illustrated in the table in Figure 3-37.

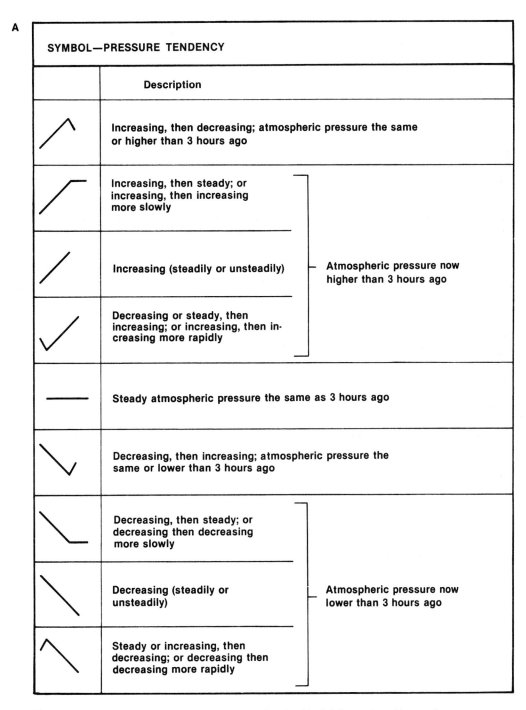

Figures 3-37 A-E. Surface Weather Analysis Station Model Symbol and Legend

B

SYMBOL——SKY COVERAGE		SYMBOL——WEATHER		SYMBOL——WEATHER	
N	Description	ww	Description	ww	Description
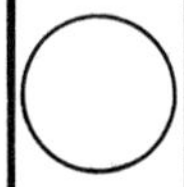 ◯	No clouds	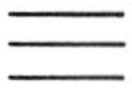 ☰	Fog	 ⃝•	Sleet
 ⦶	Less than one-tenth or one-tenth	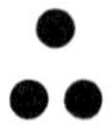 • ••	Rain Intermittent Continuous	 •▽	Rain showers
 ◔	Two and three-tenths	 ✳ ✳ ✳	Snow Intermittent Continuous	 *▽	Snow showers
 ◑	Four-tenths	 • ••	Drizzle Intermittent Continuous	 ⚡	Lightning
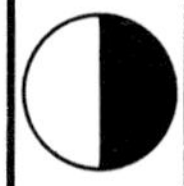 ◐	Five-tenths	 �	Thunderstorm	 ↺	Signs of tropical storm
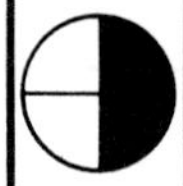 ⊖	Six-tenths	 Ƨ→	Dust or sandstorm	 ⧜	Dust devils
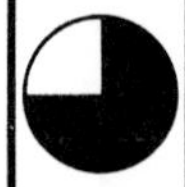 ◕	Seven and eight-tenths	 ∞	Haze	 ∿	Smoke
 ⦷	Nine-tenths or overcast with openings	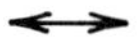 ↔	Ice crystals	 ⤉	Drifting or blowing snow
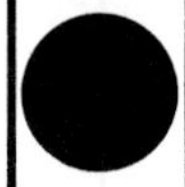 ●	Completely overcast				
 ⊗	Obscured				

82

C

SYMBOL —— LOW CLOUDS		SYMBOL —— MIDDLE CLOUDS		SYMBOL —— HIGH CLOUDS	
C_L	Description	C_M	Description	C_H	Description
(symbol)	Cumulus of fair weather little vertical development and seemingly flattened	(symbol)	Thin Altostratus (most of cloud layer semi-transparent)	(symbol)	Filaments of Cirrus or "mares tails," scattered and not increasing
(symbol)	Cumulus of considerable development, generally towering, with or without other Cumulus or Stratus bases all at same level	(symbol)	Thick Altostratus, greater part sufficiently dense to hide sun (or moon), or Nimbostratus	(symbol)	Dense Cirrus in patches or twisted sheaves, usually not increasing, sometimes like remains of Cumulonimbus, or towers or tufts
(symbol)	Cumulonimbus with tops lacking clear-cut outlines, but distinctly not cirriform or anvil-shaped; with or without Cumulus, Stratocumulus or Stratus	(symbol)	Thin Altocumulus, mostly semi-transparent; cloud elements not changing much and at a single level	(symbol)	Dense Cirrus often anvil-shaped, derived from or associated with cumulonimbus
(symbol)	Stratocumulus not formed by spreading out of Cumulus	(symbol)	Thin Altocumulus in patches; cloud elements not changing much and at a single level	(symbol)	Cirrus, often hook-shaped, gradually spreading over the sky and usually thickening as a whole
(symbol)	Stratus or Fractocumulus or both, but no Fractostratus of bad weather	(symbol)	Thin Altocumulus in bands or in a layer gradually spreading over sky and usually thickening as a whole	(symbol)	Cirrus Cirrostratus, often in converging bands, or Cirrostratus alone; generally overspreading and growing denser; the continuous layer not reaching 45° altitude
(symbol)	Fractostratus and/or Fractocumulus of bad weather (scud)	(symbol)	Altocumulus formed by the spreading out of Cumulus	(symbol)	Cirrus and Cirrostratus often in converging bands, or Cirrostratus alone; generally overspreading and growing denser; the continuous layer exceeding 45° altitude
(symbol)	Stratocumulus formed by spreading out of Cumulus; Cumulus often present also	(symbol)	Double-layered Altocumulus, or a thick layer of Altocumulus not increasing; or Altocumulus with Altostratus and/or Nimbostratus	(symbol)	Veil of Cirrostratus covering the entire sky
(symbol)	Cumulus and Stratocumulus (not formed by spreading out of Cumulus) with bases at different levels	(symbol)	Altocumulus in the form of Cumulus-shaped tufts or Altocumulus with turrets	(symbol)	Cirrostratus not increasing and not covering entire sky
(symbol)	Cumulonimbus having a clearly fibrous (cirriform) top, often anvil-shaped, with or without Cumulus, Stratocumulus or scud	(symbol)	Altocumulus of a chaotic sky, usually at different levels; patches of dense Cirrus are usually present also	(symbol)	Cirrocumulus alone or Cirrocumulus with some Cirrus or Cirrostratus but the Cirrocumulus being the main Cirroform cloud

83

D

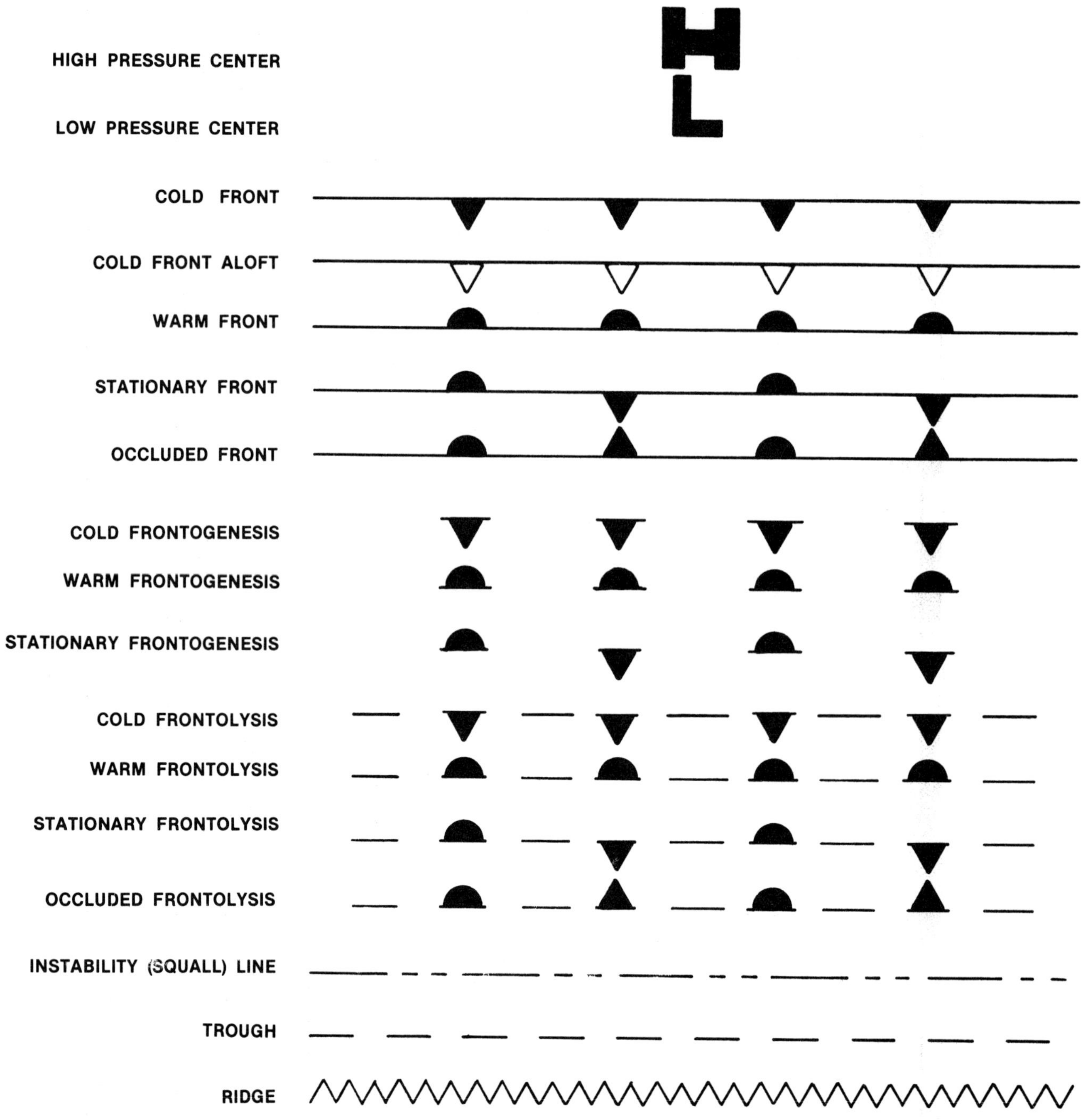

HIGH PRESSURE CENTER

LOW PRESSURE CENTER

COLD FRONT

COLD FRONT ALOFT

WARM FRONT

STATIONARY FRONT

OCCLUDED FRONT

COLD FRONTOGENESIS

WARM FRONTOGENESIS

STATIONARY FRONTOGENESIS

COLD FRONTOLYSIS

WARM FRONTOLYSIS

STATIONARY FRONTOLYSIS

OCCLUDED FRONTOLYSIS

INSTABILITY (SQUALL) LINE

TROUGH

RIDGE

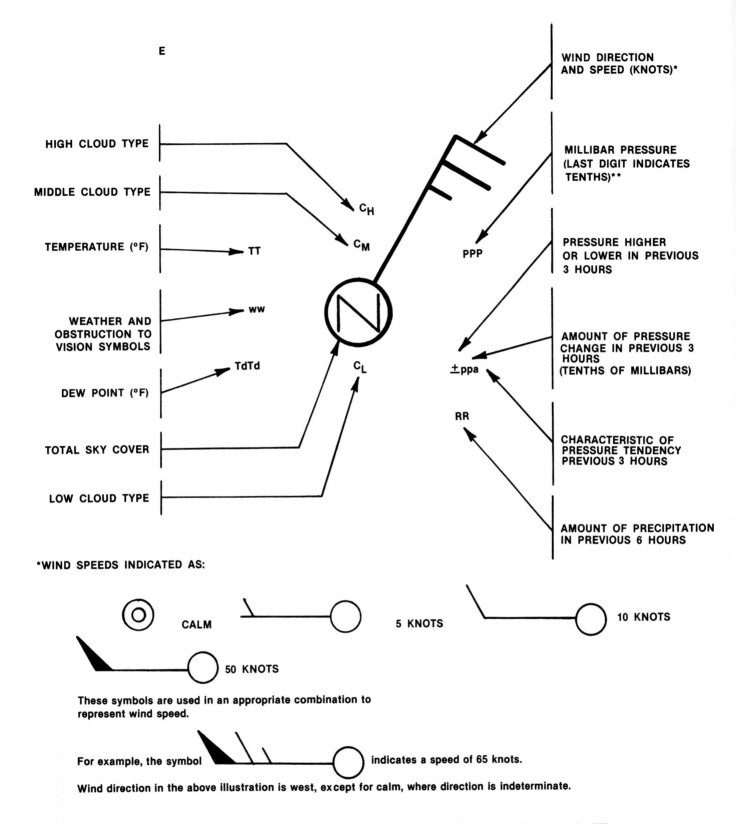

E

HIGH CLOUD TYPE → C_H

MIDDLE CLOUD TYPE → C_M

TEMPERATURE (°F) → TT

WEATHER AND OBSTRUCTION TO VISION SYMBOLS → ww

DEW POINT (°F) → TdTd

TOTAL SKY COVER

LOW CLOUD TYPE → C_L

WIND DIRECTION AND SPEED (KNOTS)*

MILLIBAR PRESSURE (LAST DIGIT INDICATES TENTHS)** → PPP

PRESSURE HIGHER OR LOWER IN PREVIOUS 3 HOURS

AMOUNT OF PRESSURE CHANGE IN PREVIOUS 3 HOURS (TENTHS OF MILLIBARS) → ±ppa

CHARACTERISTIC OF PRESSURE TENDENCY PREVIOUS 3 HOURS

RR

AMOUNT OF PRECIPITATION IN PREVIOUS 6 HOURS

*WIND SPEEDS INDICATED AS:

CALM   5 KNOTS   10 KNOTS

50 KNOTS

These symbols are used in an appropriate combination to represent wind speed.

For example, the symbol   indicates a speed of 65 knots.

Wind direction in the above illustration is west, except for calm, where direction is indeterminate.

**SAMPLE DECODE: If the PPP was 249 millibars, pressure would be in excess of 1000 millibars or 1024.9 millibars. If the PPP was 999 millibars, pressure would be less than 1000 millibars or 999.9 millibars. REMEMBER, standard sea-level pressure is 1013.2 millibars.

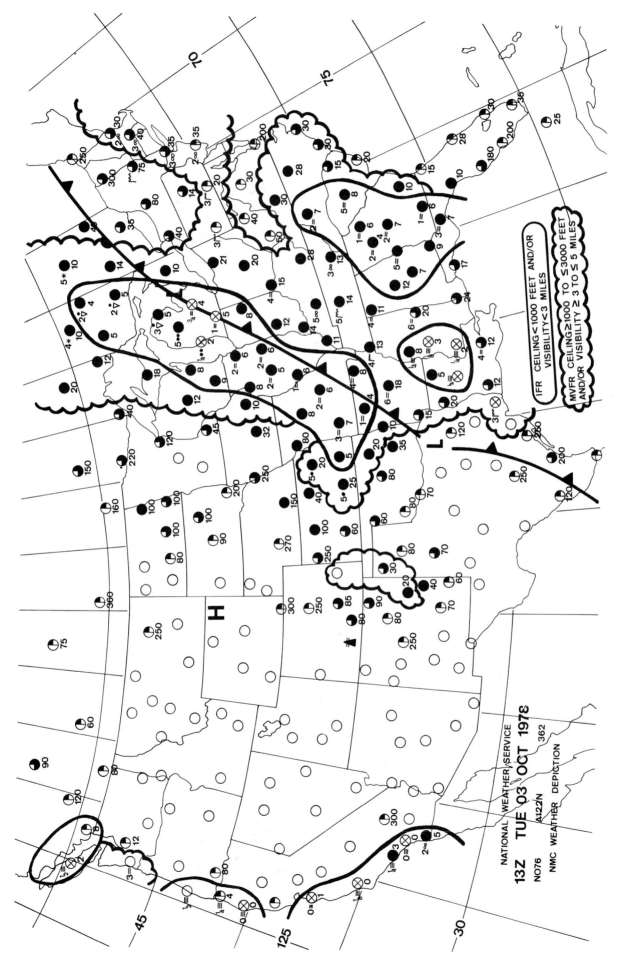

NATIONAL WEATHER SERVICE
13Z TUE 03 OCT 1978
NO76   A122N   362
NMC WEATHER DEPICTION

IFR CEILING <1000 FEET AND/OR
VISIBILITY <3 MILES

MVFR CEILING ≥1000 TO ≤3000 FEET
AND/OR VISIBILITY ≥ 3 TO ≤ 5 MILES

Figure 3-38. Sample Weather Depiction Chart

86

Weather Depiction Chart

3.160 The Weather Depiction Chart is an excellent chart to start any weather briefing since a pilot can determine general weather conditions more readily from this chart than from any other source. This chart provides the pilot with a graphic display whereby a pilot can determine if the weather is VFR, marginal VFR, or IFR. Although the Weather Depiction Chart presents an excellent picture of the weather, remember this chart shows weather conditions at the time the chart was prepared. (Figure 3-38)

3.161 Weather Depiction Charts are issued approximately every three hours. The compilation time (GMT) is recorded on the chart. The following data are depicted at each weather station (if appropriate):

1. Total sky cover.
2. Height of clouds or ceiling.
3. Weather and obstruction to vision.
4. Visibility, if less than 7 statute miles.

3.162 Cloud height is listed under the station circle. The number represents the vertical distance from the ground to the lowest cloud layer in hundreds of feet. If the total sky cover is considered to be few or scattered clouds, the listed height is the base of the lowest cloud layer. (Figure 3-39) When the total sky cover is broken, overcast, overcast with breaks, or obscured, the height is considered to be the ceiling. Absence of a height entry indicates that an obscuration is partial; or if absent before the broken, overcast with breaks, or overcast cloud layer symbols, it indicates a thin sky cover.

3.163 Weather and obstructions to vision are listed to the left of the station circle. When more than two types of weather and/or obstructions are present at the reporting station, only the one or two most significant types are entered. Whenever a station reports clouds topping ridges, a symbol unique only to the Weather Depiction Chart is listed to the left of the station circle. (Figure 3-40)

3.164 The depiction chart illustrates reported ceilings and visibilities as follows:

1. IFR conditions—Ceiling less than 1,000 feet and/or visibility less than 3 statute miles, outlined by a smooth solid line.
2. MVFR (Marginal VFR)—Ceiling 1,000 feet to 3,000 feet inclusive and/or visibility 3 to 5 statute miles inclusive, outlined by a scalloped line.
3. VFR conditions—The remaining portion of the chart not outlined contains ceilings greater than 3,000 feet or unlimited, and visibility greater than 5 statute miles.

WEATHER DEPICTION CHART—TOTAL SKY COVER TABLE

SYMBOL	TOTAL SKY COVER
	Sky Clear
	Less than 1/10 (Few)
	1/10 to 5/10 inclusive (Scattered)
	6/10 to 9/10 inclusive (Broken)
	10/10 with breaks (BINOVC)
	10/10 (Overcast)
	Sky obscured or partially obscured

Figure 3-39.

EXAMPLES OF STATION SYMBOLS AFTER PLOTTED ON THE WEATHER DEPICTION CHART

PLOTTED SYMBOL	INTERPRETED
	Few clouds, base 800 feet, visibility more than 6
	Broken sky cover, ceiling 1,200 feet, rain shower
	Thin overcast with breaks, visibility 5 in haze
	Scattered at 3,000 feet, clouds topping ridges
	Sky clear, visibility 2, ground fog or fog
	Sky partially obscured, visibility 1/2, blowing snow
	Sky obscured, ceiling 500, visibility 1/4, snow
	Overcast, ceiling 1,200 feet, thunderstorm, rain, visibility 1

Figure 3-40.

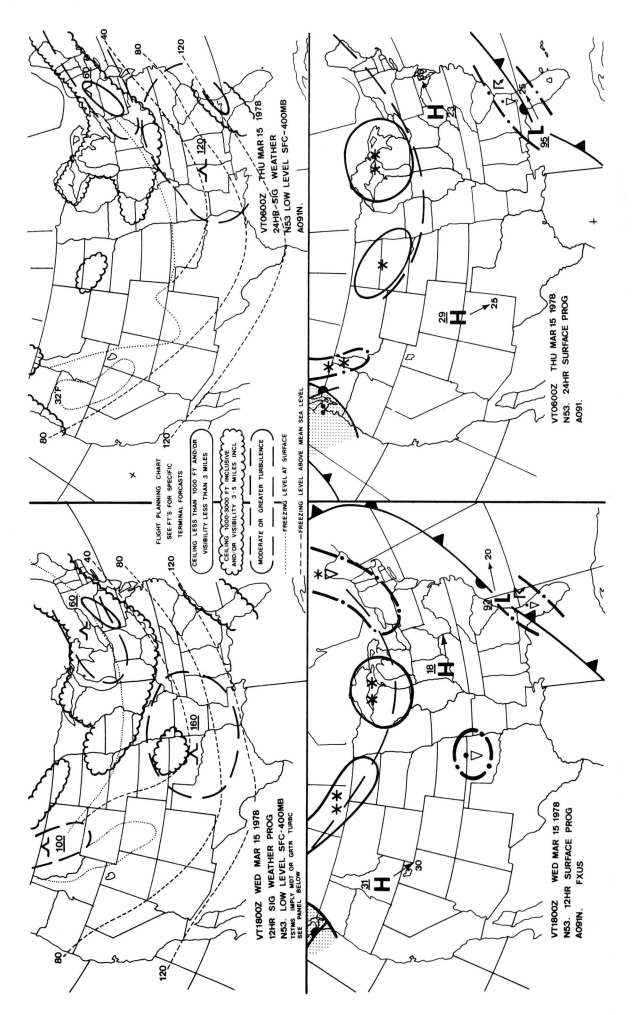

Figure 3-41. Sample Significant Weather Prognostic Chart

Significant Weather Prognostic Chart (Low Level)

3.165 Significant Weather Prognostic Charts, sometimes referred to as "progs," are generally used in long range flight planning to determine expected movement and change in weather patterns. These U.S. progs are prepared for low altitude weather (from the surface to an altitude of approximately 24,000 feet). The valid GMT time that the chart may be used is included with the prog chart legend.

3.166 The low-level prog chart consists of four panels on one chart. (Figure 3-41) On the lower half of the chart is a 12-hour and 24-hour surface prog chart. The upper half of the chart has a 12-hour and 24-hour prog chart of significant weather from the surface to a pressure level of 400 millibars (approximately 24,000 feet). These charts illustrate the conditions that are forecast for the valid time of the chart. The table in Figure 3-42 includes the standard symbols used on Significant Weather Prognostic Charts.

3.167 The two lower panels (surface prog panels) of the chart make use of the standard symbols for fronts and pressure centers as are depicted on the surface analysis chart. An arrow indicates direction and the speed (in knots) of each pressure center. Some of the 24-hour surface progs include isobars which illustrate forecast pressure patterns.

3.168 A solid line is used to identify areas of expected continuous or intermittent precipitation. Areas of showers or thunderstorms are enclosed by dash-dot lines. Shading inside the enclosed lines indicates precipitation will affect half or more of that area. The absence of shading indicates less than half of the area will receive precipitation.

3.169 The two upper panels of the Significant Weather Prognostic Chart depict areas of ceilings, limited visibility and turbulence, as well as the freezing level. As in the Weather Depiction Chart, solid lines enclose areas of forecasted IFR weather, scalloped lines enclose areas of forecasted MVFR, and VFR weather is that area not outlined.

3.170 An area which forecasts moderate or greater turbulence is identified with enclosed long-dashed lines. Forecast thunderstorms also imply that *moderate* or *greater* turbulence may be present in the storms, even though the general turbulence areas on the associated significant weather panel are not outlined. To denote turbulence intensity, one of the standard turbulence intensity symbols (as illustrated in the table in Figure 3-42) will be printed in the enclosed area. Numbers above and below a short line indicate anticipated respective tops and bases of turbulent layers (in hundreds of feet). The absence of a figure above the line indicates turbulence to the upper limit of the chart. Conversely,

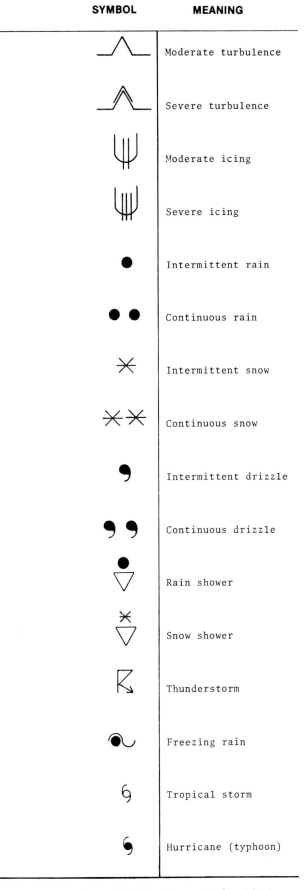

SYMBOL	MEANING
	Moderate turbulence
	Severe turbulence
	Moderate icing
	Severe icing
	Intermittent rain
	Continuous rain
	Intermittent snow
	Continuous snow
	Intermittent drizzle
	Continuous drizzle
	Rain shower
	Snow shower
	Thunderstorm
	Freezing rain
	Tropical storm
	Hurricane (typhoon)

Figure 3-42. Significant Weather Prognostic Chart Code Reference Table

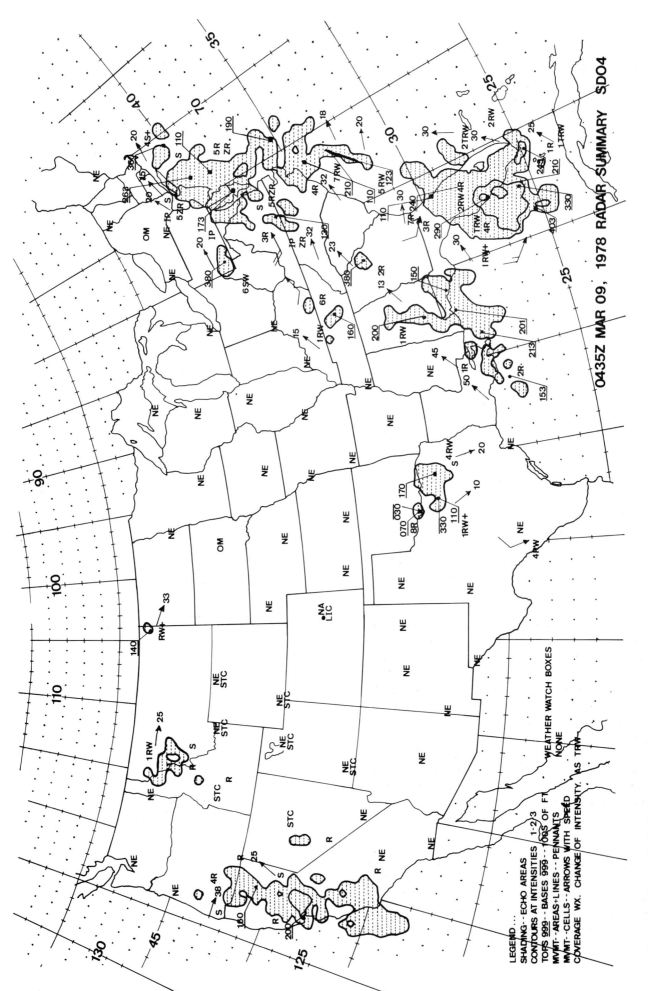

Figure 3-43. Sample Radar Summary Chart

the absence of a figure below the line indicates turbulence from the surface upwards.

3.171 A dotted line indicating the freezing level line on the surface is labeled *32°*. Short dashed lines are used to identify freezing level at various altitudes. These freezing level height contours are drawn at 4,000-foot intervals, but the 4,000-foot contour line terminates at the 4,000-foot terrain level along the Rocky Mountains. The contours are labeled in hundreds of feet MSL. Occasionally, a freezing level height contour line will cross the surface freezing level line. This condition indicates multiple freezing levels.

3.172 Aircraft *icing* is always implied in cloud and precipitation above the freezing level, although the chart does not specifically outline these areas.

Radar Summary Chart

3.173 A Radar Summary Chart displays precipitation echoes and their location, coverage, movement, and tops along with other pertinent information. (Figure 3-43) This chart is especially useful in preflight planning to determine:

1. General areas of precipitation and thunderstorm movement.

2. Increasing or decreasing intensity of weather activity.

3. Type of weather.

Pilots should note that this chart is essentially a report of past weather and not a forecast of any type.

3.174 The radar echo patterns consist of an arrangement of echoes. These echoes form a pattern that may be a line of echoes, an area of echoes, or an isolated cell. The echo pattern is indicated on the Radar Summary Chart by a contour line or series of contour lines. The table in Figure 3-44 lists the intensity level by contour and intensity level number.

3.175 Echoes of strong or very strong intensity (intensity level number 3) are depicted by one intensity contour inside another. The area described by the innermost contour line indicates the location of strong or very strong echo intensity. The area between the outermost and the inner contour line indicates an area of weak to moderate echo intensity. The same basic solution applies to deciphering echoes of intense or extreme intensity.

INTENSITY LEVEL	INTENSITY CONTOURS	ECHO INTENSITY	ESTIMATED PRECIPITATION
1		Weak to Moderate	Light to Moderate
3		Strong to Very Strong	Heavy to Very Heavy
5		Intense to Extreme	Intense to Extreme

ECHO FREE REGION		An Echo-Free Region (Unlined Region) May Exist within a Broad Precipitation Area

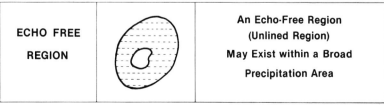

Figure 3-44. Echo Contour Intensity Table

3.176 Weather radar primarily detects particles of precipitation size within a cloud or falling from a cloud. Radar does *not* detect clouds or fog—only drops or ice particles of precipitation. Consequently the absence of echoes does not necessarily indicate clear weather conditions. Although the Radar Summary Chart indicates areas and types of precipitation, this chart *must* be used in conjunction with other reports, charts, and forecasts. The table in Figure 3-45 lists the symbols identifying the precipitation type associated with echoes.

3.177 The intensity trend of precipitation echoes is shown by either a negative sign (-) or a positive sign (+). A negative sign indicates the intensity of the echoes is decreasing. A positive sign indicates the echo intensities are increasing. Naturally, an absence of a (+) or (-) would mean no change.

3.178 Since the movement of individual echoes may differ from the movement of the overall echo pattern, an arrow with an associated number is used to represent the direction and speed (in knots) of an individual echo.

Example: An individual echo is moving southeast at a speed of 30 knots.

3.179 A line or area of echo movement is shown on the chart by an arrow with flags. A full flag indicates a speed of 10 knots and a half flag indicates a speed of 5 knots.

Example: A line or area movement is westerly at a speed of 25 knots.

3.180 Echo heights in hundreds of feet MSL are entered above and/or below a line to denote echo tops and bases respectively. Some examples of tops and bases are:

450   Tops 45,000 feet MSL.

————

120   Bases 12,000 feet MSL.

3.181 A "boxed" area enclosed by a dashed line indicates a severe weather watch is in effect. However, whenever no severe weather watch is in effect, the chart will be labeled "Weather Watch Boxes—None."

3.182 The precipitation coverage is only entered for *individual* stations. For example, 3TRW+ plotted next to a station identifier would indicate 3/10 precipitation coverage with thunderstorms and rain showers, and echo intensity increasing for that *particular* station. Whenever an area has solid sky cover, the contraction *SLD* will be plotted next to that area.

3.183 The reason a radar report for a particular station does not appear on the Radar Summary Chart is often annotated at the station location. The table in Figure 3-46 describes the symbols and their significance.

RADAR SUMMARY CHART WEATHER SYMBOLS

SYMBOL	MEANING
R	Rain
RW	Rain showers
A	Hail
S	Snow
IP	Ice pellets
SW	Snow showers
L	Drizzle
T	Thunderstorm
ZR, ZL	Freezing precipitation

Figure 3-45.

SYMBOLS INDICATING NO ECHOES

SYMBOL	MEANING
NE	No echo (equipment operating but no echoes observed)
NA	Observation not available
OM	Equipment out for maintenance

Figure 3-46.

Forecast Winds and Temperatures Aloft—Chart (FD)

3.184 Forecast Winds and Temperatures Aloft Charts are prepared for eight different altitudes on eight separate panels. A legend in the lower left corner of each panel indicates the valid time and level (altitude) of the chart. Those levels below 18,000 feet are true altitudes; levels 18,000 feet and higher are pressure altitudes (flight levels). Figure 3-47 is representative of a panel of a Winds and Temperatures Aloft Forecast.

3.185 This chart uses those arrows with barbs and pennants that are common to the surface weather map. The wind arrow is plotted to the nearest 10°, and the second digit of the coded direction is entered at the outer end of the arrow. To decode the wind direction of a plotted symbol, it is first necessary to determine the general direction (with reference to the arrow), and then use the digit to determine the wind direction to the nearest 10°. (Figure 3-47) A calm or light variable wind is indicated by 99 entered to the lower left of the station circle. The forecast temperature is plotted in two digits next to each station circle.

3.186 Occasionally it may become necessary to determine winds and temperatures for an altitude between charted levels. In such a case, it is necessary to interpolate between the charted levels.

Forecast-Report Summary Table

3.187 The numerous charts, forecasts, and reports can prove to be confusing at times, even to some of the most experienced pilots. The table in Figure 3-48 was designed to eliminate much of the confusion generated by all of the facsimile and teletype data previously discussed.

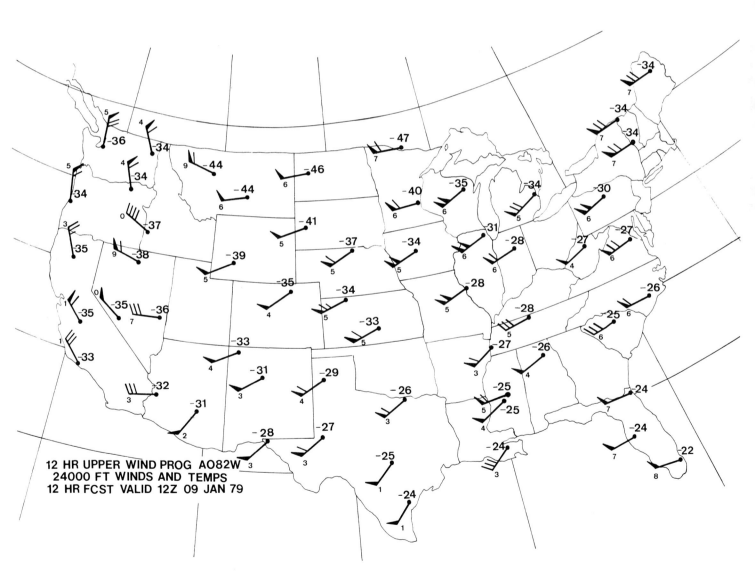

Figure 3-47. A Typical Winds and Temperatures Aloft Forecast Panel

CHAPTER THREE FORECAST-REPORT SUMMARY TABLE

NAME	CODED DESIGNATOR	DESCRIPTION	HOW OFTEN ISSUED	USE PERIOD	FACSIMILE/TELETYPE	REMARKS
Surface Aviation Weather Report	(SA)	Report	Hourly	Generally 1 hour[1]	Teletype	[1] Often called sequence report. Report could be updated every 20 minutes for a special report.
Radar Weather Report	(SD) or (RAREP)	Report	Hourly[2]	1 hour	Teletype	[2] May be issued more frequently as conditions warrant.
Terminal Forecast	(FT)	Forecast	Issued 3 times daily	Valid for 24 hours[3]	Teletype	[3] 18 hour forecast with 6 hour outlook. May be changed more frequently as conditions warrant.
Area Forecast	(FA)	Forecast	Every 12 hours	30 hours[4]	Teletype	[4] Covers 18 hour period with an additional 12 hour outlook.
Winds and Temperatures Aloft Forecast	(FD)	Forecast	Twice daily	Valid as stated	Teletype	
Convective Outlook	(AC)	Forecast	Issued 3 times daily	Valid for 24 hours	Teletype	
Convective SIGMET	(WST)	Inflight Advisory Forecast	Hourly	Valid for 2 hours	Teletype	Pilots generally receive information over radio broadcasts.
Nonconvective SIGMET	(WS)	Inflight Advisory Forecast	Unscheduled	Valid as stated	Teletype	Pilots generally receive information over radio broadcasts.
AIRMET	(WA)	Inflight Advisory Forecast	Unscheduled	Valid as stated	Teletype	Pilots generally receive information over radio broadcasts.
Surface Weather Analysis Chart		Report	Every 3 hours	3 hours	Facsimile	
Weather Depiction Chart		Report	Generally every 3 hours	Until next chart is issued	Facsimile	Issuance time may vary.
Radar Summary Chart	(SD)	Report	See remarks	Until next chart is issued	Facsimile	Issuance time may vary from every one to three hours.
Significant Weather Prognostic		Forecast	Issued 4 times daily	Valid as stated on chart[5]	Facsimile	[5] Forecast period may vary from 12 to 48 hours.
Winds and Temperatures Aloft Forecast	(FD)	Forecast	Twice daily	Valid as stated	Facsimile	

Pilot Notes:
1. All wind headings are true directions.
2. At some FSS locations some reports and forecasts may be presented by cathode ray tube displays rather than by conventional methods.

Figure 3-48.

CHAPTER 3: QUESTIONS

For answers see Appendix E

1. The 1100Z and 1300Z hourly Surface Aviation Weather Reports for MSP are listed below. Select the conclusion that can be correctly drawn from the given information.

MN 271104
MSP RS 1055 M8OVC 2F 132/41/41/1005/992
MN 271304
MSP RS 1255 M5OVC 1F 129/41/41/0000/991

1. The wind has changed to a north direction.
2. The ceiling and visibility have deteriorated.
3. The altimeter setting has increased.
4. The weather is unchanged.

2. What is the MSP 1100Z altimeter setting in question 1?

1. 30.05 inches of mercury.
2. 29.91 inches of mercury.
3. 29.92 inches of mercury.
4. 29.50 inches of mercury.

3. Which of the following statements is true in regard to the hourly sequence given for DCA?

DCA SP 1115 W2 OVC 1RF 098/43/43/1205/982/
UA OVC 32

1. The overcast is 3,200 feet thick.
2. The top of the overcast is 3,200 feet AGL.
3. The top of the overcast is 3,400 feet MSL.
4. The top of the overcast is 3,200 feet MSL.

4. On a Surface Analysis Chart the illustrated symbol (above) represents a wind from:

1. 300° at 30 knots.
2. 080° at 35 knots.
3. 260° at 35 knots.
4. 220° at 30 knots.

5. What relationship does the surface wind have with winds above the friction level?

1. The surface wind is deflected approximately 30° to the left and has a lower speed.
2. The surface wind is deflected approximately 30° to the right only.
3. The surface wind is deflected approximately 30° to the right with an increase in velocity.
4. The surface wind is deflected approximately 30° to the left with an increase in speed.

6. Air mass thunderstorms are:

1. Usually associated with cold fronts.
2. Scattered and can usually be circumnavigated.
3. The most severe of all thunderstorms.
4. Formed from stable air.

7. When flying an aircraft through a front in the Northern Hemisphere, the aircraft heading should be corrected to the:

1. Right after passing the front, regardless of the aircraft heading or type of front.
2. Left before penetrating a warm front and right after passing through the front.
3. Right before penetrating a cold front and left after passing through the front.
4. Left regardless of the type of front.

8. Turbulent air and possible icing are associated with what type of fog?

1. Upslope fog.
2. Precipitation fog.
3. Steam fog.
4. Ice fog.

9. The surface wind speed entry will be omitted from a Terminal Forecast if the wind speed is forecast to be less than:

1. 15 knots.
2. 5 knots.
3. 12 knots.
4. 10 knots.

10. Select the correct statements which describe SIGMETs and AIRMETs.

A. A SIGMET concerns weather that may be hazardous to all aircraft.
B. SIGMETs and AIRMETs are intended to cover a complete state.
C. SIGMETs and AIRMETs are included in the scheduled weather broadcast, for a 150 nautical mile radius of the reporting Flight Service Station.
D. An AIRMET concerns weather that may be hazardous to all aircraft.

1. A and B.
2. B, C, and D.
3. A, B, and C.
4. A and C.

11. Generally, tornadoes are associated with:

1. Air mass thunderstorms.
2. Cold front thunderstorms.
3. Warm front thunderstorms.
4. Squall line thunderstorms.

12. What is the 1700 Z wind forecast to be in the Terminal Forecast?

DEN 212323 C1ØBKN 3Ø OVC 5H 272Ø. Ø6Z 6Ø SCT 2625. 17Z VFR WIND . . . .
   1. Less than 10 knots.
   2. 15 knots or stronger.
   3. More than 10 knots.
   4. 25 knots or stronger.

13. With regard to the Surface Aviation Weather Report given here, what are the DEN surface weather conditions?

DEN SP 1335 M5 OVC 2R--F 166/52/51/8005/002
   1. A 500-foot overcast ceiling with 20 statute miles visibility due to rain.
   2. Visibility of 5 statute miles with heavy rain and fog.
   3. Visibility of 2 nautical miles with rain and very light fog.
   4. A measured ceiling of 500 feet overcast with 2 statute miles visibility due to very light rain and fog.

14. When warm, moist, stable air is forced to ascend up a mountain slope, what type of clouds can be expected to form?
   1. Layered clouds.
   2. Layered clouds with numerous vertical buildups.
   3. A combination of layered and vertically developed clouds.
   4. Mainly cumulus clouds.

15. The Weather Depiction Chart graphically describes:
   1. The weather conditions at the time the chart was produced.
   2. Weather conditions forecasted for the following 6 hours.
   3. Weather conditions forecasted for the following 3 hours.
   4. The current weather conditions at the time the chart is distributed.

16. Rectangular dashed areas on the Radar Summary Chart indicate:
   1. A tornado watch area.
   2. An area of widely scattered tornadoes.
   3. A severe weather watch area.
   4. An area expecting hail.

17. Temperatures and winds are reported hourly in weather reports in what standards of measurement?
   1. Temperatures in degrees Fahrenheit and winds in magnetic direction and knots.
   2. Temperatures in degrees Fahrenheit and winds in true direction and knots.
   3. Temperatures in degrees Centigrade and winds in true direction and knots.
   4. Temperatures in degrees Centigrade and winds in true direction and statute miles per hour.

18. Within what range of temperatures does the most severe and rapid accumulation of ice occur?
   1. 0°C to -10°C.
   2. 0°F to -10°F.
   3. 0°C to -15°C.
   4. 0°F to -15°F.

19. Which answer correctly lists some of the types of precipitation?
   1. Rain, snow, and frost.
   2. Snow, rain, and dew.
   3. Hail, rain, sleet, and frost.
   4. Sleet, snow, rain, and hail.

20. Weather radar is used primarily for:
   1. The detection of areas of moderate to heavy precipitation and severe storms.
   2. Tracking fronts.
   3. Determining low ceiling.
   4. Detecting tornadoes only.

21. Stability of an air mass can be increased by:
A. A warm air mass flowing over a cold surface.
B. A cold air mass flowing over a warm surface.
C. Removing water vapor from the lower atmospheric levels.
D. Sinking air.
E. The lifting of an air mass.
   1. A, C, and D.
   2. B, C, and D.
   3. A, C, and E.
   4. B, D, and E.

22. Which response identifies the reason for a reported southwesterly wind at 4,000 feet AGL and a reported southerly wind at the surface?
   1. The Coriolis force is stronger than the pressure gradient force at the surface.
   2. The isobar spacing is wider at the surface.
   3. The frictional force affects the wind at the surface.
   4. The centrifugal force is strongest at the surface.

23. What type of weather conditions are considered to be the most conducive to the formation of structural icing?
   1. Small supercooled water droplets falling from stratiform clouds.
   2. Freezing rain.
   3. Clouds at temperatures between -20°C to -30°C.
   4. Small supercooled water droplets suspended in stratiform clouds.

24. Which types of fog are dependent upon wind for subsistence?
   1. Upslope and steam fog.
   2. Advection and upslope fog.
   3. Advection and radiation fog.
   4. Upslope and ice fog.

25. In which geographic area is advection fog most likely to form?
   1. Along the coastal regions.
   2. Around large cities.
   3. Up mountain slopes.
   4. Behind slow-moving warm fronts.

26. Radar Weather Reports (SD) (RAREPS) are of particular interest to the instrument pilot since they report:
   1. Severe icing conditions.
   2. Fog and/or low ceilings.
   3. Cloud thickness.
   4. Severe storms.

27. What is a primary cause of evening fog on level inland states?
   1. Moist air cooling until it reaches the dew point temperature.
   2. A decrease in the dew point temperature after dark.
   3. Passage of a stationary front.
   4. A decrease in condensation nuclei.

28. When reviewing a Winds and Temperatures Aloft Forecast, what does 9900+10 indicate?
   1. Light and variable winds and a temperature of 10°F.
   2. Calm winds and a temperature of +10°C.
   3. Light and variable winds of less than 5 knots and a temperature of +10°C.
   4. Light and variable winds of less than 10 knots and a temperature of +10°F.

Refer to the Radar Summary Chart excerpt (below) when answering questions 29 and 30.

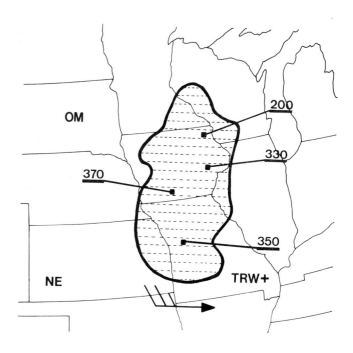

29. According to the Radar Summary Chart, the precipitation echoes over Iowa are:
   1. Moving east at 25 knots, and the highest reported cell tops are 37,000 feet.
   2. Moving east at 20 knots, and a pilot can maintain VFR at 37,000 feet.
   3. Moving east at 25 knots, and are decreasing in intensity.
   4. Moving east at 25 knots, and heavy showers are occurring.

30. What is the maximum echo intensity level indicated on the chart?
   1. Intensity level 3 (strong).
   2. Intensity level 1 (weak to moderate).
   3. Intensity level 5 (extreme).
   4. Intensity level 4 (intense).

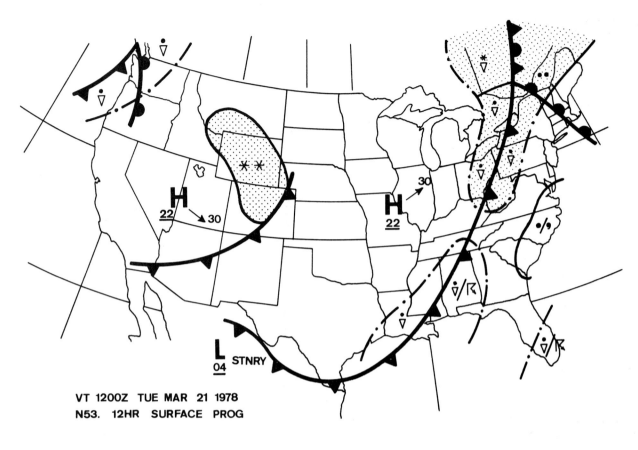

VT 1200Z TUE MAR 21 1978
N53. 12HR SURFACE PROG

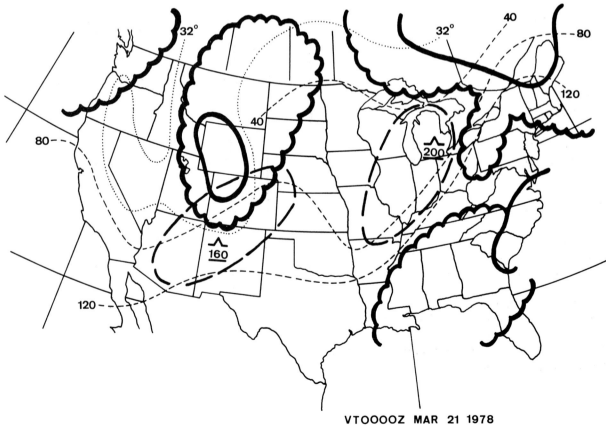

VT0000Z MAR 21 1978
12HR SIG WEATHER PROG
N29. LOW LEVEL SFC-400MB

Refer to the 12-hour Surface Prognostic Chart (page 98, top) when answering questions 31 and 32.

31. Select the correct statement regarding the illustrated 12-hour Surface Prognostic Chart.
1. Wyoming is forecast to have continuous snow.
2. Northwestern Colorado is forecast to have freezing rain.
3. Eastern Texas is forecast to have continuous rain.
4. Mississippi and Louisiana are forecast to have freezing rain.

32. Select the correct statement regarding the outlined shaded area in the northeastern part of the United States.
1. Less than half of the outlined shaded area will receive precipitation.
2. The area west of the stationary front is expected to have moderate icing.
3. The area east of the cold front is expected to have continuous snow over more than half of the area.
4. Half or more of the area is expected to have some type of shower activity.

33. The dew point is:
1. That temperature, at a given pressure and constant moisture content, to which air must be cooled to become saturated.
2. The ratio of moist air to dry air.
3. That temperature at which water vapor changes to a liquid state.
4. The ratio of the amount of water vapor in the air to the maximum amount of water vapor the air can hold at that temperature.

Refer to the low level 12-hour Significant Weather Prognostic Chart (page 98, bottom) when answering questions 34 and 35.

34. Select the correct statement relating to turbulence.
1. The eastern half of Arizona is forecast to have moderate turbulence from the surface to 16,000 feet.
2. The northwestern half of New Mexico is forecast to have moderate or greater turbulence from 16,000 feet upward.
3. The eastern half of Arizona is forecast to have severe turbulence.
4. The western half of New Mexico is forecast to have no turbulence.

35. Select the correct statement relating to the freezing level.
1. The freezing level in northern Texas is forecast to be at 12,000 feet AGL.
2. The freezing level in northern Texas is forecast to be at 10,000 feet AGL.
3. The freezing level in northeastern Texas is forecast to be at 12,000 feet MSL.
4. The freezing level in southern New Mexico is forecast to be at 1,200 feet MSL.

36. Normally, when a cold front becomes stationary, what type of weather can be expected?
1. An occluded front will form.
2. A line of thunderstorms will form.
3. The weather will become less intense but will persist longer.
4. Winds become calm.

37. Turbulence can often be expected enroute due to:
1. A warm air mass flowing over a cold air mass.
2. A temperature inversion.
3. The removal of water vapor in the lower levels of the atmosphere.
4. Convective currents in the vicinity of thunderstorms.

38. Which of the following are correct statements concerning in-flight airframe icing?

A. A rate of accumulation slightly greater than the rate of sublimation is described as a "trace."
B. The "moderate icing" accumulation rate is such that, with the occasional use of deicing equipment, icing does not present a problem.
C. The rate of accumulation of a "severe icing" condition is so great that immediate diversion is necessary.
D. The accumulation rate of icing reported as "light" may create a problem if flight is prolonged in this condition over one hour.
1. A, B, and D.
2. B and C.
3. C and D.
4. A, C, and D.

39. What is the implied surface visibility of a Terminal Forecast when the visibility entry is missing?
1. Over 3 statute miles.
2. Greater than 6 statute miles.
3. Greater than 5 statute miles.
4. Greater than 10 statute miles.

40. Which of the following would be the best indication to a pilot that his aircraft had passed through a front?
   1. A change in temperature.
   2. A change in wind direction.
   3. A decrease in indicated altitude.
   4. A change in pressure.

41. Which of the following statements are true concerning thunderstorms?

A. The greatest lightning activity in a thunderstorm is followed by the greatest rainfall at the surface.
B. Hail is more commonly found in the mature stage.
C. Downdrafts (not updrafts) characterize the dissipating stage.
D. Any thunderstorm identified as severe should be avoided by a lateral distance of at least 20 miles or a vertical distance of several thousand feet above the storm.
E. A growing thunderstorm is indicated by an increased frequency of lightning discharges.
   1. C and E.
   2. B, C, and D.
   3. A and E.
   4. All of the above statements are correct.

42. At what rate will unsaturated (dry) air heat?
   1. 5.4°F per 1,000 feet of altitude decrease.
   2. 2°F per 1,000 feet of altitude increase.
   3. 3.5°F per 1,000 feet of altitude change.
   4. 5.4°C per 1,000 feet of altitude decrease.

43. A squall line:
   1. Develops parallel to and from 50 to 300 miles behind a cold front.
   2. Is an intermittent line of thunderstorms that develops from 50 to 100 miles ahead of a cold front.
   3. Often contains severe steady state thunderstorms.
   4. Generally is a very narrow band of weather that forms from 50 to 300 miles ahead of a warm front.

44. Fog and reduced visibilities are most often encountered in industrial areas due to the:
   1. High humidity from the industrial wastes.
   2. Inversions formed by the heat released from industrial complexes.
   3. High concentration of condensation nuclei in the air.
   4. Radiation heat from the industrial complexes.

45. What does the symbol T+ indicate when it appears on a Surface Aviation Weather Report?
   1. A severe thunderstorm which has winds 50 knots or greater and/or hail ¾ inch or more in diameter.
   2. An intense thunderstorm with winds at 40 mph or greater.
   3. An extreme thunderstorm with strong winds and turbulence.
   4. A severe thunderstorm with heavy rain.

46. Choose the correct statements concerning pressure changes.

A. The pressure usually decreases rapidly as a thunderstorm approaches, then rises sharply with the onset of the first gust.
B. A squall line is always accompanied by a rise in pressure.
C. As a cold front approaches, the pressure usually falls until the front passes, then the pressure rises rapidly.
D. When crossing any front, the pressure will always rise rapidly, followed by a gradual fall in pressure after passing through the front.
   1. A, B, and C.
   2. B, C, and D.
   3. A and D.
   4. A and C.

47. Winds described in the Winds and Temperatures Aloft Forecast are stated in what terms?
   1. Speed in miles per hour and direction relative to true north.
   2. Speed in knots and direction relative to true north.
   3. Speed in knots and direction relative to magnetic north.
   4. Speed in miles per hour and direction relative to magnetic north.

48. When the letter *M* is transmitted in place of an element in the hourly sequence report, this indicates:
   1. The following element in the report was measured.
   2. That specific element (describing a condition) was missing from the report.
   3. That specific element of the report was not observed at the time of the report.
   4. That element of the report was omitted since it was not important.

49. What conditions must be present to induce the formation of a thunderstorm?

A. A lifting force.
B. Surface heating.
C. A frontal surface.
D. An unstable lapse rate.
E. A high moisture content in the atmosphere.
  1. D and E.
  2. A, B, and D.
  3. A, B, C, and E.
  4. A, D, and E.

50. The purpose of the Significant and Surface Weather Prognostic Charts is:
  1. To enable a pilot to determine the expected movement and change in weather patterns.
  2. To inform the pilot of the observed enroute weather.
  3. To graphically describe actual weather for the proposed route of flight.
  4. To depict the destination weather.

51. How is radiation fog formed?
  1. When a stable moist air mass is forced to a higher elevation.
  2. By the warming of a cold air mass which has moved over a warm surface.
  3. A moist air mass is cooled to its dew point by the earth's surface with little or no surface wind present.
  4. When evaporation from precipitation saturates cool air.

52. Which statement describes the reaction inside an aircraft when it encounters "moderate turbulence"?
  1. The occupants are forced violently against their seat belts and unsecured objects are tossed about.
  2. The occupants feel a slight strain against their seat belts and unsecured objects are displaced slightly.
  3. The occupants feel a definite strain against their seat belts and unsecured objects are dislodged.
  4. The occupants feel uncomfortable due to bumps and jolts.

53. Where may a pilot encounter wind shear?

A. In areas near the surface where a strong temperature inversion exists.
B. At any level, and it can exist in both a horizontal and vertical direction.
C. Near thunderstorms.
D. Primarily along coastal areas.

  1. B and D.
  2. B and C.
  3. A, C, and D.
  4. A, B, and C.

54. What is the approximate height of cloud bases formed by lifting action at an airport with an elevation of 500 feet, surface temperature of 74°F, and dew point of 52°F. (Assume a standard lapse rate is applicable.)
  1. 6,750 feet MSL.
  2. 5,000 feet MSL.
  3. 5,500 feet AGL.
  4. 5,500 feet MSL.

55. The amount of water vapor that air can hold is determined by:
  1. The amount of moisture the air contains.
  2. The relative humidity of the air.
  3. The temperature of the air.
  4. The dew point of the surrounding air mass.

56. Which statement correctly describes the visual range noted in the following Surface Aviation Weather Report?
DAL SA 2252 M1OVC 1/2RF 135/43/42/1807/ 993/R14LVR22V30
  1. Runway 14 left has a visual range between 200 and 400 meters.
  2. Runway 14 has a visual range between 200 and 400 feet.
  3. Runway 14 right has a visual range of 2,000 feet variable to 4,000 feet.
  4. Runway 14 left has a visual range of 2,200 feet variable to 3,000 feet.

57. Which atmospheric conditions are characteristic of unstable air?
  1. Intermittent precipitation, stratiform clouds, good visibility, and turbulence.
  2. Showery precipitation, cumuliform clouds, good visibility, and turbulence.
  3. Showery precipitation, stratiform clouds, and poor visibility.
  4. Continuous precipitation, cumuliform clouds, and poor visibility.

58. Relative humidity:
  1. Increases as the temperature-dew point spread decreases.
  2. Decreases as the temperature-dew point spread decreases.
  3. Increases as the temperature-dew point spread increases.
  4. Will remain constant as temperature and dew point change.

59. If RADAT 42Ø67 was reported in the remarks section of the hourly Surface Aviation Weather Report, a pilot could conclude:
1. Radar-observed thunderstorms are located on a true heading of 042° from the station at a distance of 67 statute miles.
2. The freezing level is 6,700 feet MSL.
3. Radar-observed thunderstorms are located on a true heading of 067° from the station at a distance of 42 statute miles.
4. The temperature is 42°F at an altitude of 6,700 feet MSL.

60. When using airborne or ground-based weather radar, a pilot should not fly between areas of strong radar echoes unless those echoes are separated by a distance of:
1. 5 to 20 miles.
2. 10 to 20 miles.
3. 25 to 35 miles.
4. 40 or more miles.

61. Prevailing visibility is:
1. The greatest horizontal visibility which is equaled or exceeded throughout half of the horizontal circle.
2. The greatest horizontal distance a pilot can see from the aircraft cockpit while on the airport surface.
3. The greatest horizontal distance a pilot can see from the aircraft cockpit while in the air.
4. The greatest horizontal distance an observer can see in any direction.

62. Runway Visual Range is an instrumentally-derived value which represents:
1. The horizontal distance a pilot will see down the runway from the approach end.
2. The slant range a pilot can see while on final approach.
3. The horizontal distance at which the control tower personnel can see a low intensity light.
4. The average slant distance which a pilot can see when positioned at the midpoint of the runway.

63. One-half statute mile visibility is equivalent to:
1. 3,600 feet RVR.
2. 2,400 feet RVR.
3. 1/2 mile RVR.
4. 2,400 yards RVR.

64. If, in the hourly Surface Aviation Weather Report, a station is reporting a scattered layer of clouds at 1,000 feet and a broken sky cover at 4,000 feet, this means:

1. At least 6/10 of the sky (as viewed from the reporting station) is concealed by clouds or other obscuring phenomena.
2. At least 5/10 of the sky (as viewed from the reporting station) is concealed by clouds.
3. That there is a layer of clouds at 1,000 feet AGL that conceals 1/10 to 5/10 of the sky, and there is also another layer of clouds at 4,000 feet AGL that conceals 6/10 to 9/10 of the sky.
4. That there is a layer of clouds at 1,000 feet MSL that conceals 5/10 of the sky and there is also another layer of clouds at 4,000 feet MSL that conceals 8/10 of the sky.

65. When referring to clouds, what does the prefix "nimbo-" or the suffix "-nimbus" indicate?
1. Precipitation.
2. Turbulence in clouds.
3. Layered clouds.
4. Vertically developed clouds.

66. The presence of ice pellets in the air or on the ground indicates:
1. Extremely cold air above.
2. A growing thunderstorm with the possibility of hail.
3. Warmer air above and probable severe icing (freezing rain).
4. Cold frontal passage.

67. An area outlined by a smooth solid line on a Weather Depiction Chart shows:
1. Ceilings less than 1,000 feet and visibilities less than 3 miles.
2. Marginal VFR conditions.
3. Ceilings 1,000 feet to 3,000 feet inclusive, and visibilities 3 to 5 miles.
4. Ceilings less than 1,000 feet and/or visibilities less than 3 miles.

68. A Convective Outlook (AC) forecasts:
1. Areas of clear air turbulence for a 12-hour period.
2. Areas of altocumulus clouds for a 6-hour period.
3. Areas of general and severe thunderstorm activity for a 24-hour period.
4. Wind shear zones for a 12-hour period.

69. Temperature inversions are found in what type of air mass?
1. Maritime tropic.
2. Unstable.
3. Conditionally unstable.
4. Stable.

70. An aircraft in flight can accumulate frost:

1. When descending from a sub-zero temperature zone into a zone of warm temperatures and higher humidity.

2. When ascending from a zone of warm temperatures into a zone of sub-zero temperatures.

3. When descending from a moist air mass into sub-zero temperatures.

4. Only when flying into an area of visible moisture.

71. If the Winds and Temperatures Aloft Forecast for DEN for an altitude of 39,000 feet is coded as *800553* this can be interpreted to mean:

1. The wind is forecast to be from a true direction of 080° at a speed of 5 mph, and the temperature is forecast to be -53°C.

2. The wind is forecast to be from a true direction of 300° at a speed of 105 knots, and the temperature is forecast to be -53°C.

3. The wind is forecast to be from a magnetic direction of 080° at a speed of 105 knots, and the temperature is forecast to be -53°C.

4. The wind is forecast to be from a magnetic direction of 080° at a speed of 5 knots, and the temperature is forecast to be -53°F.

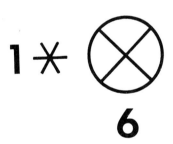

72. What is indicated by the illustrated example (above) of plotted data that might appear on a Weather Depiction Chart?

1. An obscured sky condition with a 600-foot ceiling and one mile visibility restricted by snow.

2. An obscured sky with a 100-foot ceiling and 6 miles visibility restricted by snow.

3. An overcast sky with a 600-foot ceiling and only 1 mile visibility due to rain.

4. An overcast sky with a 1,000-foot ceiling and 6 miles visibility. The obstruction to vision is snow.

73. Select the correct statement(s) regarding frost.

A. Frost forms when the temperature of the collecting surface is at or below the dew point of the adjacent air, and the dew point is below freezing.

B. Frost spoils the smooth flow of air over the airfoil, resulting in an increased stalling speed.

C. Frost forms in flight when dew freezes.

D. Frost forms when small drops of water fall on the collecting surface while the temperature of the surrounding air is at or below freezing.

1. A only.

2. A and B.

3. A, B, and C.

4. B and D.

74. What weather phenomenon is *always* associated with the passage of a frontal system?

1. An abrupt pressure decrease.

2. An abrupt temperature decrease.

3. Clouds behind the front.

4. A change in wind direction and/or speed.

75. Interpret the following Pilot Weather Report (PIREP).

UA/OV 20S PIR 1620 FL050/TP BE55/IC MDT CLEAR ICE.

1. Snow began 20 minutes past the hour at Pierre, wind 160° at 20 knots; a Beech 55 reported moderate clear ice at 5,000 feet.

2. Snow was encountered at 2,000 feet over Pierre at 1620Z; a Beech 55 encountered clear ice at 5,000 feet.

3. Twenty nautical miles south of Pierre, at 1620Z, a pilot flying a Beech 55 at 5,000 feet reported moderate clear ice.

4. At 20 minutes past the hour, south of Pierre, wind was reported as being from 160° at 20 knots; moderate clear icing began 55 minutes past the previous hour at 5,000 feet.

76. What visible signs indicate extreme turbulence in thunderstorms?

1. Roll clouds, very frequent lightning, and cumulonimbus clouds.

2. Roll clouds, lightning, low ceilings, poor visibility, and precipitation static.

3. Heavy rain, hail, and low clouds.

4. Low ceilings, reduced visibility, hail, and precipitation static.

77. In order to use the Radar Summary Chart in the most effective manner during preflight planning, pilots should:

1. Assume that the chart is the best source of information for ceilings, cloud tops, and cloud coverage between reporting stations.

2. Use the chart to determine the most accurate information relevant to cloud cover, freezing levels, and wind conditions between reporting stations.

3. Use the chart as the *only* information source regarding hazardous conditions and storms between reporting stations.

4. Compare the chart to the Weather Depiction Chart to get a three-dimensional picture of clouds and precipitation.

78. The Low Level Significant Weather Prognostic Chart depicts conditions:

1. That are forecast to be present 6 hours after the chart is prepared.

2. That are forecast to be present at a specific time shown on the chart as VT (valid time).

3. That were present approximately 3 hours before the chart was prepared.

4. That were present at the time the chart was prepared.

79. Determine the wind and temperature forecast for the depicted station (above).

1. 240° at 45 knots, -6° C.
2. 270° at 24 knots, -6° C.
3. 260° at 45 knots, -24° C.
4. 060° at 45 knots, -24° C.

80. What is the standard temperature at 20,000 feet?

1. -5° C.
2. -15° C.
3. -20° C.
4. -25° C.

4.

Aids to Navigation

4.1 A navigational aid (NAVAID) is any visual or electronic device (airborne or on the surface) which provides point to point guidance information or position data. Various types of navigation aids are in use today, each serving a special purpose in the air navigation system. These aids have varied owners and operators, namely: the Federal Aviation Administration, the military services, private organizations, and individual states. The Federal Aviation Administration, however, has the statutory authority to establish, operate, and maintain air navigation facilities and to prescribe standards for the operation of any of these aids which are used by both civil and military aircraft for instrument flight in federally controlled airspace. A discussion of those NAVAIDs that all instrument rated pilots should be familiar with is incorporated in this chapter.

VHF OMNIDIRECTIONAL RANGE (VOR)

4.2 The VOR, or omnirange, is used as the basis for navigation in the National Airspace System. These facilities are actually ground-based electronic navigation aids that transmit very high frequency navigation signals, thereby providing 360 magnetic courses from each facility. These courses are called *radials* and are oriented FROM each VOR station. (Figure 4-1) For example, aircraft A (heading 360°) when in position 1 is inbound on the 180° radial; after crossing the station (position 2), the aircraft is outbound on the 360° radial.

Figure 4-1. VOR Radials

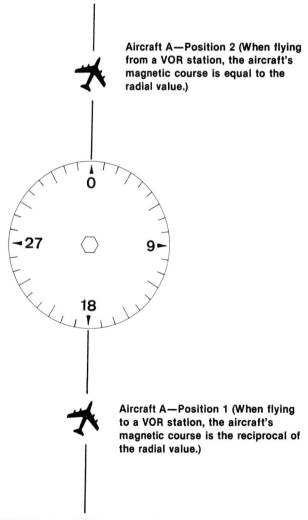

Aircraft A—Position 2 (When flying from a VOR station, the aircraft's magnetic course is equal to the radial value.)

Aircraft A—Position 1 (When flying to a VOR station, the aircraft's magnetic course is the reciprocal of the radial value.)

NOTE: The 0° radial of each omnirange is aligned with magnetic north.

VOR Frequencies/Class

4.3 VOR stations operate within the 108.0–117.95 MHz frequency band and are classified according to their operational use. The three classifications of NAVAIDs are: T (Terminal), L (Low Altitude), and H (High Altitude). It should be noted that T-VORs are located on or near an airport and are used primarily as instrument approach aids.

4.4 Each VOR facility has a power output adequate to provide coverage within its assigned operational service volume. Since the equipment is VHF it is subject to line-of-sight restriction, and its range *generally* varies proportionally to the altitude of the receiving equipment. The normal service ranges for the T, L, and H class aids are listed in the table in Figure 4-2. Certain operational requirements make it necessary to use some of these aids at greater service ranges than are listed in the table. Extended range is made possible through flight inspection determinations. Some aids also have lesser service range due to such influencing factors as location, terrain, and frequency protection. Actual restrictions to service range are listed with the NAVAID in the Airport/Facility Directory. Above and beyond certain altitude and distance limits, signal interference from other VOR facilities and signal weakening make the signal unreliable. (Areas of confusion between VOR stations can be easily recognized by an aural squeal and oscillation of the visual indicators of a VOR receiver in an aircraft.)

VOR Identification

4.5 The only positive method of identifying a VOR is by its Morse Code identification or by the recorded automatic voice identification which is always indicated by use of the word *VOR* following the range's name. Since numerous VORs are equipped for voice transmission on the VOR frequency, reliance on determining the identification of an omnirange should never be placed on listening to voice transmissions by the Flight Service Station (or approach control facility) involved. Many Flight Service Stations remotely operate several omniranges which have different names from each other and in some cases none have the name of the "parent" FSS. When voice identification has been added to a VOR station, the transmission consists of a voice announcement like "Airville VOR" alternating with the usual Morse Code identification.

4.6 *Special Note: When voice communications capability is incorporated with a VOR station, current design VOR receivers can be used to receive normal voice transmissions without interference with the navigation information being received.*

Figure 4-2. VOR/VORTAC/TACAN NAVAIDs—Normal Usable Altitude and Radius Distances

NORMAL USABLE ALTITUDES AND RADIUS DISTANCES

Class	Altitudes	Distance (miles)
(T)	12,000 feet and below	25
(L)	Below 18,000 feet	40
(H)	Below 18,000 feet	40
(H)	Within the Conterminous 48 States only, between 14,500 feet and 17,999 feet	100
(H)	18,000 feet - FL 450	130
(H)	Above FL 450	100

(H) = High   (L) = Low   (T) = Terminal

Note: An (H) facility is capable of providing (L) and (T) service volume and an (L) facility additionally provides (T) service volume.

VOR Receiving Equipment

4.7 VOR signals can be received by a variety of types of airborne equipment. Tuning equipment and visual indicators representative of most current designs are shown in Figure 4-3. Irrespective of differences in dial design, method of tuning, separation of receiver components, and multipurpose designs, all VOR receivers have at least the essential components shown in the NAV/COMM system illustrated in Figure 4-3.

Figure 4-3. A King KI 203 VOR/LOC Indicator and KX 175B NAV/COMM System

4.8 The components of a VOR receiver can be described as follows:

1. **Frequency selector**—Generally the frequency selector may be a knob or knobs, manually rotated to select any of the frequencies between 108.0 and 117.95 MHz.

2. **Course selector**—By turning the OBS (omnibearing selector), the desired course is selected. The selected course may appear in a window or under an index.

3. **Course deviation indicator (CDI)**—The deviation indicator is generally composed of a dial and a needle hinged to move laterally across the dial. The needle centers when the aircraft is on the selected radial or its reciprocal. Full needle deflection *from the center* position to either side of the dial indicates the aircraft is 10° or more off course, assuming normal needle sensitivity.

4. **TO/FROM indicator**—Also called "sense indicator" and "ambiguity indicator," the TO/FROM indicator shows whether the selected course will take the aircraft TO or FROM the station. It does *not* indicate whether the *aircraft* is *heading* to or from the station. (Figure 4-4)

5. **Flags (or other signal strength indicators)**—A warning flag (Off flag) will replace the TO/FROM indication if:

    A. The radio is turned off.

    B. The aircraft is directly over the station.

    C. The navigational signal is unreliable.

    D. The aircraft is on a VOR radial that is approximately 90° to the course set next to the course index.

Insufficient signal strength may also be indicated by a blank TO/FROM window.

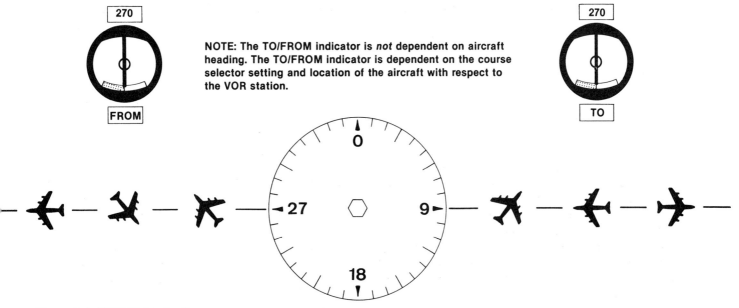

NOTE: The TO/FROM indicator is *not* dependent on aircraft heading. The TO/FROM indicator is dependent on the course selector setting and location of the aircraft with respect to the VOR station.

Figure 4-4. TO/FROM Indications

VOR Efficiency

4.9 The effectiveness of the VOR depends upon the proper use and adjustment of both ground and airborne equipment.

1. *Accuracy*—The accuracy of course alignment of the VOR is excellent, being generally plus or minus 1°.

2. *Roughness*—On some VORs, minor course roughness may be observed, evidenced by course needle or brief flag alarm activity. (Some receivers are more subject to these irregularities than others.) At a few stations, usually in mountainous terrain, the pilot may occasionally observe a brief course needle oscillation similar to the indication of "approaching station." Pilots flying over unfamiliar routes are cautioned to be on the alert for these vagaries and, in particular, to use the TO/FROM indicator to determine positive station passage. (Station passage is indicated by a *complete* reversal of the TO/FROM indicator.)

Certain propeller RPM settings can also cause the VOR course deviation indicator to fluctuate as much as + 6°. Slight changes to the RPM setting will normally smooth out this roughness. Pilots are urged to check for this propeller modulation phenomenon prior to reporting a VOR station or aircraft equipment for unsatisfactory operation.

VOR Receiver Checks

4.10 Periodic VOR receiver calibration is most important. If a receiver's Automatic Gain Control or modulation circuit deteriorates, it is possible for it to display acceptable accuracy and sensitivity close to the VOR station and display out-of-tolerance readings when located at greater distances where weaker signal areas exist. The likelihood of this deterioration varies among receivers and is generally considered a function of time. The best assurance of having an accurate receiver is periodic calibration of the instrument. Yearly intervals are recommended for this, at which time an authorized repair facility should recalibrate the receiver to the manufacturer's specifications.

4.11 The Federal Aviation Regulations provide for certain VOR equipment accuracy checks prior to flight under instrument flight rules. To comply with this requirement and to ensure satisfactory operation of the airborne system, the FAA has provided pilots with the following means of checking VOR receiver accuracy: (1) FAA VOR test facility (VOT) or a radiated test signal from an appropriately rated radio repair station; (2) certified airborne check points; and (3) certified check points on the airport surface.

4.12 The FAA VOR test facility (VOT) transmits a test signal for VOR receivers, providing users of VOR a convenient and accurate means of determining the operational status of their receivers. The facility is designed to provide a means of checking the accuracy of a VOR receiver *while the aircraft is on the ground only.* The radiated test signal is used by tuning the VOR receiver to the published frequency of the test facility. With the course deviation indicator (CDI) centered, the omni bearing selector should read 0° with the TO/FROM indication being FROM or the omni bearing selector should indicate 180° with the TO/FROM indication reading TO. Two means of identification are used with the VOR-radiated test signal. In some cases a continuous series of dots is used, while in others a continuous 1020 hertz tone will identify the test signal. Information concerning an individual test signal can be obtained from the local Flight Service Station.

4.13 A radiated VOR test signal from an appropriately rated radio repair station serves the same purpose as an FAA VOR signal, and the check is made in much the same manner. However, the frequency normally approved by the FCC is 108.0 MHz. The repair stations are also not permitted to radiate the VOR test signal continuously, and, consequently, the owner/operator must make arrangements with the repair station to have the test signal transmitted. Additionally, this service is not provided by all radio repair stations; the aircraft owner/operator must determine which repair station in his local area does provide this service. (The maximum permissible bearing errors for the various types of VOR equipment accuracy checks are further discussed in paragraph 6.24.)

4.14 In addition to the receiver tolerance checks in the Regulations, course sensitivity may be checked by noting the number of degrees of change in the course selected as the OBS is rotated to move the CDI from center to the last dot on either side. The OBS must normally be rotated between 10° and 12° of bearing change before the CDI will move from the center to the last dot on the indicator face.

VOR Orientation

4.15 CDI Interpretation. With the VOR receiver properly tuned and checked, the pilot should rotate the OBS knob until the CDI centers. For example, if the CDI centers with the 360° course under the index, the aircraft can be on any heading and at any point over the north/south reference line depicted, except over the station or close to it. (Figure 4-5) Approaching inbound from point A to point B, the CDI will deviate from side to side as the aircraft passes directly over the station where no signal is

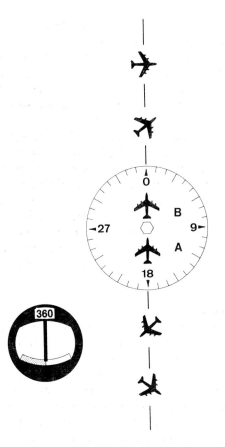

NOTE: The CDI (Course Deviation Indicator) does *not* relate to the selected course and aircraft heading. The CDI relates selected course and aircraft location.

Figure 4-5. CDI Interpretation

received. Similarly, a centered CDI with any other course shown under the index locates an aircraft over either the selected radial or its reciprocal.

4.16 TO/FROM Interpretation. With a course of 360° selected under the index, a TO indication registers, *regardless of heading*, whenever an aircraft is located within the approximate hemispherical area south of the 90/270 reference line. A FROM indication appears when the aircraft is located north of the approximate 90/270 reference line. Movement across the 90/270 area is indicated by an ambiguous TO/FROM signal. In this area, the resultant of the opposing reference and variable signals transmitted by the VOR, which actuates the TO/FROM indicator, is insufficient to produce a positive TO or FROM indication. At a speed of 150 knots, the approximate times to cross this area at various distances from the station are as follows (Figure 4-6):

Distance from Station	Width (Zone of Confusion at 3,000 feet AGL)
(In Nautical Miles)	(Time in Seconds)
1/2	8
1	10
3	25
5	50

4.17 Similarly, with any given course under the index, a FROM will register whenever an aircraft is located in the hemispherical area approximately 90° on either side of the selected course. A TO indication will register whenever an aircraft is located in the other hemisphere.

Figure 4-6. TO/FROM Interpretation

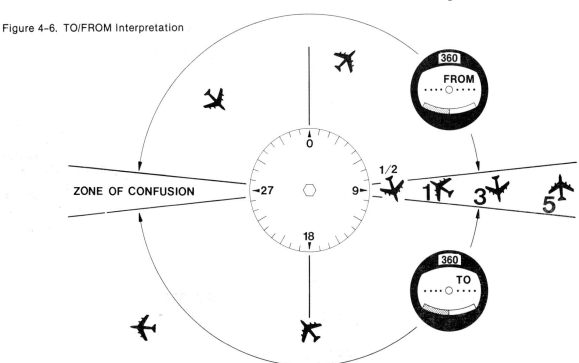

4.18 CDI and TO/FROM Interpretation. As Figure 4-7 illustrates, the position of the CDI indicates to the pilot that:

1. The aircraft is on a specific radial (or its reciprocal), *or*

2. The aircraft is to the right or left of it, *with respect to the course* selected.

4.19 Movement of the CDI, in conjunction with heading information, indicates:

1. Impending station passage.

2. Wind drift.

3. Approximate distance from the VOR station. (Drift correction and time/distance checks will be discussed later in this chapter.)

4.20 The TO/FROM indicator locates an aircraft in one of two hemispherical areas, depending on the course selected. However, the TO/FROM indicator will not provide this information in an area of weak signal strength.

4.21 *To determine the radial* on which an aircraft is located:

1. Note the TO/FROM reading.

2. If the reading is FROM, center the CDI by rotation of the OBS knob opposite the direction of CDI deflection. When the needle centers, read the radial under the Course Selector Index.

3. If the reading is TO, rotate the OBS knob in the direction of CDI deflection until FROM appears and proceed as in the previous step.

4.22 *To determine the inbound course* to the station from a present position:

1. Read the inbound magnetic course directly from the reciprocal window, following determination of the radial. (If the indicator has no reciprocal window, the inbound course should be computed arithmetically.)

2. Rotate the reciprocal to the opposite course index to change the FROM to a TO reading and the needle will center, provided the aircraft has not moved to another radial. If the aircraft has moved to another radial, recenter the needle with small adjustments, unless the aircraft is close to the station and crossing radials rapidly.

3. To proceed to the station, turn the aircraft to the magnetic heading indicated under the Course Index.

VOR Tracking

4.23 Tracking involves drift correction sufficient to maintain a direct course to or from a VOR station. The course selected for tracking inbound is shown under the course index with the TO/FROM indicator showing TO. If a pilot is off course to the left, the CDI is deflected right; if a pilot is off course to the right, the CDI is deflected to the left. Turning toward the needle returns the aircraft to the course centerline and centers the needle. (*Note:* This is a result of "PROPER SENSING." In other words, if

Figure 4-7. VOR Orientation

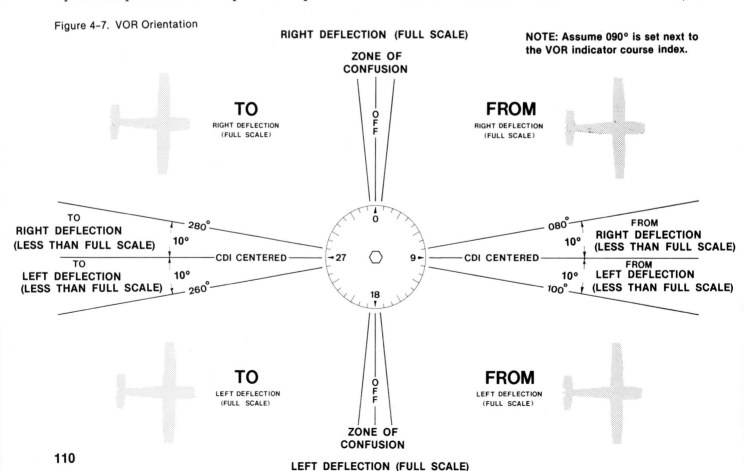

110

the CDI is to the right, the desired course is to the right; if the CDI is to the left, the desired course is to the left. A pilot can be assured of "PROPER SENSING" whenever the aircraft heading is approximately [depending on wind direction and speed] the same as the selected course [under the Course Index].)

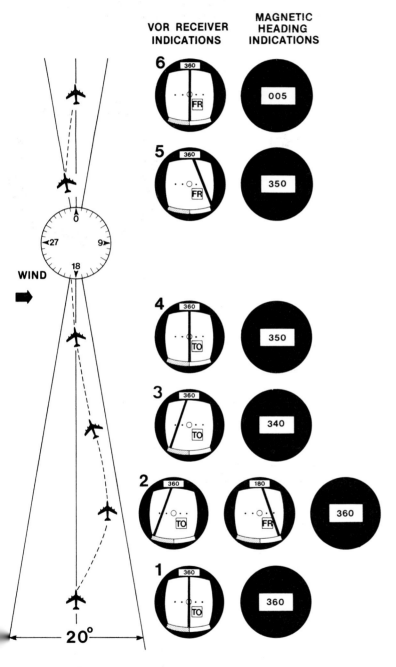

Figure 4–8. VOR Tracking

4.24 To track inbound with the wind unknown, proceed with the following steps [Figure 4-8]. Outbound tracking procedures are the same.

1. With the CDI centered, maintain the heading corresponding to the selected course.

2. As the heading is being maintained, observe the CDI for deflection to left or right. Direction of CDI deflection from centerline shows the direction of the cross-wind component. The illustration shows a left deflection, therefore left cross-wind. (Note the indications with the *reciprocal* of the inbound course set on the OBS. The indicator correctly shows FROM, indicating the aircraft is to the left of the centerline with *reference to the selected* course. Sometimes called "REVERSE SENSING," this CDI deflection indicates a turn *away* from the needle for direct return to the course centerline, and illustrates the importance of correlating heading and course selection. VOR tracking can be accomplished with "REVERSE SENSING," but errors in orientation can easily result.)

3. Turn 20° toward the needle and maintain the heading correction until the needle centers.

4. Reduce the drift correction to 10° left of the course setting, and note whether this drift-correction angle keeps the CDI centered. Subsequent left or right needle deflection indicates an excessive or insufficient drift-correction angle, requiring further bracketing. With the proper drift-correction angle established, the CDI will remain centered until the aircraft is close to the station. Approach to the station is indicated by flickering of the TO/FROM indicator and CDI as the aircraft flies into the "zone of confusion" (no-signal area). Station passage is shown by complete reversal of the TO/FROM indicator. Since the extent of the zone of confusion, an inverted cone, increases with altitude, flight through the zone of confusion varies from a few seconds at low levels to as much as two minutes at high altitudes.

5 and 6. Following station passage and TO/FROM reversal, correction to course centerline is still toward the needle. Aircraft displacement from the course centerline can be determined by the relationship of CDI displacement *and* distance from the VOR station. (Pilots should remember that VOR radials converge at the VOR station and diverge with distance away from the VOR.) Note that the extent of CDI deflection is, *by itself*, no indication of the amount of aircraft displacement from the course centerline. A large CDI deflection immediately following station passage calls for no heading correction until the CDI stabilizes; at a distance of 20 miles from a VOR station, an angular displacement of the CDI

of 4° from the center of the indicator (for example, a two-dot deflection on a five-dot center to side scale) may require a large correction angle for return to centerline.

The rate of movement of the CDI during course bracketing is thus an approximate index of distance from the station. For accurate radial interception and course following see the data presented in Figure 4-9 which illustrates these relationships.

A one degree angle is one mile wide at a distance of 57.3 miles from the angle origin.

Assuming a VOR receiver with normal course sensitivity and full-scale (center to side) deflection at 5 dots (approximately 10°): Aircraft displacement from course is approximately <u>200 feet per dot per nautical mile.</u> For example, at one nautical mile from the station, two dots (4°) of deflection indicate approximately 400 feet displacement of the aircraft from the course centerline. At 30 nautical miles from the station, two dots of deflection indicate approximately two nautical miles displacement of the aircraft from the course centerline. Similarly, at a distance of 60 nautical miles from the station, two dots of deflection indicate approximately four nautical miles of displacement of the aircraft from the course centerline.

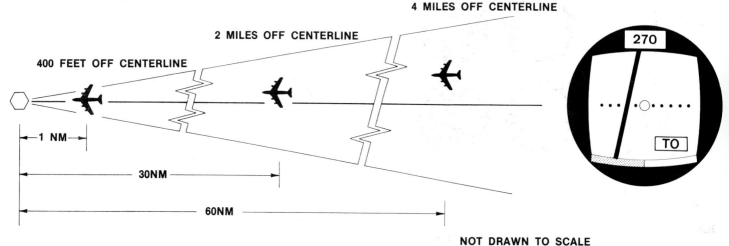

NOT DRAWN TO SCALE

Figure 4–9. CDI Deflection and Aircraft Displacement from Course

[NOTE: Other VOR receiver indicators may display a two, three, or four dot scale representing a full-scale (center to side) deflection (10°).]

VOR Time/Distance Checks

4.25 Time and distance from a VOR station can be determined by several methods involving practical application of formulas or elementary geometry. These time/distance computations are approximations since wind drift is not considered in the solutions.

Wing-Tip Bearing Change Method

4.26 The formula solution is applied to the elapsed time for a predetermined change in azimuth, or relative bearing, from the aircraft to a station located at 90° from the aircraft heading. (Figure 4-10)

4.27 Determine time/distance to station using the following steps. After tuning and identifying the VOR station:

1. Determine the radial on which the aircraft is located.

2. Turn inbound and recenter the needle if necessary.

3. Turn 80° right, or left, of the inbound course (as appropriate), rotating the OBS to the nearest

10° increment *opposite* the direction of turn.

4. Maintain heading. When the CDI centers, note the time.

5. Maintaining the same heading, rotate the OBS 10° in the same direction as in Step 3.

6. Note the elapsed time when the CDI again centers.

7. Time/distance from the station is determined using the following formulas:

$$\text{Time to station (minutes)} = \frac{60 \times \text{minutes flown between bearing change}}{\text{degrees of bearing change}}$$

$$\text{Distance to station* } = \frac{\text{TAS} \times \text{minutes flown}}{\text{degrees of bearing change}}$$

* (In NM if TAS is in knots, in SM if TAS is in MPH)

4.28 *Rule of Thumb: By analyzing the time formula, the following rules can be derived:*

Degrees of Bearing Change	Time to Station (Minutes)
5	*12 x time (in minutes) of bearing change*
10	*6 x time (in minutes) of bearing change*
20	*3 x time (in minutes) of bearing change*

4.29 The amount of bearing change flown will vary, depending upon the distance of the aircraft from the station and ground speed crossing radials. For example, 20° of bearing change may be used to compute a time/distance problem near a VOR station since the VOR radials are spaced close together. At greater distances from a VOR station, fewer degrees of bearing change are used in the computation of a time/distance problem since the radials are spaced further apart.

Isosceles Triangle Method

4.30 Time/distance to station can also be found by application of the isosceles triangle principle (that is, if two angles of a triangle are equal, two of the sides are also equal), as follows (Figure 4-11):

1. With the aircraft established on a radial, inbound, rotate the OBS 10° to the left.
2. Turn 10° to the right and note the time.
3. Maintain constant heading until the CDI centers, and note the elapsed time.
4. Time to station is the same as the time taken to complete the 10° change of bearing.

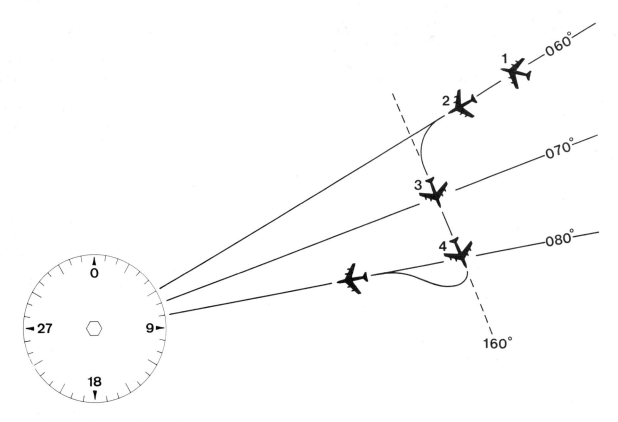

Figure 4-10. Time/Distance Check; Wing-Tip Bearing Change

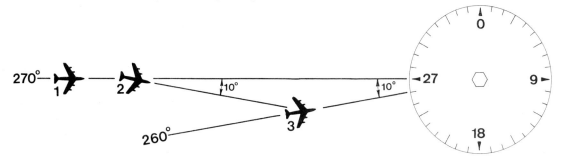

Figure 4-11. Time/Distance Check; Isosceles Triangle Method

VOR Track Interception

4.31 If an aircraft is found to be off course, the pilot must orient himself with respect to the VOR station and the course to be flown, and work a track interception problem. The following steps may be used to intercept a predetermined track, either inbound or outbound (Figure 4-12):

1. Turn to a heading to parallel the desired course, in the same direction as the course to be flown.
2. Determine the difference between the radial to be intercepted and the radial on which the plane is presently located.
3. Double the difference to determine the interception angle which should be not less than 20° or greater than 90°.
4. Rotate the OBS to the desired radial or inbound course.
5. Turn to the interception heading.
6. Hold this magnetic heading constant until the CDI centers, indicating that the aircraft is on course. (With practice in judging the varying rates of closure with the course centerline, a pilot can become proficient in leading the turn to prevent overshooting the course.)
7. Turn to the magnetic heading corresponding to the selected course, and follow tracking procedures inbound or outbound.

(*Note:* Steps 1-3 are generally omitted by experienced pilots since they turn directly to intercept a course without initially turning to parallel the desired course.)

Common Errors in the Use of the VOR

4.32 The following are common errors made by the novice instrument pilot. It should be noted that the underlying cause of most of the common errors is cockpit confusion resulting from lack of skill in the use of basic flight instruments.

1. Careless tuning and identification of VOR stations.
2. Failure to check receiver for accuracy/sensitivity.
3. Turning in the wrong direction during an orientation. This error is common until a pilot mentally visualizes aircraft position rather than just aircraft heading.
4. Failure to check the ambiguity indicator, particularly during course reversals, which results in "REVERSE SENSING" and corrections in the wrong direction.
5. Incorrect rotation of the course-selector (OBS) on a time/distance problem.
6. Overshooting and undershooting radials on interception problems.
7. Overcorrecting for incorrect aircraft heading while tracking. This is an especially common problem when tracking close to the station.
8. Misinterpretation of station passage.
9. Chasing the CDI, resulting in homing instead of tracking. Careless heading control and failure

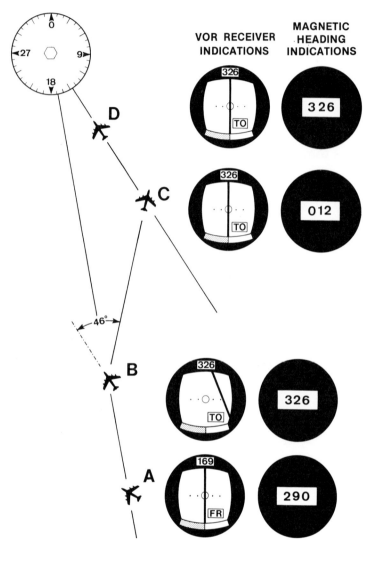

TO INTERCEPT THE 146° RADIAL AND TRACK INBOUND

A. Present position, crossing the 169° radial.

B. Turn right to parallel the inbound course. (146° plus 180° equals 326°)
The difference between 146° and 169° equals 23°. (Double 23° to determine the interception angle of 46°)
Turn to a magnetic heading of 012°. (326° plus 46°)

C. The 146° radial is intercepted when the CDI centers with the OBS set to 326°. Turn to an inbound heading of 326°.

D. Track inbound on the 146° radial.

Figure 4-12. VOR Track Interception

to bracket wind corrections make this one of the most common errors.

AUTOMATIC DIRECTION FINDER (ADF)

4.33 Knowledge of ADF procedures offers several advantages to the instrument pilot, although many seldom use ADF equipment because of the relatively simpler operation and interpretation of VHF equipment. ADF provides: (a) a back-up navigation system in the event of VHF equipment failure; (b) a means of monitoring position en route and providing data for plotting fixes; (c) a navigation system for use in areas and at altitudes where VOR "line-of-sight" signals are unreliable (since LF/MF radio waves follow the curvature of the earth from the ground transmitting facility to the receiving aircraft); (d) radio communications (receiver only) on the ground where VHF reception is impossible. Weather broadcasts and clearances can be received, for example, at points outside VHF signal range; and (e) auxiliary and standby navigation information on instrument approaches.

4.34 The ADF system (also referred to as a radio compass) is not without its disadvantages, however. A major weakness of this LF/MF means of navigation (unlike the VHF/UHF communications and navigation systems) is its susceptibility to static which is generated by atmospheric electrical disturbances. Unfortunately, the source of the static can sometimes render the typical ADF receiver useless as an aid to navigation or communications.

Figure 4-13. A King KR 85 ADF Receiver and KI 225 Indicator

Functions/Features of the ADF Receiver

4.35 Several different types of airborne direction finders are available. The essentials are common to all ADF receivers, regardless of design detail. In addition to receiving navigation signals, ADF equipment also receives voice communications from LF/MF transmitters.

4.36 A typical ADF receiver and indicator (used in light aircraft) may include the following functions/features (Figure 4-13):

1. **Frequency selector**—Permits the use of any ground transmitter, within the receiver's designed frequency range. (Most ADF receivers are capable of receiving on a frequency range of 200 kHz to 1600 kHz.)

2. **VOL (volume) control**—Controls the amplitude of the audio reception. (Volume adjustment has no effect on the ADF needle.)

3. **BFO (beat frequency oscillator) mode**—Used to obtain better reception of unmodulated signals. All U.S. commercial broadcast stations and FAA transmitting facilities that are compatible with ADF receivers transmit modulated signals. Some stations in other countries, however, broadcast unmodulated signals. Consequently, to identify an unmodulated station, the BFO mode must be used to enable the pilot to hear the Morse Code identification.

4. **ANT (antenna) mode**—Also labeled REC/receiver on some ADF receivers. Provides audio reception from the station tuned. As long as the ADF receiver is in this mode, the ADF pointer is deactivated.

5. **ADF mode**—Activates the bearing pointer (ADF needle). The bearing pointer will rotate until it points to the station being received.

6. **Test feature**—Allows the operator to check equipment reliability. The testing procedures may vary with the model of radio.

7. **Rotatable azimuth card**—Becoming a more common feature on current model ADF receivers (as opposed to fixed azimuth cards in the older models). The *rotatable* azimuth card allows the user to manually position the aircraft heading under the heading index at the top of the indicator dial. This is an aid to some pilots in determining the aircraft's position during flight.

Selection of Station

4.37 The pilot has a variety of ground transmitting facilities to choose from. The two primary types of ground transmission facilities that are complimentary with ADF receiving equipment are the nondirectional radio beacon (NDB) and the commercial broadcast station.

4.38 An NDB is a low or medium-frequency radio transmitter that transmits nondirectional signals.

These facilities normally operate in the frequency band of 200 to 415 kHz and transmit a continuous carrier with 1020 Hz modulation keyed to provide identification except during voice transmission. When a radio beacon is used in conjunction with the Instrument Landing System markers, it is called a Compass Locator. (The usable radius distances are listed in the table in Figure 4-14.)

4.39 All radio beacons except the compass locators transmit a continuous three-letter identification in code except during voice transmissions. Compass locators transmit a continuous two-letter identification in code.

CLASS	POWER (WATTS)	DISTANCE (MILES)
Compass Locator	Under 25	15
MH	Under 50	25
H	50--1999	*50
HH	2000 or more	75

*Service range of individual facilities may be less than 50 miles.

Figure 4-14. NDB Usable Radius Distance (For All Altitudes)

4.40 Commercial broadcast stations are useful for air navigation (primarily to the VFR pilot). Pilots should remember that these stations can be identified only when the broadcast is interrupted for "station identification," that some operate only during daylight hours, and that many of the low-powered stations transmit on the same frequencies, causing a potential for erratic ADF indications.

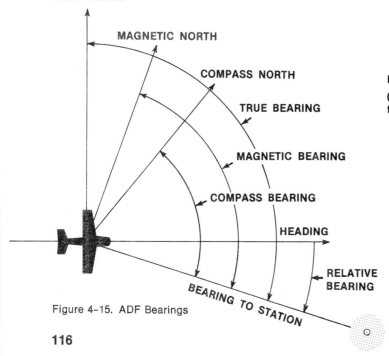

Figure 4-15. ADF Bearings

4.41 *Special Note: The use of commercial broadcast stations during inclement weather conditions is not recommended for ADF navigation purposes during any phase of instrument flight.*

ADF Orientation

4.42 Unlike the VOR receiver, which indicates magnetic bearing TO or FROM the station without reference to aircraft heading, the ADF needle points TO the station, regardless of aircraft heading or position. Therefore, the relative bearing indicated is the angular relationship between the aircraft heading and the station, measured clockwise from the nose of the aircraft.

4.43 A bearing is simply the direction of a straight line between the aircraft and station (or between the station and aircraft). The bearing line measured clockwise from the nose of the airplane is a relative bearing; measured clockwise from true north, it is a true bearing; measured clockwise from magnetic north, it is a magnetic bearing. (Figures

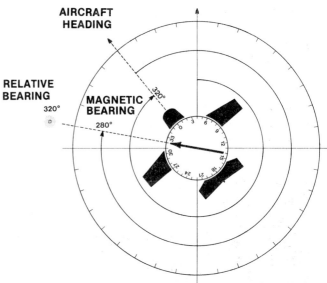

MB_{TO} = MH (320°) + RB (320°) = 640° = 280°
(NOTE: Whenever the total is greater than 360°, subtract 360 from the bearing.)

Figure 4-16. ADF Bearing Computations

FORMULAE:

True Bearing <u>to</u> Station = True Heading + Relative Bearing

Magnetic Bearing <u>to</u> Station = Magnetic Heading + Relative Bearing

True Bearing <u>from</u> Station = True Bearing <u>to</u> Station ±180°

Magnetic Bearing <u>from</u> Station = Magnetic Bearing <u>to</u> Station ±180°

4-15 and 4-16) As the illustrations show, a true, magnetic, or compass heading is measured clockwise from the appropriate north, and a relative bearing is measured clockwise from the nose of the airplane. Thus, the true, magnetic, or compass bearing to the station is the sum of true, magnetic, or compass heading, respectively, and the relative bearing.

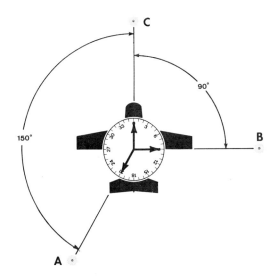

Figure 4-17. ADF Relative Bearings

4.44 Most pilots will probably orient themselves more readily if they think in terms of nose/tail and left/right needle indications, visualizing the ADF dial in terms of the longitudinal axis of the aircraft. When the needle points to 0°, the nose of the aircraft points directly to the station; with the pointer on 210°, the station is 30° to the left of the tail; with the pointer on 090°, the station is off the right wing tip. (Figure 4-17) Consequently, to turn directly toward station A, an aircraft must turn left 150° since the needle points to the left of the nose to a line 30° from the tail position. Station B is 90° to the right; therefore, the aircraft must turn right 90° to head directly toward the station.

4.45 Note that (a) the relative bearing shown on the ADF indicator does not, by itself, indicate aircraft position, and (b) the relative bearing must be related to aircraft heading to determine direction to or from the station. (Figure 4-18)

4.46 Figure 4-18 illustrates only one of several methods of determining bearings—or lines of position—between aircraft and station. By visualizing the 80° left-of-nose indication at all three positions shown, the pilot can determine the magnetic bearing to the station by subtracting the left deflection from the magnetic heading:

	A	B	C
Magnetic heading	230°	115°	340°
Minus left deflection	80°	80°	80°
Magnetic bearing (TO)	150°	035°	260°

Figure 4-18. Determining Magnetic Bearing to a Station Using ADF

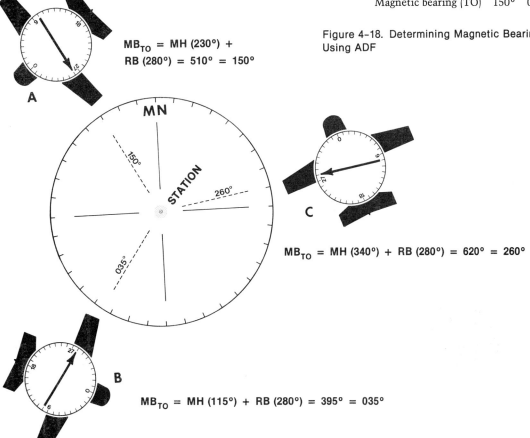

MB_{TO} = MH (230°) + RB (280°) = 510° = 150°

MB_{TO} = MH (340°) + RB (280°) = 620° = 260°

MB_{TO} = MH (115°) + RB (280°) = 395° = 035°

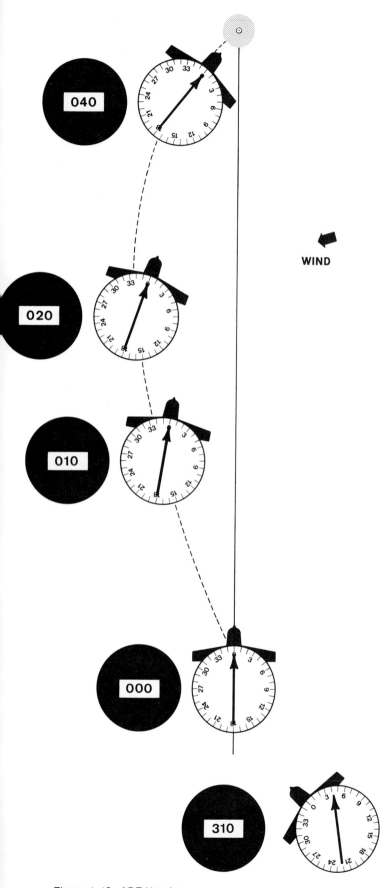

WIND

4.47 Homing. ADF homing is a procedure whereby the aircraft is flown on any heading required to keep the ADF needle on 0° until the selected station has been reached. To head the aircraft toward the station, the pilot must turn to the heading that will zero the ADF needle. The heading indicator should be used (although not necessary) in conjunction with the ADF to execute the turn. At the completion of the initial turn toward the station, the ADF needle should be checked and, if necessary, zeroed with small corrections. (Figure 4-19)

4.48 Figure 4-19 depicts an aircraft with an initial magnetic heading of 310° and a relative bearing of 42°. A right turn of approximately 40°, to a heading of 0°, should zero the needle. After the needle is zeroed, it will remain so unless the heading is changed or a crosswind affects the aircraft track. If there is no wind, the aircraft will follow a straight track to the station and assume a constant heading. If a crosswind drifts the aircraft, the homing track will be a curve while the ADF needle remains zeroed.

4.49 Approach to the station is indicated by increasingly frequent heading corrections to zero the needle (especially when a strong crosswind exists) and by side-to-side needle deflections when very close to the station. Passage directly over the station is shown by a 180° reversal of the ADF needle to the tail position; passage on either side and close to the station is indicated by a rapid swing of the needle as it continues to point to the station. Homing is easy, though seldom used during instrument flying. Competent pilots control track by more precise procedures.

4.50 Tracking. A straight geographic flight path can be followed to or from a low (or medium) frequency facility by establishing a heading, compensating for wind effect, that will maintain the desired track. ADF tracking procedures involve interpretation of the heading indicator and ADF needle to intercept and maintain a desired magnetic bearing.

4.51 Inbound Tracking. To track inbound, a pilot must turn to the heading that will zero the ADF needle. As the pilot maintains this heading, deflection of the ADF needle to the left or right indicates a crosswind (needle left/wind from left; needle right/wind from right.) When a definite change in azimuth (2°-5°) shows that the aircraft has drifted off course, a turn must be executed in the direction of needle deflection (into the wind) to re-intercept the initial inbound bearing. The angle of interception must always be greater than the number of degrees of drift, and the magnitude of any intercepting turn depends upon the observed *rate* of bearing

Figure 4-19. ADF Homing

change, true airspeed, and how quickly the pilot desires a return to course.

4.52 A rapid rate of bearing change, *while heading is constant*, indicates either a strong crosswind or close proximity to the station, or both. For example, if a pilot is 60 miles from a station and the ADF shows a 3° left deflection, the aircraft is 3 miles to the right of the desired course. In a slow aircraft, a large interception angle must be used for a quick return to the course. In a very fast aircraft, the same interception angle could result in overshooting the desired course. Similarly, the same 3° needle deflection closer to the station indicates less deviation from the desired course, and smaller angles of interception result in rapid return to course.

4.53 At a given angle of interception and with a given wind, rate of closure with the desired track varies directly with true airspeed. For example, at 150 knots TAS as compared with 100 knots TAS, the effectiveness of a given interception angle is proportionately greater for the same wind at the same distance from the station. Having determined the angle of interception for return to the desired track, a turn must be executed toward the track by that amount. As a pilot executes the turn using the heading indicator, the ADF needle rotates *opposite* the direction of turn, and, as the interception angle is established, the needle points to the side of the zero position opposite the direction of turn. As the aircraft approaches the course on a constant interception heading, the ADF needle continues to rotate as the relative bearing changes. When the needle deflection from zero equals the angle of interception, the aircraft is on the desired track. If the pilot executes the turn to the magnetic bearing of the desired track when these angles are equal, the aircraft will overshoot the track. In such a case, the aircraft can either drift back to track and then establish an estimated drift correction angle, or bracket the track with successively smaller interception angles.

4.54 A faster technique is to lead the turn to the inbound heading before the track is intercepted. The amount of lead depends upon the distance from station, rate of closure observed as the aircraft approaches the desired track, number of degrees to be turned, and rate of turn. Since these factors are variable, pilots develop effective lead estimates as they become familiar with their particular aircraft and practice ADF tracking.

4.55 Once the aircraft is back on track the pilot must maintain a sufficient drift correction angle. This can best be accomplished by maintaining an ADF needle deflection from zero, *opposite the direction of drift correction*, an amount equal to the drift correction angle. If the needle moves further from the nose position, the drift correction is excessive. The pilot must then reduce the correction angle thereby allowing the aircraft to drift back on course. This is indicated for any drift correction (or interception) angle when ADF needle deflection and drift correction angle are equal. If the estimated drift correction is insufficient, the ADF needle will move toward the nose, and a further correction to regain track is required. With careful attention to headings, effective drift correction angles can be established with very little bracketing.

4.56 Station Approach and Station Passage. The same fundamentals apply to ADF tracking as have been mentioned in connection with ADF homing. The closer an aircraft is to a station, the more aggravated are pilot errors in drift correction and basic instrument flying technique, unless the pilot recognizes station approach and acts accordingly so as not to overcontrol during the observed track deviations.

4.57 When an aircraft is close to a station, slight deviations from the desired track result in large deflections of the ADF needle. It is important, therefore, that the correct drift correction angle be established as soon as possible after interception of an inbound course. With the course "pinned down" and heading corrections kept at a minimum, the pilot will be more alert to signs of station approach than he would be if he were busy "chasing" headings and ADF deflections. Pilots should make small heading corrections (not over 5°) as soon as the needle shows a deviation from course, until it begins to rotate steadily toward a wing-tip position or shows erratic left/right oscillations. At that point, pilots should hold their last corrected heading constant and should time station passage when the needle shows either wing-tip position or settles at or near the 180° position. The time interval from the first indications of station proximity to positive station passage varies with altitude—a few seconds at low levels to 3 minutes at high altitude. Inbound tracking steps are illustrated in Figure 4-20.

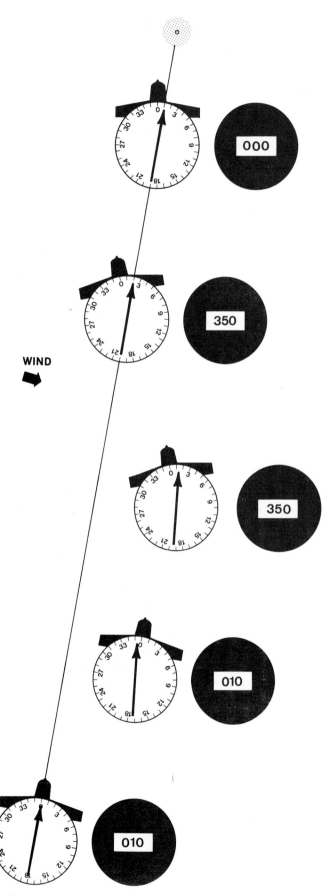

4.58 Outbound Tracking. Procedures for tracking outbound are identical to those used for inbound tracking. However, the direction of the ADF needle deflections are different from those noted during inbound track interceptions. When tracking *inbound*, a change of heading toward the desired track results in movement of the ADF needle *toward* zero. When tracking *outbound*, a change of heading toward the desired track results in needle movement further *away* from the 180° position. (Figure 4-21)

4.59 Time/Distance Checks (ADF). Time and distance to a station may be calculated with ADF procedures similar to the VOR procedures already discussed in paragraphs 4.25 through 4.29. A variety of methods commonly used are variations of the basic procedures that follow.

4.60 Wing-Tip Bearing Change. To determine the time/distance to the station, pilots should employ the following steps:

1. After tuning in the station, determine the relative bearing from the position of the ADF needle.

2. Turn the number of degrees necessary to place the needle on 090° or 270°.

3. Note the time, and fly a constant magnetic heading for a specific number of degrees of bearing change. The amount of change flown varies with the observed rate of bearing change.

4. Apply the observed time interval to the formula, or calculate the time to the station, as discussed in paragraph 4.28, if a 10° bearing change is used.

1. Turn the aircraft to zero the ADF needle. Maintain this heading until off-course drift is indicated by left or right needle deflection.

2. When a 5° change in needle deflection is observed, turn 20° in the direction of needle deflection.

3. When the needle is deflected 20° (the deflection equals the interception angle), the track has been intercepted. Lead the interception as noted in the discussion of tracking. Turn 10° toward the inbound course. The aircraft is now inbound with a 10° left drift correction angle.

4. If an off-course deflection is observed, turn once again to the original interception heading.

5. When the desired course has been reintercepted, turn 5° toward the inbound course, proceeding inbound with a 15° drift correction.

6. If the initial drift correction is excessive, as indicated by needle deflection away from the wind, turn to parallel the desired course and let the wind drift the aircraft back on course. When the needle is again zeroed, turn into the wind with a reduced drift correction angle.

Figure 4-20. ADF Tracking—Inbound

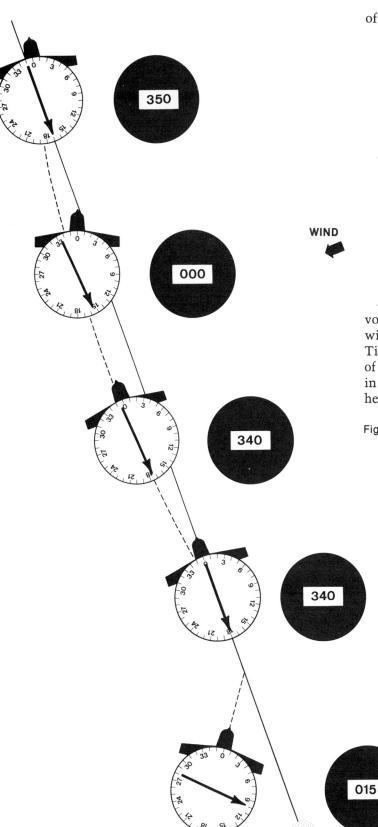

350

000

WIND

340

340

015

Assume the airplane is tracking on a 340° magnetic bearing from the station.

4.61 Other time/distance checks are applications of the isosceles triangle principle.

Bow-to-beam bearing gives time to the station by the following steps:

   1. Turn the number of degrees necessary to place the ADF needle on 045° (or 315°).

   2. Maintain heading until the needle is on 090° (or 270°).

   3. Time/distance flown equals time/distance to station.

The *double-the-angle-on-bow* method involves the following steps:

   1. Tune in a station between 10.° and 45° off the nose position, and note the relative bearing.

   2. Fly a constant magnetic heading until the angle on the nose doubles.

   3. The time/distance required to double the angle on the nose equals the time/distance to the station.

4.62 The accuracy of time/distance checks involves a number of variables, including existing wind, accuracy of timing, and heading control. Time·checks, especially those involving a rapid rate of bearing change, demand very precise techniques in basic instrument flying while the pilot maintains heading and checks elapsed time.

Figure 4-21. ADF Tracking—Outbound

Interception of Predetermined Magnetic Bearings

4.63 Basic ADF orientation, tracking, and time/distance procedures may be applied to the problem of intercepting a specified inbound or outbound magnetic bearing. To intercept an *inbound* magnetic bearing, the following steps may be used (Figure 4-22):

1. Determine the aircraft position in relation to the station by turning to the magnetic heading of the bearing to be intercepted.
2. Note whether the station is to the right or left of the nose position. Determine the number of degrees of needle deflection from the zero position, and double this amount for the interception angle.
3. Turn the aircraft toward the desired magnetic bearing the number of degrees determined for the interception angle.
4. Maintain the interception heading until the needle is deflected the same number of degrees from the zero position as the angle of interception (minus lead appropriate to the rate of bearing change).
5. Turn inbound and continue with tracking procedures. Note that this method combines inbound course interception with a time estimate to the station, since the interception leg and the inbound leg are equal sides of an isosceles triangle. The time from the completion of the turn to the interception heading (075°) until interception of the desired inbound bearing is equal to the time-to-station (double-the-angle-on-bow).

4.64 Interception of an *outbound* magnetic bearing can be accomplished by the same procedures as for the inbound intercept, except that the 180° position must be substituted for the zero position on the ADF needle.

Common Errors in the Use of the ADF

4.65 Pilots should be aware of the following common errors in using the ADF:

1. Improper tuning and station identification. As a result many students/instrument rated pilots have homed or tracked to the wrong station.
2. Dependence on homing rather than proper tracking. This commonly results from reliance on the ADF indications instead of correlating them with heading indications.
3. Poor orientation. This is due to failure to follow proper steps in orientation and tracking.
4. Improper interception angles. This is generally the result of the pilot rushing the initial orientation procedure.
5. Overshooting and undershooting predeter-

Figure 4-22. Interception of a Predetermined Magnetic Bearing

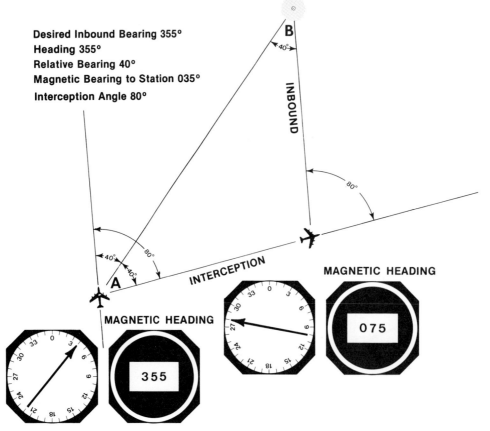

Desired Inbound Bearing 355°
Heading 355°
Relative Bearing 40°
Magnetic Bearing to Station 035°
Interception Angle 80°

mined magnetic bearings. This is often due to the pilot forgetting the course interception angles used.

6. Failure to maintain selected headings. Any heading change is accompanied by an ADF needle change. The instruments must be read in combination *before* any interpretation is made.

7. Failure to understand the limitation of the ADF and the factors that affect its use.

8. Overcontrolling track corrections close to the station (chasing the ADF needle). This is due to the pilot's failure to understand or recognize station approach.

RADIO MAGNETIC INDICATOR (RMI)

4.66 The radio magnetic indicator is an extremely versatile instrument that provides the pilot with aircraft heading and navigational bearing data. The instrument consists of a rotating compass card and one or two bearing pointers.

Figure 4-23. A King KI 226 Radio Magnetic Indicator

4.67 The single bar pointer of the RMI illustrated in Figure 4-23 is permanently connected to an automatic VOR converter and has the capability of *continually* displaying magnetic VOR bearings. The double bar pointer (of the illustrated RMI) is permanently connected electronically to an ADF receiver and continually displays magnetic ADF bearings. It should be noted that other models of RMIs may be equipped with one or two pointers. Some RMIs may also be equipped with a function switch(s) thereby allowing the operator to select the type of navigation aid (LF/MF station or VOR station) to which the pointer(s) is (are) tuned.

4.68 The head of the bearing pointers displays ADF and/or VOR magnetic bearings *TO* the selected receivable navigation aid(s). (This feature is especially useful since it eliminates the need for

any calculations involving relative bearings.) VOR radials are displayed adjacent to the tail of the respective bearing pointer(s). Magnetic bearings *FROM* an LF/MF facility are similarly displayed adjacent to the tail of the respective bearing pointer(s). Figure 4-24 further exemplifies these relationships.

4.69 The aircraft magnetic heading is continuously displayed on the compass card beneath the top index. The compass card is actuated by a remote gyro-stabilized compass system.

4.70 Should a malfunction in the compass system occur, the ADF bearing pointer(s) will continue to point to the station and display(s) *relative bearing* information only. In this situation the VOR bearing pointer(s) will still indicate bearings but the bearing information should be considered unreliable.

4.71 Like the ADF indicator, the RMI indicates passage directly over the station by a 180° reversal of the appropriate bearing pointer(s); passage on either side and close to the station is indicated by a rapid swing of the bearing pointer(s) as it (they) continues (continue) to point to the station.

4.72 *Special Note: VOR accuracy checks can be performed using an RMI. When conducting a VOR accuracy check using a VOT, the appropriate bearing pointer(s) should point to 180° regardless of aircraft heading or location with respect to the VOT facility.*

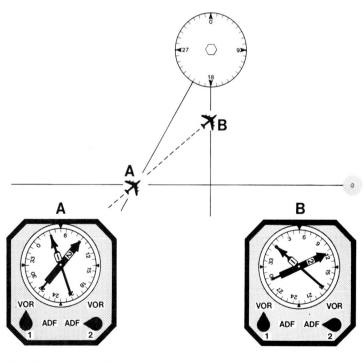

Continuous magnetic bearings to the VOR and NDB stations provide a constant observation of progress along the flight path.

Figure 4-24. RMI Applications

DISTANCE MEASURING EQUIPMENT (DME)

4.73 Distance Measuring Equipment is essentially defined as equipment used to measure, in nautical miles, the slant range distance of an aircraft from a DME navigational aid. (In addition, most current models of aircraft DME have incorporated into the equipment features such as ground speed and time to station presentation.) Distance Measuring Equipment has made it possible for the pilot to immediately determine the exact geographic position of his aircraft by observing the aircraft's VOR and DME indicating equipment. Without DME, it would normally be necessary for the instrument pilot to determine the aircraft's position by triangulation methods, using a single VOR receiver, dual VOR receivers, or a combination of VOR receivers and other low- and high-frequency navigational equipment. With the aid of DME and VOR equipment used in combination, these direct reading instruments inform the pilot of the precise distance and bearing to or from a VORTAC station. (Figure 4-25)

4.74 Distance measuring equipment normally operates in conjunction with the TACAN portion of the VORTAC station. The VORTAC station is actually a facility consisting of two components, TACAN and VOR, which provide three individual services: VOR azimuth (course), TACAN azimuth, and TACAN distance. (Civil aircraft do not use the TACAN azimuth service, however.) Although it consists of more than one component, incorporates more than one operating frequency, and uses more than one antenna system, a VORTAC is considered to be a unified navigational aid since all system components are contained at one transmitter site. Both components of a VORTAC station operate simultaneously and provide the three services at all times.

4.75 DME operates on frequencies between 962 MHz and 1213 MHz in the UHF spectrum. (Consequently, DME signals are subject to the same line-of-sight restriction as the VOR navigation system.) TACAN frequency is identified by a channel number. This channel number is used by the military. However, the frequencies of collocated VOR-TACAN (VORTAC) stations are "paired" to simplify civil airborne operations. For example, TACAN channel 73 is paired with the VOR frequency 112.6 MHz. Thus, pilots of civil aircraft, when using a VORTAC facility, tune their VOR receivers and DME units to the same frequency.

4.76 *Special Note: VOR/DME, ILS/DME, and LOC/DME navigation facilities established by the FAA also provide course and DME distance information from collocated components under the same type of frequency pairing plan. (ILS and Localizer [LOC] navigation aids are discussed later in this chapter.)*

4.77 Pilots are cautioned to identify all navigation facilities before using them. Transmitted signals from VOR and TACAN facilities are each identified by three-letter code identifications which are transmitted on a time share basis. The VOR portion of the facility is identified by a coded tone which is modulated at 1020 Hz or by a combination of code and voice. The TACAN is identified by a coded tone modulated at a higher frequency of 1350 Hz. The TACAN coded identification is transmitted one time for each three or four times that the VOR coded identification is transmitted. Whenever the VOR or TACAN portion of a VORTAC is inoperative, it is important for the pilot to recognize which identifier is retained for the operative facility. For example, a coded identification with a repetition interval of *approximately* 30 seconds indicates that only the TACAN portion of the facility is operative.

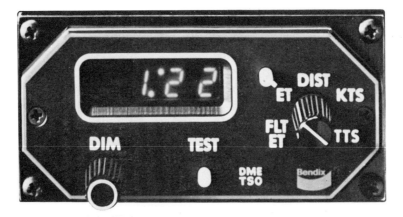

Figure 4-25. A Bendix IN-2032A (DME) Display Computer

(Note: VOR/DME, ILS/DME, and LOC/DME facilities are operated in a manner similar to that just discussed.)

4.78 The operating principle of distance measuring equipment is simple. Essentially, the transmitter portion of the aircraft DME unit initiates the process by transmitting distance interrogation pulse signals paired at a specific spacing. After receipt of these signals by the receiver portion of the ground facility, a transmitter is triggered and paired (at the same pulse spacing) distance reply pulse signals are transmitted on a different frequency. The receiver portion of the aircraft DME unit then receives the paired reply pulse signals. The time required for this round-trip-signal exchange process is then measured by the airborne DME unit and further translated into such information as distance from the aircraft to the ground station, ground speed, or time to station (depending upon the function selected on the airborne DME unit).

4.79 Reliable signals may be received at distances up to 199 NM at line-of-sight altitudes with an accuracy of better than 1/2 mile or 3% of the distance, whichever is greater. Pilots are reminded that distance information received from DME equipment is slant-range distance and *not* actual horizontal distance. The difference between a measured distance on the surface and the DME slant-range distance is known as slant-range error and is smallest at low altitude and long range. This error is greatest when the aircraft is directly over the ground facility. (Figure 4-26)

4.80 Pilots of aircraft equipped with DME can determine station passage when the DME distance readout decreases and registers the assigned altitude less NAVAID site terrain elevation. Naturally, after station passage the DME distance readout will increase as the slant-range distance increases.

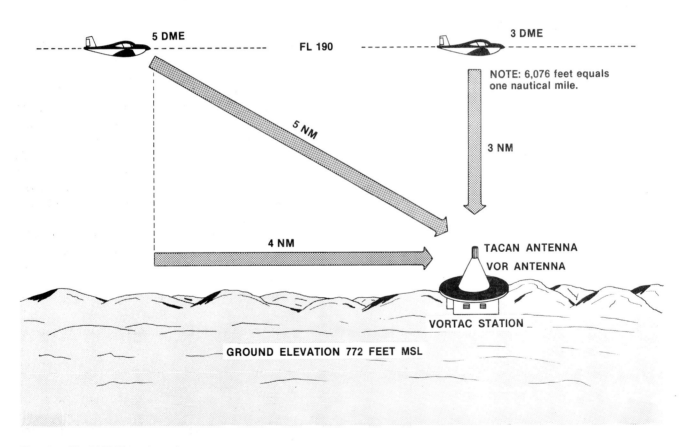

Figure 4-26. DME Distances

Flying DME Arcs

4.81 Today's instrument pilots must be familiar with the procedures and techniques for intercepting DME arcs from radials, maintaining DME arcs, and intercepting various courses from DME arcs. The following procedures and techniques for intercepting and maintaining these arcs are generally applicable to any facility which provides DME information.

4.82 Unless the pilot is highly proficient in the use of the aircraft's navigational equipment, it is recommended that DME arcs be flown *only* when RMI equipment is available.

DME Arc Interception

4.83 A DME arc interception of approximately 90° may be required when flying on a radial either inbound toward or outbound from a facility. The following steps to intercept a 10 DME arc when outbound on a radial are representative of accepted DME arc interception procedures (refer to Figure 4-27):

1. Track outbound on the SAC 325° radial, frequently checking the DME mileage readout.
2. For ground speeds below 150 knots, a .5 NM lead is usually satisfactory.
(*Note:* The following approximations can be used to determine the lead necessary to intercept a DME arc:

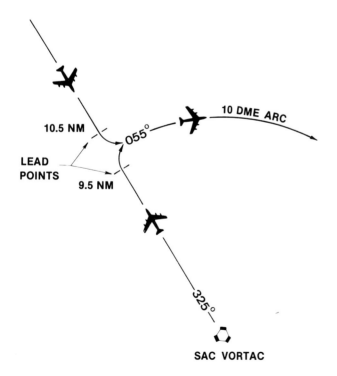

Figure 4-27. DME Arc Interception

A. For turns that approximate a 3° per second turn, lead the desired arc by 1/2% of the ground speed. For example: 100 knots ground speed x 1/2% = 1/2 nautical mile lead.

B. A second method (for faster aircraft) using ground speed in *miles per minute* minus 2 may be used to determine the lead for 30° banked turns. For example: 240 knots = 4 miles per minute, and 4 - 2 = 2 nautical miles lead.)

3. Upon reaching the lead point (9.5 NM), turn approximately 90° to the arc and set the OBS to 335° (for position determination purposes). The heading will be 055° in no-wind conditions.

4. During the last part of the intercepting turn, monitor the DME closely. If it appears the arc is being undershot, roll out of the turn early. If the arc is being overshot, continue the turn past the originally-planned rollout point.

(*Note:* The procedure for intercepting an arc when inbound on a radial is basically the same. For example, the leadout in the Figure 4-27 is 10.0 NM + .5 NM or *10.5 NM.*)

Maintaining the DME Arc

4.84 In flying the DME arc, it is important that the pilot keep a continuous mental picture of his position relative to the facility. Since the drift correction angle is constantly changing throughout the arc, wind orientation is important. In some cases, wind can be used in returning to the desired track. Arcs of large radii are easier to fly because of their "flat" curve. High ground speeds require more pilot attention because of the higher rate of deviation and correction. Maintaining the arc is simplified by keeping slightly inside the curve. Thus, the arc is always turning toward the aircraft and interception may be accomplished by holding a straight course. If the aircraft is outside the curve, the arc is "turning away" and a greater correction is required. (Figure 4-28)

1. **With an RMI,** in a no-wind condition, the pilot should theoretically be able to fly an exact circle around the facility by maintaining a relative bearing of 90° or 270°. In actual practice, a series of short legs are generally flown. To maintain the arc, proceed as follows:

A. With the bearing pointer on the wing-tip reference (90° or 270° position) and the aircraft at the desired DME range, maintain the heading and allow the bearing pointer to move 5° to 10° behind the wing tip. This will cause the range to increase slightly.

B. Next, turn toward the facility to place the bearing pointer 5° to 10° ahead of the wing-tip reference and maintain the heading until the pointer is again behind the wing tip. Continue this procedure to maintain the approximate arc.

C. If a crosswind is blowing the aircraft away from the facility, establish the reference ahead of the wing tip. If a crosswind is blowing the aircraft toward the facility, establish the reference behind the wing tip.

D. As a guide in making range corrections, change the relative bearing 10° to 20° for each 1/2 mile deviation from the desired arc. For example, under no-wind conditions, if the aircraft is 1/2 mile outside the arc and the bearing pointer is on the wing tip reference, turn the aircraft 20° toward the facility to return to the arc.

2. **Without an RMI,** orientation is more difficult since the pilot does not have a direct azimuth reference. However, a pilot can fly the procedure by using the OBS and CDI for azimuth information and the DME for arc distance. *Example* (refer to Figure 4-27):

A. If the rollout on the 055° heading places the aircraft on the arc, the DME will read 10.0 NM. If the CDI is centered (with the OBS set to 335°), the aircraft is crossing the 335° radial.

B. If the CDI reads right of center and the DME reads 10.5 NM, the aircraft is outside (left) of the arc and approaching the 335° radial. Correct heading to the right and monitor the DME for closure with the arc.

C. As the arc and the 335° radial are achieved, set the OBS ahead to 355° and correct heading 100° from the 335° radial (to a no-wind heading of 075°). Hold this heading until the 355° radial is crossed or the arc is intercepted. At this point, set the OBS ahead 20° and correct heading 100° from the radial the aircraft has intercepted. This technique will maintain a track slightly inside the desired arc (in no-wind conditions).

Intercepting a Radial from a DME Arc

4.85 The lead will vary with arc radius and ground speed. For the average general aviation aircraft, flying arcs such as are depicted on most approach charts, at speeds of 150 knots or less, the lead will be under 5°. There is no essential difference between intercepting a radial from an arc and intercepting it from a straight course.

1. **With an RMI,** the rate of bearing movement should be monitored closely while flying the arc. Set the course of the radial to be intercepted as soon as possible and determine the approximate lead radial. Upon reaching this point, start the intercepting turn.

2. **Without an RMI,** the technique for radial interception is the same except for azimuth information, which is available only from the OBS and CDI.

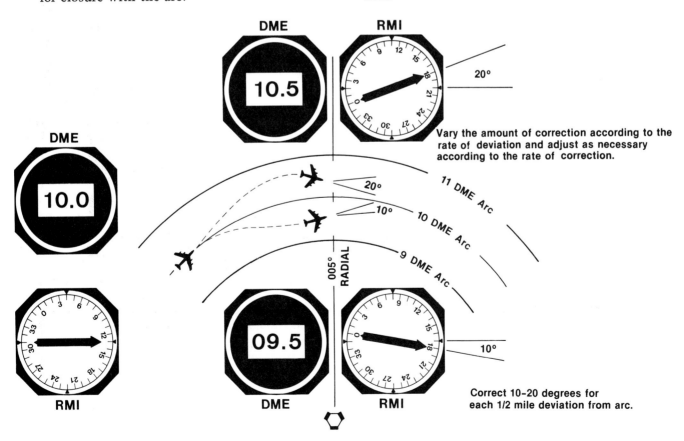

Figure 4-28. Application of DME and RMI to Maintain Arc

RADAR ALTIMETER

4.86 The radar altimeter is also often referred to as radio altimeter or ground avoidance radar. This piece of avionics accurately measures the distance (in feet) between the aircraft and the highest object on the terrain below the aircraft.

4.87 The radar altimeter is able to present an absolute altitude through the use of a microprocessor contained within the system. Essentially, the microprocessor continually measures the time interval for a short-duration signal to be transmitted and received (after the signal has been reflected from the terrain and/or object beneath the aircraft). The measured time intervals are then registered as an altitude by means of a dial or digital presentation. (Figure 4-29)

4.88 This aid is especially beneficial during the execution of instrument approaches since it offers a significant improvement in accuracy over the conventional barometric altimeter. (The accuracy of most radar altimeters is generally within a few feet at low altitudes.) The measurable indicator altitude range is generally in the order of 20 feet to 2,500 feet.

4.89 Most radar altimeters are equipped to provide the pilot with both visual and aural warning indications after a preselected descent altitude has been reached. In addition, most radar altimeters provide auxiliary outputs which can be used to supply altitude information to such other pilot conveniences as autopilots and integrated flight systems.

4.90 *Special Note: While conducting instrument approach procedures, pilots should not rely solely on the radar altimeter for altitude information. Altitude information should be derived from the barometric altimeter AND, if available, the radar altimeter.*

INSTRUMENT LANDING SYSTEM (ILS)

4.91 The instrument landing system is a "precision" instrument approach system. This system is termed a "precision" approach system since it not only provides extremely accurate horizontal (course) guidance but also provides extremely accurate vertical (slope) guidance for aircraft on final approach to a runway. (Figure 4-30)

4.92 The ILS, in comparison to all other instrument approach aids such as the VOR or non-directional beacon, is the best instrument approach aid during periods when the weather conditions are exceptionally poor for the following reasons:

1. The ILS is a more accurate approach aid than the other "nonprecision" approach aids.
2. ILS approach procedures generally allow the pilot to descend to a lower altitude during the execution of the instrument approach.
3. Pilots can often be authorized to conduct an ILS approach during conditions of reduced visibility that would normally preclude pilot authorization to conduct any nonprecision instrument approach procedure.

4.93 There are three general categories of instrument landing systems; Category I, Category II, and Category III. The Category I system is considered to be the standard ILS which provides for an approach to a height above touchdown of *not less than* 200 feet and with a runway visual range of *not less than* 1,800 feet. Category II and Category III approach procedures provide for even lower approach minimums, but special aircrew and aircraft equipment certifications (in addition to the instrument rating and an instrument equipped airplane) are required to conduct Category II and Category III approaches. Since the average instrument pilot has no need to conduct Category II or Category III approaches, further discussion of the ILS will generally be limited to the Category I ILS.

4.94 *Special Note: As a general rule, only one instrument landing system is installed per runway. However, at some locations a complete ILS is installed on each end of a runway. When this is the case, the instrument landing systems are not in service simultaneously.*

Figure 4–29. A Bonzer Radar Altimeter Indicator

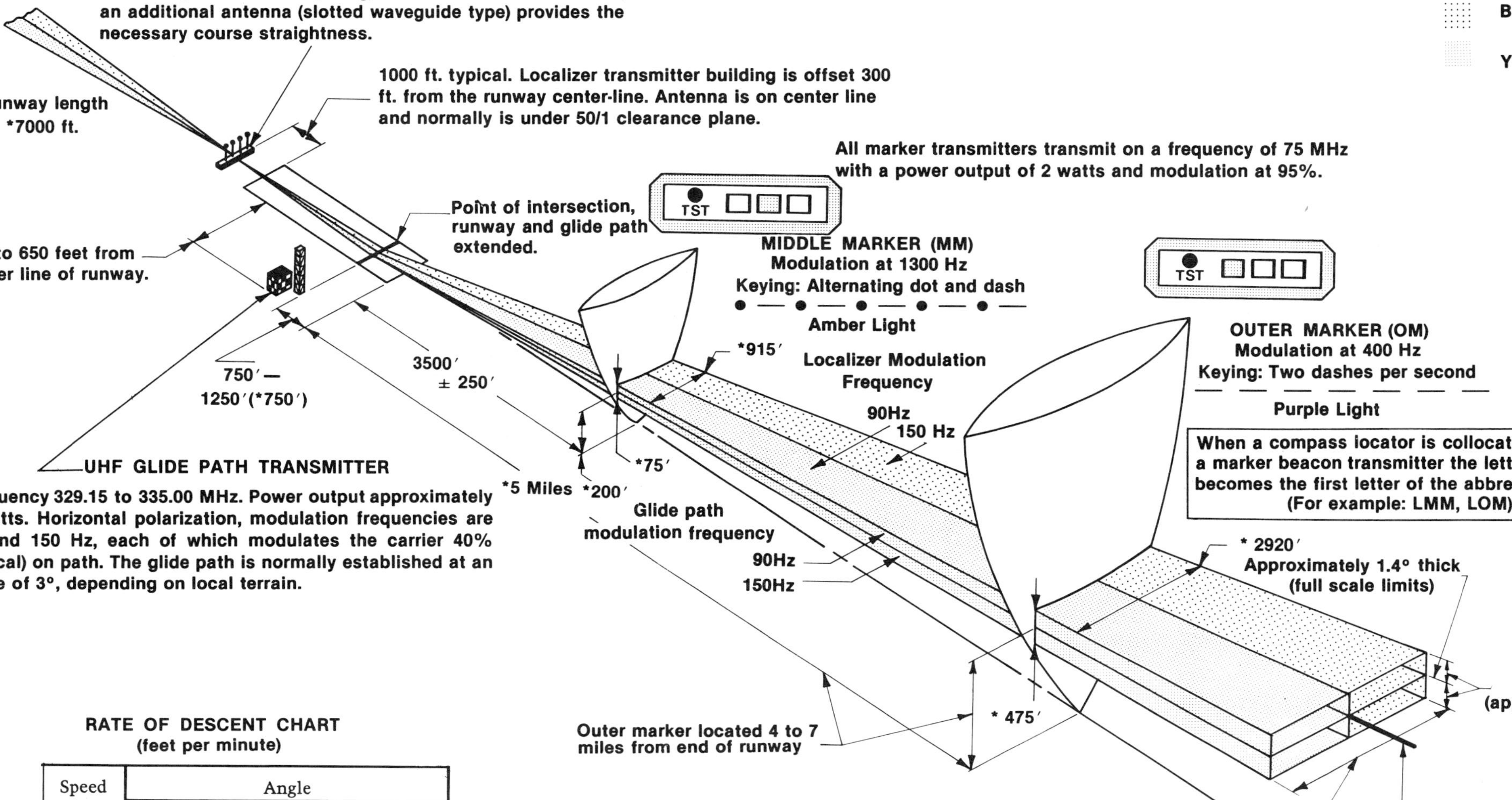

VHF LOCALIZER

108.10 to 111.95 MHz. Radiates about 100 watts. Horizontal polarization. Modulation frequencies 90 and 150 Hz. Modulation depth on course 20% for each frequency. Code identification (1020 Hz, 5%) and voice communication (modulated 50%) provided on same channel. At some localizers, where terrain (siting) difficulties are encountered, an additional antenna (slotted waveguide type) provides the necessary course straightness.

ILS approach charts should be consulted to obtain variations of individual systems.

Blue Sector

Yellow Sector

All marker transmitters transmit on a frequency of 75 MHz with a power output of 2 watts and modulation at 95%.

OUTER MARKER (OM)
Modulation at 400 Hz
Keying: Two dashes per second
——— Purple Light

When a compass locator is collocated with a marker beacon transmitter the letter "L" becomes the first letter of the abbreviation. (For example: LMM, LOM)

0.7°
(approximately)

3° above horizontal (normal)

* 2920'

Approximately 1.4° thick (full scale limits)

Course width varies; 5° at most locations (full scale limits)

MIDDLE MARKER (MM)
Modulation at 1300 Hz
Keying: Alternating dot and dash
● ▬ ● ▬ ● Amber Light

Localizer Modulation Frequency

90Hz
150 Hz

* 475'

Runway length *7000 ft.

1000 ft. typical. Localizer transmitter building is offset 300 ft. from the runway center-line. Antenna is on center line and normally is under 50/1 clearance plane.

Point of intersection, runway and glide path extended.

250 to 650 feet from center line of runway.

3500' ± 250'

750'
1250' (*750')

90Hz
150Hz

Glide path modulation frequency

*915'

*75'

*5 Miles *200'

Outer marker located 4 to 7 miles from end of runway.

UHF GLIDE PATH TRANSMITTER

Frequency 329.15 to 335.00 MHz. Power output approximately 5 watts. Horizontal polarization, modulation frequencies are 90 and 150 Hz, each of which modulates the carrier 40% (typical) on path. The glide path is normally established at an angle of 3°, depending on local terrain.

RATE OF DESCENT CHART
(feet per minute)

Speed	Angle		
(Knots)	2½°	2¾°	3°
90	400	440	475
110	485	535	585
130	575	630	690
150	665	730	795
160	707	778	849

NOTE:
Compass locators, rated at 25 watts output. 200 to 415 kHz, are installed at many outer and middle markers. A 1020 Hz tone, modulating the carrier about 95%, is keyed with the first two letters of the ILS identification on the outer locator and the last two letters on the middle locator. At some locators, simultaneous voice transmissions from the control tower are provided, with appropriate reduction in identification percentage.

* Figures marked with an asterisk are typical. Actual figures vary with deviations in distances to markers, glide angles and localizer widths.

Figure 4-30. ILS (Category I) Standard Characteristics and Terminology

Ground Components

4.95 A standard instrument landing system consists of the following components:

1. **Localizer radio transmitter**—To furnish horizontal course guidance to the runway centerline.

2. **Glide slope radio transmitter**—To furnish vertical guidance along the correct descent angle to the proper "touchdown" point on the runway.

3. **Two VHF marker beacon transmitters** (outer and middle)—To provide accurate radio fixes along the approach path to the runway.

4. **Approach lights**—Normally installed on the ILS runway to provide means for transition from instrument to visual flight.

4.96 The following supplementary elements, though not specific components of the system, may be incorporated into the system to increase safety and utility:

1. **Compass locators**—To provide transition from enroute NAVAIDs to the ILS system; to assist in holding procedures; tracking the localizer course, identifying the marker beacon sites; and to provide a final approach fix for ADF instrument approach procedures.

2. **Distance measuring equipment (DME)**— Collocated with the glide slope transmitter to provide the pilot with positive distance-to-touchdown information.

3. **Supplementary lighting systems**—To facilitate transition from instrument to outside visual references during the final stage of the approach.

Localizer

4.97 The localizer antenna array is located on the extended centerline of the instrument runway of an airport, remote enough from the opposite approach end of the runway to prevent the array from being a collision hazard.

4.98 This unit radiates a directional pattern which develops a course down the centerline of the runway toward the middle and outer markers, and a similar course along the runway centerline in the opposite direction. These courses are called the "front" and "back" courses, respectively. The localizer is designed to provide an on-course signal at a minimum distance of 18 nautical miles from the antenna between an altitude of 1,000 feet, above the highest terrain along the course line, and 4,500 feet above the elevation of the antenna site.

4.99 The radiated field pattern is modulated at two different frequencies. The right side of this pattern, looking along the normal approach path from the outer marker toward the runway, is modulated at 150 Hz. This is identified as the "blue sector" on maps and charts, as well as on some types of aircraft localizer receiver indicators. The left side of the radiated pattern is modulated at 90 Hz, and is identified as the "yellow sector." The on-course path is formed by equi-signal points between the two modulated sides of the pattern and becomes increasingly narrow as the transmitter is approached.

4.100 The localizer course width is defined as the angular displacement at any point between a full "fly-left" and a full "fly-right" indication on the localizer receiver's course deviation indicator. This course width is normally 5° (4° when associated with runways greater than 10,000 feet) and represents a lateral distance of 4,600 feet at a distance of 10 miles from the localizer array. The localizer course width at the point of aircraft touchdown is between 50 and 100 feet, depending upon the length of the runway. In addition, the localizer provides a full "fly-left" or full "fly-right" to an aircraft that is well outside the oncourse area, preventing the possibility of a "false course."

4.101 ILS Identification. Identification of each localizer facility is in International Morse Code and consists of a three-letter coded designator transmitted at frequent regular intervals. The identification is always preceded by the coded letter "I" (• •) to identify the received signal as originating at the ILS facility. For example, the ILS localizer at Bangor, Maine transmits the identifier "IBGR." The localizer includes a voice feature on its frequency for use by the associated Air Traffic Control facility in issuing approach and landing instructions. The frequency band of the localizer equipment is 108.10 to 111.95 MHz.

Glide Slope

4.102 The term "glide slope" means the complete radiation pattern generated by the glide slope facility. The term "glide path" means that portion of the glide slope that intersects the localizer. The glide slope equipment is housed in a building approximately 750 to 1,250 feet from the approach end of the runway, between 250 and 650 feet to one side of the centerline. The course projected by the glide slope equipment is essentially the same as would be generated by a localizer operating on its side, with the upper side of the course modulated at 90 Hz and the lower side 150 Hz. However, these off-course selectors are not color identified as are the localizer sectors.

4.103 The glide slope is normally adjusted at an angle of approximately 3° above the horizontal, depending upon the approach path obstructions or hazards at individual airports. Normally this will result in the interception of the glide slope with the middle marker at an elevation of about 200 feet above the runway level. At locations where standard minimum obstruction clearance cannot be obtained with the normal maximum glide slope angle, the glide slope equipment is displaced inward from the standard location if the length of the runway permits.

4.104 Unlike the localizer, the glide slope transmitter radiates signals only in the direction of the final approach on the "front course." The system provides no vertical guidance for approaches on the "back course." The glide path is normally 1.4° thick. At the normal usable distance of 10 nautical miles from the point of touchdown, this represents a vertical distance of approximately 1,500 feet, narrowing to a few feet at touchdown.

4.105 False Courses (On the Front Course). In addition to the desired course, glide slope facilities inherently produce additional courses at higher vertical angles; the angle of the lowest of these "false courses" will occur at approximately 12.5°. However, if an approach is conducted at the altitudes specified on the appropriate instrument approach procedure chart, these false courses will not be encountered.

4.106 False Courses (On the Back Course). Spurious glide slope signals may exist in the area of the localizer back course approach and can present unreliable glide slope information. Pilots should disregard all glide slope signal indications when conducting a localizer back course approach, unless a glide slope is specified on the appropriate instrument approach procedure chart.

4.107 *Special Note: Normally, a glide slope transmitter is not installed with the intent of radiating signals toward the localizer back course; however, there are a few runways at which an additional glide slope transmitter is installed to radiate signals primarily directed toward the localizer back course in order to provide vertical guidance. The two glide slope transmitters will operate on the same frequency but are interlocked to avoid simultaneous radiation and are designed to support either the front course or the back course, but not both at the same time. Approach and landing charts for the runways which have glide slopes on the localizer back course will be depicted accordingly.*

Marker Beacons

4.108 Marker beacons serve to identify a particular location in space along an airway or on the approach to an instrument runway. Two VHF marker beacons are used in the standard ILS system. These are low-powered transmitters transmitting directional signals and operating on a frequency of 75 MHz. The radiation patterns are received by aircraft flying overhead and are generally fan-shaped with an elliptical cross section; this cross section has its minor axis parallel to the approach path and its major axis at right angles to the approach path.

4.109 The **Outer Marker (OM)** normally indicates a position at which an aircraft at the appropriate altitude on the localizer course will intercept the ILS glide path. The 75 MHz carrier frequency is modulated with a 400 Hz audio tone and is keyed to emit dashes continuously at the rate of two per second.

4.110 The **Middle Marker (MM)** is located approximately 3,500 feet from the approach end of the runway, between the runway and the Outer Marker and on the centerline of the localizer course. This is also the position at which an aircraft on the glide path will be at an altitude of approximately 200 feet above the elevation of the touchdown zone. The Middle Marker's 75 MHz carrier frequency is modulated with a 1,300 Hz audio tone, keyed to transmit alternating dots and dashes at the rate of 95 dot/dash combinations per minute.

Compass Locators

4.111 As discussed previously, the Compass Locator is a low-powered nondirectional radio beacon operating in the 200-415 kHz frequency band. When used in conjunction with an ILS front course, the compass locator facilities are collocated with the Outer and/or Middle Marker facilities. The coding identification of the Outer Locator consists of the *first* two letters of the station identifier; for example, the Outer Locator at Washington National (DCA) is identified as "DC." Similarly, if a Middle Locator were established at DCA, it would be identified by the *last* two letters "CA."

Approach Lighting Systems

4.112 Normal approach and letdown on the ILS is divided into two distinct stages: the "instrument" approach using only radio guidance, and the "visual" stage, when visual contact with the ground is necessary for accuracy and safety. The most critical period of an instrument approach, particularly during low ceiling/visibility conditions, is at the point when a pilot must decide whether to land or execute a missed approach.

4.113 The purpose of the approach lighting system is to provide the pilot with lights that will penetrate the atmosphere far enough from touchdown to provide directional, distance, and glide path information for safe visual transition. With reduced visibility, rapid orientation to a strange runway can be difficult, especially during a circling approach to an airport with minimum lighting facilities, or to a large terminal airport located in the midst of distracting lights. (Specific types of approach lighting systems are discussed later in this chapter.)

ILS Receiving Equipment

4.114 For reception of electronic signals from all of the ILS transmitting and related facilities described, the airborne equipment will include the following:

1. Localizer receiver.
2. Glide slope receiver.
3. Marker beacon receiver.
4. ADF receiver (optional).
5. Distance measuring equipment (optional).

4.115 Use of the ILS does not require all of these components, however. For example, an instrument approach using the ILS system may be executed with only localizer and marker beacon receivers (sometimes called a "localizer approach"); with only localizer and ADF receivers; or with an ADF receiver only, using the compass locator as a primary approach aid. The authorized ceiling and visibility minimums will, of course, vary according to the ground and airborne equipment available and operating properly.

Localizer Receiver

4.116 Most typical light-aircraft VOR receivers are also localizer receivers with common tuning and indicating equipment. Some receivers have separate function selector switches. Otherwise, tuning of VOR and localizer frequencies is accomplished with the same knobs and switches, and the CDI indicates "on course" as it does on a VOR radial.

Glide Slope Receiver

4.117 Though some glide slope receivers are tuned separately, in a typical installation the glide slope is tuned automatically to the proper frequency when the localizer is tuned in. Each of the 40 allocated localizer channels in the 108.10 through 111.95 MHz band is associated with a corresponding glide slope frequency of the 40 UHF glide slope channels available. The paired frequencies are specified in the table in Figure 4-31.

Localizer/Glide Slope Indicator

4.118 When the localizer indicator also includes a glide slope needle, the instrument is often called a cross-pointer indicator. The crossed horizontal (glide slope) and vertical (localizer) indicators are free to move through standard 5-dot deflections to indicate position on the localizer course and glide path. (Figure 4-32)

PAIRED LOCALIZER/GLIDE SLOPE FREQUENCIES

LOCALIZER MHz	GLIDE SLOPE MHz	LOCALIZER MHz	GLIDE SLOPE MHz
108.10	334.70	110.10	334.40
108.15	334.55	110.15	334.25
108.30	334.10	110.30	335.00
108.35	333.95	110.35	334.85
108.50	329.90	110.50	329.60
108.55	329.75	110.55	329.45
108.70	330.50	110.70	330.20
108.75	330.35	110.75	330.05
108.90	329.30	110.90	330.80
108.95	329.15	110.95	330.65
109.10	331.40	111.10	331.70
109.15	331.25	111.15	331.55
109.30	332.00	111.30	332.30
109.35	331.85	111.35	332.15
109.50	332.60	111.50	332.90
109.55	332.45	111.55	332.75
109.70	333.20	111.70	333.50
109.75	333.05	111.75	333.35
109.90	333.80	111.90	331.10
109.95	333.65	111.95	330.95

Figure 4-31.

Figure 4-32. A Collins VIR-351 Navigation Receiver (top) and IND-351 VOR/LOC/GS Indicator (bottom)

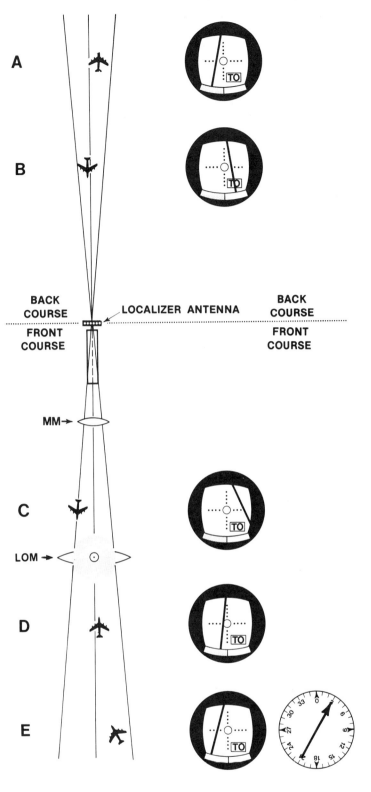

BACK COURSE
LOCALIZER ANTENNA
BACK COURSE
FRONT COURSE
FRONT COURSE

MM→

LOM→

Note that the TO/FROM indicator always registers a TO indication when the localizer receiver is receiving an adequate signal.

Figure 4–33. Localizer Receiver Indications

4.119 The *localizer needle* indicates, by deflection, the color sector in which the aircraft is flying, *regardless* of the position or heading of the aircraft. Rotation of the omni bearing selector has *no* effect on the operation of the localizer needle. Some indicators show blue and yellow sectors to the left and right of the centerline position of the needle; on instruments with no color shown, the needle deflects left in the blue sector, right in the yellow sector.

4.120 Thus, when the aircraft is inbound on the front course or outbound on the back course, the needle is deflected toward the on-course and the aircraft must turn toward the needle to correct to the appropriate track. (Refer to airplanes A and D in Figure 4-33.) Conversely, when the aircraft is inbound on the back course or outbound on the front course, the aircraft must turn away from the direction of needle deflection to reach the center of the localizer course. (Refer to airplanes B and C.) With an ADF tuned to the outer compass locator, orientation on the localizer course is simplified. (Refer to airplane E.)

4.121 The localizer course is very narrow, resulting in high sensitivity of the needle. Full-scale deflection shows when the aircraft is 2.5° to either side of the centerline. This sensitivity permits accurate orientation to the landing runway. With no more than a ¼-scale deflection maintained, an aircraft will be aligned with the runway. High needle sensitivity also tends to encourage overcontrolling, until the pilot learns to apply correct basic flying techniques for smooth control of the aircraft.

4.122 Deflection of the *glide slope needle* indicates the position of the aircraft with respect to the glide path. When the aircraft is above the glide path, the needle is deflected downward. When the aircraft is below the glide path, the needle is deflected upward. (Figure 4-34)

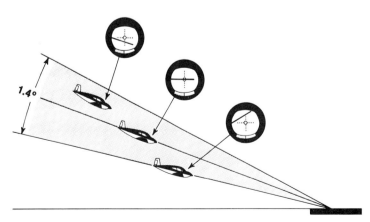

1.4°

Figure 4-34. Glide Slope Receiver Indications

4.123 When the aircraft is on the glide path, the needle is horizontal, overlying the reference dots. Since the glide path is much sharper than the localizer course (approximately 1.4° from full "up" to full "down" deflection), the needle is very sensitive to displacement of the aircraft from on-path alignment. With the proper rate of descent established on glide slope interception, very small corrections keep the aircraft aligned.

4.124 *Special Note: The localizer and glide slope warning flags disappear from view on the indicator when sufficient signal is received to actuate the needles. The flags indicate when an unstable signal or receiver malfunction occurs.*

Marker Beacon Receiver

4.125 The 75 MHz marker beacon receiver provides both aural and visual indication of passage over a VHF marker beacon. (Figure 4-35) This receiver is most often used in conjunction with instrument approaches employing outer and middle marker beacon transmitters. The purple (blue) and amber (yellow) lights identify passage over the outer and middle markers respectively along with the aural identification codes as previously discussed.

4.126 Ordinarily, there are only two marker beacons associated with an instrument landing system. However, some locations may employ a third marker beacon (inner marker) used with Category II and III instrument landing systems.

4.127 The inner marker (IM), where installed, indicates a progress point on the glide path between the middle marker and landing threshold. The IM is modulated at 3,000 Hz and identified with continuous dots keyed at the rate of six dots per second and a white marker beacon light.

4.128 Occasionally, an ILS system may be additionally equipped with a back course marker. This type of marker, where installed, normally indicates the ILS back course final approach fix where approach descent is commenced. The back course marker is modulated at 3,000 Hz and identified with two dots at a rate of 72 to 95 two-dot combinations per minute and a white marker beacon light.

Figure 4–35. A Narco Marker Beacon Receiver

4.129 Not only are inner markers and back course markers identified by a white marker beacon light and a coded 3,000 Hz tone, but fan markers are also identified in a similar manner. Fan markers (FM), although not an integral part of an instrument landing system, are generally used to provide a positive identification of a position located on a final approach course of a nonprecision approach.

4.130 *Special Note: Airborne marker beacon receivers with a selective sensitivity feature should always be operated in the "low" sensitivity position for proper reception of ILS marker beacons.*

ILS Errors

4.131 The following list of errors is common among the inexperienced *and* noncurrent instrument pilots:

1. *Failure to understand the fundamentals of ILS ground equipment, particularly the differences in course dimensions.* Since the VOR/LOC receiver indicator is used to determine the localizer course, the incorrect assumption is sometimes made that interception and tracking techniques are identical when tracking localizer courses and VOR radials. Remember that the CDI sensing of a localizer course is sharper and four to five times faster on the localizer course as compared to a VOR course at equal distance from the transmitter site.

2. *Disorientation during transition to the ILS due to poor planning and reliance on one receiver instead of on all available airborne equipment.* Pilots should use all the assistance available; a single receiver that a pilot may be relying on may fail during a critical phase of an instrument approach procedure.

3. *Disorientation on the localizer course, basically due to the first error noted.*

4. *Incorrect localizer interception angles.* A large interception angle usually results in overshooting and often in disorientation. A pilot should turn to the localizer course heading, using a small interception angle whenever possible, immediately upon the first indication of needle movement. An ADF receiver is an excellent aid to orientation during the execution of an ILS approach.

5. *Chasing the CDI and glide path needles, especially when the instrument approach procedure is not sufficiently studied prior to the flight.* Flying using the proper headings, altitudes, rate of descent, times and power configuration settings is impossible if a pilot is studying the instrument approach procedure chart during the execution of the approach.

SIMPLIFIED DIRECTIONAL FACILITY (SDF)

4.132 The Simplified Directional Facility provides a final approach course which is similar to that of the ILS localizer described in this chapter. If a pilot has a clear understanding of the ILS localizer and is aware of the additional factors listed below, he will have a complete understanding of the operational characteristics and use of the SDF.

1. The SDF transmits signals within the range of 108.10 MHz to 111.95 MHz. It provides no glide slope information.

2. For the pilot, the approach techniques and procedures used in the performance of an SDF instrument approach are essentially identical to those employed in executing a standard no-glide slope localizer approach except that the SDF course may not be aligned with the runway and the course may be wider, resulting in less precision.

3. Usable off-course indications are limited to 35° of either side of the course centerline. Instrument indications in the areas between 35° and 90° are not controlled and should be disregarded.

4. The SDF antenna may be offset from the runway centerline. Because of this, the angle of convergence between the final approach course and the runway bearing should be determined by referring to the instrument approach procedure chart. This angle is generally not more than 3°. However, it should be noted that, inasmuch as the approach course originates at the antenna site, an approach which is continued beyond the runway threshold will lead the aircraft to the SDF offset position rather than along the runway centerline.

5. The SDF signal emitted from the transmitter is fixed at either 6° or 12° as necessary to provide maximum flyability and optimum course quality.

6. Identification consists of a three-letter identifier transmitted on the SDF frequency.

THE LOCALIZER-TYPE DIRECTIONAL AID (LDA)

4.133 The localizer-type directional aid (LDA) is of comparable utility and accuracy to a localizer but is not part of a complete ILS. The LDA course usually provides a more precise approach course than the similar SDF installation. The LDA is also not aligned with the runway.

MAINTENANCE OF FAA NAVAIDs

4.134 During periods of routine or emergency maintenance, the coded identification (or code and voice, where applicable) will be removed from certain FAA NAVAIDs; namely, ILS localizers, VOR stations, nondirectional beacons, compass locators and 75 MHz marker beacons. The removal of identification serves as warning to pilots that the facility has been officially taken over by "maintenance" for tune-up or repair and may be unreliable even though it is on the air intermittently or constantly.

AREA NAVIGATION (RNAV)

4.135 Area navigation is a method of navigation which permits aircraft operation on a selected course to a predefined point *without* the need to fly directly toward or away from a navigational aid. Naturally, on a flight of even moderate length, a significant reduction of fuel consumption and en route time results. The primary navigation system which is used by general aviation for RNAV purposes is the course line computer. This system is based on azimuth and distance information generated by the present VORTAC system. (Figure 4-36)

4.136 A typical airborne area navigation system consists of a waypoint selector, a guidance display (similar to the indicator illustrated in Figure 4-32), and a vector analog computer which is the heart of the system.

4.137 Through the use of the course line computer the pilot is able to move (figuratively speaking) a VORTAC station to a desired location, thereby creating a "phantom station" called a "waypoint." (A series of waypoints make up an area navigation route.) To establish a waypoint, the pilot simply must set the distance and bearing in the appropriate waypoint selector windows. The RNAV computer and waypoint selector illustrated in Figure 4-36 have single waypoint capability. Other RNAV systems, however, may possess the capability of "storing" several waypoints for entire direct route flights.

Figure 4-36. A King KN 74 Area Navigation Computer and Waypoint Selector

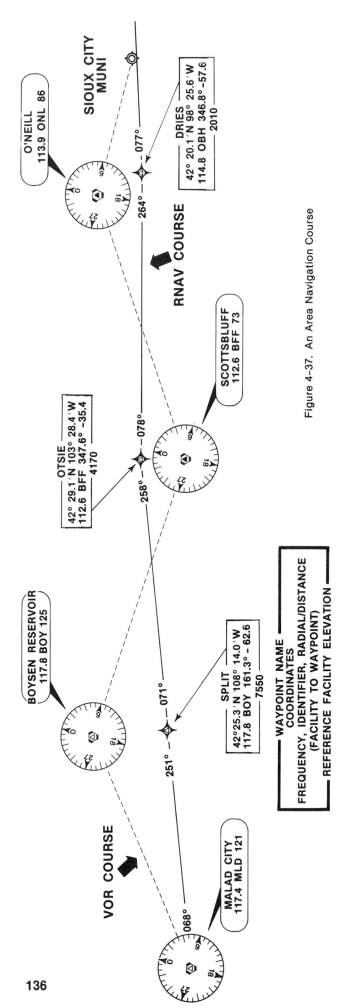

Figure 4-37. An Area Navigation Course

4.138 Figure 4-37 illustrates a typical area navigation course. It is easy to see that unnecessary doglegging is eliminated through the employment of RNAV. Although cockpit presentations of guidance information vary, in all displays, the displacement of a vertical reference indicates *distance* (not angular displacement) from a selected track (each dot on the horizontal scale may have any value, such as .25,.5,1,2, or 10 nautical miles, depending upon equipment design). Furthermore, the horizontal reference indicates the along-track distance to a selected waypoint. The intersection of the two reference indicators depicts the waypoint. Distance to the waypoint may also be read from a conventional DME indicator.

4.139 Vertical guidance is also possible with some area navigation systems. Some manufacturers provide an additional vertical navigation (VNAV) feature, which, combined with the basic two-dimensional (lateral and longitudinal) Area Navigation system, provides vertical guidance information similar to a glide slope. With this additional feature, a waypoint can be selected not only at a desired surface location but also at a desired altitude. Thus, the pilot can select and fly a predetermined vertical profile to a preselected point in space and also create and accurately follow a computed variable glide slope for instrument approaches.

INTEGRATED AUTOMATIC FLIGHT CONTROL SYSTEMS

4.140 In the past, integrated automatic control systems (integrated flight director/autopilot systems) were usually found in the heavy, more expensive aircraft. Recent monumental advances in attitude instrumentation and solid state electronics have now made it possible for even single-engine and light and medium twin engine general aviation aircraft to be equipped with integrated automatic flight control systems. Figure 4-38 illustrates a current model of an integrated automatic flight control system.

4.141 Basically, the flight director portion of this system graphically consolidates aircraft attitude and navigation data and displays computed steering commands, thereby informing the pilot how to most expeditiously fly that portion of the flight currently underway. The computed command indications also relieve the pilot of many of the mental calculations required for instrument flight. Many systems also have the capability of "flying" the aircraft from takeoff to touchdown when the autopilot is electronically "coupled" to the flight director computer. The pilot need only manipulate the control wheel to rotate the aircraft during takeoff and to flare for landing. (Such a system generally satisfies

Category II approach requirements.) The remainder of the flight is spent pushing buttons on the control panel, selecting courses, setting the throttle(s), and tuning frequencies.

4.142 The most complex integrated automatic flight control systems have the capability of flying the aircraft during the *entire* flight. These systems, obviously, are not common to even the more sophisticated general aviation aircraft. (These complex systems are primarily used in aircraft that are authorized to conduct Category III approaches.)

4.143 A typical integrated flight control system includes a mode annunciator panel, a flight director indicator (FDI), a horizontal situation indicator (HSI), a control panel, a steering computer, an instrument amplifier, and the autopilot system. The first four of these components are illustrated in Figure 4-38. A brief description of their respective functions follows:

Figure 4-38. A King KFC 200 Flight Director/Autopilot System

Mode annunciator panel—Provides the pilot with continuous information on the system's operating status.

Flight director indicator—(Also commonly referred to as attitude director indicator.) This is a basic attitude indicator and also displays computed pitch and roll "commands" required to attain and maintain a pre-selected flight condition. Integration of the flight director and autopilot system allows the pilot to manually fly the pitch and roll commands of the FDI, or to electronically couple these commands to the autopilot and monitor the performance of the autopilot on the FDI. Malfunction of an input reference system is indicated by a warning flag.

Horizontal situation indicator—Presents a plan view pictorial presentation of the aircraft's position relative to VOR radials, localizer courses, glide slope beams, and waypoints (if the aircraft is RNAV equipped). The HSI also constantly provides a gyro heading reference relative to magnetic north. Malfunctions are indicated by appropriate warning flags. (It should be noted that, although this instrument is considered to be part of an integrated automatic flight control system, aircraft not equipped with integrated automatic flight control systems are frequently equipped with HSIs.)

Control panel (mode controller)—Provides the pilot with push-button selection of all flight director/autopilot modes. When a mode is selected, the corresponding annunciator is illuminated.

4.144 *Special Note: A pilot should always refer to the appropriate equipment manual for specific information regarding a particular integrated automatic flight control system since almost every type of system incorporates different equipment features and individual methods of operation.*

RADIO DETECTION AND RANGING (RADAR)

4.145 The *fundamental* principle of radar is based on the precise timing between the transmission of a radio signal, its return "echo" from an object in the path of the beam, and the displaying of this information on the face of a cathode ray tube, referred to as a "scope." (Figures 4-39 and 4-40) *Range* is determined by measuring the time it takes for the radio signal to go out to the object and then return to the receiving antenna. The *direction* of a detected object from a radar site is determined by the position of the rotating antenna when the reflected portion of the radio signal is received.

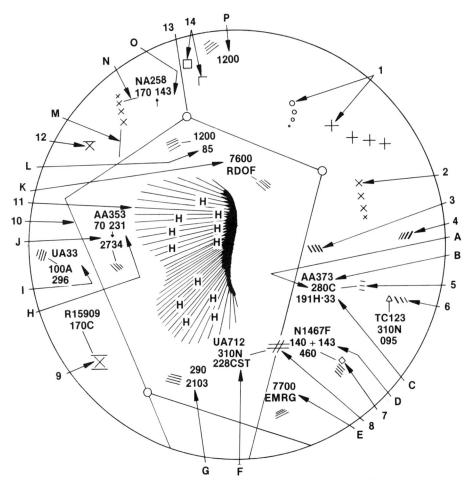

Figure 4-39. NAS Stage A Controller's Plan View Display

TARGET SYMBOLS

1. Uncorrelated primary radar target
2. * Correlated primary radar target
3. Uncorrelated beacon target
4. Correlated beacon target
5. Identing beacon target
(* Correlated means the association of radar data with the computer projected track of an identified aircraft)

POSITION SYMBOLS

6. Free track (No flight plan tracking)
7. Flat track (Flight plan tracking)
8. Coast (Beacon target lost)
9. Present position hold

OTHER SYMBOLS

10. Airway or jet route
11. Outline of weather returns based on primary radar (H's represent areas of high density precipitation which might be thunderstorms. Radial lines indicate lower density precipitation)
12. Obstruction
13. Navigational Aid
14. Airports Major: □,   Small: ⬜

THIS FIGURE ILLUSTRATES THE CONTROLLER'S RADAR SCOPE (PVD) WHEN OPERATING IN THE FULL AUTOMATION (RPD) MODE.

DATA BLOCK INFORMATION

A. * Assigned altitude FL280, mode C altitude same or within ± 200 feet assigned altitude

B. * Aircraft Identification

C. * Computer ID#191, Handoff is to Sector 33 (O-33 would mean handoff accepted) (* Letters A,B,C constitute a "full data block")

D. Aircraft is 300 feet above assigned altitude (Assigned altitude is 14,000 feet, Actual altitude is 14,300 feet)

E. Transponder set on emergency code 7700 (EMGR flashes to attract attention)

F. Computer ID# 228, CST indicates target is in Coast status

G. Assigned altitude FL290, transponder code (These two items constitute a "limited data block")

H. Assigned altitude 7,000 feet, aircraft is descending, last mode C readout (or last reported altitude was 100 feet above FL230)

I. Reported altitude (No mode C readout) same as assigned (An "N" would indicate no reported altitude)

J. Transponder code shows in full data block only when different from assigned code

K. Transponder set on Radio Failure code 7600 (RDOF flashed)

L. Code 1200 (VFR) with mode C and last altitude readout

M. Track velocity and direction vector line (Projected ahead of target)

N. Leader line connecting target symbol and data block

O. Assigned altitude 17,000 feet, aircraft is climbing, mode C readout was 14,300 when last beacon interrogation was received

P. Transponder code 1200 (VFR) with no mode C

Note: "ARTS" radar scopes combine "broadband" (primary/secondary) radar targets with alphanumeric data. Lower left hand subset displays "broadband" primary/secondary radar and ARTS III when operating without automation.

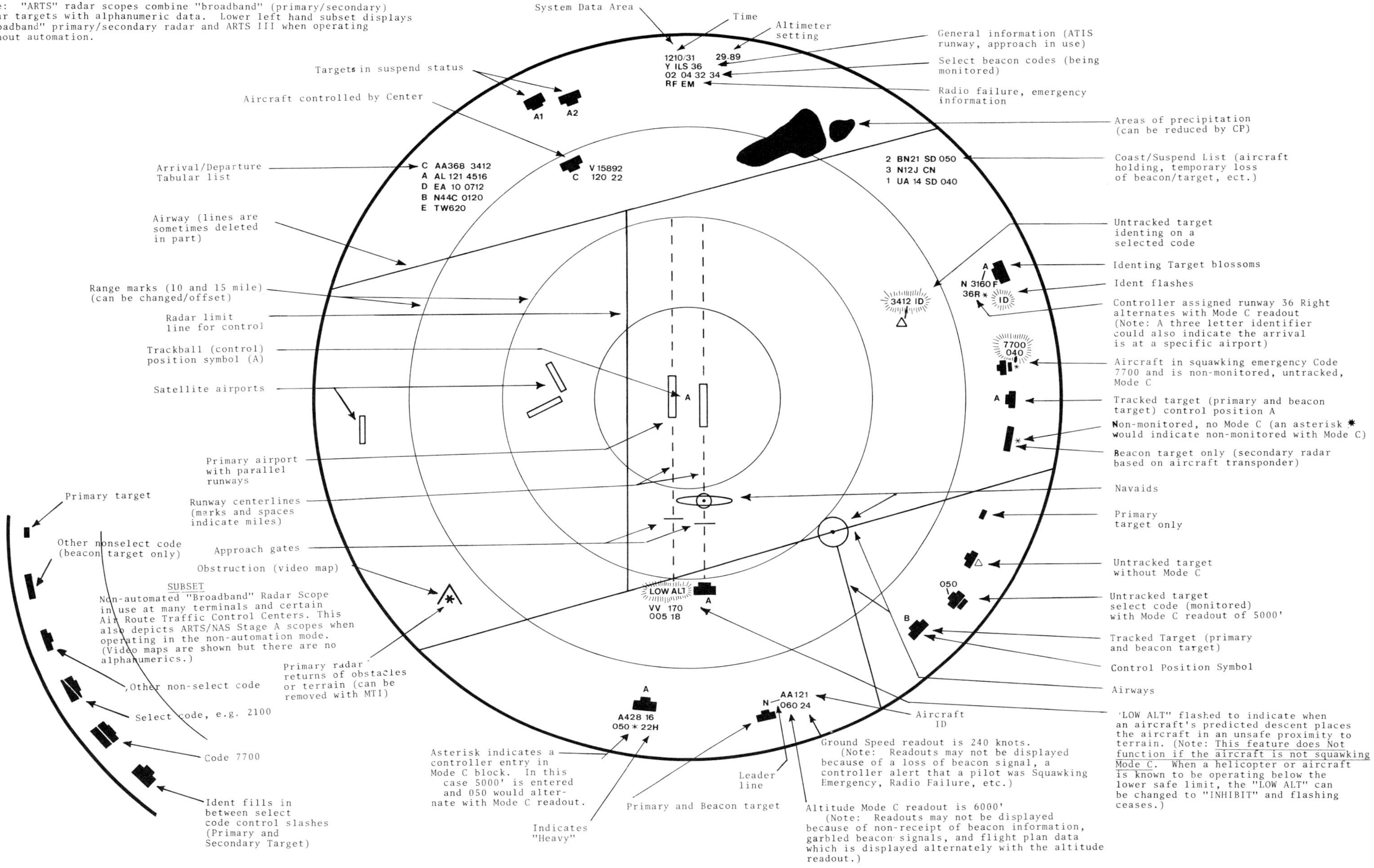

System Data Area

General information (ATIS runway, approach in use)

Select beacon codes (being monitored)

Radio failure, emergency information

Areas of precipitation (can be reduced by CP)

Coast/Suspend list (aircraft holding, temporary loss of beacon/target, ect.)

Untracked target identing on a selected code

Identing Target blossoms

Ident flashes

Controller assigned runway 36 Right alternates with Mode C readout (Note: A three letter identifier could also indicate the arrival is at a specific airport)

Aircraft in squawking emergency Code 7700 and is non-monitored, untracked, Mode C

Tracked target (primary and beacon target) control position A

Non-monitored, no Mode C (an asterisk * would indicate non-monitored with Mode C)

Beacon target only (secondary radar based on aircraft transponder)

Navaids

Primary target only

Untracked target without Mode C

Untracked target select code (monitored) with Mode C readout of 5000'

Tracked Target (primary and beacon target)

Control Position Symbol

Airways

'LOW ALT" flashed to indicate when an aircraft's predicted descent places the aircraft in an unsafe proximity to terrain. (Note: This feature does Not function if the aircraft is not squawking Mode C. When a helicopter or aircraft is known to be operating below the lower safe limit, the "LOW ALT" can be changed to "INHIBIT" and flashing ceases.)

Time

Altimeter setting

Aircraft controlled by Center

Targets in suspend status

Arrival/Departure Tabular list

Airway (lines are sometimes deleted in part)

Range marks (10 and 15 mile) (can be changed/offset)

Radar limit line for control

Trackball (control position symbol (A)

Satellite airports

Primary airport with parallel runways

Runway centerlines (marks and spaces indicate miles)

Approach gates

Obstruction (video map)

SUBSET

Non-automated "Broadband" Radar Scope in use at many terminals and certain Air Route Traffic Control Centers. This also depicts ARTS/NAS Stage A scopes when operating in the non-automation mode. (Video maps are shown but there are no alphanumerics.)

Primary radar returns of obstacles or terrain (can be removed with MTI)

Primary target

Other nonselect code (beacon target only)

Select code, e.g. 2100

,Other non-select code

Code 7700

Ident fills in between select code control slashes (Primary and Secondary Target)

Ground Speed readout is 240 knots. Readouts may not be displayed because of a loss of beacon signal, a controller alert that a pilot was Squawking Emergency, Radio Failure, etc.)

Altitude Mode C readout is 6000' (Note: Readouts may not be displayed because of non-receipt of beacon information, garbled beacon signals, and flight plan data which is displayed alternately with the altitude readout.)

Aircraft ID

Leader line

Primary and Beacon target

Indicates "Heavy"

Asterisk indicates a controller entry in Mode C block. In this case 5000' is entered and 050 would alternate with Mode C readout.

Labels within display:

1210/31
29.89
Y ILS 36
02 04 32 34
RF EM

2 BN21 SD 050
3 N12J CN
1 UA 14 SD 040

7700 040 *

A
N 3160 F
36R * ID

3412 ID

A

*

050

B

N AA121 060 24

A

LOW ALT
VV 170
005 18

A
A428 16
050 * 22H

V15892 120 22
C

A2
A1

C AA368 3412
A AL121 4516
D EA 10 0712
B N44C 0120
E TW620

Figure 4-40. ARTS III Radar Scope with Alphanumeric Data Display

Note: A number of radar terminals do not have Automated Radar Terminal Systems (ARTS) equipment. Those facilities and certain Air Route Traffic Control Centers outside the contiguous U.S. would have radar displays similar to the lower left hand subset. ARTS facilities and NAS Stage A Air Route Traffic Control Centers, when operating in the non-automation mode would also have similar displays and certain services based on automation may not be available.

139

4.146 The basic types of radar systems used by the FAA are:

1. **Airport Surface Detection Equipment (ASDE)**—ASDE is specifically designed to detect all principal features on the surface of an airport, including aircraft and vehicular traffic, and to present the entire image on a radar indicator console in the control tower. This equipment is used to augment visual observation by tower personnel of aircraft and/or vehicular movements on runways and taxiways.

2. **Air Route Surveillance Radar (ARSR)**—Air route surveillance radar is primarily used to detect and display an aircraft's position while en route between terminal areas. The ARSR enables controllers to provide radar air traffic control service when aircraft are within the ARSR coverage (up to 200 miles under optimum conditions). By means of a Microwave Link Relay System, an unlimited number of radar transmitter sites can be remoted from the control center to provide navigational guidance along the air routes.

3. **Airport Surveillance Radar (ASR)**—This radar system is designed to provide relatively short range coverage in the general vicinity of an airport and to serve as an expeditious means of handling terminal area traffic through observation of precise aircraft locations on a radar scope. The ASR can also be used as an instrument approach aid. ASR provides range (up to 60 miles) and azimuth information, but does *not* provide elevation data.

4. **Precision Approach Radar (PAR)**—This radar equipment is used to detect and display the azimuth, range, *and elevation* of an aircraft on the final approach course to a runway (rather than as an aid for sequencing and spacing aircraft). The term "precision" is used to describe this type of radar system because this system, like the ILS, provides accurate vertical (glide slope) information. Unlike surveillance radar, two antennas are used in the PAR array, one scanning a vertical plane, and the other scanning horizontally. Since the range of PAR is limited to 10 miles, azimuth to 20 degrees, and elevation to 7 degrees, *only* the final approach area is scanned. Each scope is divided into two parts: the upper half presents altitude and distance information, and the lower half presents azimuth and distance information.

Primary and Secondary Radar

4.147 Radar can be further categorized as primary or secondary. The *primary* radar surveillance system provides the controller with a map-like presentation based upon all the radar echoes (often referred to as "skin paint" or "blips") of aircraft within detection range of the radar facility. Since there is no direct method of initially identifying a particular aircraft (the echoes do not have identifying features) controllers often request pilots to execute turns to specific headings for aircraft identification. By means of electronically generated range marks and 360° azimuth-indicating devices, each radar target can be located with respect to the radar facility, or can be located with respect to another radar target. The bearing and range of one aircraft target with respect to another can be determined from direct readings presented on the control panel.

4.148 Secondary surveillance radar is also referred to as the Air Traffic Control Radar Beacon System (ATCRBS). Secondary radar relies on the exchange of electronic signals between ground-based equipment (interrogator) and airborne equipment (transponder). The *interrogator*, a ground based radar beacon transmitter-receiver, scans in synchronism with the primary radar and transmits ultra high frequency pulsed radio signals (on 1030 MHz). The interrogator repetitiously requests all transponders, on the mode being used, to reply. This airborne transmitter-receiver automatically receives the signals from the interrogator, interprets them, and selectively replies by transmitting (on a frequency of 1090 MHz) with a specific preselected reply pulse or pulse group (code) only to those interrogations being received on the mode to which it is set to respond. These replies are independent of, and much stronger than a primary radar return. The replies are received by the interrogator, are decoded, and are then displayed on the radar scope in a *distinct* pattern (normally two short parallel lines). Primary returns are also displayed on the same scope.

4.149 A mode is the letter or number assigned to a specific pulse spacing of radio signals transmitted or received by ground interrogator or airborne transponder components of the Air Traffic Control Radar Beacon System (ATCRBS). At present, there are six modes. Modes 1 and 2 are used exclusively by the military services. Mode A in the civil system is the same as military Mode 3 and is used exclusively for air traffic control. It is commonly designated Mode A/3. Modes B and D are still unassigned. Mode C is used for automatic altitude reporting in the NAS Stage A (en route) and the ARTS III (terminal) systems.

4.150 Some transponders are interfaced with a special encoding altimeter or blind encoder and are, therefore, equipped with a Mode C automatic altitude reporting capability. This system converts aircraft altitude, in 100 foot increments, to coded digital information which is transmitted together with Mode C framing pulses to the interrogating radar facility. The manner in which transponder panels are designed differs; therefore, a pilot should be thoroughly familiar with the operation of his transponder so that its full capabilities may be realized.

4.151 The transponder is basically quite easy to operate. The following discussion describes some of the basic features of the transponder illustrated in Figure 4-41:

1. Any one of the 4096 Mode A/3 *codes* can be selected by simply switching the appropriate code into the code windows. (Since there are no eights or nines used, the numerical value of the codes range from 0000 to 7777.)

2. The *IDENT* button is depressed when positive aircraft identification is necessary. When a transponder's IDENT feature is activated, a Special Position Identification pulse (SPI) is transmitted. The space between the parallel lines of the target on the radar scope will then fill in, identifying the aircraft unmistakably.

3. The *STY* (standby) function maintains the transponder in a warm-up state. In other words, the transponder will not reply to interrogation.

4. When the transponder is switched to the ON position it will reply (with the preselected code) to Mode A/3 interrogations.

5. The *ALT* (altitude) function activates the Mode C capability of a transponder (assuming an encoder is connected to the transponder).

Figure 4-41. A King KT 76 Transponder (top) and KEA 125 Encoding Altimeter (bottom)

4.152 After analyzing the secondary radar system, it can be concluded that aircraft transponders greatly improve the effectiveness of radar systems through the reinforcement of radar targets, rapid target identification, and the extension of the radar coverage area.

Limitations of Radar

4.153 It is very important for the instrument pilot to recognize the fact that there are limitations to radar service. Some of the limitations are:

1. The characteristics of radio waves are such that they normally travel in a continuous straight line unless they are:

   A. "Bent" by abnormal atmospheric phenomena such as temperature inversions;

   B. Reflected or attenuated by dense objects such as heavy clouds, precipitation, ground obstacles, and mountains; or

   C. Screened by high terrain features.

2. The bending of radar pulses, often called anomalous propagation or ducting, may cause many extraneous blips to appear on the radar operator's display if the pulses have not been bent toward the ground or may decrease the detection range if the pulses are bent upward. It is difficult to solve the effects of anomalous propagation, but, by using beacon radar and electronically eliminating stationary and slow moving targets by a method called moving target indicator (MTI), the problem is usually eliminated.

3. Radar energy that strikes dense objects will be reflected and displayed on the operator's scope, thereby blocking out aircraft at the same range and greatly weakening or completely eliminating the display of targets at a greater range. Again, the transponder/interrogator and MTI are very effectively used to combat ground clutter and weather phenomena, and a method of circularly polarizing the radar beam will eliminate some weather returns. A negative characteristic of MTI is that an aircraft flying at a speed that coincides with the canceling signal of the MTI (tangential or "blind" speed) may not be displayed to the radar controller.

4. Relatively low altitude aircraft will not be detected if they are screened by mountains or are below the radar beam due to earth curvature. The only solution to screening is the installation of strategically placed multiple radars which has been done in some areas.

5. Since the transponder's coverage is limited to "line of sight," low altitude or aircraft antenna shielding by the aircraft itself may result in reduced range. Range can be improved by the aircraft climbing to a higher altitude. It may be

possible to minimize antenna shielding by locating the antenna where dead spots are only noticed during abnormal flight attitudes.

6. The amount of reflective surface of an aircraft will determine the amount of the radar return. Consequently, a small light aircraft will be more difficult to detect by radar as compared to a large commercial jet. Once again, the use of a radar beacon is invaluable if the aircraft is equipped with an airborne transponder.

7. The example shown in Figure 4-42 illustrates the possible error in radar traffic advisories when it is necessary for a pilot to apply drift correction to maintain a specific track. The pilot of aircraft A in Figure 4-42 would be advised that traffic was at the 2 o'clock position. Since it is not necessary for the pilot of aircraft A to apply wind correction (crab) to make good his track, the actual position of the traffic issued would be correct. Traffic information would be issued to the pilot of aircraft B as in the 10 o'clock position. However, the actual position of the traffic as seen by the pilot of aircraft B would be 9 o'clock. Since the radar controller can only observe aircraft track (course) on the radar display, traffic advisories must be issued accordingly, and pilots should give due consideration to this fact when looking for reported traffic.

When the aircraft's track is equal to the aircraft's heading radar traffic information is correct with respect to the nose of the aircraft and the track.

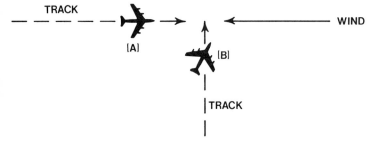

When the aircraft is crabbing into the wind radar traffic information is correct with respect to the track only.

Figure 4-42. An Example of Radar Traffic Information Error

LIGHTING AIDS

4.154 The following section contains pertinent information relative to lighting aids. As a general rule, pilots, in the past, have taken a rather passive attitude toward the "specifics" of lighting aids. Today's instrument pilot, however, must thoroughly understand the various types of lighting aids since, during poor weather conditions, these visual NAVAIDs play an increasingly significant role.

Rotating Beacon

4.155 The rotating beacon has a vertical light distribution making it most effective at angles of one to three degrees above the horizontal from its site; however, it can be seen well above and below this peak spread. Rotation is in a clockwise direction when viewed from above. It is always rotated at a constant speed which produces the visual effect of flashes at regular intervals.

4.156 In control zones, operation of the rotating beacon during the hours of daylight may indicate that the ground visibility is less than 3 miles and/or the ceiling is less than 1,000 feet. Pilots should not rely solely on the operation of the rotating beacon to indicate weather conditions (IFR versus VFR). If controls are provided at locations with control towers ATC personnel turn the beacon on. However, at many airports throughout the country, the rotating beacon is turned on by a photoelectric cell or time clocks and ATC personnel have no control as to when it is turned on. Also, there is no regulatory requirement for daylight operation.

Instrument Approach Light Systems

4.157 Instrument approach light systems provide the basic means for transition from instrument flight using electronic approach aids to visual flight and landing. Operational requirements dictate the sophistication and configuration of the approach light system for any particular airport. The common instrument approach lighting aids that instrument pilots should be familiar with are illustrated in Figure 4-43.

4.158 *Special Note: Condenser-Discharge Sequenced Flashing Light Systems are installed in conjunction with the instrument approach light system at some airports which have U.S. Standard "A" approach lights as a further aid to pilots making instrument approaches. The system consists of a series of brilliant blue-white bursts of light flashing in sequence along the approach lights. It gives the effect of a ball of light traveling towards the runway. An impression of the system as a pilot first observes the flashing lights when making an approach is that of large tracer shells rapidly fired from a point in space toward the runway.*

A DOT "●" PORTRAYED WITH APPROACH LIGHTING
LETTER IDENTIFIER INDICATES SEQUENCED FLASHING
LIGHTS (F) INSTALLED WITH THE APPROACH LIGHTING
SYSTEM.
EXAMPLE: (Ⓐ₁)

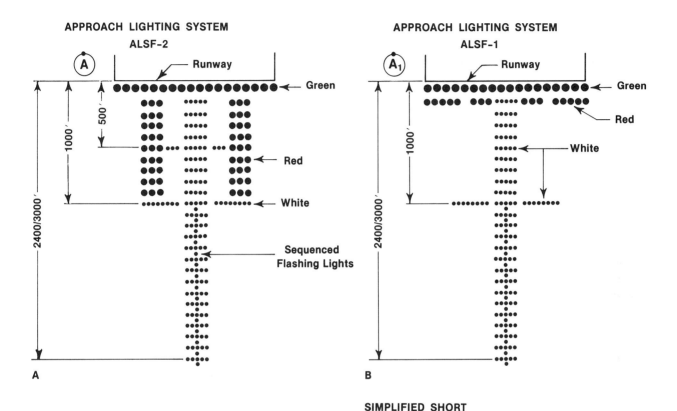

A — APPROACH LIGHTING SYSTEM ALSF-2

B — APPROACH LIGHTING SYSTEM ALSF-1

C — SHORT APPROACH LIGHTING SYSTEM SALS (High Intensity)

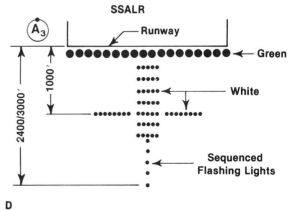

D — SIMPLIFIED SHORT APPROACH LIGHTING SYSTEM with Runway Alignment Indicator Lights SSALR

Figure 4-43 A to H. Legend of Approach Lighting Systems

MEDIUM INTENSITY (MALS AND MALSF) OR SIMPLIFIED SHORT (SSALS AND SSALF) APPROACH LIGHTING SYSTEMS

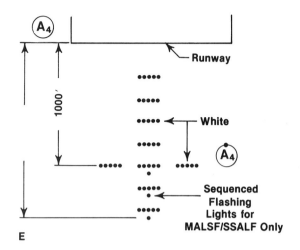

E

MEDIUM INTENSITY APPROACH LIGHTING SYSTEM with Runway Alignment Indicator Lights MALSR

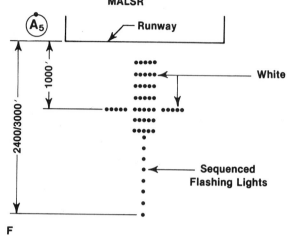

F

OMNIDIRECTIONAL APPROACH LIGHTING SYSTEM ODALS

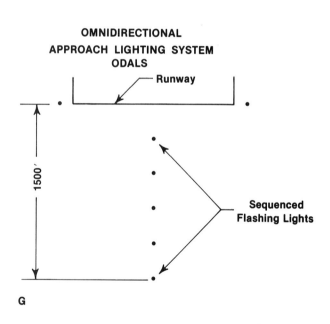

G

VISUAL APPROACH SLOPE INDICATOR VASI

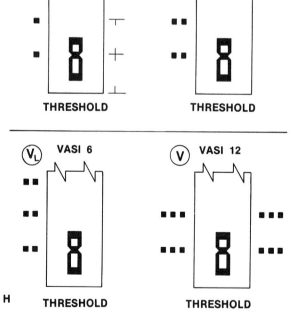

H

Ⓥ VISUAL APPROACH SLOPE INDICATOR WITH STANDARD THRESHOLD CLEARANCE PROVIDED

Ⓥ₋L VISUAL APPROACH SLOPE INDICATOR WITH A THRESHOLD CROSSING HEIGHT TO ACCOMMODATE LONG BODIED OR JUMBO AIRCRAFT

Runway Edge Light Systems

4.159 Runway edge lights are used to outline the edges of runways during periods of darkness and restricted visibility conditions. These light systems are classified according to the intensity or brightness they are capable of producing; they are the High Intensity Runway Lights (HIRL), Medium Intensity Runway Lights (MIRL), and the Low Intensity Runway Lights (LIRL). The HIRL and MIRL systems have variable intensity controls, whereas the LIRLs normally have one intensity setting.

4.160 The runway edge lights are white except that on instrument runways aviation yellow replaces white on the last 2,000 feet or half the runway length, whichever is less, to form a caution zone for landings. The lights marking the longitudinal limits of the runway emit red light toward the runway to indicate the end of runway to departing aircraft and emit green outward from the runway end to indicate the threshold to landing aircraft.

In-Runway Lighting

4.161 Touchdown zone lighting and runway centerline lighting are installed on some precision approach runways to facilitate landing under adverse visibility conditions. Taxiway turnoff lights may also be added to expedite movement of aircraft from the runway.

4.162 A brief description of the various types of in-runway lighting follows:

1. **Touchdown Zone Lighting (TDZ)**—Two rows of transverse light bars disposed symmetrically about the runway centerline in the runway touchdown zone. The system starts 100 feet from the landing threshold and extends to 3,000 feet from the threshold or the midpoint of the runway, whichever is the lesser.

2. **Runway Centerline Lighting System or Centerline Lighting (RCLS or CL)**—Flush centerline lights spaced at 50-foot intervals beginning 75 feet from the landing threshold and extending to within 75 feet of the opposite end of the runway.

3. **Runway Remaining Lighting (RRL)**—Is applied to centerline lighting systems in the final 3,000 feet as viewed from the takeoff or approach position. Alternate red and white lights are seen from the 3,000-foot points to the 1,000-foot points, and all red lights are seen for the last 1,000 feet of the runway. From the opposite direction, these lights are seen as white lights.

4. **Taxiway Turnoff Lights**—Flush lights spaced at 50-foot intervals, defining the curved path of aircraft travel from the runway centerline to a point on the taxiway.

Runway End Identifier Lights (REIL)

4.163 Runway End Identifier Lights are installed at many airfields to provide rapid and positive identification of the approach end of a particular runway. The system consists of a pair of synchronized flashing lights, one of which is located laterally on each side of the runway threshold facing the approach area. REILs may be located longitudinally 200 feet either upwind or downwind from the runway threshold. They are effective for:

1. Identification of a runway surrounded by a preponderance of other lighting.

2. Identification of a runway which lacks contrast with surrounding terrain.

3. Identification of a runway during reduced visibility.

Displaced Threshold Lighting

4.164 A displaced threshold is a threshold that is located at a point on the runway other than the designated beginning of the runway. Figure 4-44 illustrates some typical examples of displaced threshold lighting. The rules pertaining to displaced threshold lighting are as follows:

1. No landings are permitted short of displaced threshold lights.

2. No aircraft operations are permitted short of the displaced threshold lights if edge-of-runway lights (white or colored) are absent.

3. Takeoffs are permitted in the area short of displaced threshold lights if edge-of-runway lights appear as:

   A. Red, when takeoff is toward the visible displaced threshold lights.

   B. White (normal), and no displaced threshold is visible (due to 180° obstructions of lights).

4. Taxiing only is permitted in the area short of displaced threshold lights, if edge-of-runway lights appear as blue (taxiways and runway areas designated as taxiways are bounded by blue lights).

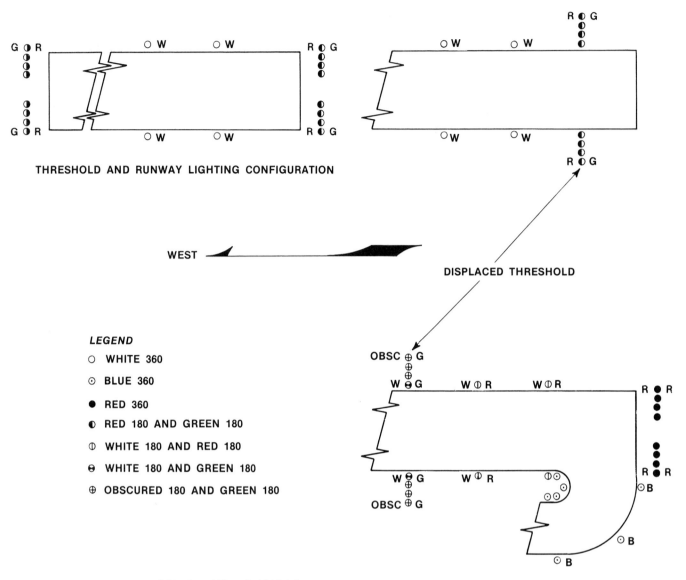

THRESHOLD AND RUNWAY LIGHTING CONFIGURATION

WEST

DISPLACED THRESHOLD

LEGEND

○ WHITE 360

⊙ BLUE 360

● RED 360

◑ RED 180 AND GREEN 180

◐ WHITE 180 AND RED 180

⊖ WHITE 180 AND GREEN 180

⊕ OBSCURED 180 AND GREEN 180

Figure 4–44. Examples of Displaced Threshold Lighting as Compared to a Typical Runway Lighting Configuration

Visual Approach Slope Indicator (VASI)

4.165 The VASI is a ground-based system of lights which are arranged to provide visual descent guidance information during the approach to a runway, thereby insuring obstruction clearance in the final approach area only. These lights are visible from the air at distances of 3 to 5 miles during the day and up to 20 miles or more at night. The visual glide path (light path) of the VASI provides safe obstruction clearance within + 10° of the extended runway centerline and up to 4 nautical miles from the runway threshold. Descent, using the VASI, should not be initiated until the aircraft is visually aligned with the runway. Lateral course guidance to assure runway alignment should be obtained by referring to the runway lights, the runway, or by other approach aids. (Figure 4-45)

4.166 VASI installations may consist of 2, 4, 6, 12, or 16 light units arranged in bars referred to as near, middle, and far bars. Most VASI installations consist of two bars, near and far, and may consist of 2, 4, or 12 light units. Some airports have VASIs consisting of 3 bars (near, middle, and far) which provide an additional visual glide path for use by high cockpit aircraft. This installation may consist of either 6 or 16 light units. VASI installations consisting of 2, 4, or 6 light units are located on one side of the runway, usually the left. Where the installation consists of 12 or 16 light units, the light units are located on both sides of the runway.

4.167 Two bar VASI installations provide one visual glide path which is normally set at 3°. Three bar VASI installations provide two visual glide paths. The lower glide path is provided by the near

146

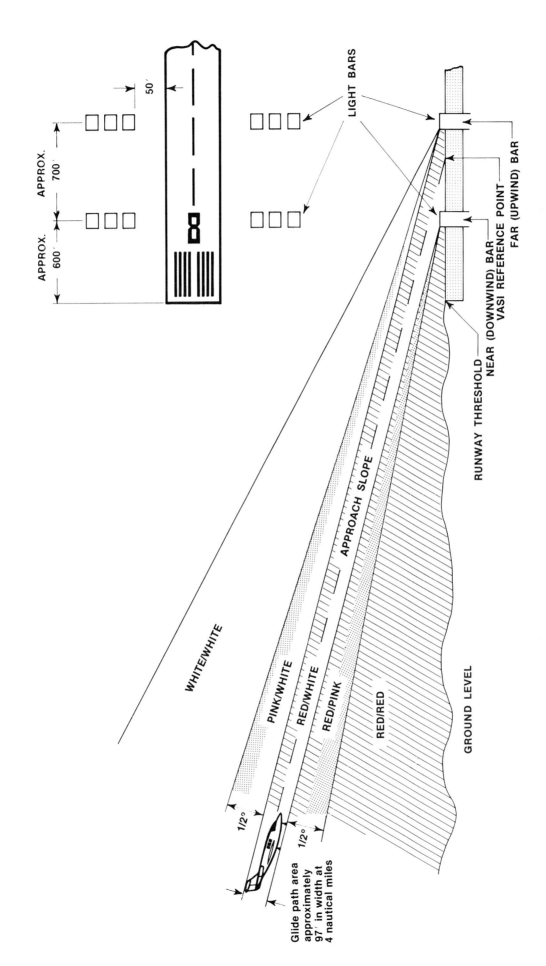

Figure 4–45. Typical VASI Color Indication Profile

and middle bars and is normally set at 3°, while the upper glide path, provided by the middle and far bars, is normally ¼° higher. This higher glide path is generally intended for use only by high cockpit aircraft to provide a sufficient threshold crossing height. Although normal glide path angles are 3°, angles at some locations may be as high as 4.5° to give proper obstacle clearance. Pilots of high performance aircraft are cautioned that use of VASI angles in excess of 3.5° may cause an increase in runway length required for landing and rollout.

4.168 The following information is provided for pilots who are unfamiliar with the principles and operation of this system and pilot technique required. The basic principle of the VASI is that of color differentiation between red and white. Each light unit projects a beam of light having a white

	LIGHT BAR	COLOR
(a) Below glide path	Far	Red
	Near	Red
(b) On glide path	Far	Red
	Near	White
(c) Above glide path	Far	White
	Near	White

Figure 4-46. Possible Two Bar VASI Light Combinations

	LIGHT BAR	COLOR
(a) Below both glide paths	Far	Red
	Middle	Red
	Near	Red
(b) On lower glide path	Far	Red
	Middle	Red
	Near	White
(c) On upper glide path	Far	Red
	Middle	White
	Near	White
(d) Above both glide paths	Far	White
	Middle	White
	Near	White

Figure 4-47. Possible Three Bar VASI Light Combinations

segment in the upper part of the beam and a red segment in the lower part of the beam. The light units are arranged so that the pilot using the VASIs during an approach will see the combination of lights as depicted in the tables in Figures 4-46 and 4-47.

4.169 When on the proper path of a two bar VASI, the pilot will view the near bar as white and the far bar as red. From a position below the glide path, the pilot will see both bars as red. In moving up to the glide path, the pilot will see the color of the near bar change from red to pink to white. From a position above the glide path, the pilot will see both bars as white. In moving down to the glide path, the pilot will see the color of the far bar change from white to pink to red. When the pilot is below the glide path, the red bars tend to merge into one distinct red signal, and a safe obstruction clearance may not exist under this condition.

4.170 When using a three bar VASI, it is not necessary to use all three bars. The near and middle bars constitute a two bar VASI for using the lower glide path. Also, the middle and far bars constitute a two bar VASI for using the upper glide path.

4.171 In haze or dust conditions or when the approach is made into the sun, the white lights may appear yellowish. This is also true at night, when the VASI is operated at a low intensity. Certain atmospheric debris may give the white lights an orange or brownish tint; however, the red lights are not affected and the principle of color differentiation is still applicable.

4.172 *Special Notes:*
1. *Some deterioration of system guidance may occur as an aircraft approaches the runway threshold; this is due to the spread of light sources and narrowing of individual colors. Since deterioration of system guidance occurs close in, the VASI should be used as an approach aid rather than a landing aid.*
2. *Federal Aviation Regulation 91.87 (d) (3) requires aircraft approaching to land on runways served by visual approach slope indicators to maintain an altitude at or above the glide slope until a lower altitude is necessary for a safe landing. However, this regulation does not prohibit normal bracketing maneuvers, above or below the glide slope, that are conducted for the purpose of remaining on the glide slope.*

Tri-color Visual Approach Slope Indicator

4.173 Tri-color Visual Approach Slope Indicators have been installed at many airports. The Tri-color Approach Slope Indicator normally consists of a single light unit, projecting a three-color visual approach path into the final approach area of the runway upon which the system is installed. In all of these systems, a below glide path indication is red, the above glide path indication is amber (yellow) and the on glide path indication is green.

4.174 Currently installed Tri-color Visual Approach Slope Indicators are low candlepower projector-type systems. Research tests indicate that these systems generally have a daytime useful range of approximately ½ to 1 mile. Nighttime useful range, depending upon visibility conditions, varies from 1 to 5 miles. Projector-type Visual Approach Slope Indicators may be initially difficult to locate in flight due to their small light source. Once the light source is sighted, however, it will provide accurate *vertical* guidance to the runway. Pilots should be aware that this yellow-green-red configuration produces a yellow-green transition light beam between the yellow and green primary light segments and a yellow transition light beam (that is inconsistant with what would naturally be expected) between the green and red primary light segments. Obviously, this yellow transition light beam can be confused with the primary yellow (too high) signal.

Control of Lighting Systems

4.175 Operation of approach light systems and runway lighting is controlled by the control tower. At some locations, the FSS may control the lights where there is no control tower in operation.

4.176 Pilots may request that lights be turned on or off. Runway edge lights, in-pavement lights, and approach lights also have intensity controls which may be varied to meet the pilot's requests. Sequenced flashing lights may be turned on and off. Some sequenced flashing systems also have intensity controls.

Pilot Control of Airport Lighting

4.177 The Federal Aviation Administration has installed controls on selected airport lights to provide pilots of aircraft while airborne or on the ground with the ability to control lights by keying the microphone. These controls are available at all times at selected locations that do not have a tower or flight service station. Airports served by part-time towers or flight service stations have the control system activated when the tower or station is not operating. Control of the lights is possible when aircraft are within 15 miles of the airport. Where a single runway is served by both approach lights and runway edge lights, priority will be given to the approach light system for pilot control. If no approach lights are installed, priority will be given to runway edge lights over other lighting systems such as REIL and VASI.

4.178 FAA-approved control systems provide for the installation of three types of radio controls:

A three step system that provides low, medium, or high intensity; a two step system that provides low or high intensity; and a control to turn on a light system without regard to intensity. Each activation or change of intensity will start a timer to maintain the selected light intensity step of 15 minutes (which should be adequate time to complete an approach, landing, and necessary taxiing).

4.179 Currently, all lighting systems serving an airport are designed to be controlled on a single radio frequency.

4.180 The two step control may be activated to provide either low or high intensity initially. Similarly, the three step control may be activated to provide either low, medium, or high intensity initially.

4.181 Suggested usage would be to always activate the control by keying the microphone five times to ensure that the lights are activated. All controls, regardless of the system, can be activated by keying the microphone five times. Adjustment can then be made to high or low intensity as appropriate or desired at a later time. (Refer to the table in Figure 4-48.)

4.182 Where the airport is not served by an instrument approach procedure, it may have either the standard FAA-approved control system or an independent type system of different specification installed by the airport sponsor. The Airport/Facility Directory contains descriptions of pilot controlled lighting systems for each airport having these systems and explains the type of lights, method of control, and operating frequency in clear text. (This is further discussed in chapter 7.)

RADIO CONTROL SYSTEM	KEY MICROPHONE	INTENSITY
3 Step Approach Light System	7 times in 5 seconds	High
	5 times in 5 seconds	Medium
	3 times in 5 seconds	Low
2 Step Approach Light System	7 times in 5 seconds	High
	3 times in 5 seconds	Low
ACTIVATE (Rwy lights, REIL, or VASI)	5 times in 5 seconds	Lights On

NOTE: Instrument Approach Procedures Charts include data identifying airports that are equipped with pilot control lighting systems, lighting system and runway identification, and the system control frequency.

Figure 4-48. Legend for Light Controls

AIRPORT MARKINGS

4.183 In the interest of safety and efficiency, airport markings have been provided to afford the pilot visual cues of possible airport operations. Figure 4-49 illustrates some of the more common standardized runway and taxiway markings.

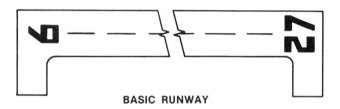

BASIC RUNWAY

BASIC RUNWAY MARKING—Markings used for operations under Visual Flight Rules: centerline marking and runway direction numbers.

NOTE: Runway numbers and letters are determined from the approach direction. The number is the whole number nearest one-tenth the magnetic azimuth of the centerline of the runway, measured clockwise from the magnetic north. The letter or letters differentiate between parallel runways:

For two parallel runways "L" "R"

For three parallel runways "L" "C" "R"

BASIC RUNWAY

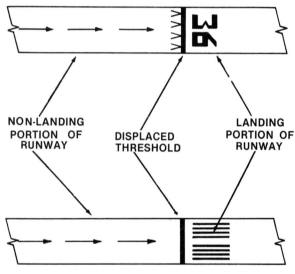

PRECISION/NON-PRECISION RUNWAY

DISPLACED THRESHOLD RUNWAY MARKINGS

THRESHOLD—A line perpendicular to the runway centerline designating the beginning of that portion of a runway usable for landing.

NOTE: A displaced threshold is not at the beginning of the full strength runway pavement. The paved area behind the displaced runway threshold is available for taxiing, the landing rollout, and the takeoff of aircraft.

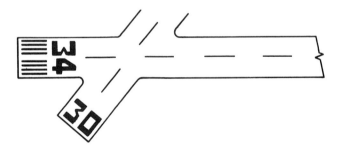

NON-PRECISION INSTRUMENT RUNWAY (RUNWAY 34)

NON-PRECISION INSTRUMENT RUNWAY MARKING—Markings on runways served by a non-visual non-precision approach aid and intended for landings under instrument weather conditions: basic runway markings plus threshold marking.

Figure 4-49. Common Runway and Taxiway Markings

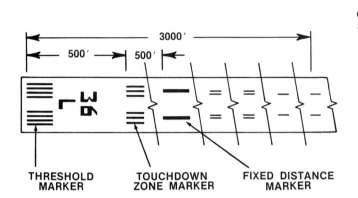

THRESHOLD MARKER   TOUCHDOWN ZONE MARKER   FIXED DISTANCE MARKER

PRECISION INSTRUMENT RUNWAY

PRECISION INSTRUMENT RUNWAY MARKING—Markings on runways served by non-visual precision approach aids and on runways having special operational requirements, non-precision instrument runway marking, touchdown zone marking, fixed distance marking, plus side stripes.

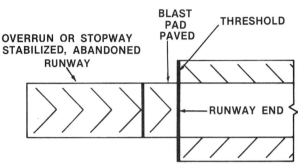

OVERRUN/STOPWAY AND BLAST PAD AREA

CLOSED OR OVERRUN/STOPWAY AREA—Any surface or area which appears usable but which, due to the nature of its structure, is unusable.

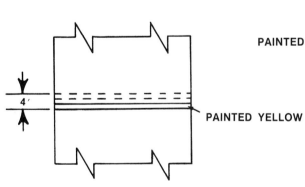

PAINTED YELLOW

CONVENTIONAL TAXIWAY HOLDING LINE

CONVENTIONAL HOLDING LINES—Taxiway markings placed not less than 100 feet and not more than 200 feet from the nearest edge of the runway.

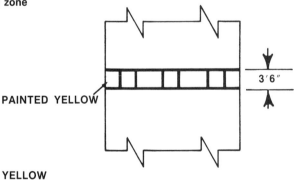

PAINTED YELLOW

CATEGORY II TAXIWAY HOLDING LINE

CATEGORY II HOLDING LINES—Taxiway markings generally placed 400 feet from runway centerline at airports equipped to handle ILS Category II operations.

NOTE: While Category II approaches are being conducted aircraft holding for a departure clearance should remain behind the Category II holding lines to avoid the possibility of interfering with ILS guidance signals.

CHAPTER 4: QUESTIONS

For answers see Appendix E

1. How can passage of a VORTAC station be determined by the use of a DME?

    1. A momentary indicator flag is displayed during station passage.

    2. The range indicator will read zero upon station passage.

    3. The range indicator will stop decreasing at ¼ mile from the station and will start increasing at ¼ mile past the station.

    4. The range indicator will register a decrease in range until displaying the height above the station as the aircraft passes over the station; following station passage, an increase in range will be displayed.

2. SSALR is the abbreviation for:

    1. Simplified short approach light system with runway alignment indicator lights.

    2. Simplified short approach lead-in surveillance radar.

    3. High intensity runway lights systems.

    4. Short approach light system.

3. Select the correct statement regarding a three bar VASI system.

    1. This system provides two visual glide paths.

    2. A three-color approach path is projected in the final approach area.

    3. The middle and far light bars constitute a two bar VASI for using the lower glide path.

    4. All of the above.

Refer to the runway illustration (left) when answering questions 4 and 5.

4. Which marking is the touchdown zone marking for the illustrated precision instrument approach runway, and what is the distance from the end of the runway to the touchdown zone marking?

    1. A – 17 feet.

    2. B – 500 feet.

    3. C – 750 feet.

    4. D – 1,500 feet.

5. Which marking is the fixed distance marker and what is the distance from the end of the runway to this marker?

    1. A – 17 feet.

    2. B – 750 feet.

    3. C – 1,000 feet.

    4. D – 1,250 feet.

6. If an airplane's VOR equipment is tuned to a VOR station with the OBS set to 75°, when would the indicator not have a TO or a FROM indication?

1. When the airplane crosses over the 255° radial.

2. When the airplane crosses over the 75° radial.

3. When the airplane crosses over the 165° radial or the 345° radial.

4. There is always either a TO or a FROM indication.

7. While Category II approaches are being conducted, aircraft holding for a departure clearance should remain behind the second set of yellow taxiway holding lines (Category II holding lines) to avoid:

1. A possible collision with landing aircraft.

2. Possible confusion to the pilot on runway location.

3. The possibility of interfering with precision approach radar signals.

4. The possibility of interfering with ILS guidance signals.

8. The Rapid City (RAP) ILS facility transmits the following identifiers:

1. I-RAP on the localizer frequency.

2. RA on the outer marker frequency.

3. AP on the middle marker frequency.

4. All of the above are correct.

9. What distance is displayed by the DME indicator?

1. Line of sight direct distance from the aircraft to the VORTAC station in statute miles.

2. Ground track distance in nautical miles.

3. Slant range distance in statute miles.

4. Slant range distance in nautical miles.

10. When should departing aircraft hold behind Category II taxiway holding lines?

1. Whenever Category II operations are being conducted.

2. Whenever the departure airport is equipped for Category II operations.

3. During VFR weather conditions only.

4. Whenever the existing weather conditions are below prescribed VFR weather minimums.

11. ATC requested a pilot to fly a magnetic heading of 010° until intercepting the 350° outbound bearing from an NDB station. What will be the relative bearing at the point of interception?

1. 360°.

2. 160°.

3. 200°.

4. 180°.

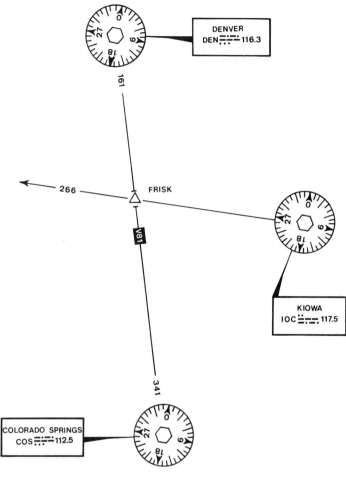

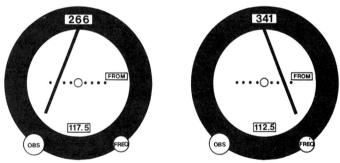

12. With reference to the two VOR indicators shown (above), what is the aircraft's position with respect to FRISK Intersection if the aircraft is flying on V-81 from Colorado Springs to Denver?

1. South of FRISK Intersection and east of course.

2. Over FRISK Intersection and west of course.

3. South of FRISK Intersection and west of course.

4. North of FRISK Intersection and west of course.

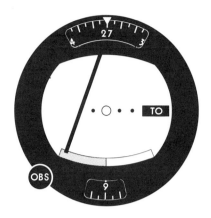

13. Referring to the VOR indicator shown in the illustration (above), the approximate position of the aircraft:
1. Cannot be determined without knowing the aircraft heading.
2. Is west of the station and north of course.
3. Is west of the station and south of course.
4. Is east of the station and north of course.

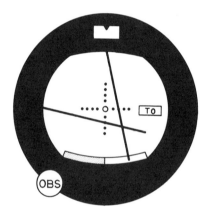

14. Determine the aircraft's position by analyzing the ILS indicator depicted in the illustration (above).
1. The aircraft is below the glide path and right of the localizer course.
2. The aircraft is above the glide path and left of the localizer course.
3. The aircraft is above the glide path and right of the localizer course.
4. The aircraft is below the glide path and left of the localizer course.

15. Select the statement that correctly describes how an SDF differs from an ILS.
1. The outer and middle markers are not included in an SDF approach.
2. The SDF signal course width is fixed at either 6° or 12°.
3. SDF provides glide slope information.
4. The SDF course is always aligned 3° off the runway centerline.

16. A pilot established on the proper glide path while using a two bar VASI system will observe:
1. Red over white.
2. Pink over pink.
3. White over red.
4. Pink over red.

17. What will accurately-tuned VOR equipment indicate during a VOR accuracy check using a VOT facility?
1. The CDI will be centered and the TO/FROM indicator will register a *TO* indication with the OBS set on either 0° or 180°.
2. The CDI will be centered and the OBS should either be set on 180° with the TO/FROM indicator registering a *TO* indication, or 360° with the TO/FROM indicator registering a *FROM* indication.
3. The CDI will be centered, and the TO/FROM indicator will register a *TO* indication if south of the VOT with OBS set on 0°.
4. The OBS should read 180° with a *FROM* indication.

18. What does the operation of an airport rotating beacon during the daylight hours indicate?
1. The ground visibility is less than 3 miles and/or the ceiling is less than 1,000 feet in the control zone.
2. The prevailing visibility is less than 2 miles within the airport traffic area.
3. The beacon is located at a military airfield.
4. The inflight visibility is less than 3 miles and the ceiling is less than 1,500 feet within the control zone.

19. Assume an aircraft is tracking to an NDB on an inbound magnetic bearing of 090°. If the wind direction is from the south, what would be a representative relative bearing?
1. 360°.
2. 350°.
3. 270°.
4. 010°.

20. The Tri-Color Approach Slope Indicator normally consists of:
1. A single light unit which projects a three-color visual approach path.
2. Three independent light units which together project a three-color visual approach path.
3. The same system as the VASI with an extra light bar upwind.
4. The same system as the VASI with an extra light bar downwind.

21. Which statement correctly describes how an LDA system differs from an ILS system?
  1. The LDA system has no marker beacons or glide slope transmitter.
  2. The LDA approach is always aligned within 3° of the runway.
  3. The LDA course width is either 6° or 12°.
  4. The LDA approach is comparable to a localizer approach in accuracy and utility, but is not aligned with the runway centerline.

22. A full-scale right to left VOR CDI deflection represents:
  1. 5°.
  2. 10°.
  3. 2.5°.
  4. A minimum of 20°.

23. A pilot whose aircraft is tracking outbound from a VOR, on a constant heading, notes that the CDI needle remains at a constant one dot right deflection. This is an indication that the aircraft is:
  1. 10° from the selected VOR radial.
  2. Moving closer to the selected radial.
  3. Parallel to the selected radial.
  4. Moving away from the selected radial.

24. When an aircraft is flying in an area of heavy rain, a transponder is of primary importance to the pilot because:
  1. It aids the controller in locating the aircraft.
  2. It gives the pilot priority over other aircraft.
  3. ATC can automatically authorize a Contact Approach.
  4. When in radar contact, the pilot can deviate from the assigned altitude.

25. A pilot using DME and RMI equipment in conjunction with a VORTAC station is tracking on a 15 DME arc. If the wind is from the west, what position should the bearing pointer reflect when the aircraft is flying from the 140° radial counterclockwise to the 090° radial?
  1. Behind the left wingtip reference.
  2. Ahead of the left wingtip reference.
  3. Ahead of the right wingtip reference.
  4. Behind the right wingtip reference.

26. The corresponding visual and aural codes used to identify an aircraft's position when over the outer, middle, and inner markers are:

Outer Marker	Middle Marker	Inner Marker
1. Purple ——	Amber •—•—	White ••••
2. Amber •—	White ••••	Amber ——
3. White ••••	Purple —•	Purple —•
4. Purple •—	Amber ——	White •—•—

27. A pilot wishes to intercept the 200° outbound bearing of an NDB while maintaining a 350° magnetic heading. What will the ADF indicate when the aircraft intercepts the 200° outbound bearing of the NDB?
  1. 210°.
  2. 335°.
  3. 225°.
  4. 30°.

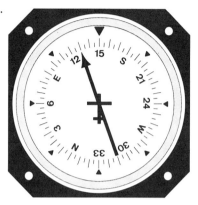

28. With reference to the instrument indications (above), what is the aircraft's position while tracking on the 310° outbound bearing *to* an NDB station?
  1. Right of course and south of the station.
  2. On course northwest of the station.
  3. Left of course and north of the station.
  4. On course southeast of the station.

29. What is a waypoint?
  1. A preselected geographical position used to define an RNAV route.
  2. A compulsory reporting point.
  3. A fan marker reporting point.
  4. A VOR used to define an airway fix.

30. What magnetic heading and relative bearing are necessary to maintain a track on the 080° outbound bearing from an NDB station, assuming a 12° right drift correction angle?
  1. MH 080°, RB 180°.
  2. MH 092°, RB 168°.
  3. MH 092°, RB 180°.
  4. MH 168°, RB 192°.

31. Which of the following statements are correct if a pilot attempts to home to an NDB station using an ADF receiver without the aid of a heading indicator?
  1. The ADF receiver is unusable without a compass.
  2. A pilot can home to the NDB station by simply centering the ADF needle on 0°.
  3. A pilot cannot home to an NDB station because the RB will change.
  4. This procedure can only be used with an RMI.

32. How does a pilot know that a VOR is being repaired or aligned?
1. ATC will notify the pilot as the aircraft converges toward the VOR.
2. Code and voice identification are omitted from the aural signal.
3. The VOR TO/FROM indicator will display an ''Off'' flag.
4. The information will be broadcast over the VOR by voice transmission.

33. What DME distance reading would be registered when an aircraft cruising at 11,000 feet MSL crosses over a VORTAC station? (Assume the VORTAC has an elevation of 1,278 feet MSL.)
1. 0.0 NM.
2. 1.6 NM.
3. 1.4 NM.
4. 1.8 NM.

34. If an ATC radar controller advises a pilot of traffic at 8 o'clock, where should the traffic be located?
1. 120° to the right of the nose of the airplane.
2. On a right true course of 120°.
3. 120° to the left of the aircraft's direction of travel.
4. 90° to the left of the nose.

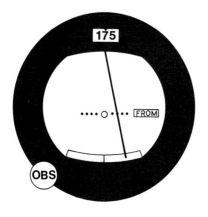

35. Determine the aircraft's position by examining the VOR course deviation indicator shown in the illustration (above).
1. The aircraft is east of course on the 170° radial.
2. The aircraft is west of course on the 190° radial.
3. The aircraft's position cannot be determined.
4. The aircraft is east of course on the 175° radial.

36. What can be assumed if a coded three-letter identifier is broadcast approximately every 30

seconds from a VORTAC station?
1. The VOR facility is operating properly.
2. Only the DME is operating.
3. The VORTAC is operating properly.
4. The complete VORTAC is decommissioned for maintenance.

37. The coded identification group of a particular localizer is I-DAL. What is the identification of the associated marker locator?
1. The compass locator identification for the middle marker is AL.
2. The compass locator identification for the inner marker is IDA.
3. The compass locator identification for the outer marker is AL.
4. The compass locator identification for the outer marker is I-DAL.

38. Assume a pilot has tuned his RMI receiver to a VOR station. Determine, from the RMI indication in the illustration (above), on which radial the aircraft is located and the aircraft heading.
1. 10° radial and MH of 315°.
2. 190° radial and MH of 315°.
3. 315° radial and MH of 190°.
4. 135° radial and MH of 10°.

39. A *back course* marker can be identified by:
1. A flashing purple light and an aural signal of alternate dots and dashes.
2. A flashing amber light and an aural signal of two dots per second.
3. A flashing white light and an aural signal of 72 to 95 two-dot combinations per minute.
4. A flashing white light and an aural signal of four dashes per second.

40. Which combination of lights correctly denotes the aircraft location with respect to the glide slope when using the tri-color VASI system?

Below the Glide Slope	On the Glide Slope	Above the Glide Slope
1. Red	White	Amber
2. Red	Green	Amber
3. Red	Pink	White
4. Red	Green	White

41. Many airports are equipped with runway end identifier lights (REIL) to provide the pilot with:
1. An outline of the runway.
2. An identification of the touchdown zone lights.
3. Rapid and positive identification of the approach end of an instrument runway.
4. An identification of the runway remaining lighting.

42. MALSR is the abbreviation for:
1. Medium approach lighting system with runway end identifier lights.
2. Minimum approach lighting system with RAIL.
3. Minimum alignment lights short runway.
4. Medium intensity approach light system with runway alignment indicator lights.

43. REIL approach lights are a pair of synchronized flashing lights that are located on:
1. The far end of sequenced flashing lights.
2. Each side of the runway threshold facing the approach area.
3. The far end of the runway.
4. Each side of the roll bars 1,000 feet from the approach end of the runway.

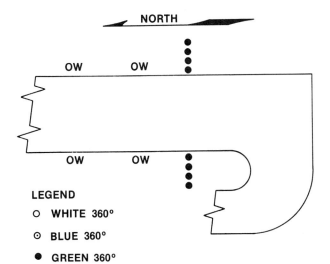

LEGEND

○ WHITE 360°

◉ BLUE 360°

● GREEN 360°

44. The displaced threshold lights on the illustrated runway (above) indicate:
1. All aircraft operations south of the threshold lights are prohibited.

2. Aircraft can taxi in both directions.
3. Aircraft can taxi and take off in a north direction.
4. Aircraft can taxi north but cannot take off until passing the threshold lights.

45. How does the scale sensitivity of a VOR receiver indicator compare to the scale sensitivity of most localizer receiver indicators?
1. Approximately the same sensitivity as a localizer receiver indicator.
2. Approximately half the sensitivity of a localizer receiver indicator.
3. Approximately twice the sensitivity of a localizer receiver indicator.
4. Approximately one-fourth the sensitivity of a localizer receiver indicator.

46. What flight path altitudes should be maintained by a fixed wing aircraft approaching a runway served with a VASI system?
1. Remain on or above the glide path until a point one-half mile from the runway threshold.
2. Remain on or above the glide path until arrival over the 500 foot runway marker.
3. Remain on or below the glide path until passing over the runway threshold.
4. Remain on or above the glide path until passing over the runway threshold.

47. Select the correct statements concerning radar.

A. Primary radar relies on signals to be reflected back from aircraft.
B. The ATCRBS or secondary radar displays codes received from airborne transponders.
C. Secondary radar relies on signals to be reflected back from aircraft.
D. Primary radar displays codes received from airborne transponders.
E. One advantage of ATCRBS is its capability to rapidly identify radar targets.
1. C and D.
2. A, B, and E.
3. A, C, and E.
4. C, D, and E.

48. When a pilot is executing a localizer back course approach and the CDI reflects a left deflection, the aircraft is:
1. To the left of the localizer course when inbound.
2. To the right of the localizer course when inbound.
3. To the left of the localizer course when outbound.
4. Above the glide path but on course.

49. Select the correct statement(s) regarding the ILS glide slope.

A. The normal glide path projection angle is approximately 3°.
B. The glide path beam is approximately 1.4° thick.
C. False glide slope signals may be received below the glide path projection angle.
D. Spurious glide slope signals, which could result in unreliable glide slope information, may exist in the area of the localizer back course approach.
E. Controller communications are commonly received on the glide slope frequency.
   1. A, B, C, D, and E.
   2. A only.
   3. C and E.
   4. A, B, and D.

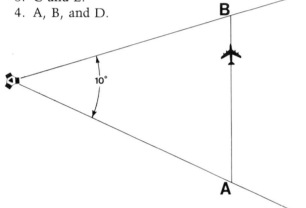

50. Determine the time necessary for an aircraft to fly over a navigational facility assuming it takes the illustrated aircraft (above) 1 minute and 25 seconds to fly from position A to position B.
   1. 8 minutes 50 seconds.
   2. 8 minutes 30 seconds.
   3. 6 minutes 25 seconds.
   4. 6 minutes 30 seconds.

51. Which of the following statements are correct regarding the ILS?

A. The OBS setting has no effect on the localizer needle.
B. The TO/FROM indicator will indicate TO when the localizer receiver is receiving a signal.
C. The transmitted coded identification is removed when maintenance is being performed on the facility.
D. A compass locator is a required element of an ILS.
E. Pilots may receive controller transmissions on the localizer frequency.
   1. A, B, and D.
   2. A, B, C, and E.
   3. B, C, and E.
   4. A, C, and E.

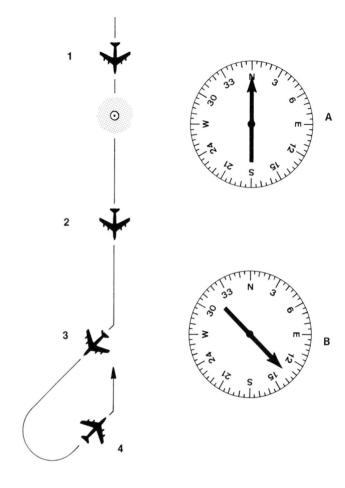

52. Match the ADF indications in the illustration (above) with the respective airplane positions.
   1. Airplane 2–Indicator A, and Airplane 4–Indicator B.
   2. Airplane 1–Indicator A, and Airplane 4–Indicator B.
   3. Airplane 2–Indicator A, and Airplane 3–Indicator B.
   4. Airplane 1–Indicator A, and Airplane 3–Indicator B.

Refer to illustrated DME arc (page 159) for questions 53 and 54.

53. Assume a pilot is flying a DME arc in a no-wind condition as depicted by the airplane in the illustration. When passing over the 200° radial (position 4), the pilot notices that the DME is registering 19 NM. What corrective steps are necessary to resume course on the 20 DME arc if the airplane's magnetic heading is 290°?
   1. Set the OBS to 210° and maintain the same heading until the DME registers 20 NM.
   2. Set the OBS to 220° and maintain a heading of 300° until the DME registers 20 NM.
   3. Set the OBS to 190° and maintain a heading of 290° until the DME registers 20 NM.
   4. Leave the OBS set to 200° and maintain the same heading until the DME registers 20 NM.

54. What radial of the VORTAC station will the airplane be crossing before the CDI begins to move from a full-scale right deflection if the OBS setting is 210°? (Refer to the illustration.)

    1. 220°.

    2. 200°.

    3. 195°.

    4. It is not possible to determine, since no VOR receivers have a standard minimum receiver sensitivity level.

55. What RMI indications would register when a pilot performs an operational check of dual VORs using a VOT? (Assume the navigation equipment is accurate.)

    1. Both RMI bearing indicators will point to 180°.

    2. Both RMI bearing indicators will point to 360°.

    3. One RMI bearing indicator will point to 180° and the other RMI bearing indicator will point to 360°.

    4. RMI equipment is only used in conjunction with low frequency radio transmitters.

56. What is assured when an aircraft remains on the proper glide path during an approach aided by a VASI system?

    1. Touchdown on the runway threshold.

    2. Obstruction clearance in the final approach area.

    3. Course guidance to the runway centerline.

    4. Touchdown on the runway numbers.

57. How is a displaced threshold marked on an instrument runway?

    1. Red chevron marks are painted on the non-landing portion of the runway.

    2. Arrows lead to the threshold marking.

    3. There is an *X* painted in the non-landing portion of the runway.

    4. A Maltese Cross is painted on the displaced threshold area.

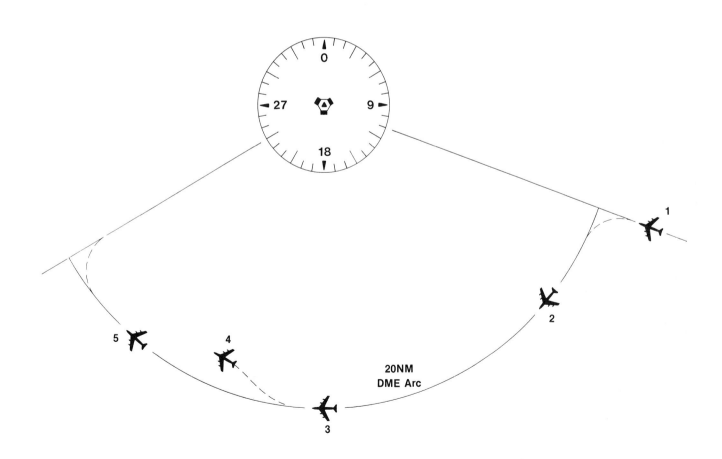

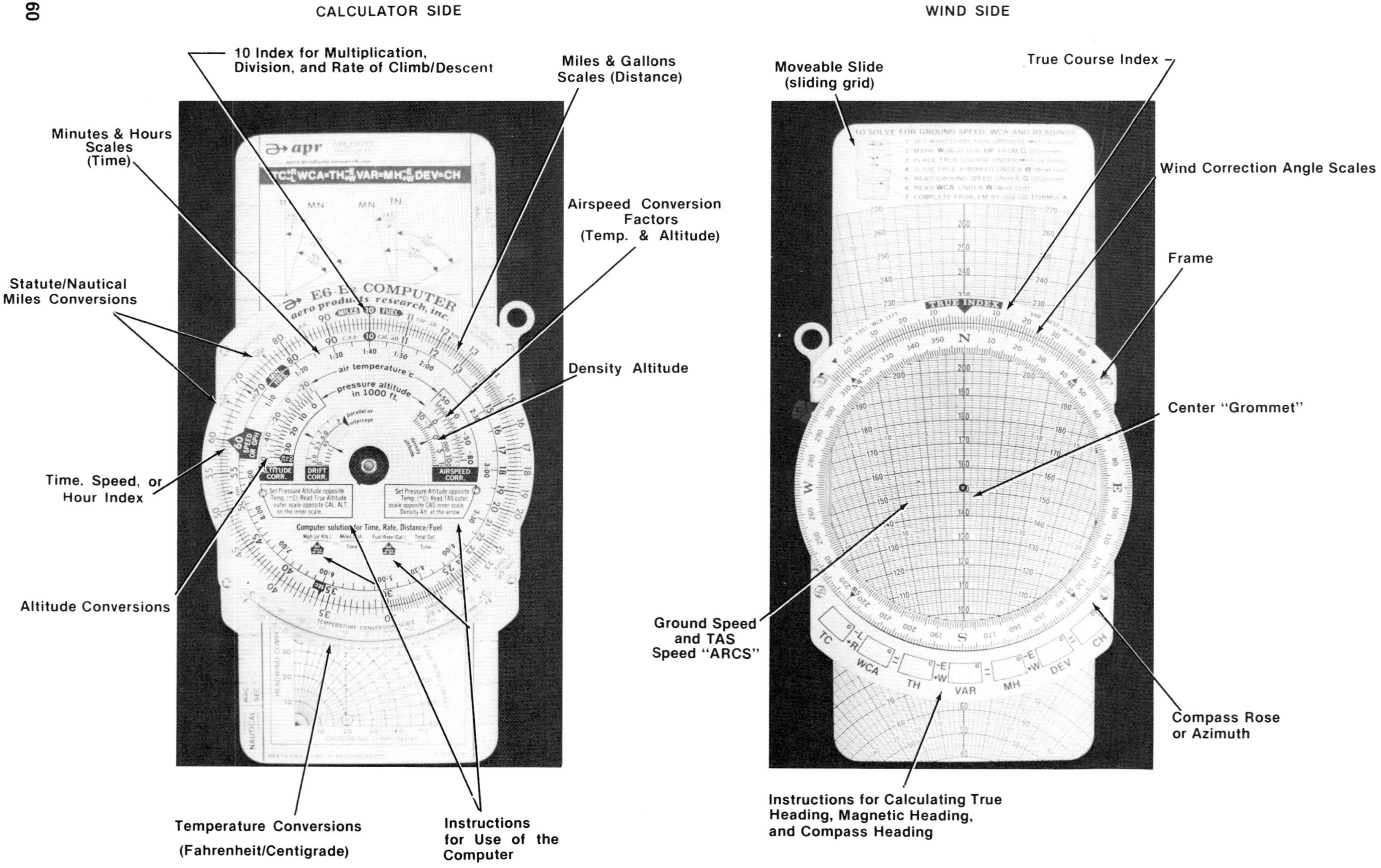

WIND SIDE

CALCULATOR SIDE

True Course Index

Wind Correction Angle Scales

Frame

Center "Grommet"

Compass Rose or Azimuth

Moveable Slide (sliding grid)

Instructions for Calculating True Heading, Magnetic Heading, and Compass Heading

Ground Speed and TAS Speed "ARCS"

Miles & Gallons Scales (Distance)

Airspeed Conversion Factors (Temp. & Altitude)

Density Altitude

10 Index for Multiplication, Division, and Rate of Climb/Descent

Instructions for Use of the Computer

Minutes & Hours Scales (Time)

Temperature Conversions (Fahrenheit/Centigrade)

Statute/Nautical Miles Conversions

Time, Speed, or Hour Index

Altitude Conversions

Figure 5-1. Calculator and Wind Sides of the E6-B Type Computer

160

5.

Flight Computer and Performance Charts

5.1 There is a seemingly endless number of different types of computer problems and performance charts. Naturally, it would not be feasible to catalogue and describe each type of computation that is possible. This chapter does, however, describe the most common types of computers and computer problems along with a representative sampling of the more common types of performance charts that should be understood by the average general aviation instrument-rated pilot.

INTRODUCTION TO THE FLIGHT COMPUTER

5.2 Most pilots use their flight computers for a few elementary computations. This chapter, however, presents a thorough review of the computer in order that the instrument pilot may be able to fully utilize the flight computer to his advantage for a wide range of computations. Included in the chapter are examples of most types of computer problems that an instrument pilot will generally need to calculate in order to complete an accurate instrument flight plan.

5.3 There is an abundance of different types and sizes of flight computers available. A large E6-B type of computer is recommended simply because it is generally easier to set up problems and read the most precise answers on the E6-B type as compared to many of the smaller computers. The E6-B type is designed with a different face on each side. One side of the computer (calculator side) is designed to solve many types of ratio and performance problems by means of a circular slide rule. The opposite side is designed to solve wind problems by means of resolving wind triangle vectors on the computer grid. (Figure 5-1)

Time–Speed–Distance Computations

5.4 The calculator side of the computer has two scales. The fixed outer scale is often called the miles and gallons scale (distance). The movable middle and inner disc scale is called the minutes and hours scale (time). Each scale has a reference index (**10**) called the 10 Index. The movable scale, in addition to the 10 Index, has a black arrowhead (▬▲▬), commonly called the Time, Speed, or Hour Index, which is found at the 60-minute mark.

5.5 The outer and middle scales are graduated into identical increments. Much of the skill in using the computer is dependent upon the accurate interpretation of the graduations that are not numbered. Remember, the number *10*, for example, may represent .10, 1.0, 10.0, 100, or 1,000. Consequently, the graduated marks between different numbers can have different values. (Figure 5-2)

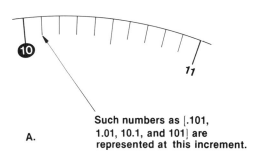

A.

Such numbers as (.101, 1.01, 10.1, and 101) are represented at this increment.

Figure 5–2 A-D. Scale Graduations on the Computer Sometimes Represent Different Increment Values

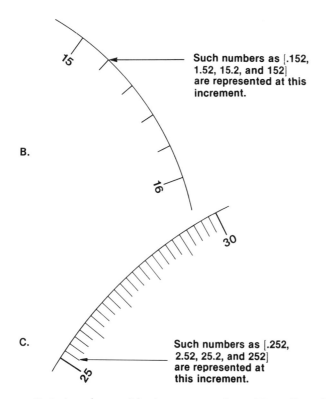

B.

Such numbers as [.152, 1.52, 15.2, and 152] are represented at this increment.

C.

Such numbers as [.252, 2.52, 25.2, and 252] are represented at this increment.

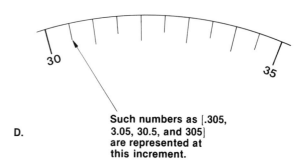

D.

Such numbers as [.305, 3.05, 30.5, and 305] are represented at this increment.

5.6 Another aid in computing Time-Speed-Distance problems is the hour scale. (Figure 5-3) This scale provides easy conversion from minutes to hours and minutes.

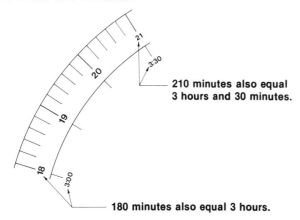

210 minutes also equal 3 hours and 30 minutes.

180 minutes also equal 3 hours.

Figure 5-3. The Inner Computer Scale Converting Minutes to Hours and Minutes

5.7 The calculator side of the computer is designed to set up proportions (ratios). (Figure 5-4) In setting up any computer ratio problem, the pilot is essentially going from the "known" to solve for the "unknown." In this proportion, three known numbers are used to find the unknown number. The following ratio is set into the computer to solve for the unknown time, speed, or distance:

$$\frac{\text{Speed (Outer Scale)}}{\text{Hour Index (Middle Scale)}} = \frac{\text{Distance (Outer Scale)}}{\text{Time (Middle Scale)}}$$

5.8 *Special Notes:*
1. *In Time-Speed-Distance problems, the units of speed and distance are labeled in like units (i.e., if statute miles [SM] are used as the units of distance, the speed will be expressed in miles per hour [MPH]; if nautical miles per hour [KTS] are used as the units to describe speed, the distance will be expressed in nautical miles [NM]).*
2. *Generally, seconds are not involved in a ratio problem unless a distance is less than 10 miles or a time element is less than 10 minutes. In either of the two cases, it is perhaps easiest to convert the seconds to tenths of a minute. This can easily be accomplished by dividing the number of seconds by 6. For example: 1 minute 36 seconds equals 1.6 minutes.*

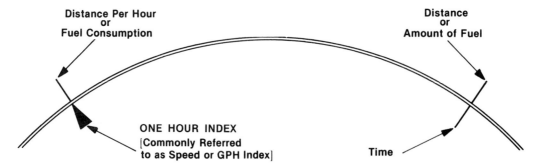

Distance Per Hour or Fuel Consumption

Distance or Amount of Fuel

ONE HOUR INDEX [Commonly Referred to as Speed or GPH Index]

Time

Figure 5-4. An Example of How Ratios Are Used to Solve Time, Speed, Distance, and Fuel Problems

5.9 The following examples demonstrate these Time-Speed-Distance relationships. Figure 5-5 illustrates the solution for a typical unknown distance problem. In this problem, an aircraft's ground speed is 130 MPH. To determine the miles that can be travelled in 70 minutes, the Hour Index (middle scale) was moved opposite the 13 on the outer scale. The correct answer (152 SM) on the outer scale is then read opposite the 70 on the middle scale.

5.10 Figure 5-6 illustrates the solution for a typical unknown speed problem. In this problem an aircraft flew 200 statute miles in 120 minutes. After setting 20 on the outer scale opposite the 12 on the middle scale, the unknown speed (100 MPH) can be determined by reading the speed on the outer scale opposite the Hour Index.

5.11 Figure 5-7 illustrates the solution for a typical unknown time problem. In this problem an aircraft's speed is 180 knots. To determine the time to fly 330 NMs, the Hour Index was positioned opposite the 18 on the outer scale. The answer (110 minutes) found on the middle scale is opposite the 33 on the outer scale.

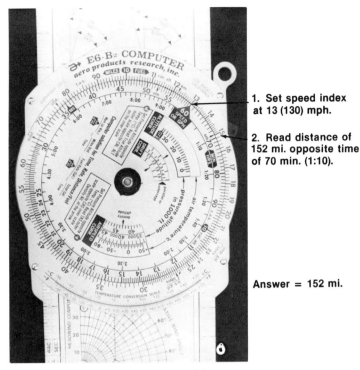

1. Set speed index at 13 (130) mph.

2. Read distance of 152 mi. opposite time of 70 min. (1:10).

Answer = 152 mi.

Figure 5-5. Computing an Unknown Distance

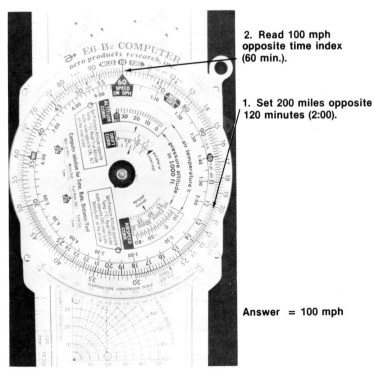

2. Read 100 mph opposite time index (60 min.).

1. Set 200 miles opposite 120 minutes (2:00).

Answer = 100 mph

Figure 5-6. Computing an Unknown Speed

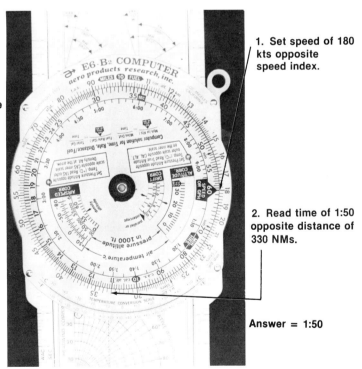

1. Set speed of 180 kts opposite speed index.

2. Read time of 1:50 opposite distance of 330 NMs.

Answer = 1:50

Figure 5-7. Computing an Unknown Time

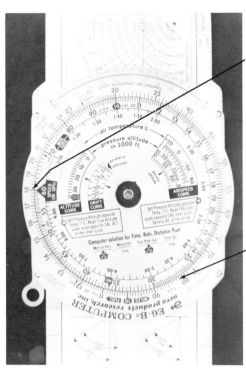

1. Set speed index at 18 (180) mph.

2. Read distance of 8.1 mi. opposite time of 2.7 minutes (2 minutes and 42 seconds).

Answer = 8.1 mi.

Figure 5-8. Computing an Unknown Distance Using Minutes and Seconds

5.12 Figure 5-8 illustrates the solution for a problem in which seconds is one of the known factors.

Given: Ground speed—180 MPH.
Time from point A to point B: 2 minutes 42 seconds.

Find: Distance from point A to point B.

In this example, 2 minutes 42 seconds was converted to 2.7 minutes. The Hour Index was moved opposite the 18 on the outer scale. The correct answer (8.1 SM) on the outer scale is read opposite the 2.7 on the middle scale.

Exercise A. Solve for the unknown.*

	Time	Speed	Distance
1.	:____	149 MPH	87 SM
2.	2:30	172 KTS	____NM
3.	1:23	____MPH	200 SM
4.	0:52	____KTS	158 NM
5.	:____	185 KTS	380 NM
6.	0:20	105 MPH	____SM
7.	:____	192 KTS	768 NM
8.	1:10	____MPH	210 SM
9.	0:02:48	180 MPH	____SM

Fuel Consumption Computations

5.13 Fuel consumption problems are solved by the same procedure as Time-Speed-Distance problems, except that gallons or pounds of fuel are substituted for distances. The following ratio is set into the computer to solve for the unknown time, rate, or fuel:

$$\frac{\text{Fuel Rate (Outer Scale)}}{\text{Hour Index (Middle Scale)}} = \frac{\text{Total Fuel (Outer Scale)}}{\text{Total Time (Middle Scale)}}$$

5.14 The following examples demonstrate these fuel consumption relationships. Figure 5-9 illustrates the solution for an unknown total fuel problem. In this problem an airplane's flow rate is 13 GPH. To determine the total fuel used in 90 minutes, the Hour Index (middle scale) was moved opposite the 13 on the outer scale. The correct answer (19.5 gallons) on the outer scale is read opposite the 90-minute mark on the middle scale.

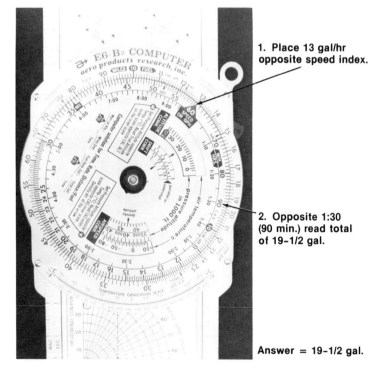

1. Place 13 gal/hr opposite speed index.

2. Opposite 1:30 (90 min.) read total of 19-1/2 gal.

Answer = 19-1/2 gal.

Figure 5-9. Computing an Unknown Fuel Quantity

* Answers for Exercises A—O are found in Appendix E.

164

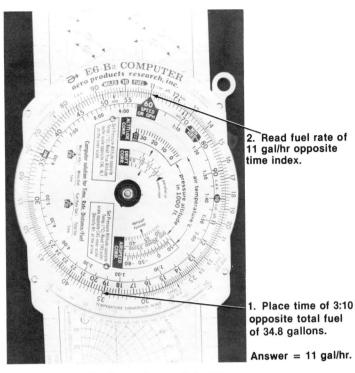

2. Read fuel rate of 11 gal/hr opposite time index.

1. Place time of 3:10 opposite total fuel of 34.8 gallons.

Answer = 11 gal/hr.

Figure 5-10. Computing an Unknown Fuel Rate

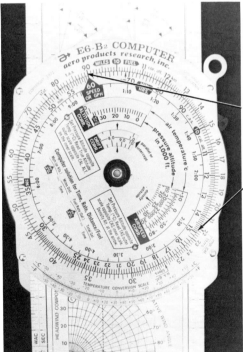

1. Place 9 (90) gallons opposite the time index.

2. Opposite 22 gallons find time of 147 min. or 2:27.

Answer = 2:27

Figure 5-11. Computing an Unknown Time

5.15 Figure 5-10 illustrates the solution for an unknown fuel rate problem. In this problem, an airplane has spent 34.8 gallons of fuel in 3 hours and 10 minutes. After positioning the 19 (190 minutes = 3 hours and 10 minutes) on the middle scale opposite the approximate value of 34.8 on the outer scale, the fuel rate can be determined. The unknown quantity (11 GPH) can be read on the outer scale opposite the Hour Index.

5.16 Figure 5-11 illustrates the solution for an unknown time problem. In this problem, an airplane's fuel consumption is 9 GPH. To determine the flying time needed to use 22 gallons of fuel, the Hour Index (middle scale) was positioned opposite the 90 on the outer scale. The correct answer (147 minutes) is located on the middle scale opposite the 22 on the outer scale.

Excercise B. Solve for the unknowns.

	Time	Fuel Rate	Quantity
10.	2:32	15 GPH	___gal.
11.	0:40	___GPH	9 gal.
12.	_:_	24 GPH	100 gal.
13.	4:10	___PPH	600 lbs.
14.	0:40	90 PPH	___lbs.
15.	_:_	75 PPH	360 lbs.

Finding the Rate of Climb

5.17 Rate-of-climb problems can be solved by using the outer (miles) and middle (minutes) scale for multiplication and division. In a sample problem (Figure 5-12), a pilot plans to climb 8,000 feet at an average rate of climb of 400 feet per minute (FPM) as indicated by the aircraft's performance charts. This type of problem is solved by simple division, where 8,000 (the dividend) is being divided by 400 (the divisor). To find the time to climb, 40 (400 FPM) is set on the middle (minutes) scale opposite the 80 (8,000 feet) on the outer (miles) scale. The quotient-answer (20 or 20 minutes) is found on the outside scale opposite the **⑩** Index (middle scale).

5.18 The following ratio should be used when dividing on the E6-B type computer:

$$\frac{\text{Dividend}}{\text{Divisor}} = \frac{\text{Quotient}}{⑩}$$

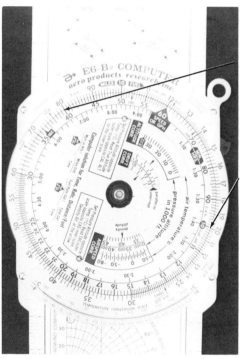

1. Place 80 (8,000) feet opposite average rate of climb 40 (400) FPM.

2. Opposite the 10 index read the time-to-climb 20 minutes on the outside scale.

Figure 5-12. Computing Time to Climb

Exercise C. Solve for the unknowns.

	Altitude Change	Rate of Climb	Time
16.	4,200 ft.	840 FPM	_____
17.	8,400 ft.	700 FPM	_____
18.	3,300 ft.	_____	6 min.
19.	1,500 ft.	_____	3 min.
20.	2,100 ft.	420 FPM	_____

Temperature Conversion (Centigrade/Fahrenheit)

5.19 Most computers are equipped with a conversion scale to convert from Centigrade to Fahrenheit or from Fahrenheit to Centigrade. (Figure 5-13)

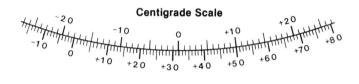

Centigrade Scale

Fahrenheit Scale

Figure 5–13. Converting Degrees Centigrade — Degrees Fahrenheit

Distance Conversion (Statute/Nautical)

5.20 Another useful scale, that most of the E6-B type computers have, is the statute to nautical (or nautical to statute) mile conversion scale. (Figure 5-14) The conversion process is elementary. Simply position the nautical miles on the middle scale opposite the "naut" arrow on the outer scale. Then read the statute miles (middle scale) under the "stat" arrow on the outer scale. Naturally, the process may be reversed to convert from statute to nautical miles. Figure 5-14 demonstrates the conversion from 100 nautical miles to the equivalent of 115 statute miles.

Exercise D. Convert the distances and speeds to the appropriate values.

	Nautical	Statute
21.	60 NM	_____ SM
22.	400 NM	_____ SM
23.	_____ NM	240 SM
24.	130 NM	_____ SM
25.	_____ NM	4.5 SM
26.	110 KTS	_____ MPH
27.	_____ KTS	190 MPH
28.	_____ KTS	155 MPH
29.	444 KTS	_____ MPH
30.	_____ KTS	255 MPH

True Airspeed Computations (E6-B Type Computers)

5.21 The airspeed indicator is engineered to provide accurate indications at sea level under standard atmospheric conditions. Since these conditions are rarely found at altitude, pilots that fly aircraft at airspeeds below 200 knots must correct calibrated airspeed for nonstandard pressure and temperature variations to determine the true airspeed. To calculate the true airspeed, it is necessary to find the scale labeled For Airspeed Corrections. Pressure altitude, outside air temperature, and calibrated airspeed must be used in the TAS computations in order to calculate the exact airspeed. Since the error is so slight, indicated altitude is sometimes substituted for pressure altitude. Indicated airspeed is also generally substituted for calibrated airspeed.

5.22 The true airspeed can be found by setting the pressure altitude (or indicated altitude if the pressure altitude is not available) opposite the outside free air temperature. The TAS on the outer (distance) scale is then read opposite the indicated airspeed or calibrated airspeed on the middle (minute) scale.

5.23 Figure 5-15 demonstrates how to find the TAS using the E6-B type computer. The procedure is to set the indicated altitude (10,000 feet) opposite the temperature (+12° C) on the airspeed correction scale. The TAS (180 MPH or KTS) on the outer scale is then read opposite the indicated airspeed (150 MPH or KTS) on the middle scale. The procedure can also be used to determine IAS from TAS.

5.24 Again, the units for measuring speed may be either miles per hour or knots. Remember, if the indicated airspeed (or true airspeed) were in MPH, for example, the computed true airspeed (or indicated airspeed) would be expressed in the same unit values.

5.25 Error caused by compressibility is another element to consider when computing true airspeeds *above* 200 knots for flight at the *higher* altitudes. Compressibility results from a buildup of molecules on the leading edge of the wing at high airspeeds. This restraining pressure produces an extra ram effect on the pitot system, causing a *higher* airspeed to be reflected on the airspeed indicator than the actual airspeed warrants. A higher temperature is also registered on the outside air temperature gauge, when compressibility is a factor, due to molecular friction. Compressibility error is normally compensated for by:

    1. Multiplying a compressibility factor times the uncorrected true airspeed, *or*

    2. Subtracting a compressibility error (generally less than 10 knots) from the CAS and temperature error from the outside air temperature (OAT) before calculating the problem on the computer.

5.26 *Special Note: The pressure altitude scale is expressed in units of 1,000's of feet, not 100's of feet. The temperature scale is expressed in degrees Centigrade, not degrees Fahrenheit. Two examples of common mistakes which lead to computer error are:*

Attempting to set a 1,500 ft. pressure altitude in the 15,000 ft. pressure altitude position on the computer.

Attempting to set °F in the °C temperature position. (Not converting the degrees Fahrenheit to degrees Centigrade.)

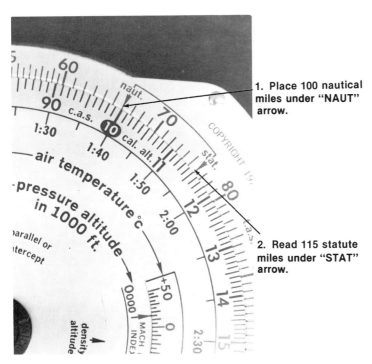

1. Place 100 nautical miles under "NAUT" arrow.

2. Read 115 statute miles under "STAT" arrow.

Figure 5-14. Converting Statute Miles
— Nautical Miles

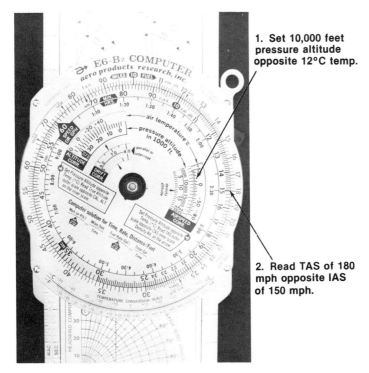

1. Set 10,000 feet pressure altitude opposite 12°C temp.

2. Read TAS of 180 mph opposite IAS of 150 mph.

Figure 5-15. Computing True Airspeed

Computing Density Altitude

5.27 Finding the density altitude involves approximately the same procedure as determining true airspeed. Using this procedure, set the pressure altitude opposite the outside free air temperature on the airspeed correction and density altitude scale. Read the density altitude from the scale inside the density altitude window. In Figure 5-16 the density altitude is computed by setting the pressure altitude (10,000 feet) opposite the temperature (+12° C), and reading the density altitude from the density altitude scale. In this example, the density altitude is computed to be 11,800 feet.

5.28 *Special Note: The density altitude scale is expressed in units of 1,000 feet.*

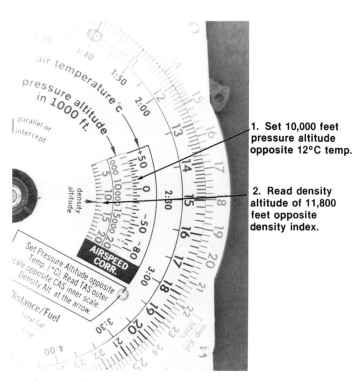

1. Set 10,000 feet pressure altitude opposite 12°C temp.

2. Read density altitude of 11,800 feet opposite density index.

Figure 5-16. Computing Density Altitude

Determining the Wind Correction Angle and Ground Speed (E6-B Type Computer)

5.29 Unfortunately, air masses (wind) are almost always moving, so pilots should not fly from point to point without first considering the effects of wind. The resolution of the problem involving wind depends upon the solution of the wind triangle.

5.30 Three simple vectors with fixed elements comprise the wind triangle. These vectors are:

1. **Wind vector**—Composed of the direction and speed of the wind.

2. **Ground vector**—Composed of the true course (track) and the ground speed. This vector represents the movement of the aircraft with respect to the ground.

3. **Air vector**—Composed of the true heading and the true airspeed. This vector represents the movement of the aircraft with respect to the air mass.

5.31 Each of the vectors in the triangle has a direction and length. The direction is measured from true north, and the length is measured by some standard scale, usually MPH or KTS. The standard unit of time, represented by each vector, is 60 minutes.

5.32 The wind triangle is solved using the E6-B computer by plotting the wind vector on the transparent circular plate; the other vectors of the triangle constitute parts of the grid. A graphic solution of a wind triangle using the E6-B type computer is illustrated in Figure 5-17.

5.33 Familiarity with the following terms is essential in understanding the wind side of the computer and solving wind triangle problems:

True Course (TC)—The ground track (course) of an aircraft measured with reference to true north.

True Heading (TH)—The longitudinal axis (heading) of the aircraft measured with reference to true north.

Magnetic Course (MC)—The ground track (course) of an aircraft measured with reference to magnetic north.

Wind Correction Angle (WCA)—The angle between the aircraft heading and the aircraft track, which is equal to the wind drift.

Exercise E. Solve for the unknown answers.

	Pressure Altitude	Temperature	IAS(KTS)	TAS(KTS)	Density Altitude
31.	3,500 ft.	-15°C	150	____	____
32.	9,500 ft.	+20°C	____	190	____
33.	22,000 ft.	-14°F	140	____	____
34.	13,500 ft.	-25°C	____	250	____
35.	7,000 ft.	+77°F	130	____	____

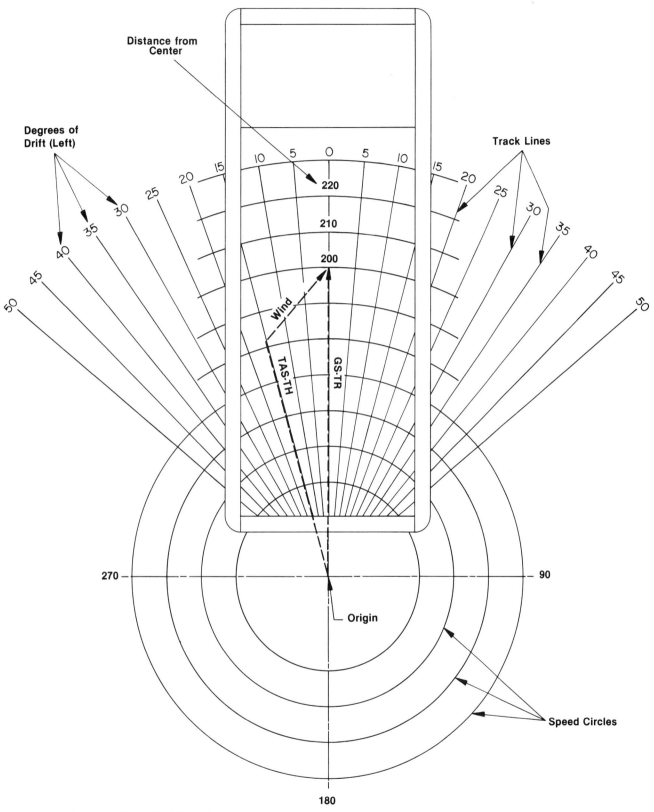

Figure 5-17. Solution of the Wind Triangle

5.34 The wind side of the E6-B type computer is a simple arrangement depicting the wind vector triangles. Most wind face sides of E6-B type computers have three basic parts:

1. A frame.
2. A transparent circular plate that can be rotated.
3. A grid plate that can be moved up and down.

5.35 On the top of the frame is a drift scale graduated 50° to the left and 50° to the right with a *True Index* in the center. The circular plate is graduated into 360 units which can be used to set a desired direction measured from true north opposite the True Index. Placed in the center of the circular plate is a small black circle called the grommet. Upon examining the grid, a pilot will find it divided into areas of concentric arcs called speed circles; each arc (or division) is displaced by two units of distance. Through the center of the grid is a line that intersects the True Index and the center grommet. On each side of the grid are a series of converging straight lines which meet at a point outside the grid. These converging lines on the grid are called "track lines" since they depict the number of degrees by which the true course (track) differs from the true heading.

5.36 A sample problem is illustrated to review the procedure involved in finding ground speed and wind correction angle.

Given:

Planned true course, 340°.
Forecast wind, 035°/30 KTS.
Planned true airspeed, 140 KTS.
Variation, 13° East.

Solution:

1. The first step is to set the true wind direction (035°) under the True Index. (Figure 5-18A)
2. Next slide the grid up or down until a convenient figure (such as the 120 unit speed curve) is located under the grommet.
3. Place a pencil dot (30 units) *above* the grommet towards the True Index. (In this particular problem, the pencil dot should coincide with the 150 unit speed curve.) (Figure 5-18B)
4. Now rotate the center disc until the true course (340°) appears under the True Index as shown in Figure 5-18C.
5. Then slide the grid until the wind dot appears over the TAS (140 knot speed circle).

6. The drift will be the number of degrees (track lines) the wind dot is right or left of the centerline (which is 10° Right).
7. The ground speed (120 KTS) is the value under the grommet. (Figure 5-18D)
8. There are two remaining unknowns, the true heading (TH) and the magnetic heading (MH), which are an essential part of the flight planning process. The true heading is easily determined by adding (for right drift) or subtracting (for left drift) the drift correction angle from the true course. In Figure 5-18D the wind dot is located 10° to the right of the center reference line. The true heading (350°) is calculated in this example by applying the WCA (+10° for Right WCA) to the true course (340°).
9. Finally, the magnetic heading can be calculated by selecting the degrees of variation (13°E) from the appropriate navigational chart and applying it to the true heading. This rule is sometimes expressed: "When converting from true to magnetic, east is least, and west is best," which means that if the variation is easterly, it will be subtracted from the true heading, or if the variation is westerly, it will be added to the true heading. (Therefore, the magnetic heading is 350° - 13° = 337°.) To sum up the complete formulas:

TC (+R) WCA = TH
$\qquad$ or
$\qquad$ (-L)

TH (+W) VAR = MH
$\qquad$ or
$\qquad$ (-E)

5.37 *Special Notes:*

1. *Occasionally, it may become necessary to calculate the true course using the magnetic course and variation. Remember, the rule "east is least, and west is best" pertains to calculations from true course or heading to magnetic course or heading only. When converting from a magnetic course or heading to a true course or heading, westerly variation is subtracted, or easterly variation is added, as appropriate.*

2. *If the wind speed and true airspeed are expressed in different unit values, either the true airspeed or the wind speed must be converted so that both speeds are expressed in terms of the same unit values.*

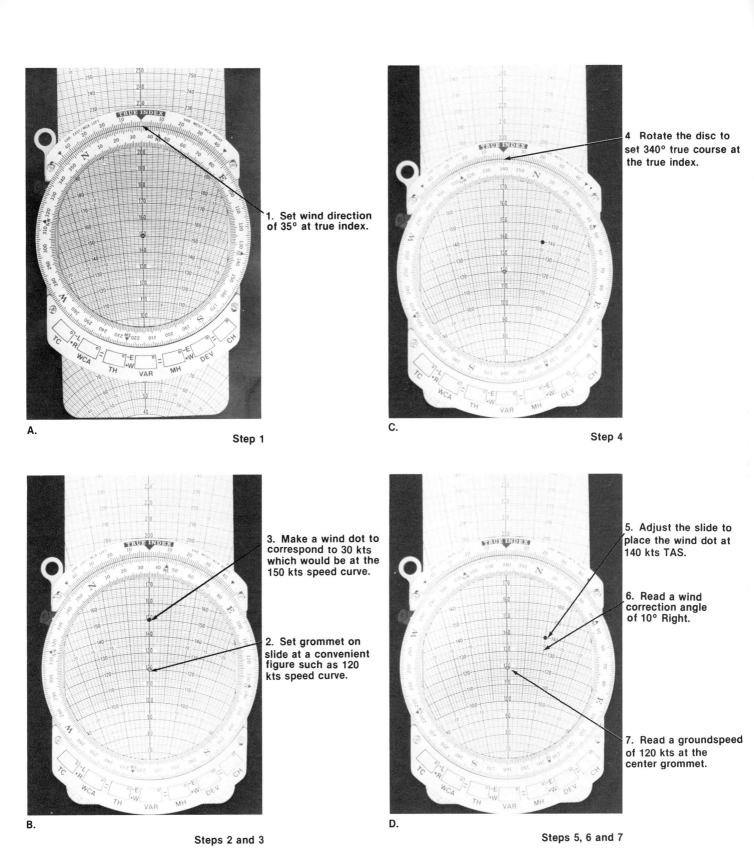

A.   Step 1

1. Set wind direction of 35° at true index.

C.   Step 4

4 Rotate the disc to set 340° true course at the true index.

B.   Steps 2 and 3

3. Make a wind dot to correspond to 30 kts which would be at the 150 kts speed curve.

2. Set grommet on slide at a convenient figure such as 120 kts speed curve.

D.   Steps 5, 6 and 7

5. Adjust the slide to place the wind dot at 140 kts TAS.

6. Read a wind correction angle of 10° Right.

7. Read a groundspeed of 120 kts at the center grommet.

Figure 5–18 A-D. Steps Involved in Solving a Wind Vector Problem

5.38 Common wind problem computer errors include:

1. Setting the grommet rather than the pencil dot on the TAS when determining ground speed (GS) and WCA (Step 5).
2. Not using wind speeds and true airspeeds with similar unit values (Steps 3 and 5).
3. Placing the wind speed dot below the grommet (Step 3).
4. Neglecting to slide the grid until the TAS appears under the pencil dot (Step 5).

Solving the Wind Triangle on a Circular Computer (Finding Wind Correction Angle and Ground Speed)

5.39 Most circular computer problem (front) sides are quite similar to the problem side of the E6-B type computer. For this reason, no discussion is necessary for the problem side of the circular computer. However, the wind side of the circular computer is sufficiently different from the wind side of the E6-B type computer to merit the following discussion.

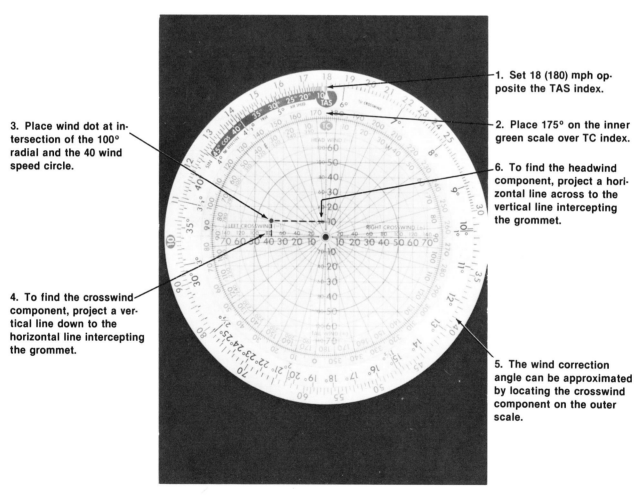

3. Place wind dot at intersection of the 100° radial and the 40 wind speed circle.

4. To find the crosswind component, project a vertical line down to the horizontal line intercepting the grommet.

1. Set 18 (180) mph opposite the TAS index.

2. Place 175° on the inner green scale over TC index.

6. To find the headwind component, project a horizontal line across to the vertical line intercepting the grommet.

5. The wind correction angle can be approximated by locating the crosswind component on the outer scale.

Figure 5–19. Solution for Wind Correction Angle and Ground Speed on the Circular Computer

172

5.40 The procedure to use in finding the wind correction angle and ground speed on a circular computer is as follows (refer to Figure 5-19):

Given: TAS 180 MPH.
TC 175°.
Wind 100° True/40 MPH.

Solution:

1 and 2. Set the true airspeed (180) on the outside scale opposite the TAS index (▲) on the middle scale. Then position the true course (175°) on the inner green scale over the TC index (**TC**).

3. Locate the wind direction (100°) on the green scale where the wind direction "radial" intersects the wind speed (40) circle. Place the pencil (wind) dot at the interception point.

4. To determine the crosswind component, project a vertical line from the wind dot down (or up) to the horizontal line intersecting the center grommet and read the wind component (39 MPH left).

5. On the outer scale locate the wind component from Step 3 and read the wind correction angle opposite on the middle scale (-12°). The correction angle must be *added* to the true course to determine true heading if the wind dot is *right* of center. If the wind dot is *left* of center, then the correction angle must be *subtracted* from the true course to determine true heading (175° TC - 12° WCA = 163° TH).

6. To determine the component of headwind or tailwind, project a horizontal line from the wind dot across to the center vertical line intersecting the center grommet and read the component (-10 MPH) to be added or subtracted from the TAS. To determine the ground speed, the wind component must be *subtracted* from the TAS if the wind dot is *above* center, or *added* if the wind dot is *below* center (180 MPH - 10 MPH = 170 MPH GS).

PERFORMANCE CHARTS

5.41 Performance charts depict aircraft performance under varying sets of conditions. These charts are usually found in the FAA-approved Airplane Flight Manual and in the Owner's Manual or Handbook prepared by the aircraft manufacturer. Although the format and specific ground rules will vary with the manufacturer, the obtainable information usually covers the relative values of the three major factors affecting aircraft performance: density altitude, gross weight, and wind.

5.42 A pilot should refer to performance charts if there is a doubt about:

1. The condition of the runway.
2. A relatively high density altitude.
3. The pilot's skill and familiarity with the aircraft and its equipment.

5.43 Always remember that the performance data on the charts were obtained from new, ideally loaded and serviced aircraft. Thus, the information on the performance charts holds true for an individual pilot only if that pilot's aircraft is kept in peak operating condition. A safe pilot will consider the airplane's performance to be somewhat less than that predicted by the charts. Because the charts can contribute to a sometimes critical margin of safety, they are always covered in the written examinations. This section discusses and reviews charts in logical order, from pre-takeoff to landing procedures.

Significant Terms

5.44 The following terms are often used during the course of aircraft performance discussions. Commit these terms to memory:

Maximum take-off power—The maximum allowable take-off power as rated by the manufacturer. Prolonged operation at or above this power level will most likely result in damage to the engine.

Maximum except take-off (METO) power—The maximum power that can be maintained for continuous operation.

Exercise F. Solve the following problems for MH, WCA, GS, and TH.

	TC	WIND	TAS	VARIATION	MH	WCA	GS(KTS)	TH
36.	240°	190°/20 KTS	120 KTS	5°E	___	___	___	___
37.	160°	090°/40 KTS	190 KTS	10°W	___	___	___	___
38.	320°	240°/35 KTS	230 MPH	7°W	___	___	___	___
39.	280°	360°/25 KTS	140 KTS	4°E	___	___	___	___
40.	200°	310°/30 KTS	150 MPH	11°W	___	___	___	___

Cruise climb power—The maximum power recommended by the manufacturer for a cruise climb.

Maximum cruise power—The highest power setting recommended by the manufacturer for cruise.

Recommended cruise power—The intermediate power settings suggested by the manufacturer.

Economy cruise power—The cruise power setting which will yield the maximum distance per unit of fuel.

Service ceiling—The highest pressure altitude at which an aircraft has the capability of climbing at a maximum rate of 50 feet per minute.

Critical altitude—The highest altitude at which an aircraft can maintain METO power. A further increase in altitude (above critical altitude with a wide open throttle) will result in a further decrease in power below the METO power level.

Pressure Altitude Chart

5.45 Many performance problems incorporate pressure altitude as one of the necessary variables. The chart in Figure 5-20 provides an easy method of computing pressure altitude. For example:

Given: Indicated Altitude (or field elevation), 3,795 feet.
Altimeter Setting, 29.70'' Hg.

Find: Pressure Altitude.

5.46 It can be determined from the chart that a correction factor of 205 feet must be added to the indicated altitude (field elevation) to compute the pressure altitude. Therefore, the pressure altitude is 4,000 feet (3,795 feet + 205 feet = 4,000 feet P.A.). In many instances the altimeter setting will not correspond exactly with one of the numbers on the altimeter setting list. In such cases it is necessary to interpolate in order to obtain the exact correction factor. (Refer to Figure 5-21 in the density altitude discussion.)

5.47 If the pressure altitude conversion chart is not available, another "rule of thumb" method of calculating pressure altitude is to find the difference between the correct altimeter setting and 29.92'' Hg (29.92 - 29.70 = .22'' Hg). Multiply the pressure difference by 1,000 (.22 x 1,000 = 220) and subtract the product from the indicated altitude if the current altimeter setting is more than 29.92'' Hg, or add the product to the indicated altitude if the altimeter setting is less than 29.92'' Hg (3,795 feet + 220 feet = 4,015 feet approximate pressure altitude). Although this method is not as accurate as the pressure altitude conversion chart, it provides a good "ballpark figure" of the pressure altitude.

Altimeter Setting in. Hg.	Altitude Addition For Obtaining Pressure Altitude
28.3...	1,535
28.4...	1,435
28.5...	1,340
28.6...	1,245
28.7...	1,150
28.8...	1,050
28.9...	955
29.0...	865
29.1...	770
29.2...	675
29.3...	580
29.4...	485
29.5...	390
29.6...	300
→ 29.7...	........205 ◄
29.8...	110
29.9...	20
29.92..	0
30.0...	........-75
30.1...	.......-165
30.2...	.......-255
30.3...	.......-350
30.4...	.......-440
30.5...	.......-530
30.6...	.......-620
30.7...	.......-710
30.8...	.......-805

Figure 5-20. Conversion Chart to Find Pressure Altitude

Density Altitude Graphs

5.48 Most aircraft performance charts are based upon density altitude. Figure 5-21 is a density altitude graph with an example problem. To calculate density altitude, find the temperature (in degrees Centigrade) at the bottom of the graph. Extend a line from the approximate temperature vertically until it intersects the approximate pressure altitude line. The next step is to extend a line from the intersection of the temperature line and pressure altitude line horizontally to the density altitude scale. Density altitude can be found numbered vertically on the left side of the graph.

Exercise G. Solve the following problems for pressure altitude and density altitude.

	Altimeter Setting	Field Elevation	Temperature	Pressure Altitude (Ft.)	Density Altitude (Ft.)
41.	29.92	sea level	59°F	_____	_____
42.	30.00	3,075 ft.	30°C	_____	_____
43.	29.00	3,935 ft.	32°F	_____	_____
44.	29.55	1,500 ft.	94°F	_____	_____
45.	30.80	500 ft.	0°C	_____	_____

SET ALTIMETER TO 29.92 IN.HG.

WHEN READING PRESSURE ALTITUDE

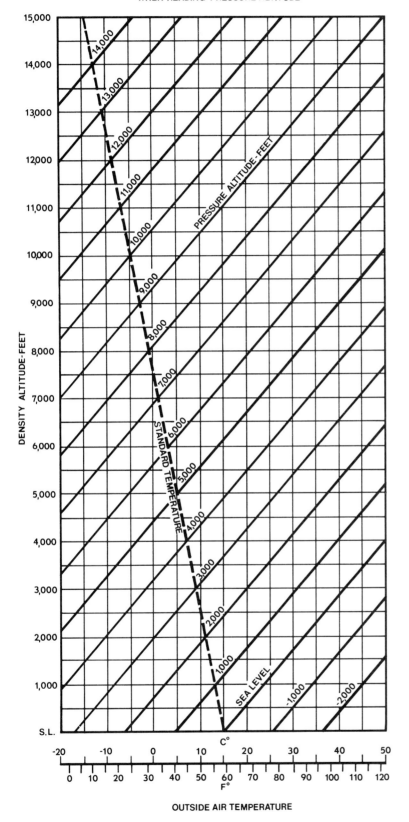

OUTSIDE AIR TEMPERATURE

PRESSURE ALTITUDE (PA) CAN BE OBTAINED

FROM THE ALTIMETER SETTING.

(Refer to sample problem below.)

ALTIMETER SETTING IN.HG.	ALTITUDE ADDITION CORRECTION FACTOR (CF) FOR OBTAINING PRESSURE ALTITUDE
28.0	1,825
28.1	1,725
28.2	1,630
28.3	1,535
28.4	1,435
28.5	1,340
28.6	1,245
28.7	1,150
28.8	1,050
28.9	955
29.0	865
29.1	770
29.2	675
29.3	580
29.4	485
29.5	390
29.6	300
29.7	205
29.8	110
29.9	20
29.92	0
30.0	- 75
30.1	-165
30.2	-255
30.3	-350
30.4	-440
30.5	-530
30.6	-620
30.7	-710 ←
30.8	-805 ←
30.9	-895
31.0	-965

EXAMPLE

GIVEN:

Altimeter Setting   30.73 IN. HG.
Field Elevation (FE)   1,250 Ft.

SOLUTION:

The solution is obtained by using the Pressure Altitude formula:

$$PA = FE + CF$$

Note the altitude addition correction factors of -710 and -805 feet, from the chart above, for altimeter settings of 30.70 and 30.80 IN. HG., respectively.

To determine the exact correction factor, interpolation is necessary as follows:

$$
\begin{array}{lll}
30.70 \\
30.73 \quad \}\ 3\ \Big\}\ 10 \quad & -710 \\
30.80 & -805
\end{array}\ \Big\}\ -95
$$

$$-95 \times 3/10 = -28.5$$
$$-710 + (-28.5) = -739$$

After the correction factor has been determined the answer can then be found using the PA formula.

$$1,250 + (-739) = 511 \text{ Ft.}$$

Density Altitude Graph

Figure 5-21. Density Altitude Graph

Accelerate-Stop Distance Graph

5.49 Prior to takeoff, pilots should consider the possibility of aborting during the takeoff roll due to some unsafe or emergency condition. The accelerate-stop distance is the total distance from break release accelerating to decision speed and decelerating to a full stop. The general factors used to determine the accelerate-stop distance are outside air temperature, pressure altitude, gross weight, and the headwind/tailwind component. Most graphs assume a paved and level runway; therefore, a pilot should take into consideration such additional factors as grass, rain, ice, snow, and/or runway slope.

1. To solve a typical accelerate-stop distance problem, locate the outside air temperature (15°C) on the bottom left side of the graph in Figure 5-22.

2. Extend a vertical line up to the appropriate pressure altitude line (5,650 feet). (This portion of the graph is simply a density altitude chart resembling the previously described density altitude graph.)

3. From the intersection of the vertical temperature line and the pressure altitude curve, a horizontal line is extended to the right to the weight reference line (5,400 pound line).

4. A sloping line is then, generally, extended downward to the right, from the intersection of the horizontal line and weight reference line, parallel to the sloping guide lines until intercepting the vertical gross weight line (5,400 pounds).

5. A horizontal line is then extended to the right, from the vertical gross weight line (5,400 pound line), to the zero wind reference line.

6. Then, paralleling the sloping guide lines, a slanted line is extended downward (or upward, if applicable), to the right until intersecting the appropriate headwind/tailwind line (9.5 KTS headwind).

7. A horizontal line is then extended to the right from the intersection of the slanted line and the appropriate headwind/tailwind line.

8. The accelerate-stop distance is read from the intersection of the final horizontal line and the scale at the right hand side of the graph (3,960 feet).

ACCELERATE - STOP DISTANCE

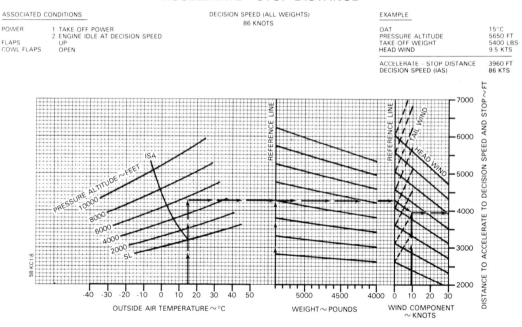

Figure 5-22. Accelerate - Stop Distance Graph

Exercise H. Solve for the accelerate-stop distance.

	Outside Air Temperature	Pressure Altitude	Gross Weight	Wind Component	Accelerate-Stop Distance (Ft.)
46.	-10°C	sea level	5,400 lbs.	23 MPH headwind	_____
47.	32°F	2,000 ft.	4,500 lbs.	10 KTS tailwind	_____
48.	8°C	4,000 ft.	5,000 lbs.	20 KTS headwind	_____
49.	20°C	8,000 ft.	4,000 lbs.	30 KTS headwind	_____
50.	30°C	2,000 ft.	4,300 lbs.	0 calm wind	_____

176

5.50 *Special Note: In this particular example problem, the take-off weight vertical line was also the weight reference line; therefore, it was not necessary to extend a parallel sloping line to the right from the weight reference line to intersect the appropriate vertical weight line (Step 4).*

Takeoff Distance over 50-Foot Obstacle Graph

5.51 There are a multitude of different types of takeoff distance graphs (charts). The following discussion is representative of the factors influencing the design of those graphs.

5.52 Figure 5-23 illustrates a typical 50-foot obstacle performance graph. This type of graph incorporates such factors as ambient temperature, pressure altitude, aircraft gross weight, and headwind component.

5.53 In the example illustrated in Figure 5-23, the ambient temperature (70°F) is located on the bottom scale of the graph. A vertical line is extended to the appropriate pressure altitude curve (Point A, 2,000 feet pressure altitude). A horizontal line is then extended to Point B, which is the initial gross weight vertical reference line. Next, a slanted line is extended to the right, parallel to the curved

weight lines (Point C, 2,900 pounds). Next, a horizontal line is further extended to the right from Point C to Point D. Point D is the initial headwind vertical reference line. From Point D a slanted line is extended to the right parallel to the curved headwind lines (Point E, 10 MPH). The final step is completed when a line is extended horizontally to the right from Point E to Point F. The take-off distance over a 50-foot obstacle (1,450 feet) is then read at Point F.

Exercise I. Solve the following problems for takeoff distance over a 50-foot obstacle.

	Temperature	Pressure Altitude (Ft.)	Weight (Lbs.)	Headwind	Take-Off Distance (Ft.)
51.	20°F	2,000	3,100	10 MPH	_____
52.	40°F	4,000	2,900	30 KTS	_____
53.	61°C	1,000	2,700	Calm	_____
54.	50°F	3,000	2,600	20 MPH	_____
55.	53°C	4,000	2,500	15 MPH	_____

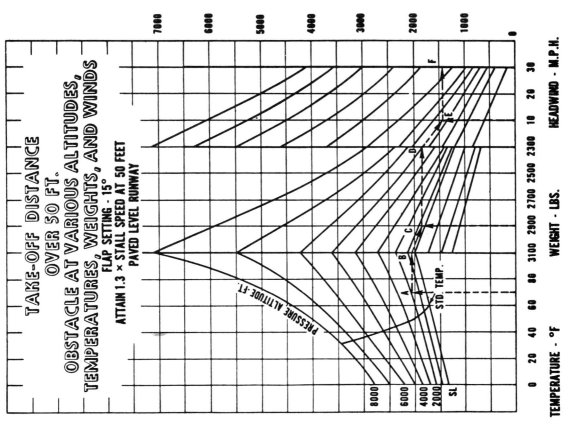

Figure 5-23. Takeoff Distance Over 50-Foot Obstacle Graph

Time-Fuel-Distance to Climb Graph

5.54 Figure 5-24 is a typical Time-Fuel-Distance to Climb Graph. This graph is useful during the course of everyday flying to find time, fuel, and distance needed to climb from one altitude to another.

5.55 The information necessary to use a graph of this type generally consists of the following:

1. Outside air temperature (OAT) at the initial climb altitude and the OAT at the cruise altitude.
2. Pressure altitude at the start of the climb and the pressure altitude at the cruising altitude.
3. The initial climb weight.

5.56 In this example, an aircraft has climbed from an initial pressure altitude of 5,650 feet to a cruising pressure altitude of 11,500 feet. This is essentially a two-part graph problem. Following the two sets of arrows on the graph, it is easy to determine the time and fuel needed to climb to the initial pressure altitude and to the cruise pressure altitude. The time, fuel, and distance to climb information obtained from the graph is based on a climb from a sea level pressure altitude; therefore, it is necessary to subtract the time, fuel, and distance to climb information derived for the initial climb altitude from the cruise pressure altitude time, fuel, and distance to climb information.

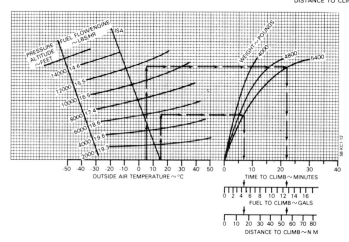

Figure 5–24. Example Problem on a Time-Fuel-Distance to Climb Graph

---

Exercise J. Solve the following problems for time, fuel and distance to climb.

	Initial Climb Weight (Lbs.)	OAT (°C) Initial Climb Altitude	Pressure Altitude Initial Climb Altitude	OAT (°C) Cruise Altitude	Cruise Pressure Altitude	Time To Climb (Min.)	Fuel To Climb (Gal.)	Distance To Climb (NM)
56.	4,000	25	2,000	15	10,000	_____	_____	_____
57.	4,800	20	5,000	8	11,000	_____	_____	_____
58.	5,400	15	4,000	5	10,500	_____	_____	_____
59.	4,800	10	6,000	0	12,000	_____	_____	_____
60.	5,400	15	5,500	4	9,500	_____	_____	_____

Best Rate and Best Angle of Climb Graph

5.57 Figure 5-25 is a representative illustration of a Best Rate and Best Angle of Climb Graph for a single-engine aircraft. In this example, density altitude must already be computed from the outside air temperature and pressure altitude. An aircraft with a gross weight of 2,500 pounds, climbing at a density altitude of 7,500 feet (see Point A), has a best angle of climb speed of 84 MPH. Note that the same aircraft with gear extended and flaps extended 15° (see Point B) has a best angle of climb speed of 73 MPH.

5.58 An aircraft with a gross weight of 3,100 pounds and with gear and flaps retracted, climbing at a density altitude of 3,500 feet (see Point C), has a best rate of climb speed of 109 MPH. Note that the same aircraft with gear extended and flaps extended 15° (see Point D) has a best rate of climb speed of 94 MPH.

Exercise K. Compute the unknowns using Figure 5-25.

61. What is the best angle of climb speed for an aircraft weighing 3,100 pounds, flying at a density altitude of 2,000 feet, with gear and flaps retracted? _____ MPH.

62. What is the best rate of climb speed for an aircraft weighing 3,100 pounds flying at a density altitude of 2,000 feet with gear extended and flaps extended 15°? _____ MPH.

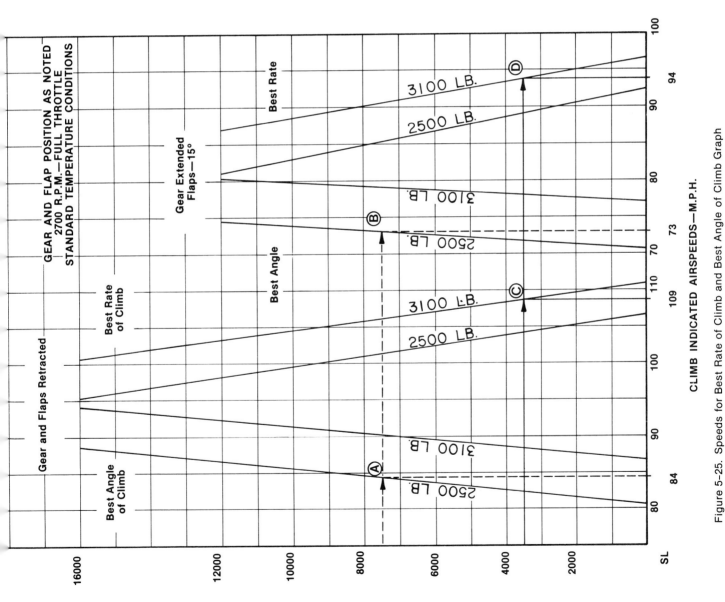

Figure 5-25. Speeds for Best Rate of Climb and Best Angle of Climb Graph

Climb—One Engine Inoperative Graph

5.59 Figure 5-26 is representative of a Climb—One Engine Inoperative Graph used for a multiengine aircraft. The procedure for determining the climb rate and gradient is again similar to the procedure for determining the accelerate–stop distance from the Accelerate–Stop Distance Graph. (Figure 5-26)

Fuel Flow vs. Brake Horsepower Graph

5.60 Figure 5-27 is a common type of Fuel Flow vs. Brake Horsepower Graph. Although there are different variations to this particular graph, the graph illustrated is similar to many of the Fuel Flow vs. Brake Horsepower Graphs currently in use.

5.61 *Example:* Assume a pilot is operating a twin-engine aircraft and wishes to know how much

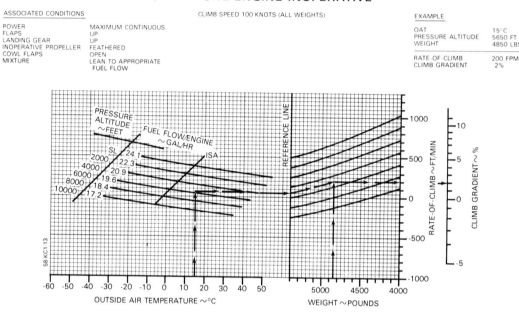

Figure 5-26. Climb—One Engine Inoperative Graph

Exercise L. What is the rate of climb and the takeoff climb gradient for a multiengine aircraft with one engine inoperative under the following conditions? (Refer to Figure 5-26.) Assume the following:

Power—Maximum Continuous
Flaps—Up Position
Landing Gear—Up Position
Inoperative Propeller—Feathered Position
Cowl Flaps—Open Position
Mixture—Lean to Appropriate Fuel Flow.

	Outside Air Temperature (°C)	Pressure Altitude (Ft.)	Weight (Lbs.)	Climb Gradient (%)	Rate of Climb (Ft./min.)
63.	10	3,000	5,000	_____	_____
64.	0	6,000	4,700	_____	_____
65.	-10	10,000	4,500	_____	_____

fuel could be conserved in a period of one hour if the power settings were changed from 70% "takeoff and climb" power to 60% "cruise (lean)" power.

1. Using the graph illustrated in Figure 5-27, it is first necessary to locate the intersection of the diagonal curve labeled "Takeoff and Climb" and the vertical 70% "Maximum Continuous Power Line."

2. After locating the intersection, a horizontal line should be drawn to the left scale.

3. The fuel flow, 17.1 gallons per hour, of each engine can be read from the scale.

4. Remember, since this graph is fuel flow per engine per hour, the fuel flow must be multiplied by the number of operating engines.

5.62 Again using the same procedure with the diagonal curve labeled "Cruise (Lean)" and the 60% "Maximum Continuous Power Line," it can be

determined that the fuel flow per hour for *both* engines is 24.8 gallons. The resultant change in fuel flow per hour per engine will conserve a total of 9.4 gallons of fuel per hour.

Exercise M (Refer to Figure 5-27 to solve the following problems.) What would be the total savings of fuel for a twin-engine aircraft if:

66. The power setting is changed from 75% "Take-off and Climb" to 65% "Cruise (Lean)" and the air-craft is flown for one hour? _____ gallons.

67. The power setting is changed from 65% "Take-off and Climb" to 55% "Cruise (Lean)" and the air-craft is flown for two hours? _____ gallons.

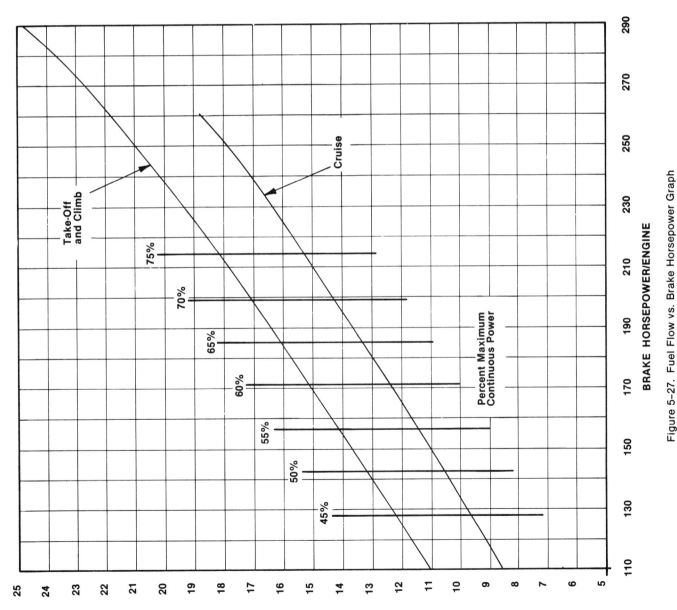

Figure 5-27. Fuel Flow vs. Brake Horsepower Graph

Cruise Power Settings Chart

5.63 The Cruise Power Settings Chart is perhaps one of the most overlooked charts for light aircraft today. This *type* of chart is often disguised (like other types of charts) with a different sounding name and in some cases one or two additional parameters added to the chart. The Cruise Power Setting Chart is quite handy for those pilots who are becoming acquainted with a new aircraft or for those pilots who are renewing an ''old acquaintance.'' (Figure 5-28)

5.64 Not only can a pilot determine what true airspeed to expect at altitude, but also what the aircraft's fuel consumption at specific power settings will be.

5.65 *Example:* At a pressure altitude of 4,000 feet with an outside air temperature of 16°F, a pilot can anticipate a TAS of 192 KTS at 2,500 RPM's and 24.5 inches of manifold pressure.

Climb-Balked Landing Graph

5.66 The Climb-Balked Landing Graph is useful in determining aircraft performance in the event the pilot of an aircraft must execute a ''missed approach'' or a ''go-around,'' (discussed further in chapters 9 and 10). The ''associated conditions'' for a situation of this nature vary with the aircraft design. Figure 5-29, however, is representative of the design considerations of a typical light twin aircraft. Review this graph and sample problem.

CRUISE POWER SETTINGS

CRUISE POWER SETTINGS
MAXIMUM CRUISE POWER
24.5 IN. HG. @ 2500 RPM (OR FULL THROTTLE)
5200 LBS.

PRESS. ALT.	ISA −36°F (−20°C)							STANDARD DAY (ISA)							ISA +36°F (+20°C)						
	OAT		ENGINE SPEED	MAN. PRESS	FUEL FLOW/ ENGINE		TAS	CAS	OAT		ENGINE SPEED	MAN. PRESS	FUEL FLOW/ ENGINE		TAS	CAS	OAT		ENGINE SPEED	MAN. PRESS	FUEL FLOW/ ENGINE		TAS	CAS
FEET	°F	°C	RPM	IN HG	PPH	GPH	KTS	KTS	°F	°C	RPM	IN HG	PPH	GPH	KTS	KTS	°F	°C	RPM	IN HG	PPH	GPH	KTS	KTS
SL	28	−2	2500	24.5	96	16.0	186	193	64	18	2500	24.5	93	15.4	188	188	100	38	2500	24.5	90	14.8	189	183
2000	21	−6	2500	24.5	98	15.9	192	193	57	14	2500	24.5	95	15.8	193	188	95	35	2500	24.5	91	15.2	195	183
4000	16	−9	2500	24.5	100	16.7	197	192	52	11	2500	24.5	96	16.1	199	187	88	31	2500	24.5	93	15.5	200	182
6000	9	−13	2500	23.4	97	16.2	198	188	45	7	2500	23.4	93	15.6	200	183	81	27	2500	23.4	90	15.0	201	178
8000	1	−17	2500	22.0	90	15.0	196	181	37	3	2500	22.0	87	14.5	197	176	73	23	2500	22.0	84	14.0	199	170
10000	−6	−21	2500	20.0	84	14.0	194	174	30	−1	2500	20.0	82	13.6	195	168	66	19	2500	20.0	79	13.1	196	163
12000	−13	−25	2500	18.3	78	13.1	191	166	23	−5	2500	18.3	76	12.7	192	161	59	15	2500	18.3	73	12.2	193	155
14000	−20	−29	2500	16.8	73	12.2	188	158	16	−9	2500	16.8	71	11.8	189	153	52	11	2500	16.8	69	11.4	189	148
16000	−29	−34	2500	15.5	68	11.3	184	150	7	−14	2500	15.5	66	11.0	195	145	43	6	2500	15.5	64	10.6	185	139

NOTES:
1. Full Throttle Manifold Pressure Settings are approximate.
2. Shaded area represents operation with full throttle.
3. ISA (International Standard Atmosphere) is based upon the sea-level standard and normal lapse rate (as discussed in paragraphs 3.3 and 3.5). ISA temperature can be computed mathematically as discussed in paragraph 3.4.

Figure 5-28. Cruise Power Settings Chart

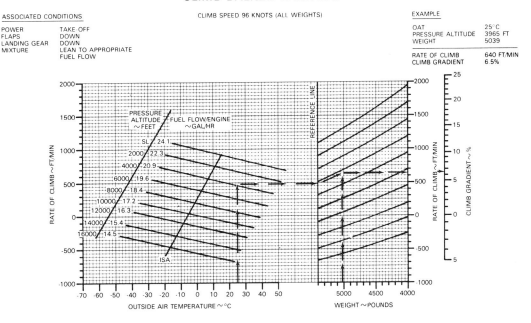

CLIMB-BALKED LANDING

CLIMB SPEED 96 KNOTS (ALL WEIGHTS)

ASSOCIATED CONDITIONS

POWER	TAKE-OFF
FLAPS	DOWN
LANDING GEAR	DOWN
MIXTURE	LEAN TO APPROPRIATE FUEL FLOW

EXAMPLE

OAT	25°C
PRESSURE ALTITUDE	3965 FT
WEIGHT	5039
RATE OF CLIMB	640 FT/MIN
CLIMB GRADIENT	6.5%

Figure 5–29. Climb-Balked Landing Graph

Exercise N. Assume associated conditions of:
  Power—Takeoff.
  Flaps—Down Position.
  Landing Gear—Down Position.
  Mixture—Leaned to Appropriate Fuel Flow.

Find the rate of climb and climb gradient for the following conditions:

	Outside Air Temperature (°C)	Pressure Altitude (Ft.)	Weight (Lbs.)	Rate of Climb (Ft./Min.)	Climb Gradient (%)
68.	0	2,000	4,500	_____	_____
69.	15	4,000	4,700	_____	_____
70.	30	7,000	5,400	_____	_____

Oxygen Duration Chart

5.67 Within the past few years, oxygen breathing systems have gained wide acceptance for general aviation aircraft. The type of oxygen system employed generally depends upon the type of aircraft being flown and the aircraft operating altitude. The three types of systems available to general aviation aircraft are: Continuous-Flow—used up to 25,000 feet; Demand—used up to 35,000 feet; and Pressure-Demand—used up to 40,000 feet. Of the three types of oxygen breathing systems being used today, the Continuous-Flow type is used by most general aviation aircraft. The more sophisticated high altitude general aviation aircraft employ the Pressure-Demand type system for the crew members and the Continuous-Flow type for the passengers.

5.68 Since there is a variety of oxygen breathing systems to choose from and a wide range of operation variables, Oxygen Duration Charts are designed with many different operational parameters in mind. Many Oxygen Duration Charts may take into consideration such variables as:
  1. Cabin altitude.
  2. Numbers of persons breathing oxygen.
  3. Minutes of oxygen useable.
  4. Percent of occupancy of oxygen in cylinders.
  5. Oxygen cylinder pressure.
  6. Flow of oxygen (normal or 100%).
  7. Cylinder volume.
Refer to Figure 5-30 for a typical Oxygen Duration Chart and sample problem.

MINUTES OF OXYGEN AT THE DESIGNATED ALTITUDES

CYLINDER VOLUME	OCCUPANTS RECEIVING	12,500	15,000	20,000
39.2 CU. FT.	1	811	597	406
	2	406	298	202
	3	270	198	135
	4	202	149	101
	5	162	119	81
	6	135	99	67
52.8 CU. FT.	1	1075	790	538
	2	538	395	269
	3	358	263	179
	4	271	198	134
	5	214	158	107
	6	179	131	90

A.

Exercise O. Compute the minutes of oxygen duration under the following conditions (Refer to Figure 5-30):

	Cylinder Volume (Cu.Ft.)	Occupants Receiving Oxygen	Planned Altitude (Ft.)	Gauge Pressure (PSI)	Oxygen Duration (Min.)
71.	52.8	6	15,000	1,600	_____
72.	39.2	4	12,500	880	_____
73.	52.8	3	20,000	1,400	_____
74.	39.2	5	15,000	1,120	_____

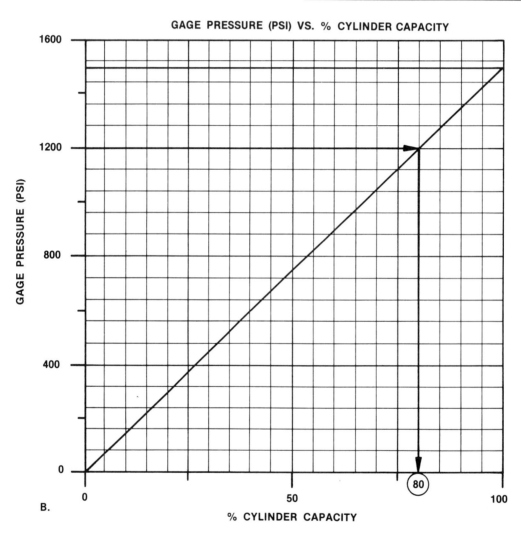

GAGE PRESSURE (PSI) VS. % CYLINDER CAPACITY

B.

Figure 5-30 A-C. Oxygen Duration Chart.

C.

PREFLIGHT:
1. Read oxygen pressure from Oxygen Pressure Gage.
2. Determine percent capacity of system.
3. Multiply percent capacity by minutes of oxygen duration.

EXAMPLE:
Occupants Receiving Oxygen 4
Gage Pressure . . . . 1200 psi
Percent Cylinder Capacity (Refer to Chart) 80%
Total Cylinder Capacity . . . . 39.2 cu. ft.
Proposed Flight Altitude . . . . 12,500 feet
Duration (Full Cylinder) . . . . 202 minutes
Duration (80% Cylinder Capacity) . . . . . 162 minutes

CHAPTER 5: QUESTIONS

For answers see Appendix E

1. What rate of climb must an aircraft maintain to climb from an altitude of 3,200 feet to an altitude of 8,000 feet in 7½ minutes?
1. 360 feet per minute.
2. 385 feet per minute.
3. 640 feet per minute.
4. 800 feet per minute.

2. Assume that the flight time between two VOR-TACs was 49 minutes, and that the fuel consumption rate was 72.0 pounds per hour. How much fuel was consumed?
1. 58.8 pounds.
2. 46.5 pounds.
3. 35.2 pounds.
4. 70.1 pounds.

3. The highest altitude at which METO power can be attained is defined as:
1. True altitude.
2. Maximum brake altitude.
3. Service altitude.
4. Critical altitude.

4. What would an aircraft's magnetic heading be if the magnetic course being flown was 072°, variation was 13°E, wind was from 340° (true) at 20 knots, and the TAS was 219 MPH?
1. 079°.
2. 066°.
3. 053°.
4. 040°.

5. Find the CAS that would produce a TAS of 160 KTS at a pressure altitude of 8,000 feet and +10°C temperature.
1. 139 knots.
2. 184 knots.
3. 144 knots.
4. 136 knots.

6. A pilot arrives at a chosen alternate airport with 45 minutes of fuel. If the pilot reduces the aircraft's fuel consumption from 26 gallons per hour to 18 gallons per hour, how long can the pilot fly and still have a 45-minute fuel reserve?
1. 16½ minutes.
2. 22½ minutes.
3. 14½ minutes.
4. 20 minutes.

7. True airspeed (at speeds below 200 knots, where compressibility is not a factor) can be computed by correcting:
1. Calibrated airspeed for density altitude and temperature.
2. Indicated airspeed for density altitude and temperature.
3. Indicated airspeed for indicated altitude and temperature.
4. Calibrated airspeed for pressure altitude and temperature.

8. Assume an airplane with a TAS of 165 KTS is flying a true course of 060°. The forecast wind is from 350° (true) at 20 KTS, and the distance to be traveled is 68 nautical miles. Compute the estimated time enroute (ETE).
1. 26 minutes.
2. 28½ minutes.
3. 23 minutes.
4. 24½ minutes.

9. Find the magnetic heading for the aircraft in the previous problem if the variation is 10°W.
1. 060°.
2. 054°.
3. 070°.
4. 064°.

10. Refer to the Density Altitude Graph (page 186, top) and determine the density altitude for the following conditions: Airport elevation = 1,240 feet; Temperature = +30°F; Altimeter setting = 30.20'' Hg.
1. 2,600 feet.
2. Below sea level.
3. 2,300 feet.
4. 900 feet.

11. Refer to the Fuel Flow vs. Brake Horsepower Graph (page 186, bottom). What is the increase in the total amount of fuel consumed when a pilot increases the aircraft's power setting from the 160 brake horsepower (BHP) ''Cruise (Lean)'' power setting to the 210 BHP ''Take-off and Climb'' power setting? (Assume the aircraft flown is a twin-engine aircraft.)
1. 3.0 gallons per hour.
2. 6.3 gallons per hour.
3. 12.6 gallons per hour.
4. 2.8 gallons per hour.

DENSITY ALTITUDE CHART

EXAMPLE: IF AMBIENT TEMP. IS -15°C
AND PRESSURE ALT. IS 6000 FEET,
THE DENSITY ALT. IS 4000 FEET

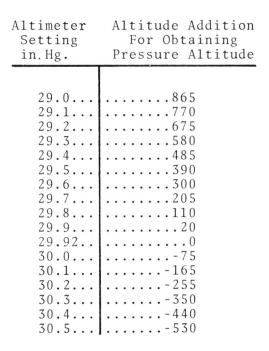

Altimeter Setting in. Hg.	Altitude Addition For Obtaining Pressure Altitude
29.0...	865
29.1...	770
29.2...	675
29.3...	580
29.4...	485
29.5...	390
29.6...	300
29.7...	205
29.8...	110
29.9...	20
29.92..	0
30.0...	.......-75
30.1...	.......-165
30.2...	.......-255
30.3...	.......-350
30.4...	.......-440
30.5...	.......-530

FUEL FLOW vs BRAKE HORSEPOWER

EXAMPLE:

FUEL FLOW/ENGINE CONDITION'	11 7 LBS/GAL LEVEL FLIGHT CRUISE LEAN
BRAKE HORSEPOWER PER ENGINE	160 HP

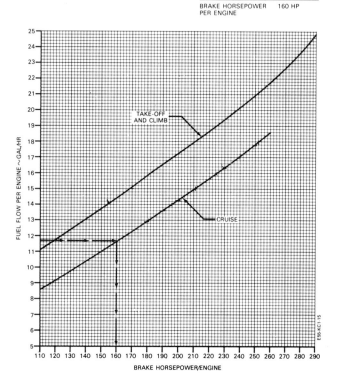

186

TIME, FUEL AND DISTANCE TO CLIMB

ASSOCIATED CONDITIONS
POWER   25 IN HG. OR
                FULL THROTTLE, 2500 RPM   CLIMB SPEED 139 KNOTS
FUEL DENSITY 6.0 LB/GAL
MIXTURE   LEAN TO APPROPRIATE FUEL FLOW
COWL FLAPS CLOSED

EXAMPLE
OAT AT TAKE-OFF	15°C
OAT AT CRUISE	5°C
AIRPORT PRESSURE ALTITUDE	5650 FT
CRUISE PRESSURE ALTITUDE	11500 FT
INITIAL CLIMB WEIGHT	5400 LBS
TIME TO CLIMB	(22-7) = 15 MIN
FUEL TO CLIMB	(12.7-4.7) = 8 GAL
DISTANCE TO CLIMB	(55-17) = 38 NM

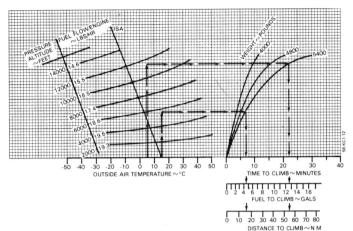

12. Refer to the Time-Fuel-Distance to Climb Graph (above). Determine the time, fuel, and distance required to climb from a pressure altitude of 5,200 feet to a pressure altitude of 13,000 feet. Assume that the temperature is standard, and the initial aircraft climb weight is 4,800 pounds.

  1. 16 minutes, 8.5 gallons, and 40 nautical miles.

  2. 20 minutes, 11.5 gallons, and 50 nautical miles.

  3. 24 minutes, 14.5 gallons, and 60 nautical miles.

  4. 16 minutes, 11.5 gallons, and 60 nautical miles.

13. An aircraft with an IAS of 185 KTS is flying at a pressure altitude of 11,000 feet, where the outside air temperature is +10°C. What is the TAS?

  1. 274 knots.

  2. 225 knots.

  3. 196 knots.

  4. 217 knots.

14. Refer to the Pressure Altitude Chart (right). Find the pressure altitude of an airport that has a field elevation of 2,500 feet MSL and an altimeter setting of 30.30'' Hg.

  1. 2,530 feet.

  2. 2,850 feet.

  3. 2,150 feet.

  4. 2,500 feet.

Altimeter Setting in. Hg.	Altitude Addition For Obtaining Pressure Altitude
28.3...	1,535
28.4...	1,435
28.5...	1,340
28.6...	1,245
28.7...	1,150
28.8...	1,050
28.9...	955
29.0...	865
29.1...	770
29.2...	675
29.3...	580
29.4...	485
29.5...	390
29.6...	300
29.7...	205
29.8...	110
29.9...	20
29.92...	0
30.0...	..........-75
30.1...	.........-165
30.2...	.........-255
30.3...	.........-350
30.4...	.........-440
30.5...	.........-530
30.6...	.........-620
30.7...	.........-710
30.8...	.........-805

15. Refer to the Climb-Two Engine Graph (below, top). Find the rate of climb for an aircraft at a pressure altitude of 7,500 feet, a temperature of 20°C, and a gross weight of 4,400 pounds.

1. 1,600 feet per minute.
2. 900 feet per minute.
3. 1,400 feet per minute.
4. 850 feet per minute.

16. Using the Landing Distance Graph (below, bottom), find the landing distance *over a 50-foot obstacle*, assuming: a pressure altitude of 1,100 feet, outside air temperature of 5°C, gross weight of 4,000 pounds, and no wind.

1. 1,800 feet.
2. 1,650 feet.
3. 1,400 feet.
4. 2,500 feet.

CLIMB - TWO ENGINE

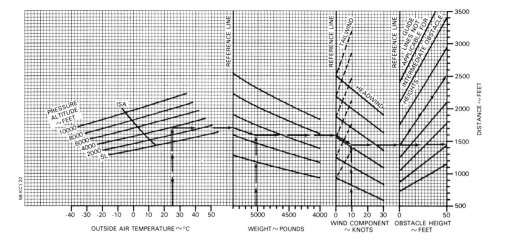

CLIMB SPEED 104 KNOTS (ALL WEIGHTS)

ASSOCIATED CONDITIONS:

POWER	MAXIMUM CONTINUOUS
FLAPS	UP
LANDING GEAR	UP
COWL FLAPS	OPEN
MIXTURE	LEAN TO APPROPRIATE FUEL FLOW

EXAMPLE

OAT	15°C
PRESSURE ALTITUDE	11500 FEET
WEIGHT	5352 LBS
RATE OF CLIMB	550 FPM
CLIMB GRADIENT	4%

LANDING DISTANCE

ASSOCIATED CONDITIONS:

POWER	RETARDED TO MAINTAIN 800 FT/MIN ON FINAL APPROACH
FLAPS	DOWN
LANDING GEAR	DOWN
APPROACH SPEED	IAS AS TABULATED
BRAKING	MAXIMUM
RUNWAY	PAVED, LEVEL, DRY SURFACE

WEIGHT ~ POUNDS	SPEED AT 50 FT KNOTS
5400	96
5000	91
4600	87
4000	81

EXAMPLE

OAT	25°C
PRESSURE ALTITUDE	3965 FT
WEIGHT	5039 LBS
WIND COMPONENT	9.5 KTS
GROUND ROLL	1450 FT
TOTAL OVER 50 FT OBSTACLE	2500 FT
APPROACH SPEED	91 KTS

TIME, FUEL AND DISTANCE TO DESCEND

ASSOCIATED CONDITIONS:

POWER	AS REQUIRED TO MAINTAIN 500 FT/MIN RATE-OF-DESCENT
LANDING GEAR	UP
FLAPS	UP

EXAMPLE:

INITIAL ALTITUDE	11500 FT
FINAL ALTITUDE	3965 FT
TIME TO DESCEND	(23-8) = 15 MIN
FUEL TO DESCEND	(9.7-3.3) = 6.4 GAL
DISTANCE TO DESCEND	(72-25) = 47 NM

DESCENT SPEED
175 KNOTS

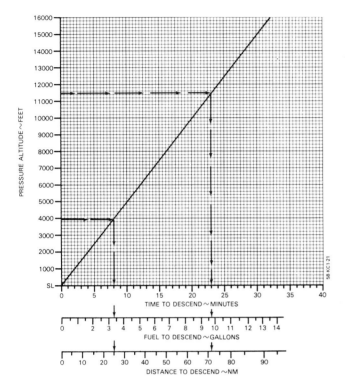

17. Refer to the Time Fuel Distance to Descend Graph (left). Find the time and distance to descend given the initial descent pressure altitude of 13,000 feet and the final leveling off pressure altitude of 2,500 feet.

1. 23 minutes and 72 nautical miles.
2. 26 minutes and 80 nautical miles.
3. 23 minutes and 80 nautical miles.
4. 21 minutes and 64 nautical miles.

18. Using the Takeoff Distance Graph (below), find the ground roll and the total distance required to fly over a 50-foot obstacle if the pressure altitude is 3,000 feet, outside air temperature is 10°C, takeoff weight is 5,000 pounds, and the headwind is 20 knots.

1. 1,520 feet ground roll and 2,300 feet over a 50-foot obstacle.
2. 1,650 feet ground roll and 2,500 feet over a 50-foot obstacle.
3. 1,420 feet ground roll and 1,420 feet over a 50-foot obstacle.
4. 1,320 feet ground roll and 2,100 feet over a 50-foot obstacle.

TAKE-OFF DISTANCE

ASSOCIATED CONDITION

POWER	TAKE-OFF POWER
MIXTURE	LEAN TO APPROPRIATE FUEL FLOW
FLAPS	UP
LANDING GEAR	RETRACT AFTER POSITIVE CLIMB ESTABLISHED
COWL FLAPS	OPEN

TAKE-OFF SPEEDS (ALL WEIGHTS)
LIFT-OFF 86 KNOTS
50 FEET 94 KNOTS

EXAMPLE

OAT	15°C (59°F)
PRESSURE ALTITUDE	5650 FEET
TAKE-OFF WEIGHT	5400 LBS
HEAD WIND COMPONENT	9.5 KNOTS
GROUND ROLL	1900 FEET
TOTAL DISTANCE OVER 50 FT OBSTACLE	3090 FEET
TAKE-OFF SPEED AT LIFT-OFF	86 KTS
50 FT	94 KTS

58 KC1 7

6.

Preflight Regulations

6.1 This chapter reviews those regulations that an instrument pilot should be aware of during preflight planning. Also included in this chapter are many regulations that all private and commercial pilots should be familiar with. Since most regulations are quite lengthy in their entirety, some of the superfluous (for the purpose of this text) elements of these regulations have been edited to make the regulations more clear. Naturally, as in any textbook, some portions of this book may become obsolete with time. Consequently, all serious pilots must obtain current copies of the appropriate regulations from the Superintendant of Documents, Government Printing Office Bookstore or any other outlet where the most recent issue of the Federal Aviation Regulations can be purchased. It is recommended that the appropriate current regulations be studied as the regulations in this chapter and other chapters are being reviewed.

PILOT REQUIREMENTS

Preflight Action (FAR 91.5 a,b)

6.2 The following regulations (edited) apply to preflight action:

Each pilot in command shall, before beginning a flight, familiarize himself with all available information concerning that flight. This information must include:
(a) For a flight under IFR or a flight not in the vicinity of an airport, weather reports and forecasts, fuel requirements, alternatives available if the planned flight cannot be completed, and any known traffic delays of which he has been advised by Air Traffic Control (ATC).

(b) For any flight, runway lengths at airports of intended use, and the available aircraft takeoff and landing distance information.

Pilot Certificates and Ratings (FAR 61.5 a,b)

6.3 Many pilots (students through professionals) are often confused while reading regulations containing the words certificate, rating, class, category, and type. The following edited excerpt from FAR 61.5 should eliminate any confusion completely:

(a) The following *certificates* are issued under FAR Part 61:
  (1) Pilot certificates:
    Student pilot.
    Private pilot.
    Commercial pilot.
    Airline transport pilot.
  (2) Flight instructor certificates.
(b) The following *ratings* are placed on pilot certificates (other than student pilot) where applicable:
  (1) Aircraft *category* ratings:
    Airplane.
    Rotorcraft.
    Glider.
    Lighter-than-air.
  (2) Airplane *class* ratings:
    Single-engine land.
    Multiengine land.
    Single-engine sea.
    Multiengine sea.
  (5) Aircraft *type* ratings include:
    Large aircraft (maximum certificated gross weight of *more* than 12,500 pounds), other than lighter-than-air.

Small turbojet-powered airplanes.
Small helicopters for operations requiring an airline transport pilot certificate.
Other aircraft type ratings specified by the Administrator through aircraft type certificate procedures.

(6) Instrument *ratings* (on private and commercial pilot certificates only):
Instrument—airplanes.
Instrument—helicopter.

Pilot Certification (FAR 61.3 a,c,e)

6.4 The following edited regulation is a general summation of necessary pilot certification for the instrument pilot:

(a) *Pilot Certificate.* No person may act as pilot in command or in any other capacity as a required pilot flight crewmember of a civil aircraft of United States registry unless he has in his personal possession a current pilot certificate issued to him.

(c) *Medical Certificate.* No person may act as pilot in command or in any other capacity as a required pilot flight crewmember of an aircraft under a certificate issued to him, unless he has in his personal possession an appropriate current medical certificate.

(e) *Instrument Rating.* No person may act as pilot in command of a civil aircraft under instrument flight rules, or in weather conditions less than the minimums prescribed for VFR flight unless, in the case of an airplane, he holds a minimum of an instrument rating.

Medical Requirements (FAR 61.23)

6.5 Pilots are often confused about the duration of their medical certificates. It can often be a confusing situation when a pilot engages in more than one type of flying operation. The following regulations and examples will provide the necessary information to satisfy any questions concerning the duration of medical certificates:

Duration of Medical Certificates:

(a) A first-class medical certificate expires at the end of the last day of:

(1) The 6th month after the month of the date of examination shown on the certificate, for operations requiring an airline transport pilot certificate;

(2) The 12th month after the month of the date of examination shown on the certificate, for operations requiring only a commercial pilot certificate; *and*

(3) The 24th month after the month of the date of examination shown on the certificate, for operations requiring only a private or student pilot certificate.

(b) A second-class medical certificate expires at the end of the last day of:

(1) The 12th month after the month of the date of examination shown on the certificate, for operations requiring a commercial pilot certificate; and

(2) The 24th month after the month of the date of examination shown on the certificate, for operations requiring only a private or student pilot certificate.

(c) A third-class medical certificate expires at the end of the last day of the 24th month after the month of the date of examination shown on the certificate, for operations requiring a private or student pilot certificate.

6.6 A consolidated chart (Figure 6-1) indicates the class of medical certificate needed for the appropriate type of flying activity that a pilot may be planning. Examples of expired dates on medical certificates are listed as follows: A first-class medical certificate issued on July 8, 1979, will expire midnight January 31, 1980, but if used as a second-class medical certificate, it will expire midnight July 31, 1980, and if used as a third-class medical certificate, it will expire midnight July 31, 1981. A second-class medical certificate issued on July 8, 1979, will expire on July 31, 1980, but if the medical certificate is used as a third-class certificate, it will expire on July 31, 1981. A third-class medical certificate issued on July 8, 1979, will expire on July 31, 1981.

6.7 *Special Note: A pilot, holding a private pilot certificate or commercial pilot certificate, may have an instrument rating endorsement on that certificate. The class of medical certificate required, however, is based upon the type of flying activity (private or commercial operations) and not the type of certification rating held. For example: A pilot holding a commercial pilot certificate with an instrument rating needs only a third-class medical certificate to conduct an IFR pleasure flight.*

CERTIFICATE	CLASS	OPERATION	DURATION
ATP	I	Air Carrier	6 Months
	I	Commercial	12 Months
	I	Private	24 Months
Commercial	II	Commercial	12 Months
	II	Private	24 Months
Private	III	Private	24 Months

Figure 6-1. Table of the Medical Certificate Duration Based on the Type of Flying Activity

Recent Flight Experience: Pilot in Command (FAR 61.57)

6.8 Today more than ever before, pilots are faced with the responsibility of complying with a seemingly endless number of regulations concerning recent flight experience requirements. However, the regulations are not as complicated as they may seem upon initial survey. The following regulations (edited) explain in detail the recent flight experience requirements for an instrument pilot:

(a) *Flight Review.* (Often called Biennial Flight Review.) After November 1, 1974, no person may act as pilot in command of an aircraft unless, within the preceding 24 months, he has:

(1) Accomplished a flight review given to him, in an aircraft for which he is rated, by an appropriately certificated instructor or other person designated by the Administrator; and

(2) Had his logbook endorsed by the person who gave him the review certifying that he has satisfactorily accomplished the flight review.

However, a person who has, within the preceding 24 months, satisfactorily completed a pilot proficiency check conducted by the FAA, an approved pilot check airman or a U.S. Armed Force for a pilot certificate, rating or operating privilege, need not accomplish the flight review required by this section.

(b) *Meaning of Flight Review.* As used in this section, a flight review consists of:

(1) A review of the current general operating and flight rules of FAR Part 91; and

(2) A review of those maneuvers and procedures which in the discretion of the person giving the review are necessary for the pilot to demonstrate that he can safely exercise the privileges of his pilot certificate.

(c) *General Experience.* No person may act as pilot in command of an aircraft carrying passengers, nor of an aircraft certificated for more than one required pilot flight crewmember, unless within the preceding 90 days, he has made three takeoffs and three landings as the sole manipulator of the flight controls in an aircraft of the same *category* and *class* and, if a type rating is required, of the same *type*. If the aircraft is a tailwheel airplane, the landings must have been made to a full stop in a tailwheel airplane. For the purpose of meeting the requirements of the paragraph a person may act as pilot-in-command of a flight under day VFR or day IFR if no persons or property other than as necessary for his compliance thereunder, are carried. This paragraph does not apply to operations requiring an airline transport pilot certificate, or to operations conducted under FAR Part 135.

(d) *Night Experience.* No private or commercial pilot may act as pilot in command of an aircraft carrying passengers during the period beginning 1 hour *after* sunset and ending 1 hour *before* sunrise (as published in the American Air Almanac) unless, within the preceding 90 days, he has made at least 3 takeoffs and 3 landings to a full stop during that period in the *category* and *class* of aircraft to be used.

(e) *Instrument.*

(1) *Recent IFR Experience.* No pilot, of an airplane, may act as pilot in command under IFR, nor in weather conditions less than the minimums prescribed for VFR, unless he has, within the past 6 months:

Logged at least 6 hours of instrument time under actual or simulated IFR conditions, at least 3 of which were in flight in the category of aircraft involved, including at least 6 instrument approaches, or passed an instrument competency check in the category of aircraft involved.

(2) *Instrument Competency Check.* A pilot who does not meet the recent instrument experience requirements of the preceding paragraph during the prescribed time or 6 months thereafter may not serve as pilot in command under IFR, nor in weather conditions less than the minimums prescribed for VFR, until he passes an instrument competency check in the category of aircraft involved, given by an FAA inspector, a member of an Armed Force of the United States authorized to conduct flight tests, an FAA-approved check pilot, or a certificated instrument flight instructor. The Administrator may authorize the conduct of part or all of this check in a pilot ground trainer equipped for instruments or an aircraft simulator.

6.9 *Special Note: Remember, 3 hours of instrument flight (hood or actual) of the 6 required hours, must be in the category of aircraft involved. The remaining 3 hours of instrument time could be completed in a rotorcraft, glider, airship, or an instrument ground trainer. The 6 instrument approaches could be accomplished in either an aircraft or simulator.*

Flight Time (FAR Part 1.1)

6.10 Flight time is defined as that time from the moment the aircraft first moves under its own power for the purpose of flight until it comes to rest at the next point of landing (commonly referred to as "block-to-block" time).

Pilot Logbooks (FAR 61.51 a,c)

6.11 According to FAR 61.51 a, a pilot must record all aeronautical training and experience used to meet the requirements for a certificate, rating, or recent flight experience. The logging of other flight time is not required. FAR 61.51 c (edited) states that:

Pilot-In-Command Flight Time. A private or commercial pilot may log as pilot-in-command time only that flight time during which he is the sole manipulator of the controls of an aircraft for which he is rated, or when he is the sole occupant of the aircraft, or when he acts as pilot in command of an aircraft requiring more than one pilot.

Instrument Flight Time. A pilot may log as instrument flight time only that time during which he operates the aircraft solely by reference to instruments, under actual or simulated instrument flight conditions.

> **Example:** A pilot initiated the aircraft taxi at 1212, departed 1220, entered the clouds at 1308, flew out of the clouds at 1420, landed at 1550, and came to rest at 1600. The pilot-in-command time that would be logged would be 3.8 hours, and the logged instrument time would be 1.2 hours.

Flight Instruction; Simulated Instrument Flight (FAR 91.21 a, b)

6.12 There is often some confusion regarding the use of a functioning throwover control wheel and who may act as a safety pilot during simulated instrument flight. The following regulation and example should clarify both points:

(a) No person may operate a civil aircraft (except a manned free balloon) that is being used for flight instruction unless that aircraft has fully functioning, dual controls. However, instrument flight instruction may be given in a single-engine airplane equipped with a single, functioning throwover control wheel, in place of fixed, dual controls of the elevator and ailerons, when:

    (1) The instructor has determined that the flight can be conducted safely; and

    (2) The person manipulating the controls has at least a private pilot certificate with appropriate category and class ratings.

(b) No person may operate a civil aircraft in simulated instrument flight unless:

    (1) An appropriately rated pilot occupies the other control seat as a safety pilot;

    (2) The safety pilot has adequate vision forward and to each side of the aircraft, or a competent observer in the aircraft adequately supplements the vision of the safety pilot; and

    (3) Except in the case of lighter-than-air aircraft, that aircraft is equipped with fully functioning dual controls. However, simulated instrument flight may be conducted in a single-engine airplane, equipped with a single, functioning, throwover control wheel, in place of fixed, dual controls of the elevator and ailerons, when:

    (i) The safety pilot has determined that the flight can be conducted safely; and

    (ii) The person manipulating the control has at least a private pilot certificate with appropriate category and class ratings.

Example: A safety pilot in a multiengine aircraft is required to have a multiengine rating on his pilot certificate.

General Limitations (FAR 61.31 c,d,e)

6.13 Although FAR 61.31 c,d,e is nothing more than a review for any pilot, it is incorporated into this text (edited) for the purpose of insuring an adequate understanding of regulations concerning general limitations for pilots.

(c) *Category and Class Rating: Carrying Another Person or Operating for Compensation or Hire.* Unless he holds a category and class rating for that aircraft, a person may not act as pilot in command of an aircraft that is carrying another person or is operated for compensation or hire. In addition, he may not act as pilot in command of that aircraft for compensation or hire.

(d) *Category and Class Rating: Other Operations.* No person may act as pilot in command of an aircraft in solo flight in operations not subject to the previous paragraph, unless he meets at least one of the following:

    (1) He holds a category and class rating appropriate to that aircraft.

    (2) He has received flight instruction in the pilot operations required by this part, appropriate to the category and class of aircraft for first solo, given to him by a certificated flight instructor who found him competent to solo that category and class of aircraft and has so endorsed his logbook.

    (3) He has soloed and logged pilot-in-command time in that category and class of aircraft before November 1, 1973.

(e) *High Performance Airplanes.* A person holding a private or commercial pilot certificate may not act as pilot in command of an airplane that has more than 200 horsepower, or that has a retractable landing gear, flaps, and a controllable propeller, unless he has received flight instruction from an authorized flight instructor who has certified in his logbook that he is competent to pilot an airplane that has more than 200 horsepower, or that has a retractable landing gear, flaps, and a controllable propeller, as the case may be. However, this instruction is not required if he has logged flight time as pilot in command in high performance airplanes before November 1, 1973.

AIRCRAFT REQUIREMENTS

Responsibility of Maintenance (FAR 91.163 a, 91.165)

6.14 The owner or operator of an aircraft is primarily responsible, according to FAR 91.163a, for maintaining that aircraft in an airworthy condition. In addition, as stated in FAR 91.165, the owner or operator shall ensure that maintenance personnel make appropriate entries in the aircraft and maintenance records indicating the aircraft has been released to service.

Inspections (FAR 91.169)

6.15 All pilots should be familiar with annual 100-hour and progressive inspection requirements. Thus the following regulation (edited) is incorporated into this text to avoid confusion regarding aircraft inspection:

(a) Except as provided in paragraph (c) of this section, no person may operate an aircraft unless, within the preceding 12 calendar months, it has had:
  (1) An annual inspection and has been approved for return to service; or
  (2) An inspection for the issue of an airworthiness certificate.
No inspection performed under paragraph (b) of this section may be substituted for any inspection required by this paragraph unless it is performed by a person authorized to perform annual inspections, and is entered as an ''annual'' inspection in the required maintenance records.
(b) Except as provided in paragraph (c) of this section, no person may operate an aircraft carrying any person (other than a crewmember) for hire, and no person may give flight instructions for hire in an aircraft which that person provides, unless within the preceding 100 hours of time in service it has received an annual or 100-hour inspection and been approved for return to service, or received an inspection for the issuance of an airworthiness certificate. The 100-hour limitation may be exceeded by not more than 10 hours if necessary to reach a place at which the inspection can be done. The excess time, however, is included in computing the next 100 hours of time in service.

(c) Paragraphs (a) and (b) of this section do not apply to:
  (1) Any aircraft for which its registered owner or operator complies with the progressive inspection requirements; or
  (2) An aircraft that carries a special flight permit or a current experimental or provisional certificate.

Civil Aircraft: Certifications Required (FAR 91.27a,b)

6.16 Although the following regulation (edited) should already be common knowledge to all general aviation pilots, it is included in this text as a review to the instrument rating applicant.

(a) Except as provided for special flight authorizations, no person may operate a civil aircraft unless it has within it the following:
  (1) An appropriate and current airworthiness certificate.
  (2) A registration certificate issued to its owner.
(b) No person may operate a civil aircraft unless the airworthiness certificate or special flight authorization is displayed at the cabin or cockpit entrance so that it is legible to passengers or crew.

Civil Aircraft Airworthiness (FAR 91.29)

6.17 Like the preceding regulation the following regulation concerning airworthiness serves as an additional regulation review.

(a) No person may operate a civil aircraft unless it is in an airworthy condition.
(b) The pilot in command of a civil aircraft is responsible for determining whether that aircraft is in condition for safe flight. He shall discontinue the flight when unairworthy mechanical or structural conditions occur.

Civil Aircraft Operating Limitation and Marking Requirements (FAR 91.31 b)

6.18 The following is an edited excerpt of FAR 91.31:

(b) No person may operate a U.S. registered civil aircraft unless there is available in the aircraft a current Airplane Flight Manual, approved manual material, markings, and placards, or any combination thereof, containing each operating limitation prescribed for that aircraft, including the following:
  (1) Powerplant (e.g., r.p.m., manifold pressure, gas temperature, etc.).
  (2) Airspeeds (e.g., normal operating speed,

flaps extended speed, etc.).

(3) Aircraft weight, center of gravity, and weight distribution, including the composition of the useful load in those combinations and ranges intended to insure that the weight and center of gravity position will remain within approved limits (e.g., combinations and ranges of crew, oil, fuel, and baggage).

(4) Minimum flight crew.

(5) Kinds of operation.

(6) Maximum operating altitude.

(7) Maneuvering flight load factors.

6.19 *Special Notes:*

1. Normal, utility, acrobatic, and transport are categories of standard airworthiness certificates that are issued for new aircraft. Normally, a new aircraft is issued a standard airworthiness certificate. However, another airworthiness certificate may have to be issued if the aircraft is damaged to the extent that it requires major repair.

2. Restricted, experimental, limited, and provisional airworthiness certificates are special airworthiness certificates that are issued for specific purposes. Special flight permits (*FAR 21.197) may also be issued for aircraft that are capable of safe flight, but may not meet applicable airworthiness standards. For example, a special flight permit may be substituted for the standard airworthiness certificate in order that an aircraft with an expired annual inspection may be flown to a location where the airplane can have an annual inspection performed.

Instrument and Equipment Requirements (FAR 91.33 a,b,c,d,e)

6.20 When studying FAR 91.33 instrument pilots should be fully aware that the instrument and equipment requirements for VFR flight for daytime and nighttime operations are also part of the instrument and equipment requirements for IFR flight operations. The following is an edited excerpt of this regulation:

(a) *General.* Except as provided in paragraphs (c) (3) and (e) of this section, no person may operate a powered civil aircraft with a standard category U.S. airworthiness certificate in any operation described in paragraphs (b) through (e) of this section unless that aircraft contains the instruments and equipment specified in those paragraphs (or FAA-approved equivalents) for that type of operation, and those instruments and items of equipment are in operable condition.

(b) *Visual flight rules (day).* For VFR flight during the day the following instruments and equipment are required:

(1) Airspeed indicator.

(2) Altimeter.

(3) Magnetic direction indicator.

(4) Tachometer for each engine.

(5) Oil pressure gauge for each engine using pressure system.

(6) Temperature gauge for each liquid-cooled engine.

(7) Oil temperature gauge for each air-cooled engine.

(8) Manifold pressure gauge for each altitude engine.

(9) Fuel gauge indicating the quantity of fuel in each tank.

(10) Landing gear position indicator, if the aircraft has a retractable landing gear.

(11) If the aircraft is operated for hire over water and beyond power-off gliding distance from shore, approved flotation gear readily available to each occupant, and at least one pyrotechnic signaling device.

(12) Approved safety belts for all occupants who have reached their second birthday.

(13) For small civil airplanes manufactured after July 18, 1978, an approved shoulder harness for each front seat. The shoulder harness must be designed to protect the occupant from serious head injury when the occupant experiences substantial inertia forces. Each shoulder harness installed at a flight crewmember station must permit the crewmember, when seated and with his safety belt and shoulder harness fastened, to perform all functions necessary for flight operations.

(c) *Visual flight rules (night).* For VFR flight at night the following instruments and equipment are required:

(1) Instruments and equipment specified for visual flight rules (day) of this section.

(2) Approved position lights.

(3) An approved aviation red or aviation white anti-collision light system on all U.S. registered civil aircraft. In the event of failure of any light of the anti-collision light system, operations with the aircraft may be continued to a stop where repairs or replacement can be made.

(4) If the aircraft is operated for hire, one electric landing light.

(5) An adequate source of electrical energy for all installed electric and radio equipment.

(6) One spare set of fuses, or 3 spare fuses of each kind required.

(d) *Instrument flight rules.* For IFR flight the following instruments and equipment are required:

(1) Instruments and equipment specified for

visual flight rules (day and night).

(2) Two-way radio communications system and navigational equipment appropriate to the ground facilities to be used.

(3) Gyroscopic rate-of-turn indicator.

(4) Slip-skid indicator.

(5) Sensitive altimeter adjustable for barometric pressure.

(6) A clock displaying hours, minutes, and seconds with a sweep-second pointer or digital presentation.

(7) Generator of adequate capacity.

(8) Gyroscopic bank and pitch indicator (artificial horizon).

(9) Gyroscopic direction indicator (directional gyro or equivalent).

(e) *Flight at and above 24,000 feet MSL.* If VOR Navigational equipment is required, no person may operate a U.S. registered civil aircraft within the 50 states, and the District of Columbia, at or above 24,000 feet MSL unless that aircraft is equipped with approved distance measuring equipment (DME). When DME required by this paragraph fails at and above 24,000 feet MSL, the pilot in command of the aircraft shall notify ATC immediately, and may then continue operations at and above 24,000 feet MSL to the next airport of intended landing at which repairs or replacement of the equipment can be made.

Aircraft Lights (FAR 91.73 a,b,d)

6.21 The following is an excerpt of FAR 91.73:

No person may, during a period from *sunset* to *sunrise* (or, in Alaska, during the period a prominent unlighted object cannot be seen from a distance of 3 statute miles or the sun is more than 6 degrees below the horizon):

(a) Operate an aircraft unless it has lighted position lights;

(b) Park or move an aircraft in, or in dangerous proximity to, a night flight operations area of an airport unless the aircraft:

(1) Is clearly illuminated;

(2) Has lighted position lights; or

(3) Is in an area which is marked by obstruction lights.

(d) Operate an aircraft, required to be equipped with an anticollision light system, unless it has approved and lighted aviation red or aviation white anticollision lights. However, the anticollision lights need not be lighted when the pilot in command determines that, because of operating conditions, it would be in the interest of safety to turn the lights off.

Altimeter System Tests and Inspections (FAR 91.170 a,c)

6.22 FAR 91.170 a,c should not be considered just another regulation but should be considered sound advice for the instrument pilot. The following is an edited excerpt:

(a) No person may operate an airplane in controlled airspace under IFR unless, within the preceding 24 calendar months, each static pressure system and each altimeter instrument has been tested and inspected and found to comply with specified standards. The static pressure system and altimeter instrument tests and inspections may be conducted by:

(1) The manufacturer of the airplane on which the tests and inspections are to be performed;

(2) A certificated repair station properly equipped to perform these functions; or

(3) A certificated mechanic with an airframe rating (static pressure system tests and inspections only).

(c) No person may operate an airplane in controlled airspace under IFR at an altitude above the maximum altitude to which an altimeter of that airplane has been tested.

Emergency Locator Transmitter (ELT) (FAR 91.52 a,b,d,e,f)

6.23 After reviewing FAR 91.52, almost all general aviation instrument pilots find themselves in the category of being required to have an ELT attached to their aircraft. However, occasionally there are situations that prove to be exceptions to the rule, so it would be prudent to review this regulation (edited):

(a,b) No person may operate a U.S. registered civil airplane unless there is attached to the airplane an automatic type emergency locator transmitter that is in operable condition and meets the applicable FAR requirements.

(d) Batteries used in the emergency locator transmitters required by paragraphs (a) and (b) of this section must be replaced (or recharged, if the battery is rechargeable):

(1) When the transmitter has been in use for more than one cumulative hour; or

(2) When 50 percent of their useful life (or for rechargeable batteries, 50 percent of their useful life of charge), as established by the transmitter manufacturer, has expired.

(e) Notwithstanding paragraphs (a) and (b) of this section, a person may:

(1) Ferry a newly acquired airplane from the place where possession of it was taken to a

place where the emergency locator transmitter is to be installed; and

(2) Ferry an airplane with an inoperative emergency locator transmitter from a place where repairs or replacement cannot be made to a place where they can be made.

(f) However, the following aircraft are not required to have an ELT aboard in flight:

(1) Turbojet-powered aircraft;

(2) Aircraft while engaged in scheduled flights by scheduled air carriers certificated by the Civil Aeronautics Board;

(3) Aircraft while engaged in training operations conducted entirely within a 50-mile radius of the airport from which such local flight operations began;

(4) Aircraft while engaged in flight operations incident to design and testing;

(5) New aircraft while engaged in flight operations incident to their manufacture, preparation, and delivery;

(6) Aircraft while engaged in flight operations incident to the aerial application of chemicals and other substances for agricultural purposes;

(7) Aircraft certificated by the Administrator for research and development purposes;

(8) Aircraft while used for showing compliance with regulations, crew training, exhibition, air racing, or market surveys; and

(9) Aircraft equipped to carry not more than one person.

(10) An aircraft during any period for which the transmitter has been temporarily removed for inspection, repair, modification or replacement, subject to the following:

(i) No person may operate the aircraft unless the aircraft records contain an entry which includes the date of initial removal, the make, model, serial number and reason for removal of the transmitter, and a placard is located in view of the pilot to show ''ELT not installed.''

(ii) No person may operate the aircraft more than 90 days after the ELT is initially removed from the aircraft.

VOR Equipment Check for IFR Operations (FAR 91.25)

6.24 Not only is a VOR equipment check a safe practice for the instrument pilot, but the equipment check is also a good operating practice for the VFR pilot. Since there are different methods of checking VOR equipment and different limits of the permissible indicated bearing error, this regulation (edited) must be reviewed until a thorough understanding is attained.

(a) No person may operate a civil aircraft under IFR using the VOR system of radio navigation unless the VOR equipment of that aircraft:

(1) Is maintained, checked, and inspected under an approved procedure; or

(2) Has been operationally checked within the preceding 30 days, and was found to be within the limits of the permissible indicated bearing error set forth in paragraph (b) or (c) of this section.

(b) Except as provided in paragraph (c) of this section, each person conducting a VOR check under paragraph (a) (2) of this section shall:

(1) Use, at the airport of intended departure, an FAA operated or approved test signal (*VOT*) or a test signal radiated by a certificated and appropriately rated radio repair station or, outside the United States, a test signal operated or approved by appropriate authority, to check the VOR equipment (the maximum permissible indicated bearing error is plus or minus 4 degrees);

(2) If a test signal is not available at the airport of intended departure, use a point on an airport surface designated as a VOR system checkpoint by the Administrator or, outside the United States, by appropriate authority (the maximum permissible bearing error is plus or minus 4 degrees);

(3) If neither a test signal nor a designated checkpoint on the surface is available, use an airborne checkpoint designated by the Administrator or, outside the United States, by appropriate authority (the maximum permissible bearing error is plus or minus 6 degrees); or

(4) If no check signal or point is available, while in flight:

(i) Select a VOR radial that lies along the centerline of an established VOR airway;

(ii) Select a prominent ground point along the selected radial preferably more than 20 miles from the VOR ground facility and maneuver the aircraft directly over the point at a reasonably low altitude; and

(iii) Note the VOR bearing indicated by the receiver when over the ground point (the maximum permissible variation between the published radial and the indicated bearing is 6 degrees).

(c) If dual system VOR (units independent of each other except for the antenna) is installed in the aircraft, the person checking the equipment may check one system against the other in place of the check procedures specified in paragraph (b) of this section. He shall tune both systems to the same VOR ground facility and note the indicated bearings to that station. The maximum permissible variation between the two indicated bearings is 4 degrees. (Figure 6-2)

(d) Each person making the VOR operational check as specified in paragraph (b) or (c) of this section shall enter the date, place, bearing error, and sign the aircraft log or other record. In addition, if a test signal radiated by a repair station, as specified in paragraph (b) (1) of this section, is used, an entry must be made in the aircraft log or other record by the repair station certificate holder or the certificate holder's representative certifying to the bearing transmitted by the repair station for the check and the date of transmission.

6.25 *Special Note: Figure 6-3 illustrates a typical VOR operational check log. Note that there is no special provision on this log for the recording of Tach time since FAR 91.25 specifies that the VOR equipment must be operationally checked only within the preceding 30 days.*

ATC Transponder Equipment (FAR 91.24 b,c)

6.26 The following regulation (edited) provides a condensed view of airspace transponder requirements and authorized deviations:

(b) *Controlled airspace: all aircraft.* No person may operate an airplane in controlled airspace unless that aircraft is equipped with an operable coded radar beacon transponder having a Mode 3/A 4096 code capability, replying to Mode 3/A interrogation with the code specified by ATC, and is equipped with automatic pressure altitude reporting equipment having a Mode C capability that automatically replies to Mode C interrogations by transmitting pressure altitude information in 100-foot increments. This requirement applies:

In Group I Terminal Control Areas; and
In all controlled airspace of the 48 contiguous States and the District of Columbia, above 12,500 feet MSL, excluding the airspace at and below 2,500 feet AGL.

METHOD OF VOR CHECK	MAXIMUM PERMISSIBLE ERROR
TEST SIGNAL (VOT OR REPAIR STATION TEST SIGNAL)......	.......±4 DEGREES
DESIGNATED AIRPORT GROUND CHECKPOINT.................	.......±4 DEGREES
DUAL VOR RECEIVERS (ONE COMPARED TO THE OTHER).......	.......4 DEGREES
AIRBORNE CHECKPOINT (DESIGNATED OR PILOT-SELECTED)...	.......±6 DEGREES

Figure 6-2. Maximum Permissible VOR Receiver Bearing Error

DATE	LOCATION	BEARING ERROR REC. #1	BEARING ERROR REC. #2	REMARKS	SIGNATURE
5/10/78	OMAHA AIRBORNE 310° RADIAL	TO +3° / FROM +2°	TO 0° / FROM -1°	TACH 142.7	Edward D. Becker
5/20/78	BOSTON-LOGAN VOT	TO +2° / FROM +2°	TO -1° / FROM -1°	TACH 148.0	Edward D. Becker
5/23/78	OAKLAND GND 023° RADIAL	TO +3° / FROM +2°	TO 0° / FROM 0°	TACH 157.8	Edward D. Becker
		TO / FROM	TO / FROM		

Figure 6-3. A Typical VOR Operational Check Log

Group II Terminal Control Areas, however, only require an operable coded radar beacon transponder having a Mode 3/A 4096 code capability, replying to Mode 3/A interrogation with the code specified by ATC.

(c) *ATC authorized deviations.* ATC may authorize deviations from paragraph (b) of this section:

(1) Immediately, to allow an aircraft with an inoperative transponder to continue to the airport of ultimate destination, including any intermediate stops, or to proceed to a place where suitable repairs can be made, or both;

(2) Immediately, for operations of aircraft with an operating transponder but without operating automatic pressure altitude reporting equipment having a Mode C capability; and

(3) On a continuing basis, or, for individual flights, for operations of aircraft without a transponder, in which case the request for a deviation must be submitted to the ATC facility having jurisdiction over the airspace concerned at least four hours before the proposed operation.

ATC Transponder Tests and Inspections (FAR 91.177)

6.27 FAR 91.177 states that no person may use an ATC transponder that is specified in FAR 91.24, of this chapter, unless, within the preceding 24 calendar months, that ATC transponder has been tested and inspected and found to comply with specified standards. The tests and inspections may be conducted by: A certificated repair station properly equipped to perform those functions and holding an appropriate rating; or the manufacturer of the aircraft on which the transponder to be tested is installed, if the transponder was installed by that manufacturer.

Data Correspondence Between Automatically Reported Pressure Altitude Data and the Pilot's Altitude Reference (FAR 91.36 a,b,c)

6.28 The following regulation (edited) should be thoroughly reviewed since it concerns equipment that is playing an ever increasingly important role in today's air traffic system:

No person may operate any automatic pressure altitude reporting equipment associated with a radar beacon transponder:

(a) When deactivation of that equipment is directed by ATC;

(b) Unless, as installed, that equipment was tested and calibrated to transmit altitude data corresponding within 125 feet (on a 95-percent prob-

ability basis) of the indicated or calibrated datum of the altimeter normally used to maintain flight altitude, with that altimeter referenced to 29.92 inches of mercury for altitudes from sea level to the maximum operating altitude of the aircraft; or

(c) After September 1, 1979, unless the altimeters and digitizers in that equipment meet the standards in applicable technical standard orders.

TERMINAL CONTROL AREAS (TCA) (FAR 91.90 a,b)

6.29 Even though all private and commercial pilots should be intimately familiar with Terminal Control Area functions, a brief review of TCAs might aid in the understanding of FAR 91.90. A Terminal Control Area consists of controlled airspace extending upward from the surface or higher to specified altitudes. TCAs often resemble the shape of an upside-down wedding cake. Group I Terminal Control Areas are located at the nation's busiest airports. Consequently, it is necessary for reasons of safety to have rigid regulations concerning operating rules, pilot requirements, and equipment requirements for operations within these areas. Group II TCAs are located at less busy locations. Nevertheless, many operating rules, pilot requirements, and equipment requirements are still necessary, although not as demanding as those requirements for Group I TCAs. The following is the regulation (edited):

(a) *Group I Terminal Control Areas*

(1) *Operating rules.* No person may operate an aircraft within a Group I Terminal Control Area designated in Part 71* of this chapter except in compliance with the following rules:

(i) No person may operate an aircraft within a Group I Terminal Control Area unless he has received an appropriate authorization from ATC prior to the operation of that aircraft in that area.

(ii) Unless otherwise authorized by ATC, each person operating a large turbine engine powered airplane to or from a primary airport shall operate at or above the designated floors while within the lateral limits of the Terminal Control Area.

(2) *Pilot requirements.* The pilot in command of a civil aircraft may not land or take off that aircraft from an airport within a Group I Terminal Control Area unless he holds at least a private pilot certificate.

* Part 71 not included in this text.

		GROUP I TCA	GROUP II TCA
P I L O T	**R E Q U I R E M E N T S**	1. Minimum of a Private Pilot certificate in order to land or takeoff from an airport within the TCA.	1. No special pilot ratings required.
E Q U I P M E N T	**R E Q U I R E M E N T S**	1. Operable VOR or TACAN receiver. 2. Operable two-way radio capable of communication on the appropriate frequencies. 3. An operable 4096 code transponder with mode C altitude reporting cability.	1. Same. 2. Same. 3. A 4096 code transponder except for IFR flights operating to or from an airport outside of but in close proximity to the TCA when the commonly used transition, approach, or departure procedures to such airport require flight within the TCA.
O P E R A T I N G	**R U L E S**	1. ATC authorization required. 2. Maximum indicated airspeed below 10,000 feet MSL-250 knots. 3. Maximum indicated airspeed in airspace underlying a TCA, or in a VFR corridor designated through a TCA-200 knots. 4. Large turbine powered aircraft operating to or from a primary airport shall operate at or above the designated floors while within the lateral limits of the TCA.	1. Same. 2. Same. 3. Same. 4. Same.

S P E C I A L	**N O T E**	ATC MAY AUTHORIZE DEVIATIONS:
		    1. Immediately for an aircraft with an inoperative transponder.
		    2. Immediately for an aircraft with an operative transponder but without an operative encoding altimeter.
		    3. With four hours advance notice for operations of aircraft without a transponder.	

Figure 6-4. Table of the TCA Operating Rules and Pilot and Equipment Requirements

(3) *Equipment requirements.* Unless otherwise authorized by ATC in the case of in-flight VOR, TACAN, or two-way radio failure; or unless otherwise authorized by ATC in the case of a transponder failure occurring at any time, no person may operate an aircraft within a Group I Terminal Control Area unless that airplane is equipped with:

(i) An operable VOR or TACAN receiver;

(ii) An operable two-way radio capable of communicating with ATC on appropriate frequencies for that Terminal Control Area; and

(iii) An operable coded radar beacon transponder having a Mode 3/A 4096 code capability, replying to Mode 3/A interrogation with the code specified by ATC, and is equipped with automatic pressure altitude reporting equipment having Mode C capability.

(b) *Group II Terminal Control Areas*

(1) *Operating rules.* No person may operate an aircraft within a Group II Terminal Control Area designated in Part 71 of this chapter except in compliance with the following rules:

(i) No person may operate an aircraft within a Group II Terminal Control Area unless he has received an appropriate authorization from ATC prior to operation of that aircraft in that area, and unless two-way radio communications are maintained, within that area, between that aircraft and the ATC facility.

(ii) Unless otherwise authorized by ATC, each person operating a large turbine engine powered airplane to or from a primary airport shall operate at or above the designated floors while within the lateral limits of the Terminal Control Area.

(2) *Equipment requirements.* Unless otherwise authorized by ATC in the case of inflight VOR, TACAN, or two-way radio failure; or unless otherwise authorized by ATC in the case of a transponder failure occurring at any time, no person may operate an airplane within a Group II Terminal Control Area unless that aircraft is equipped with:

(i) An operable VOR or TACAN receiver;

(ii) An operable two-way radio capable of communicating with ATC on the appropriate frequencies for that Terminal Control Area; and

(iii) An operable coded radar beacon transponder having a Mode 3/A 4096 code capability. However, a transponder is not required for flights operating to or from an airport outside of but in close proximity to the Terminal Control Area, when the commonly used transition, approach, or departure procedure to such airports requires flight within the Terminal Control Area.

POSITIVE CONTROL AREAS (PCA) AND ROUTE SEGMENTS (FAR 91.97)

6.30 FAR 91.97 (edited) concerns aircraft operations within the defined limits of the Positive Control Area. The vertical extent of PCA is from 18,000 feet to and including Flight Level 600 throughout most of the conterminous United States and Alaska.

(a) Except as provided in paragraph (b) of this section, no person may operate an aircraft within a Positive Control Area, or positive control route segment designated in Part 71 of this chapter, unless that aircraft is:

(1) Operated under IFR at a specific flight level assigned by ATC;

(2) Equipped with instruments and equipment required for IFR operations;

(3) Flown by a pilot rated for instrument flight; and

(4) Equipped, when in a Positive Control Area, with:

(i) An operable coded radar beacon transponder, having at least a Mode 3/A 4096 code capability, replying to Mode 3/A interrogation with the code specified by ATC, and is equipped with automatic pressure altitude reporting equipment having a Mode C capability that automatically replies to Mode C interrogations by transmitting pressure altitude information in 100-foot increments.

(ii) A radio providing direct pilot/controller communication on the frequency specified by ATC for the area concerned.

(b) ATC may authorize deviations from the requirements of paragraph (a) of this section. In the case of an inoperative transponder, ATC may immediately approve an operation within a Positive Control Area allowing flight to continue, if desired, to the airport of ultimate destination, including any intermediate stops, or to proceed to a place where suitable repairs can be made, or both. A request for authorization to deviate from a requirement of paragraph (a) of this section, other than for operation with an inoperative transponder as outlined above, must be submitted at least 4 days before the proposed operation, in writing, to the ATC center having jurisdiction over the Positive Control Area concerned. ATC may authorize a deviation on a continuing basis or for an individual flight, as appropriate.

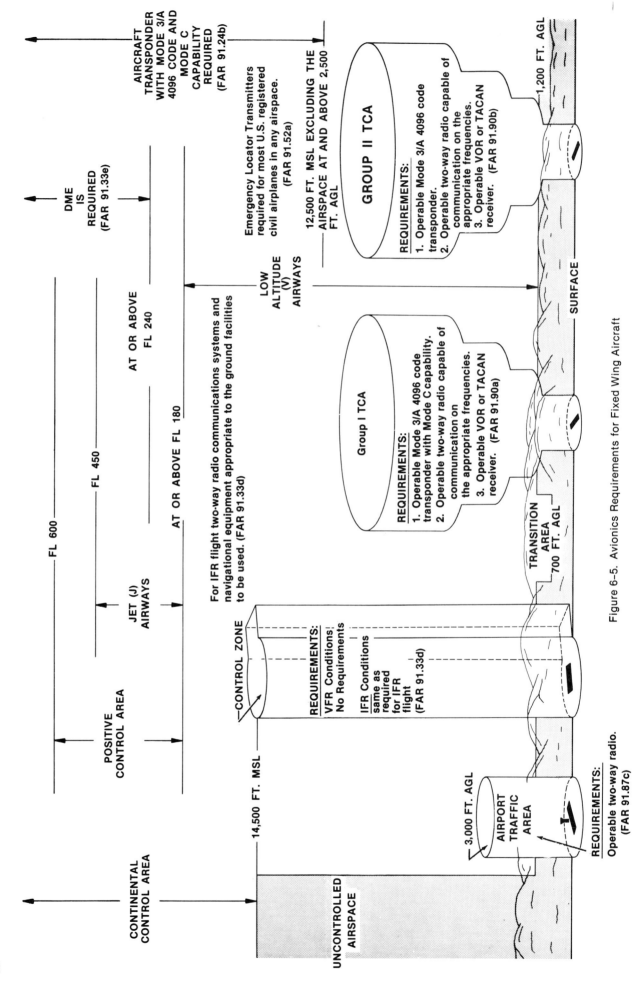

Figure 6-5. Avionics Requirements for Fixed Wing Aircraft

6.31 Figure 6-5 depicts avionics requirements for fixed wing aircraft. This chart should serve as an adequate tool for visualizing the avionics needs for a particular type of airspace. This illustration incorporates many elements of regulations previously discussed.

FUEL REQUIREMENTS FOR FLIGHT IN IFR CONDITIONS (FAR 91.23)

6.32 FAR 91.23 is of particular interest to the instrument pilot during the preflight planning process since fuel is such a critical factor. Pilots are reminded that this regulation specifies a *minimum* fuel requirement, and that it is often advantageous to carry more than the required minimum fuel.

(a) Except as provided in paragraph (b) of this section, no person may operate a civil aircraft in IFR conditions unless it carries enough fuel (considering weather reports and forecasts, and weather conditions) to:

(1) Complete the flight to the first airport of intended landing;

(2) Fly from that airport to the alternate airport; and

(3) Fly after that for 45 minutes at normal cruising speed.

(b) Paragraph (a)(2) of this section does not apply if:

(1) * Part 97 of this subchapter prescribes a standard instrument approach procedure for the first airport of intended landing; and

(2) For at least one hour before and one hour after the estimated time of arrival at the airport, the weather reports or forecasts or any combination of them, indicate:

(i) The ceiling will be at least 2,000 feet above the airport elevation; and

(ii) Visibility will be at least 3 miles.

FLIGHT PLAN; INFORMATION REQUIRED (FAR 91.83 b,c)

6.33 The similarities concerning time, ceiling, and visibility requirements should be noted between the previous and following regulation (edited) so possible future confusion can be avoided.

(b) An alternate airport for an IFR flight plan is not required if part 97 of this subchapter prescribes a standard instrument approach procedure for the first airport of intended landing and, for at least one hour before and one hour after the estimated time of arrival, the weather reports or forecasts or any combination of them, indicate:

(1) The ceiling will be at least 2,000 feet above the airport elevation; and

(2) Visibility will be at least 3 miles.

(c) *IFR alternate airport weather minimums.* Unless otherwise authorized by the Administrator, no person may include an alternate airport in an IFR flight plan unless current weather forecasts indicate that, at the estimated time of arrival at the alternate airport, the ceiling and visibility at the airport will be at or above the following alternate airport weather minimums:

(1) If an instrument approach procedure has been published in Part 97 of this chapter for that airport, the alternate airport minimums specified in that procedure or, if none are so specified, the following minimums:

(i) Precision approach procedure:
Ceiling 600 feet and visibility 2 statute miles.

(ii) Nonprecision approach procedure:
Ceiling 800 feet and visibility 2 statute miles.

(2) If no instrument approach procedure has been published in Part 97 of this chapter for that airport, the ceiling and visibility minimums are those allowing descent from the ** MEA, approach, and landing, under basic VFR.

SUPPLEMENTAL OXYGEN (FAR 91.32)

6.34 When reviewing the regulation governing oxygen requirements, it would be advantageous to inspect Figure 6–6 so that a more accurate interpretation of the regulation can be obtained.

(a) *General.* No person may operate a civil aircraft of U.S. registry:

(1) At cabin pressure altitudes above 12,500 feet MSL up to and including 14,000 feet MSL, unless the required minimum flight crew is provided with and uses supplemental oxygen for that part of the flight at those altitudes that is of more than 30 minutes duration;

(2) At cabin pressure altitudes above 14,000 feet MSL, unless the required minimum flight crew is provided with and uses supplemental oxygen during the entire flight time at those altitudes; and

(3) At cabin pressure altitudes above 15,000 feet MSL, unless each occupant of the aircraft is provided with supplemental oxygen.

(b) *Pressurized cabin aircraft.*

(1) No person may operate a civil aircraft of U.S. registry with a pressurized cabin:

(i) At flight altitudes above Flight Level 250, unless at least a 10-minute supply of sup-

---

* Part 97 not included in this text.

** The definition of MEA is thoroughly discussed in chapter 7.

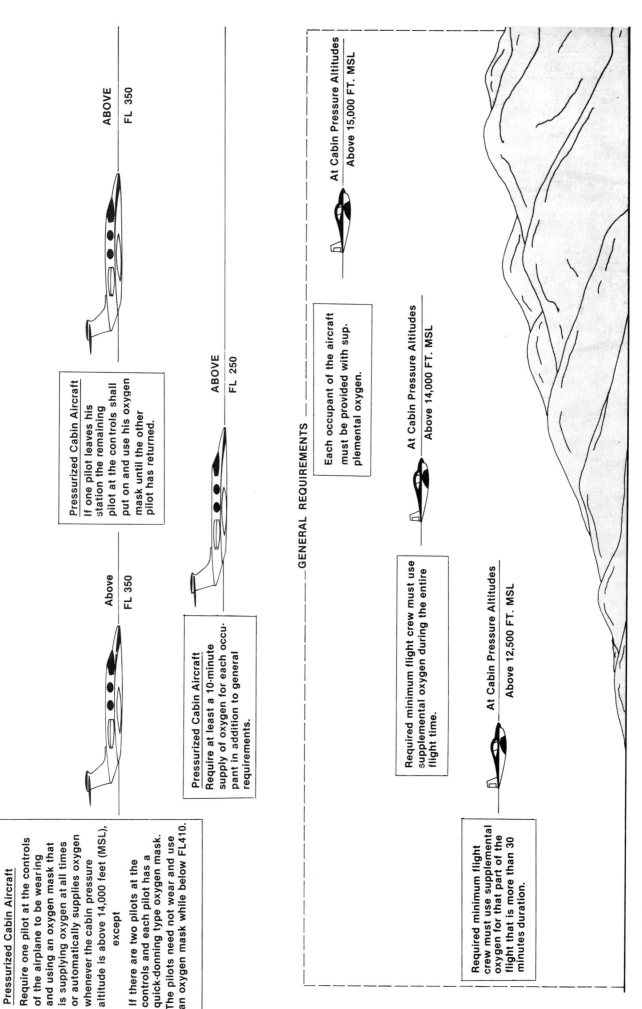

Figure 6-6. Supplemental Oxygen Requirements

Pressurized Cabin Aircraft

Require one pilot at the controls of the airplane to be wearing and using an oxygen mask that is supplying oxygen at all times or automatically supplies oxygen whenever the cabin pressure altitude is above 14,000 feet (MSL), except

If there are two pilots at the controls and each pilot has a quick-donning type oxygen mask. The pilots need not wear and use an oxygen mask while below FL410.

Above FL 350

Pressurized Cabin Aircraft

If one pilot leaves his station the remaining pilot at the controls shall put on and use his oxygen mask until the other pilot has returned.

ABOVE FL 350

Pressurized Cabin Aircraft

Require at least a 10-minute supply of oxygen for each occupant in addition to general requirements.

ABOVE FL 250

GENERAL REQUIREMENTS

Each occupant of the aircraft must be provided with supplemental oxygen.

At Cabin Pressure Altitudes Above 15,000 FT. MSL

Required minimum flight crew must use supplemental oxygen during the entire flight time.

At Cabin Pressure Altitudes Above 14,000 FT. MSL

Required minimum flight crew must use supplemental oxygen for that part of the flight that is more than 30 minutes duration.

At Cabin Pressure Altitudes Above 12,500 FT. MSL

plemental oxygen in addition to any oxygen required to satisfy paragraph (a) of this section, is available for each occupant of the aircraft for use in the event that a descent is necessitated by loss of cabin pressurization; and

(ii) At flight altitudes above Flight Level 350, unless one pilot at the controls of the airplane is wearing and using an oxygen mask that is secured and sealed, and that either supplies at all times or automatically supplies oxygen whenever the cabin pressure altitude of the airplane exceeds 14,000 feet MSL, except that the one pilot need not wear and use an oxygen mask while at or below Flight Level 410 if there are two pilots at the controls and each pilot has a quick-donning type of oxygen mask that can be placed on the face with one hand from the ready position within five seconds, supplying oxygen and properly secured and sealed.

(2) Notwithstanding subparagraph (1) (ii) of this paragraph, if for any reason at any time it is necessary for one pilot to leave his station at the controls of the aircraft when operating at flight altitudes above Flight Level 350, the remaining pilot at the controls shall put on and use his oxygen mask until the other pilot has returned to his station.

PORTABLE ELECTRONIC DEVICES (FAR 91.19)

6.35 Regulation 91.19 is of particular interest to the instrument pilot since instrument flight relies heavily on electronic guidance and in-flight pilot/controller communications.

(a) Except as provided in paragraph (b) of this section, no person may operate, nor may any operator or pilot in command of an aircraft allow the operation of, any portable electronic device on any of the following U.S. registered civil aircraft:
(1) Aircraft operated by an air carrier or commercial operator; or
(2) Any other aircraft while it is operated under IFR.
(b) Paragraph (a) of this section does not apply to:
(1) Portable voice recorders;
(2) Hearing aids;
(3) Heart pacemakers;
(4) Electric shavers; or
(5) Any other portable electronic device that the operator of the aircraft has determined will not cause interference with the navigation or communication system of the aircraft on which it is to be used.

(c) In the case of an aircraft operated by an air carrier or commercial operator, the determination required by paragraph (b) (5) of this section shall be made by the air carrier or commercial operator of the aircraft on which the particular device is to be used. In the case of other aircraft, the determination may be made by the pilot in command or other operator of the aircraft.

LIQUOR AND DRUGS (FAR 91.11)

6.36 The following regulation is often thought of by pilots as the ''8-hour alcohol rule,'' however, pilots should not overlook the message in (2).

(a) No person may act as a crewmember of a civil aircraft:
(1) Within 8 hours after the consumption of any alcoholic beverage;
(2) While under the influence of alcohol; or
(3) While using any drug that affects his faculties in any way contrary to safety.
(b) Except in an emergency, no pilot of civil aircraft may allow a person who is obviously under the influence of intoxicating liquors or drugs (except a medical patient under proper care) to be carried in that aircraft.

ATC CLEARANCE AND FLIGHT PLAN REQUIRED (FAR 91.115)

6.37 FAR 91.115 states that:
No person may operate an aircraft in controlled airspace under IFR unless:
(a) He has filed an IFR flight plan; and
(b) He has received an appropriate ATC clearance.

BASIC AND SPECIAL VFR WEATHER MINIMUMS FOR FIXED WING AIRCRAFT (FAR 91.105 AND FAR 91.107)

6.38 Every aviator should be knowledgeable of the basic VFR weather minimums in the interest of safety and to determine if a flight must be conducted under instrument flight rules. These basic VFR weather minimums change with altitude and type of airspace—controlled or uncontrolled.

6.39 The minimum flight visibilities and distances from clouds for a pilot to remain VFR are shown in Figure 6-7. The importance of *understanding* and *memorizing* the basic VFR weather minimums from Figure 6-7 cannot be overemphasized because the usual routine prior to flight planning is to assess the weather for the intended route to determine if it is above VFR minimums.

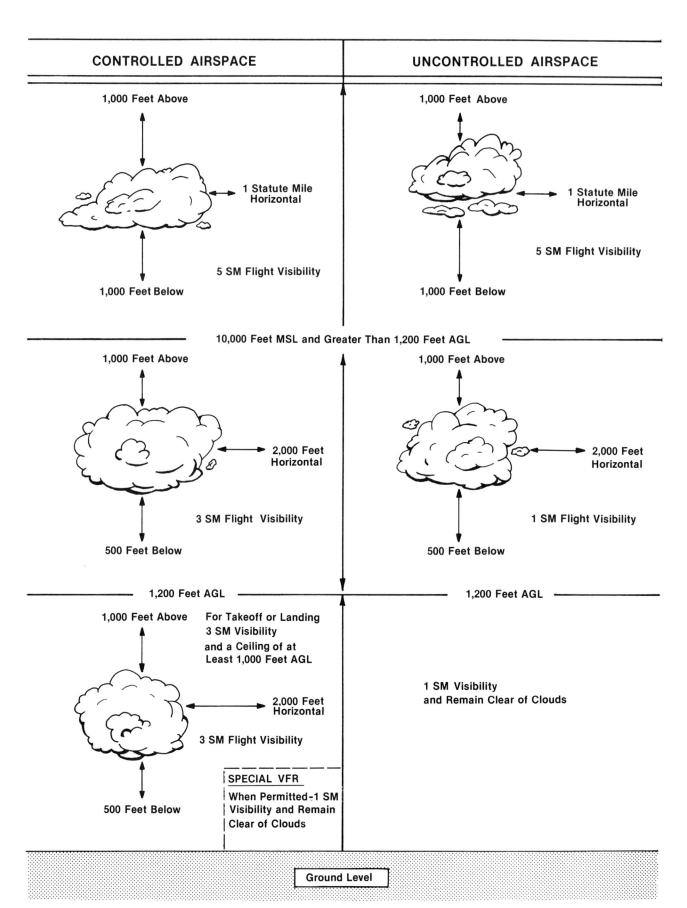

Figure 6-7. VFR Weather Minimums for Fixed Wing Aircraft

For answers see Appendix E.

1. A current airworthiness certificate should be maintained by:
1. The pilot.
2. The chief mechanic.
3. The co-pilot.
4. The owner or operator.

2. A private pilot is proposing a day flight carrying two passengers. Prior to departing on this flight the pilot must have acquired at least:
1. Three takeoffs and landings (day) or 5 takeoffs and landings (night) in the same category and class within the preceding 90 days.
2. Three takeoffs and landings (day) or 3 takeoffs and landings (night) in the same category and class within the preceding 90 days.
3. Five takeoffs and landings (day) or 3 takeoffs and landings (night) in the same category within the preceding 90 days.
4. Three takeoffs and landings (day or night) in the same category within the preceding 90 days.

3. A pilot is maintaining currency in single and multiengine aircraft. In the last 90 days, the pilot has made 4 takeoffs and landings in a multiengine aircraft, with 2 takeoffs and landings in the single-engine aircraft. The pilot has also logged 6 hours of instrument time and 3 approaches in the multiengine aircraft, and 1 hour of instrument time and 2 approaches in the single-engine aircraft in the past 6 months. In order to legally conduct an instrument flight in the single-engine aircraft with passengers, the pilot must also have accomplished:
1. Five hours of instrument flight time, 4 approaches, and 1 takeoff and landing in the single-engine airplane.
2. One approach only.
3. One takeoff and landing in the single-engine airplane.
4. One approach and 1 takeoff and landing in the single-engine airplane.

4. To meet recent instrument flight experience within the past 6 months, a pilot must have:
1. Passed an instrument competency check.
2. Logged 6 hours of instrument flight time in the same category of aircraft and 6 approaches.
3. Logged 3 hours of instrument flight time in the same category of aircraft, and 3 hours of instrument time and 6 approaches in a simulator.
4. All the above choices are correct.

5. The forecasted destination weather at the ETA for a proposed IFR flight is predicted to be a ceiling of 1,200 feet and 5 miles visibility. The required fuel supply for this flight is:
1. Sufficient fuel to fly to the destination airport only.
2. Sufficient fuel to fly to the destination airport, then to the alternate airport, plus 45 minutes at normal cruise speed.
3. Sufficient fuel to fly to the destination airport plus 45 minutes at the most economical cruise speed.
4. Sufficient fuel to fly to the destination airport plus one hour at normal cruise speed.

6. When making a VOR accuracy check using a VOT, which is the correct combination of OBS setting, flag indication, and maximum allowable bearing error shown below?

	OBS Setting	Flag	Maximum Error
1.	000°	To	±4°
2.	180°	To	±4°
3.	000°	From	±6°
4.	180°	From	±6°

7. What are the standard IFR alternate airport weather minimums?

A. A ceiling of 600 feet and a visibility of 2 statute miles for a precision approach.
B. A ceiling of 800 feet and a visibility of 2 statute miles for a nonprecision approach.
C. A ceiling and visibility allowing a descent from MEA, approach, and landing, if the airport does not have a published instrument approach procedure.
D. A ceiling of 1,000 feet and a visibility of 3 statute miles for all approaches.
1. D only.
2. A, B, and C.
3. A, B, C, and D.
4. A and B.

8. A pilot is planning to file an IFR flight plan, but the weather en route is VFR. Select the correct response in regard to the VOR accuracy check.

A. A VOR accuracy check is not required because the weather is VFR.
B. The maximum permissible indicated bearing error using a designated ground checkpoint is +4°.
C. The maximum permissible indicated bearing error using an airborne checkpoint is +6°.
D. The maximum permissible indicated bearing error checking one VOR against the other is 4°.
1. B, C, and D.
2. A only.
3. A, B, and C.
4. A, B, C, and D.

9. No pilot may operate his aircraft in controlled airspace under IFR rules, unless the static pressure system and altimeter have been tested and inspected within:
1. 10 days and 10 hours of flight time.
2. 12 calendar months.
3. 90 days.
4. 24 calendar months.

10. The relevancy of a pilot's medical certificate depends upon:
1. The category of the aircraft flown.
2. The type of rating or certificate a pilot holds.
3. The type of operation conducted.
4. The type of flight plan a pilot intends to file.

11. An aircraft presently does not meet applicable airworthiness requirements. What may be substituted for an airworthiness certificate?
1. A special flight permit.
2. An FAA examiner's signature in the aircraft logbook.
3. A certified mechanic's signature in the aircraft logbook.
4. An amended airworthiness certificate.

12. What class of medical certificate may a private pilot conducting IFR flight operations hold?
1. A first-class medical certificate that is valid for 12 months.
2. A second-class medical certificate that is valid for 6 months.
3. A third-class medical certificate that is valid for 12 months.
4. A first, second, or third-class medical certificate that expires at the end of the last day of the 24th month after the month of the date of examination.

13. A VOR equipment check should be recorded:
1. In the aircraft log or other record with the date, place, bearing error, and signature of the person conducting the VOR operational check.
2. In the aircraft log with the date and error.
3. In the aircraft log or other permanent record with the date, place, Tach time, bearing error, and the signature of the person conducting the check.
4. In any permanent record with the date and signature of the person conducting the check.

14. Within what period of time must the VOR equipment be operationally checked prior to making an IFR flight? (Assume that the VOR equipment is not maintained, checked, and inspected under an approved procedure.)

1. The preceding 30 days before flight.
2. The preceding 10 hours of flight time and within 10 days before flight.
3. The preceding 10 days before flight.
4. The preceding 10 hours of flight time or within 30 days before flight.

15. The airworthiness certificate must be:
1. In the pilot's possession.
2. With the aircraft's logbooks.
3. Displayed at the cabin or cockpit entrance.
4. Maintained with the service records.

16. What pilot-in-command and instrument flight time should be logged from the following information?

Start taxi	0700	Exit clouds	0845
Departure	0710	Land	0950
Enter clouds	0715	Stop taxi	0955

1. PIC 2.9 hours, Instrument time 1.5 hours.
2. PIC 2.5 hours, Instrument time 2.5 hours.
3. PIC 2.5 hours, Instrument time 1.5 hours.
4. PIC 2.7 hours, Instrument time 2.5 hours.

17. Who may act as a safety pilot in simulated instrument flight?
1. A flight instructor.
2. Any pilot who holds an instrument rating.
3. An appropriately rated pilot.
4. Any pilot.

18. A pilot is planning an IFR flight to an airport that is forecasted to have no ceiling and 20 miles visibility from one hour before to one hour after the flight's estimated time of arrival. The pilot should plan sufficient fuel to fly to the:
1. Destination airport plus one hour reserve fuel at cruising speed.
2. First airport of intended landing plus 45 minutes reserve fuel at normal cruising speed.
3. Destination airport, then to the alternate airport, plus 45 minutes reserve fuel at normal cruising speed.
4. Destination airport plus 45 minutes reserve fuel at best holding speed.

19. Assume a pilot is operating an aircraft that consumes 15 gallons of fuel per hour, and the flight time to the destination airport is 2 hours and 30 minutes. If the weather at the destination airport is below prescribed instrument approach weather minimums, how long can the pilot fly a holding pattern over the VOR if the flying time to the alternate airport is 40 minutes and the total usable fuel is 64

gallons?
   1. 21 minutes.
   2. 1 hour and 1 minute.
   3. 1 hour and 7 minutes.
   4. 45 minutes.

20. Select the correct statement concerning flight at FL 200.
   1. The pilot must hold an instrument rating, and the aircraft must be equipped with a transponder and a DME.
   2. The pilot must hold an instrument rating, be on an IFR flight plan, and the aircraft must be equipped with the required instruments and equipment for IFR flight, and in addition the aircraft must be equipped with a transponder having at least a 64 code capability.
   3. The pilot must hold an instrument rating, be on an IFR flight plan, and the aircraft must be equipped with the required instruments and equipment for IFR flight including a transponder with at least a 4096 code and altitude reporting capability, and a radio providing direct pilot/controller communication on specified ATC frequencies.
   4. The aircraft must be equipped with a transponder having at least a 64 code capability.

21. According to Federal Aviation Regulations, which of the following are required to be carried aboard the aircraft in flight?
   1. Aircraft registration, airworthiness certificate, and engine and aircraft logbooks.
   2. Aircraft registration, airworthiness certificate, and a radio transmitter form.
   3. Aircraft registration, airworthiness certificate, and unapproved owners manual.
   4. Aircraft registration, airworthiness certificate, and appropriate operating limitations.

22. Which of the following discrepancies must be corrected prior to an IFR departure? (Assume flight below FL 240.)

A. A generator not charging to adequate capacity.
B. An inoperative DME.
C. A vertical speed indicator that reads 100 feet on the ground.
D. An inoperative second hand on the clock.
E. An inoperative turn and slip indicator.
   1. A, C, D, and E.
   2. A, B, and E.
   3. B, C, and D.
   4. A, D, and E.

23. Which of the following portable electronic devices cannot be operated in the aircraft during an IFR flight?
   1. Portable voice recorder.
   2. FM radio.
   3. Electric shaver.
   4. Heart pacemaker.

24. Which of the following statements concerning the use of oxygen are correct?

A. Each occupant must be provided with supplemental oxygen above a cabin pressure altitude of 14,000 feet MSL.
B. Below a cabin pressure altitude of 12,500 feet MSL, no oxygen is required.
C. Oxygen is not required on a flight at a cabin pressure altitude of 13,500 feet MSL if this flight is less than 30 minutes in duration at that altitude.
D. Above Flight Level 250 (in a pressurized aircraft), a minimum of a 10-minute supply of oxygen is required for each occupant.
   1. C only.
   2. A, C, and D.
   3. B, C, and D.
   4. A, B, and D.

25. If a pilot was issued a second-class medical certificate February 2, 1979 and wishes to exercise the privileges of a private pilot, that medical certificate is valid until:
   1. March 1, 1981.
   2. February 2, 1981.
   3. February 28, 1981.
   4. January 31, 1981.

26. Assume a pilot flies an aircraft directly over an airborne VOR receiver checkpoint which is north of a VOR station. Select the correct VOR receiver setting and indications for such a situation.

A. 180°.
B. 360°.
C. To.
D. From.
E. Maximum indicated bearing error +6°.
F. Maximum indicated bearing error +4°.
   1. B, C, and E.
   2. A, C, and F.
   3. B, D, and E.
   4. A, D, and E.

27. The pilot in command of a civil aircraft must possess an instrument rating *only* when conducting flight operations:
   1. In controlled airspace under instrument flight rules.
   2. In weather conditions less than the minimum prescribed for VFR flight.
   3. In weather conditions less than the minimum

prescribed for VFR flight in controlled airspace.

4. Under instrument flight rules, in weather conditions less than the minimum prescribed for VFR flight, and in a Positive Control Area or positive route segment.

28. For which of the following operations must the pilot in command of a civil aircraft possess an instrument rating?

1. Flight above a solid overcast at any altitude.
2. Flight in VFR conditions on an IFR flight plan.
3. Flight on a Victor airway conducted under simulated instrument conditions.
4. Any flight above an altitude of 1,200 feet AGL, when the visibility is less than 3 statute miles.

29. What tests, inspections, or checks are required for an aircraft in order for it to be operated on an instrument flight not carrying persons for instruction or hire?

1. Transponder test, altimeter system test, annual inspection, and VOR accuracy check.
2. Altimeter system test, 100-hour inspection, and VOR accuracy check.
3. Altimeter system test, annual inspection, 100-hour inspection, and VOR accuracy check.
4. Transponder test, altimeter system test, weight and balance test, annual inspection, 100-hour inspection, and VOR accuracy check.

30. How much time does a pilot have after recent instrument experience requirements lapse before it is necessary to pass an instrument competency check to act as pilot in command under IFR?

1. 90 days.
2. 6 months.
3. 12 months.
4. 24 months.

31. Prior to the departure of any IFR flight conducted in controlled airspace, the pilot in command must become familiar with all available information concerning that flight. This information must include fuel requirements, known traffic delays, weather reports and forecasts, and landing distance information. In addition, the pilot in command must:

1. Include an alternate airport on the flight plan and determine if the aircraft is airworthy.
2. Determine if the aircraft is airworthy by checking all of the aircraft maintenance records.
3. Be familiar with the runway lengths at airports of intended use, and the alternatives available if the planned flight cannot be completed.
4. Include an alternate airport on the flight plan and become familiar with the instrument ap-

proaches at airports of intended use.

32. Encoding altimeters are required:

A. In Group I TCAs.
B. In Positive Control Areas.
C. In control zones at any altitude.
D. Above 12,500 feet MSL in controlled airspace except at and below 2,500 feet AGL.

1. A and C only.
2. A, B, and C.
3. B and D only.
4. A, B, and D.

33. What pilot action is necessary if DME failure occurs at an altitude above 24,000 feet MSL?

1. Notify ATC immediately and continue the flight to the next airport of intended landing where the DME can be repaired or replaced.
2. Notify ATC that it is necessary to descend to a lower altitude due to DME failure.
3. Notify ATC immediately and land at the nearest airport where the DME can be repaired or replaced.
4. Continue to the destination airport and request an altitude below 24,000 feet MSL.

34. What are the basic VFR weather minimums for flight in controlled airspace below 10,000 feet MSL?

1. One statute mile surface visibility; the aircraft must remain clear of clouds.
2. Three statute miles flight visibility; the aircraft must remain at least 500 feet below, 1,000 feet above, or 2,000 feet horizontally from clouds.
3. One statute mile flight visibility; the aircraft must remain at least 500 feet below, 1,000 feet above, or 2,000 feet horizontally from clouds.
4. Three statute miles flight visibility; the aircraft must remain clear of clouds.

35. No pilot may include an alternate airport in an IFR flight plan unless the alternate airport has:

1. An operational FSS or control tower.
2. An operational control tower.
3. A 5,000-foot paved runway.
4. A current weather forecast.

36. A pilot is planning to depart an uncontrolled airport. If there is a 900-foot overcast ceiling and the floor of the overlaying controlled airspace is 1,200 feet AGL, an ATC clearance must be obtained prior to:

1. Taxiing.
2. Entering IFR weather conditions.
3. Departure.
4. Entering the controlled airspace.

37. A pilot must have an IFR clearance before entering:

    1. Any airspace whenever the visibility is less than one statute mile.

    2. A Terminal Control Area, Continental Control Area, and any airspace where the visibility is less than one statute mile.

    3. Controlled airspace with IFR weather conditions and the Positive Control Area.

    4. Any airspace above 1,200 feet AGL where the visibility is less than one statute mile.

38. Where is an IFR clearance necessary to conduct a flight operation during VFR weather conditions?

    1. Group I and II TCAs.

    2. Positive Control Area.

    3. Continental Control Area.

    4. Positive Control Area and Continental Control Area.

39. What are the vertical dimensions of the Positive Control Area in the area of the conterminous United States?

    1. From 18,000 feet MSL to and including FL 410.

    2. From 14,500 feet MSL to and including FL 450.

    3. From 14,500 feet MSL to and including FL 410.

    4. From 18,000 feet MSL to and including FL 600.

7.

Flight Planning

7.1 What constitutes a sound flight plan? To design a sound flight plan, a pilot must consider the type of aircraft and equipment to be used for the proposed flight, the forecast weather, pilot capabilities, and pilot familiarity with the particular route to be flown, to name a few factors. This chapter examines the essential information that an instrument-rated pilot needs to utilize in order to compose a sound flight plan. Also included in this chapter is an example of a properly constructed IFR flight plan.

7.2 While selecting the route of flight, a pilot must consider all pertinent weather information (as discussed in chapter 3), aircraft performance (as discussed in chapters 1 and 5), and various pilot and equipment requirements (as discussed in chapters 2, 4, and 6). After all of this information has been analyzed by the pilot, a written plan of action, which includes an alternate course of action if the flight cannot be completed as planned, should be constructed.

PUBLICATIONS

7.3 There are several publications that are of paramount importance for the pilot to consult during the flight planning process. They include the Airman's Information Manual, the Airport/Facility Directory, and the Graphic Notices of Operational Data.

Airman's Information Manual—Basic Flight Information and ATC Procedures (AIM)

7.4 The Airman's Information Manual is often considered to be the pilot's bible—a major source of pertinent flying information. It is published by the U.S. Department of Transportation Federal Aviation Administration, and is sold by the Superintendent of Documents. It is issued semiannually and contains the fundamental procedures required in order to fly in the United States National Airspace System. AIM also contains information concerning factors affecting safety of flight, items of interest to pilots concerning health and medical facts, ATC rules, a glossary of terms used in the air traffic control system, Air Defense Identification Zones (ADIZ), mountainous areas, good operating practices, and emergency procedures.

Airport/Facility Directory

7.5 The Airport/Facility Directory is a seven-part publication that is published and distributed every eight weeks; it is available by subscription from the National Ocean Survey. It is designed to be used with aeronautical charts covering the conterminous United States, Puerto Rico, and the Virgin Islands.

7.6 This publication is of great value to the instrument pilot since it contains many subjects necessary to review during the flight planning process. *Some* of the sections it contains are:
1. The Airport/Facility Directory.
2. VOR Receiver Check Points.
3. Air Route Traffic Control Centers, and
4. Preferred IFR Routes.

Figures 7–1 through 7–4 are excerpted from the Airport/Facility Directory. Each figure should be carefully reviewed.

DIRECTORY LEGEND

LEGEND

This Directory is an alphabetical listing of data on record with the FAA on all airports that are open to the public, associated terminal control facilities, air route traffic control centers and radio aids to navigation within the conterminous United States, Puerto Rico and the Virgin Islands. Airports are listed alphabetically by associated city name and cross referenced by airport name. Facilities associated with an airport, but with a different name, are listed individually under their own name, as well as under the airport with which they are associated.

The listing of an airport in this directory merely indicates the airport operator's willingness to accommodate transient aircraft, and does not represent that the facility conforms with any Federal or local standards, or that it has been approved for use on the part of the general public.

The information on obstructions is taken from reports submitted to the FAA. It has not been verified in all cases. Pilots are cautioned that objects not indicated in this tabulation (or on charts) may exist which can create a hazard to flight operation.

Detailed specifics concerning services and facilities tabulated within this directory are contained in Airman's Information Manual, Basic Flight Information and ATC Procedures.

The legend items that follow explain in detail the contents of this Directory and are keyed to the circled numbers on the sample on the preceding page.

① CITY/AIRPORT NAME

Airports and facilities in this directory are listed alphabetically by associated city and state. Where the city name is different than the airport name the city name will appear on the line above the airport name. Airports with the same associated city name will be listed alphabetically by airport name and will be separated by a dashed rule line. All others will be separated by a solid rule line.

② NOTAM SERVICE

The symbol § preceding the airport name indicates NOTAM Service is provided. Notam service is available only at airports with established instrument approach procedures, or high volume VFR activity.

③ LOCATION IDENTIFIER

A three or four character code assigned to airports. These identifiers are used by ATC in lieu of the airport name in flight plans, flight strips and other written records and computer operations.

④ AIRPORT LOCATION

Airport location is expressed as distance and direction from the center of the associated city in nautical miles and cardinal points, i.e., 3.5 NE.

⑤ TIME CONVERSION

Hours of operation of all facilities are expressed in Greenwich Mean Time (GMT) and shown as "Z" time. The directory indicates the number of hours to be subtracted from GMT to obtain local standard time and local daylight saving time GMT-5(-4DT). The symbol ‡ indicates that during periods of Daylight Saving Time effective hours will be one hour earlier than shown. In those areas where daylight saving time is not observed that (-4DT) and ‡ will not be shown.

⑥ GEOGRAPHIC POSITION OF AIRPORT

⑦ CHARTS

The Sectional Chart and Low and High Altitude Enroute Chart and panel on which the airport or facility is located.

⑧ INSTRUMENT APPROACH PROCEDURES

IAP indicates an airport for which a prescribed (Public Use) FAA Instrument Approach Procedure has been published.

⑨ ELEVATION

Elevation is given in feet above mean sea level and is the highest point on the landing surface. When elevation is sea level it will be indicated as (00). When elevation is below sea level a minus (-) sign will precede the figure.

⑩ ROTATING LIGHT BEACON

B indicates rotating beacon is available. Rotating beacons operate dusk to dawn unless otherwise indicated in AIRPORT REMARKS.

⑪ SERVICING

S1: Minor airframe repairs.
S2: Minor airframe and minor powerplant repairs.
S3: Major airframe and minor powerplant repairs.
S4: Major airframe and major powerplant repairs.

B.

DIRECTORY LEGEND
SAMPLE

① **CITY NAME**
§ ② ③ ④ ⑤ ⑥
AIRPORT NAME (ORL) 2.6 E GMT-5(-4DT) 28°32'43"N 81°20'10"W   **JACKSONVILLE**
⑨ ⑩ ⑪ ⑫ ⑬ ⑭ ⑮ ⑯   **H-4G, L-19C** ⑦
113 B S4 FUEL 100 JET A OX 1, 2, 3 TPA 800' AOE CFR Index A ⑧ IAP

⑰ RWY 07-25: H6000X150 (ASPH) S-90, D-160, DT-300 HIRL
   RWY 07: ALSF1 Trees 1700' from thld   RWY 25: REIL Rgt tfc
   RWY 13-31: H4620X100 (ASPH) HIRL
   RWY 13: VASI Pole 600' from thld 385' ovrn   RWY 31: VASI Rgt tfc ttc 569' ovrn. Brush 200' from thld
⑱ AIRPORT REMARKS: Acft 100,000 lbs or over ctc Director of Aviation for approval (305) 894-9831. Fee for all airline charters, travel clubs and certain revenue producing acft
⑲ COMMUNICATIONS: ATIS 127.25 UNICOM 123.0
   NME FSS (ORL) on fld 123.65 122.65 122.2 122.1R 112.2T (305) 894-0861
Ⓡ NAME APP CON 124.8 (337°-179°) 120.15 (180°-336°)
   TOWER 118.7 GND CON 121.7 CLNC DEL 125.55
   STAGE I SVC ctc ORLANDO APP CON
⑳ RADIO AIDS TO NAVIGATION:
   NAME (H) VORTAC 112.2 ORL Chan 59 28°32'33"N 81°20'07"W at fld.
     VOR unusable 050°-060° beyond 5000'
   ILS 109.9 I-ORL Rwy 07. LOM Henry 221 OR
   ASR
㉑ COMM/NAVAID REMARKS: Tower operates 1200-0400‡

AIRPORT NAME (X30) 7 W GMT-5(-4DT) 28°31'50"N 81°32'26"W   **JACKSONVILLE**
130 S4 FUEL 100 OX 2
RWY 18-36: 2430X150 (TURF) LIRL
   RWY 18: Thld dspld 215'   RWY 36: Thld dspld 270'
AIRPORT REMARKS: Attended dawn-0300‡
COMMUNICATIONS: UNICOM 122.8
   NME FSS (ORL)

AIRPORT NAME (MCO) 6.1 SE GMT-5(-4DT) 28°25'53"N 81°19'29"W   **JACKSONVILLE**
96 B FUEL 100, JET A CFR Index D   **H-4G, L-19C**
RWY 18R-36L: H12004X300 (CONC) S-100, D-200, DT-400 HIRL   IAP
   RWY 18R: ALSF1, REIL Rgt ttc   RWY 36L: ALSF1
RWY 18L-36R: H12004X200 (ASPH) S-165, D-200, DT-400 HIRL
   RWY 18L: ALSF1 Thld dspld 990'   RWY 36R: ALSF1 Rgt tfc
AIRPORT REMARKS: Attended 1200-0300‡. 1000' ovrns all rwys
COMMUNICATIONS: UNICOM 123.0
   NAME FSS (ORL) on Herndon
Ⓡ APP CON 124.8 (337°-179°) 120.1 (180°-336°)
   TOWER 124.3 GND CON 121.85 CLNC DEL 134.7
   DEP CON 124.8 (337°-179°) 120.1 (180°-336°)
   STAGE III SVC ctc APP CON
RADIO AIDS TO NAVIGATION:
   (H) VORTAC 112.2 ORL Chan 59 28°32'33"N 81°20'07"W 173° 5.7 NM to fld
     VOR unusable 050°-060° beyond 15 NM below 5000'
   ILS 109.3 I-MCO Rwy 36 BC unusable
   ASR

AIRPORT NAME (See PLYMOUTH)

A.

Figure 7-1 A.F. Airport/Facility Directory Legend

213

DIRECTORY LEGEND

⑫ FUEL

FUEL	
CODE	PRODUCT
80	Grade 80 gasoline (Red)
100	Grade 100 gasoline (Green)
100LL	Grade 100LL gasoline (low lead) (Blue)
115	Grade 115 gasoline
A	Jet A-Kerosene freeze point—40° C.
A1	Jet A-1—Kerosene, freeze point—50° C.
A1 +	Jet A-1—Kerosene with icing inhibitor, freeze point—50° C.
B	Jet B—Wide-cut turbine fuel, freeze point—50° C.
B +	Jet B—Wide-cut turbine fuel with icing inhibitor, freeze point—50° C.

⑬ OXYGEN

OX 1   High Pressure
OX 2   Low Pressure
OX 3   High Pressure—Replacement Bottles
OX 4   Low Pressure—Replacement Bottles

⑭ TRAFFIC PATTERN ALTITUDE

TPA—Traffic Pattern Altitude is provided only for those airports without a 24 hour operating control tower. "Altitudes shown are Above Ground Level (AGL)"

⑮ AIRPORT OF ENTRY AND LANDING RIGHTS AIRPORTS

AOE—Airport of Entry-A customs Airport of Entry where permission from U.S. Customs is not required, however, at least one hour advance notice of arrival must be furnished.

LRA—Landing Rights Airport-Application for permission to land must be submitted in advance to U.S. Customs. At least one hour advance notice of arrival must be furnished.

NOTE: Advance notice of arrival at both an AOE and LRA airport may be included in the flight plan when filed in Canada or Mexico, if destination is an airport where flight notification service is available. This notice will also be treated as an application for permission to land in the case of an LRA. (See Customs, Immigration and Naturalization, Public Health and Agriculture Department requirements in the International Flight Information Manual for further details.)

⑯ CERTIFICATED AIRPORT (FAR 139) and FAA INSPECTION

Airport serving Civil Aeronautics Board certified carriers and certified under FAR. Part 139 are indicated by the CFR Index i.e., CFR Index A, which relates to the availability of Crash, Fire, Rescue equipment.

All airports not inspected by FAA will be identified by the note: Not insp. This indicates that the airport information has been provided by the owner or operator of the field.

Airports serving Civil Aeronautics Board certified carriers and certified under FAR, Part 139, are indicated by the CFR index; i.e., CFR index A, which relates to the availability of crash, fire, rescue equipment.

FAR—PART 139 CERTIFICATED AIRPORTS
INDICES AND FIRE FIGHTING AND RESCUE EQUIPMENT REQUIREMENTS

Airport Index	Required No. Vehicles	Aircraft Length	Scheduled Departures	Agent + Water for Protein Foam
A	1	≲90'	≲1	500#DC or 450#DC + 50 gal H²0
		⟩90', ≲126'	⟨5	300#DC + 500 gal H²0
B	2	⟩90', ≲126'	≲5	Index A + 1500 gal H²0
		⟩126', ≲160'	⟨5	
C	3	⟩126', ≲160'	≲5	Index A + 3000 gal H²0
		⟩160', ≲200'	⟨5	
D	3	⟩160', ≲200'	≲5	Index A + 4000 gal H²0
		⟩200'	⟨5	
E	3	⟩200'	≲5	Index A + 6000 gal H²0
Ltd.	Vehicle and capacity requirements for airports limited operating certificates are determined on a case by case basis.			

⟩ Greater Than: ⟨ Less Than   ≲ Equal or Greater Than: ≲ Equal or Less Than; H²0—Water; DC—Dry Chemical.

NOTE: If AFFF (Aqueous Film Forming Foam) is used in lieu of Protein Foam, the water quantities listed for Indices A thru E can be reduced 33-1/3%.

⑰ RUNWAY DATA

Runway information is shown on two lines. That information common to the entire runway is shown on the first line while information concerning the runway ends are shown on the second or following line. Lengthy information will be footnoted and placed in the Airport Remarks.

Runway direction, surface, length, width, weight bearing capacity, lighting, gradient (when gradient exceeds 0.3 percent) and appropriate remarks are shown for each runway. Direction, length, width, lighting and remarks are shown for sealanes.

C.

DIRECTORY LEGEND

RUNWAY SURFACE AND LENGTH

Runway lengths prefixed by the letter "H" indicate that the runways are hard surfaced (concrete, asphalt). If the runway length is not prefixed, the surface is sold, clay, etc. The runway surface composition is indicated in parentheses after runway length as follows:

(ASPH)–Asphalt   (GRVL)–Gravel, or cinders
(CONC)–Concrete   (TURF)–Sod
(DIRT)–Dirt

The full dimensions of helipads are shown, i.e., 50X50.

RUNWAY WEIGHT BEARING CAPACITY

Runway strength data shown in this publication is derived from available information and is a realistic estimate of capability at an average level of activity. It is not intended as a maximum allowable weight or as an operating limitation. Many airport pavements are capable of supporting limited operations with gross weights of 25-50% in excess of the published figures. Permissible operating weights, insofar as runway strengths are concerned, are a matter of agreement between the owner and user. When desiring to operate into any airport at weights in excess of those published in the publication, users should contact the airport management for permission. Add 000 to figure following S, D, DT, DDT and MAX for gross weight capacity:

    S—Runway weight bearing capacity for aircraft with single-wheel type landing gear, (DC-3), etc.
    D—Runway weight bearing capacity for aircraft with dual-wheel type landing gear, (DC-6),etc.
    DT—Runway weight bearing capacity for aircraft with dual-tandem type landing gear, (707), etc.
    DDT—Runway weight bearing capacity for aircraft with double dual-tandem type landing gear, (747), etc.

Quadricycle and dual-tandem are considered virtually equal for runway weight bearing consideration. as are single-tandem and dual-wheel.

Omission of weight bearing capacity indicates information unknown.

RUNWAY LIGHTING

Lights are in operation sunset to sunrise. Lighting available by prior arrangement only or operating part of the night only and/or pilot controlled and with specific operating hours are indicated under airport remarks as footnotes. Since obstructions are usually lighted, obstruction lighting is not included in this code. Unlighted obstructions on or surrounding an airport will be noted in airport remarks.

Temporary, emergency or limited runway edge lighting such as flares, smudge pots, lanterns or portable runway lights will also be shown in airport remarks, instead of being designated by code numbers.

Types of lighting are shown with the runway or runway end they serve.

LIRL—Low intensity Runway Lights
MIRL—Medium Intensity Runway Lights
HIRL—High Intensity Runway Lights
REIL—Runway End Identifier Lights
C/L—Centerline Lights
TDZ—Touchdown Zone Lights
ODALS—Omni Directional Approach Lighting System.
USAF OVRN—Air Force Overrun 1000' Standard Approach Lighting System.
LDIN—Lead-In Lighting System.
MALS—Medium Intensity Approach Lighting System.
MALSF—Medium Intensity Approach Lighting System with Sequenced Flasher Lights.
MALSR—Medium Intensity Approach Lighting System with Runway Alignment Indicator Lights.

SALS—Short Approach Lighting System.
SALSF—Short Approach Lighting System with Sequenced Flashing Lights.
SSALS—Simplified Short Approach Lighting System.
SSALF—Simplified Short Approach Lighting System with Sequenced Flashing Lights.
SSALR—Simplified Short Approach Lighting System with Runway Alignment Indicator Lights.
ALSF1—High Intensity Approach Lighting System with Sequenced Flashing Lights, Category I, Configuration.
ALSF2—High Intensity Approach Lighting System with Sequenced Flashing Lights, Category II, Configuration.
VASI—Visual Approach Slope Indicator Systems

VASI approach slope angle and TCH will be shown only when slope angle exceeds 3°.

RUNWAY GRADIENT

Runway gradient will be shown only when it is 0.3 percent or more. When available the direction of slope upward will be indicated. i.e., 0.5% up NW.

RUNWAY END DATA

Lighting systems such as VASI, MALSR, REIL; obstructions; displaced thresholds will be shown on the specific runway end. "Rgt tfc"–Right traffic indicates right turns should be made on landing and takeoff for specified runway end.

⑱ AIRPORT REMARKS

"Landing Fee" indicates landing charges for private or non-revenue producing aircraft, in addition, fees may be charged for planes that remain over a couple of hours and buy no services, or at major airline terminals for all aircraft.

Obstructions—Because of space limitations only the more prominent obstacles are indicated. Natural obstruction, such as trees, clearly discernible for contact operations are not included. On the other hand, all obstructions within at least a 20:1 approach ratio are indicated.

Remarks—Data is confined to operational items affecting the status and usability of the airport.

⑲ COMMUNICATIONS

Communications will be listed in sequence in the order shown below:

Automatic Terminal Information Service (ATIS) and Private Aeronautical Stations (UNICOM) along with their frequency is shown, where available, on the line following the heading "COMMUNICATIONS".

Flight Service Station (FSS) information. The associated FSS will be shown followed by the identifier and information concerning availability of telephone service, e.g. Direct Line (DL). Local Call (LC), etc. Where the airport NOTAM File identifier is different then the associated FSS it will be shown as "NOTAM File DCA". Where the FSS is located

D.

DIRECTORY LEGEND

on the field it will be indicated as "on arpt" following the identifier. Frequencies available will follow. The FSS telephone number will follow along with any significant operational information. FSS's whose name is not the same as the airport on which located will also be listed in the normal alphabetical name listing for the state in which located. Limited Remote Communication Outlet (LRCO) or Remote Communications Outlet (RCO) providing service to the airport followed by the frequency and name of the Controlling FSS.

FSS's and CS/Ts provide information on airport conditions, radio aids and other facilities, and process flight plans. Airport Advisory Service is provided at the pilot's request on 123.6 or 123.65 by FSS's located at non-tower airports or when the tower is not in operation. (See AIM Part 1, ADVISORIES AT NON TOWER AIRPORTS.)

Aviation weather briefing service is provided by FSS's and CS/T's: however, CS/T personnel are not certified weather briefers and therefore provide only factual data from weather reports and forecasts. Flight and weather briefing services are also available by calling the telephone numbers listed.

Limited Remote Communications Outlet (LRCO)—Unmanned satellite air/ground communications facility, which may be associated with a VOR. These outlets effectively extend service range of the FSS and provide greater communications reliability.

Remote Communications Outlet (RCO)—An unmanned satellite air to ground communication stations remotely controlled and providing UHF and VHF communications capability to extend the service range of an FSS.

Civil communications frequencies used in the FSS air/ground system are now operated simplex on 122.0, 122.2, 122.3, 122.4, 122.6, 123.6; emergency 121.5; plus receive-only on 122.05, 122.1, 122.15 and 123.6.

    a.   122.0 is assigned as the Enroute Flight Advisory Service channel at selected FSS's.

    b.   122.2 is assigned to all FSS's as a common enroute simplex service.

    c.   123.6 is assigned as the airport advisory channel at non-tower FSS locations, however, it is still in commission at some FSS's collocated with towers to provide part-time Airport Advisory Service.

    d.   122.1 is the primary receive-only frequency at VORs. 122.05, 122.15 and 123.6 are assigned at selected VORs meeting certain criteria.

    e.   Some FSS's are assigned 50kHz channels for simplex operation in the 122-123 MHz band (e.g. 122.35). Pilots using the FSS A/G system should refer to this directory or appropriate charts to determine frequencies available at the FSS or remoted facility through which they wish to communicate.

Part time FSS hours of operation are shown in remarks under facility name.

   Emergency frequency 121.5 is available at all Flight Service Stations. Towers, Approach Control and RADAR facilities, unless indicated as not available.

TERMINAL SERVICES

ATIS—A continuous broadcast of recorded non-control information in selected areas of high activity.

UNICOM—A non-government air/ground radio communications facility utilized to provide general airport advisory service.

APP CON—Approach Control. The symbol Ⓡ indicates radar approach control.

TOWER—Control tower

GND CON—Ground Control

DEP CON—Departure Control. The symbol Ⓡ indicates radar departure control.

CLNC DEL—Clearance Delivery.

VFR ADVSY SVC—VFR Advisory Service. Service provided by Non-Radar Approach Control.

STAGE I SVC—Radar Advisory Service for VFR aircraft

STAGE II SVC—Radar Advisory and Sequencing Service for VFR aircraft

STAGE III SVC—Radar Sequencing and Separation Service for participating VFR Aircraft within a Terminal Radar Service Area (TRSA)

TCA—Radar Sequencing and Separation Service for all aircraft in a Terminal Control Area (TCA)

⑳ RADIO AIDS TO NAVIGATION

The Airport/Facility Directory lists by facility name all Radio Aids to Navigation in the National Airspace System and those upon which the FAA has approved an instrument approach. Private or military Radio Aids to Navigation not in the National Airspace System are not tabulated.

All VOR, VORTAC and ILS equipment in the National Airspace System has an automatic monitoring and shutdown feature in the event of malfunction. Unmonitored as used in the publication means that FSS or tower personnel cannot observe the malfunction or shutdown signal.

NAVAID information is tabulated as indicated in the following sample:

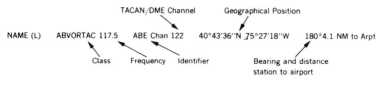

```
                          TACAN/DME Channel        Geographical Position
                              ↘                      ↙
NAME (L)    ABVORTAC 117.5    ABE Chan 122    40°43'36"N 75°27'18"W    180°4.1 NM to Arpt
                  ↗        ↖        ↑                                    ↑
               Class    Frequency  Identifier                      Bearing and distance
                                                                   station to airport

                        VOR unusable 020°-060° beyond 26 NM below 3500'
                                              ↗
                                          Restrictions
```

ASR—indicates that civil radar instrument approach minimums are published.

E.

DIRECTORY LEGEND

RADIO CLASS DESIGNATIONS

Identification of VOR/VORTAC/TACAN Stations by Class (Operational Limitations):

Normal Usable Altitudes and Radius Distances

Class	Altitudes	Distance (miles)
(T)	12,000' and below	25
(L)	Below 18,000'	40
(H)	Below 18,000'	40
(H)	Within the Conterminous 48 States only, between 14,500' and 17,999'	100
(H)	18,000'-FL 450	130
(H)	Above FL 450	100

(H) = High   (L) = Low   (T) = Terminal

NOTE: An (H) facility is capable of providing (L) and (T) service volume and an (L) facility additionally provides (T) service volume.

The term VOR is, operationally, a general term covering the VHF omnidirectional bearing type of facility without regard to the fact that the power, the frequency-protected service volume, the equipment configuration, and operational requirements may vary between facilities at different locations.

AB	Automatic Weather Broadcast (also shown with ▪ following frequency.)
B	Scheduled Broadcast Station (broadcasts weather at 15 minutes after the hour.)
DME	UHF standard (TACAN compatible) distance measuring equipment.
H	Non-directional radio beacon (homing), power 50 watts to less than 2,000 watts.
HH	Non-directional radio beacon (homing), power 2,000 watts or more.
H-SAB	Non-directional radio beacons providing automatic transcribed weather service.
ILS	Instrument Landing System (voice, where available, on localizer channel).
LDA	Localizer Directional Aid.
LMM	Compass locator station when installed at middle marker site.
LOM	Compass locator station when installed at outer marker site.
MH	Non-directional radio beacon (homing) power less than 50 watts.
S	Simultaneous range homing signal and/or voice.
SABH	Non-directional radio beacon not authorized for IFR or ATC. Provides automatic weather broadcasts.
SDF	Simplified Direction Facility.
TACAN	UHF navigational facility-omnidirectional course and distance information.
VOR	VHF navigational facility-omnidirectional course only.
VOR/DME	Collocated VOR navigational facility and UHF standard distance measuring equipment.
VORTAC	Collected VOR and TACAN navigational facilities.
W	Without voice on radio facility frequency.
Z	VHF station on location marker at a LF radio facility.

(21) COMM/NAVAID REMARKS:
Pertinent remarks concerning communications and NAVAIDS.

F.

VOR RECEIVER CHECK POINTS
VOR/VORTAC

The list of VOR airborne and ground check points are included in this section. Use of these check points is explained in Part 1, Airman's Information Manual

NOTE: Under column headed "Type Check Pt. Gnd. AB/ALT", G stands for ground, A/ stands for airborne followed by a number (2300) indicating the altitude above mean sea level at which the check should be conducted. Facilities are listed in alphabetical order, in the state where the check points are located.

Facility Name (Arpt Name)	Freq/Ident	Type Check Pt. Gnd. AB/ALT	Azimuth from Fac. Mag	Dist. from Fac. N.M.	Check Point Description

ARKANSAS

Facility Name (Arpt Name)	Freq/Ident	Type Check Pt. Gnd. AB/ALT	Azimuth from Fac. Mag	Dist. from Fac. N.M.	Check Point Description
El Dorado (Goodwin Field)	108.2/ELD	G	228	3.8	On parking ramp at center twy.
Fayetteville (Drake Fld)	116.4/FYV	A/2500	182	14.3	Over white circle on arpt.
Flippin	115.1/FLP	A/1900	053	5.0	Over water tower at Mountain Home.
Fort Smith (Fort Smith Muni)	110.4/FSM	A/1500	233	5.2	Over water tank at W edge of arpt.
Gosnell	111.8/GOJ	A/1700	099	7.3	Over railroad bridge at Armorel.
Harrison (Boone County)	112.5/HRO	G	131	4.3	At int of N/S and E/W twys in front of trml bldg.
Jonesboro (Jonesboro Muni)	108.6/JBR	G	226	3.9	On SE corner of terminal ramp.
Little Rock (Adams Field)	113.9/LIT	G	315	4.5	On twy adjacent to junction rwy 14-32.
Monticello	111.6/MON	A/1500	305	5.7	Over white water tower.
Pine Bluff (Grider Field)	116.0/PBF	G	178	4.5	On center twys W of N/S rwy.
Texarkana	116.3/TXK	A/1500	164	6.0	Over water tower west of downtown.
Walnut Ridge (Walnut Ridge Regional)	114.5/ARG	G	051	1.7	On twy at parking ramp adjacent to tetrahedron.

Figure 7-2. VOR Receiver Check Points Excerpt from the Airport/Facility Directory

AIR ROUTE TRAFFIC CONTROL CENTERS

Air Route Traffic Control Center frequencies and their remoted transmitter sites are listed below for the coverage of this volume. Bold face type indicates high altitude frequencies, light face type indicates low altitude frequencies.

Ⓡ **CHICAGO CENTER**   H-1-3, L-10-11-12-21-23, A-1
  Burlington – 135.6
  Cedar Rapids – 121.4
  Des Moines – 127.05
  Dubuque – **128.65** 127.0 121.05 118.55 ①
  Washington – **133.85 132.8** 127.85
  CENTER REMARKS – ① Ultra hi alt freq above FL 350.

Ⓡ **DENVER CENTER** – **133.85 132.85** 126.5   H-1-2-3, L-5-6-7-8-9-10-11
  Crawford – **133.5** 127.2
  Goodland – **133.3 132.5** 127.65
  Grand Island – 132.7
  Hayes – **135.5**
  Natoma – 132.5
  Ogallala – **134.4** 132.7
  O'Neill – 132.7 **133.5**
  Rapid City – **134.65** 127.2

Ⓡ **KANSAS CITY CENTER** – 135.3   H-1-2-3, L-6-11-21-23, A-2
  Anthony – **134.3** 118.8
  Blue Springs – **134.7** 125.25 119.65
  Columbia – **135.4 134.5** 118.4
  Emporia – **132.25** 125.3 120.2
  Farmington – **132.65 128.4** 124.55
  Garden City – **133.45** 126.95 **126.35** 125.2 124.4
  Hutchinson – **135.9** 125.9 118.8
  Joplin – 128.6
  Kirksville – **135.0** 132.6
  Natoma – **132.95** 124.4
  Olathe – **135.3 134.7 126.8** 125.25 123.8 120.5 119.7
  Richland – **133.8** 124.1
  St. Charles – **133.4** 125.9 121.25
  St. Joseph – 127.9
  St. Louis – 128.1 125.5
  Salina – 134.9
  Springfield – **132.9** 127.5 **126.85**
  Stilwell – 125.55
  Topeka – 123.8 120.5

Ⓡ **MINNEAPOLIS CENTER** – **134.45** 125.5 120.3   H-1-3, L-10-11-12
  Aberdeen – 120.6
  Alexandria – **133.4** 126.1
  Bemidji – 134.74
  Brainerd – 118.05
  Clark – **135.8 133.8**
  Darwin – 125.5
  Des Moines – **132.4** 126.55 118.15
  Dickinson – **133.55 126.8**
  Duluth – **134.55** 127.9
  Fairmont – 127.75
  Fargo – **127.35**
  Farmington – **135.7** 125.9
  Ft. Dodge – **134.0**
  Grand Forks – **132.15** 127.8
  Grand Island – **135.1** 119.4
  Jamestown – 125.6 **124.2**
  International Falls – 120.9
  Lincoln – 124.8
  Marysville – **133.1** 126.4
  Mason City – **134.25** 127.3
  Minneapolis – **134.45** 125.5 120.3
  Minot – **127.6** 118.9
  Omaha – **134.35 128.75** 119.6
  Omaha – **134.35 128.75** 119.6
  Omaha RAPCON – 346.3
  O'Neill – 128.0
  Pierre – **134.8** 125.1
  Redwood Falls – **133.65** 127.1
  Rochester – 132.35
  Sioux City – **128.55 127.85** 124.1
  Sioux Falls – **135.45** 132.1
  CENTER REMARKS – Enroute radar svc avbl subject to flw ltd; ① Not avbl N of a line fr 46°30''N. 96°00''W drct to Hibbing VOR drct to Houghton VOR drct to 47°40''N 86°46''W. ② Radar wx advsy svc avbl only within a 290 NM pad of Minneapolis, NM and Omaha, NE.

Figure 7–3. Air Route Traffic Control Centers Excerpt from the Airport/Facility Directory

PREFERRED IFR ROUTES

A system of preferred routes has been established to guide pilots in planning their routes of flight, to minimize route changes during the operational phase of flight, and to aid in the efficient orderly management of the air traffic using federal airways. The preferred IFR routes which follow are designed to serve the needs of airspace users and to provide for a systematic flow of air traffic in the major terminal and en route flight environments. Cooperation by all pilots in filing preferred routes will result in fewer traffic delays and will better provide for efficient departure, en route and arrival air traffic service.

The following lists contain preferred IFR routes for the low altitude stratum and the high altitude stratum. The high altitude list is in two sections; the first section showing terminal to terminal routes and the second section showing single direction route segments. Also, on some high altitude routes low altitude airways are included as transition routes.

The following will explain the terms/abbreviations used in the listing:

1. Preferred routes beginning/ending with an airway number indicate that the airway essentially overlies the airport and flight are normally cleared directly on the airway.

2. Preferred IFR routes beginning/ending with a fix indicate that aircraft may be routed to/from these fixes via a Standard Instrument Departure (SID) route, radar vectors (RV), or a Standard Terminal Arrival Route (STAR).

3. Preferred IFR routes for major terminals selected are listed alphabetically under the name of the departure airport. Where several airports are in proximity they are listed under the principal airport and categorized as a metropolitan area; e.g., New York Metro Area.

4. Preferred IFR routes used in one direction only for selected segments, irrespective of point of departure or destination, are listed numerically showing the segment fixes and the direction and times effective.

5. Where more than one route is listed the routes have equal priority for use.

6. Official location identifiers are used in the route description for VOR/VORTAC navaids.

7. Intersection names are spelled out.

8. Navaid radial and distance fixes (e.g., ARD201113) have been used in the route description in an expediency and intersection names will be assigned as soon as routine processing can be accomplished. Navaid radial (no distance stated) may be used to describe a route to intercept a specified airway (e.g., MIV MIV101 V39; another navaid radial (e.g., UIM UIM255 GSW081); or an intersection (e.g., GSW081 Fitch).

9. Where two navaids, an intersection and a navaid, a navaid and a navaid radial and distance point, or any navigable combination of these route descriptions follow in succession, the route is direct.

10. The effective times for the routes are in GMT. Pilots planning flight between the terminals or route segments listed should file for the appropriate preferred IFR route.

11. (90-170 incl) altitude flight level assignment in hundred of feet.

12. The notations "pressurized" and "unpressurized" for certain low altitude preferred routes to Kennedy Airport indicate the preferred route based on aircraft preformance.

PREFERRED ROUTES—LOW

Terminals	Route	Effective Times (GMT)
DALLAS/FORT WORTH AREA		
Atlanta	V18 UIM V54 TXK V278 BHM V18N	
	MAYES V325 DALAS ATL	0000-2359
Houston	ENNIS LOA322 LOA V477W TNV	0000-2359
Memphis	V18 UIM V16 RAMSY	1200-1400
		1800-0000
Midway	DFW017 MLC202 MLC V63 UIN V116 JOT	0000-2359
New Orleans	V18 UIM V114 VEILS	0000-2359
O'Hare	DFW017 MLC202 MLC V63 UIN V116	
	PIA V262 BDF V10 VAINS	0000-2359
San Antonio	V358 ACT V17 WINKS	0000-2359
HOUSTON METRO AREA		
Dallas	V477 SCY SCY296 SEAGO	0000-2359
NEW ORLEANS METRO AREA		
Dallas	Walker V114N AEX V114 GGG V94 SCY	
	SCY296 SEAGO	0000-2359

PREFERRED ROUTES—HIGH

Terminals	Route	Effective Times (GMT)
ALBUQUERQUE		
Chicago Midway	J18 LVS J19 J26 BDF JOT	0000-2359
Chicago O'Hare	J18 LVS J19 J26 BDF BDF052 ORD235	
	VAINS	0000-2359
DALLAS/FORT WORTH METRO AREA		
Detroit Metro	DFW075 TXK240 TXK J131 EVV IND	
	FWA V11 V100 MOTOR	1100-0300
Kennedy	DFW075 TXK240 TXK LIT J6 BWG	
	BWG075 BKW263 BKW J147 GVE J37	
	J55 TWIGG ACY241 ACY ACY058	
	DPK221 SATES	1100-0300
La Guardia	DFW075 TXK240 TXK LIT J6 CRW J8	
	EWT EWT067 RBV249 RBV	1100-0300
Midway	DFW017 MLC202 MLC FYV J105 BDF JOT	1100-0300
Newark	DFW075 TXK240 TXK LIT J6 CRW J8	
	EWT EWT052 ARD234 ARD V433	
	HARRY	1100-0300

Figure 7-4. Preferred IFR Routes Excerpt from the Airport/Facility Directory

INFORMATION CURRENT AS OF APRIL 18, 1978

THIS SECTION CONTAINS NOTICES TO AIRMEN THAT ARE EXPECTED TO REMAIN IN EFFECT FOR AT LEAST SEVEN DAYS.
NOTE: NOTICES ARE ARRANGED IN ALPHABETICAL ORDER BY STATE (AND WITHIN STATE BY CITY OR LOCALITY). NEW OR REVISED DATA: NEW OR REVISED DATA ARE INDICATED BY BOLD ITALICIZING THE AIRPORT NAME.
NOTE: ALL TIMES ARE LOCAL UNLESS OTHERWISE INDICATED.

ALABAMA

BIRMINGHAM MUNI ARPT: ALS rwy 23 OTS. Tower 640 ft AGL 5.6 miles SW unlighted. Rwy 5–23 clsd 2300–0700 daily. ILS LOC rwy 5 OTS 2300–0700 daily. (3/78)
DOTHAN ARPT: UNICOM freq 123.0 cmsnd. (4/78)
EUTAW MUNI ARPT: Tower 525 ft MSL 3 miles SW unlighted. (5/78)
FAIRHOPE MUNI ARPT: Threshold lights OTS. (3/78)
GADSDEN MUNI ARPT: Rwy lights rwy 6–24 OTS. (5/78)
GROVE HILL MUNI ARPT: Tower 218 ft AGL 2 miles NNW unlighted. (5/78)
MOBILE, BATES FIELD: Rwy 18–36 wt brg capacity S – 26000 lbs. Rwy 18–36 closed over 26000 lbs. (4/78)
SELMA, SELFIELD ARPT: Rwy 18–36 closed permly. (3/78–2)
TUSKEGEE MOTON FIELD: Rwy lights operate dusk-2400. (4/78)

ALASKA

For complete information on Alaska consult the Alaska Supplement.

ARIZONA

SPECIAL NOTICE: The Grand Canyon Caverns Area. Quarry located 3 miles west-southwest of Grand Canyon Caverns Landing Strip. Acft are cautioned to avoid this area during daylight hours, if necessary to fly over the area maintain a minimum alt of 4000 ft AGL due to possible damage from flying rocks or turbulence caused by blasting. (3/78)
GRAND CANYON AND PETRIFIED FOREST NATIONAL PARKS: All pilots are requested to avoid flying below the canyon rim and to maintain a distance 1500 ft above and horizontally from all scenic overlooks, parks, and trails. (10/74)
GRAND CANYON NATIONAL PARK: ATCT hours 0700–1900. (5/78–5)
HUNT GREEN VALLEY ARPT: Arpt closed. (11/76)
PARKER MUNI ARPT:: VASI rwy 1 and rwy 19 OTS. TPA 800 ft AGL. Rwy 1 open full length. (4/78)
PAYSON ARPT: TPA 1044 ft AGL. (3/78–2)
PHOENIX SKY HARBOR INTL ARPT: ILS rwy 8R and rwy 26L OTS except IFR weather. (4/78)
RIMROCK ARPT: TPA 625 ft AGL. (3/78–2)
SCOTTSDALE MUNI ARPT: Prior permission required for transient acft parking due to construction, adjacent parallel twy and acft parking area until June 30. (5/78)
WICKENBURG MUNI ARPT:: Rwy 5–23 now 5050 ft. TPA 1000 ft AGL. (4/78)
WILLIAMS MUNI ARPT: Rwy lights rwy 2–20 52 ft off edge of rwy. (5/78–2)
WINSLOW MUNI ARPT: Rwy 4–22 closed jet/ turbine acft. (5/78)

ARKANSAS

ARKADELPHIA MUNI ARPT: Rwy lights OTS. (4/78)
BATESVILLE REGIONAL ARPT: Rwy lights rwy 17–35 OTS. (4/78)
LITTLE ROCK, ADAMS FIELD: ILS OM rwy 22 OTS until Jun 1. (4/78)
MALVERN MUNI ARPT: Rotating beacon OTS. (10/77–2)
NASHVILLE HOWARD COUNTY ARPT: Rotating beacon and low intensity rwy lights OTS until July 1. (2/78)
POCAHONTAS MUNI ARPT: VASI rwy 18 OTS. (5/78)
ROGERS: NDB "ROG" OTS. (3/78)
SILOAM SPRINGS, SMITH FIELD: Threshold rwy 18 dsplcd 305 ft. (2/78)

CALIFORNIA

SPECIAL NOTICE: Do not mistake dirt strip on large island, Lake Berryessa, lctd lat 38–34 long 122–13 for airport. Strip is unauthorized and unsafe. (10/74)
SPECIAL NOTICE: The MELONES RESERVOIR/DAM AREA, lctd about 5 to 12 miles SW of Columbia Arpt and about 8 miles S of Frog Town Arpt at Angels Camps:acft are cautioned to avoid the area, if necessary to fly over the area maintain a minimum alt of 4000 ft, due to possible damage from flying rock or turbulence caused by continuous blasting for dam construction until 1979.
SPECIAL NOTICE: Avoid flying below 1000 ft over a 400 acre Wildlife Refuge along the south side of the mouth of the Salinas River and ocean shoreline eastward. (1/76)
ANO NUEVO ISLAND: Avoid low flying in the vicinity and over island. Biological research of wild life in progress. (10/74)
APPLE VALLEY ARPT: VASI rwy 36 cmsnd. (3/78–2)
AVALON, CATALINA ARPT: UNICOM now freq 122.7. (4/78)
COLTON AIRPARK: Arpt closed permly. (5/78–5)
CORONA MUNI ARPT: Tower 828 ft MSL 3 miles east unlighted. Rwy lights rwy 7–25 and rotating beacon OTS. (4/78)
COVELO, ROUND VALLEY ARPT: Rwy lights rwy 10–28 OTS thru May 6. (9/77)
DAGGETT, BARSTOW-DAGGETT ARPT: Rwy lights operate dusk-2200, after 2200 contact Daggett FSS. (3/78–2)
DELANO MUNI ARPT: Rwy 14–32 closed, parallel twy open non-turbojet acft 12500 lbs and under. (3/78)
FULLERTON MUNI ARPT: RAIL rwy 24 OTS. (3/77)
HALF MOON BAY ARPT: VASI rwy 30 cmsnd. (3/78–2)
HOLLISTER MUNI ARPT: UNICOM freq 123.0 cmsnd. (4/78)
LOS ANGELES ARTCC: The use of 720 channel communication equipment is required for continued unrestricted IFR operations in the Los Angeles ARTCC high altitude sectors. (4/78)
LOS ANGELES INTL ARPT: ALS rwy 25R now simplified short apch light system with RAILS. (5/78–5)
MAMMOTH LAKES ARPT: Arpt closed nights, rwy lights OTS. (3/78)
NAPA COUNTY ARPT: Flocks of gulls in vicinity of arpt and on rwys primarily during rainy weather. (4/78)
NEEDLES ARPT: TPA 1000 ft AGL. (4/78)
OAKLAND ARTCC: The use of 720 channel communication equipment is required for continued unrestricted IFR operations in the Oakland ARTCC high altitude sectors. (4/78)

Figure 7-5. Excerpt of NOTAM (D) Data Found in the Notices to Airmen Publication

Graphic Notices of Operational Data

7.7 Although this quarterly publication (available by subscription from the Superintendent of Documents) is not used as extensively by instrument pilots as the two previously mentioned publications, it should, nevertheless, be consulted during the flight planning process. Information which is located in this publication includes:

1. A tabulation of parachute jump areas.
2. Special Notice Area Graphics.
3. Terminal Area Graphics.
4. Terminal Radar Service Area (TRSA) Graphics.
5. Olive Branch Routes.
6. Other similar data, as required, not subject to frequent change.

Notices to Airmen (NOTAMs)

7.8 Prior to any instrument flight, pilots should review the *most current* en route and destination flight information *at the local Flight Service Station.* NOTAMs are an excellent source for determining some of this information, and are categorized as follows: Landing Area NOTAMs, Lighting Aid NOTAMs, Air Navigation Aid NOTAMs, Special Data NOTAMs, and Regulatory (FDC) NOTAMs. The types of NOTAMs that contain the above categorized information are discussed in the following paragraphs.

NOTAMs (D)

7.9 Information which is of a critical nature that could affect the safety of flight operations is considered NOTAM (D) data. This data is prepared for *distant* dissemination by FSS personnel, and is transmitted over the teletype circuits and appended to the hourly Surface Aviation Weather Reports (discussed in 3.130) when such information cannot be immediately included in the Airport/Facility Directory or aeronautical charts. When NOTAM (D) data is expected to remain in effect for seven days or longer, it is then also included in the Notices to Airmen publication which is issued every 14 days by the Superintendent of Documents. (Figure 7-5) For NOTAM (D) data of a more permanent nature, the changes may also be published on appropriate aeronautical charts.

NOTAMs (L)

7.10 Information that is of a less critical nature, and does not meet NOTAM (D) criteria, is disseminated by FSS personnel as NOTAM (L) data. This data is only reported *locally* by means of telautograph, telephone, control towers, Flight Service Stations, and local ATIS broadcasts. Unlike NOTAM (D) data, NOTAM (L) data is not appended to the hourly Surface Aviation Weather Reports, nor is it included in the hourly NOSUM.

FDC NOTAMs

7.11 Data relating to changes, regulatory in nature, that affect the en route structure or instrument approach procedures are disseminated by the National Flight Data Center (NFDC) as FDC NOTAMs. Initially these NOTAMs are reported through "all circuit" dissemination. Furthermore, the FDC NOTAMs will appear in the Notices to Airmen publication if the data is still in effect at the date of publication. (Figure 7-6)

7.12 FDC NOTAMs are identified (on teletype transmissions and in the NOTAM publication) as Flight Information/Permanent (FI/P) and as Flight Information/Temporary (FI/T). The identifier FI/P implies NOTAM conditions are expected to continue for more than 45 days; FI/T implies NOTAM conditions are expected to exist for a period *less* than 45 days.

FEDERAL AIRWAY SYSTEMS

7.13 There are different types of route structures that a pilot may plan to fly in the Federal Airway System. A Federal Airway is controlled airspace in the form of a corridor, the centerline of which is defined by the use of radio navigation aids. Three primary route systems have been established for air navigation purposes. These three route systems are:

1. VOR Route System (referred to as Victor airways).
2. Jet Route System (referred to as Jet airways).
3. Area Navigation (RNAV) Route System.

7.14 The **VOR Route (Airway) System** consists of airways designated from 1,200 feet above the surface (or in some instances higher) up to but not including 18,000 feet MSL. The VOR Airway System is designed to serve aircraft which operate at these altitudes. These Low Altitude Airways which compose the VOR Airway System are predicated primarily on VOR/VORTAC navigation aids and are depicted on En Route Low Altitude Charts. In addition to outlining the VOR Airway System, En Route Low Altitude Charts also include information relative to limits of controlled airspace, position identification and frequencies of radio aids, selected airports, minimum en route and minimum obstruction clearance altitudes, airway distances, reporting points, restricted areas, and related data.

7.15 The **Jet Route System** consists of high altitude routes established from 18,000 feet MSL to FL 450 inclusively. This route system is designed to serve those high performance aircraft which operate at or between these altitudes. En Route High Alti-

F.A.A. NATIONAL FLIGHT DATA CENTER

FDC NOTAMS

THE LISTING BELOW INCLUDES, IN PART, CHANGES IN FLIGHT DATA, PARTICULARLY OF A REGULATORY NATURE, WHICH AFFECT STANDARD INSTRUMENT APPROACH PROCEDURES, AERONAUTICAL CHARTS AND SELECTED FLIGHT RESTRICTIONS, PRIOR TO THEIR NORMAL PUBLICATION CYCLE. THEREFORE, THEY SHOULD BE REVIEWED DURING PRE-FLIGHT PLANNING. THIS LISTING INCLUDES ALL FDC NOTAMS CURRENT THRU FDC NOTAM NUMBER SHOWN BELOW.

LEGEND

FDC ------- NATIONAL FLIGHT DATA CENTER
6/103 ----- ACCOUNTABILITY NUMBER ASSIGNED TO THE MESSAGE ORIGINATOR BY FDC
FI/T ------ FLIGHT INFORMATION/TEMPORARY
FI/P ------ FLIGHT INFORMATION/PERMANENT
--------- NEW NOTAM

THE FOLLOWING LISTING CONTAINS FDC NOTAMS
THRU FDC 8/482

EAST CENTRAL

ILLINOIS

FDC 8/141 FI/T CHICAGOLAND CHICAGO/WHEELING ILL. TAKEOFF MINIMUMS RWY 13 200 FOOT CEILING 1 MILE VISIBILITY REQUIRED.

#FDC 8/466 FI/T MT VERNON-OUTLAND MT VERNON IL. ILS RWY 23 AMDT 2 STRAIGHT-IN DECISION HEIGHT 721 FEET VISIBILITY 3/4 MILE HEIGHT ABOVE TOUCHDOWN 250 FEET ALL CATEGORIES. STRAIGHT-IN LOCALIZER VISIBILITY 3/4 MILE CATEGORY A B AND C. VOR RWY 23 AMDT 7 STRAIGHT-IN VISIBILITY 3/4 MILE CATEOGRY A AND B.

INDIANA

FDC 8/250 FI/T MADISON MUNICIPAL MADISON IN. NDB RWY 3 AMDT 3 AND VOR/DME RWY 3 AMDT 2 IFR DEPARTURE PROCEDURE RWY 3 AND RWY 21 CLIMB RUNWAY HEADING TO 1500 FEET BEFORE TURNING SOUTHEAST.

KENTUCKY

FDC 8/412 FI/T US GOVERNMENT ENROUTE LOW ALTITUDE CHART L21 PANEL D FROTH INT KY SHOULD BE DESCRIBED AS BWG VORTAC R-258/44 AND CCT VORTAC R-183/35.

MICHIGAN

FDC 7/1121 FI/T LUCE COUNTY NEWBERRY MI. VOR RWY 11 AMDT 4 VOR RWY 29 AMDT 4 USE SAULT STE MARIE MICHIGAN ALTIMETER SETTING.

FDC 7/1407 FI/T MUSKEGON COUNTY MUSKEGON MI. ILS RWY 32 AMDT 9 STRAIGHT-IN RWY 32 DECISION HEIGHT 877 FEET HEIGHT ABOVE TOUCHDOWN 250 FEET VISIBILITY RVR 4000 FEET ALL CATEGORIES. STRAIGHT-IN LOCALIZER RWY 32 VISIBILITY RVR 4000 FEET ALL CATEGORIES. RADAR-1 AMDT 2 RWY 32 VISIBILITY RVR 4000 FEET CATEGORIES A B AND C. TAKEOFF MINIMUMS RWY 32 RVR 4000 FEET AUTHORIZED FOR FAR 135 OPERATORS.

FDC 7/1431 FI/T KALAMAZOO MUNI KALAMAZOO MI. NDB RWY 35 AMDT 9 MISSED APPROACH POINT 5.6 MILES AFTER PASSING AZ LOM. STRAIGHT-IN RWY 35 HEIGHT ABOVE TOUCHDOWN 452 FEET ALL CATEGORIES. TOUCHDOWN ZONE ELEVATION RWY 35 868 FEET.

FDC 7/1487 FI/T KALAMAZOO MUNI KALAMAZOO MI. ILS RWY 35 AMDT 11 DISTANCE FINAL APPROACH FIX TO MISSED APPROACH POINT 5.6 MILES FINAL APPROACH FIX TO THRESHOLD 5.6 MILES. DISTANCE TO THRESHOLD FROM OUTER MARKER 5.6 MILES: FROM MIDDLE MARKER 0.4 MILES: FROM GLIDE SLOPE ANTENNA 1150 FEET. THRESHOLD CROSSING HEIGHT 57 FEET. TOUCHDOWN ZONE ELEVATION 868 FEET. STRAIGHT-IN ILS RWY 35 DECISION HEIGHT 1068 FEET ALL CATEGORIES. STRAIGHT-IN LOCALIZER RWY 35 HEIGHT ABOVE TOUCHDOWN 392 FEET ALL CATEGORIES. MISSED APPROACH LOCALIZER 5.6 MILES AFTER PASSING AZ LOM. LOC BC RWY 17 AMDT 9 DISTANCE FINAL APPROACH FIX TO MISSED APPROACH POINT AND THRESHOLD 3.9 MILES.

Figure 7-6. Excerpt of FDC NOTAM Information Found in Notices to Airmen Publication

tude Charts are used to describe the Jet Route System and provide much information similar to the information presented on the En Route Low Altitude Charts.

7.16 At present, the **RNAV Route System** is a high altitude route system established from and including 18,000 feet MSL to FL 450, covering the 48 adjacent states. Only properly equipped and certificated aircraft may use these routes. (The presence of RNAV routes, however, should not be interpreted to signify that RNAV equipment is to be used exclusively for these routes. RNAV equipment may also be used to navigate Victor airways, many Terminal Arrival/Departure routes, and even *some* RNAV-approved instrument approach procedures.) Area Navigation (RNAV) High Altitude Charts define the RNAV Route System. Information depicted on the Area Navigation (RNAV) High Altitude Charts includes: RNAV routes, waypoints, trackangle, changeover points, distances, selected navigational aids and airports, special use airspace, oceanic routes, and transitional information.

7.17 *Special Notes:*
1. *Future en route chart discussion will be generally limited to the En Route Low Altitude Charts since much of the nomenclature presented on all the en route charts is the same. En Route Low Altitude Charts are the most widely used aeronautical charts for en route instrument navigation.*
2. *Although detailed information concerning area charts, profile descent procedures, SIDs, STARs, IFR departure procedures, and instrument approach procedure charts is not incorporated in this chapter (they are discussed in chapters 8 and 9), these charts are also considered to be important considerations in the flight planning process.*

IFR WALL PLANNING CHARTS (PUBLISHED BY NATIONAL OCEAN SURVEY)

7.18 If the East and West IFR Wall Planning Charts are available, a pilot should use them to plan the route of flight when the proposed cross-country flight covers a substantial distance. These charts only display *low altitude airways* utilizing VOR facilities and *oceanic routes* off coastal areas. Included on the IFR Wall Planning Charts are Air Route Traffic Control Center (ARTCC) boundaries, state boundaries, Special Use Airspace, time zone lines, and outlines and identification of En Route Low Altitude Charts. Figure 7-7 illustrates an excerpt from an IFR Wall Planning Chart.

EN ROUTE LOW ALTITUDE CHARTS

7.19 There are twenty-eight (U.S. series L-1 through L-28) Low Altitude Instrument En Route Charts published by the National Ocean Survey covering the entire United States.

7.20 Low Altitude Charts are printed and distributed every 56 days (to ensure that depicted data are current and reliable), and the effective use dates of the charts are printed on the front cover. (Figure 7-8) In addition, all of the terminal frequencies (for civil airports) of approach and departure control, ATIS, VOTs, control towers, and VORs, as well as additional information when space prohibits placement on the chart, are printed on the end covers of the charts (in the communication index).

7.21 *Special Note: Pilots are urged to use only the latest issue of aeronautical charts for flight planning and conducting flight operations.*

En Route Low Altitude Chart—Legend

7.22 A complete colored legend of the En Route Low Altitude Chart with an excerpt from an En Route Low Altitude Chart is located in the Appendix of this text (Figures G-2 and G-3). This legend should be thoroughly reviewed before continuing the study of this chapter.

Chart Depiction of Airspace

7.23 Aircraft operations conducted in controlled and uncontrolled airspace are varied. Due to the nature of some of the operations conducted, necessary restrictions must be placed upon other aircraft operations for safety reasons.

7.24 Controlled airspace is defined as airspace, designated as a **Continental Control Area, control area, control zone, Terminal Control Area, or transition area,** within which some or all aircraft may be subject to Air Traffic Control. One of the primary purposes of controlled airspace is to preclude VFR traffic from entering this airspace when the weather is below VFR minimums. Thus, all aircraft in controlled airspace on instrument flight plans with ATC are guaranteed lateral and vertical separation when the weather is below basic VFR weather minimums. (When the weather is VFR, however, pilots with IFR clearances must provide their own separation from VFR aircraft.)

7.25 Controlled airspace which is outlined on the En Route Low Altitude Chart includes Terminal Control Areas, Victor airways, and control zones. Color codes, symbols, and airspace information boxes are used to distinguish between controlled and uncontrolled airspace (as illustrated in the Appendix). It would be of great benefit to review Figure 6-5 during parts of the following discussion of the more important different types of airspace.

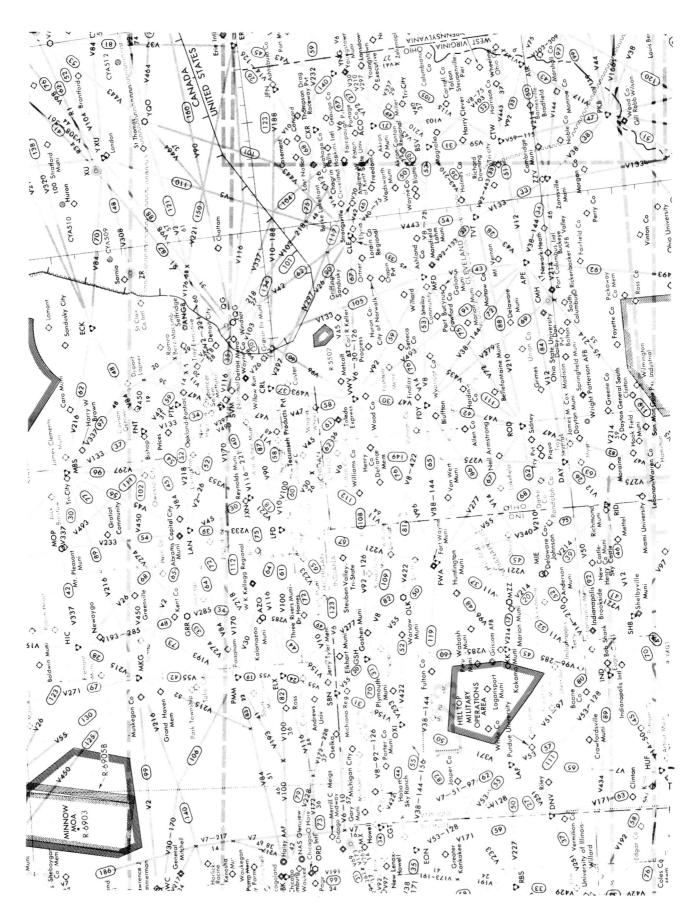

Figure 7-7. Excerpt from an IFR Wall Planning Chart

7.26 The **Air Defense Identification Zone** (ADIZ) is defined as the area of airspace over land or water, extending upward from the surface, within which the ready identification, the location, and the control of aircraft are required in the interest of national security. The types of ADIZ are:

1. Domestic Air Defense Identification Zone—an ADIZ within the United States along an international boundary of the United States.
2. Coastal Air Defense Identification Zone—an ADIZ over the coastal water of the United States.
3. Distant Early Warning Identification Zone (DEWIZ)—an ADIZ over the coastal waters of the state of Alaska. Air Defense Identification Zones are depicted on charts by the continuous pattern (••••••) forming a line.

7.27 Airport traffic areas are generally defined as that airspace within a horizontal radius of 5 statute miles from the geographical center of any airport at which a control tower is *operating*, extending from the surface up to, but not including, an altitude of 3,000 feet above the elevation of the airport. Unless otherwise authorized or required by ATC, no person may operate an aircraft within an airport traffic area except for the purpose of landing at, or taking off from, an airport within that area. Airport traffic areas are *not* depicted on En Route Low Altitude Charts; however, pilots may determine if an airport has an airport traffic area by consulting the front cover of the chart and noting if the airport is equipped with a control tower.

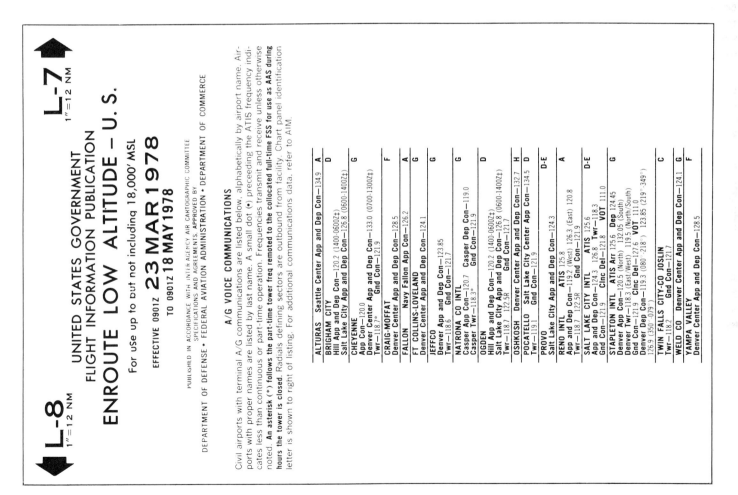

Figure 7-8. A Typical Front Cover of an En Route Low Altitude Chart

7.28 The **Continental Control Area** consists of the airspace of the 48 contiguous states, the District of Columbia, and Alaska (excluding the Alaska peninsula west of Longitude 160°00'00''W), at and above 14,500 feet MSL, but does not include:

1. The airspace less than 1,500 feet above the surface of the earth; or
2. Prohibited and restricted areas, other than the restricted areas listed in * FAR Part 71 Subpart D.

The Continental Control Area is *not* depicted on En Route Low Altitude Charts.

7.29 **Control areas** are considered to be that airspace designated as Colored Federal Airways, VOR Federal Airways, Terminal Control Areas, Additional Control Areas, and Control Area Extensions, but not including the Continental Control Area. Unless otherwise designated, control areas also include the airspace between a segment of a main VOR airway and its associated alternate segments.

7.30 **Control zones** are defined as controlled airspace which extends upward from the surface and terminates at the base of the Continental Control Area. Control zones that do not underlie the Continental Control Area have no upper limit. A control zone may include one or more airports and is normally a circular area within a radius of 5 statute miles and any extensions necessary to include instrument departure and arrival paths. Most control zones are depicted on En Route Low Altitude Charts by a broken blue line (similar to the control zone symbol depicted on sectional charts) except in the case when fixed-wing aircraft are prohibited from special VFR flight. In this situation, control zones are identified by a series of *T* symbols outlining the control zone. When a control zone is not continuously in effect, the fact is appropriately noted on the chart near the control zone symbol.

7.31 The **Positive Control Area** is *not* described on En Route Low Altitude Charts simply because the upper limit of these charts underlies the lower limit of the Positive Control Area. (Refer to paragraph 6.30 for a dimensional description of the Positive Control Area.)

7.32 **Special Use Airspace** is airspace of defined dimensions identified by an area on the surface of the earth wherein activities must be confined because of their nature, and/or wherein limitations may be imposed upon aircraft operations that are not a part of those activities. The types of Special Use Airspace are:

1. **Alert Area**—Airspace which may contain a high volume of pilot training activities or an unusual type of aerial activity—neither of which is hazardous to aircraft. Alert Areas are depicted on aeronautical charts for the information of non-participating pilots. All activities within an Alert Area are conducted in accordance with Federal Aviation Regulations, and pilots of participating aircraft as well as pilots transiting the area are equally responsible for collision avoidance.

2. **Controlled Firing Area**—Airspace wherein activities are conducted under conditions so controlled as to eliminate hazards to nonparticipating aircraft and to ensure the safety of persons and property on the ground.

3. **Military Operations Area (MOA)**—An MOA is an airspace assignment of defined vertical and lateral dimensions established outside Positive Control Areas to separate/segregate certain military activities from IFR traffic and to identify for VFR traffic where these activities are conducted.

4. **Prohibited Area**—Designated airspace within which the flight of aircraft is prohibited.

5. **Restricted Area**—Airspace within which the flight of aircraft, while not wholly prohibited, is subject to restriction. Most restricted areas are designated joint use, and IFR/VFR operations in the area may be authorized by the controlling ATC facility when it is not being utilized by the using agency. Restricted areas are depicted on en route charts. Where joint use is authorized, the name of the ATC controlling facility is also shown.

6. **Warning Area**—Airspace which may contain hazards to nonparticipating aircraft in international airspace.

7.33 Areas of Special Use Airspace are enclosed by color-coded crosshatching (▨▨▨). Normally these areas are color coded in blue, but Military Operations Areas are color coded in a dark brown color. Information that *may* be included in Special Use Airspace areas consists of: area identification, effective altitudes, operation times, weather conditions during which the area is in operation, and the voice call of the controlling agency. When a Victor airway penetrates Special Use Airspace, it is indicated by the pattern (▦) overlaying part of the airway. (Refer to the legend in Appendix G of this text.)

7.34 **Terminal Control Areas** are indicated on the En Route Low Altitude Chart by an area of light blue shading in the area of the TCA. A special TCA identification box is another distinguishing feature of Terminal Controlled Airspace. (Refer to paragraph 6.29 for a TCA dimensional description.)

7.35 **Transition areas** are defined as controlled airspace extending upward from 700 feet or more above the surface of the earth when designated in

---

* FAR Part 71 Subpart D is not contained in this text.

conjunction with an airport for which an approved instrument approach procedure has been prescribed, or from 1,200 feet or more above the surface of the earth when designated in conjunction with airway route structures or segments. Unless otherwise limited, transition areas terminate at the base of the overlying controlled airspace. Transition areas are designed to contain IFR operations in controlled airspace during portions of the terminal operation and while transiting between the terminal and en route environment. Transition areas are *not* illustrated on En Route Low Altitude Charts.

7.36 A **Victor airway** is defined as a control area, or portion thereof, established in the form of a corridor, the centerline of which is defined by radio navigational aids. The VOR airways are predicated solely on VOR/VORTAC navigation aids, except in Alaska, and are depicted on aeronautical charts by a *V* ("Victor") followed by the airway number, for example V–26. Segments of Victor airways in Alaska are based on LF/MF navigation aids and charted in a brown color instead of blue on en route charts. These airways are numbered similarly to U.S. highways. As in the highway numbering system, a segment of an airway which is common to two or more routes carries the numbers of all the airways which coincide for that segment. When such is the case, a pilot, in filing a flight plan, needs to indicate only that airway number of the route which he is using. **Alternate airways** are identified by their location with respect to the associated main airway. "Victor 11 East" indicates an alternate airway associated with, and lying to the east of, Victor 11.

7.37 Uncontrolled airspace is that portion of the airspace that has not been designated as Continental Control Area, control area, control zone, Terminal Control Area, or transition area, and within which ATC has neither the authority nor the responsibility for exercising control over air traffic. Uncontrolled airspace is indicated on En Route Low Altitude Charts by a light brown shading overlaying the areas of uncontrolled airspace. This shading, thereby, distinguishes uncontrolled airspace from areas of controlled airspace (which are generally open white areas). Pilots should inspect brown shaded areas carefully to avoid misinterpreting the brown shaded outline of bodies of water (such as the Great Lakes) for areas of uncontrolled airspace. Bodies of water can easily be distinguished from uncontrolled airspace since the shading for bodies of water outlines the water and is a darker shading than that used for uncontrolled airspace.

7.38 Instrument pilots should remember that the highest altitude that uncontrolled airspace extends to is generally 14,500 feet MSL since the Continental Control Area blankets most of the United States.

En Route Low Altitude Chart—IFR Altitude Designations

7.39 Another consideration during flight planning, in addition to airspace, is charted altitudes. The Federal Aviation Administration establishes IFR altitudes along Federal airways in controlled airspace after consideration of:

1. Obstruction clearance criteria;
2. Navigation signal coverage for accurate navigation; *and*
3. Two-way radio communications.

7.40 Knowledge of the following definitions is essential in the interpretation of charted altitudes. (Refer to Figure 7–9 when studying the following definitions.)

1. **Maximum Authorized Altitude (MAA)**—A published altitude representing the maximum useable altitude or flight level for an airspace structure or route segment. It is the highest charted altitude for which an MEA is designated at which adequate reception of navigation signals is assured. (An MAA designation is primarily due to interference from VOR navigation signals on the same frequency at altitudes above the MAA.)

2. **Minimum Crossing Altitude (MCA)**—The minimum altitude at which certain radio facilities or intersections must be crossed in specified directions of flight. If a normal climb, commenced immediately after passing a fix beyond which a higher MEA applies, would *not* assure adequate obstruction clearance, an MCA is specified. The designated MCA symbol indicates that the MCA must be reached *prior to* passing the symbol location. Located next to the symbol will be the name of the location (or intersection), the airway number(s), the minimum crossing altitude(s), and the direction(s) of flight to which the MCA pertains. (Note: A fix, as previously mentioned, is a geographical position determined by reference to one or more radio NAVAIDs.)

3. **Minimum En Route Altitude (MEA)**—The lowest published altitude between radio fixes which assures acceptable navigational signal coverage and meets obstacle clearance requirements between those fixes. The MEA prescribed for a Federal airway, or segment thereof, applies to the entire width of the airway, segment, or route between the radio fixes defining the airway, segment or route. In Figure 7–9, note the two numbers (altitudes) printed next to the airway line. The top altitude depicted is the MEA. If only one altitude is listed, it is the MEA. The MEA is also occa-

sionally different for opposite directions along an airway due to rising or lowering terrain.

4. **Minimum Obstruction Clearance Altitude (MOCA)**—The lowest published altitude in effect between radio fixes on VOR airways, off-airway routes, or route segments, which meets obstacle clearance requirements for the entire route segment and which assures acceptable navigation signal coverage only within 22 nautical miles of a VOR. The obstruction clearance that is normally afforded is at least 1,000 feet (2,000 feet in mountainous areas) above the highest terrain or obstruction within a horizontal distance of 5 statute miles on either side of the centerline of the airway or route. The MOCA is printed directly below the MEA and is identified by an asterisk (*). The designation of a MOCA indicates that a higher MEA has been established for that particular airway or segment because of signal reception requirements. When no MOCA is shown on the chart, the MEA and MOCA are considered to be the same. A flight altitude at the MOCA may be requested by a pilot, or assigned by ATC for traffic control purposes, for use within 22 nautical miles of the VOR. The MOCA may be assigned beyond 22 nautical miles provided certain special conditions exist. Beyond 22 nautical miles, the MOCA assures only obstruction clearance.

5. **Minimum Reception Altitude (MRA)**—The lowest altitude required to receive adequate signals to determine specific fixes. This altitude is identified on En Route Low Altitude Charts by a flag containing an "R." Reception of signals from a radio facility located off the airway being flown may be inadequate at the designated MEA, in which case an MRA is designated for the fix. A DME fix arrow (| ➔ or ▭▷ |) at a fix where an MRA is given indicates that the fix may also be identified with DME. If DME is used to identify the fix, the MRA does not apply since it is not necessary to receive the facility off the airway.

Maximum Authorized Altitude (MAA)

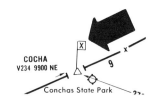

Minimum Crossing Altitude (MCA)

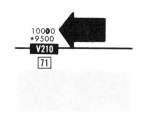

Minimum Enroute Altitude (MEA)

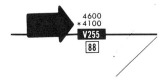

Minimum Obstruction Clearance Altitude (MOCA)

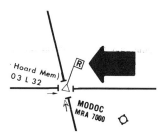

Minimum Reception Altitude (MRA)

Figure 7-9. NOS En Route Low Altitude Chart - Altitude Nomenclature

En Route Low Altitude Chart—ARTCC Boundaries/Symbols

7.41 The Air Traffic Control System is extensive. Consequently, Air Route Traffic Control Centers (ARTCC) have been established throughout the United States for the primary purpose of providing service to aircraft operating on IFR flight plans within controlled airspace. These areas controlled by the centers are identified on NOS En Route Charts by the pattern (⎍⎍⎍), with the names of the Air Route Traffic Control Centers on their respective sides of the pattern. (Figure 7–10)

7.42 Many Air Route Traffic Control Centers regulate areas of several hundreds of miles from the main center facilities. As a result, the areas served by these centers are divided into sectors, and each sector is managed by one or a team of controllers. Center controllers are capable of directly communicating with IFR air traffic on certain frequencies, and maximum communications coverage is only possible through the employment of Remote Center Air/Ground (RCAG) sites. Each sector has its own

frequency, so as an IFR flight progresses from one sector to another, the pilot is requested to change to the next sector's discrete frequency. Also as an IFR flight progresses, that particular flight's data is passed along from sector to sector within each Center, and from Center to Center along the route, thereby insuring the orderly flow of traffic from area to area. Figure 7–10 illustrates a typical ARTCC remoted site symbol.

Radio Aids to Navigation and Communication Data Boxes

7.43 Information that can be derived from Radio Aids to Navigation and Communication data boxes is remarkably abundant. The legend which appears on the En Route Low Altitude Chart (and in the Appendix of this text), although reasonably thorough, does not provide detailed examples. In order to supplement the information in the legend, Figure 7–11 is provided to illustrate some examples of several common types of information that can be obtained from the Radio Aids to Navigation data boxes.

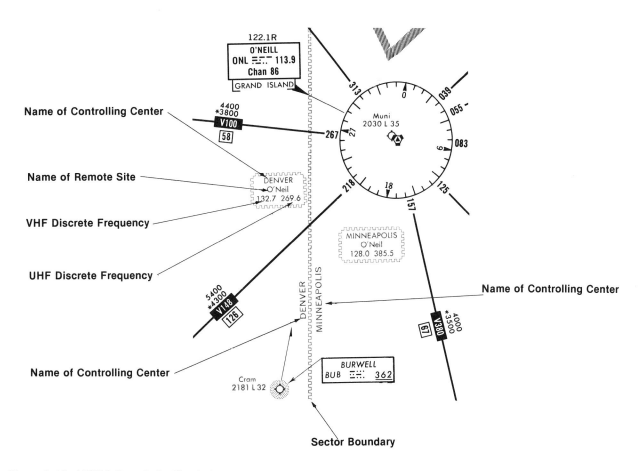

Figure 7-10. ARTCC Boundaries/Symbols

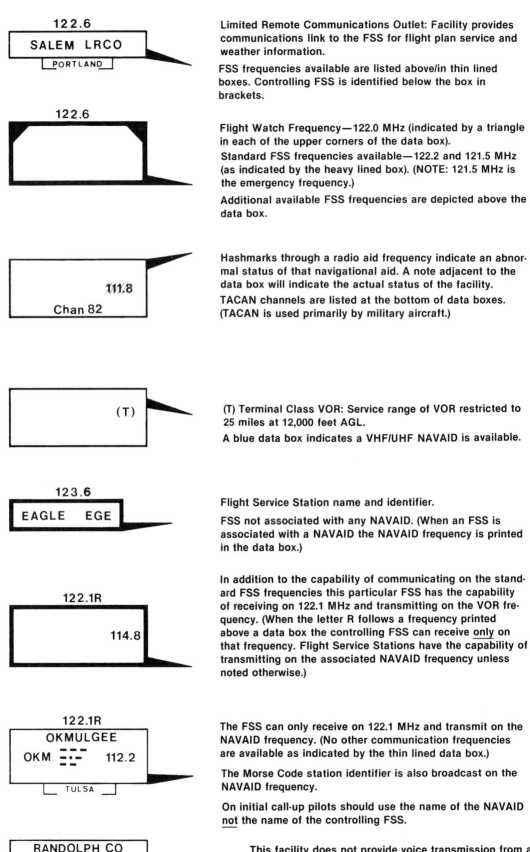

122.6

SALEM LRCO

PORTLAND

Limited Remote Communications Outlet: Facility provides communications link to the FSS for flight plan service and weather information.

FSS frequencies available are listed above/in thin lined boxes. Controlling FSS is identified below the box in brackets.

122.6

Flight Watch Frequency—122.0 MHz (indicated by a triangle in each of the upper corners of the data box).

Standard FSS frequencies available—122.2 and 121.5 MHz (as indicated by the heavy lined box). (NOTE: 121.5 MHz is the emergency frequency.)

Additional available FSS frequencies are depicted above the data box.

111.8

Chan 82

Hashmarks through a radio aid frequency indicate an abnormal status of that navigational aid. A note adjacent to the data box will indicate the actual status of the facility.

TACAN channels are listed at the bottom of data boxes. (TACAN is used primarily by military aircraft.)

(T)

(T) Terminal Class VOR: Service range of VOR restricted to 25 miles at 12,000 feet AGL.

A blue data box indicates a VHF/UHF NAVAID is available.

123.6

EAGLE   EGE

Flight Service Station name and identifier.

FSS not associated with any NAVAID. (When an FSS is associated with a NAVAID the NAVAID frequency is printed in the data box.)

122.1R

114.8

In addition to the capability of communicating on the standard FSS frequencies this particular FSS has the capability of receiving on 122.1 MHz and transmitting on the VOR frequency. (When the letter R follows a frequency printed above a data box the controlling FSS can receive <u>only</u> on that frequency. Flight Service Stations have the capability of transmitting on the associated NAVAID frequency unless noted otherwise.)

122.1R

OKMULGEE

OKM   112.2

TULSA

The FSS can only receive on 122.1 MHz and transmit on the NAVAID frequency. (No other communication frequencies are available as indicated by the thin lined data box.)

The Morse Code station identifier is also broadcast on the NAVAID frequency.

On initial call-up pilots should use the name of the NAVAID <u>not</u> the name of the controlling FSS.

RANDOLPH CO

RQY   <u>284</u>

This facility does not provide voice transmission from any FSS. (A NAVAID frequency that is underlined indicates that voice transmission by the controlling agency is not possible through that particular NAVAID.)

The NDB frequency of the illustrated data box is 284 kHz. [A brown data box is an indication of a LF/MF NAVAID facility. LF/MF NAVAID information (printed in brown) may also be included in blue navigation and communication data boxes.]

Figure 7-11. Distinguishing Features of Radio Aids to Navigation and Communication Data Boxes

Chart Representation of ILS, Localizer, and SDF Symbols

7.44 When reviewing the En Route Low Altitude Charts, some pilots become quite confused when trying to determine if an airport has a published ILS, Localizer, or SDF instrument approach procedure. Figure 7-12 illustrates these symbols and their specific functions.

7.45 An ILS localizer or SDF localizer is often used (in addition to providing course guidance) in conjunction with another NAVAID to establish an intersection or reporting point. When used to establish an intersection or reporting point, the localizer is said to be providing an "ATC function" and is so symbolically noted on the En Route Low Altitude Chart.

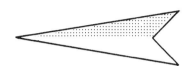

Published ILS and/or Localizer Procedure Available

Published SDF Procedure Available

ILS Localizer Course with ATC Function—Feathered Side Indicates Blue Sector

Back Course Localizer with ATC Function

SDF Localizer Course with ATC Function

Figure 7-12. Chart Representation of ILS, Localizer, and SDF Symbols

Chart Depiction of Compulsory and Non-compulsory Reporting Points

7.46 The safety and effectiveness of traffic control depends to a great extent on the proper separation of air traffic. Air Traffic Control must be able to accurately estimate the progress of every aircraft operating on an IFR flight plan in order to provide handling in a safe and expeditious manner.

7.47 Federal Aviation Regulations require pilots operating on IFR flight plans to furnish position reports when passing certain reporting points, except when in "Radar Contact." Reporting points are indicated on en route charts. The designated *compulsory* reporting point symbol is the solid triangle (▲); the "On Request" non-compulsory reporting point symbol is an open triangle (△). (Reports when passing an "On Request" reporting point are only necessary when requested by ATC.)

7.48 These reporting points are positioned on en route charts in intersections and over NAVAIDs. Even if a pilot is completely familiar with chart NAVAID symbols, it can still prove to be confusing when a solid or open triangle is placed on a NAVAID symbol. It would be wise to study the excerpt of the En Route Low Altitude Chart in Appendix G and note how the various NAVAID symbols change in appearance with the placement of a solid or open triangle on them.

Changeover Point (COP)

7.49 A Changeover Point is a point along the route or airway segment between two adjacent navigation facilities (or waypoints in the case when RNAV is employed) where change in navigation guidance should occur. Pilots should change the navigation receiver frequency from the NAVAID station behind the aircraft to the NAVAID station ahead of the aircraft when located at a COP. The symbol (Γ) is used on en route charts to indicate the COP when the navigation receiver frequency change should occur at a position other than the midway point along straight route segments. When the COP symbol is not printed on en route charts, it is understood that the COP is midway between the navigation facilities for straight route segments, or at the intersection of radials or courses forming a dogleg in the case of dogleg route segments. COPs are established for the purpose of preventing frequency interference from other navigation facilities and to aid the pilot in determining the proper NAVAID to use to obtain the most precise course information.

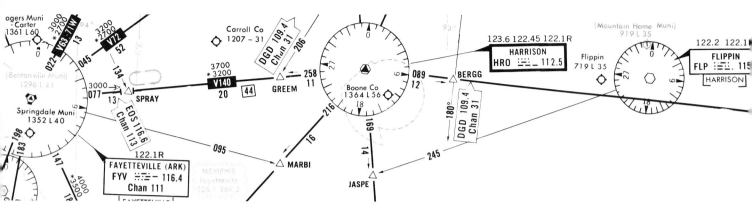

Figure 7-13. Intersection Identification Using VOR Receivers

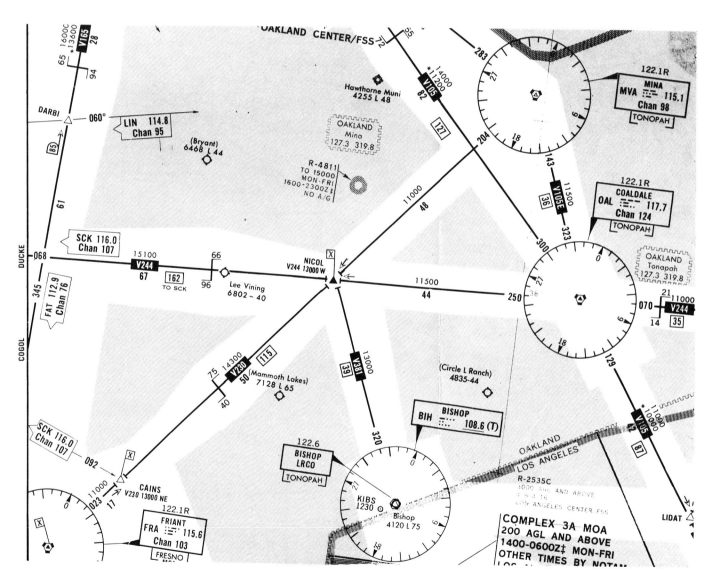

Figure 7-14. Intersection Identification with Distance
Measuring Equipment and VOR Receivers

Intersection Formation and Identification (VOR, VORTAC, and NDB)

7.50 Intersections can be defined by two intersecting VOR or NDB radials, or by one VORTAC radial when DME equipment is employed. The name of each intersection is also printed on en route charts along with a triangle in the center of each intersection, designating whether the intersection is a compulsory or an "On Request" reporting point.

7.51 To distinguish which NAVAIDs are to be used for the identification of particular intersections, open tip and solid tip arrows are printed next to the radial forming the intersection, and arrows are also drawn from NAVAIDs to intersections. An arrow used in conjunction with a VHF facility depicts an *outbound* radial; an arrow used in conjunction with an LF/MF facility depicts an *inbound* bearing. For an example, refer to Figure 7-13. MARBI Intersection can be identified by the use of the 216° radial of HARRISON VORTAC and the 095° radial of FAYETTEVILLE VORTAC as noted by the two small solid tip arrows. (GREEM, JASPE, and BERGG Intersections can be identified in a similar manner.)

7.52 The larger open tip arrow found on the two DME types that appear in the En Route Low Altitude Chart Legend in Appendix G designates that an intersection can be identified with the use of a VOR receiver and Distance Measuring Equipment. NICOL Intersection in Figure 7-14, for example, can be identified (with Distance Measuring Equipment and a VOR receiver) by the identification of the 204° radial of MINA VORTAC at a DME-measured distance of 48 nautical miles. (NICOL Intersection can also be identified in a similar manner using COALDALE VORTAC.)

7.53 In the case where an aircraft is not DME equipped, the radial that is aligned with the DME arrow may be used to identify an intersection with the use of a VOR receiver if two or more identifiable radials form that intersection. NICOL Intersection can be identified (with a VOR receiver) by the use of the 204° radial of MINA VORTAC and the 250° radial of COALDALE VORTAC. (Note that NICOL Intersection can also be considered a compulsory reporting point, VOR Changeover Point, and DME fix.)

SELECTING AND FLIGHT PLANNING THE ROUTE

7.54 Assume a selected route of flight is from Joliet Municipal Airport, Illinois, to Lorain County Regional Airport, Ohio. Mansfield Lahm Municipal Airport, Ohio is the required alternate airport. To select the appropriate En Route Low Altitude Chart (L-23) for this flight, a pilot should first consult an IFR Wall Planning Chart.

7.55 Included in Appendix G along with the legend of the En Route Low Altitude Chart is an excerpt of Chart L-23. A flight planned route with associated information will be extrapolated from this chart excerpt throughout the remaining discussion on flight planning.

7.56 The construction of an IFR flight time analysis is quite similar in format to that of a VFR flight analysis. (Figure 7-15) If a pilot uses the strategy of "going from the known to the unknown" and constructs a flight analysis in an organized manner, the possibility of making any mistakes is greatly reduced.

7.57 Once the departure and destination airports have been determined, the most practical route should be selected. Generally, the most practical route is the most direct airway route except when such conditions as icing and thunderstorms enter into flight planning considerations. This flight route, however, is the shortest route of flight along Victor airways. (V-92 to VWV then V-6.)

7.58 After all of the obvious essential "known" information is derived from such sources as Aircraft Flight Manuals, weather reports and forecasts, and the appropriate navigation charts, that information should be listed on the flight analysis sheet. It is then an easy task to solve for the "unknowns."

7.59 One of the categories of unknowns that must be solved in an early stage of the flight analysis is the determination of the true courses. Since all radials and bearings that appear on this chart are magnetic courses, variation must be applied in the appropriate manner (as discussed in chapter 5) to obtain the true course. (Figure 7-16)

7.60 *Special Note: Since variation values are only printed on the inside of the borders of the chart, it is best to project a line between corresponding variation reference points to accurately determine the variation for particular routes of flight depicted in the center of the chart.*

7.61 The route leg distances required to complete the flight analysis can be readily obtained from the en route chart using the total mileage boxes. However, since the mileage from Joliet Municipal Airport to CGT VORTAC is less than the 34 nautical miles listed from JOT VORTAC to CGT VORTAC, a plotter must be used. After measuring the distance from the departure airport to a 45° intercept of the airway and from the point of interception to CGT VORTAC, it can be determined that the distance of the first leg of flight is approximately 31 nautical miles. The succeeding route legs are 70, 107, and 67 nautical miles respectively.

7.62 Altitude planning is another important factor in the IFR flight planning process. The pilot

FLIGHT TIME ANALYSIS

CHECK POINT FROM	TO	ROUTE CRUISE ALT/FLT LEVEL	TRUE COURSE	WINDS ALOFT / TEMP °C	AIRSPEED IAS	AIRSPEED TAS	GROUND SPEED	DRIFT CORR ANGLE	DIST (NM)	TIME LEG	TIME TOTAL	FUEL CONSUMED (LBS) LEG	FUEL CONSUMED (LBS) TOTAL	MISC.
Joliet Muni Airport	CGT	V92 Climbing	092	280°/12 Kts 5°C	122	130	143	1°L	31	+13		51		Fuel—Includes Taxi and Runup
CGT	GSH	V92 9000	087	300°/20 Kts -3°C	161	184	201	3°L	70	+21	+34	52	103	
GSH	VWV	V92 9000	090	300°/12 Kts -3°C	161	184	195	2°L	107	+33	1+07	83	186	
VWV	CLE	V/6 9000	092	300°/08 Kts -3°C	161	184	191	1°L	67	+21	1+28	52	238	

ALTERNATE ROUTE

CHECK POINT FROM	TO	ROUTE CRUISE ALT/FLT LEVEL	TRUE COURSE	WINDS ALOFT / TEMP °C	AIRSPEED IAS	AIRSPEED TAS	GROUND SPEED	DRIFT CORR ANGLE	DIST (NM)	TIME LEG
CLE	MFD	V5 8000	212	300°/10 Kts -1°C	163	184	183	3°R	35	+12

Figure 7-15. A Typical Flight Time Analysis

FUEL SUMMARY

	TIME	FUEL
EN ROUTE	1+28	238#
ALTERNATE	+12	30#
RESERVE	+45	113#
TOTAL	2+25	381#

CHECK POINT FROM	TO	MAGNETIC COURSE (FROM THE EN ROUTE CHART)	VARIATION (FROM THE EN ROUTE CHART)	TRUE COURSE (DETERMINED BY THE ALGEBRAIC SUM OF THE MC AND VAR)
Joliet Airport	CGT	091°	+1 (1°E)	092°
CGT	GSH	087°	0	087°
GSH	VWV	092°	-2 (2°W)	090°
VWV	CLE	096°	-4 (4°W)	092°
ALTERNATE ROUTE				
CLE	MFD	217°	-5 (5°W)	212°

Figure 7-16. Magnetic Course to True Course Conversion Table

must not only consider present and forecast weather conditions and the aircraft's performance capability, but must also consider magnetic courses and obstruction clearance requirements.

7.63 A pilot operating an aircraft in accordance with Instrument Flight Rules in level cruising flight in *controlled* airspace is required to maintain the altitude or flight level assigned that aircraft by ATC. (There is an exception to this rule. If ATC assigns a VFR Conditions on Top clearance, pilots are expected to operate in accordance with those altitudes appropriate for this type of clearance, as discussed in chapter 8.)

7.64 Pilots planning flights in accordance with Instrument Flight Rules in *uncontrolled* airspace should observe those altitude requirements defined in the table in Figure 7–17. (Pilots planning IFR flights in controlled airspace also generally adhere to those same altitudes as described in Figure 7–17.)

7.65 *Special Note: The highest IFR altitude to which an instrument rated pilot can generally expect to be cleared to fly when conducting flight operations on a Victor airway is 17,000 feet MSL.*

7.66 One of the last but most important areas in the computation of a flight time analysis is the planned fuel requirement, as discussed in chapter 6. After the required fuel for the planned route is computed, the pilot must determine the fuel needed to fly to the alternate airport, if an alternate airport is required, and still have a 45-minute fuel reserve. Since fuel is such an important consideration, all pilots should recheck all computations to insure that their aircraft have more than adequate supplies of fuel.

THE FAA FLIGHT PLAN

7.67 As previously stated, prior to departure from within, or prior to entering, controlled airspace, a pilot must submit a complete flight plan and receive an IFR clearance if weather conditions are below VFR minimums. Instrument flight plans may be submitted to the nearest Flight Service station or airport traffic control tower either in person or by telephone (or by radio if no other means are available). Pilots should file IFR flight plans at least 30 minutes prior to estimated time of departure to preclude possible delay in receiving a departure clearance from ATC. Otherwise, a 30-minute delay is not unusual in receiving an ATC clearance because of time spent in processing flight plan data. Traffic saturation frequently prevents control personnel from accepting flight plans by radio. In such cases, the pilot is advised to contact the nearest Flight Service Station for the purpose of filing the flight plan.

7.68 Air Traffic Control computers have been programmed to delete non-activated proposed departure flight plans. Most centers have this parameter set in order to delete these flight plans a minimum of one hour after the proposed departure time. To ensure their flight plans remain active, pilots whose actual departure time will be delayed one hour or more beyond their filed departure time are requested to notify ATC of their revised departure time.

7.69 Figure 7–18 is the FAA flight plan form currently in use. A brief summation of the information necessary to complete each block of the flight plan form follows:

Block 1. Check the type of flight plan. Check both the VFR and IFR blocks if it is a composite (VFR/IFR) flight plan.

Block 2. Enter the complete aircraft identification including the prefix *N* if applicable.

Block 3. Enter the designator for the aircraft (for example, C-182) or, if the designator is unknown, the aircraft manufacturer's name (Cessna), followed by a slant (/) and the representative equipment code letter as specified in Figure 7–19. (It is recommended that pilots file the maximum transponder/navigation capability of their aircraft in the equipment suffix. This will provide air traf-

If the magnetic course (ground track) is	Below 18,000 feet MSL fly	At or above 18,000 feet MSL but below FL 290, fly	At or above FL 290, fly 4000-foot intervals
0° to 179°	Odd thousands, MSL (3000, 5000, 7000, etc.)	Odd Flight Levels, (FL 190, 210, 230, etc.)	Beginning at FL 290 (FL 290, 330, 370, etc.)
180° to 359°	Even thousands, MSL (2000, 4000, 6000, etc.)	Even Flight Levels (FL 180, 200, 220, etc.)	Beginning at FL 310 (FL 310, 350, 390, etc.)

Figure 7-17. Uncontrolled Airspace—IFR Altitudes and Flight Levels

FLIGHT PLAN

DEPARTMENT OF TRANSPORTATION— FEDERAL AVIATION ADMINISTRATION

Form Approved
OMB No. 04-R0072

1. TYPE	2. AIRCRAFT IDENTIFICATION	3. AIRCRAFT TYPE/ SPECIAL EQUIPMENT	4. TRUE AIRSPEED	5. DEPARTURE POINT	6. DEPARTURE TIME		7. CRUISING ALTITUDE
VFR IFR DVFR			KTS		PROPOSED (Z)	ACTUAL (Z)	

8. ROUTE OF FLIGHT

9. DESTINATION (Name of airport and city)	10. EST. TIME ENROUTE		11. REMARKS
	HOURS	MINUTES	

12. FUEL ON BOARD		13. ALTERNATE AIRPORT (S)	14. PILOT'S NAME, ADDRESS & TELEPHONE NUMBER & AIRCRAFT HOME BASE	15. NUMBER ABOARD
HOURS	MINUTES			

16. COLOR OF AIRCRAFT

CLOSE VFR FLIGHT PLAN WITH_____FSS ON ARRIVAL

FAA Form 7233-1 (5-72)

*1976-G.P.O.-1703M-674-857-197

Figure 7-18. The FAA Flight Plan Form

/X   No transponder

/T   Transponder with no altitude encoding capability

/U   Transponder with altitude encoding capability

/D   DME, no transponder

/B   DME, transponder with no altitude encoding capability

/A   DME, transponder with altitude encoding capability

/M   TACAN-only, no transponder

/N   TACAN-only, transponder with no altitude encoding capability

/P   TACAN-only, transponder with altitude encoding capability

/C   Certificated RNAV, transponder with no altitude encoding capability

/F   Certificated RNAV, transponder with altitude encoding capability

/W   Certificated RNAV, no transponder

Figure 7-19. FAA Flight Plan Form—Equipment Code Letters

fic control with the necessary information to utilize all facets of navigational equipment and transponder capabilities available. In the case of appropriately certificated area navigation equipped aircraft, pilots should file on the flight plan the /C, /F, or /W capability of the aircraft even though an area navigation route has not been requested. This will ensure ATC awareness in the event an area navigation route is available and may be utilized to expedite the flight.)

Block 4. Enter the computed true airspeed.

Block 5. Enter the departure point/airport identifier code (or the name if the identifier is unknown). (Note: Use of identifier codes will expedite the processing of the flight plan.)

Block 6. Enter the proposed departure time in Greenwich Mean Time (GMT) (Z). If airborne, specify the actual or proposed departure time as appropriate.

Block 7. Enter the requested en route altitude or flight level. When more than one altitude/flight level is desired along the route of flight, it is best to make a subsequent request directly to the controller.

Block 8. Define the route of flight by using NAVAID/identifier codes (or names if the code is unknown), airways, jet routes, and waypoints (for RNAV). Use NAVAIDs or waypoints to define direct routes and radials/bearings to define other unpublished routes. A pilot who intends to make an airway flight using VOR facilities, for example, will simply specify the appropriate Victor airway(s) and transition point(s), by name(s) and location identifier(s), in the flight plan. *Example:* MSP V2 FAR V181 GFK. If a flight is to be conducted in part by means of LF/MF navigation aids and in part on omniranges, specifications of the appropriate airways in the flight plan will indicate which types of facilities will be used along the described routes and permit ATC to issue a traffic clearance accordingly. A route may also be described by specifying the station over which the flight will pass, but in this case since many VOR's and LF/MF aids have the same name, the pilot must be careful to indicate which aid will be used at a particular location. This will be indicated by specifying the type of facility to be used after the location name in the following manner: Newark LF/MF, Allentown VOR.

Block 9. Enter the destination airport identifier code (or name if the identifier is unknown). Include the city name (or even the state name) if needed for clarity.

Block 10. Enter the estimated time en route based on the latest forecast winds.

Block 11. Enter only those remarks pertinent to ATC or to the clarification of other flight plan information. Items of a personal nature are not accepted. Do not assume that remarks will be automatically transmitted to every controller. Specific requests should be made to the appropriate controller.

Block 12. Specify the fuel on board computed from the departure point.

Block 13. Specify an alternate airport if desired or required. (Do NOT include routing.)

Block 14. Enter the pilot's complete name, address, and telephone number. Enter sufficient information to identify home base, airport, or operator. This information would be essential in the event of a search and rescue operation.

Block 15. Enter the total number of persons on board including crew.

Block 16. Enter the predominant aircraft color(s).

COMPOSITE FLIGHT PLANS

7.70 Flight plans which specify VFR operations for one portion of a flight and IFR operations for another portion of the flight, are called composite flight plans. This type of flight plan will be accepted by the FSS at the point of departure. If VFR flight is conducted for the first portion of the flight, the pilot should report the departure time to the FSS with which the VFR/IFR flight plan was filed. Subsequently, before arriving at the proposed point for change to IFR or before flying into IFR conditions, the pilot should contact the nearest FSS and request the IFR clearance, then cancel the VFR portion of the flight plan. Regardless of the type facility the pilot is communicating with (FSS, center, or tower), it is the pilot's responsibility to request that facility to "close the VFR flight plan." The pilot must remain in VFR weather conditions until operating in accordance with the IFR clearance.

7.71 When a flight plan indicates IFR for the first portion of flight and VFR for the latter portion, the pilot will normally be cleared to the point at which the change is proposed. Once the pilot has reported over the clearance limit and does not desire further IFR clearance, Air Traffic Control should be advised to cancel the IFR portion of the flight plan. Further clearance will not be necessary for VFR flight beyond that point. If the pilot desires to continue the IFR flight plan beyond the clearance limit, Air Traffic Control should be contacted at least five minutes prior to the clearance limit and further IFR clearance should be requested.

7.72 *Special Note: When a composite flight plan is filed, the fix or other location identifier at which the flight plan changes from VFR to IFR or from IFR to VFR should be carefully noted on the flight plan.*

DIRECT ROUTE FLIGHTS

7.73 Whenever a flight is conducted off airway routes in a straight line between two navigational aids, fixes, points, or any combination thereof, it is called a "direct route flight." When flight planning, all or any portions of the route which will not be flown on the radials/courses of established airways or routes, for example, direct route flights, must be defined by indicating the radio fixes over which the flight will pass. Fixes selected to define the route shall be those over which the position of the aircraft can be accurately determined. Such fixes automatically become compulsory reporting points for the flight, unless ATC advises the pilot otherwise. Only those navigational aids established for use in a particular structure, that is, in the Low or High structures, may be used to define the en route phase of a direct flight within that structure.

7.74 The azimuth feature of VOR aids and the azimuth and distance (DME) features of VORTAC aids are assigned certain frequency-protected areas of airspace. These NAVAIDs are intended for application to established airway and route use, and to provide guidance for planning flights outside of established airways or routes. These areas of airspace are expressed in terms of cylindrical service volumes of specified dimensions called "class limits" or "categories." An operational service volume has been established for each class in which adequate signal coverage and frequency protection can be assured. To facilitate use, consistent with operational service volume limits of VOR or VORTAC aids, pilots, while flight planning, should remember that use of such aids for defining a direct route of flight in controlled airspace should not exceed the following:

1. *Operations above Flight Level 450*—Use aids not more than 200 nautical miles apart. These aids are depicted on En Route High Altitude Charts—U.S.
2. *Operations off established routes from 18,000 feet MSL to Flight Level 450*—Use aids not more than 260 nautical miles apart. These aids are depicted on En Route High Altitude Charts—U.S.
3. *Operations off established airways below 18,000 feet MSL*—Use aids not more than 80 nautical miles apart. These aids are depicted on En Route Low Altitude Charts–U.S.
4. *Operations off established airways between 14,500 feet MSL and 17,999 feet MSL in the conterminous United States*—(H) facilities not more than 200 nautical miles apart may be used.

7.75 Increasing use of self-contained airborne navigational systems which do not rely on the VOR/VORTAC system has resulted in pilot requests for direct routes which exceed NAVAID service volume limits. These direct route requests will be approved *only in a radar environment*, with approval based on pilot responsibility for navigation on the authorized direct route. "Radar flight following" will be provided by ATC for air traffic control purposes. At times, ATC will initiate a direct route in a radar environment which exceeds NAVAID service volume limits. In such cases ATC will provide radar monitoring and navigational assistance as necessary.

7.76 Pilots are reminded that they are responsible for adhering to obstruction clearance requirements on those segments of direct routes that are outside of controlled airspace. The MEAs and other altitudes shown on low altitude IFR en route charts pertain to those route segments within controlled airspace, and those altitudes may not meet obstruction clearance criteria for flight operations off those routes. When planning a direct flight where no applicable minimum altitudes are prescribed, the following minimum IFR altitudes apply:

1. In designated mountainous areas, 2,000 feet above the highest obstacle within a horizontal distance of 5 statute miles from the course to be flown; or
2. Other than mountainous areas, 1,000 feet above the highest obstacle within a horizontal distance of 5 statute miles from the course to be flown; or
3. As otherwise authorized by the Administrator or assigned by ATC.

7.77 *Special Note: The best procedure to follow to determine obstruction heights for a particular direct route flight is to simply plot the course of the proposed flight on sectional or other VFR charts and inspect the area along the route of flight.*

RNAV FLIGHT PLANNING

7.78 Pilots of RNAV certificated aircraft have the option of filing and operating in accordance with established or designated route criteria or filing for random (impromptu) RNAV routes. The complexities involved in determining route width, with reference to facility usable distance, require that random RNAV routes only be approved in a radar environment. ATC will radar monitor each flight; however, navigation on the random RNAV route is the responsibility of the pilot. Factors that will be considered by ATC in approving random RNAV routes include the capability to provide radar monitoring and compatibility with traffic volume and flow. When operationally feasible, pilots are urged to file established or designated RNAV routes in lieu of random RNAV routes.

7.79 Pilots requesting ATC clearance for random RNAV routes are expected to do the following:

1. File airport to airport flight plans prior to departure.

2. File the appropriate RNAV capability certification suffix in the flight plan.

3. Plan the random route portion of the flight plan to begin and end over appropriate arrival/departure transition fixes or over appropriate navigation aids for the altitude stratum within which the flight will be conducted.

4. File route structure transitions to and from the random route portion in the flight plan. The use of normal preferred departure and arrival routes is recommended.

5. Define random routes by waypoints. File route description waypoints by using degree/distance in reference to navigation aids for the appropriate altitude stratum.

6. File a minimum of one route description waypoint for each Air Route Traffic Control Center's area over which the random portion of flight will be conducted. Such waypoints must be located within 200 nautical miles of the boundary of the preceding center's flight advisory area.

7. File an additional route description waypoint for each turnpoint in the route.

8. Though not required in the flight plan, plan additional waypoints necessary to ensure accurate navigation via the filed route of flight. Navigation is the pilot's responsibility unless ATC assistance is requested.

9. Plan the route of flight in order to avoid Prohibited and Nonjoint use of Restricted Airspace unless pilots have obtained permission to operate in that airspace and so inform the appropriate ATC facility. Avoid flight planning through other uncontrolled airspace unless specifically desiring flight through such airspace.

CHAPTER 7: QUESTIONS

For answers see Appendix E

1. What is the purpose of FDC NOTAMs, and where are they found?
   1. The Notices to Airmen publication contains the FDC NOTAMs which list changes of flight data of a regulatory nature, affecting standard instrument approach procedures, aeronautical charts, and selected flight restrictions, prior to their normal publication cycle.
   2. FDC NOTAMs are attached to the hourly weather, and they contain changes in airport data.
   3. AIM contains the FDC NOTAMs which list all the safety-of-flight information, and sectional and world aeronautical charts.
   4. All NOTAMs are attached to hourly weather

sequence reports and list all the safety-of-flight information.

2. Why have preferred IFR routes been established?
   1. To insure that aircraft will be adequately protected in uncontrolled airspace.
   2. To insure that all aircraft will remain in radar contact.
   3. For more efficient use of the NAVAID facilities.
   4. To minimize route changes during the operational phase of flight, thereby providing efficient departure, en route, and arrival air traffic services.

Refer to the illustrated En Route Low Altitude Chart excerpt (page 240) when answering questions 3, 4, 5, 6, and 7.

3. Select the correct statement(s) regarding the charted altitudes.

A. The maximum reception altitude for VEGA (a) Intersection is 6,500 feet MSL.
B. The minimum reception altitude for CANYON (b) Intersection is 7,000 feet AGL.
C. The minimum crossing altitude for SUMMER (c) Intersection is 9,000 feet MSL.
D. The minimum en route altitude for airway V-12N (d) is 6,500 feet MSL.
   1. A, C, and D.
   2. B only.
   3. C and D.
   4. D only.

4. Select the correct statement(s) regarding intersection identification.

A. SUMMER (c) Intersection can be identified by the 78 DME fix of the 033° radial of TXO VORTAC.
B. MOSER (e) Intersection can be identified by the 010° radial of TXO VORTAC and the 241° radial of AMA VORTAC.
C. EXELL (f) Intersection can be identified by the 31 DME fix of the 307° radial of AMA VORTAC.
D. FLUTY (g) Intersection can be identified by the 170° radial of TCC VORTAC and the 278° radial of TXO VORTAC.
   1. B, C, and D.
   2. A, B, and C.
   3. A, C, and D.
   4. A, B, and D.

5. From the illustration, determine the location of the VOR changeover point of airway V-12 (h).
   1. 52 nautical miles from Amarillo.
   2. 45 statute miles from Tucumcari.
   3. 57 nautical miles from Tucumcari.
   4. 44 statute miles from Amarillo.

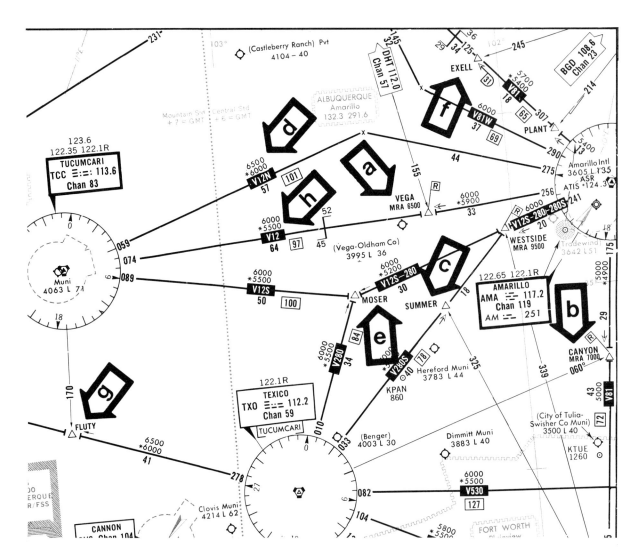

6. What is the estimated time en route from AMARILLO VORTAC to TUCUMCARI VORTAC via V–12 (h) assuming the following conditions?

Cruising altitude—10,000 feet MSL
TAS—177 knots
Variation—10° 30′ East
Winds and temperatures aloft—9,000 ft.   12,000 ft.
                                          2926–06   3232–09

1. 43 minutes.
2. 41 minutes.
3. 38 minutes.
4. 48 minutes.

7. What VFR communications frequencies can a pilot expect to be monitored by Amarillo FSS?
1. 122.1 MHz and 123.6 MHz.
2. 122.5 MHz, 122.0 MHz, 122.65 MHz, and 123.6 MHz.
3. 122.1 MHz, 122.2 MHz, 122.65 MHz, and 121.5 MHz.
4. 121.5 MHz, 122.1 MHz, 122.65 MHz, and 123.6 MHz.

Refer to the illustrated En Route Low Altitude Chart excerpt (page 241) when answering questions 8 and 9.

8. The illustrated symbol (a) —O—O—O— is used to denote that the route from GUC VORTAC south is:
1. An airway that should only be used during emergency situations.
2. An LF/MF airway.
3. A substitute route structure.
4. A preferred route airway.

9. What is the status of Durango VOR (b)?
1. The VOR is shut down through August 1.
2. The VOR is undergoing maintenance.
3. A frequency change is in progress.
4. The navigation signals are unreliable.

10. VOT frequencies are printed in the Airport/Facility Directory and:
1. In the communication listing on En Route Low Altitude Charts.
2. In the communication listing on STAR charts.
3. In FAR Part 91.25.
4. In all of the above.

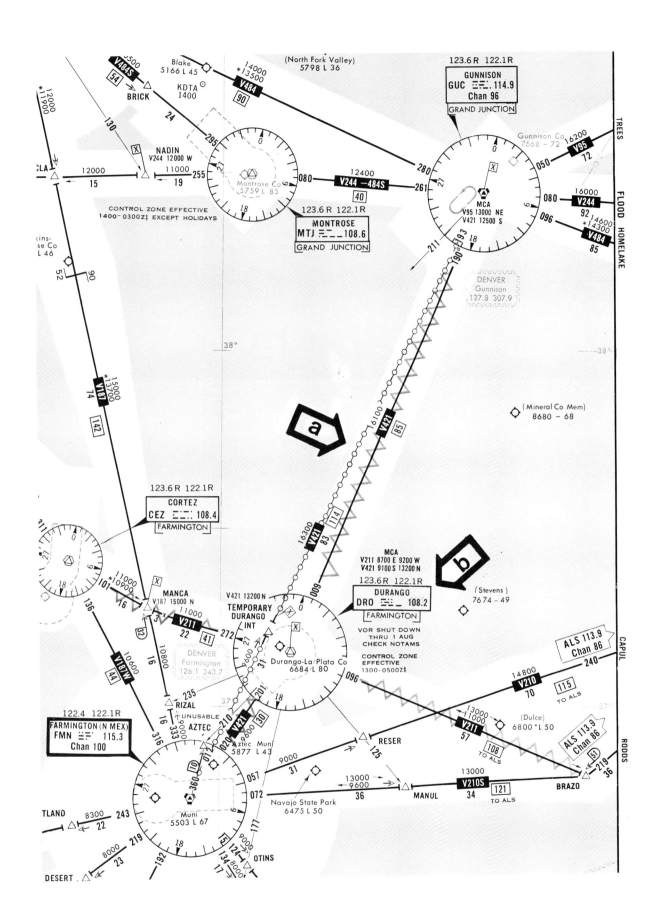

Terminals	Route	Effective Times (GMT)
MOLINE		
Fort Wayne	MLI V156 V38 FWA	0000-2359
South Bend	MLI V156 SBN	0000-2359
ROCKFORD		
Fort Wayne	V227 V156 V38 FWA	0000-2359
South Bend	V227 V156 SBN	0000-2359
SOUTH BEND		
Moline	SBN V156 MLI	0000-2359
Rockford	V156 V227 RFD	0000-2359
SPRINGFIELD		
Midway	V63 UIN V116 JOT	0000-2359
O'Hare	V63 UIN V116 PIA V262 BDF V10 VAINS	0000-2359

Refer to the excerpt from the Airport/Facility Directory (above) when answering question 11.

11. What may a pilot filing a preferred route from South Bend to Rockford expect after reaching RFD?
1. A SID.
2. Radar vectors or a STAR.
3. A cruise clearance.
4. An abbreviated clearance.

12. Minimum en route altitude (MEA) is the lowest published altitude between fixes that:
1. Provides 1,000 feet of terrain clearance and assures two-way radio communications.
2. Assures navigation signal coverage and provides 1,500 feet of obstruction clearance.
3. Provides 2,000 feet of terrain clearance and adequate signal coverage for voice communications and DME information.
4. Meets obstruction clearance requirements and assures acceptable navigational signal coverage.

KANSAS

COLBY: NDB "CBK" OTS. (11/76)
BIRD CITY COMMUNITY ARPT: Rotating beacon cmsnd. (2/77-2)
ELKHART-MORTON COUNTY ARPT: VASI rwy 17 and rwy 35 cmsnd. (12/76-2)
GOODLAND, RENNER FLD/GOODLAND MUNI ARPT: OM rwy 30 cmsnd. (2/77-3)
HERINGTON MUNI ARPT: N 2550ft rwy 17-35 closed. (12/76-2)
HUTCHINSON MUNI ARPT: Rwy lights rwy 3-21 OTS. (2/76)
KANSAS CITY, FAIRFAX ARPT: Commercial FM radio station interference may affect radio communication immediate vicinity of arpt. (7/76)
MANHATTAN MUNI ARPT: VASI rwy 21 cmsnd. (12/76-2)
SYLVIA, ROBERTS AIRFIELD: Rwy 17-35 2250 ft turf. Rotating beacon, UNICOM freq 122.8. (11/76-2)
TOPEKA: CTLZ hours 0600-2200. (12/76-3)
WICHITA RAWDON FIELD: Arpt closed. (9/76)
ULYSSES ARPT: VASI rwy 17 and rwy 35 OTS. (5/76-2)

13. When reviewing the illustrated excerpt (above) of NOTAMs found in the Notices to Airmen publication, a pilot should discover that:
1. The Hutchinson Municipal Airport is out of service.

2. Commercial FM radio station interference may affect radio communications in the immediate vicinity of Fairfax Airport.
3. The VASI to Runway 21 at Manhattan Municipal is currently out of service.
4. The Topeka Airport control tower is in operation from 0600 to 2000 hours.

14. Where can the most recent NOTAMs concerning ATC facilities be located?
1. Notices to Airmen Section in the AIM.
2. FDC NOTAMs Section in the AIM.
3. Notices to Airmen, which are issued by mail service biweekly.
4. FSS NOTAMs.

Refer to the illustrated Airport/Facility Directory excerpt (page 243, top) when answering question 15.

15. If a pilot is preflight planning at Santa Fe County Airport and desires a weather briefing, the proper action would be to:
1. Call the Santa Fe FSS on the field.
2. Call the Santa Fe tower on 119.5 MHz.
3. Make a long distance call to Albuquerque FSS.
4. Make a local call to Albuquerque FSS.

Refer to the illustrated En Route Low Altitude Chart excerpt (page 243, bottom) when answering questions 16 and 17.

16. What is the maximum altitude ATC will assign a pilot en route from TUS VORTAC to DUG VORTAC on airway V–66 (a)?
1. 13,000 feet MSL.
2. 9,500 feet MSL.
3. 18,000 feet MSL.
4. 9,000 feet MSL.

17. What is the distance from CIE VORTAC to TUS VORTAC via airway V–16S (b)?
1. 75 nautical miles.
2. 59 nautical miles.
3. 84 statute miles.
4. 54 nautical miles.

§ **SANTA FE COUNTY MUNI** (SAF) 8.7 SW GMT-7(-6DT) 35°37'01"N 106°05'20"W   **ALBUQUERQUE**
6344   B   S4   **FUEL** 100, JET A   OX 1, 2, 3, 4   **H-2G, L-4G, L-6E**
  RWY 02-20: H8322X150 (ASPH) S-48, D-65, DT-105 MIRL .81% up N   **IAP**
  RWY 15-33: H6304X150 (ASPH) S-46, D-65, DT-105 MIRL .73% up SE
  RWY 10-28: H6297X100 (ASPH) S-25 .45% up E
  AIRPORT REMARKS: Attended continuously. Control Zone effective 1300-0500Z‡
    Rwy 10-28 closed to acft 17,000 lbs and over
  COMMUNICATIONS: UNICOM 123.0
    ALBUQUERQUE FSS (ABQ) LC 982-3871
    SANTA FE LRCO 122.1R 110.6T (ALBUQUERQUE FSS)
  ® **ALBUQUERQUE CENTER APP CON** 124.7
    TOWER 119.5 opr 1300-0500Z‡   **GND CON** 124.7
  ® **ALBUQUERQUE CENTER DEP CON** 124.7
  RADIO AIDS TO NAVIGATION:
    (L) **BVORTAC** 110.6 SAF Chan 43   35°22'25.9"N 106°03'51.7"W   332° 4.2 NM to fld.
    VORTAC unusable 015°-030° beyond 30 NM below 14,600'

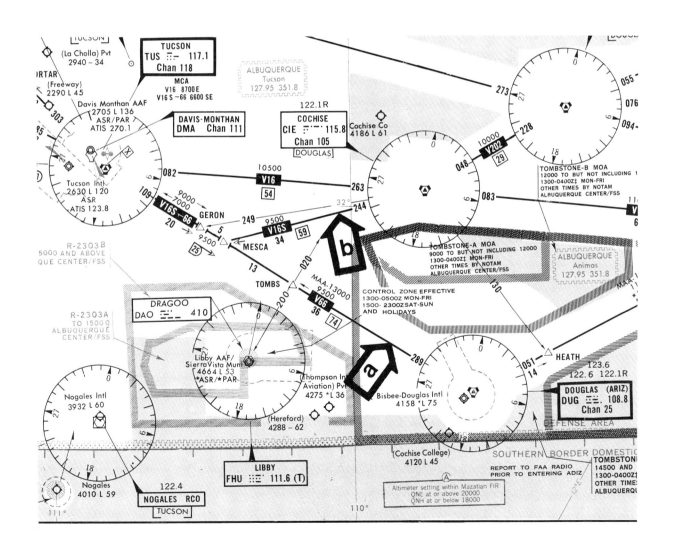

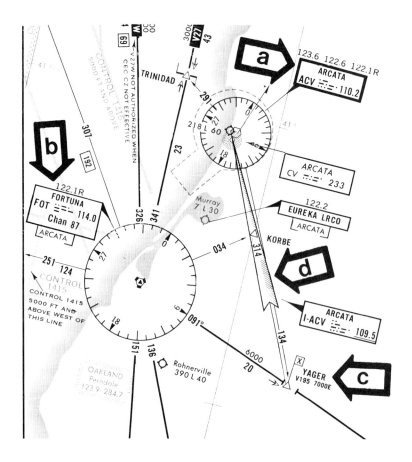

Refer to the illustrated En Route Low Altitude Chart excerpt (above) when answering questions 18, 19, 20, and 21.

18. The symbols for ARCATA (a) and FORTUNA (b) radio aids indicate that:

1. ARCATA VOR has DME capability and FORTUNA is TACAN-equipped.
2. FORTUNA is equipped with a TACAN, and the ARCATA navigation aid is a VORTAC.
3. FORTUNA is equipped with a VORTAC and the ARCATA navigation aid is a VOR.
4. FORTUNA is equipped with a VOR and the ARCATA navigation aid is a VORTAC.

19. Select the response(s) that correctly describe(s) YAGER (c) Intersection.

A. YAGER Intersection can be identified by the FOT 091° radial at a distance of 20 DME.
B. YAGER Intersection is formed by the FOT 091° radial and the ACV 314° radial.
C. YAGER Intersection is formed by the FOT 091° radial and the ACV 134° radial.
D. YAGER Intersection is formed by the FOT 271° radial·and the Back Course of the ACV ILS.

1. A and C.
2. D only.
3. A and B.
4. A, B, and D.

20. Select the correct response from the information provided on YAGER Intersection.

1. The MOCA at YAGER Intersection is 6,000 feet MSL when traveling in an easterly direction.
2. The MCA at YAGER Intersection is 7,000 feet MSL when traveling in any direction.
3. The MCA at YAGER Intersection is 7,000 feet MSL when traveling in a westerly direction.
4. The MCA at YAGER Intersection is 7,000 feet MSL when traveling in an easterly direction on airway V–195.

21. What is the meaning of the ILS symbol (d) depicted on the illustrated En Route Low Altitude Chart excerpt?

1. A published SDF approach is available.
2. In addition to providing course guidance for an ILS approach, the localizer provides an ATC function.
3. Only course guidance for a Back Course localizer approach is provided.
4. A VOR approach is available at that airport.

22. Where can a pilot find the *latest* FDC NOTAMs?

1. In the Notices to Airmen publication.
2. Any control tower.
3. With the NOS Instrument Approach Procedure Chart revisions.
4. Any FAA Flight Service Station.

23. The symbol §, when plotted next to an airport name in the Airport/Facility Directory, denotes the availability of:

1. Pre-taxi clearance delivery service.
2. NOTAM service.
3. Transcribed weather broadcasts.
4. A VOT.

24. An airport printed in brown on the En Route Low Altitude Chart signifies that:

1. The airport does not have a published instrument approach procedure.
2. The airport has an LF radio facility.
3. The airport does not have a control tower.
4. The airport does not have a hard-surfaced runway.

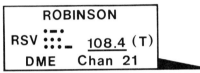

25. What does the symbol (T) shown in the illustrated navigation data box excerpt (above) indicate?

1. ATC voice transmissions may be received on the VOR frequency.
2. FSS voice transmissions may be received on the VOR frequency.
3. The useable range of the VOR is 80 nautical miles.
4. The useable range of the VOR is 25 nautical miles.

26. Refer to the Airport/Facility Directory excerpt (below) for Kansas City Downtown (MKC) Airport and select the correct responses.

A. The ground control frequency is 121.9 MHz.
B. The longest runway is 7,580 feet.
C. A pilot may listen to scheduled weather broadcasts on LF facilities between 2200–0500 local time.

D. The FSS is located on the field.
E. The longest runway is 9,500 feet.
F. Radar services are available.

1. B, C, and D.
2. A, D, and F.
3. B, C, D, and F.
4. B and F.

27. The minimum obstruction clearance altitude (MOCA) assures instrument pilots:

1. A 1,000-foot obstruction clearance within the airway.
2. Continued radar contact.
3. Adequate obstruction clearance for the route segment and acceptable navigation signal coverage only within 22 nautical miles of a VOR.
4. Acceptable navigation signal coverage and obstruction clearance within 25 nautical miles of a VOR.

28. Which types of controlled airspace are featured on En Route Low Altitude Charts?

1. Airways and control zones only.
2. That airspace below 14,500 feet MSL.
3. Control zones, Victor airways, and Terminal Control Areas up to but not including 18,000 feet MSL.
4. Victor airways and that airspace above 10,000 feet MSL but less than 18,000 feet MSL.

29. What type of equipment is designated by a "U" placed in Block 3 (Aircraft Type/Special Equipment Section) of an FAA flight plan form?

1. Transponder with altitude encoding capability.
2. DME only.
3. Transponder with altitude encoding capability and DME.
4. Transponder with altitude encoding capability, area navigation equipment, and DME.

MISSOURI   101

§ **KANSAS CITY DOWNTOWN** (MKC) 0 NW GMT-6(-5DT) 39°07'23"N 94°35'33"W   **KANSAS CITY**
758 B S4 **FUEL** 80, 100, 115, JET A OX 1, 2, 3, 4 LRA   **H-1D, 3A, L-6H, 21A, A-2E**
RWY 18-36: H7000X150 (ASPH-CONC) S-75, D-150, DT-300 HIRL   **IAP**
   RWY 18: Road SALSF   **RWY 36:** Antenna RAIL
RWY 03-21: H5052X150 (ASPH) S-48, D-73, DT-136 HIRL
   RWY 03: Levee   **RWY 21:** Railroad thld dsplcd 700'
AIRPORT REMARKS: Attended continuously. Standard grooving entire length Rwy 18-36.
COMMUNICATIONS: ATIS 124.6 **UNICOM** 123.0
   KANSAS CITY FSS (MKC) on arpt 122.6 122.2 122.1R 112.6T (816) GR1-7565
Ⓡ **APP CON** 120.95
   DOWNTOWN TWR 126.8 **GND CON** 121.9 **CLNC DEL** 121.9 **PRE-TAXI CLNC** 121.9 Freq 121.5 not available
Ⓡ **DEP CON** 120.95
   STAGE II SVC ctc **APP CON** within 25 NM on 121.1
RADIO AIDS TO NAVIGATION: VOT 108.6
   (H) BVORTAC 112.6 MKC Chan 73 39°16'46"N 94°35'28"W 171° 8.7 NM to fld
   RIVERSIDE (T) VORW 111.4 RIS 39°07'14"N 94°35'47"W at fld
      VOR unusable beyond 15 NM below 2400' 125°-170° 252°-260° 300°-310°
      all other azimuths beyond 15 NM below 2400'
      Also unusable above 10,000'
   MACKENZIE NDB (LOM) 344 MK 39°13'15"N 94°33'51"W 185° 5.4 NM to fld
   ILS 109.9 I-MKC Rwy 18 GS unusable below 1014' LOM MACKENZIE NDB
COMM/NAVAID REMARKS: Interference from FM radio station may affect communication in the immediate vicinity
   of arpt. Flight watch 1200-0400Z‡. No scheduled weather broadcast on VORTAC 0400-1100Z‡

30. When the NAVAID service volume limits are exceeded, ATC will approve direct flights in:
1. Airspace above 10,000 feet MSL only.
2. Uncontrolled airspace only.
3. Airspace above 18,000 feet MSL only.
4. A radar environment only.

31. What is the maximum IFR altitude an instrument pilot can expect to be cleared to fly when operating on a Victor airway?
1. 17,000 feet MSL.
2. 18,000 feet MSL.
3. 24,500 feet MSL.
4. FL 450.

32. When a direct IFR off-airway flight is conducted over mountainous terrain, the cruising altitude should be:

1. Any odd thousand-foot altitude when operating below 18,000 feet MSL on a magnetic course of 180° through 359°.
2. Determined by the highest MOCA from the surrounding airways.
3. 2,000 feet above the highest obstacle within a horizontal distance of 5 statute miles from the course to be flown as depicted on the appropriate Sectional or other VFR navigation chart.
4. 2,000 feet higher than the highest obstruction within a horizontal distance of 5 nautical miles as depicted on the appropriate En Route Low Altitude Chart.

Refer to the illustrated En Route Low Altitude Chart excerpt (below) when answering questions 33, 34, 35, and 36.

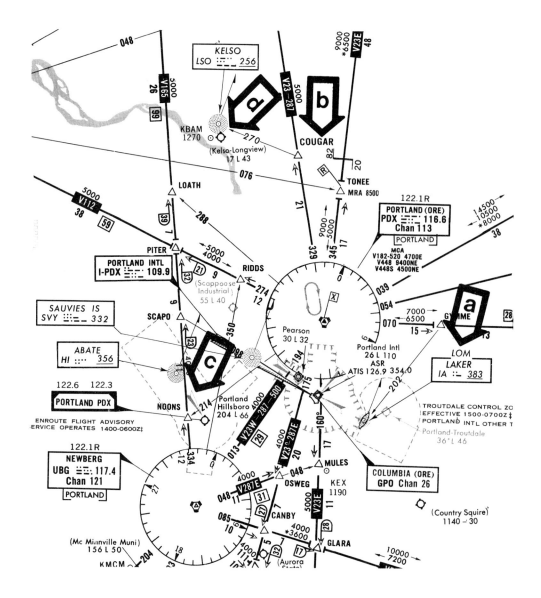

246

33. Select the correct statement describing the function of Lake radio beacon (a) located east of Portland VORTAC.

1. It is a locator outer marker and mandatory reporting point.
2. It is a mandatory reporting point and has no voice.
3. It is a locator outer marker and has no voice.
4. It is a compulsory reporting point and provides a bearing to GROVES Intersection.

34. COUGER Intersection (b), located just north of Portland VORTAC, is formed by:

1. The 270° outbound bearing from LSO and the 345° radial from PDX.
2. The 270° inbound bearing to LSO and the 329° radial from PDX.
3. The 090° outbound bearing from LSO and the 345° radial from PDX.
4. The 090° inbound bearing to LSO and the 159° radial from PDX.

35. Referring to the Portland Hillsboro Airport, from the symbol (c) ⊳⎯⎯ a pilot should know that this airport is equipped with:

1. A Back Course ILS approach.
2. An ILS approach.
3. An SDF approach.
4. An LDA approach.

36. What type of airspace is designated below the airway structure at Kelso Long View Airport (d)?

1. Uncontrolled.
2. Airport traffic area only.
3. Control zone and airport traffic area.
4. Control zone only.

Refer to the En Route Low Altitude Chart excerpts in Appendix G when answering questions 37 and 38.

37. What is the distance from Findlay VORTAC via airway V–422, Chicago Heights VORTAC via airway V–8 to Joliet VORTAC?

1. 247 nautical miles.
2. 274 nautical miles.
3. 211 statute miles.
4. 211 nautical miles.

38. For planning purposes, how much fuel is required for the previously mentioned flight from Findlay Airport to Joliet Municipal Airport with O'Hare (ORD) as the required alternate? Assume the TAS is 142 knots with an average 34-knot headwind component to Joliet Municipal and an average tailwind component of 10 knots from Joliet Municipal to O'Hare. Use a fuel consumption of 15 gallons per hour and allow 5 gallons of fuel consumption for taxi, climb, and descent.

1. 295.8 lbs.
2. 49.3 lbs.
3. 265.8 lbs.
4. 237.5 lbs.

Refer to the illustrated En Route Low Altitude Chart excerpt (below) when answering questions 39 and 40.

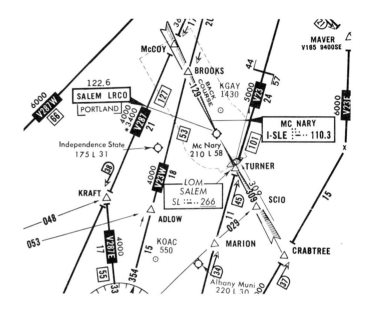

39. What facility with communications capability for flight plan service is provided at McNary Airport?

1. A remote Flight Service Station.
2. A long range control facility.
3. A Limited Remote Communications outlet.
4. A Flight Service Station.

40. What is the frequency of the NDB located near the McNary Airport?

1. 266 KHz.
2. 210 KHz.
3. 110.3 MHz.
4. 309 KHz.

41. Select the correct statement(s) pertaining to composite flight plans.

A. All IFR and VFR composite flight plans are opened by the tower.
B. A composite flight plan must specify VFR the first leg of the flight.
C. A pilot filing a composite flight plan should check both the IFR and VFR boxes in Block 1 of the FAA flight plan form.
D. A pilot should check the IFR box only in Block 1

when filing a composite flight plan.
1. C only.
2. A, B, and C.
3. B and D.
4. A, B, and D.

42. Pilots conducting IFR flights off established airways should use VOR or VORTAC aids that are:
1. Depicted on En Route High Altitude Charts and not more than 200 nautical miles apart for operations from 18,000 feet MSL to FL 450.
2. Depicted on En Route Low Altitude Charts and not more than 80 nautical miles apart for operations below 18,000 feet MSL.
3. Depicted on En Route Low Altitude Charts and not more than 260 nautical miles apart for operations at altitudes between 14,500 feet MSL and 17,999 feet MSL.
4. Depicted on En Route Low Altitude Charts and not more than 120 nautical miles apart for operations below 18,000 feet MSL.

43. If an aircraft cruised at a higher altitude than the MAA specified for that route or segment:
1. Interference from a nearby VOR, on the same frequency, could render the navigation signal unusable.
2. Radar services and pilot/controller communications would be impaired.
3. Only the terminal (T) class VOR facility would provide acceptable course guidance.
4. Pilot/controller communications would be intermittent.

44. What are the appropriate IFR cruising altitudes for flights in uncontrolled airspace below 18,000 feet MSL?
1. Even thousand-foot MSL altitudes when on a magnetic heading of 0° through 179°; odd thousand-foot MSL altitudes when on a magnetic heading of 180° through 359°.
2. An instrument pilot may fly any altitude in uncontrolled airspace.
3. The altitude must be assigned by ATC.
4. Even thousand-foot MSL altitudes when on a magnetic course of 0° through 179°; odd thousand-foot MSL altitudes when on a magnetic course of 180° through 359°

45. Choose the response that correctly identifies when IFR flight plans should be filed and when non-activated IFR flight plans may be deleted.
1. IFR flight plans should be filed at least 30 minutes prior to the estimated time of departure and may be deleted by ATC after 1 hour past proposed departure time.

2. IFR flight plans should be filed at least 30 minutes prior to the estimated time of departure and may be deleted by ATC after 30 minutes past proposed departure time.
3. IFR flight plans should be filed within 30 minutes of the estimated time of departure and may be deleted by ATC within 1 hour after filing the flight plan.
4. IFR flight plans should be filed within 30 minutes of the estimated time of departure and may be deleted by ATC within 30 minutes after filing the flight plan.

Refer to the excerpt from the Airport/Facility Directory (page 249) when answering question 46.

46. What is the correct procedure for performing an operational check of the VOR equipment at Houghton (Houghton County Memorial Airport)?
1. Tune to a VOT frequency, and check to see if the OBS is within 4° of the 0° setting when the CDI is centered and the TO/FROM indicator registers a FROM indication.
2. Fly over a smoke stack 12 nautical miles from the VOR, tune to the local VOR, and check to see if the CDI is centered when the OBS is between 070° and 078° and the TO/FROM indicator registers a TO indication.
3. Fly over a smoke stack 12 nautical miles from the VOR, tune to the local VOR, and check to see if the CDI is centered when the OBS is between 068° and 080° and the TO/FROM indicator registers a TO indication.
4. Taxi on the terminal ramp in front of the Flight Service Station, tune to the local VOR, center the CDI and check to see if the OBS is between 097° and 105° with a FROM indication registering on the TO/FROM indicator.

47. Which of the following types of airspace are included on IFR wall planning charts?
1. All RNAV routes and low altitude airways.
2. All low altitude airway routes using VOR facilities.
3. All high altitude airways and associated VOR facilities.
4. All jet routes, RNAV routes, and low altitude airways.

48. The terms *MEA GAP* as viewed on an airway course line of an En Route Low Altitude Chart indicate:
1. There is *no* MEA established in that area.
2. The navigation signal is unreliable when at the MEA in that area.
3. The MEA is *not* established, but is assigned upon request.

Facility Name (Arpt Name)	Freq/Ident	Type Check Pt. Gnd. AB/ALT	Azimuth from Fac. Mag	Dist. from Fac. N.M.	Check Point Description
			MICHIGAN		
Alpena	108.8/APN	A/2100	256	10.3	Over dam NE corner of Fletchers Pond.
Alpena (Phelps Collins)	108.8/APN	G	198	0.7	On painted circle on runup area for dsplcd thld of Rwy 36.
Battle Creek	109.4/BTL	A/2000	262	11	Over power house stacks 1 NM E of Comstock.
Escanaba	110.8/ESC	A/2000	002	14	Over microwave twr 1 NM S of Perkins.
Flint (Bishop)	116.9/FNT	G	299	0.53	On runup area Rwy 9.
Grand Rapids	110.2/GRR	A/2500	228	10.5	Over intersection of N/S hwy & E/W road 1 NM W of Wayland.
Houghton (Houghton County Memorial)	112.8/CMX	A/2500	074	12	Over smoke stack.
	112.8/CMX	G	281	0.62	On terminal ramp in front of FSS.
Kalamazoo (Kalamazoo Muni)	109.8/AZO	G	168	0.7	On middle of warmup area Rwy 35.
Keeler (Ross Field)	115.1/ELX	A/1600	266	13.3	Over intersection of N/S and E/W rwys.
Lansing (Abrams Muni)	110.8/LAN	A/2500	343	5.5	Over int NW/SE & N/S hwys 1.7 NM N arpt.
Lansing (Capital City)	110.8/LAN	G	053	5.4	At center of apch end Rwy 06.
Litchfield (Jackson County-Reynolds Field)	111.2/LFD	A/2000	050	18	Over intersection of NE/SW and NW/SE rwys.
Manistee (Manistee Co.-Blacker)	111.4/MBL	G	275	1.1	On center of twy leading to Rwy 09-27.
Marquette (Marquette County)	109.8/MQT	G	236	0.5	On 5000' twy entrance to Rwy 08.
Muskegon (Muskegon County)	115.2/MKG	A/1500	272	8.2	Over intersection of NW/SE and NE/SW rwys.
Newberry	108.2/ERY	A/2500	088	14	Over int of E/W & N/S hwys 1.5 NM S of Hubert.
Peck (St Clair County Intl)	114.0/ECK	A/2000	163	23	Over apch end Rwy 04.
Pellston (Emmet County)	111.8/PLN	G	239	6.5	At intersection of N/S and E/W twys.
Pontiac (Oakland-Pontiac)	111.0/PTK	G	115	5.7	On circle on warmup pad apch end Rwy 27L.
	111.0/PTK	G	120	5.0	On circle on warmup pad apch end Rwy 09R.
Saginaw	112.9/MBS	A/1700	058	6.7	Over intersection US 10 and I-75.
Sault Ste Marie (Sault Ste. Marie City-County)	112.2/SSM	A/2100	336	4.25	Over intersection E/W and NW/SE rwys.
Traverse City (Cherry Capital)	114.6/TVC	G	347	4.7	At intersection of E/W twy and Rwy 23 twy.
Willow Run (Willow Run)	110.0/YIP	G	283	0.8	At NE corner of ramp near center twy.

4. The MEA does not provide obstruction clearance in that area.

49. When the symbol ▷ is plotted next to an airport symbol on an En Route Low Altitude Chart, this indicates:
   1. The airport has a published ILS procedure.
   2. The airport has a published LOC procedure.
   3. The airport has a published SDF procedure.
   4. The airport has a published LDA procedure.

50. What, in addition to the pilot properly filing an IFR flight plan and the aircraft being RNAV certificated, is a necessary condition for ATC to approve an IFR random RNAV route?
   1. The aircraft must be equipped with two operable RNAV receivers.
   2. The proposed flight plan route must be in radar environment.
   3. The flight plan must be filed at least 1 hour prior to the expected time of departure.
   4. The proposed RNAV waypoints must be established fixes.

51. How long is an FDC NOTAM in effect if it is of a temporary nature?
   1. 10 days.
   2. More than 45 days.
   3. Until it is removed from future lists.
   4. 90 days.

52. What information should be listed in Block 8 (Route of Flight Section) if an IFR flight plan is filed for a route of flight off airways or by area navigation?
   1. The departure and arrival fixes and only one waypoint or navigation facility in each ARTCC sector.
   2. Navigation facilities or waypoints separated by distances less than 200 nautical miles.
   3. Each navigation facility or waypoint that will be used for navigation.
   4. Only those navigation facilities depicted as compulsory reporting points on En Route Low Altitude Charts.

53. Why should a pilot review the latest FDC NOTAMs while preflight planning for an IFR flight?
   1. To check if any changes have occurred that may affect an instrument approach procedure that may be executed.
   2. To obtain current information relative to the status of en route navigation facilities.
   3. To obtain current information relative to the IFR routes that would provide the best service due to existing weather conditions.
   4. To obtain the latest flight safety information.

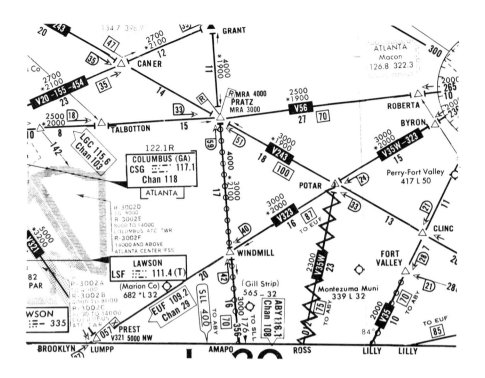

Refer to the illustrated En Route Low Altitude Chart excerpt (above) when answering question 54.

54. Which navigation facility forms the substitute route structure south of PRATZ Intersection?

1. SASSER (SLL) VOR.
2. ATLANTA (ATL) VORTAC.
3. ALBANY (ABY) VORTAC.
4. SASSER (SLL) NDB.

55. A "transition area" can be described as:

A. Controlled airspace extending upward from 700 feet or more above the surface when designated in conjunction with an airport for which an instrument approach procedure has been prescribed.

B. Controlled airspace extending upward from 1,200 feet or more above the surface when designated in conjunction with airway route structures or segments.

C. Controlled airspace extending from 14,500 feet MSL up to but not including FL 450.

D. Controlled airspace extending from the surface up to 700 feet MSL when designated in conjunction with airway route structures.

1. A only.
2. B only.
3. A and B.
4. C and D.

56. A control zone that lies within the 48 contiguous states can be described as:

1. Controlled airspace that extends from the surface up to the base of the Continental Control Area.

2. Controlled airspace that normally extends from 1,200 feet AGL up to but not including 10,000 feet MSL.

3. Controlled airspace that normally extends from the surface up to but not including 3,000 feet AGL.

4. Controlled airspace that normally extends from 1,200 feet AGL up to and including 18,000 feet MSL.

Refer to the illustrated En Route Low Altitude Chart excerpt (below) when answering question 57.

57. During what time period is the control zone effective at Lake Tahoe Airport?

1. From 1500Z to 0600Z.
2. From 2300Z to 1400Z.
3. From 0600 to 1000 local time.
4. 24 hours a day.

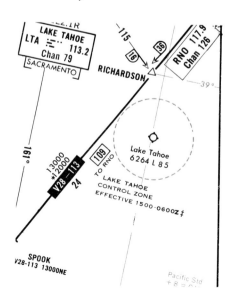

Refer to the illustrated symbol (above) when answering question 58.

58. What information can be derived from the figure?

   1. The figure represents the boundaries of a TCA.

   2. All aircraft are required to have an operable transponder when operating in the depicted area.

   3. Special VFR flight (for fixed-wing aircraft) is not permitted within the control zone.

   4. The control zone is in effect during specified periods of time.

Refer to the illustrated En Route Low Altitude Chart excerpt (below) when answering questions 59 and 60.

59. An aircraft flying on an IFR flight plan from TAOS VORTAC north on airway V–83 will be under the control of:

   1. Albuquerque Center.

   2. Denver Center.

   3. Alamosa Center.

   4. Albuquerque Center, then Denver Center.

60. When would RODDS Intersection be considered a compulsory reporting point?

A. When TAOS VORTAC is inoperative.

B. When ATC loses radar contact with the aircraft.

C. Any time the intersection is used to determine a route segment for a direct IFR flight.

D. When required by ATC.

   1. A, B, and C.

   2. B, C, and D.

   3. C and D.

   4. B and D.

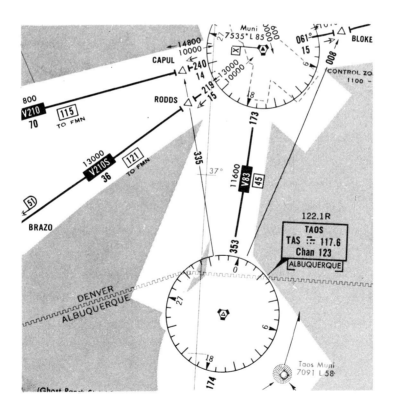

8.

Departure and En Route Procedures

8.1 This chapter discusses those facilities, services, and procedures that are available to most pilots conducting flight operations in accordance with Instrument Flight Rules.

CLEARANCES

8.2 The FAA establishes the prescribed standards for the operation of navigational aids, Air Route Traffic Control Centers, and airspace limits. When the weather is below basic VFR weather minimums, ATC provides the following for each aircraft that is in controlled airspace operating on an IFR clearance: directional guidance, terrain clearance, and safe separation between other aircraft that are also operating in accordance with ATC clearances. This is accomplished through the use of Air Route Traffic Control Centers and navigational aids.

8.3 An IFR clearance which is provided by ATC is authorization for a pilot and aircraft to proceed into controlled airspace under specified rules. Such airspace is controlled for the purpose of preventing collisions between known IFR traffic. Pilots on IFR clearances must execute the appropriate maneuvers at precise times, at specified altitudes, over designated routes and geographic positions, and in an orderly sequence with other aircraft.

8.4 Any clearance that is issued by ATC is predicated on known IFR traffic and physical airport conditions. An IFR clearance may be received at the departure point or while en route, and normally contains:

1. Aircraft identification.
2. A clearance limit to the airport of intended landing. (A clearance limit is the fix, point, or location to which an aircraft is cleared when

issued an air traffic clearance.) However, under certain conditions, at some locations a short range clearance procedure is utilized whereby a clearance is issued to a fix within or just outside of the terminal area and the pilot is advised of the frequency on which to receive the long range clearance direct from the center controller.
3. A departure procedure (often in the form of headings and altitudes, to separate aircraft in the terminal area).
4. The route of flight filed by the pilot. (In some cases, due to traffic conditions or inoperative NAVAIDs, ATC may specify a different route.)
5. A specific altitude or flight level while the aircraft is in controlled airspace. (ATC may also assign an altitude different from the requested altitude.)
6. Holding pattern instructions (if required).
7. Any special information (if required).

Cruise Clearances

8.5 When an altitude is assigned, the word *maintain* is often used in a clearance. Occasionally, the controller may substitute the word *cruise* for the word *maintain* when assigning altitudes for relatively short flights in noncongested areas. The word *cruise* is used in an ATC clearance to authorize a pilot to conduct flight at any altitude from the minimum IFR altitude up to and including the altitude specified in the clearance. The pilot may level off at any intermediary altitude within this block of airspace. Climb/descent within the block is to be made at the discretion of the pilot. However, once the pilot starts descent and reports leaving an altitude in the block, that pilot may not return to that altitude without additional ATC clearance. Further, cruise is approval for the pilot to proceed to and execute an instrument approach procedure at the destination airport and can be used in conjunction with:

1. An airport clearance limit at locations *with* a standard/special instrument approach procedure (the FARs require that, if an instrument letdown to an airport is necessary, the pilot shall make the letdown in accordance with a standard/special instrument approach procedure for that airport); *or,*

2. An airport clearance limit at locations that are within/below/outside controlled airspace and *without* a standard/special instrument approach procedure. Such a clearance is *not authorization* for the pilot to descend under IFR conditions below the applicable minimum IFR altitude nor does it imply that ATC is exercising control over aircraft in uncontrolled airspace; however, it provides a means for the aircraft to proceed to the destination airport, and descend and land in accordance with applicable FARs governing VFR flight operations.

Abbreviated IFR Departure Clearance

8.6 An IFR clearance that contains the words "cleared as filed" is an abbreviated clearance. An abbreviated IFR departure clearance is based upon the *route* of flight filed in the IFR flight plan, provided the filed route can be approved with little or no revision. The abbreviated clearance procedures are based on the following conditions:

1. The aircraft must be on the ground or in VFR conditions while airborne.

2. The pilot will not accept an abbreviated clearance if the route or destination of a flight plan filed with ATC has been changed by him before departure.

3. It is the responsibility of the pilot to inform ATC in the initial call-up (for clearance) when the filed flight plan has been (a) amended or (b) canceled and replaced with a new filed flight plan. Note: The facility issuing a clearance may not have received the revised route or the revised flight plan by the time a pilot requests clearance. The controller will then issue a detailed clearance when he has knowledge that the original filed flight plan has been changed or when the pilot requests a full route clearance.

8.7 *Special Notes:*

1. *An abbreviated clearance does not include the en route altitude. Therefore, an en route altitude will be stated in an abbreviated clearance or the pilot will be advised to expect an assigned/filed altitude within a given time frame or at a certain point after departure.*

2. *The clearance, as issued, will be considered as a clearance to the destination airport filed in the flight plan.*

RECEIVING AN IFR CLEARANCE

8.8 An IFR clearance is issued by the ARTCC which controls the airspace at the requesting pilot's location. The actual clearance, however, may be relayed to the pilot from any one of a number of FAA facilities or directly from the appropriate ARTCC.

Clearance Delivery—High Density Airports

8.9 At certain high density airports, a pre-taxi clearance delivery frequency is established for departing IFR aircraft. Before taxiing, pilots of departing IFR aircraft may elect to receive their clearance from pre-taxi clearance delivery, assuming the following:

1. Pilot participation is not mandatory.

2. Participating pilots should call clearance delivery or ground control not more than 10 minutes prior to proposed taxi time. (This normally is the first communication contact a pilot will make on the aircraft radio before the flight.)

3. IFR clearance or delay information will be issued at the time of this initial radio contact.

4. After receiving a clearance on a pre-taxi clearance delivery frequency, a pilot should contact ground control for taxi instructions when ready to taxi.

5. Normally, pilots are not required to inform ground control that the IFR clearance was received on a pre-taxi clearance delivery frequency.

6. If a pilot wishes to taxi without having already received a clearance, ground control should be informed accordingly.

Clearance Receipt—Airports Served by a Control Tower Not Providing Pre-taxi Clearance Delivery Service

8.10 At airports served by a control tower, a pilot may request an IFR clearance on initial contact with ground control when a pre-taxi clearance delivery service is not provided.

Clearance Receipt—Airports Served by a Flight Service Station

8.11 At an airport served only by a Flight Service Station, a pilot may request an IFR clearance from the FSS prior to or during taxi. Pilots of aircraft departing from airports served by a part time control tower and a full time FSS may also receive an IFR clearance from the FSS when the control tower is not in operation.

Clearance Receipt—Other Airports

8.12 A pilot departing an airport not served by a Flight Service Station or control tower may receive a clearance by calling a nearby FSS on the telephone prior to takeoff, or by contacting a nearby ARTCC facility while on the ground or after the aircraft is airborne. However, a clearance obtained through FSS in this manner may have a restricted departure time, for example: "Clearance void if not off by 0810Z."

Clearance Receipt—En Route

8.13 Once en route, a pilot may elect to receive a clearance by filing an IFR flight plan through an FSS. When the FSS reads back a clearance, the clearance will normally contain an en route frequency on which to contact ATC.

8.14 An IFR flight plan may also be filed and received directly from ATC through a remote facility while an aircraft is en route. Pilots are reminded that contacting ATC directly to file a flight plan is not the recommended procedure because it increases the work load of the controllers.

8.15 *Special Note: The phrase, "clearance on request," may be used by clearance delivery, ground control, or FSS when the clearance is not ready but has been requested from ATC.*

AMENDED CLEARANCES

8.16 Amendments to the initial clearance will be issued at any time an air traffic controller deems such action necessary to avoid possible confliction between aircraft during routine and emergency situations. Clearances will require that a flight "hold" or change altitude prior to reaching the point where standard separation from other IFR traffic would no longer exist. Some pilots have questioned this action and requested "traffic information" and were at a loss when the reply indicated "no traffic reported." In such cases the controller has taken action to prevent a traffic confliction which would have occurred at a distant point.

8.17 The pilot has the privilege of requesting a different clearance from that which has been issued by ATC if:

1. The pilot feels that he has information which would make another course of action more practicable; *or*
2. If aircraft equipment limitations forbid compliance with the clearance issued; *or*
3. If the issued clearance would cause a pilot to deviate from an FAA regulation.

8.18 Pilots should observe the following rules concerning amended clearances.

1. When a clearance is amended, the most recent ATC clearance has precedence over *all related items* of the previous ATC clearance. (A clearance which amends only the altitude portion does not change the route portion in the previous clearance. Similarly, a clearance which amends only the route portion, whether based upon vectors or ground NAVAIDs, does not change the altitude portion of the previous clearance.)
2. If the amended route no longer requires a flight to cross a specified fix/radial for which an associated crossing altitude was previously issued, the crossing altitude cannot apply, and the previous crossing altitudes for such fixes/radials are no longer in effect.
3. When the route or altitude in a previously issued clearance is amended, the controller will restate applicable *altitude restrictions*. (If previously issued altitude restrictions are omitted from an amended clearance, those *altitude restrictions* are cancelled and any charted restrictions will apply thereafter.)
4. Pilots should pay particular attention to the clearance and not assume that the route and altitude/flight level are the same as requested in the flight plan.
5. If any portion of a clearance or amendment is not clearly understood, pilots should request verification from ATC.

ADHERENCES TO CLEARANCES

8.19 After obtaining an ATC clearance under either Visual or Instrument Flight Rules, the pilot in command shall not deviate from that clearance unless an amended clearance is obtained. Furthermore, the addition of a VFR or other restriction does not authorize a pilot to deviate from the route of flight or any other provision of the Air Traffic Control clearance.

VFR RESTRICTIONS

8.20 ATC will *not* issue a clearance to an IFR flight specifying that climb, descent, or any portion of the flight be conducted in VFR conditions, unless one of the following conditions exists:

1. The pilot requests the VFR restriction.
2. For noise abatement benefits, where part of the IFR departure route does not conform with an FAA-approved noise abatement route or altitude.

8.21 If a pilot is operating on an IFR flight plan and is issued a VFR restriction, the pilot is responsible for avoiding other aircraft. (ATC will not apply IFR separation during the VFR restriction portion of the flight.)

8.22 *Special Note: If a pilot receiving a VFR restriction finds that compliance with the clearance* *is not feasible, that pilot should maintain VFR conditions and request an amended clearance.*

SPECIAL VFR CLEARANCES

8.23 Instrument rated pilots must remember that under certain conditions non-instrument rated pilots may request and be granted clearances by ATC to enter, leave, or operate within most control zones when the weather is less than that required for VFR flight. Special VFR clearances may be issued when:

1. The traffic permits.
2. The flight will not delay IFR operations.
3. The visibility and cloud clearance requirements can be met (as depicted in Figure 6-7).

8.24 Although instrument rated pilots generally do not request Special VFR clearances, nevertheless the following considerations should be thoroughly reviewed to improve piloting effectiveness and safety within control zones.

1. The controller may require a pilot on a Special VFR clearance to fly at or below a certain altitude due to other traffic. In addition, at locations equipped with radar, VFR flights may be vectored.
2. ATC will provide separation between Special VFR and other IFR flights.
3. Special VFR operations by fixed-wing aircraft are prohibited in some control zones (as noted on aeronautical charts) due to the volume of IFR traffic.
4. Special VFR operations by fixed-wing aircraft are prohibited between sunset and sunrise, unless the pilot is instrument rated, and the aircraft is equipped for IFR flight.
5. Special VFR clearances are effective within control zones only. For example, ATC does not provide separation after an aircraft leaves the control zone on a Special VFR clearance.

ATC CLEARANCE/INSTRUCTION READBACK

8.25 Pilots should make a written record of each ATC clearance as it is received, since the specified conditions which are part of an ATC clearance are occasionally different from those conditions stated in proposed flight plans. Additionally, ATC may deem it necessary to add to or amend a clearance.

8.26 After having received and recorded an IFR clearance, the pilot should study the clearance to determine if he can comply (or wishes to comply) with the clearance. It is then the responsibility of the pilot to accept or refuse the clearance as issued.

8.27 It is suggested that pilots as a general procedure verify, by a readback, any portions of a clearance that are complex or about which any doubt exists. Pilots of airborne aircraft should read back those parts of ATC clearances/instructions containing altitude assignments or vectors. *The readback procedure is an invaluable aid in reducing communications errors.*

8.28 When a pilot reads a clearance/instruction back to a controller, the following procedures should be observed:

1. Precede all readbacks/acknowledgments with the aircraft identification. The controllers can thereby determine that the correct aircraft received the clearance/instruction. The requirement to include aircraft identification in all readbacks/acknowledgments becomes more important when frequency congestion increases and when aircraft with similar call signs are on the same frequency.
2. Read back altitudes, altitude restrictions, and vectors in the same sequence as they are issued in the clearance/instruction.
3. Altitudes contained in charted procedures should not be read back unless they are specifically stated by the controller.

AUTOMATIC TERMINAL INFORMATION SERVICE (ATIS)

8.29 Automatic Terminal Information Service is the continuous broadcast of recorded *noncontrol* information in designated high activity terminal areas. Its purpose is to improve controller effectiveness, and to relieve frequency congestion by automating the repetitive transmission of essential but routine information. ATIS is continuously broadcast on the voice feature of a TVOR/VOR/VORTAC located on or near the airport, or on a discrete UHF/VHF frequency.

8.30 The information that is included in a typical ATIS broadcast consists of:

1. Airport identification.
2. Time of weather sequence.
3. Ceiling (generally only if the ceiling is below 5,000 feet AGL).
4. Visibility (generally only if the visibility is less than 5 statute miles).
5. Obstructions to visibility.
6. Temperature.
7. Wind direction (magnetic) and velocity (knots).
8. Altimeter settings.
9. Pertinent remarks.
10. Instrument approach and runways in use. (Departure runway(s) will only be broadcast by ATIS if different from the landing runway(s), except at locations having a separate ATIS for departure. Where VFR arrival aircraft are expected to make initial contact with approach control, this fact and the appropriate frequencies may be

broadcast on ATIS.)

11. Phonetic letter identifier.

8.31 These ATIS broadcasts are normally updated hourly with each weather observation. However, they will be updated more frequently should a significant change occur in the information. In addition, each broadcast is coded with a letter of the phonetic alphabet, and each time the message is updated, the next phonetic alphabet code letter will be appended to the broadcast.

8.32 Landing or departing pilots should monitor ATIS whenever possible to relieve frequency congestion. However, each pilot should notify controllers that the ATIS message was received by repeating the alphabetical code letter appended to the broadcast. For example, the words "information Delta received" signify that the pilot has received the ATIS information alphabetically coded "Delta."

8.33 Some pilots use the phrase "have the numbers," in communications with control towers. This phrase indicates that the pilot has received wind and runway information *only* and that the tower does not need to repeat this information. Since the phrase does not indicate receipt of an ATIS broadcast, it should never be used to indicate receipt of an ATIS broadcast.

8.34 *Special Note: Controllers will issue pertinent information to pilots who do not acknowledge receipt of a broadcast or who acknowledge receipt of a broadcast which is not current.*

TRANSPONDER OPERATION

8.35 Proper application of transponder procedures will provide both VFR and IFR air traffic with a higher degree of safety in a high density traffic environment. As noted in chapter 4, transponders substantially increase the capability of radar to detect aircraft. The Mode C feature further enables the controller to rapidly determine where potential traffic conflicts may exist. Even pilots of aircraft conducting VFR flight operations are afforded greater protection from IFR aircraft and VFR aircraft which are receiving traffic advisories. Even though navigation through the employment of such aids as radar stations and transponder-equipped aircraft make the skies a safer place to fly, pilots should never relax their visual scanning vigilance (when possible) for other aircraft.

8.36 Pilots of transponder-equipped aircraft should adjust the transponder while airborne to reply on the Mode A/3 code specified by ATC and, if so equipped, to reply on Mode C with altitude reporting *capability activated* unless deactivation is directed by ATC, or unless the installed aircraft equipment has not been tested and calibrated in accordance with FAR 91.36.

8.37 When ATC assigns a transponder code to an aircraft, one or a combination of the 4096 discrete codes *four-digit code designation* will be used. For example, Code 2100 will be expressed as "two one zero zero."

8.38 Occasionally a misinformed pilot will activate the IDENT feature after an assigned code has been set in the transponder. The transponder should be operated *only* as specified by ATC. The IDENT feature should only be activated at the *request* of an ATC controller.

Transponder Setting

8.39 Pilots of aircraft equipped with a transponder on an IFR flight should, prior to departure:

1. Adjust the transponder to the standby mode. (Remember that many transponders require from 30 seconds to a minute for warm-up.)
2. Set in the assigned code.
3. Switch the transponder to the "on" or normal operating position as late as practicable prior to takeoff (and to "off" or "standby" as soon as practicable after completing landing roll unless the change to "standby" has been accomplished previously at the request of ATC).

Transponder Phraseology

8.40 Both civil and military air traffic controllers will use the following phraseology when referring to operation of the transponder. Instructions by Air Traffic Control refer only to Mode A/3 or Mode C operations and do not affect the operation of the transponder on other modes.

Squawk (number)—Operate radar beacon transponder on designated code in Mode A/3.

Squawk IDENT—Depress the IDENT button momentarily.

Squawk standby—Switch transponder to standby position.

Squawk low/normal—Operate transponder on low or normal sensitivity as specified. The transponder is operated in "normal" position unless ATC specified "low." ("On" is used instead of "normal" as a master control label on some types of transponders.)

Squawk altitude—Activate Mode C with automatic altitude reporting.

Stop squawk altitude—Turn off altitude reporting switch and continue transmitting Mode C framing pulses. If the equipment does not have this capability, turn off Mode C.

Squawk mayday—Operate transponder on Code 7700.

Squawk VFR—Operate transponder in the emergency position regardless of altitude.

Stop squawk—Switch off transponder.
Stop squawk (mode in use)—Switch off specified mode.

Transponder Codes

8.41 Pilots should be familiar with the following transponder codes, to be used in the described situation:

Code 1200—For flight operations, at any altitude, conducted in accordance with Visual Flight Rules. (Instrument pilots must remember that if an IFR flight plan is cancelled while en route, the transponder should be adjusted accordingly.)

Code 7700 *—For emergency situations.

Code 7600 *—For radio failure.

Code 7500 *—For hijack.

8.42 *Special Notes:*

1. *Pilots of civil aircraft should never, under any circumstances, operate transponders on Code 0000. (This code is reserved for military interceptor operations.)*

2. *When making routine code changes, pilots should avoid inadvertent selection of Codes 7500, 7600 through 7677, or 7700 through 7777, thereby triggering false alarms at automated ATC ground radar facilities. (For example, when switching from Code 2700 to Code 7200, switch first to 2200 then 7200, NOT to 7700 and then 7200.)*

STANDARD INSTRUMENT DEPARTURES (SIDs)

8.43 The FAA has established special departure and arrival procedures for application at certain airports (located in areas of high traffic activity) to simplify clearance delivery procedures. These procedures are called SIDs and STARs (Standard terminal arrival routes). Both types of procedures are charted in a similar manner. STARs are discussed further in chapter 9. Figure 8–1 illustrates a SID for the Metropolitan Oakland International Airport.

8.44 Pilots of civil aircraft operating from locations where SID procedures are effective may expect ATC clearances containing a SID. Use of a SID requires pilot possession of at least the textual description of the approved effective SID. All effective SIDs are published in textual and graphic form by the National Ocean Survey in Eastern United States and Western United States SID booklets.

8.45 If the pilot does not possess a preprinted SID description, or if for any other reason does not wish to use a SID, the pilot is expected to advise ATC.

* Discussed in greater detail in chapter 10.

Pilots who do not wish to use a SID should notify ATC verbally if they have not previously written "No SID" in the remarks section of their filed flight plan form.

8.46 In many cases, obstruction avoidance procedures are incorporated into established SIDs and the SID is referenced as the obstruction avoidance procedure. In this case, when a pilot desires to utilize the SID, it should be filed in the flight plan as the first item of the requested routing.

8.47 Crossing restrictions used in a SID may be established for traffic separation or to assist the pilot in obstacle avoidance. When a crossing restriction is established for either reason, pilots are expected to cross the fix as charted and continue to make good a minimum climb of 152 feet per mile after crossing the fix until reaching the MEA or assigned altitude.

8.48 ATC procedures require controllers to state the name, current number, and transition name of each SID for *all* departure clearances (including abbreviated clearances) when a SID or SID transition is to be employed. This procedure applies even when the SID routing is incorporated in the filed flight plan. (Pilots occasionally confuse SID procedures with STAR procedures. Pilots should note, however, that STARs, when filed in a flight plan, are considered a part of the filed route of flight and will not normally be stated in an initial departure clearance.)

Example: "Cessna three six one three Juliett cleared as filed, Englewood Two Departure, Elwood Transition, maintain Flight Level two nine zero, squawk two one zero zero."

FLIGHT PLAN ACTIVATION

8.49 Pilots of aircraft departing on IFR flights from airports served by operational control towers will have their flight plans activated automatically (without pilot request). But pilots of aircraft departing airports that do *not* have operational control towers must contact the nearest Flight Service Station or other ATC facility by radio to notify them of the aircraft departure time.

NAVIGATION FROM TAKEOFF TO THE EN ROUTE PHASE OF FLIGHT

8.50 Normal departure procedures will vary according to the proposed route, the traffic environment, and the ATC facilities controlling the flight. Some IFR flights are conducted under radar surveillance and control from takeoff to touchdown, while other IFR flights are conducted entirely by pilot navigation.

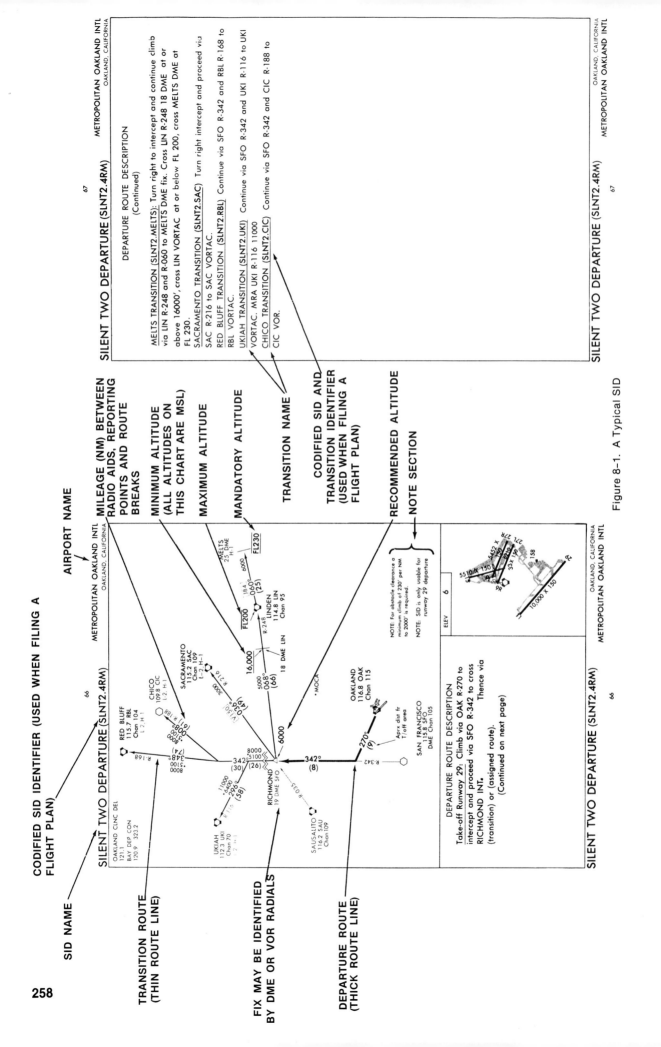

Figure 8-1. A Typical SID

258

Departure—From an Airport in Uncontrolled Airspace

8.51 Where ATC has no jurisdiction, no IFR clearance will be issued. Consequently, ATC has no control over IFR flights conducted in uncontrolled airspace and therefore the pilot must assume the responsibility of separation from other traffic. Generally, it is up to the pilot to provide his own navigation without the aid of ATC for flight in uncontrolled airspace.

8.52 With the rapid expansion of controlled airspace within the National Airspace System, the amount of uncontrolled airspace is diminishing. (This is the primary reason that the average instrument pilot will normally file an IFR flight plan via airways during periods of inclement weather conditions.) Pilots are reminded that the advantages are few and the hazards are many while flying in uncontrolled airspace.

Departure—From an Airport Served by Departure Control

8.53 Departure Control is an ATC service provided by a facility (in congested areas) that is responsible for ensuring separation between arrival and departure aircraft. In order to expedite the handling of departures, Departure Control may suggest a takeoff direction other than that which may normally have been used under VFR handling. Many times it is preferred to offer the pilot a runway that will require the fewest turns after takeoff to place the pilot on his filed course or selected departure route as quickly as possible. At many locations, particular attention is paid to the use of preferential runways for local noise abatement programs and route departures away from congested areas.

8.54 Departure Control utilizing radar will normally clear aircraft out of the terminal area using standard instrument departures via radio navigation aids. When a departure is to be vectored immediately following takeoff, the pilot will be advised prior to takeoff of the initial heading to be flown, but may not be advised of the purpose of the heading. When given a vector taking his aircraft off a previously assigned nonradar route, the pilot will be advised briefly what the vector is to achieve. Thereafter, radar service will be provided until the aircraft has been reestablished "on-course" using an appropriate navigation aid and the pilot has been advised of his position; or, a handoff is made to another radar controller with further surveillance capabilities. (A handoff [radar handoff] is the transfer of radar identification of an aircraft from one controller to another, either within the same facility or interfacility. Actual transfer of control responsibility may occur at the time of the handoff, or at a specified time, point, or altitude.)

8.55 Controllers will inform pilots of the departure control frequencies and, if appropriate, the transponder code before takeoff.

Departure—From an Airport in Controlled Airspace Not Served by Departure Control

8.56 There are many airports in controlled airspace that are not served by a Departure Control. In these cases, after a clearance has been received and the cleared aircraft has taken off, the pilot is expected to proceed on course via the most direct route if no specific departure instructions were issued with the clearance. The pilot is generally expected to provide his own navigation except in some areas where ARTCC may provide radar vectors to the en route course.

COMMUNICATIONS

8.57 The pilot's ability to communicate with the appropriate facility at the proper time is a critical factor in flight safety. The following communications procedures should be reviewed occasionally to insure maximum proficiency of IFR communications skills.

Departure Communications

8.58 Pilots are often confused as to which frequencies to use and when to use them. Most flights conducted in accordance with Instrument Flight Rules will have different routes of flight and departure airports. Naturally the types of facilities to be contacted and times that they are contacted will vary significantly and will dictate the necessary pilot action. Many pilots on IFR flights will not use any communications frequency from the time their IFR clearance is received until contacting the appropriate Air Route Traffic Control Center. Still, pilots of aircraft on IFR clearances departing major airports are required to change communication frequencies several times in the proper sequence.

8.59 As previously discussed, the correct frequencies needed to depart a controlled airport may be found in the communication section on the En Route Low Altitude Chart or in the Airport/Facility Directory. After determining the proper communication frequencies, the correct sequence of use during the departure from a major metropolitan airport is:

1. ATIS.
2. Clearance delivery.
3. Ground control.
4. Tower.
5. Departure control.

8.60 *Rules of Thumb: The following guidelines help a pilot determine when to transition from one frequency to another: While a departing aircraft is on the ground, the frequency change is generally initiated at the pilot's discretion. Once the aircraft is in the air, however, the controller originates the frequency change.*

En Route Communications with Air Traffic Control

8.61 Pilots of departing aircraft will generally be assigned a frequency on which an ARTCC facility may be contacted either prior to or after takeoff. If for some reason a pilot cannot establish radio contact or reestablish radio contact after changing frequencies in the air, the pilot should:

1. Attempt to reestablish contact with ARTCC on the communications frequency previously used or on any other known frequencies; *or*
2. Contact an FSS; *or*
3. If both procedures fail, use the emergency frequency 121.5 MHz to reestablish communications.

8.62 ARTCC communication frequencies are designed *strictly* for communications pertinent to the control of IFR aircraft. Filing of flight plans, en route weather, or weather forecasts should be requested through the appropriate Flight Service Station.

MANDATORY REPORTS (IFR, RADIO COMMUNICATIONS - FAR 91.125)

8.63 The pilot in command of each aircraft operated under IFR in controlled airspace *shall* have a continuous watch maintained on the appropriate frequency and shall report the following by radio as soon as possible:

1. The time and altitude of passing each designated reporting point, or the reporting points specified by ATC (refer to paragraphs 7.47 and 7.73), except while the aircraft is under radar control, in which case only the passing of those reporting points specifically requested by ATC need be reported;
2. Any unforecast weather conditions encountered; and
3. Any other information relating to the safety of flight.

ADDITIONAL EN ROUTE REPORTS

8.64 The following reports *should* be made to ATC or FSS facilities without request:

1. The time and altitude/flight level upon reaching a holding fix or point to which cleared. (Not required when in "radar contact.")
2. When vacating any previously assigned altitude/flight level for a newly assigned altitude/flight level.
3. When leaving any assigned holding fix or point. (Not required when in "radar contact.")
4. A corrected estimate at any time it becomes apparent that an estimate as previously submitted is in error in excess of 3 minutes. (Not required when in "radar contact.")
5. When an altitude change will be made if operating on a clearance specifying "VFR Conditions on Top."
6. When an aircraft's average true airspeed at cruising altitude between reporting points varies or is expected to vary plus or minus 5 percent, or 10 knots, whichever is greater, from the airspeed given in the flight plan. (Not required when in "radar contact.")

POSITION REPORTS

8.65 Position reports should include the following information:

1. Aircraft identification.
2. Aircraft position at the time of the report.
3. Time at that position.
4. Altitude or flight level (including actual altitude when operating on a VFR Conditions on Top clearance).
5. Type of flight plan (not required in an IFR position report made directly to ARTCC or approach control).
6. Name of, and estimated time of arrival at, the next reporting point.
7. Name only of the next succeeding reporting point along the route of flight.
8. Pertinent remarks.

PILOT/CONTROLLER PHRASEOLOGY

8.66 The following phrases are a summation of examples of the proper manner in which pilots should use ground station call signs:

Airport Unicom—"PHILIP UNICOM"

FAA Flight Service Station—"RAPID CITY RADIO"

FAA Flight Service Station (En Route Flight Advisory Service Weather)— "SEATTLE FLIGHT WATCH"

Airport Traffic Control Tower—"BILLINGS TOWER"

Clearance Delivery Position (IFR)—"DALLAS CLEARANCE DELIVERY"

Ground Control Position in Tower—"MIAMI GROUND"

Radar or Nonradar Approach Control Position— "OKLAHOMA CITY APPROACH"

Radar Departure Control Position—"ST. LOUIS DEPARTURE"

FAA Air Route Traffic Control Center—"WASHINGTON CENTER"

8.67 Phraseology used by controllers to effect a frequency change will most generally follow these guidelines: "(Aircraft identification) CONTACT (facility name or location name and terminal function) (frequency) AT (time, fix, or altitude) OVER."

8.68 The following phraseology should be utilized by pilots for establishing contact with the designated ATC facility:

1. When a position report will be made: "(Name) CENTER, (aircraft identification), (position), OVER."

2. When no position report will be made: "(Name) CENTER, (aircraft identification) ESTIMATING (reporting point), (time) AT (altitude/ flight level) CLIMBING/DESCENDING TO MAINTAIN (altitude/flight level) OVER."

3. When operating in a radar environment and no position report is required: "(Name) CENTER, (aircraft identification) AT (exact altitude/flight level); or, if appropriate, LEAVING (exact altitude/flight level) CLIMBING/DESCENDING TO MAINTAIN (altitude/flight level) OVER."

8.69 The safety of the Air Traffic Control System depends largely on the use of radar to separate aircraft. Therefore, when the controller informs a pilot that the aircraft is in "radar contact," this means the controller has identified the aircraft in the ATC system. (Once the controller has established radar contact, this fact will not be repeated when the aircraft's identifying code on the radar scope is handed off to another controller.)

8.70 When the controller states "radar contact" and gives the pilot relative position from a NAVAID, the pilot is expected to confirm the aircraft's position. If not tuned to the same NAVAID, the pilot will be expected to ask for another position relative to the NAVAID from which the aircraft radio is receiving.

8.71 A pilot may be given radar vectors during the departure, en route, and/or final approach stages of flight. But, generally, once an aircraft has been established close to the planned route, ATC will inform the pilot to "resume normal navigation." The phrase "resume normal navigation" signifies that the pilot is responsible for maintaining the specified route of flight.

8.72 "Radar contact lost" is the phraseology used by ATC controllers to inform a pilot that radar identification of the pilot's aircraft is not possible at the present time. The phrase "radar service terminated" is used by ATC to inform a pilot that any of the services that could be received while under

radar contact will no longer be provided.

8.73 *Special Notes:*

1. When ATC advises "radar contact lost" or "radar service terminated," pilots should resume normal reporting procedures.

2. When advised by ATC to change frequencies, pilots should acknowledge the instructions. If a pilot selects the new frequency without an acknowledgment, the controller's workload is increased since the controller has no way of knowing if the pilot received the instruction or lost use of the aircraft radios.

EN ROUTE WEATHER INFORMATION

8.74 It is often necessary for pilots to check en route and destination weather during most IFR flights. Pilots should be familiar with some of the different types of en route weather information services available in addition to the In-Flight Weather Advisories discussed in paragraphs 3.149 through 3.153.

Transcribed Weather Broadcasts

8.75 Meteorological and Notice to Airmen data are recorded on tapes and broadcast continuously over the low-frequency (200–415 KHz) navigational aids (LF/MF range or H facilities) and VORs at *selected* Flight Service Stations. The taped information consists of station identification, general forecast weather conditions in the area, pilot reports, radar reports when available, winds aloft data, and weather conditions at selected locations within a 400-mile radius of the broadcasting station. The taped information is updated as necessary.

Scheduled Weather Broadcasts

8.76 *Most* Flight Service Stations having VORs or NDBs with voice capability broadcast weather reports and Notice to Airmen information at 15 minutes past each hour from reporting points within a radius of approximately 150 miles of the broadcast station. (Unscheduled broadcasts will also be made at random times as necessary. Information contained in unscheduled broadcasts is generally of a more important nature than the information contained in scheduled broadcasts.)

En Route Flight Advisory Service (Flight Watch/EFAS)

8.77 If a pilot requires weather information other than that broadcast over NAVAIDs, the En Route Flight Advisory Service or the appropriate Flight Service Station should be contacted. EFAS is a nationwide service specifically designed to provide en route aircraft with timely and meaningful weather information pertinent to the type of flight, route of flight, and altitude. This service is provided by specialists, particularly trained, from selected Flight Service Stations controlling one or more remote communications outlets covering a large geographical area. As previously noted, all EFAS communications are conducted on the designated frequency of 122.0 MHz.

8.78 Pilots of aircraft on IFR flight plans will be provided weather reports for the proposed route of flight, and for the destination and/or alternate airport; they will be provided with terminal forecasts for the destination and/or alternate airport upon request. Pilots are reminded that EFAS *is not* intended to be used for position reporting, filing or closing flight plans, obtaining complete preflight weather briefings, or obtaining random weather reports and forecasts.

ATC Weather Dissemination

8.79 Certain ATC Centers are staffed with one or more meteorologists. Pilots benefit from the meteorologists' presence since the controllers are briefed by the meteorologists; the controllers, in turn, *may* relate *critical* weather information to pilots or use the information to better plan flight operations during troublesome weather conditions. Remember, as stated in paragraph 8.62, pilots should not make *routine* weather requests to ATC.

EN ROUTE ALTIMETER SETTINGS

8.80 Proper vertical separation between aircraft depends on accurate altimeter settings. For this reason, it is of utmost concern that all pilots maintain a current altimeter setting. Aircraft on IFR flight plans are normally furnished the correct altimeter settings while en route by ATC.

8.81 FAR Part 91.81, which outlines regulations governing altimeter settings, states that: Each person operating an aircraft shall maintain the cruising altitude or flight level of that aircraft, as the case may be, by reference to an altimeter that is set, when operating as follows:

1. Below 18,000 feet MSL, to the current reported altimeter setting of a station along the route and within 100 nautical miles of the aircraft. If there is no station along the route and within 100 nautical miles of the aircraft, then to the current reported altimeter setting of an appropriate available station.

2. At or above 18,000 feet MSL, to 29.92" Hg. The lowest usable flight level is determined by the atmospheric pressure in the area of operation, as shown in the following table:

Current Altimeter Setting	Lowest Usable Flight Level
29.92 or higher	180
29.91 through 29.42	185
29.41 through 28.92	190
28.91 through 28.42	195
28.41 through 27.92	200
27.91 through 27.42	205
27.41 through 26.92	210

HOLDING PATTERNS

8.82 A holding pattern is a predetermined maneuver which keeps aircraft within a specified airspace while awaiting further clearance from Air Traffic Control. (Figure 8–2) Whenever an aircraft has been cleared to a point other than the destination airport, it is the responsibility of the ATC controller to furnish the pilot with an additional clearance prior to the time the aircraft arrives at the clearance limit. A further clearance may authorize flight beyond the clearance limit or may contain specific holding instructions for the aircraft. However, when such a clearance is not received by the time the aircraft is 3 minutes from the clearance limit, the pilot is expected to effect a speed reduction in order to cross the clearance limit initially *at or below the maximum holding speed* (unless subsequent clearance prior to reaching the clearance limit permits flight beyond it) and:

1. When reaching the clearance limit, begin holding in accordance with the holding pattern depicted on the appropriate FAA approved chart (for example, En Route Low or High Altitude Chart) for the clearance limit, maintaining the last assigned altitude/flight level; *or*

2. If no holding pattern is charted, the pilot is expected to begin holding in a *standard* holding pattern on the course on which the aircraft approaches the fix and immediately request further clearance.

(The altitude/flight level of the aircraft at this clearance limit will be protected so that separation will exist in the event the aircraft holds awaiting further clearance.)

8.83 When an ATC clearance requires that an aircraft be held at a holding point where the pattern is not depicted, the clearance will include the following information:

1. The direction to hold from the holding point. (The direction to hold with relation to the holding fix will be specified as one of eight general directions, such as north, northeast, east, and so forth.)

2. Holding fix (for example, an airway intersection, DME fix, VOR, or NDB). (Refer to Figures 8–3, 8–4, and 8–5.)

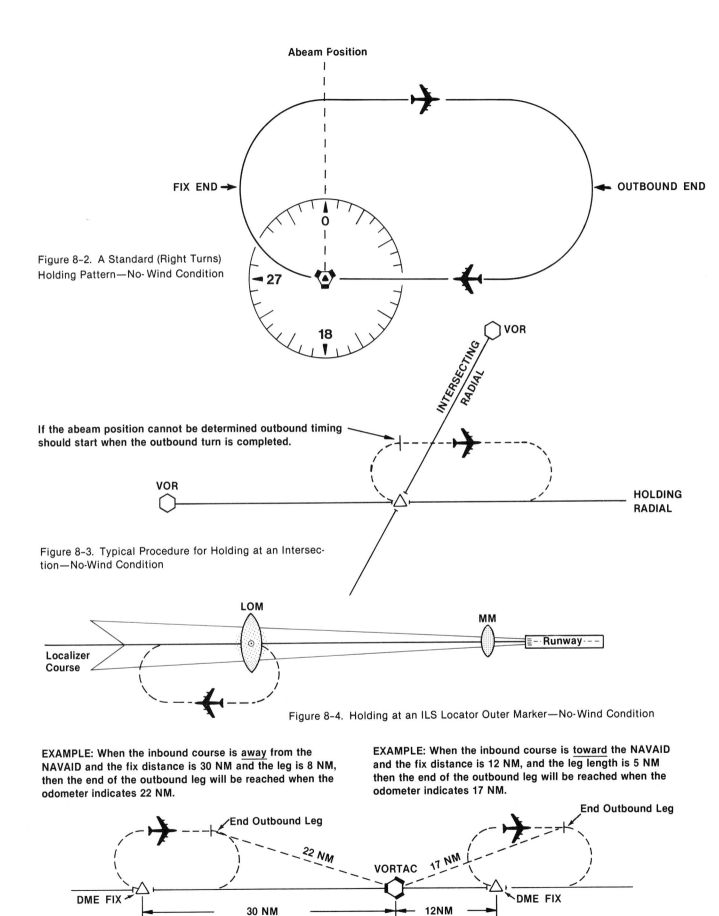

Figure 8-2. A Standard (Right Turns) Holding Pattern—No-Wind Condition

If the abeam position cannot be determined outbound timing should start when the outbound turn is completed.

Figure 8-3. Typical Procedure for Holding at an Intersection—No-Wind Condition

Figure 8-4. Holding at an ILS Locator Outer Marker—No-Wind Condition

EXAMPLE: When the inbound course is <u>away</u> from the NAVAID and the fix distance is 30 NM and the leg is 8 NM, then the end of the outbound leg will be reached when the odometer indicates 22 NM.

EXAMPLE: When the inbound course is <u>toward</u> the NAVAID and the fix distance is 12 NM, and the leg length is 5 NM then the end of the outbound leg will be reached when the odometer indicates 17 NM.

Holding Course Away from NAVAID

Holding Course Toward NAVAID

Figure 8-5. Typical DME Holding Patterns—No-Wind Condition

3. Specified radial, course, magnetic bearing, airway number, or jet route.

4. Outbound leg length in nautical miles if DME is to be employed, or minutes if DME is not employed.

5. Left turns, if a nonstandard holding pattern is to be executed or right turns if a standard holding pattern is to be executed. (Or, the controller may not specify the type of holding pattern. In that case the holding pattern is understood to be standard.)

6. Time to expect a further clearance, or time to expect an approach clearance.

Holding Pattern Entry

8.84 Holding is one procedure that causes uncertainty for some pilots, but, with a minimum of effort, holding procedures can be easily mastered. The type of entry procedure to use when entering a holding pattern is based on the aircraft's heading upon arrival at the holding fix. Figure 8–6 is representative of the holding procedures for *standard* holding patterns. Note that the entry procedures are oriented to a line at a 70° angle with the inbound course. The three procedures used for a standard holding pattern entry are:

1. For a **parallel entry procedure,** parallel the holding course after passing the fix, turn left, and return to the holding fix, or intercept the holding course and fly the pattern. (Figure 8–7)

2. For a **teardrop entry procedure,** proceed outbound on a track of 30° (or less) to the holding course, turn right to intercept the holding course, and fly the pattern. (Figure 8–8)

3. For a **direct entry procedure,** intercept the course or holding fix, turn right after passing the fix, and fly the pattern. (Figure 8–9)

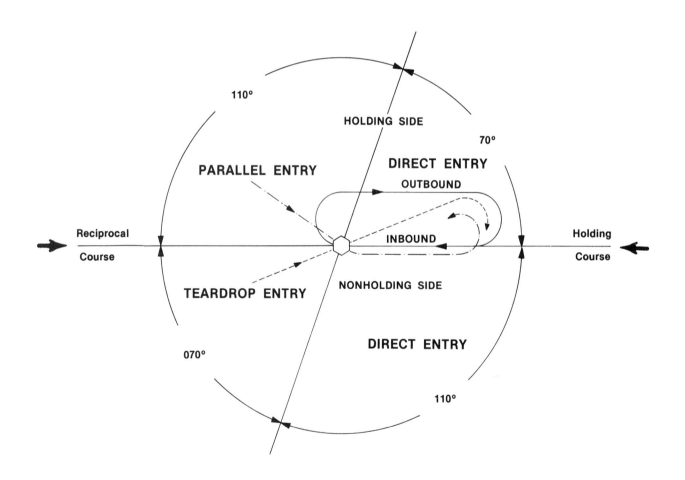

Figure 8-6. Standard Holding Pattern Entry Procedures

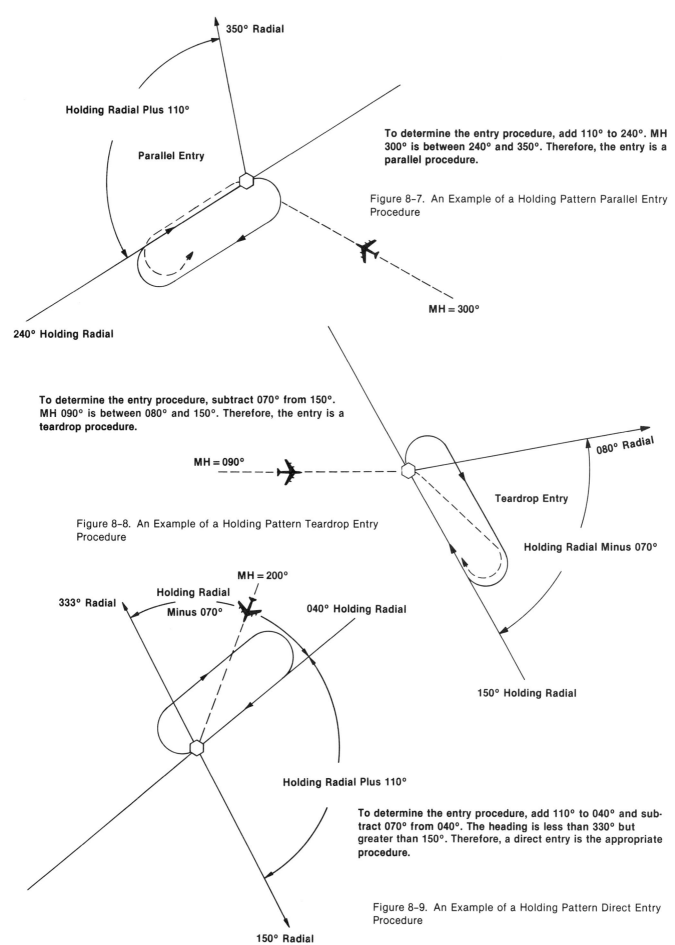

350° Radial

Holding Radial Plus 110°

Parallel Entry

To determine the entry procedure, add 110° to 240°. MH 300° is between 240° and 350°. Therefore, the entry is a parallel procedure.

Figure 8-7. An Example of a Holding Pattern Parallel Entry Procedure

MH = 300°

240° Holding Radial

To determine the entry procedure, subtract 070° from 150°. MH 090° is between 080° and 150°. Therefore, the entry is a teardrop procedure.

080° Radial

MH = 090°

Teardrop Entry

Figure 8-8. An Example of a Holding Pattern Teardrop Entry Procedure

Holding Radial Minus 070°

MH = 200°

Holding Radial Minus 070°

333° Radial

040° Holding Radial

150° Holding Radial

Holding Radial Plus 110°

To determine the entry procedure, add 110° to 040° and subtract 070° from 040°. The heading is less than 330° but greater than 150°. Therefore, a direct entry is the appropriate procedure.

Figure 8-9. An Example of a Holding Pattern Direct Entry Procedure

150° Radial

8.85 Nonstandard holding patterns are similar to the standard holding patterns except that the fix end and outbound end turns are made to the left. Entry procedures to a nonstandard pattern are oriented in relation to the 70° line on the holding side just as in the standard holding pattern. (Figure 8–10)

8.86 A simplified guide for determining the type of entry procedure to execute for a standard holding pattern is:

1. If the aircraft's magnetic heading is between the holding radial's bearing and 110° *more* than the holding radial bearing, the procedure is a parallel entry. (Figure 8–7)

2. If the aircraft's magnetic heading is at or between the holding radial's bearing and 70° *less* than the holding radial bearing, the procedure is a teardrop entry. (Figure 8–8)

3. All other headings to the holding fix determine a direct entry. (Figure 8–9)

8.87 When flying a nonstandard holding pattern, the guide for determining the type of entry procedure is only slightly different.

1. If the aircraft's magnetic heading is between the holding radial's bearing and 110° *less* than the holding radial bearing, the procedure is a parallel entry.

2. If the aircraft's magnetic heading is at or between the holding radial's bearing and 70° *more* than the holding radial bearing, the procedure is a teardrop entry.

3. All other headings to the holding fix determine a direct entry.

8.88 Pilots are expected to make all turns during entry (and while in the holding pattern) at whichever of the following requires the lesser degree of bank:

1. 3° per second rate of turn.

2. 30° bank angle.

3. 25° bank angle provided a flight director system is used during the maneuver.

(A rate of turn of 3° per second requires the lesser degree of bank for aircraft holding at speeds below 175 knots.)

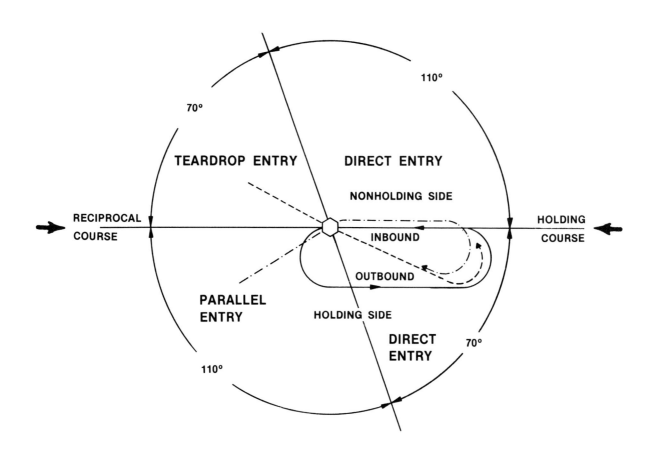

Figure 8–10. Nonstandard Holding Pattern Entry Procedures

Holding Pattern Dimensions

8.89 *At or below 14,000 feet MSL,* the standard holding pattern consists of a racetrack pattern requiring approximately 4 minutes to execute in a no-wind condition. The aircraft follows the specified course inbound to the holding fix, turns 180° to the right, flies a parallel straight course outbound for one minute, turns 180° to the right, and flies the inbound course *(for one minute)* to the fix.

8.90 The inbound leg of a holding pattern is not always one minute in duration (length). At altitudes above 14,000 feet MSL, the length of the inbound leg must be 1½ minutes in duration (length). Also when Distance Measuring Equipment is used, at any altitude, the length (instead of time) of the outbound leg (outbound course) will be specified by the controller and, naturally, the inbound leg will vary in length. (Figure 8-5)

Holding Pattern Timing

8.91 The symmetrical racetrack pattern cannot be precisely tracked when a wind exists. Therefore, pilots must compensate for the effects of a known wind, except when turning. The effect of the wind is counteracted by correcting for drift on the inbound and outbound legs, and by applying time allowances. For example, the outbound leg of a timed holding pattern may be lengthened in order for the inbound leg to be exactly one minute in length. (Figure 8-11)

8.92 Outbound timing of a holding pattern begins *over* or *abeam* the fix, whichever occurs later. The method used to determine the abeam position of a holding pattern varies with location and type of NAVAID used to execute the maneuver. For example:

1. When holding over a VOR facility, the outbound timing begins when the TO-FROM indicator reverses *after* the aircraft has turned to the outbound leg.

2. When holding over a compass locator, the outbound timing for a standard pattern starts when the ADF relative bearing is 90° plus or minus the drift correction angle.

When the abeam position cannot be determined, the outbound timing should be started at the completion of the turn to the outbound leg.

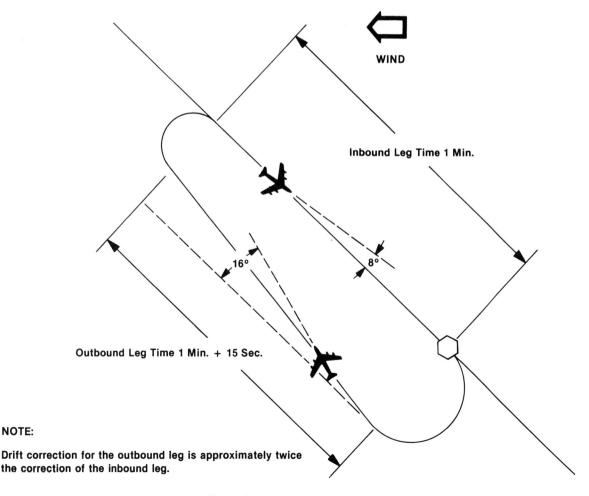

WIND

Inbound Leg Time 1 Min.

16°

8°

Outbound Leg Time 1 Min. + 15 Sec.

NOTE:

Drift correction for the outbound leg is approximately twice the correction of the inbound leg.

Figure 8-11. Holding Pattern Drift Correction

Maximum Holding Speeds

8.93 The maximum airspeed at which a pilot is expected to hold is:

1. Propeller-driven aircraft—175 knots IAS.
2. Civil turbo jets
   A. Minimum holding altitude through 6,000 feet—200 knots IAS.
   B. Above 6,000 feet through 14,000 feet—210 knots IAS.
   C. Above 14,000 feet—230 knots IAS.

8.94 *Special Notes:*

1. Minimum holding altitude (MHA) is defined as the lowest altitude, prescribed for a holding pattern, which assures navigational signal coverage, communications, and which meets obstacle clearance requirements.

2. When holding at a fix and instructions are received specifying the time of departure from the fix, the pilot should adjust his flight path within the limits of the established holding pattern in order to leave the fix at the exact time specified. After departing the holding fix, normal speed is to be resumed with respect to other governing speed requirements (such as terminal area speed limits) and to specific ATC requests.

AMENDING FLIGHT PLANS WHILE EN ROUTE

8.95 If, while en route, a pilot should desire to change the destination originally designated on the IFR flight plan, obtaining a changed route clearance involves the same procedure as filing and receiving the original clearance.

8.96 Pilots should also note that if an IFR flight plan is cancelled and a VFR flight plan is opened while en route, a pilot should switch the transponder to the VFR Code (1200) and descend/climb to an appropriate VFR altitude. At this same time, ATC will usually clear the pilot to switch from Center to en route VFR frequencies.

AIRCRAFT SPEED

8.97 FAR 91.70 states:

(a) Unless otherwise authorized by the Administrator, no person may operate an aircraft below 10,000 feet MSL at an indicated airspeed of more than 250 knots (288 MPH).

(b) Unless otherwise authorized or required by ATC, no person may operate an aircraft within an airport traffic area at an indicated airspeed of more than:

   (1) In the case of a reciprocating engine aircraft, 156 knots (180 MPH); or

   (2) In the case of a turbine-powered aircraft, 200 knots (230 MPH).

Part (b) does not apply to any operations within a Terminal Control Area. Such operations shall comply with part (a).

(c) No person may operate an aircraft in the airspace underlying a Terminal Control Area, or in a VFR corridor designated through a Terminal Control Area, at an indicated airspeed of more than 200 knots (230 MPH).

8.98 *Special Note: Pilots retain the prerogative of rejecting the application of speed adjustment by ATC if the minimum safe airspeed for any particular operation is greater than the speed adjustment. In such cases, pilots are expected to advise ATC of the speed that will be used.*

EN ROUTE ALTITUDE CHANGES

8.99 Pilots are generally expected to initiate a climb, when necessary, to a higher minimum IFR altitude *immediately after* passing the charted point (such as an intersection or NAVAID) beyond which that minimum altitude applies. The exception to the rule occurs when ground obstructions intervene, in which case the point (as charted) beyond which the higher minimum altitude applies shall be *crossed at or above* the applicable MCA (as the definition for MCA implies in paragraph 7.40).

8.100 When ATC issues a clearance, pilots are expected to execute the provisions of the clearance upon acceptance. The phrase "at pilot's discretion" when included in the altitude information of an ATC clearance signifies that ATC has offered the pilot the option to initiate a climb/descent when the pilot wishes. The pilot is further authorized to conduct the climb/descent at any rate, and to temporarily level off at any intermediate altitude. However, once the pilot has vacated an altitude, the pilot may not return to that altitude without an additional clearance.

8.101 If the altitude information contained in an ATC *descent* clearance includes a provision to "cross (fix) at/at or above/below (altitude)," the manner in which the descent is executed to comply with the crossing altitude is at the pilot's discretion. This authorization to descend at pilot's discretion is only applicable to that portion of the flight to which the crossing altitude restriction applies, and the pilot is expected to comply with the crossing altitude as a provision of the clearance. Any other clearance in which the pilot's execution is optional will state "at pilot's discretion."

8.102 When ATC has not used the phrase "at pilot's discretion" or imposed any climb/descent restrictions, pilots should initiate a climb/descent promptly upon acknowledgment of the clearance. The descent or climb should be executed at an optimum rate consistent with the operating characteristics of the aircraft to within 1,000 feet above or below the assigned altitude, and then attempt to descend or climb at a rate of 500 feet per minute until the assigned altitude is reached. If at any time the pilot is unable to climb/descend at a rate of at least 500 feet per minute, ATC should be advised. If it is *necessary* to level off at an intermediate altitude during a climb or descent ATC should be advised; the exception is for a level off at 10,000 feet MSL on descent or 3,000 feet above airport elevation (prior to entering an airport traffic area) when required for speed reduction procedures consistent with FAR 91.70 (paragraph 8.97). (*Note*: Leveling off at 10,000 feet MSL on descent or 3,000 feet above airport elevation [prior to entering an airport traffic area] is a routine practice. Controllers anticipate this action and plan accordingly.)

8.103 Air Traffic Control, in certain situations will include the term "immediately" in an instruction to impress the urgency of an imminent situation, and *expeditious* compliance by the pilot is expected and necessary for flight safety.

8.104 Occasionally pilots become confused while flying a published procedure (such as a SID) containing altitude restrictions and then receiving additional altitude restrictions in an ATC clearance. In this situation, both sets of altitude restrictions apply. If another clearance is issued by ATC stating "altitude restrictions are cancelled," the altitude restrictions issued in the previous clearance(s) are cancelled, but any restrictions contained in a published procedure *still* apply.

8.105 *Special Note: If a pilot discovers that an incorrect altitude is being maintained, the pilot should inform ATC of the actual altitude being maintained and REMAIN at that altitude until ATC issues a clearance containing an altitude change.*

AIRWAY/ROUTE COURSE CHANGES

8.106 Pilots of aircraft on IFR flight plans are required to fly the centerline of airways or, on any other route, along the direct course between the navigational aids or fixes defining that route. This requirement pertains to *all* aircraft, whether climbing, descending, or maintaining altitude. This requirement, however, does not prohibit maneuvering the aircraft:

1. To pass well clear of other air traffic or in VFR conditions, to clear the intended flight path both before and during climb or descent; *or*

2. When ATC authorizes otherwise.

8.107 Special attention must be given to this requirement during course changes. An early turn, as illustrated in Figure 8–12, is one method of adhering to airways/routes. Other instruments, such as Distance Measuring Equipment, may be used by the pilot to lead a turn when initiating course changes.

8.108 Turns which are initiated at or after fix passage may exceed airway/route boundaries, depending on such factors as the amount of course change required, wind direction and velocity, and pilot technique. Consequently, if pilots do not lead turns, they are expected to take other actions, as considered necessary, during course changes.

VFR CONDITIONS ON TOP CLEARANCE

8.109 A VFR Conditions on Top/VFR on Top Clearance is an IFR clearance term, used in lieu of a specific altitude assignment upon an instrument rated pilot's request, which authorizes the aircraft to be flown *in VFR weather conditions* (above a cloud, haze, smoke or other meteorological formation) at an appropriate VFR altitude/flight level which is not below the minimum IFR altitude, but

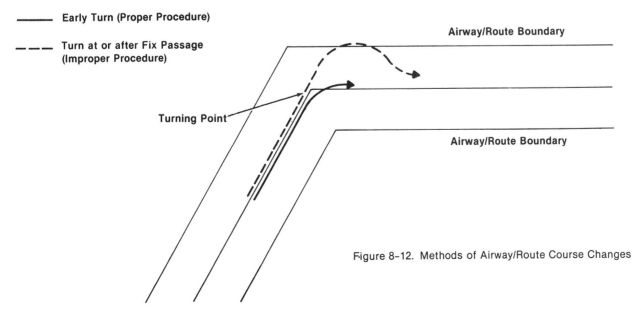

———— Early Turn (Proper Procedure)

— — — Turn at or after Fix Passage (Improper Procedure)

Airway/Route Boundary

Turning Point

Airway/Route Boundary

Figure 8–12. Methods of Airway/Route Course Changes

is at least 1,000 feet above any meteorological condition. This procedure provides a practical means of permitting the pilot to select altitude(s)/flight level(s) of his choice, thereby bypassing such inconveniences as turbulence, unfavorable ground speeds, icing in clouds, and delays due to other traffic.

8.110 Pilots with authorization from ATC to maintain VFR Conditions on Top should be aware of the following:

1. The pilot must adhere to applicable *IFR and VFR* flight rules.

2. If operating more than 3,000 feet above the surface, the pilot is expected to fly at a VFR altitude/flight level appropriate for the direction of flight and to keep ATC advised of the altitude/flight level. (Figure 8-13)

3. ATC may issue traffic information on other pertinent IFR traffic, however, ATC does not provide separation between the VFR on Top aircraft and other traffic. It is the pilot's responsibility to see and avoid other aircraft when operating in VFR weather conditions or on a VFR Conditions on Top clearance.

4. A VFR Conditions on Top clearance does not relieve the pilot of the responsibility of: flight at or above minimum IFR altitudes, position reporting procedures, radio communications, notification of ATC concerning any change in the flight plan, or adherence to ATC clearances.

5. ATC will not authorize a VFR Conditions on Top operation in Positive Control Areas.

6. The pilot must maintain the transponder code as assigned by ATC.

7. Pilots desiring a VFR on Top clearance may—

A. Write VFR on Top in Block 7 of the FAA flight plan form prior to departure; *or*

B. Request the VFR on Top clearance in addition to the IFR clearance after departure.

TO VFR CONDITIONS ON TOP CLEARANCE

8.111 Departing instrument-rated pilots who wish an IFR clearance *only to climb through* a layer of overcast or reduced visibility and then continue flight VFR may request ATC clearance *To* VFR Conditions on Top. This request may be made through a Flight Service Station, by telephone to ATC, or by request to the tower before taxiing out. The clearance, which authorizes IFR flight through the cloud layer, will contain a nearby clearance limit, routing, and a request to report reaching VFR Conditions on Top. When the pilot reaches VFR Conditions on Top and desires to cancel the IFR portion of the flight, he should so state. This type of operation can be combined with a VFR flight plan to the destination airport.

8.112 *Special Note: Pilots often confuse VFR Conditions on Top and To VFR Conditions on Top clearances with the VFR Over the Top operations. A VFR Over the Top operation is generally considered to be the operation of an aircraft over the top of a cloud layer (or area of reduced visibility) in accordance with Visual Flight Rules and not on an IFR flight plan.*

FLIGHT IN RESTRICTED AIRSPACE

8.113 ATC facilities use the following procedures when aircraft are operating on IFR clearances (including those aircraft operating on a VFR Conditions on Top clearance) along a route which lies within joint-use restricted airspace:

1. Before an aircraft enters the restricted airspace, ATC will coordinate with the controlling agency to obtain permission for that aircraft to operate in the restricted airspace.

2. If ATC obtains permission for that aircraft to operate in the restricted airspace, no specific clearance will be issued, and no specific action is required of the pilot.

If the magnetic course is	More than 3,000 feet above the surface but below 18,000 feet MSL fly	Above 18,000 feet MSL to FL 290 (except within Positive Control Area) fly	Above FL 290 (except within Positive Control Area) fly 4,000 foot intervals
0° to 179°	Odd thousands, MSL, plus 500 feet (3500, 5500, 7500, etc)	Odd Flight Levels plus 500 feet (FL 195, 215, 235, etc)	Beginning at FL 300 (FL 300, 340, 380, etc)
180° to 359°	Even thousands, MSL, plus 500 feet (4500, 6500, 8500, etc)	Even Flight Levels plus 500 feet (FL 185, 205, 225, etc)	Beginning at FL 320 (FL 320, 360, 400, etc)

Figure 8-13. Controlled and Uncontrolled Airspace VFR Altitudes and Flight Levels

3. If the ATC facility cannot obtain permission, ATC will issue an amended clearance, so the aircraft will avoid the restricted airspace.

IFR SEPARATION STANDARDS

8.114 Air Traffic Control effects separation of aircraft vertically by assigning different altitudes; longitudinally by providing an interval expressed in time or distance between aircraft on the same, converging, or crossing courses; and laterally, by assigning different flight paths. Standard separation will be provided between all aircraft operating on IFR flight plans except:

1. When VFR Conditions on Top has been requested by a pilot and authorized by ATC in lieu of a specific cruising or holding altitude; *and*

2. When clearances specifying that climb or descent or any portion of the flight shall be conducted in VFR Conditions are issued.

8.115 When radar is employed in the separation of aircraft at the same altitude, a minimum of 3 miles separation is provided between aircraft operating within 40 miles of the radar antenna site, and 5 miles between aircraft operating farther than 40 miles from the antenna site. These minimums may be increased or decreased in certain specific situations.

8.116 Controllers may vector aircraft within controlled airspace for separation purposes, noise abatement considerations, when an operational advantage will be realized by the pilot or the controller, or when requested by the pilot. Vectors outside of controlled airspace will be provided only on pilot request. Pilots will be advised as to what the vector is to achieve when the vector is controller-initiated and will take the aircraft off a previously assigned nonradar route. To the extent possible, aircraft operating on RNAV routes will be allowed to remain on their own navigation.

CHAPTER 8: QUESTIONS

For answers see Appendix E

1. An ATC clearance to maintain VFR Conditions on Top:
1. Guarantees instrument pilots normal IFR separation.
2. Cancels the IFR flight plan.
3. Must be suggested by the ATC controller.
4. Does not guarantee vertical separation and the pilot is responsible for avoiding other aircraft.

2. What code should a pilot set into the transponder after receiving a clearance to maintain VFR Conditions on Top when at an altitude of 11,500 feet MSL? (The previously assigned code was 1125.)
1. Code 1200.
2. Code 1150.
3. Code 1400.
4. Code 1125 should remain set in the transponder.

3. If, while on an IFR clearance, a pilot is assigned a higher altitude by ATC, the pilot should:
1. Initiate a climb immediately and report arriving at the assigned altitude.
2. Report leaving the previously assigned altitude and climb at 500 feet per minute to the newly assigned altitude.
3. Report leaving the previously assigned altitude, climb as rapidly as practical to an altitude within 1,000 feet of the newly assigned altitude, then climb at a rate of 500 feet per minute until the assigned altitude is reached.
4. Climb as rapidly as possible to within 1,000 feet of the newly assigned altitude, then climb at a rate of 500 feet per minute until reaching the assigned altitude, and report reaching the newly assigned altitude.

4. When will ATC issue a clearance to an IFR flight specifying that a climb, descent or any portion of the flight be conducted in VFR conditions?
1. When the pilot requests the VFR restriction, or for noise abatement purposes.
2. When the visibility is expected to be ½ statute mile or greater.
3. Only inside of a Terminal Control Area.
4. When the aircraft is in uncontrolled airspace.

5. A clearance to maintain VFR Conditions on Top will not be approved by ATC in which controlled airspace?
1. Positive Control Area.
2. Continental Control Area.
3. Control zone.
4. Transition area.

6. What altitude should a pilot maintain with a VFR Conditions on Top clearance?
1. An altitude appropriate for VFR flight, that is at least 1,000 feet above any meteorological conditions, and at or above the MEA, or MOCA, if appropriate.
2. An altitude at or above the MEA or MOCA.
3. An altitude 1,000 feet above the MEA, MOCA, or any meteorological conditions.
4. An altitude of 500 feet or more above the MEA or MOCA.

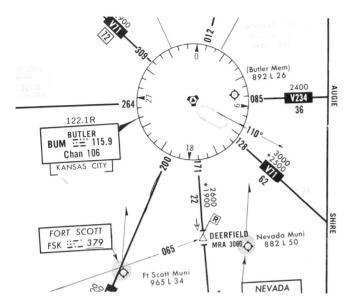

Refer to the illustrated En Route Low Altitude Chart excerpt (above) when answering questions 7 and 8.

7. Which type of entry is appropriate if a pilot tracking inbound on the 264° radial on a magnetic heading of 090° is issued a clearance to hold over BUTLER VORTAC?

    1. A direct entry to hold on the inbound 264° radial of BUTLER VORTAC.

    2. A parallel entry to establish a holding pattern on the 110° radial of BUTLER VORTAC.

    3. A parallel entry to establish a holding pattern on the 290° radial of BUTLER VORTAC.

    4. A teardrop entry to hold on the 110° radial of BUTLER VORTAC.

8. A pilot has been cleared from the BUTLER VORTAC via the 171° radial to hold south of DEERFIELD Intersection-left turns. What type of entry procedure is appropriate if the aircraft heading, when approaching the intersection, is 175°?

    1. A direct entry.

    2. A parallel entry.

    3. A teardrop entry.

    4. A teardrop or parallel entry.

9. While en route on an IFR flight plan, a pilot should, without request, report to ATC a change in airspeed (given in the flight plan) of more than:

    1. Plus or minus 10 percent, or 5 knots, whichever is greater.

    2. Plus or minus 5 percent, or 10 knots, whichever is greater.

    3. 10 MPH.

    4. 20 knots.

10. Which type of VFR operation requires pilot possession of an instrument rating?

    1. VFR Conditions Over the Top.

    2. Special VFR—daytime operation.

    3. DVFR.

    4. VFR Conditions on Top.

11. What procedure is normally used to obtain an altimeter setting when pilots on IFR flight plans are conducting flight operations in controlled airspace below 18,000 feet MSL?

    1. Contact the nearest FSS when passing each VOR en route for the altimeter setting.

    2. Request an altimeter setting from ARTCC every 100 nautical miles.

    3. None. The altimeter setting is given by ATC periodically.

    4. Monitor the en route NAVAIDs for the scheduled weather broadcasts.

12. Choose the statement(s) that correctly describe(s) cruise clearance.

A. A pilot may climb to or descend from the assigned altitude without further clearance.

B. A cruise clearance authorizes the pilot to proceed to and make an approach at the destination airport.

C. The term "cruise" will be used instead of "maintain."

D. A cruise clearance is normally issued for short flights into congested areas.

    1. A, C, and D.

    2. A, B, and D.

    3. A, B, and C.

    4. B, C, and D.

13. What is indicated by the absence of a sky condition/ceiling and visibility in the ATIS message?

    1. The airport served by ATIS is VFR.

    2. The hourly weather has not been observed.

    3. There is a ceiling of 3,000 feet or higher and the visibility is 3 statute miles or more.

    4. There is a ceiling/sky condition of 5,000 feet or higher and the visibility is 5 statute miles or more.

14. When an ATC controller requests a pilot to "Squawk IDENT," what is the appropriate pilot action?

    1. Place the transponder in the standby position.

    2. Depress the "IDENT" button for 30 seconds.

    3. Depress the "IDENT" button momentarily.

    4. Execute a 45° turn either to the right or to the left.

15. If a pilot's aircraft is found to be cruising at an altitude other than the assigned altitude, the correct pilot action would be to:

1. Inform ATC of the present altitude, but maintain the present altitude until ATC authorizes a change in altitude.
2. Request a clearance to the assigned altitude.
3. Immediately climb or descend as necessary to the assigned altitude.
4. Report leaving the present altitude, initiate a climb or descent as appropriate to the assigned altitude, and then report reaching the assigned altitude.

16. When a controller advises a pilot to "resume normal navigation" after being radar vectored, this means:

1. The pilot should track directly to the closest VOR.
2. The pilot should set the transponder to the standby position.
3. Radar contact is lost.
4. The pilot is now responsible for his own navigation.

17. If ATC requests a pilot to "squawk altitude," the pilot should:

1. Report his altitude to ATC.
2. Set the transponder to the Mode C position.
3. Set 29.92 in the Kollsman Window of the altimeter.
4. Depress the "IDENT" button of the transponder.

18. When departing on an IFR flight, when should a pilot switch from the control tower frequency to the departure control frequency?

1. At the control tower's request.
2. Immediately after takeoff.
3. On takeoff roll.
4. Prior to entering IFR conditions.

19. Select the response that correctly exemplifies the recommended phraseology for a pilot establishing contact with an ATC facility when conducting an IFR flight in a radar environment. Assume no position report is required.

1. "Denver Center, Cessna two zero four three Sierra, at one zero thousand feet, over."
2. "Denver Center, Cessna two zero four three Sierra, over."
3. "Denver Center, Cessna four three Sierra, ten thousand feet, squawking 1123, over."
4. "Air Route Traffic Control, four three Sierra, ten thousand, estimating GILL at four zero, over."

20. A pilot who does not want to be issued a SID for an IFR departure should:

1. Write "no SID" in the remarks section of the flight plan form.
2. State "no STAR" to ground control when taxiing for departure.
3. Know that no action by the pilot is required since the pilot must request a SID before a SID is issued.
4. Know that SIDs are not issued to general aviation aircraft.

21. When should outbound timing in a holding pattern begin?

A. Upon roll-out to the outbound heading if the abeam position of a holding fix cannot be determined.
B. At the pilot's discretion.
C. Abeam or over the fix, whichever occurs later.
D. Only the inbound leg is timed.

1. B only.
2. A and C.
3. A, B, and C.
4. D only.

22. Select the correct statement(s) concerning speed restrictions.

A. 250 knots IAS is the maximum speed at which an aircraft may fly below 10,000 feet MSL.
B. 200 knots IAS is the maximum speed at which an aircraft may fly beneath the lateral limits of a TCA.
C. 250 knots IAS is the maximum speed at which an aircraft may fly within a TCA.
D. 156 knots IAS is the maximum speed at which a reciprocating engine aircraft may fly within an airport traffic area.

1. A, B, C, and D.
2. A and B.
3. D only.
4. B only.

23. The phrase "radar contact" as used by ATC means:

1. The aircraft transponder is operating properly.
2. ATC will provide separation from all aircraft.
3. The aircraft is identified on the controller's radar display.
4. The aircraft is cleared to climb or descend at the discretion of the pilot.

24. Select the correct statement(s) regarding pre-taxi clearance procedures.

A. Pilots should contact clearance delivery/ground control no more than 10 minutes before proposed taxi time.

B. Pilots should contact clearance delivery/ground control at least 15 minutes before proposed taxi time.

C. Pilot participation is not mandatory.

D. Delay information may be issued upon initial call-up.

   1. B only.
   2. A, C, and D.
   3. B, C, and D.
   4. B and C.

25. What pilot technique should be employed when initiating a course change from one airway to another?

   1. A standard rate turn to the new course should be initiated upon reaching the fix.

   2. A 30° banked turn to the new course should be executed upon passing over the intersection.

   3. A turn should be made after reaching the intersecting airway using the appropriate angle of bank so the aircraft remains within 4 nautical miles of course.

   4. An early turn should be executed to assure that the aircraft rolls out on the center of the outbound airway.

26. What pilot action is required while conducting an IFR flight on a Victor airway that enters restricted airspace?

   1. No special pilot action is necessary unless ATC advises that the restricted airspace is not penetrable.

   2. Pilots should contact ATC and request a vector around the restricted area.

   3. Pilots should contact the nearest FSS for permission to enter the restricted area.

   4. If ATC does not grant permission to enter the restricted airspace, the correct procedure is to fly the shortest route around the area.

27. The maximum airspeed that a propeller-driven aircraft may maintain in a holding pattern is:

   1. 175 knots TAS.
   2. 175 knots IAS.
   3. 200 knots IAS.
   4. 210 knots TAS.

28. Select the correct information concerning transponder codes.

A. When cancelling an IFR flight plan above 14,000 feet MSL, the proper transponder code is 1400.

B. The VFR transponder code for an altitude of 13,500 feet MSL is 1200.

C. The VFR transponder code below 10,000 feet MSL is 1200.

D. The hijack transponder code is 7500.

   1. A, B, and D.
   2. A and C.
   3. B, C, and D.
   4. A, B, C, and D.

29. A pilot operating in accordance with IFR rules should, without request, report which of the following to ATC? (Assume the aircraft is *not* in radar contact.)

A. Vacating any previously assigned altitude/flight level for a newly assigned altitude/flight level.

B. The time and altitude/flight level upon reaching a holding fix or point to which cleared.

C. Leaving any assigned holding fix or point.

D. Making an altitude change if operating on a clearance specifying VFR Conditions on Top.

E. An ETA in error in excess of 3 minutes.

F. Encountering weather conditions that have not been forecast.

   1. A, B, and E.
   2. C, D, and E.
   3. A, B, C, and F.
   4. All responses are correct.

30. What action is required by the pilot to activate an IFR flight plan?

   1. The pilot must call the tower or FSS as appropriate and report the departure time.

   2. None when departing a tower-controlled field, since the tower activates the flight plan automatically.

   3. None. The FSS or control tower activates the flight plan automatically.

   4. None. The flight plan is automatically activated when the pilot reads back the IFR clearance.

31. If ATC issues an abbreviated IFR departure clearance, that clearance will always contain:

   1. An expect further clearance time.

   2. A final fix.

   3. An en route altitude, or a time or certain point after departure at which the pilot can expect to receive an assigned/filed altitude.

   4. A destination airport.

32. Which of the following statements pertaining to IFR clearances are correct?

A. A pilot should always refuse an IFR clearance whenever it differs from the route or altitude of the proposed flight plan.
B. An IFR clearance guarantees a pilot the minimum separation from all other aircraft.
C. Pilot participation in the pre-taxi clearance delivery program is not mandatory.
D. If an IFR clearance would cause a pilot to deviate from an FAA regulation, the pilot should request an amended clearance.
  1. D only.
  2. A and B.
  3. A, C, and D.
  4. C and D.

33. What frequency should a pilot use to contact En Route Flight Advisory Service/Flight Watch?
  1. Any standard FSS frequency.
  2. 123.6 or 122.6 MHz.
  3. 122.0 MHz only.
  4. Transmit on 122.1 and receive over the local VOR station.

Refer to the Porte One Departure SID for San Francisco International Airport (page 276) when answering questions 34, 35, 36, and 37.

34. What are the altitude restrictions for the Porte One Departure and Panoche Transition? (Assume takeoff from Runway 10R.)
  1. Cross the 4 DME fix on the 350° radial of SFO VOR at or above 1,600 feet MSL; cross PORTE DME fix at or above 9,000 feet MSL; climb to at least 13,000 feet MSL before crossing PESCADERO DME fix; and cross WAGES DME fix at or above FL 200 or at a lower assigned altitude/flight level.
  2. At the intersection of the 095° radial of the SFO VOR and the 135° radial of OAK VORTAC an aircraft must be at or above 5,000 feet MSL and at or below 7,000 feet MSL; when at the 25 DME fix on the 135° radial of OAK VORTAC an aircraft must be at or above 9,000 feet MSL and at or below 11,000 feet MSL; when at WAGES DME fix an aircraft must be at or above FL 200 or at a lower altitude/flight level if assigned.
  3. After takeoff, climb at least 300 feet per nautical mile to the 4 DME fix on the 350° radial of the SFO VOR; cross PESCA Intersection above 13,000 feet MSL; cross WAGES DME fix above FL 200.

4. At the intersection of the 095° radial of the SFO VOR and the 135° radial of OAK VORTAC an aircraft must be at or above 5,000 feet AGL and at or below 7,000 feet AGL; when at the 25 DME fix on the 135° radial of OAK VORTAC an aircraft must be at or above 9,000 feet AGL and at or below 11,000 feet AGL; when at WAGES DME fix an aircraft must be at or above FL 200 or at a lower altitude/flight level if assigned.

35. What is the approximate distance depicted for the Porte One Departure and the Fresno Transition? (Assume takeoff from Runway 1L.)
  1. 179 nautical miles.
  2. 166 nautical miles.
  3. 183 nautical miles.
  4. 162 nautical miles.

36. What is the purpose of the left turn after takeoff on Runways 19L and 19R?
  1. To avoid the steeply rising terrain south of the airport.
  2. To avoid steeply rising terrain north of the airport.
  3. To avoid obstacles on the west side of the airport.
  4. To intercept the 350° radial of the San Francisco VOR.

37. What is the minimum rate of climb required if an aircraft maintains a groundspeed of 120 knots and takes off on Runway 28R?
  1. 300 feet per minute.
  2. 600 feet per nautical mile.
  3. 600 feet per minute.
  4. 450 feet per nautical mile.

38. Which report should a pilot make without request, to ATC, when conducting an IFR operation in controlled airspace? (Assume the aircraft is in radar contact.)
  1. The time and altitude/flight level reaching a holding fix.
  2. When leaving any assigned holding fix.
  3. A corrected estimate at any time it becomes apparent that a previous estimate is in error in excess of 3 minutes.
  4. When vacating any previously assigned altitude/flight level for a newly assigned altitude/flight level.

DEPARTURE ROUTE DESCRIPTION
(Continued)

Take-off Runway 28L/R: Climb via the SAN FRANCISCO VOR R-281 so as to cross the 6 DME FIX at or above 2500', then turn left heading 180° so as to intercept and proceed via the POINT REYES R-135 to cross PORTE DME FIX (POINT REYES R-135 40 DME) at or above 9000' and PESCADERO DME FIX (POINT REYES R-135 55 DME) at or above 13,000'. Then turn left heading 090° to intercept and proceed via the WOODSIDE R-116 to cross WAGES DME FIX (WOODSIDE R-116 36 DME) at or above FL 200 or at assigned lower altitude/flight level. Thence via (transition) or (assigned route).

Take-off Runways 10/R and 19L/R: Climb via SAN FRANCISCO VOR R-095 to intercept the OAKLAND VORTAC R-135 at or above 5000' and at or below 7000'. Continue climb via Oakland R-135 to cross the 25 DME fix at or above 9000' and at or below 11,000' and WAGES DME Fix (OAKLAND R-135 50 DME) at or above FL 200 or at assigned lower altitude/flight level. Thence via (transition) or (assigned route). When San Francisco VOR/DME is inoperative, Rwy 28 departures shall climb via the west course of San Francisco Rwy 28 ILS localizer for a radar vector to POINT REYES R-135 then resume SID.

AVENAL TRANSITION (PORTE1.AVE): Via AVENAL R-297 to AVENAL VORTAC. Cross the AVENAL R-297 93 DME FIX at or above FL 240 or at assigned lower altitude/flight level.
FRESNO TRANSITION (PORTE1.FAT): Via FRESNO R-257 to FRESNO VORTAC.
PANOCHE TRANSITION (PORTE1.PXN): Via PANOCHE R-275 to PANOCHE VORTAC.

SAN FRANCISCO CLNC DEL
121.4
BAY DEP CON
120.9   323.2

*Aprx dist fr T/off area

POINT REYES
113.7 PYE
Chan 84

R-350

1600'

2500'

4 DME
200°
281°
101°
6 DME
180°

R-281

LOCALIZER
109.5 I-SFO

SAN FRANCISCO
115.8 SFO
DME Chan 105

PORTE
40 DME

OAKLAND
116.8 OAK
Chan 115

R-135

7000
5,000

R-095

095°
(13)

135°
(15)

WOODSIDE
113.9 OSI
Chan 86

R-116

090°
(17)

135°
(15)

9000

PESCA
55 DME PYE

R-180

13,000

11,000
9000

25 DME

(25)

116°
(18)

FL 200
or assigned lower alt/FL

WAGES
50 DME OAK
36 DME OSI
117 DME AVE

R-275

(24)

077°
(93)

R-257

FRESNO
112.9 FAT
Chan 76
L-2, H-2

095°
(49)

PANOCHE
112.6 PXN
Chan 73
L-2, H-2

R-297

117°
(93)

AVENAL
117.1 AVE
Chan 118
L-2, H-2

93 DME AVE
FL 240
or assigned lower alt/FL

NOTE: Rwy 28L/R:
For obstacle clearance a minimum
climb rate of 300' per NM to 2000
is required.

NOTE: Rwy 19L/R Departures
Turn left as soon as practicable
due to steeply rising terrain
to 2000' immediately south
of airport.

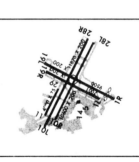

ELEV   11

DEPARTURE ROUTE DESCRIPTION

Take-off Runway 1L/R: Climb via the SAN FRANCISCO VOR R-350 so as to cross the 4 DME at or above 1600', then turn left heading 200° to intercept and proceed via the POINT REYES R-135 to cross PORTE DME FIX (POINT REYES R-135 40 DME) at or above 9000' and the PESCADERO DME FIX (POINT REYES R-135 55 DME) at or above 13,000'. Then turn left heading 090° to intercept and proceed via the WOODSIDE R-116 to cross WAGES DME FIX (WOODSIDE R-116 36 DME) at or above FL 200 or at assigned lower altitude/flight level. Thence via (transition) or (assigned route).

(Continued on next page)

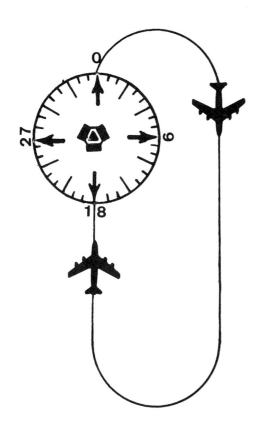

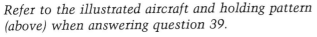

Refer to the illustrated aircraft and holding pattern (above) when answering question 39.

39. What type of entry should be executed by the pilot of the aircraft in order to enter into the depicted holding pattern?

1. A right turn when over the VORTAC and then fly the pattern (direct entry).
2. A left turn when arriving over the VORTAC to parallel the holding course, another left turn and return to the holding fix or intercept the holding course (parallel entry).
3. A left turn when over the holding fix, then track on the holding radial, another left turn, and return to the holding fix (teardrop entry).
4. Track outbound on the 210° radial, then turn left to intercept the holding course (teardrop entry).

40. Assume it is necessary to maintain a magnetic heading of 260° when tracking on the inbound leg of a holding pattern established on the 090° radial of a VOR station. What should the approximate *outbound* magnetic heading be?

1. 110°.
2. 080°.
3. 070°.
4. 100°.

41. Select the correct response(s) regarding the possible alternative(s) for the pilot whenever the pilot's aircraft has reached its clearance limit without a further clearance.

A. Begin holding in accordance with the holding pattern depicted on the appropriate chart.
B. Land as soon as possible if the weather is VFR, and notify ATC immediately.
C. Continue on the flight planned route and request further clearance.
D. Begin holding in a standard holding pattern on the course on which the aircraft approaches the fix if no holding pattern is charted.

1. A only.
2. B only.
3. C only.
4. A and D.

42. When flying on Victor airways, aircraft with instrument clearances are required to:

1. Remain right of the airway centerline when climbing.
2. Remain right of the airway centerline when climbing or descending.
3. Remain on the airway centerline except to avoid other aircraft or when ATC authorizes otherwise.
4. Remain right of the airway centerline when climbing and left of the airway centerline when descending.

43. What would be the appropriate altitude(s) for an instrument flight that has a VFR Conditions on Top clearance? Assume the magnetic course is 242°, the MEA of the airway is 12,000 feet MSL, and the top of the overcast cloud layer is 6,800 feet MSL.

A. 12,500 feet MSL.
B. 14,000 feet MSL.
C. 8,500 feet MSL.
D. 18,500 feet MSL.

1. A only.
2. B only.
3. A and D.
4. A, C, and D.

44. What is the appropriate pilot action when ATC issues an IFR clearance to an airborne aircraft?

1. The pilot *must* read back the entire clearance as issued.

2. None; clearance readback (by airborne aircraft) is not necessary.

3. The pilot should read back those parts of an ATC clearance containing altitude assignments or vectors.

4. The pilot should read back an amended clearance only.

45. Aircraft avoidance is the responsibility of pilots on IFR flight plans:

1. At all times.

2. Only when weather conditions allow visual contact.

3. Only when advised by center/approach control.

4. From takeoff until established on a Federal airway if not in a radar environment.

46. What action is warranted if a pilot receives a speed adjustment clearance from ATC that is lower than the aircraft's minimum safe airspeed?

1. The pilot must attempt to maintain the speed within 10 knots.

2. The pilot should cancel the IFR flight plan.

3. The pilot may turn off the airway or descend to the MEA.

4. The pilot is expected to advise ATC of the speed that will be maintained.

47. Where may Standard Instrument Departures (SIDs) be found?

1. In graphic chart form with En Route High Altitude Charts.

2. In textual form in the Airport/Facility Directory.

3. In textual and graphic form in East and West SID booklets.

4. In textual form in the Instrument Flying Handbook.

48. When making routine transponder code changes, pilots should avoid inadvertent selection of such codes as:

1. 2707, 7600, and 7700.

2. 3100, 7700, and 7777.

3. 4200, 7600, and 7700.

4. 7500, 7600, and 7700.

9.

Terminal Procedures

9.1 Perhaps the most important phases of instrument flight are those of the transition from the en route stage through the instrument approach. This chapter presents the various aspects of the final stages of instrument flight. Familiarity with the following definitions will be necessary during the course of the discussion on terminal procedures.

Approach gate—The point on the final approach course which is one mile from the final approach fix on the side away from the airport, or 5 miles from landing threshold, whichever is farther from the landing threshold. This is an imaginary point used within ATC as a basis for final approach course interception for aircraft being vectored to the final approach course. (Refer to Figure G-4 in the Appendix.)

Decision height (DH)—The height, with respect to the operation of aircraft, at which a decision must be made during an ILS or PAR instrument approach to either continue the approach or to execute a missed approach if the required visual reference has not been established. This height is expressed in feet above mean sea level (MSL) above the highest runway elevation in the touchdown zone. For Category II ILS operation the decision height is additionally expressed as a radio altimeter setting.

Final approach fix (FAF)—The designated fix from or over which the final instrument approach to an airport is executed. The FAF identifies the beginning of the final approach segment of the instrument approach.

Final approach—The flight path of an aircraft which is inbound to an airport on a final instrument approach course, beginning at the final approach fix or point and extending to the airport or the point where a circle-to-land maneuver or a missed approach is executed.

Minimum descent altitude (MDA)—The lowest altitude, expressed in feet above mean sea level, to which descent is authorized on final approach, where no electronic glide slope is provided, or during circle-to-land maneuvering in execution of a standard instrument approach procedure.

Height above airport (HAA)—The height of the MDA above the published airport elevation. HAA is published in conjunction with circling minimums for all types of approaches.

Height above touchdown (HAT)—The height of the DH or MDA above the highest runway elevation in the touchdown zone (first 3,000 feet of runway). HAT is published in conjunction with straight-in minimums.

Minimum safe altitudes (MSA)—These are published for emergency use on approach procedure charts utilizing NDB or VOR type facilities. The altitude shown provides at least 1,000 feet of clearance above the highest obstacle in the defined sector to a distance of 25 NM from the facility.

Minimum vectoring altitude (MVA)—The lowest MSL altitude at which an IFR aircraft will be vectored by a radar controller, except as otherwise authorized for radar approaches, departures and missed approaches. The altitude meets IFR obstacle clearance criteria.

Circle to land (circling) maneuver—A maneuver necessary to position the aircraft with the landing runway when a straight-in landing is not desirable or possible at the conclusion of an instrument approach procedure. Conditions such as wind direction and velocity may influence the decision to execute a circling maneuver.

Timed approach—A procedure that is used primarily by high performance aircraft at high density airports that are served by operational control towers. It is essentially a timed holding pattern over an approach fix and is used in lieu of a procedure turn to reduce flying time.

STANDARD TERMINAL ARRIVAL ROUTES (STARs)

9.2 A standard terminal arrival route (STAR) is an Air Traffic Control coded IFR arrival route established for application to arriving IFR aircraft destined for certain airports. Its purpose is to simplify clearance delivery procedures. (Figure 9-1)

9.3 Pilots of IFR civil aircraft destined to locations for which STARs have been published may be issued a clearance containing a STAR whenever ATC deems it appropriate. Use of STARs requires pilot possession of at least the approved textual description. As with any ATC clearance or portion thereof, it is the responsibility of each pilot to accept or refuse an issued STAR. Pilots should notify ATC verbally if they do not wish to use a STAR and have not previously written "no STAR" in the remarks section of the flight plan.

9.4 A bound booklet containing all STAR charts is available by subscription from the National Ocean Survey. STARs implemented on an urgent/emergency basis will be published in textual form in the Notices to Airmen publication.

PROFILE DESCENT PROCEDURES

9.5 A Profile Descent is basically an uninterrupted descent (except where level flight is required for speed adjustment) from cruising altitude to interception of a minimum altitude specified for the initial or intermediate segment of an instrument approach. (Figure 9-2)

9.6 This procedure was primarily designed to minimize the amount of time that high performance aircraft (turbojet aircraft and turboprop aircraft weighing more than 12,500 pounds) operate at low altitudes and around terminal areas. This is ac-

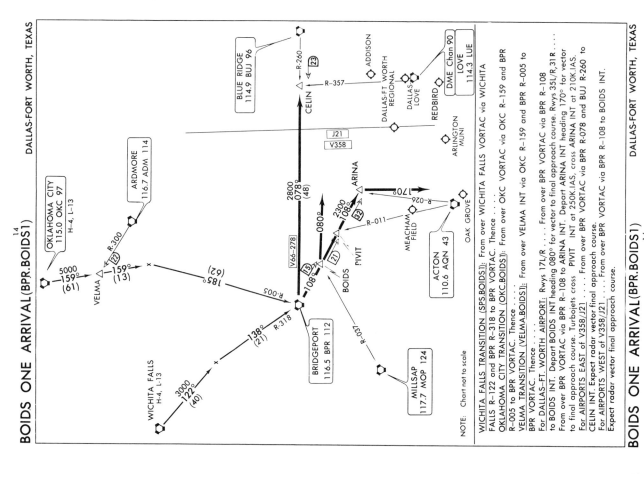

Figure 9–1. A Typical STAR Chart

complished by permitting *economical* descent gradients (approximately 300 feet per NM). Actual altitude loss will vary depending on aircraft characteristics and the most economical descent for specific flights.

9.7 Some of the benefits of Profile Descent procedures are:

1. Increased flight safety by reducing exposure time between controlled and uncontrolled aircraft at lower altitudes around airports.

2. Significant fuel savings in support of national energy conservation programs.

3. Reduction of aircaft noise in the proximity of airports.

4. Standardized arrival procedures for high performance aircraft, and equitable distribution of arrival delays.

9.8 Pilots should possess a copy of the appropriate Runway Profile Descent Chart in order to comply with a published Runway Profile Descent clearance issued by the controller. Pilots are expected to advise ATC if they do not have Profile Descent Charts or if they are unable to comply with a Profile Descent clearance. Profile Descent Charts are available by subscription from the National Ocean Survey and should be reviewed before flight.

9.9 Profile Descent clearances are subject to traffic conditions and may be altered by ATC, as necessary. An ATC clearance must be received in order for a pilot to execute a Profile Descent. Acceptance, by the pilot, of a Profile Descent clearance requires the pilot to adhere to altitudes, speeds, and headings as depicted on the Profile Descent Procedure Chart. Any subsequent clearance received, such as a new assigned altitude, voids all altitudes depicted on the Profile Descent Procedure Chart, but the pilot must continue to adhere to the speeds and headings as depicted. Similarly, any clearance which changes a speed restriction or depicted vector heading would not affect the depicted altitude. When crossing altitudes and speed restrictions are depicted on Profile Descent Charts or issued verbally, ATC will expect the pilot to descend first to the crossing altitude and then reduce speed. Pilots will be cleared initially to fly a specified STAR and advised which Runway Profile Descent procedure to expect.

9.10 *Special Note: A Profile Descent clearance constitutes an ATC clearance. This clearance does not, however, constitute clearance to fly an instrument approach procedure. The last "maintain altitude" specified in the Profile Descent procedure constitutes the "last ATC assigned altitude." The pilot should maintain such altitude until he is cleared to another altitude or cleared for an approach and is established on a published route segment of the instrument approach procedure.*

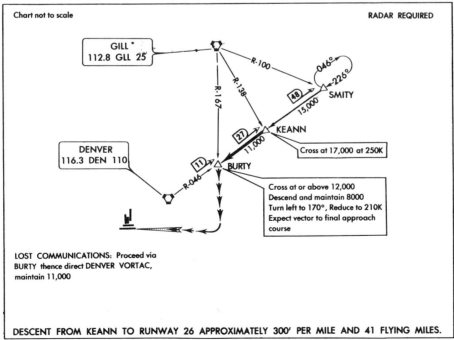

Figure 9-2. A Typical Profile Descent Procedure Chart

TRANSITIONING TO AREA CHARTS

9.11 As pilots approach certain high density areas, they should refer to area charts if an area chart is available for the specific terminal area. If an area chart is published (by NOS) for a specific area, it is so indicated on the applicable En Route Low Altitude Chart. These area charts are designed to aid pilots in flight operations in certain congested terminal areas. The format of the area chart is basically the same as that of the en route chart except that the scales of an area chart permit an enlarged view of the local area.

APPROACH CONTROL

9.12 Many airports have an approach control facility which is responsible for controlling all instrument flights operating within its defined service area. Approach control may serve one or more airfields, and control is exercised primarily by direct pilot/controller communications. ARTCC will specify a frequency for arriving pilots to contact approach control.

9.13 When landing at an airport with approach control services and where two or more instrument approach procedures are published, pilots will be provided with information in advance of their arrival. The pilot will be informed of the type of approach to expect, or will be notified that radar vectors may be issued for a Visual Approach. The two instances when information will *not* be furnished are:

1. When visibility at the airport is 3 statute miles or better and the ceiling is at or above the highest initial approach altitude established for any low altitude instrument approach procedure for the airport.

2. When ATIS is provided for the airport and the pilot indicates having received the ATIS information.

Advance information to the pilot is intended to aid the pilot in planning arrival actions. It does not, however, constitute an ATC clearance or commitment, and is subject to change. Conditions such as fluctuating weather, shifting winds, or a blocked runway may result in changes to approach information already received.

RADAR APPROACH CONTROL

9.14 Where radar is approved for approach control service, it is used not only for radar approaches (ASR and PAR) but is also used to provide vectors in conjunction with published non-radar approaches based on radio NAVAIDs (ILS, VOR, NDB, TACAN). Radar vectors can provide course guidance and expedite traffic to the final approach course of any established instrument approach pro-

cedure or to the traffic pattern for a Visual Approach. Approach control facilities that provide this radar service will operate in the following manner.

9.15 Controllers may exercise either of two approach clearance options for arriving aircraft. One option is to clear arriving aircraft to an outer fix most appropriate to the route being flown with vertical separation and, if required, to give holding information. A second option would occur when radar handoffs are effected between the ARTCC and approach control, or between two approach control facilities. In that case, aircraft are cleared to the airport or to a fix so located that the handoff will be completed prior to the time the aircraft reaches the fix. When radar handoffs are utilized, successive arriving flights may be handed off to approach control with radar separation in lieu of vertical separation. After release to approach control, aircraft are vectored to the appropriate final approach course, such as ILS, VOR, ADF, or others. Radar vectors and altitude/flight levels will be issued as required for spacing and separating aircraft. *For this reason, pilots must not deviate from the headings issued by approach control.* Aircraft will normally be informed when it is necessary to vector across the final approach course for spacing or other reasons. If approach course crossing is imminent and the pilot has not been informed that vectors for crossing the final approach course will be issued, the controller should be questioned promptly. The pilot is not expected to turn inbound on the final approach course unless an approach clearance has been issued. This clearance will normally be issued with the final vector for interception of the final approach course, and the vector will be such as to enable the pilot to establish the aircraft on the final approach course prior to reaching the final approach fix. When established inbound on the final approach course, radar separation will be maintained and the pilot will be expected to complete the approach utilizing the approach aid designated in the clearance as the primary means of navigation. It is imperative that, once established on the final approach course, pilots must not deviate from it unless a clearance to do so is received from Air Traffic Control. After passing the final approach fix on final approach, aircraft are expected to continue inbound on the final approach course and complete the approach or execute the missed approach procedure published for that airport.

APPROACH CLEARANCE

9.16 An aircraft that is issued an approach clearance prior to reaching a clearance holding fix has not received a new routing. Although an approach clearance may have been issued prior to the aircraft reaching the holding fix, the pilot is expected to proceed via the holding fix (the last assigned route), through a transition if one exists, and then to the appropriate initial approach fix to initiate the instrument approach procedure. However, if a transition fix is located along the clearance route prior to the holding fix, and an approach clearance is received, the pilot should commence the approach from the transition fix if the aircraft has not already passed the transition fix.

9.17 When an Air Traffic Controller wishes to route an aircraft directly to the initial approach fix, the words "direct. . . ," "proceed direct. . . " (or a similar phrase) will be stated by the controller; this can be interpreted without question by the pilot. Pilots uncertain of *any* clearance should question ATC immediately.

9.18 Pilots are reminded that while operating on an unpublished route or while being radar vectored, the pilot, when an approach clearance is received, shall, in addition to complying with the minimum altitudes for IFR operations, maintain his last assigned altitude:

1. Unless a different altitude is assigned by ATC, *or*
2. Until the aircraft is established on a segment of a published route or instrument approach procedure.

After the aircraft is so established, published altitudes apply to descent within each succeeding route or approach segment unless a different altitude is assigned by ATC. Notwithstanding this pilot responsibility, for aircraft operating on unpublished routes or while being radar vectored, ATC will, except when conducting a radar approach, issue an IFR approach clearance only after the aircraft is:

1. Established on a segment of a published route or instrument approach procedure, or
2. Assigned an altitude to maintain until the aircraft is established on a segment of a published route or instrument approach procedure.

The altitude assigned will assure IFR obstruction clearance from the point at which the approach clearance is issued until established on a segment of a published route or instrument approach procedure.

9.19 Several instrument approach procedures using various navigation/approach aids may be authorized for an airport. ATC may advise that a particular approach procedure is being used, primarily to expedite traffic. If a pilot is issued a clearance that specifies a particular approach procedure, the pilot is expected to notify ATC immediately if a different approach procedure is desired. In this event, it may be necessary for ATC to withhold clearance for the different approach until such time as traffic

conditions permit. However, if involved in an emergency situation, the pilot will be given priority.

9.20 If the pilot is not familiar with the specific approach procedure, ATC should be advised and they will provide detailed information on how to execute the procedure.

9.21 At times ATC may not specify a particular approach procedure in the clearance but will state "cleared for the approach." Such clearance indicates that the pilot may execute any of the authorized instrument approach procedures for that airport.

9.22 When cleared for a specifically prescribed instrument approach procedure, for example, "cleared for ILS runway one niner approach" or when "cleared for the approach," that is, execution of any procedure prescribed for the airport, pilots shall execute the entire procedure as described on the instrument approach procedure chart unless an appropriate new or revised ATC clearance is received, or the IFR flight plan is cancelled.

LANDING CLEARANCE

9.23 Whenever the reported weather is below the published minimums for a particular approach, the controller will so advise the pilot and request the pilot's intentions. Clearance to land will be based solely on the pilot's stated intentions and the traffic situations. If a pilot requests landing clearance, the controller will qualify the landing clearance as follows: "cleared to land if you have landing minimums." Consequently, the decision to land with the weather below landing minimums is the pilot's responsibility. Pilots are reminded that such an action by a pilot could result in an FAA violation.

TERMINAL RADAR PROGRAMS FOR VFR AIRCRAFT

9.24 Radar services not only play an important role in the advising, sequencing, and separation of IFR aircraft but have an important function in providing similar services to VFR aircraft as well. Instrument pilots should be aware of the terminal radar programs for VFR aircraft so they may develop the necessary insight to conduct flight operations in terminal areas with VFR aircraft.

Stage I Service (Radar Advisory Service for VFR Aircraft)

9.25 Stage I service is available at airports served by an approach control equipped with radar. Stage I facilities provide traffic information and limited vectoring to VFR aircraft on a workload-permitting basis in addition to the control of IFR aircraft. Vectoring service may be furnished if requested by the

VFR pilot or if accepted by the pilot when suggested by ATC.

Stage II Service (Radar Advisory and Sequencing for VFR Aircraft)

9.26 Stage II service is available only at *certain* terminal areas served by an approach control. The purpose of the Stage II service is to adjust the flow of arriving VFR and IFR aircraft into the traffic pattern in a safe and orderly manner, and to provide radar traffic information to departing VFR aircraft. On initial contact by VFR aircraft, approach control will assume that Stage II service is requested unless advised otherwise. Approach control will provide the VFR pilot with information, including such items as wind and runway information and routings, as necessary, for proper sequencing with other participating VFR and IFR traffic en route to the airport. After radar contact is established, the VFR pilot may navigate without assistance into the traffic pattern, or depending on traffic conditions, may be directed to fly specific headings to position the flight behind a preceding aircraft in the approach sequence.

9.27 Standard radar separation will be provided between IFR aircraft until such time as the aircraft is sequenced and the pilot is in visual contact with the traffic to be followed. Standard radar separation between VFR, or between VFR and IFR aircraft, will not be provided.

Stage III Service (Radar Sequencing and Separation Service for VFR Aircraft)

9.28 Like Stage II service, Stage III service is provided only at *certain* terminal locations. The purpose of this service is to provide separation between all *participating* VFR aircraft and all IFR aircraft operating within the airspace defined as the Terminal Radar Service Area (TRSA).

9.29 Visual separation is exercised when prevailing conditions permit, and it will be applied as follows:

1. When a VFR flight is positioned behind the preceding aircraft and the pilot reports having that aircraft in sight, the pilot will be directed to follow it.
2. When IFR flights are being sequenced with other traffic and the pilot reports the aircraft to be followed is in sight, the pilot may be directed to follow it and will be cleared for a "visual approach."
3. If other "non-participating" or "local" aircraft are in the traffic pattern, the tower will issue a landing sequence.
4. Departing VFR aircraft may be asked if they can visually follow a preceding departure out of

the TRSA. If the pilot concurs, the controller will direct the pilot to follow the preceding aircraft until leaving the TRSA.

9.30 Until visual separation is obtained, standard vertical or radar separation will be provided in the following manner:

1. Vertical separation of 1,000 feet may be used between IFR aircraft.
2. Vertical separation of 500 feet may be used between VFR aircraft, or between a VFR and IFR aircraft.
3. Radar separation varies, depending on size of aircraft and aircraft distance from the radar antenna. The minimum separation used will be 1½ miles for most VFR aircraft under 12,500 pounds GWT. If an aircraft is being separated from larger aircraft, the minimum is increased appropriately. Pilots operating VFR in a TRSA:

   A. Must maintain an altitude when assigned by ATC unless the altitude assignment is to maintain at or below a specified altitude and
   B. When not assigned an altitude should coordinate with ATC prior to any altitude change.

9.31 Within the TRSA, traffic information on observed but unidentified targets will be provided, to the extent possible, to all IFR and participating VFR aircraft.

9.32 *Special Note: Information concerning locations and frequencies of the Stage I, II, and III services is contained in the Airport/Facility Directory. Remember, TRSA charts with a description of the services provided, flight procedures, and ATC procedures, are contained in the Graphic Notices and Operational Data publication. Pilot (VFR) participation is suggested but not mandatory.*

RADAR APPROACHES

9.33 A radar approach may be given to any aircraft upon request; it may be offered to pilots of aircraft in distress or to expedite traffic. A surveillance approach, however, might not be approved unless there is an ATC operational requirement, or an unusual or emergency situation. Acceptance of a precision or surveillance approach by a pilot does not waive the prescribed weather minimums for the airport or for the particular aircraft operator concerned.

Precision Approach (PAR)

9.34 In addition to receiving azimuth and elevation information, pilots are told to anticipate glide path interception approximately 10 to 30 seconds before it occurs and are also told when to start descent. The published decision height (DH) will be given only if the pilot requests it. If the aircraft is observed to deviate above or below the glide path, the pilot is informed of the relative amount of deviation by use of terms "slightly" or "well" and is expected to adjust the aircraft's rate of descent to return to the glide path. Range from touchdown is given at least once each mile. If an aircraft is observed by the controller to proceed outside of specified safety zone limits in azimuth and/or elevation, and it continues to operate outside these prescribed limits, the pilot will be directed to execute a missed approach or to fly a specified course, unless the runway environment is in sight. Navigational guidance in azimuth and elevation is provided for the pilot until the aircraft reaches the published DH. Advisory course and glidepath information is furnished by the controller until the aircraft passes over the landing threshold, at which point the pilot is advised of any deviation from the runway centerline. Radar service is automatically terminated upon completion of the approach.

Surveillance Approach (ASR)

9.35 Since the radar information used for a surveillance approach is considerably less precise than that used for a precision approach, the accuracy of the approach will not be as great and higher minimums will apply. Although guidance in elevation is not possible, pilots will be advised when to commence descent to the minimum descent altitude (MDA) or, if appropriate, to an intermediate stepdown fix minimum crossing altitude and subsequently to the prescribed MDA. In addition, the pilot will be advised of the location of the missed approach point (MAP) prescribed for the procedure and his position each mile on final approach from the runway, airport, or MAP, as appropriate. *If requested* by the pilot, recommended altitudes will be issued at each mile, based on the descent gradient established for the procedure, down to the last mile that is at or above the MDA. Normally, navigational guidance will be provided until the aircraft reaches the MAP. Controllers will terminate guidance and instruct the pilot to execute a missed approach, unless, at the MAP, the pilot has the runway in sight. Also, if at any time during the approach the controller considers that safe guidance for the remainder of the approach cannot be provided, the controller will terminate guidance and instruct the pilot to execute a missed approach. Similarly, guidance termination and missed approach will be effected upon pilot request, and controllers may terminate guidance when the pilot reports the runway in sight or otherwise indicates that continued guidance is not required. Radar service is automatically terminated at the completion of a radar approach.

9.36 The published MDA for straight-in approaches will be given to the pilot before the descent begins; however, if the circling MDA is required it will be given only on request.

No-Gyro Approach

9.37 A No-Gyro approach is available to a pilot under radar control who experiences circumstances wherein the aircraft's directional gyro or other stabilized compass is inoperative or inaccurate. When this occurs, the pilot should so advise Air Traffic Control and request a No-Gyro vector and approach. Pilots of aircraft not equipped with a directional gyro or other stabilized compass who desire radar handling may also request a No-Gyro vector or approach. The pilot should make the turn at standard rate and should execute the turn immediately upon receipt of instructions, for example, "turn right," "stop turn." When a surveillance or precision approach is made, and after the aircraft has been established on final approach, the pilot will be advised to execute turns at half standard rate.

9.38 *Special Note: Remember, PAR approaches provide precise navigational guidance in terms of azimuth and elevation. ASR approaches provide navigational guidance in azimuth only.*

SIMULTANEOUS ILS APPROACHES

9.39 Simultaneous ILS approaches are provided at many airports having parallel runways which are separated by at least 4,300 feet between centerlines. Integral parts of the total system are: ILS, radar, communications, ATC procedures, and appropriate airborne equipment. An approach procedure chart permitting simultaneous approaches will contain a note like "simultaneous approach authorized rwys 32L and 32R" identifying the appropriate runways, as the case may be. When advised that simultaneous ILS approaches are in progress, pilots shall advise approach control immediately of malfunctioning or inoperative receivers, or if a simultaneous approach is not desired. (Figure 9–3)

9.40 Radar Monitoring Service is provided for each ILS to insure prescribed lateral separation during approaches. Pilots will be assigned frequencies to receive advisories and instructions. (Aircraft deviating from either localizer course to the point where the no transgression zone may be penetrated will be instructed to take corrective action.) If an aircraft fails to respond to such instructions, the aircraft on the adjacent localizer may be instructed to alter course.

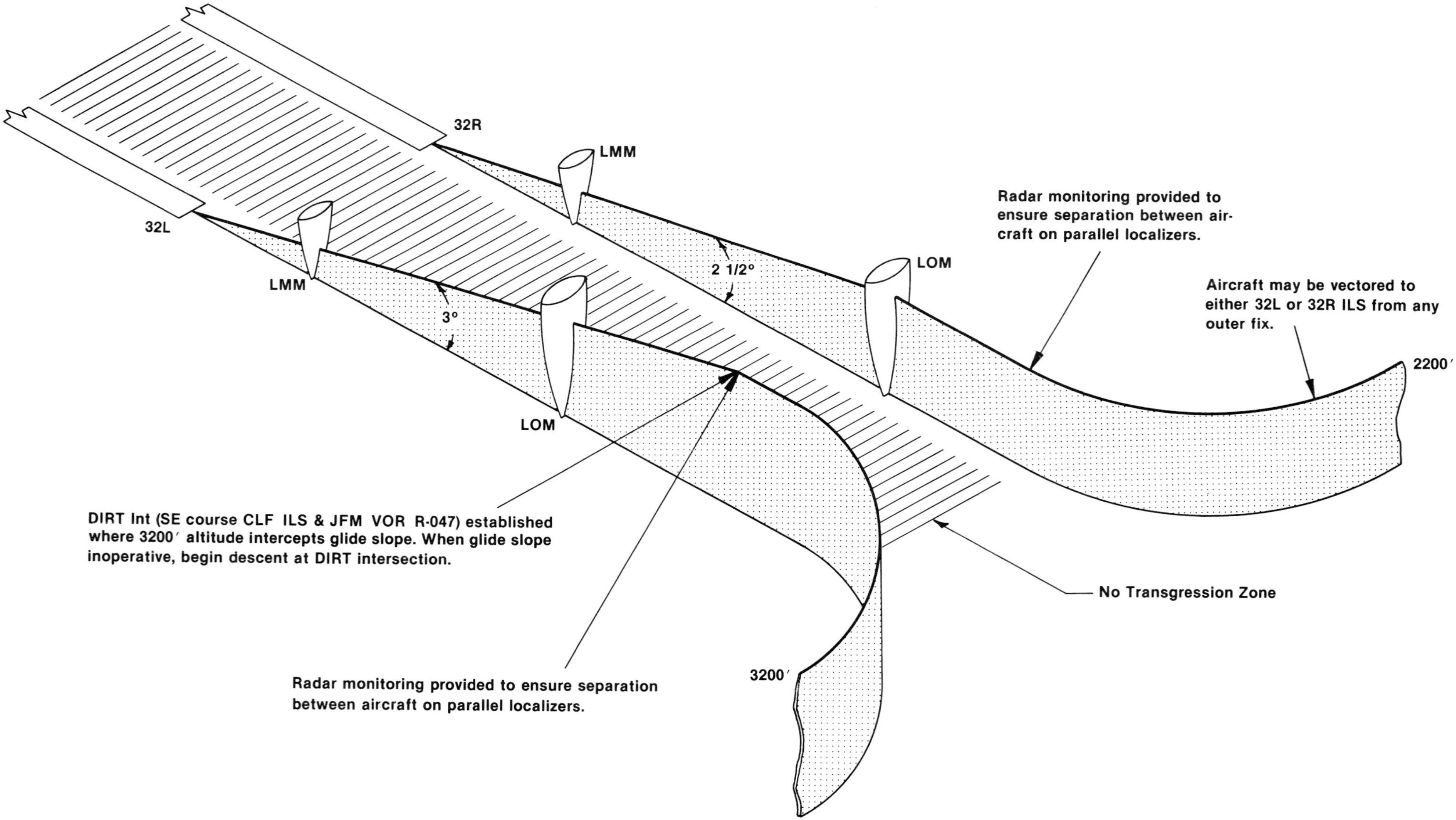

2200'

Aircraft may be vectored to
either 32L or 32R ILS from any
outer fix.

Radar monitoring provided to
ensure separation between aircraft on parallel localizers.

No Transgression Zone

LOM

2 1/2°

3°

LMM

32R

LOM

LMM

32L

3200'

Radar monitoring provided to ensure separation
between aircraft on parallel localizers.

DIRT Int (SE course CLF ILS & JFM VOR R-047) established
where 3200' altitude intercepts glide slope. When glide slope
inoperative, begin descent at DIRT intersection.

286

Figure 9-3. Simultaneous ILS Approaches

9.41 Whenever simultaneous ILS approaches are in progress, radar advisories will be provided on the tower frequency, and instrument pilots should be aware of the following:

1. The monitor controller will have the capability of overriding the tower controller on the tower frequency.

2. The pilot will be advised to monitor the tower frequency.

3. The monitor will automatically be terminated at one mile, or if procedurally required at a specific location, at the ILS middle marker.

4. The monitor controller will *not* advise when the monitor is terminated.

RADAR MONITORING OF INSTRUMENT APPROACHES

9.42 When approaches are being monitored by radar, the radar advisories serve only as a secondary aid, since the pilot has selected the ILS or other navigational aid as the primary aid for the approach.

9.43 Instrument approaches will be monitored at a few FAA radar locations and at military airfields. This is done when approaches are conducted using navigational aids that provide course guidance from the final approach fix to the runway, coinciding with the PAR course. Radar advisories will also be furnished to the pilot whenever the reported weather is below basic VFR minimums (1,000-foot ceiling and 3 statute miles visibility), at night, or on pilot request.

9.44 Prior to starting final approach, the pilot will be advised of the frequency on which the advisories will be transmitted. At some airports it may be the ILS localizer voice channel. If, for any reason, radar advisories cannot be furnished, the pilot will be so advised.

9.45 Advisory information, derived from radar observations, includes information on:

1. Passing the final approach fix. (At this point, the pilot may be requested to report sighting the approach lights or the runway.)

2. Trend advisories with respect to elevation and/or azimuth radar position and movement. Whenever the aircraft nears the PAR safety limit, the pilot will be advised that the aircraft is well above or below the glidepath, or well left or right of course.

LANDING PRIORITY

9.46 A clearance for a specific type of approach (ILS, ADF, VOR or Straight-in Approach) to an aircraft operating on an IFR flight plan does not mean that landing priority will be given over other traffic. Traffic control towers handle all aircraft, *regardless of the type of flight plan*, on a "first-come, first-

served" basis. Sometimes, because of local traffic or runway in use, it may be necessary for the controller, in the interest of safety, to provide a different landing sequence. In any case, a landing sequence will be issued each aircraft as soon as possible to enable the pilot to properly adjust the aircraft's flight path.

VISUAL APPROACH

9.47 The Visual Approach is a procedure which is used by ATC (during adequate *VFR* weather conditions) to expedite traffic flow by eliminating the necessity of executing a complete standard or special instrument approach procedure. When a pilot accepts authorization for a "visual approach," it is assumed that the clearance acceptance also includes:

1. Responsibility to visually maintain adequate spacing from the preceding aircraft, which the pilot is instructed to follow, *and*

2. Responsibility for adequate wake turbulence separation.

9.48 ATC may *authorize* an aircraft to conduct a Visual Approach to an airport when:

1. Flight to and landing at the airport can be accomplished in VFR conditions.

2. The pilot has the airport in sight and is number one in the approach sequence, or has reported the preceding aircraft in sight and has been instructed to follow it.

3. In the case of *Non-Radar* approach control facilities and certain towers, if visual separation can be provided by the tower between the IFR departures and aircraft cleared for a Visual Approach.

4. In the case of *radar*-controlled aircraft:

A. Potential traffic conflicts with other aircraft under Air Traffic Control have been resolved.

B. At tower controlled airports if the succeeding aircraft is instructed to land on a parallel runway separated by less than 2,500 feet from the runway being used by the other aircraft, both aircraft are informed of the aircraft using the other runway; *or*

Radar separation is maintained or both aircraft are sighted by the tower and the local controller will provide visual separation; *or*

Parallel runways separated by 2,500 feet or more, or converging runways are in use—all aircraft involved are informed that other arriving aircraft are using the other runway.

9.49 ATC may *vector* aircraft for a Visual Approach to the airport of intended landing in the following situations:

1. At airports *with* weather reporting service: If the reported ceiling at the airport of intended

landing is 500 feet above the minimum vectoring altitude and visibility is 3 miles or more; or

2. At airports *without* weather reporting service: If the pilot reports that descent and flight to the airport can be made in VFR conditions.

9.50 *Special Notes:*

1. *Radar service is automatically terminated, without advising the pilot, when the aircraft is instructed to contact the tower or Flight Service Station.*

2. *Authorization to conduct a Visual Approach is an IFR authorization and does not alter IFR flight plan cancellation responsibility.*

CONTACT APPROACH

9.51 The Contact Approach is a procedure similar to the Visual Approach, and may be used by a pilot (with prior authorization from ATC) in lieu of conducting a standard or special instrument approach procedure to an airport. However, instrument pilots should realize that a Contact Approach is an *IFR* operation that is allowed in *VFR* and *IFR* weather conditions, whereas a Visual Approach is an *IFR* operation that is conducted only in *VFR* weather conditions.

9.52 Pilots operating in accordance with an IFR flight plan, provided they are clear of clouds and have at least one-mile flight visibility and can reasonably expect to continue to the destination airport in those conditions, may request ATC authorization for a Contact Approach.

9.53 Controllers may authorize a Contact Approach provided:

1. The Contact Approach is specifically requested by the pilot. *ATC cannot initiate this approach.*

2. The reported ground visibility at the destination airport is at least one statute mile.

3. The Contact Approach must be conducted to an airport having a standard or special instrument approach procedure.

4. Approved separation is applied between aircraft cleared for a Contact Approach, as well as between these aircraft and other IFR or special VFR aircraft.

9.54 A Contact Approach is not intended for use by a pilot on an IFR flight clearance to operate to an airport not having an authorized instrument approach procedure. Nor is it intended for an aircraft to conduct an instrument approach to one airport and then, when "in the clear," to discontinue that approach and proceed to another airport. In the execution of a Contact Approach, the pilot assumes the responsibility for obstruction clearance. When the pilot is told to contact the tower, radar service is automatically terminated.

9.55 *Special Note: Upon careful examination, several differences can be noted between Visual and Contact Approaches. All instrument pilots and applicants should thoroughly review both of these procedures and note the differences.*

INSTRUMENT APPROACH PROCEDURES (PUBLISHED)

9.56 According to FAR 91.116, each person operating an aircraft shall, when an instrument letdown to an airport is necessary, use a standard instrument approach procedures chart prescribed for that airport.

9.57 If "cleared for the approach," a pilot has many approach options available. The instrument approach procedures can be divided into two categories, non-precision and precision.

9.58 Non-precision approach charts are published for the following types of facilities:

1. NDB
2. VOR
3. VORTAC or VOR/DME
4. ASR

9.59 Precision approach charts are published for the following types of facilities:

1. ILS
2. PAR

9.60 *Some* of the variables that a pilot should consider when selecting the appropriate approach procedure are the existing weather conditions, the aircraft instrumentation, the approach and ground navigation facilities available, the type aircraft used, and last but not least *the pilot's ability*.

9.61 Civil Instrument Approach Procedures are established by the Federal Aviation Administration after careful analysis of obstructions, terrain features and navigational facilities. Based on this information, the National Ocean Survey and other charting agencies publish instrument approach charts as a service to the instrument pilot. Appropriate maneuvers, which include altitudes, courses, and other limitations, are prescribed in these procedures. It is important that all pilots thoroughly understand these procedures and their use. The following are parts of the government-produced instrument approach procedure charts.

Legend Pages

9.62 Legend Pages contain the Plan View Symbols, Profile Information, Aerodrome Sketch Information, and General Information and Abbreviations. The following Figures 9–4, 9–5, and 9–6 show Legend Pages to the NOS instrument approach procedure charts.

LEGEND

INSTRUMENT APPROACH PROCEDURES (CHARTS)

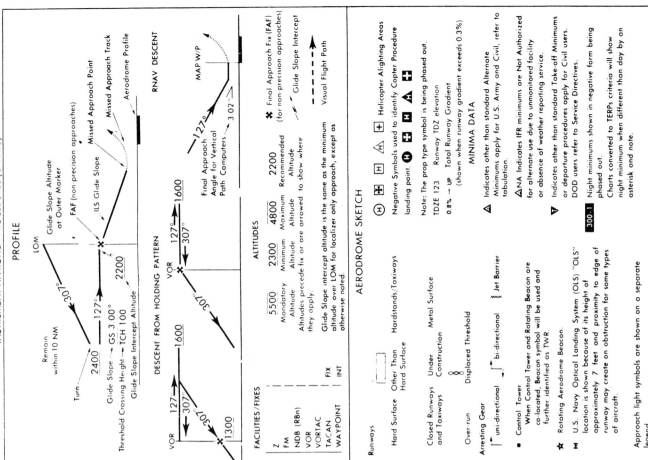

PUBLISHED BY NOS, NOAA, TO IACC SPECIFICATIONS

Figure 9-5. Legend NOS Instrument Approach Procedure Chart Profile Section

---

INSTRUMENT APPROACH PROCEDURES (CHARTS)

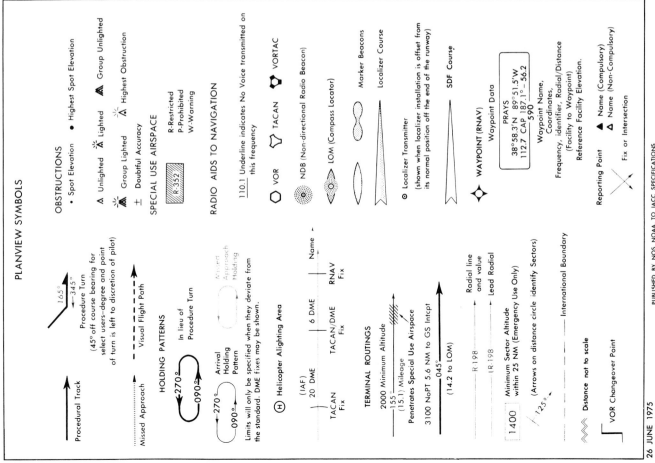

PUBLISHED BY NOS, NOAA, TO IACC SPECIFICATIONS

Figure 9-4. Legend NOS Instrument Approach Procedure Chart Plan View Symbols

GENERAL INFORMATION & ABBREVIATIONS

★ Indicates control tower operates non-continuously. All distances in nautical miles (except Visibility Data which is in statute miles, and Runway Visual Range which is in hundreds of feet). Runway dimensions in feet. Elevations in feet Mean Sea Level. All radials/bearings are Magnetic.

ADF	Automatic Direction Finder	MALS/R	Medium Intensity Approach Light Systems /with RAIL
ALS	Approach Light System	MAP	Missed Approach Point
APP CON	Approach Control	MDA	Minimum Descent Altitude
ARR	Arrival	MIRL	Medium Intensity Runway Lights
ASR/PAR	Published Radar Minimums at this Aerodrome.	NA	Not Authorized
ATIS	Automatic Terminal Information Service	NDB	Non-directional Radio Beacon
		NoPT	No Procedure Turn Required (Procedure Turn shall not be executed without ATC clearance)
BC	Back Course	RA	Radio Altimeter Height
C	Circling	Radar Required	Radar vectoring required for this approach
CAT	Category	Radar Vectoring	May be expected through any portion of the Nav Aid Approach, except final.
CHAN	Channel		
CLNC DEL	Clearance Delivery	RAIL	Runway Alignment Indicator Lights
DH	Decision Height	RBn	Radio Beacon
DME	Distance Measuring Equipment	REIL	Runway End Identifier Lights
DR	Dead Reckoning	RCLS	Runway Centerline Light System
ELEV	Airport Elevation	RNAV	Area Navigation
FAF	Final Approach Fix	RRL	Runway Remaining Lights
FM	Fan Marker	RTB	Return To Base
GPI	Ground Point of Interception	Runway Touchdown Zone	First 3000' of Runway.
GS	Glide Slope	RVR	Runway Visual Range
HAA	Height Above Aerodrome	S	Straight-in
HAL	Height Above Landing	SALS	Short Approach Light System
HAT	Height Above Touchdown	(S) SALS/R	(Simplified) Short Approach Light System /with RAIL
HIRL	High Intensity Runway Lights	SDF	Simplified Directional Facility
IAF	Initial Approach Fix	TA	Transition Altitude
ICAO	International Civil Aviation Organization	TAC	TACAN
Intcp	Intercept	TCH	Threshold Crossing Height (Height in feet Above Ground Level)
INT, INTXN	Intersection		
LDA	Localizer Type Directional Aid	TDZ	Touchdown Zone
Ldg	Landing	TDZE	Touchdown Zone Elevation
LIRL	Low Intensity Runway Lights	TDZL	Touchdown Zone Lights
LDIN	Lead in Light System	TLv	Transition Level
LOC	Localizer	W.P.	Waypoint (RNAV)
LR	Lead Radial Provides at least 2 NM (Copter 1 NM) of lead to assist in turning onto the intermediate/final course.		
MALS	Medium Intensity Approach Light System		

LANDING MINIMA FORMAT

In this example airport elevation is 1179, and runway touchdown zone elevation is 1152.

All minimums in parentheses not applicable to Civil Pilots. Military Pilots refer to appropriate regulations.

CATEGORY	A	B	C	D
S-ILS-27	1352/24			
S-LOC-27	1440/24 288	1640-1 461(500-1)	1640-1½ 461(500-1½)	1740-2 561(600-2)
CIRCLING	1540-1 361(400-1)	288 200 (200-½)	200 (300-½)	1440/50 288(300-1)

Aircraft Approach Category
Visibility (RVR 100's of feet)
Visibility in Statute Miles
DH · HAT · MDA · HAA

Straight-in ILS to Runway 27
Straight-in with Glide Slope inoperative or not used to Runway 27

26 JUNE 1975   PUBLISHED BY NOS, NOAA, TO IACC SPECIFICATIONS

Figure 9-6. Legend NOS Instrument Approach Procedure Chart General Information and Abbreviations

---

Format for Government-Produced Instrument Approach Procedure Charts

9.63 Each chart consists of five sections: (1) Margin Identification; (2) Plan View; (3) Profile View; (4) Landing Minimum section (and notes); and (5) Aerodrome Sketch. (Figure 9–7)

Margin Identification (Section 1 of Government-Produced Instrument Approach Procedure Charts)

9.64 The procedure identification (Figure 9–8) is derived from the type of facility providing final approach course guidance, and:

1. Runway number, when the approach course is *within 30°* of the runway centerline, for example, ILS Rwy 14; *or*

2. Sequential letter for the airport, when the approach course is *more than 30°* from runway centerline, for example, VOR–A, VOR–B.

9.65 Nondirectional Beacon (NDB), Localizer (LOC), and Localizer-Type Directional Aid (LDA) are used to identify more accurately the type of facility providing final approach course guidance.

1. An NDB procedure indicates that a Nondirec-

tional Beacon provides course guidance.

2. An LOC procedure number indicates that a localizer provides course guidance and glide slope (ground facility) has not been installed.

3. An LDA procedure is similar to a localizer, but is not aligned with the runway centerline. The approach chart should be examined to determine the direction and degrees of alignment away from the runway centerline.

9.66 A VOR/DME procedure number or letter indicates that both operative VOR and DME receivers and ground equipment in normal operation are required to use the procedure. When either the VOR *or* DME is inoperative, this procedure is not authorized.

9.67 When DME arcs and DME fixes are authorized in a procedure and the procedure identification does not include the three letter DME-type of facility in the margin identification, the procedure may be used without utilizing the DME equipment.

9.68 VORTAC-type procedure is a VOR/DME procedure that is authorized for an aircraft equipped with either VOR/DME or TACAN receiver.

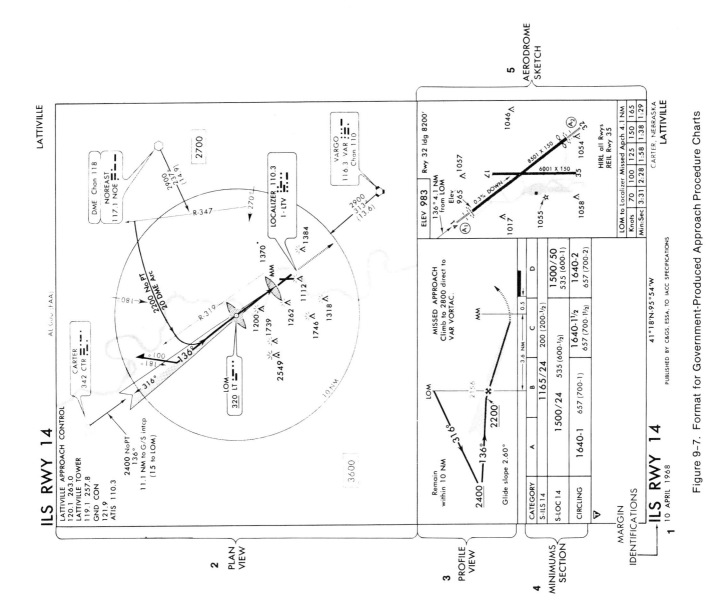

Figure 9-7. Format for Government-Produced Approach Procedure Charts

TOP MARGIN IDENTIFICATION

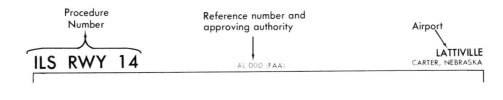

BOTTOM MARGIN IDENTIFICATION

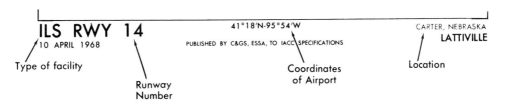

Figure 9-8. Top and Bottom Margin Identification

Plan View (Section 2 of Government-Produced Instrument Approach Procedure Charts)

9.69 The Plan View provides an aerial view of the entire approach procedure. Information pertaining to the initial approach segment, including procedure turn, minimum safe altitude for each sector, courses prescribed for the final approach segment, and obstructions, is portrayed in this section. Navigation and communication frequencies are also listed on the Plan View. The instrument pilot must understand the following aspects of the plan view:

1. Composition.
2. En Route Facilities Ring.
3. Feeder Facilities Ring.
4. Radar.
5. Initial Approach.
6. Procedure Turn.
7. ILS approach procedures that do not require a procedure turn.

Composition

9.70 Normally, all information within the Plan View is shown to scale. Data shown within the 10 NM distance circle is always shown to scale. (Figure 9-9) The dashed circles, called concentric rings, are used when all information necessary to the procedure will not fit to scale within the limits of the Plan View area. These circles then serve as a means to systematically arrange this information in its relative position outside and beyond the 10 NM distance circle. These concentric rings are labeled En Route Facilities and Feeder Facilities.

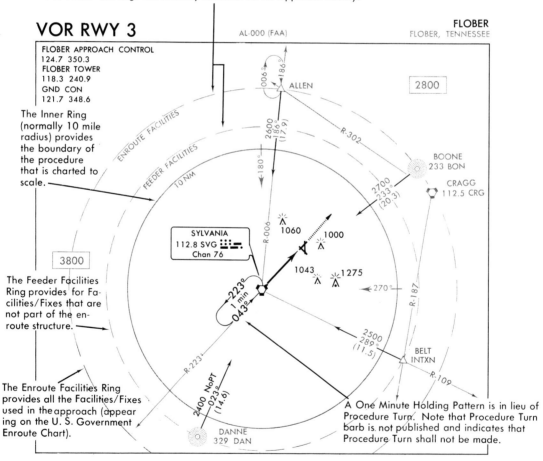

Figure 9-9. A Plan View of an Instrument Approach Procedure Chart Illustrating Basic Format With Concentric Rings

Figure 9-10. A Plan View of an Instrument Approach Procedure Chart Illustrating Basic Format

En Route Facilities Ring

9.71 Radio aids to navigation, fixes and intersections that are part of the En Route Low Altitude airway structure and used in the approach procedure are shown in their relative position on this En Route Facilities Ring. (Figure 9–9.)

Feeder Facilities Ring

9.72 Radio aids to navigation, fixes, and intersections used by the air traffic controller to direct aircraft to intervening facilities/fixes between the en route structure and the initial approach fix are shown in their relative positions on the Feeder Facilities Ring.

Radar

9.73 The availability of RADAR (refer to Figure 9–11) is indicated below the communications information by the appropriate and applicable letters: ASR, PAR, ASR/PAR, or Radar Vectoring. These terms are applied as follows:

ASR—Indicates Airport Surveillance Radar instrument approach procedures are available at the airport, and also that Radar Vectoring is available for the procedures.

PAR—Indicate Precision Approach Radar instrument approach procedures are available.

Radar Vectoring—Indicates Radar Vectoring is available but radar instrument approach procedures are not available.

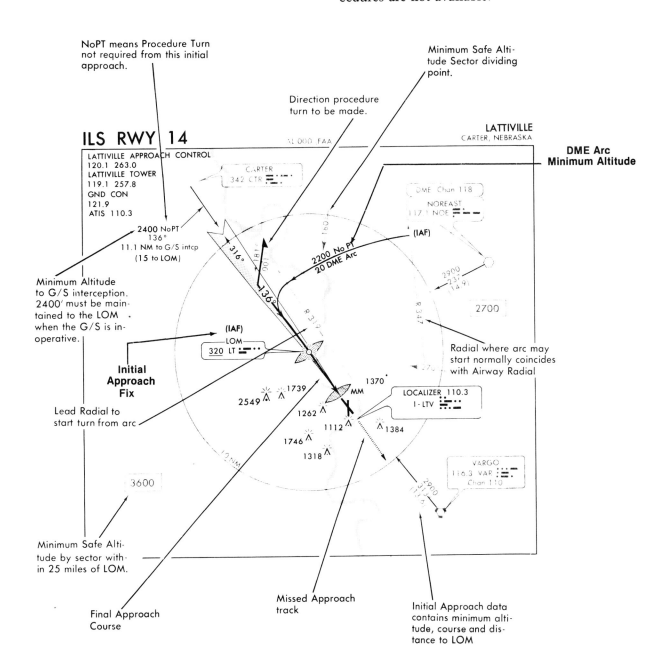

293

Initial Approach

9.74 Initial approach information is portrayed in the Plan View of instrument approach charts by course lines, with an arrow indicating the direction. Minimum altitude and distance between fixes is also shown with the magnetic course.

9.75 An initial approach may be made along prescribed routes within the terminal area which may be along an arc, radial, course, heading, radar vector, or a combination thereof. Procedure turns and high altitude teardrop penetrations are initial approach segments.

9.76 In the initial approach, the aircraft has departed the en route phase of flight, and is maneuvering to enter an intermediate or final segment of the instrument approach (refer to Figures 9–10 and 9–11).

9.77 When the term *NoPT* appears on the Plan View, an intermediate approach is provided. These altitudes shown with the term *NoPT* cannot be used as an initial approach altitude for the purpose of determining alternate airports' requirements.

Concerning ATC Services: If no ATC services are available, there will be an absence of frequency information.

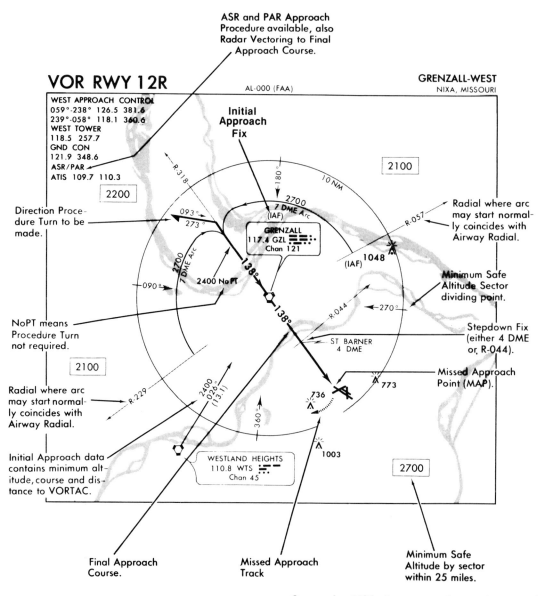

Figure 9–11. A Plan View of an Instrument Approach Procedure Chart Illustrating Basic Format With Radar Services

Concerning MSA: As many as four sectors may be depicted with different altitudes for each sector displayed in rectangular boxes in the Plan View. A single altitude for the entire area may be shown in the lower right portion of the Plan View. <u>Navigational course guidance is not assured at the MSA within these sectors.</u>

Procedure Turn

9.78 A procedure turn is specified on instrument approach procedure charts when it is necessary to reverse direction to establish an aircraft inbound on an intermediate or final approach course (refer to Figure 9-11). The instrument approach procedure specifies the outbound and inbound courses, the distance within which the procedure turn shall be completed, and the side of the inbound course (by the magnetic compass direction) on which the turn should be made. A barb indicates the direction or side of the outbound course on which the procedure turn is made. Headings are provided for course reversal using the 45°-type procedure turn. The type and rate of the turn and the point at which the turn is begun is left to the discretion of the pilot (refer to Figure 9-12). The maneuver must be completed within the prescribed procedure turn distance. The altitude prescribed for the procedure turn is a *minimum* altitude until the aircraft is established on the inbound course (refer to Figures 9-13 and 9-14).

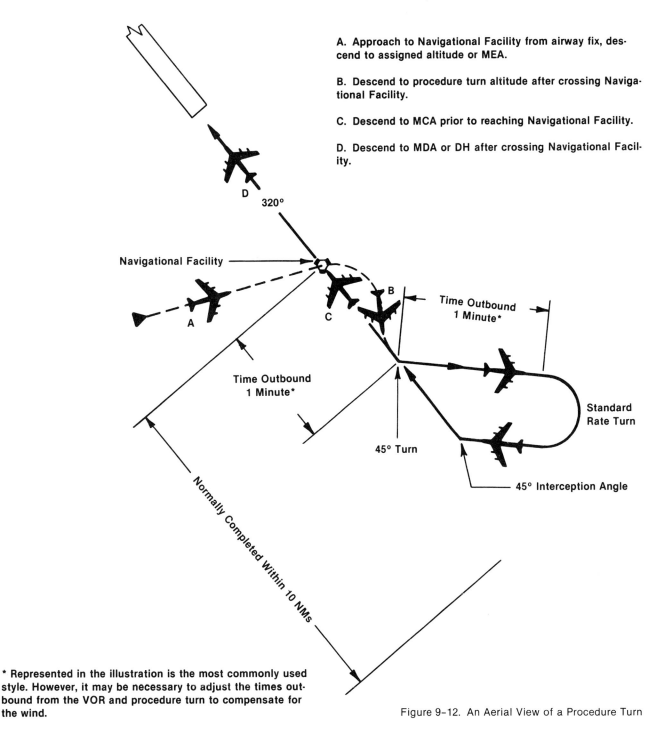

A. Approach to Navigational Facility from airway fix, descend to assigned altitude or MEA.

B. Descend to procedure turn altitude after crossing Navigational Facility.

C. Descend to MCA prior to reaching Navigational Facility.

D. Descend to MDA or DH after crossing Navigational Facility.

* Represented in the illustration is the most commonly used style. However, it may be necessary to adjust the times outbound from the VOR and procedure turn to compensate for the wind.

Figure 9-12. An Aerial View of a Procedure Turn

9.79 A teardrop procedure/penetration turn may be specified in some procedures for a required course reversal. The teardrop procedure consists of departure from an initial approach fix on an outbound course followed by a turn toward and interception of the inbound course at or prior to the intermediate fix or point. Its purpose is to permit an aircraft to reverse direction and lose considerable altitude within reasonably limited airspace. When no fix is available to mark the beginning of the intermediate segment, it shall be assumed to commence at a point 10 miles prior to the final approach fix. When the facility is located on the airport, an aircraft is considered to be on final approach upon completion of the penetration turn. However, the final approach segment begins on the final approach course 10 miles from the facility.

9.80 A procedure turn may not be established when an approach can be made from a properly aligned holding pattern. In such cases, the holding pattern is established over an intermediate fix or a final approach fix and, as in the procedure turn, the descent from the minimum holding pattern altitude to the final approach fix altitude may not commence until the aircraft is established on the inbound course.

9.81 A procedure turn is not required when an approach can be made directly from a specified intermediate fix to the final approach fix. In such cases, the term *NoPT* is used with the appropriate course and altitude to denote that the procedure turn is not required. When a procedure turn is desired, and when cleared to do so by ATC, descent below the procedure turn altitude should not be made until the aircraft is established on the inbound course, since some NoPT altitudes may be lower than the procedure turn altitude.

9.82 There are some limitations that exist on a pilot's use of the procedure turn. Aviators should be well aware of these, which include the following:

1. In the case of a radar initial approach to a final approach fix or position, or a timed approach from a holding fix, or where the procedure specifies *NoPT*, no pilot may make a procedure turn unless, when the pilot receives the final approach clearance, ATC is so advised and a clearance is received.

2. When a teardrop procedure turn is depicted and a course reversal is required, this type turn must be executed.

3. When a one-minute holding pattern replaces the procedure turn, the standard entry and the holding pattern must be followed except when *Radar Vectoring* is provided or when NoPT is shown on the approach course.

4. Procedure turns are limited as otherwise restricted by notes and symbols on the procedure charts.

ILS Approach Procedures That Do Not Require A Procedure Turn

9.83 When an approach course is published for an ILS procedure that does not require a procedure turn (NoPT), the following applies:

1. In the case of a dog-leg track with no fix depicted at the point of interception on the localizer course, the total distance is shown from the facility or fix to the LOM, or to an NDB associated with the ILS.

2. The minimum altitude applies until the glide slope is intercepted, at which point the aircraft descends on the glide slope.

3. When the glide slope is not utilized, this minimum altitude is maintained to the LOM (or to the NDB if appropriate).

4. In isolated instances, when proceeding NoPT to the LOM and when the glide slope cannot be utilized, a procedure turn will be required to descend for a straight-in approach and landing. In these cases, the requirement for a procedure turn will be annotated on the Plan View of the procedure chart.

Profile View (Section 3 of Government-Produced Instrument Approach Procedure Charts)

9.84 The Profile View shows a side view of the procedure. This view includes the *minimum* altitude and maximum distance for the procedure turn, altitudes over prescribed fixes, distances between fixes, and the missed approach procedure. Instrument pilots must be thoroughly familiar with the following aspects of the Profile View Section:

1. Precison approach glide slope intercept altitudes.

2. Stepdown fixes in non-precision procedures.

3. Missed approach points.

4. Visual descent points. (Refer to Figures 9–13 and 9–14.)

Precision Approach Glide Slope Intercept Altitude

9.85 This is a minimum altitude for glide slope interception after completion of a procedure turn. It applies to precision approaches and, except where otherwise prescribed, it also applies as a minimum altitude for crossing the final approach fix in case the glide slope is inoperative or not used.

Stepdown Fixes in Non-Precision Procedures

9.86 A stepdown fix may be provided on the final approach, for example, between the final approach fix (FAF) and the airport, for the purpose of au-

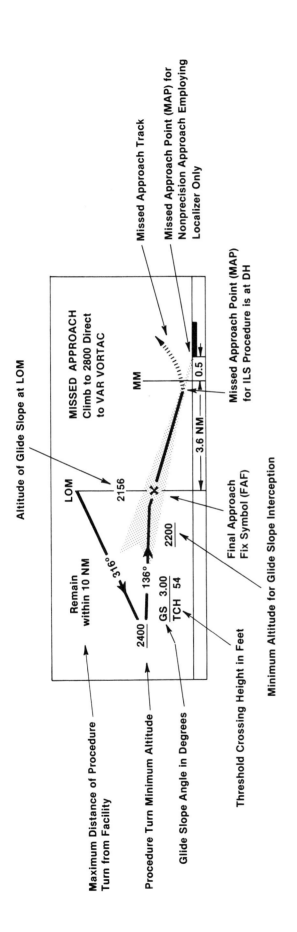

Maximum Distance of Procedure Turn from Facility

Altitude of Glide Slope at LOM

Procedure Turn Minimum Altitude

Glide Slope Angle in Degrees

Threshold Crossing Height in Feet

Minimum Altitude for Glide Slope Interception

Final Approach Fix Symbol (FAF)

Missed Approach Track

Missed Approach Point (MAP) for Nonprecision Approach Employing Localizer Only

Missed Approach Point (MAP) for ILS Procedure is at DH

MISSED APPROACH Climb to 2800 Direct to VAR VORTAC

Remain within 10 NM

LOM
2156

2400   316°   136°

GS 3.00
TCH 54

2200

MM

3.6 NM   0.5

Figure 9–13. A Profile View of a Precision Instrument Approach Procedure

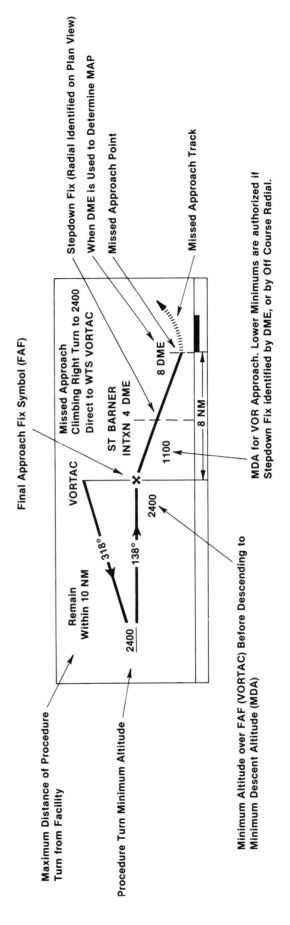

Maximum Distance of Procedure Turn from Facility

Procedure Turn Minimum Altitude

Final Approach Fix Symbol (FAF)

Minimum Altitude over FAF (VORTAC) Before Descending to Minimum Descent Altitude (MDA)

Stepdown Fix (Radial Identified on Plan View)

When DME is Used to Determine MAP

Missed Approach Point

Missed Approach Track

MDA for VOR Approach. Lower Minimums are authorized if Stepdown Fix identified by DME, or by Off Course Radial.

Missed Approach Climbing Right Turn to 2400 Direct to WTS VORTAC

ST BARNER INTXN 4 DME

VORTAC

Remain Within 10 NM

2400   318°   138°

2400

1100

8 DME

8 NM

Figure 9–14. A Profile View of a Non-Precision Instrument Approach Procedure

297

thorizing a lower MDA after passing an obstruction. This stepdown fix may be made by an NDB bearing, fan marker, radar fix, radial from another VOR, or by a DME when provided for (as shown in Figure 9–14). Normally, there is only one stepdown fix between the FAF and the MAP. If the stepdown fix cannot be identified for any reason, the altitude at the stepdown fix becomes the MDA for a straight-in landing. However, when circling under this condition, a pilot must refer to the Minimums Section of the procedure for the applicable circling minimum. (Figure 9–16)

Missed Approach Point

9.87 It should be specifically noted that the missed approach points are different for the complete ILS (with glide slope) and for the localizer only approach. The MAP for the ILS is at the *decision height* while the "localizer only" MAP is usually over the (straight-in) *runway threshold.* In some nonprecision procedures, the MAP may be arrived at prior to reaching the runway threshold in order to clear obstructions in the missed approach climb-out area. In non-precision procedures, the pilot determines when the MAP has been reached by timing from the FAF. The FAF has been clearly identified by use of the maltese cross symbol in the profile section. The distance from the FAF to the MAP and the time and speed table are found below the aerodrome sketches (refer to Figure 9–18). This does not apply to VOR/DME procedures, or when the facility is on the airport and the facility is the MAP.

Visual Descent Point (VDP)

9.88 The VDP is a defined position on the final approach course of certain *non-precision straight-in approach procedures* from which normal descent from the MDA to the runway touchdown point may be commenced, provided that required visual reference is established. When VDPs are provided, the location of the VDP and the type of electronic navigational aid identifying the VDP will be indicated on the profile view of the approach chart by the symbol **V** . DME will normally be used as the VDP identification aid for VOR/DME and localizer Back Course approaches that incorporate a VDP. Similarly, a 75 MHz marker will be used for NDB approaches (that incorporate a VDP) and where DME cannot be implemented. VDPs will not normally be established for runways served by precision approach aids. VDPs are *not* a mandatory part of approach procedures but are intended to provide additional guidance where they are implemented. A VASI will normally be installed on those runways served by a non-precision approach that incorporates a VDP.

9.89 The pilot should not descend below the MDA prior to reaching the VDP. Acquisition of the required visual reference prior to reaching the VDP should alert the pilot that the point from which a normal descent path (approximately 3°) intersects the MDA has not yet been reached. Conversely, reaching the VDP prior to acquiring the required visual reference should alert the pilot to the likelihood of a missed approach. Aircraft not equipped to identify the VDP should fly the procedure as though no VDP had been provided.

Landing Minimum Section (Section 4 of Government-Produced Instrument Approach Procedure Charts)

9.90 The Landing Minimum Section of government-produced instrument approach charts can be initially confusing to the instrument applicant. The following discussion covers in detail those basic facts and many specific elements that a pilot must understand in order to properly interpret the Landing Minimum Section. For this reason, conscientious study of this particular subject is essential.

Aircraft Approach Categories

9.91 Minimums are specified for the various aircraft speeds. Speeds are based upon a value 1.3 times the stalling speed of the aircraft in the *landing* configuration at *maximum* certificated *landing weight.* Thus, they are *computed* values. Naturally, an aircraft can fit into only one category. However, if it is necessary to maneuver at speeds in excess of the upper limit of the speed range for a particular category, the landing minimums for the next higher approach category should be used. For example, an aircraft which falls into Category A but is circling to land at a speed in excess of 91 knots, should use the approach Category B minimums when circling to land. Refer to the following category limits and reference table in Figure 9–17.

Straight-In Minimums

9.92 Straight-in minimums are shown on instrument approach procedure charts when the final approach course of the instrument approach procedure is within 30° of the runway alignment, and a normal descent can be made from the IFR altitude shown on the instrument approach procedures to the runway surface. When either the normal rate of descent or the runway alignment factor of 30° is exceeded, a straight-in minimum is not published and a circling minimum applies. The fact that a straight-in minimum is not published does not preclude the pilot from landing straight-in if the active runway is in sight of the pilot in sufficient time to make a normal landing. Under such condi-

MINIMUMS SECTION (and notes).

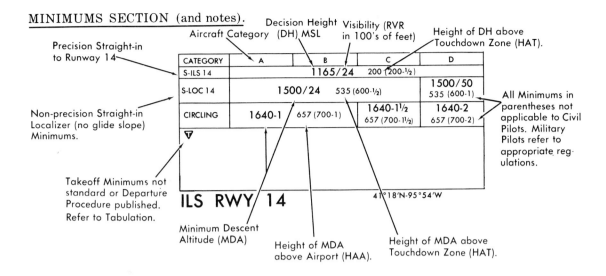

Figure 9-15. A Sample Minimum Section of a Precision Instrument Approach Procedure Chart

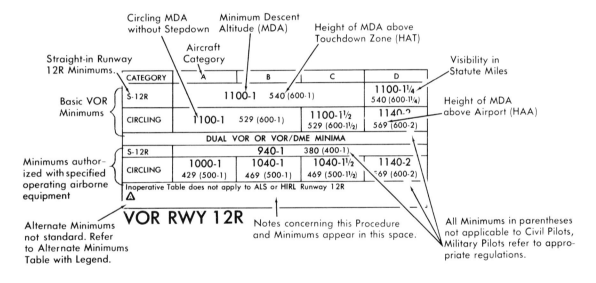

Figure 9-16. A Sample Minimum Section of a Non-Precision Instrument Approach Procedure Chart

APPROACH CATEGORY	SPEED
A	Speed less than 91 knots.
B	Speed 91 knots or more but less than 121 knots.
C	Speed 121 knots or more but less than 141 knots.
D	Speed 141 knots or more but less than 166 knots.
E	Speed 166 knots or more.

Figure 9-17. Aircraft Approach Category Limits and Reference Table

tions, and when Air Traffic Control has issued a landing clearance on the active runway, a pilot is not expected to circle even though only circling minimums are published. Pilots wishing to circle at a controlled airport should advise ATC.

Circling Minimums

9.93 The circling minimums published on the instrument approach chart provide adequate obstruction clearance; the pilot should not descend below the circling altitude until the aircraft is in a position to make final descent for landing. Sound judgment and knowledge of pilot and aircraft capabilities should be used to determine the exact maneuver in each instance, since the airport design, the aircraft position, altitude, and airspeed must all be considered. The following basic rules apply to circling approaches:

1. Pilots should fly the shortest path to the base or downwind leg as appropriate under minimum weather conditions. There is no restriction from passing over the airport or other runways.

2. It should be recognized that many circling maneuvers may be conducted while VFR flying is in progress at the airport. Standard left turns or specific instruction from the controller for maneuvering must be considered when circling to land.

3. At airports without a control tower, it may be desirable to fly over the airport to determine wind and turn indicators, and to observe other traffic which may be on the runway or flying in the vicinity of the airport.

Minimum Descent Altitude (MDA)/Decision Height (DH) Concept

9.94 *IFR landing minimums.* Ceiling minimums are not prescribed in approach procedures as a landing limit. The published visibility is the required weather condition for landing. Regulations allow approaches down to the prescribed MDA or DH, as appropriate to the procedure being executed, *without regard to reported ceiling.*

9.95 *Descent below minimum descent altitude or decision height.* No person may operate an aircraft below the prescribed MDA or continue an approach below the DH unless:

1. The aircraft is in a position from which a normal approach can be made to the runway of intended landing; and

2. The approach threshold of that runway, or approach lights or other markings identifiable with the approach end of the runway, are clearly visible to the pilot; and

3. If, upon arrival at the MAP, or at any time thereafter, any of the above requirements are not met, the pilot shall immediately execute the appropriate missed approach procedure.

Publication of Landing Minimums

9.96 The government-produced approach procedure charts always contain the following information listed in this order: MDA or DH, visibility, HAA or HAT, and military minimums (ceiling and visibility) for each aircraft approach category. Since the chart is used by both civil and military pilots, the ceiling, as well as visibility, required by the military will be published in parentheses. Civil operators should disregard this information.

Examples of Published Landing Minimums

(The following examples have been taken from the government-produced approach procedure chart shown in Figure 9-7.)

9.97 *Straight-in precision.* An example of straight-in ILS minimums is shown below. The touchdown zone elevation is 965 feet, whereas the airport elevation is 983 feet.

STRAIGHT-IN TO RUNWAY 14	DH	VIS	HAT	MILITARY
S-ILS 14	1165	/ 24	200	(200–1/2)

It should be noted that the visibility is separated from the DH by a slant line (/) when it is RVR, and separated by a hyphen (-) when it is meteorological visibility. This will help differentiate the two visibility values. Remember, RVR is indicated in hundreds of feet, and meteorological visibility is indicated in statute miles. If RVR were not authorized, it would appear 1165-1/2.

9.98 *Straight-in non-precision.* When the ILS approach procedure is used but the aircraft does not have a glide slope receiver or the glide slope ground equipment is out of service, localizer minimums apply to the straight-in landing on that runway.

	MDA	VIS	HAT	MILITARY
S-LOC 14	1500	/ 24	535	(600–1/2)

9.99 *Circling.* Visibility for circling is always in a meteorological value of statute miles. Height of the MDA above the airport elevation is provided by HAA.

	MDA	VIS	HAA	MILITARY
CIRCLING	1640	– 1	657	(700–1)

Additional Facts Concerning the Landing Minimum Section

9.100 The same minimums apply to both day and night operations unless different minimums are specified at the bottom of the minimum box in the space provided for symbols or notes.

9.101 The minimums for straight-in and circling appear directly under each aircraft category. When there is no division line between minimums for each category on the straight-in or circling lines, the minimums apply to two or more categories under the A, B, C, or D. (*Example:* In Figure 9-15, the S-ILS 14 minimums apply to all four categories. The S-LOC 14 minimums are the same for Cate-gories A, B, and C, and different for Category D. The circling minimums are the same for Categories A and B and different for Categories C and for D.)

9.102 Occasionally, an approach procedure may authorize two different sets of minimums for aircraft equipped to different degrees of navigational equipment. An example of this is the Nixa, Missouri, Grenzall West Airport, VOR Rwy 12R procedure (Figures 9-14 and 9-16) which authorizes minimums for aircraft with one VOR receiver. Lower minimums are authorized if the aircraft also has DME or dual VOR receivers and ST. BARNER Intersection is identified. (Refer to Figure 9-16 for dual minimums.)

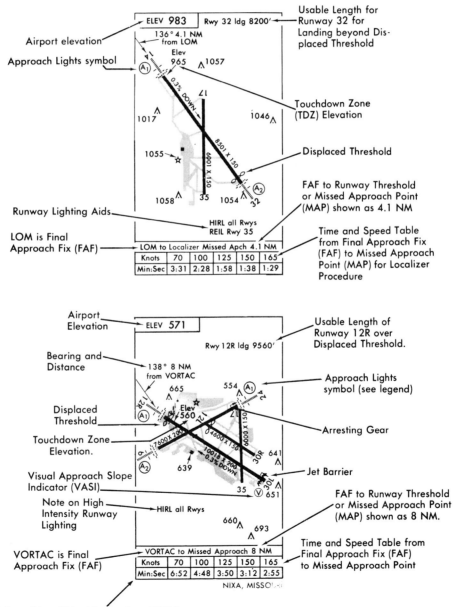

The time section of the table will be blank when DME is used to determine the MAP or when the navigational facility is located on the airport.

Figure 9-18. Two Sample Aerodrome Sketch Sections from Two Instrument Approach Procedure Charts

The Aerodrome Sketch (Section 5 of Government-Produced Instrument Approach Procedure Charts)

9.103 Although the Aerodrome Sketch section of an instrument approach procedure chart appears to be, and is, simple, there are still a few facts and considerations (in addition to what is shown in the legend) that an instrument pilot should assess.

9.104 One item to consider first is that the speed (knots) used to determine the time from the final approach fix to the missed approach point is a *ground speed*. Too many pilots suffer the misconception that this speed is a true, indicated, equivalent, or some other type of airspeed. Pilots are reminded that if the ground speed is increased during an instrument approach, the rate of descent should also be increased. Conversely, if the ground speed is decreased, the rate of descent should also be decreased.

9.105 Another consideration is that the airport elevation is not necessarily the same as the Touchdown Zone (TDZ) elevation.

9.106 Pilots should also remember that the legend for the approach light systems (see chapter 4) should be consulted when examining a particular approach lights symbol.

Inoperative Components or Visual Aids Table

9.107 Generally, most air navigation facilities have a very low out-of-service time. Consequently, the lowest landing minimums with all components and visual aids operating are published. However, an Inoperative Components or Visual Aids Table is published to determine landing minimums when components or aids of the system are inoperative *or are not utilized.* In order to apply the Inoperative Components or Visual Aids Table, it is necessary that the pilot correctly identify the components or visual aids applicable to the particular approach being flown and the approach category of the aircraft. Whenever there are Inoperative Components or Visual Aids, it will be publicized by NOTAM and/or ATC advisories. (Figure 9–19.)

Application of the Inoperative Components or Visual Aids Table

9.108 When using instrument approach procedure charts, the minimums must be adjusted in accordance with the Inoperative Components or Visual Aids Table. This will be done when a ground component or visual aid *pertinent* to the procedure is inoperative or not utilized.

9.109 With two or more components inoperative, only the greater or greatest increase in altitude or visibility is required, and the increases are *not* cumulative. When a visual aid has been installed, but reduced visibility minimums have not been authorized, the Inoperative Components or Visual Aids Table would not be used. The following type of note would then appear below the minimums section (Figure 9–16):

"Inoperative table does not apply to ALS or HIRL Runway 12R."

9.110 The general rules below will always apply to inoperative components:

1. Operative runway lights are required for night operation.

2. When the facility providing course guidance is inoperative, the procedure is not authorized. On VOR/DME procedures, when either VOR or DME is inoperative, the procedure is not authorized.

3. When the ILS glide slope is inoperative or not utilized, the published straight-in localizer minimum applies.

4. Compass locator or precision radar may be substituted for the ILS outer or middle marker.

5. Surveillance radar may be substituted for the ILS outer marker. DME, at the glide slope site, may be substituted for the outer marker when published on the ILS procedure.

6. Facilities that establish a stepdown fix (such as 75 MHz FM, off course VOR radial, and others) are not components of the basic approach procedure, and applicable minimums for use, both with or without identifying the stepdown fix, are published in the minimums section. (Figure 9–16)

7. Additional methods of identifying a fix may be used when authorized on the procedure.

8. To authorize Runway Visual Range minimums, the following components and visual aids must be available in addition to basic components of the approach procedure:

A. Precision approach procedures: RVR reported for the runway; HIRL; all-weather runway markings.

B. Non-precision approach procedures: RVR reported for the runway; HIRL; instrument runway markings.

C. Inoperative RVR minimums. Where RVR visibility minimums are published and the runway markings become unusable, the necessary adjustment will be accomplished by NOTAM and by air traffic advisory. If RVR minimums are published in an instrument approach procedure, but RVR is inoperative and cannot be reported for the runway at that time, it is necessary that the RVR minimums which are specified in the procedure be converted and applied as ground visibility in accordance with the table found in Figure 3–27.

Instrument Approach Procedures (Charts)
INOPERATIVE COMPONENTS OR VISUAL AIDS TABLE
Civil Pilots see FAR 91.117(c)

Landing minimums published on instrument approach procedure charts are based upon full operation of all components and visual aids associated with the particular instrument approach chart being used. Higher minimums are required with inoperative components or visual aids as indicated below. If more than one component is inoperative, each minimum is raised to the highest minimum required by any single component that is inoperative. ILS glide slope inoperative minimums are published on instrument approach charts as localizer minimums. This table may be amended by notes on the approach chart. Such notes apply only to the particular approach category(ies) as stated. See legend page for description of components indicated below.

(1) ILS, MLS, and PAR

Inoperative Component or Aid	Approach Category	Increase DH	Increase Visibility
MM*	ABC	50 feet	None
MM*	D	50 feet	¼ mile
ALSF 1 & 2, MALSR, & SSALR	ABCD	None	¼ mile

*Not applicable to PAR

(2) ILS with visibility minimum of 1,800 or 2,000 RVR.

Inoperative Component or Aid	Approach Category	Increase DH	Increase Visibility
MM	ABC	50 feet	To 2400 RVR
MM	D	50 feet	To 4000 RVR
ALSF 1 & 2, MALSR, & SSALR	ABCD	None	To 4000 RVR
TDZL, RCLS	ABCD	None	To 2400 RVR
RVR	ABCD	None	To ½ mile

(3) VOR, VOR/DME, VORTAC, VOR (TAC), VOR/DME (TAC), LOC, LOC/DME, LDA, LDA/DME, SDF, SDF/DME, RNAV, and ASR

Inoperative Visual Aid	Approach Category	Increase MDA	Increase Visibility
ALSF 1 & 2, MALSR, & SSALR	ABCD	None	½ mile
SSALS, MALS & ODALS	ABC	None	¼ mile

(4) NDB

Inoperative Visual Aid	Approach Category	Increase MDA	Increase Visibility
ALSF 1 & 2, MALSR, & SSALR	C	None	½ mile
	ABD	None	¼ mile
MALS, SSALS, ODALS	ABC	None	¼ mile

PUBLISHED BY NOS, NOAA, TO IACC SPECIFICATIONS
14 APRIL 1977

Figure 9-19. Inoperative Components or Visual Aids Table

Nonstandard Alternate Minimums Chart

9.111 As discussed in chapter 6, *standard* alternate minimums (forecast two hours before to two hours after the estimated time of arrival) for nonprecision approaches are an 800-foot ceiling and 2 statute miles visibility, and for precision approaches are a 600-foot ceiling and 2 statute miles visibility. Some approach charts may have the symbol △ shown in the note section of the approach chart. (Figure 9-16) This symbol indicates that alternate minimums other than standard alternate minimums are authorized. Consequently, when pilots are planning a flight, it is essential that the instrument approach procedure charts be checked to determine if standard alternate minimums apply. If the symbol △ is shown on the chart, the IFR Alternate Minimums Listing must be consulted to determine the appropriate *nonstandard* alternate minimums. (Refer to Figure 9-20.)

9.112 The letters *NA* may be shown on some approach charts in the note section following the △ symbol. These letters indicate that the airport is not authorized for use as an alternate due to an unmonitored facility or absence of a weather reporting service.

9.113 *Special Note: In the event that a pilot elects to proceed to a selected alternate airport, the ceiling and visibility minimums required to establish that airport as an alternate are disregarded, and the published landing minimum (on the instrument approach procedure chart) becomes applicable for the new destination utilizing facilities as appropriate to the procedure. In other words, the alternate airport becomes a new destination, and the pilot uses the landing minimum appropriate to the type of procedure selected.*

IFR Takeoff Minimums and Departure Procedures

9.114 The symbol ▽ shown in the note section of an instrument approach procedure chart indicates that only aircraft operating under FAR Part 121, 123, 129, and 135 must comply with prescribed takeoff minimums for that particular departure airport. (Figure 9-15) Although operators of aircraft not engaged in a commercial activity *do not* have any IFR takeoff minimums, it is, nevertheless, necessary to review the appropriate IFR Takeoff Minimums and Departure Procedures Listing. All pilots should review these listings *during preflight planning* to determine if an IFR departure procedure for obstruction avoidance has been established for the climbout phase of flight. (Figure 9-21)

Civil Radar Instrument Approach Minimums

9.115 Also included with the NOS instrument approach procedure charts is a listing of radar approach minimums for the respective airports. Instrument pilots should consult the appropriate listing prior to the initiation of a radar instrument approach. (Figure 9-22)

Figure 9-21 (top)

AERODROME NAME	TAKE-OFF MINIMUMS
WEST CENTRAL UNITED STATES (Continued from page 3)	
FESTUS MEMORIAL, Festus, Missouri	Rwys 18, 36: E bound departures, when weather is below 500-1, climb to 1500 on runway heading before turning on course.
FLOYD W. JONES LEBANON, Lebanon, Missouri	Rwy 36, 200-1 — Rwys 27, 36, maintain runway heading until reaching 2000 before turning on course.
FORNEY AAF, Fort Leonard Wood, Missouri	Rwys 14, 32, ¾ mile* — Rwys 14, 32, when planned route of flight is S-bound, climb to 2500 on assigned heading before proceeding on course.
FORT COLLINS-LOVELAND, Fort Collins-Loveland, Colorado	Take-off Rwys 6, 24 NA. Climb to 7000 via GLL R-248 to Neffs Int, or climb to 8000 in holding pattern on LLD NDB, continue climb via 320° bearing and GLL R-258 to Libel Int to cross at or above 10,000.
FORT DODGE MUNI, Fort Dodge, Iowa	Rwy 18, 700-1; Rwy 6, ½ mile* — Rwys 12, 24, 30, when weather is below 700-1 climb on runway heading to 1500 before turning. *(FAR 135)
FREMONT MUNI, Fremont, Nebraska	Rwy 18, 600-1. IFR DEPARTURE PROCEDURE: Rwys 8, 13, 26, 31 and 36: When weather below 1000-1, climb runway heading to 1800 before turning.
FULTON MUNI, Fulton, Missouri	Rwy 5, 500-1
GALLATIN FIELD, Bozeman, Montana	Rwy 12, ½ mile. *(FAR 135) Climb W bound on R-284 BZN VOR within 15 NM to cross BZN VOR at or above: NW bound V2, 4900; S bound V343 7200; SE bound V2/86, 8100'.
GATEWAY NORTH INDUSTRIAL, Anoka, Minnesota	Rwy 9, 400-1
GENERAL BREES FIELD, Laramie, Wyoming	Climb direct LAR VORTAC before proceeding on course.
GLACIER PARK INTL, Kalispell, Montana	Rwy 1, ¾ mile*; Rwy 7, 800-1. Rwys 1, 25, 29 turn left, Rwys 7,11, turn right. Climb direct FCA VOR. Continue climb to 6200 on FCA R-146 then climbing right turn direct FCA VOR to cross FCA VOR at or above: SW bound V448, 7000; SE bound V536, 7000; E bound V536, 8300. *(FAR 135)
GORDON MUNI, Gordon, Nebraska	Rwy 22, 700-1. IFR DEPARTURE PROCEDURE: Rwys 4, 11 and 29 climb runway heading to 4200 before turning.
GRAND FORKS INTL, Grand Forks, North Dakota	Rwy 35, ½ mile* *(FAR 135)
GRAND RAPIDS ITASCA COUNTY, Grand Rapids, Minnesota	Rwy 28, 300-1. Rwys 16, 22: When weather is below 300-1 climb runway heading to 1600 before turning W bound.
GREAT FALLS INTL, Great Falls, Montana	Rwys 3, 34, ½ mile* *(FAR 135)
GUNNISON COUNTY, Gunnison, Colorado	Rwys 6, 17, 24, 35, 1400-2. Climb visually over airport to 9000, continue climbing direct to GUC VORTAC. Depart at or above 12,400, except if NE-bound on J-10/128 or V-95 depart at or above 13,000.
GWINNER MUNI, Gwinner, North Dakota	Rwys 23, 34 when weather is below 200-1, climb runway heading to 1500 before turning.
HALL COUNTY REGIONAL, Grand Island, Nebraska	Rwy 35, ½ mile* *(FAR 135)
HALLOCK MUNI, Hallock, Minnesota	Rwys 13, 31 when weather is below 500-1, climb to 1300 on runway heading before turning.
HAMPTON MUNI, Hampton, Iowa	Rwy 17, 400-1
HANNIBAL MUNI, Hannibal, Missouri	Rwys 16, 34, when weather is below 400-1, maintain runway heading until 1200 before proceeding E-bound.
HASTINGS MUNI, Hastings, Nebraska	Rwys 14, 32 climb runway heading to 2800 before turning.
HAYS MUNI, Hays, Kansas	All runways, W bound departures: When weather is below 900-1 climb runway heading to 2900 before turning.
HECTOR, Fargo, North Dakota	Rwy 35, RVR/24*; Rwy 3, 13, 200-1 *(FAR 135)

(Continued on page 5)

       PUBLISHED BY NOS NOAA TO IACC SPECIFICATIONS

Figure 9-21. IFR Takeoff Minimums and Departure Procedures Chart

Figure 9-20 (bottom)

AERODROME NAME	ALTERNATE MINIMUMS
WEST CENTRAL UNITED STATES (Continued from page 3)	
RENNER FIELD GOODLAND MUNI, Goodland, Kansas	VOR Rwy 30, 1100-2* *Standard for VOR/DME approach.
ROCK SPRINGS SWEETWATER COUNTY, Rock Springs, Wyoming	VOR-A, 1200-2
ROSEAU MUNI, Roseau, Minnesota	VOR Rwy 16, NA*; VOR Rwy 34, NA* *Standard for operators with approved weather reporting service.
ROSECRANS MEM, St. Joseph, Missouri	NDB Rwy 17*; NDB Rwy 35*; ILS Rwy 35*†; VOR Rwy 17, 1000-2%; RNAV Rwy 17%; LOC(BC) Rwy 17* †ILS, Cat D 700-2 *NA for all operators when control zone not effective. %NA when control zone not effective, except for operators with approved weather reporting service.
ST. PAUL DOWNTOWN HOLMAN FIELD, St. Paul, Minnesota	VOR Rwy 30, 900-2; LOC Rwy 30, 900-2 NA when control zone not effective.
SIDNEY-RICHLAND MUNI, Sidney, Montana	NDB Rwy 19, 1200-2*; NDB Rwy 1, 1100-2* *For operators with approved weather reporting service.
SIOUX CITY MUNI, Sioux City, Iowa	ILS Rwy 31*; VOR Rwy 31 (TAC); VORTAC Rwy 13*; LOC BC Rwy 13*; RNAV Rwy 35, 900-2 *Category: E, 900-2
SPENCER MUNI, Spencer, Iowa	NDB Rwy 29 NA* *Standard for operators with approved weather reporting service.
SPIRIT OF ST. LOUIS, St. Louis, Missouri	VOR Rwy 7, 1000-2*; LOC BC Rwy 25, 900-2*; NDB Rwy 7, 1200-2; ILS Rwy 7† *NA when control zone not effective, except for operators with approved weather reporting service †ILS, 700-2, LOC, 1000-2
STAPLETON INTL, Denver, Colorado	ILS BC Rwy 8R* *LOC 1000-2
WALKER FIELD, Grand Junction, Colorado	ILS Rwy 11, 700-2
WATERLOO MUNI, Waterloo, Iowa	ILS Rwy 12*†; NDB Rwy 12*; LOC/DME BC Rwy 30* †ILS Category D, 700-2 *NA when control tower not in operation.
WATERTOWN MUNI, Watertown, South Dakota	ILS/DME Rwy 35 Category D, 700-2
WICHITA MID-CONTINENT, Wichita, Kansas	ILS Rwy 19R*; Radar 1, 1200-2 *S-LOC, 900-2
WILLMAR MUNI, Willmar, Minnesota	VOR Rwy 10, NA*; VOR Rwy 28, NA* *Standard for operators with approved weather reporting service.
WINDOM MUNI, Windom, Minnesota	NDB (ADF) Rwy 17, NA* *Standard for operators with approved weather reporting service.
WINONA MUNI MAX CONRAD FIELD, Winona, Minnesota	VOR-A, 1200-2*; VOR Rwy 29, 1400-2* *NA when control zone not effective except for operators with approved weather reporting service.
WOLFPOINT INTL, Wolfpoint, Montana	NDB-A NA* *1400-2 for operators with approved weather reporting service.
WORTHINGTON MUNI, Worthington, Minnesota	VOR Rwy 17; VOR Rwy 35 NA when control zone not effective except operators with approved weather reporting service.
YELLOWSTONE, West Yellowstone, Montana	NDB Rwy 1 NA*; ILS Rwy 1 NA† *1700-2 for operators with approved weather reporting service. †1200-2 for operators with approved weather reporting service.

       PUBLISHED BY NOS, NOAA TO IACC SPECIFICATIONS

Figure 9-20. IFR Alternate Minimums Listing

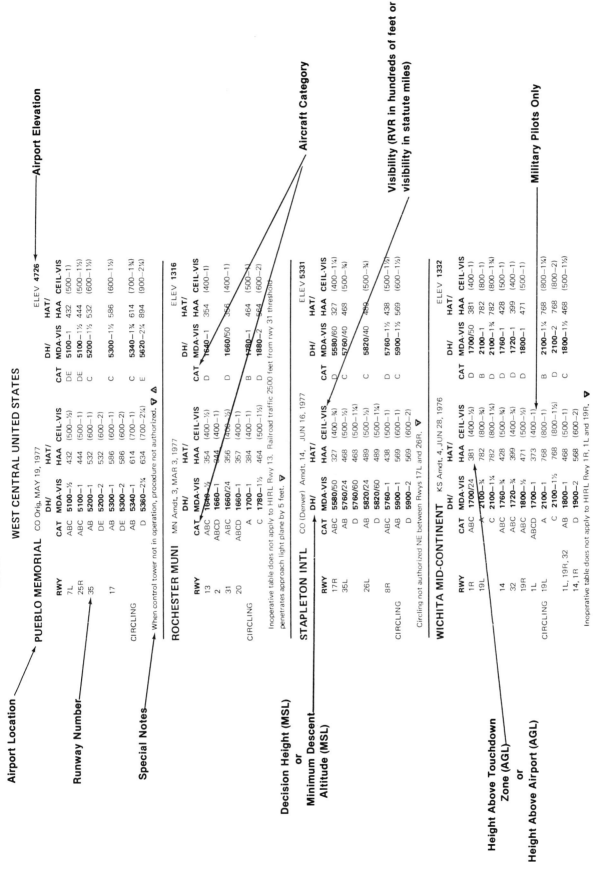

Figure 9-22. A Sample Listing of Civil Radar Instrument Approach Minimums

TIMED APPROACHES FROM A HOLDING FIX

9.116 Timed approaches may be conducted when the following conditions are met:

1. A control tower is in operation at the airport where the approaches are conducted.

2. Direct communications are maintained between the pilot and the center/approach controller until the pilot is instructed to contact the tower.

3. A course reversal must not be part of the missed approach procedure if more than one missed approach procedure is available.

4. If only one missed approach procedure is available, the following conditions must be met:

   A. Course reversal is not required; and,

   B. Reported ceiling and visibility are equal to or greater than the highest prescribed circling minimums for the instrument approach procedure.

5. When cleared for the approach, pilots shall not execute a procedure turn.

9.117 Although the controller will not specifically state that "timed approaches are in progress," the assignment of a time to depart the final approach fix inbound is indicative that timed approach procedures are being utilized; also, in lieu of holding, the controller may use radar vectors to the final approach course to establish a mileage interval, between aircraft, that will insure the appropriate time sequence between the final approach fix and the airport.

9.118 Each pilot in an approach sequence will be given advance notice as to the time to leave the holding point on approach to the airport. When a time to leave the holding point has been received, the pilot should adjust the aircraft flight path to leave the fix as closely as possible to the designated time.

9.119 Figure 9–23 depicts a final approach procedure from a holding pattern at a final approach fix. At 11:45 local time, a pilot who is holding receives instructions to leave the fix inbound at 11:49. These instructions are received just as the pilot has completed the turn at the outbound end of the holding pattern and is proceeding inbound towards the fix. Arriving back over the fix, the pilot notes that the time is 11:46 and that there are three minutes to lose in order to leave the fix at the assigned time. Since the time remaining is more than two minutes, the pilot plans to fly a race-track pattern rather than a 360° turn, which would use up two minutes. The turns at the ends of the race-track pattern will consume approximately two minutes. Three minutes to go, minus two minutes required for turns, leaves one minute for level flight. Since two portions of level flight will be required to get

back to the fix inbound, the pilot halves the one minute remaining and plans to fly level for 30 seconds outbound before initiating a turn toward the fix on final approach. If the winds were negligible at flight altitude, this procedure would bring the pilot inbound across the fix precisely at the specified time of 11:49. However, if the pilot expects a headwind on final approach, the 30-second outbound course should be shortened somewhat, since the wind will carry the aircraft away from the fix faster while outbound and decrease the ground speed while returning to the fix. If the pilot knows there will be a tailwind on final approach, the calculated 30-second outbound heading should be lengthened somewhat, since the wind will tend to hold the aircraft closer to the fix while outbound and increase the ground speed while returning to the fix.

SIDE-STEP MANEUVER

9.120 Air Traffic Control may authorize an approach procedure which serves either one of two parallel runways that are separated by 1,200 feet or less, to be followed by a straight-in landing on the adjacent runway. Aircraft that will execute a side-step maneuver will be cleared for a specified approach and landing on the adjacent parallel runway. For example, the controller would say, "Cleared for ILS runway 07 left approach, side-step to runway 07 right." Pilots are expected to commence the side-step maneuver as soon as possible after the runway or runway environment is in sight. Landing minimums to the adjacent runway will be higher than the minimums to the primary runway, but will normally be lower than the published circling minimums. ATC will not clear aircraft for landing on an adjacent runway unless weather conditions will permit successful completion of the side-step maneuver.

MISSED APPROACH PROCEDURES

9.121 A pilot must comply with the appropriate missed approach instructions when:

1. Instructed to do so by ATC; or

2. When it is determined that at any time it is unsafe to continue the approach or that a safe landing is not possible; or

3. When arriving at the DH, MAP, or any point thereafter, it is determined that visual reference to the runway environment is insufficient to complete the landing; or

4. If communication is lost for more than 5 seconds on final of a PAR approach or for more than 15 seconds on final of an ASR approach and the pilot is unable to take over visually.

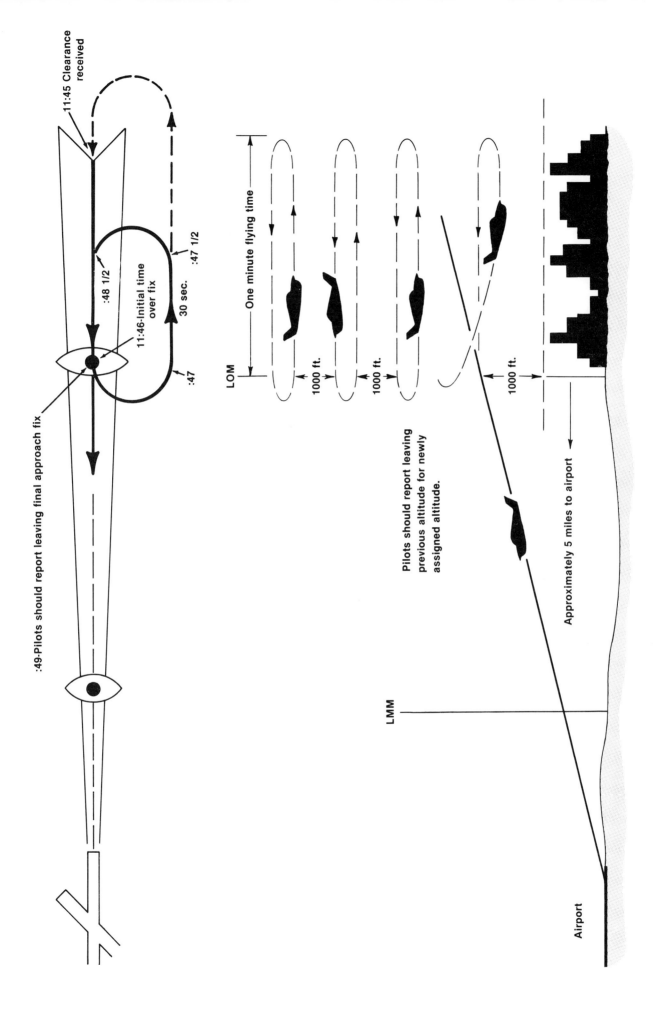

:49-Pilots should report leaving final approach fix

11:45 Clearance received

:48 1/2

:47 1/2

11:46-Initial time over fix

30 sec.

:47

LOM

One minute flying time

1000 ft.

1000 ft.

1000 ft.

LMM

Pilots should report leaving previous altitude for newly assigned altitude.

Approximately 5 miles to airport

Airport

Figure 9-23. A Typical Timed Approach

The appropriate missed approach instructions include:

1. The published missed approach instructions specified for the particular procedure being executed (refer to the Profile View Section of Figure 9-7), unless alternate missed approach instructions are issued by ATC; or

2. If executing a missed approach from a radar approach, the missed approach procedure previously issued, which should be followed unless the controller specifies a new altitude to climb to and a new heading to fly.

9.122 Whenever a pilot executes an early missed approach, the entire published instrument approach procedure (to the MAP) should be flown at or above the DH or MDA *before* initiating a turning maneuver. This is essential because instrument approach procedures are based on the assumption that missed approaches will be initiated at the MAP not lower than the DH or MDA. Although design consideration is given to normal maneuvers during the course of instrument approaches, compensation is not made for *abnormally early* turns during a missed approach.

9.123 In the event visual reference cannot be maintained while circling to land from an instrument approach, the pilot should initiate a climbing turn toward the landing runway and continue turning until established on the missed approach course. Adherence to this procedure will insure that aircraft will remain within the circling and missed approach obstruction clearance areas.

9.124 *Special Note: Instrument pilots are often confused about when to execute a missed approach during a non-precision instrument approach procedure. The missed approach should be executed at the MAP if the runway environment is not in sight and not at the MDA if the MDA is reached prior to reaching the MAP. The MDA should be maintained until the MAP is reached.*

COMMUNICATIONS

Reports to ATC or FSS Facilities

9.125 In addition to those required and suggested reports discussed in chapter 8, the following reports should be made to ATC or Flight Service Station facilities, without request, during terminal area operations. Pilots should report:

1. When departing the final approach fix inbound on final approach. This report is not required, however, while aircraft are in radar contact.

2. When an approach has been missed. This is, naturally, a necessary report since the pilot must receive an additional clearance, for example, to proceed to an alternate airport or to execute another instrument approach procedure.

Cancelling the IFR Flight Plan

9.126 It is the instrument pilot's responsibility to initiate the cancellation of the IFR flight plan except when landing at an airport with a functioning control tower, in which case the IFR flight plan is automatically closed upon landing. A pilot may cancel an IFR flight plan at any time in which the aircraft is in VFR conditions, *except* when operating in Positive Controlled Airspace.

9.127 A pilot may close an IFR flight plan by:

1. Communicating with the local FSS in person or by radio after landing; or

2. Radio, *weather conditions permitting*, while still airborne and able to communicate to ATC in the event there is no FSS at the arrival airport and air/ground communications with ATC are not possible below a certain altitude; or

3. A telephone call to the nearest FSS or ATC facility after landing if the arrival airport is not served by an FSS.

Traffic Advisories

9.128 At airports equipped with a full time FSS but a part time control tower, the FSS service will, in addition to its regular services, issue traffic advisories when the control tower is not in operation.

CHAPTER 9: QUESTIONS

For answers see Appendix E

1. A procedure turn is a required maneuver used to establish an aircraft inbound on an intermediate or final approach course except:

A. When the symbol *NoPT* is depicted.
B. When Radar Vectoring is provided.
C. When a one-minute holding pattern is published in lieu of a procedure turn.
D. When the procedure turn is not authorized.

    1. A and C.
    2. B and C.
    3. A, B, C, and D.
    4. B and D.

2. Under what conditions may a pilot who is operating on an IFR flight plan obtain a Contact Approach?

    1. Only if ATC specifically assigns a Contact Approach and the visibility is at least one statute mile.
    2. Only if the pilot requests a Contact Approach and is clear of clouds, and the reported visibility is at least one statute mile.
    3. Only if the pilot requests a Contact Approach and the airport is reporting VFR conditions.
    4. Only if ATC assigns a Contact Approach and the airport is reporting VFR conditions.

3. Refer to the ILS Rwy 31 instrument approach procedure chart (below) for Aberdeen Regional to determine the altitude of an aircraft when on the glide path over the outer marker.

    1. 2,641 feet MSL.
    2. 2,700 feet MSL.
    3. 2,750 feet MSL.
    4. 1,499 feet MSL.

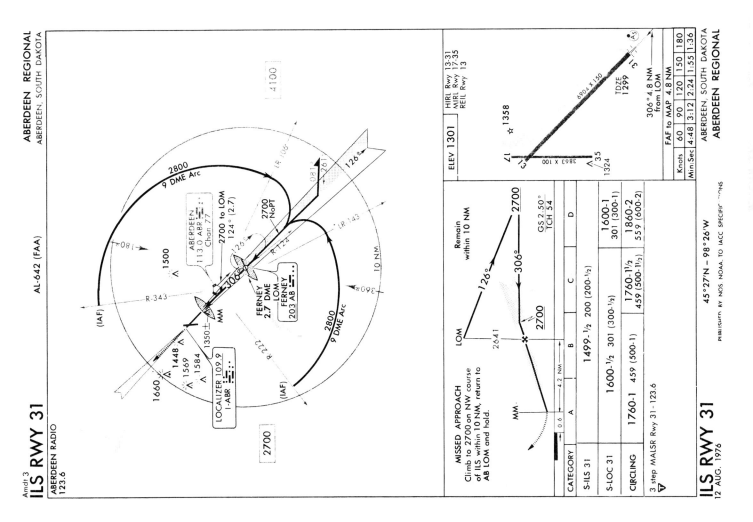

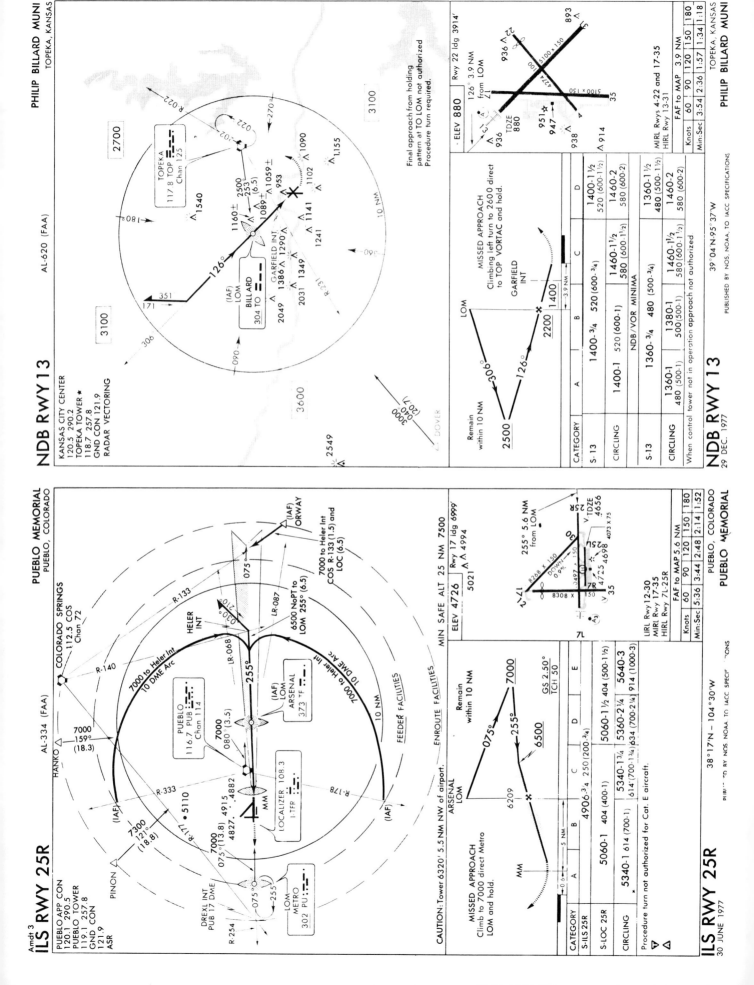

NDB RWY 13 — PHILIP BILLARD MUNI, TOPEKA, KANSAS

Amdt 3
AL-620 (FAA)

KANSAS CITY CENTER
120.5 290.2
TOPEKA TOWER ★
118.7 257.8
GND CON 121.9
RADAR VECTORING

TOPEKA
117.8 TOP Chan 125

(IAF) LOM
BILLARD
304 TO

Final approach from holding
pattern at TO LOM not authorized.
Procedure turn required.

ELEV 880

Rwy 22 ldg 3914'
126° 3.9 NM from LOM

TDZE 880

MIRL Rwys 4-22 and 17-35
HIRL Rwy 13-31

MISSED APPROACH
Climbing left turn to 2600 direct
to TOP VORTAC and hold.

Remain within 10 NM

CATEGORY	A	B	C	D
S-13	1400-1	1400-¾ 520 (600-¾)	1460-1½ 580 (600-1½)	1400-1½ 520 (600-1½)
CIRCLING	1400-1	1460-1½ 580 (600-1½)	1460-2 580 (600-2)

NDB/VOR MINIMA

S-13	1360-1 480 (500-1)	1360-¾ 480 (500-¾)	1460-1½ 580 (600-1½)	1360-1½ 480 (500-1½)
CIRCLING	1360-1 480 (500-1)	1380-1 500 (500-1)	1460-1½ 580 (600-1½)	1460-2 580 (600-2)

When control tower not in operation approach not authorized.

Knots	60	90	120	150	180
Min:Sec	3:54	2:36	1:57	1:34	1:18

FAF to MAP 3.9 NM

NDB RWY 13
29 DEC. 1977

PHILIP BILLARD MUNI
TOPEKA, KANSAS

PUBLISHED BY NOS, NOAA, TO IACC SPECIFICATIONS

39°04'N-95°37'W

ILS RWY 25R — PUEBLO MEMORIAL, PUEBLO, COLORADO

Amdt 3
AL-334 (FAA)

PUEBLO APP CON
120.1 290.5
PUEBLO TOWER
119.1 257.8
GND CON
121.9
ASR

COLORADO SPRINGS
112.5 COS Chan 72

(IAF) ORWAY

7000 to Heler Int
COS R-133 (1.5) and
LOC (6.5)

6500 NoPT to
LOM 255° (6.5)

HELER INT

PUEBLO
116.7 PUB Chan 114

(IAF) LOM
ARSENAL
373 °F

LOCALIZER 108.3

LOM
METRO
302 PU

DREXL INT
PUB 17 DME

PINON

HANKO
159°
(18.3)

7000 to Heler Int
10 DME Arc

7000 to Heler Int

FEEDER FACILITIES

ENROUTE FACILITIES

CAUTION: Tower 6320' 5.5 NM NW of airport.

MIN SAFE ALT 25 NM 7500

ELEV 4726   Rwy 17 ldg 6999'

TDZE 4656

MISSED APPROACH
Climb to 7000 direct Metro
LOM and hold.

Remain within 10 NM

CATEGORY	A	B	C	D	E
S-ILS 25R	4906-¾ 250 (200-¾)				
S-LOC 25R	5060-1 404 (400-1)	5060-1½ 404 (500-1½)	5640-3
CIRCLING	5340-1 614 (700-1)	5340-1¾ 614 (700-1¾)	5360-2¼ 634 (700-2¼)	914 (1000-3)

Procedure turn not authorized for Cat. E aircraft.

Knots	60	90	120	150	180
Min:Sec	5:36	3:44	2:48	2:14	1:52

FAF to MAP 5.6 NM

LIRL Rwy 12-30
MIRL Rwy 17-35
HIRL Rwy 7L-25R

GS 2.50°
TCH 50

ILS RWY 25R
30 JUNE 1977

PUEBLO MEMORIAL
PUEBLO, COLORADO

38°17'N – 104°30'W

PUBLISHED BY NOS NOAA TO IACC SPECIFICATIONS

Refer to the NDB Rwy 13 instrument approach procedure chart (page 310, top) for Philip Billard Municipal Airport when answering questions 4, 5, and 6.

4. A pilot is cleared for an NDB Rwy 13 approach at Philip Billard Municipal Airport. If the airplane has operable VOR and NDB receivers, what is the MDA and minimum required visibility for this approach? Assume: The aircraft used for this approach falls into the "Category A" approach category.
1. An MDA of 1400 feet MSL and a 3/4 statute mile visibility.
2. An MDA of 1400 feet MSL and a 1 nautical mile visibility.
3. An MDA of 1360 feet MSL and a 3/4 statute mile visibility.
4. An MDA of 1360 feet MSL and a 3/4 nautical mile visibility.

5. What would be the time to the MAP for an NDB Rwy 13 approach assuming final approach speed is 103 MPH and the reported wind is 130° at 30 knots?
1. 2 minutes and 36 seconds after passing the LOM.
2. 3 minutes and 54 seconds after passing the LOM.
3. 2 minutes and 36 seconds after passing GARFIELD Intersection.
4. 3 minutes and 54 seconds after passing GARFIELD Intersection.

6. Under what circumstances would an NDB Rwy 13 approach clearance to Philip Billard Municipal Airport be denied by ATC?
A. When the reported ceiling is below 500 feet.
B. When the control tower is not in operation.
C. When the Billard LOM is not in operation.
D. When the Topeka VORTAC is not in operation.
1. B and D.
2. A, B, C, and D.
3. C and D.
4. B and C.

7. The speeds listed in the Time and Speed Table on instrument approach procedure charts are:
1. Equivalent Airspeeds.
2. True Airspeeds.
3. Ground speeds.
4. Indicated Airspeeds (estimated).

Refer to the ILS Rwy 25R instrument approach procedure chart (page 310, bottom) for Pueblo Memorial Airport when answering questions 8, 9, and 10.

8. A pilot has been cleared to HELER Intersection via ORWAY Intersection. After passing ORWAY Intersection at 9,000 feet MSL, ATC clears the pilot for an ILS approach to Rwy 25R. The pilot should:
1. Descend to 7,000 feet MSL and remain at that altitude until intercepting the glide path.
2. Maintain 9,000 feet MSL until passing HELER Intersection, then descend to 6,500 feet MSL until intercepting the glide path.
3. Descend to 7,000 feet MSL and remain at that altitude until passing HELER Intersection, then descend to 6,500 feet MSL until intercepting the localizer course, and execute the ILS approach as depicted on the approach chart.
4. Descend to 6,500 feet MSL and remain at that altitude until passing HELER Intersection.

9. The minimum safe altitude shown on the approach chart provides the pilot with a clearance of:
1. 1,000 feet above all terrain within 25 statute miles of the airport.
2. 1,000 feet above all obstructions within 25 nautical miles of the LOM.
3. 1,000 feet above all terrain within 25 nautical miles of the Pueblo VORTAC.
4. 1,000 feet above all obstructions within 22 nautical miles of the airport.

10. What course of action is necessary when a pilot experiences a complete loss of the navigational receivers after being cleared for an ILS Rwy 25 approach at Pueblo? (Assume the reported visibility is 1 statute mile and the reported ceiling is 500 feet.)
1. Advise approach control that the aircraft is descending to VFR conditions on the runway heading.
2. Advise approach control of the problem and request a radar vector to an area of VFR conditions.
3. Advise approach control of the problem and request a PAR approach.
4. Advise approach control of the problem and request an ASR approach.

11. The rate of descent that should be maintained during an instrument approach is governed by:
1. Ground speed.
2. TAS.
3. EAS.
4. IAS.

12. What type of radar service is provided by the Stage III Terminal Radar Program?

1. Radar sequencing and separation service for participating VFR aircraft and all IFR aircraft operating within a TRSA.
2. Radar advisory service for all aircraft operating within a TCA.
3. Radar advisory and sequencing for VFR aircraft.
4. Radar vectoring to the runway only.

13. At airports equipped with a full-time Flight Service Station but a part-time tower, what tower function does the Flight Service Station acquire during hours when the control tower is not in operation?

1. The Flight Service Station will issue traffic advisories.
2. The Flight Service Station will clear all aircraft for takeoff and landing.
3. The Flight Service Station will issue all IFR clearances.
4. The Flight Service Station will acquire all tower functions.

14. Who is responsible for closing an IFR flight plan at an airport which only has a Flight Service Station?

1. Air Traffic Control.
2. Flight Service Station.
3. The pilot.
4. The nearest tower.

Refer to the ILS-A instrument approach procedure chart (below) for Fairfax Municipal Airport when answering questions 15, 16, and 17.

15. If a pilot is flying the 7 DME Arc into Fairfax, it can be determined from the chart that:

1. 2,600 feet is a recommended altitude.
2. 2,600 feet is a maximum altitude.
3. 2,600 feet is a minimum altitude.
4. 2,600 feet is a mandatory altitude.

16. What is the initial approach fix for an ILS-A approach when an aircraft is inbound on the 086° radial of the Kansas City VORTAC?

1. The MKC 086° radial at 25 DME.
2. Over the Mackenzie LOM.
3. Over the MKC VORTAC.
4. The MKC 086° radial at 7 DME.

17. What is the distance from the missed approach point to the runway on an ILS-A approach to Fairfax Municipal Airport?

1. .8 NM.

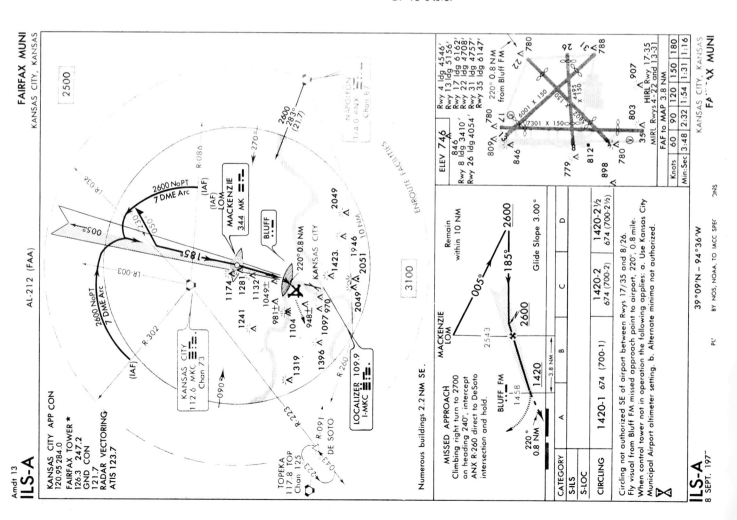

2. 1/2 NM.
3. 1 NM.
4. 1,420 feet.

18. Which of the following are correct statements in regard to missed approach points?

A. The missed approach point for an ILS approach is at the DH.
B. The missed approach point for a VOR approach is at the MDA.
C. The missed approach point of an NDB approach is determined by the timing from the final approach fix when the NDB facility is not on the airport.
D. DME is used to determine the missed approach point at certain airports.
  1. A, B, and D.
  2. A, B, C, and D.
  3. A, C, and D.
  4. B and C.

19. All turns during a No-Gyro approach are:
  1. 1/2 standard rate.
  2. Standard rate.
  3. At a 28° angle of bank.
  4. Standard rate except on final approach when they are to be 1/2 standard rate.

20. What is the correct landing priority for arriving aircraft at a tower-controlled airport?
  1. IFR flights, VFR flights in the traffic pattern, and then VFR flights entering the traffic pattern.
  2. "First come, first served" basis.
  3. IFR flights, then VFR flights.
  4. Gliders, airplanes, and then helicopters.

21. What may a pilot substitute for a middle marker during an ILS approach?
  1. A VORTAC radial.
  2. A compass locator or precision radar.
  3. DME.
  4. A compass locator or DME.

22. How are initial approach fixes identified on instrument approach procedure charts?
  1. By fixes labeled with an *IAF*.
  2. By fixes labeled with a ▲ .
  3. Any routes within the 10 NM ring are initial approach fixes.
  4. By fixes labeled with a *NoPT*.

23. From the list below, select the correct statements regarding timed approaches from a holding fix.

A. When cleared for the approach, pilots shall not execute a procedure turn.

B. A control tower must be in operation where the approaches are conducted.
C. Direct communications must be maintained between the pilot and the center/approach controller until the pilot is instructed to contact the tower.
D. A control tower does not need to be in operation where the approaches are conducted.
  1. A and B.
  2. A and D.
  3. A, B, and C.
  4. C and D.

24. The words Radar Vectoring listed on the plan view of the instrument approach chart mean:
  1. ASR, PAR and Radar Vectoring procedures are available.
  2. Only ASR vectoring is available.
  3. ASR and Radar Vectoring procedures are available.
  4. Radar Vectoring is available but radar instrument approach procedures are not available.

Refer to the LOC BC Rwy 26 instrument approach procedure chart (page 314, top) for Cedar Rapids Municipal Airport when answering questions 25, 26, and 27.

25. What is the distance from IOW VORTAC to QUAKER Intersection?
  1. 15 statute miles.
  2. 15 nautical miles.
  3. 25 nautical miles.
  4. 21.9 nautical miles.

26. What is the minimum authorized altitude which a pilot may descend to when cleared from CID VORTAC to QUAKER Intersection?
  1. 2,000 feet MSL.
  2. 1,240 feet MSL.
  3. 2,500 feet MSL.
  4. 2,650 feet MSL.

27. Select the correct statements in regard to the Cedar Rapids aerodrome sketch.

A. The elevation of Rwy 26 is 860 feet MSL.
B. Runway 13 has a downward gradient of 0.3%.
C. Runway 13 has a displaced threshold.
D. Runway 8 is equipped with VASI.
E. Runway 13 has 5,450 feet available for landing aircraft.
F. All runways are equipped with REIL.
  1. A, D, and E.
  2. C only.
  3. A, C, and E.
  4. A, C, E, and F.

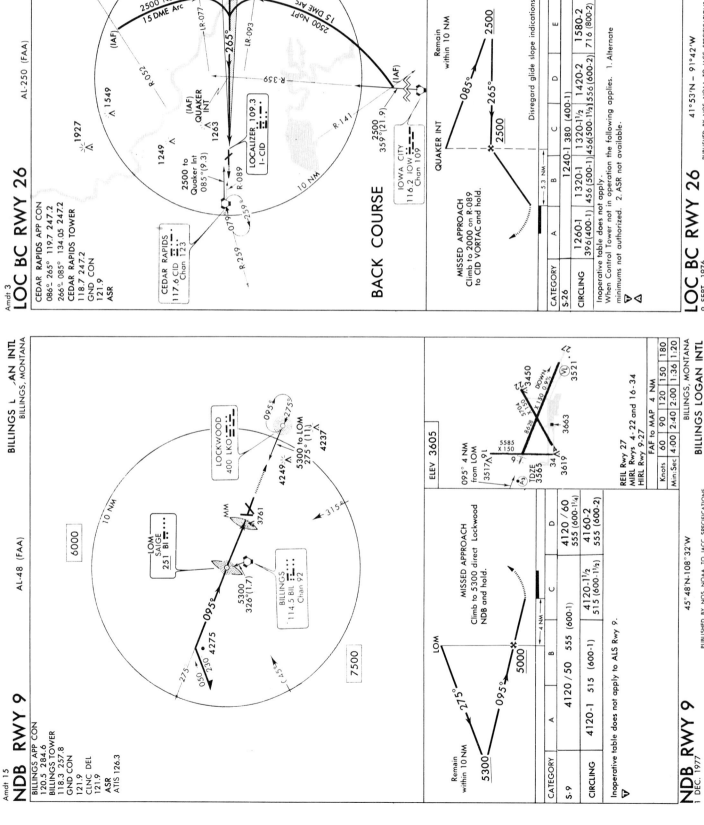

CEDAR RAPIDS MUNI
CEDAR RAPIDS, IOWA

Amdt 3
LOC BC RWY 26

AL-250 (FAA)

CEDAR RAPIDS APP CON
086° 265° 119.7 247.2
266°-085° 134.05 247.2
CEDAR RAPIDS TOWER
118.7 247.2
GND CON
121.9
ASR

LOCALIZER 109.3
I-CID

IOWA CITY
116.2 IOW
Chan 109

CEDAR RAPIDS
117.6 CID
Chan 123

BACK COURSE

MISSED APPROACH
Climb to 2000 on R-089
to CID VORTAC and hold.

Remain within 10 NM

Disregard glide slope indications.

CATEGORY	A	B	C	D	E
S-26	1240-1 380 (400-1)				
CIRCLING	1260-1 396(400-1)	1320-1 456(500-1)	1320-1½ 456(500-1½)	1420-2 556(600-2)	1580-2 716 (800-2)

Inoperative table does not apply.
When Control Tower not in operation the following applies. 1. Alternate
minimums not authorized. 2. ASR not available.

Trees to 900', 800' East and
500' South of threshold
Rwy 26.

ELEV 864 | Rwy 13 ldg 5110'

265° 5.3 NM
from Quaker Int

MIRL Rwy 13-31
HIRL Rwys 8-26
REIL Rwys 13 and 26

Knots	60	90	120	150	180
Min:Sec	5:18	3:32	2:39	2:07	1:46

FAF to MAP 5.3 NM

41°53'N – 91°42'W

LOC BC RWY 26
9 SEPT. 1976

CEDAR RAPIDS, IOWA
CEDAR RAPIDS MUNI

PUBLISHED BY NOS, NOAA, TO IACC SPECIFICATIONS

BILLINGS LOGAN INTL
BILLINGS, MONTANA

Amdt 15
NDB RWY 9

AL-48 (FAA)

BILLINGS APP CON
120.5 284.6
BILLINGS TOWER
118.3 257.8
GND CON
121.9
CLNC DEL
121.9
ASR
ATIS 126.3

LOCKWOOD
400 LKO

LOM
SAIGE 251 BI

BILLINGS
114.5 BIL
Chan 92

MISSED APPROACH
Climb to 5300 direct Lockwood
NDB and hold.

Remain within 10 NM

CATEGORY	A	B	C	D
S-9	4120-1 515 (600-1)	4120-1 515 (600-1)	4120-1½ 515 (600-1½)	4160-2 555 (600-2)
CIRCLING	4120/50 555 (600-1)	4120/50 555 (600-1)	4120-1½ 515 (600-1½)	4120/60 555 (600-1¼)

Inoperative table does not apply to ALS Rwy 9.

ELEV 3605

095° 4 NM
from LOM

REIL Rwy 27
MIRL Rwys 4-22 and 16-34
HIRL Rwy 9-27

Knots	60	90	120	150	180
Min:Sec	4:00	2:40	2:00	1:36	1:20

FAF to MAP 4 NM

45°48'N-108°32'W

NDB RWY 9
1 DEC. 1977

BILLINGS, MONTANA
BILLINGS LOGAN INTL

PUBLISHED BY NOS, NOAA, TO IACC SPECIFICATIONS

Refer to the NDB Rwy 9 instrument approach procedure chart (page 314, bottom) for Billings Logan International Airport when answering question 28.

28. What are the required weather minimums for a straight-in approach to Rwy 09 for an aircraft meeting approach Category A specifications?
1. A ceiling of 555 feet and an RVR of 5,000 feet.
2. A ceiling of 600 feet and 1 statute mile visibility.
3. A ceiling of 555 feet and an RVR of 6,000 feet.
4. An RVR of 5,000 feet only.

29. The Visual Descent Point is a defined point:

A. At which the missed approach should be initiated during a precision approach procedure.
B. At which a pilot should be able to see the runway environment on all approaches.
C. Which coincides with the DH on an ILS approach.
D. On the final approach course of a non-precision straight-in approach procedure from which normal descent from the MDA to the runway touchdown point may be commenced.
   1. A, B, and D.
   2. A and B.
   3. B, C, and D.
   4. D only.

30. Select the statements that correctly describe Profile Descent Procedures.

A. Profile Descent Procedures are primarily designed for turbojet aircraft and turboprop aircraft weighing more than 12,500 pounds.
B. Profile Descent Procedures enhance flight safety through a reduction of low altitude flight activity by high performance aircraft.
C. Profile Descent Procedures contribute to the reduction of fuel consumption by allowing aircraft to remain at higher altitudes for longer periods of time before final descent.
D. Profile Descent Procedures reduce the noise level for areas adjacent to airports.

1. A only.
2. A, B, C, and D.
3. B, C, and D.
4. C and D.

31. Aircraft approach categories are based upon what factors?
1. A value of 1.3 times the stalling speed in cruise configuration and maximum certificated gross landing weight.
2. A value of 1.3 times the stalling speed of the aircraft in the landing configuration.
3. Empty weight and stalling speed.
4. Zero fuel weight and 1.4 times the stalling speed of the aircraft in the landing configuration.

32. Which type of approach must be requested by the pilot before ATC will issue a clearance?
1. Contact.
2. Visual.
3. Landing.
4. ILS.

33. During an ILS approach, a pilot may descend below the DH when the pilot has the runway clearly in sight and:
1. Has passed the middle marker.
2. The glide slope needle is centered.
3. The aircraft is above the glide path.
4. Is in position to make a normal approach and land on the intended runway.

34. With reference to the Civil Radar Instrument Approach Minimums Chart Excerpt (below) what are the minimum descent altitude and visibility required for an ASR approach to Rwy 21 at Duluth International Airport? Assume: The aircraft used for this falls into the "Category A" approach category.
1. 1,627 feet MSL and an RVR of 2,400 feet.
2. 1,627 feet MSL and a 1/2 statute mile visibility.
3. 500 feet MSL and 1 statute mile visibility.
4. 1,820 feet MSL and 1 statute mile visibility.

CIVIL RADAR INSTRUMENT APPROACH MINIMUMS CHART

	RWY	CAT	DH/ MDA-VIS	HAT/ HAA	CEIL-VIS	CAT	DH/ MDA-VIS	HAT/ HAA	CEIL-VIS
PAR	9	ABCDE	1627/24	200	(200–½)				
ASR	27	ABC	1820/24	399	(400–½)	DE	1820/50	399	(400–1)
	9	ABC	1840/24	413	(500–½)	DE	1840/50	413	(500–1)
	3	ABC	1820–1	401	(500–1)	DE	1820–1½	401	(500–1½)
	21	ABC	1820–1	405	(500–1)	DE	1820–1½	405	(500–1½)
CIRCLING		AB	1880–1	452	(500–1)	C	1880–1½	452	(500–1½)
		D	1980–2	552	(600–2)	E	2360–3	932	(1000–3)

DULUTH INTL MN Amdt. 12, JUN 9, 1977   ELEV **1428**

▽ △

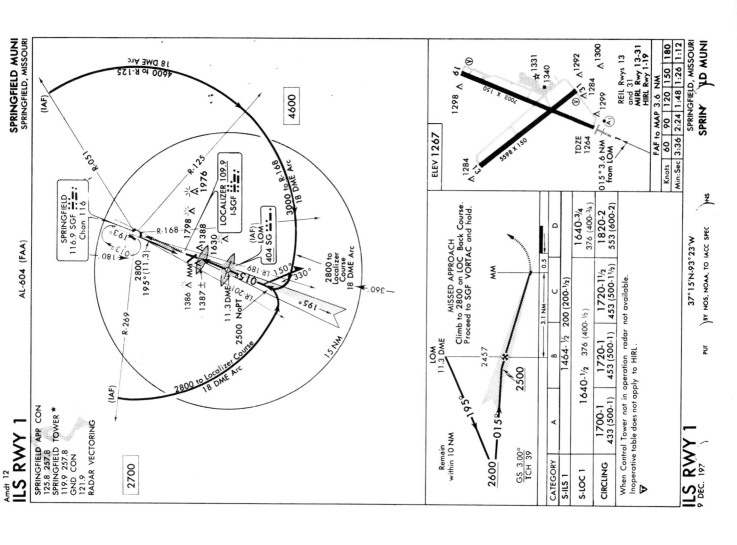

Instrument Approach Procedures (Charts)
INOPERATIVE COMPONENTS OR VISUAL AIDS TABLE
Civil Pilots see FAR 91.117(c)

Landing minimums published on instrument approach procedure charts are based upon full operation of all components and visual aids associated with the particular instrument approach chart being used. Higher minimums are required with inoperative components or visual aids as indicated below. If more than one component is inoperative, each minimum is raised to the highest minimum required by any single component that is inoperative. ILS glide slope inoperative minimums are published on instrument approach charts as localizer minimums. This table may be amended by notes on the approach chart. Such notes apply only to the particular approach category(ies) as stated. See legend page for description of components indicated below.

(1) ILS, MLS, and PAR.

Inoperative Component or Aid	Approach Category	Increase DH	Increase Visibility
MM*	ABC	50 feet	None
MM*	D	50 feet	¼ mile
ALSF 1 & 2, MALSR, & SSALR	ABCD	None	¼ mile

*Not applicable to PAR

(2) ILS with visibility minimum of 1,800 or 2,000 RVR.

Inoperative Component or Aid	Approach Category	Increase DH	Increase Visibility
MM	ABC	50 feet	To 2400 RVR
MM	D	50 feet	To 4000 RVR
ALSF 1 & 2, MALSR, & SSALR	ABCD	None	To 4000 RVR
TDZL, RCLS	ABCD	None	To 2400 RVR
RVR	ABCD	None	To ½ mile

(3) VOR, VOR/DME, VORTAC, VOR (TAC), VOR/DME (TAC), LOC, LOC/DME, LDA, LDA/DME, SDF, SDF/DME, RNAV, and ASR

Inoperative Visual Aid	Approach Category	Increase MDA	Increase Visibility
ALSF 1 & 2, MALSR, & SSALR	ABCD	None	½ mile
SSALS, MALS & ODALS	ABC	None	¼ mile

(4) NDB

Inoperative Visual Aid	Approach Category	Increase MDA	Increase Visibility
ALSF 1 & 2, MALSR, & SSALR	C	None	½ mile
	ABD	None	¼ mile
MALS, SSALS, ODALS	ABC	None	¼ mile

14 APRIL 1977

PUBLISHED BY NOS, NOAA, TO IACC SPECIFICATIONS

Refer to the ILS Rwy 1 instrument approach procedure chart (page 316, top) for Springfield Municipal Airport when answering questions 35, 36, 37, and 38.

35. At what altitude and location should a pilot conducting a localizer approach to Rwy 1 execute a missed approach if the aircraft is maintaining a ground speed of 120 knots?
   1. At 1,464 feet MSL over the middle marker.
   2. At 1,700 feet MSL over the approach end of the runway.
   3. At 1,464 feet MSL over the approach end of the runway.
   4. At 1,640 feet MSL and 1 minute and 48 seconds flying time from the outer marker.

36. On which runway(s) are VASI lights located?
   1. Rwy 19 and Rwy 31.
   2. Rwy 13.
   3. Rwy 01.
   4. Rwy 16.

37. TCH 39, as depicted on the profile view of the Springfield Approach Procedure Chart, represents:
   1. A touchdown point of 390 feet from the end of the runway.
   2. A threshold crossing height of 39 feet.
   3. A TACAN crossing height of 3,900 feet.
   4. A touchdown circling height of 390 feet.

38. At what point during the instrument approach procedure will the glide slope be intercepted?
   1. At 3.6 NMs from the end of the runway.
   2. After passing the outer marker.
   3. Over the outer marker.
   4. Prior to the outer marker.

39. Select the correct response regarding Visual Approaches.

A. A pilot must request a Visual Approach.
B. On a Visual Approach, when the pilot is instructed to contact the tower, radar service is automatically terminated.
C. ATC may authorize a Visual Approach only if VFR weather conditions can be maintained.
D. Authorization to conduct a Visual Approach constitutes the cancellation of the IFR flight plan.
   1. A, B, and C.
   2. A and D.
   3. B, C, and D.
   4. B and C.

40. What is the minimum visibility required for a Contact Approach?
   1. Three statute miles flight visibility.
   2. One statute mile ground visibility.
   3. One statute mile flight or ground visibility.
   4. Three statute miles flight or ground visibility.

41. What course of action should a pilot follow when the MDA is reached during a VOR approach?
   1. Maintain the MDA to the missed approach point.
   2. Commence a missed approach in accordance with the instrument approach procedure chart.
   3. Start timing to the missed approach point.
   4. Reduce power to the proper descent power setting and lower the landing gear.

42. With reference to the Inoperative Components or Visual Aids Table (page 316, bottom), what should the DH and visibility be increased to with an inoperative middle marker and an ALSF-1 system for an ILS approach with a DH of 1,150 feet MSL and an RVR of 2,400 feet? (Assume a Category A aircraft is used for this approach.)
   1. A DH of 1,200 feet MSL and an RVR of 2,400 feet.
   2. A DH of 1,200 feet MSL and a visibility of 3/4 statute mile.
   3. A DH of 1,200 feet MSL and a visibility of one statute mile.
   4. A DH of 1,250 feet MSL and a visibility of 3/4 statute mile.

43. Referring to the Crowe One Arrival STAR (page 318, top), the correct route for the Hanksville transition is:
   1. From over HANKSVILLE VORTAC via Hanksville R-213, GFS R-026 and LAS R-075/ILS localizer to CROWE DME fix.
   2. From over HANKSVILLE VORTAC via Hanksville R-213 BLD R-043, GFS R-026 and LAS R-075/ILS localizer to CROWE DME fix with radar vectors.
   3. From over HANKSVILLE VORTAC via Hanksville R-213, BLD R-043, GFS R-026 and LAS R-075/ILS localizer to CROWE DME fix LAS ILS localizer to EAGLE Intersection.
   4. From over HANKSVILLE VORTAC via Hanksville R-213, BLD R-043, LAS R-075/ILS localizer to CROWE DME fix.

CROWE ONE ARRIVAL (CROWE.CROWE 1)

McCARRAN INTERNATIONAL
LAS VEGAS, NEVADA

LAS VEGAS APP CON
NORTH 121.1 353.6
WEST, SOUTH 125.9 353.6
NORTHEAST, EAST 119.4 353.6
ATIS 125.6

HANKSVILLE
H-2, L-5

BRYCE
CANYON
H-2, L-5

MILFORD
H-2, L-5

213° (81)
24000

208° (81)
24000

177° (102)
24000

WOLF

223° (61)

108 DME

TUBA CITY
113.5 TBC 82

65 R-254

SUPAI

R-254
254° (50)
16500

PEACH SPRINGS
H-2, L-5

R-043

176° 205°

80
14500

HIGGS

103

208°
12000

255° 10000

PIERCE

74

MILL

290° (47)
9000

GOFFS
114.4 GFS 91

R-026

CROWE
7300

49

17

39

255° (22)
6400

EAGLE

LAS VEGAS
116.9 LAS 116

LOCALIZER
110.3 I-LAS

R-075

R-016

BOULDER CITY
116.7 BLD 114

NOTE: Expect to cross Crowe DME
fix at or below 16000'.

NOTE: Chart not to scale

BRYCE CANYON TRANSITION (BCE.CROWE1): From over BRYCE CANYON VORTAC
via BRYCE CANYON R-208, GFS R-026 and LAS R-075/ILS Localizer to CROWE DME
fix . . . . .
HANKSVILLE TRANSITION (HVE.CROWE1): From over HANKSVILLE VORTAC via
HANKSVILLE R-213, BLD R-043, GFS R-043 and LAS R-075/ILS Localizer to CROWE DME
fix . . . . .
MILFORD TRANSITION (MLF.CROWE1): From over MILFORD VORTAC via MILFORD
R-177, GFS R-026 and LAS R-075/ILS Localizer to CROWE DME fix . . . . .
PEACH SPRINGS TRANSITION (PGS.CROWE1): From over PEACH SPRINGS VORTAC
via PEACH SPRINGS R-290 to CROWE DME fix . . . . .
SUPAI TRANSITION (SUPAI.CROWE1): From over SUPAI DME fix via TBC R-254 and
LAS R-075/ILS Localizer to CROWE DME fix . . . . .
. . . From CROWE DME fix LAS ILS Localizer to EAGLE INT.
Runways 1, 7, and 19: From EAGLE INT except vectors to final approach course to
McCarran Airport.
Runway 25: From EAGLE INT expect ILS approach procedure to McCarran Airport.

CROWE ONE ARRIVAL (CROWE.CROWE 1)

LAS VEGAS, NEVADA
McCARRAN INTERNATIONAL

Amdt 2
NDB RWY 36

SEDALIA MEMORIAL
SEDALIA, MISSOURI

AL-5584 (FAA)

KANSAS CITY CENTER
119.65 285.6

ENROUTE FACILITIES

BOONVILLE
(23.8)
2500

2500
320°
(36.4)

ODESSA

10 NM

R 073

1271
1279
1166
1390

SEDALIA
DMO
281

350°

WRAYS INT

170°

125°
305°

170°

2500
320°
(35.7)
ROACH

WHITEMAN
109.0 SZL

(18.1)
2500

AUGIE

MIN SAFE ALT 25 NM 3000

ELEV 909

Use Whiteman AFB, Missouri altimeter setting.
When not available use Columbia, Missouri altimeter setting
and the following applies: 1. All MDAs increase 140 feet.
2. Increase visibilities S-36 Single Minima Cats. B, C and D and
circling Cat. B ¼ mile; Dual Minima S-36 Cats C and D ¼ mile.

MISSED APPROACH
Climbing right turn to 2500,
return to DMO NDB and hold.

18

5000 X 100

23

TDZE
909

36

980
3600 x 50

350° to
DMO NDB

MIRL Rwys 5-23 and 18-36

Knots	60	90	120	150	180
Min:Sec					

NDB

170°

WRAYS INT

350°

1540

Remain
within 10 NM

2500

*1680 when using
Columbia, Missouri
altimeter setting.

3.6 NM

CATEGORY	A	B	C	D
S-36	1540-1 631 (700-1)	1540-1 631 (700-1)	1540-1¼ 631 (700-1¼)	1540-1½ 631 (700-1½)
CIRCLING	1540-1 631 (700-1)		1540-1½ 631 (700-1½)	1540-2 631 (700-2)

NDB/VOR MINIMA

	1360-1 451 (500-1)			
S-36				
CIRCLING	1360-1 451 (500-1)	1360-1½ 451 (500-1½)	1360-2 551 (600-2)	

NA

38°42'N – 93°11'W

D BY NOS, NOAA. TO IACC SPEC

ONS

NDB RWY 36
9 SEPT. 1

SEDALIA, MISSOURI
SEDALIA MEMORIAL

44. Which of the following statements are correct concerning missed approaches?

A. Pilots should comply with published missed approach instructions unless alternate missed approach instructions are issued by ATC.

B. If a pilot elects to initiate a missed approach prior to reaching the DH, he may execute a turning maneuver immediately.

C. If communication is lost for more than 5 seconds on final of a PAR approach, pilots should execute a missed approach if unable to take over visually.

D. If communication is lost for more than 15 seconds on final of an ASR approach, pilots should execute a missed approach if unable to take over visually.

   1. All of the above.
   2. B and C.
   3. A, C, and D.
   4. A and B.

Refer to the NDB Rwy 36 instrument approach procedure chart (page 318, bottom) for Sedalia Memorial Municipal Airport when answering questions 45, 46, and 47.

45. After landing at Sedalia, Missouri, a pilot realized he had neglected to close his IFR flight plan while airborne. The pilot may close the flight plan by:

   1. Transmitting and receiving on 119.65 MHz to Kansas City Radio.
   2. Telephoning the nearest FSS or ATC facility.
   3. Transmitting to Kansas City Center on 119.65 MHz and receiving on the Sedalia NDB.
   4. Transmitting to Kansas City Radio on 122.1 and receiving on the Sedalia NDB.

46. At what point should a missed approach be executed if a pilot fails to see the runway environment at the appropriate time during the instrument approach procedure?

   1. At the first indication of station passage.
   2. After the procedure turn inbound.
   3. Two minutes and twenty-four seconds after passing WRAYS Intersection.
   4. Over WRAYS Intersection.

47. What is the MDA for a straight-in approach, assuming the Columbia altimeter setting is used and WRAYS intersection can be determined during the approach procedure?

   1. 1,680 feet MSL.
   2. 1,540 feet MSL.
   3. 631 feet AGL.
   4. 1,500 feet MSL.

48. Which of the following components and/or visual aids, when inoperative, increase the DH during an ILS approach procedure?

A. Middle Marker.
B. Outer Marker.
C. ODALS.
D. ALSF-1.
E. SSALR.
F. ALS.
G. REIL/RAIL.
   1. A only.
   2. A and B.
   3. B, C, D, E, F, and G.
   4. A, B, and F.

49. Which of the following statements pertaining to the Contact Approach are true?

A. The Contact Approach provides both IFR and special VFR aircraft separation.

B. The Contact Approach is only used when no instrument approach procedure is published.

C. The pilot assumes responsibility for obstruction clearance.

D. ATC may assign a Contact Approach without the pilot requesting the approach.

   1. A and B.
   2. B, C, and D.
   3. A, B, and C.
   4. A and C.

50. Select the correct statements concerning Standard Terminal Arrival Routes.

A. STARs are coded Air Traffic Control IFR arrival routes.

B. The purpose of a STAR chart is to simplify clearance delivery procedures.

C. Pilots of IFR civil aircraft may be issued a clearance containing a STAR whenever ATC deems it appropriate.

D. Use of STAR charts requires pilot possession of at least the approved textual description.

E. Pilot acceptance of a STAR is mandatory.

   1. A, B, and D.
   2. A, B, C, and D.
   3. A, C, and E.
   4. C and D.

51. Which statement(s) below is (are) correct regarding ASR approaches?

A. The pilot will be advised of the location of the missed approach point and the aircraft's position each mile on the final approach.

B. *If requested* by the pilot, recommended altitudes will be issued at each mile on final approach after commencing descent.

C. Navigational guidance will generally be provided until the aircraft reaches the MDA.

D. Both altitude and distance information is provided during ASR approaches.

    1. A, C, and D.
    2. A, B, and C.
    3. C only.
    4. D only.

52. What ceiling and visibility requirements must be met before a radar equipped approach control facility can vector an aircraft for a Visual Approach if the arrival airport is not served by a control tower but has weather reporting services?

    1. The reported ceiling at the airport of intended landing must be 500 feet or more above the minimum vectoring altitude or the visibility must be 3 miles or more.

    2. The reported ceiling at the airport of intended landing must be 500 feet or more above the minimum vectoring altitude and the visibility must be 3 miles or more.

    3. The reported ceiling at the airport of intended landing must be at least 1,000 feet AGL and the visibility must be 3 miles or more.

    4. The reported ceiling at the airport of intended landing must be at least 500 feet AGL and the visibility must be at least 1 mile.

53. Select the correct statements in regard to Contact and Visual Approaches.

A. Visual Approaches are only conducted in a radar environment.

B. The Contact Approach is specifically designed for military aircraft.

C. Contact Approaches are conducted during VFR and IFR conditions in radar and non-radar environments.

D. A Visual Approach clearance cannot be issued unless the arrival airport has a prescribed instrument approach procedure.

    1. A, C, and D.
    2. A, B, and D.
    3. A and C.
    4. C only.

54. How should a pilot become established on the prescribed missed approach procedure course if he loses visual contact with the airport during a circling approach?

    1. Execute a climbing turn in the direction of the landing runway.

    2. Execute a climbing turn away from the landing runway.

    3. Climb to an altitude of 2,000 feet AGL.

    4. Continue the prescribed approach procedure maintaining an altitude of 200 feet above circling minimums.

Refer to the VOR Rwy 31 instrument approach procedure chart (page 321) for Sioux City Municipal Airport when answering questions 55, 56, 57, and 58.

55. Assume a pilot has executed a missed approach procedure and has entered the depicted holding pattern. After receiving another VOR Rwy 25 approach clearance, the pilot should:

    1. Proceed outbound on the 132° radial of the SUX VOR, make a procedure turn, and complete the approach as depicted.

    2. Fly outbound on the 037° radial to the 10 DME Arc and complete the approach as depicted.

    3. Start the VOR approach when on the inbound leg of the holding pattern on a heading of 312°.

    4. Start the VOR approach when over the VOR inbound.

56. What is the HAA for a Category D aircraft making a VOR Rwy 31 approach at Sioux City Municipal Airport?

    1. 562 feet AGL.
    2. 345 feet MSL.
    3. 240 feet.
    4. 1,440 feet MSL.

57. Assume an aircraft is 22 NMs out on the 266° radial of the SUX VORTAC at an altitude of 5,000 feet MSL and is cleared for a VOR Rwy 31 approach. The pilot should descend to:

    1. 3,100 feet MSL, proceed directly to the VORTAC, track outbound on the 132° radial while descending to 2,900 feet, and complete the approach using a procedure turn.

    2. 4,400 feet MSL and fly the 20 DME Arc approach procedure.

    3. 2,900 feet MSL and fly the 20 DME Arc approach procedure.

    4. 4,400 feet MSL, proceed directly to the VORTAC until within 15 NMs of the VORTAC, then descend to 2,900 feet MSL and complete the approach procedure using a procedure turn.

58. Determine the MDA and MAP for an aircraft that has been cleared for a VOR Rwy 31 approach and circle to land on Runway 13 assuming the following conditions:

Ceiling—measured 700 feet overcast
Visibility—one statute mile
Wind—130° at 16 knots
Aircraft approach speed—102 MPH

1. 1,620 feet MSL and 2 minutes 26 seconds from the VOR.

2. 1,440 feet MSL and 1 minute 50 seconds from the VORTAC.

3. 1,620 feet MSL and 2 minutes 6 seconds from the VORTAC.

4. 1,620 feet MSL and 1 minute 50 seconds from the VORTAC.

59. While conducting an ILS approach, what would be the appropriate action if the glide slope warning flag appears after the aircraft has passed over the outer marker inbound?

1. Continue the approach maintaining the same rate of descent until the DH is reached.

2. Immediately initiate a missed approach.

3. Attempt to re-establish a glide slope indication

by readjusting the NAV receiver frequency selector.

4. Continue the approach descending to the MDA for the localizer approach procedure.

60. Select the correct statement regarding missed approaches.

1. A pilot should *only* initiate a missed approach after arriving at the MDA or DH.

2. If conditions become unsafe at *any* time during an instrument approach a missed approach should be executed.

3. If a missed approach is initiated prior to the MAP, a turning maneuver can be executed at the time the missed approach is initiated.

4. The side-step maneuver is often used in place of the missed approach procedure.

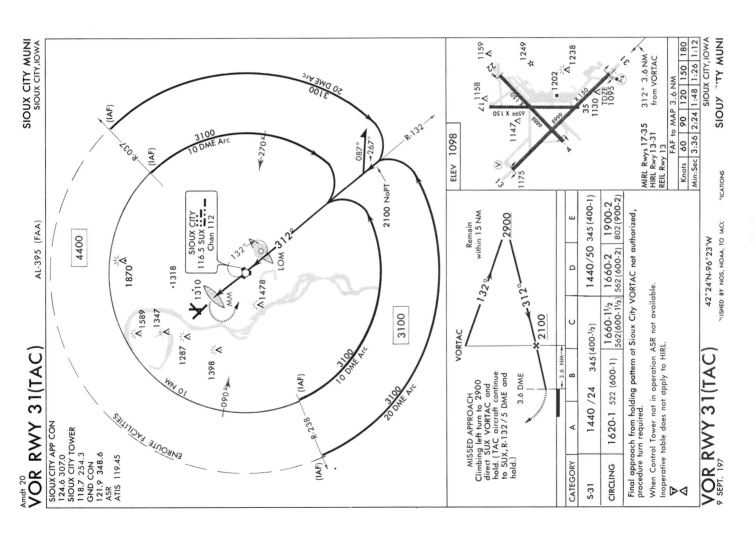

ALBUQUERQUE APP CON
124.4 301.5
ATIS 118.0

ALBUQUERQUE
113.2 ABQ 79

CHILI

270° (73)

R-090

265° (100)

TEXICO
H-2, L-4

270°

27

270°

R-024

SOCORRO
116.8 ONM 115

NOTE: Chart not to scale

From over TEXICO VORTAC via TEXICO R-265 and ALBUQUERQUE R-090 to CHILI DME Fix. Depart CHILI DME Fix heading 270° for vector to final approach.

AERODROME NAME	TAKE-OFF MINIMUMS

WEST CENTRAL UNITED STATES
(Continued from page 8)

MONTICELLO MUNI .... Rwy 31, 300-1
Monticello, Iowa

MONTROSE COUNTY ...... Rwys 2, 12, 20, 300-1
Montrose, Colorado
IFR DEPARTURE PROCEDURE: Rwy 30, NW-bound V-484S: Climb on course to GJT VORTAC. All other departures: climb on MTJ R-295 to 7000. Climbing right turn back to MTJ VOR, to depart at airway MEA.

NATRONA COUNTY INTL ...... Rwy 7, ½ mile*
Casper, Wyoming
SE bound V-19 and V-85 and S bound V26/85 W climb direct CPR VORTAC before proceeding on course, or comply with published Casper SID's.
*(FAR 135)

NEODESHA MUNI
Neodesha, Kansas
All Runways: When weather is below 600-1, W bound departures maintain runway heading to 1200 before turning.

NEOSHO MEMORIAL
Neosho, Missouri
IFR DEPARTURE PROCEDURE: Rwy 18, climb runway heading to 1500 before turning eastbound.

NEW ULM MUNI .... Rwy 13, 400-1
New Ulm, Minnesota
Rwy 13, make immediate right turn to 1900 on 220° bearing from ULM NDB before turning E. Restriction due to 1399 tower 1.2 NM SE.

OLIVIA MUNI .... Rwy 12, 200-1
Olivia, Minnesota

ORANGE CITY MUNI .... Rwy 34, 200-1
Orange City, Iowa

ORR PUBLIC .... Rwy 13, 500-1
Orr, Minnesota

OTTUMWA INDUSTRIAL .... Rwy 31, ½ mile*
Ottumwa, Iowa
*(FAR 135)

PHILLIPSBURG MUNI .... Rwy 3, 500-1
Phillipsburg, Kansas
Rwys 13, 21, 31: When planned route of flight is N or NE-bound, climb runway heading to 2400 before turning.

AERODROME NAME	TAKE-OFF MINIMUMS

PIERRE MUNI .... Rwy 31, ½ mile*
Pierre, South Dakota
*(FAR 135)

PIPESTONE MUNI
Pipestone, Minnesota
IFR DEPARTURE PROCEDURE: Rwys 9, 27, 36, when weather is below 200-1 climb runway heading to 1900 before turning.

POCAHONTAS MUNI .... Rwy 18, 200-1
Pocahontas, Iowa
Rwys 11, 29, 36, climb to 2000 on runway heading before turning S bound.

PUEBLO MEMORIAL .... Rwy 7L, ½ mile*
Pueblo, Colorado   Rwy 25R, ¾ mile*
Climb direct to PUB VORTAC, continue climb on airways to assigned altitude; except SW-bound between R-200 CW to R-245 climb in holding pattern (244° inbound, right turns) to depart at 9000; NW-bound R-309 depart at 5700.
*(FAR 135)

RAPID CITY REGIONAL .... Rwy 32, ½ mile*
Rapid City, South Dakota
Rwys 1, 14, 19, 32 departing SW on V-26 climb to 4200 runway heading before proceeding on course.
*(FAR 135)

RAWDON FIELD
Wichita, Kansas
All runways: Plan IFR departure to avoid 1814 Tower 1.8 NM NW.

RAWLINS MUNI
Rawlins, Wyoming
Rwy 22 turn left; Rwy 29 turn right; climb direct SIR NDB before proceeding on course.

RED OAK MUNI
Red Oak, Iowa
Rwys 13, 17, 22 when weather is below 500-1 climb runway heading to 1500 before proceeding on course.

RENNER FIELD (GOODLAND MUNI) .Rwy 17, 900-1
Goodland, Kansas
IFR DEPARTURE PROCEDURE: All runways, when weather is below 1000-2, maintain runway heading until reaching 4500 before turning on course.

(Continued on page 10)

61. When flying the Texico One Arrival, where is the VOR changeover point between TEXICO VOR-TAC and ALBUQUERQUE VORTAC? Refer to the Texico One Arrival STAR (page 322, top).

    1. At CHILI Intersection.

    2. 27 DME miles from CHILI Intersection.

    3. 73 miles from TEXICO VORTAC.

    4. 100 miles from TEXICO VORTAC.

62. What conditions and/or procedures apply for takeoff and departure in a single engine aircraft operating under FAR Part 91 on an IFR flight from Red Oak Municipal and departing on Runway 17? Refer to the IFR takeoff minimums and departure procedures excerpt (page 322, bottom).

    1. There are no minimum ceiling and visibility requirements; however, if conditions are less than 500-1, a climb (on the runway heading) must be made to 1,500 feet before proceeding on course.

    2. The reported visibility must be at least one statute mile. Ceiling minimums are not applicable.

    3. The reported visibility must be at least one statute mile and the ceiling must be at least 500 feet.

    4. The reported ceiling must be at least 500 feet. Visibility minimums are not applicable.

63. Which report should a pilot make without request (to ATC) when conducting an IFR operation in controlled airspace? (Assume the aircraft is in radar contact.)

    1. When departing the final approach fix inbound on final approach.

    2. While on final approach.

    3. When an approach has been missed.

    4. When the runway is in sight at the completion of an instrument approach.

10.

Emergency Procedures and Good Operating Practices for Instrument Pilots

10.1 This chapter does not attempt to catalog all possible in-flight emergencies. Rather, it concentrates specifically upon emergency procedures and good operating practices that are of particular interest to the instrument pilot.

EMERGENCY PROCEDURES

10.2 If an emergency should arise in which a pilot needs assistance, the pilot should:

1. Contact a controlling agency and indicate the nature of the distress and the intentions of the pilot. If unable to establish contact on an assigned frequency, the pilot should use an emergency frequency (121.5 MHz or 243.0 MHz).

2. Set the transponder to Mode A/3, Code 7700 if unable to establish voice communications with any air traffic control facility.

3. Actuate the locator beacon (if the plane is so equipped) if a crash is imminent.

Radio Communications Failure

10.3 Radio communications failure is a rare occurrence. However, when such a failure does occur, it may precipitate an emergency which affects the safety of everyone using the airspace. Only the pilot can determine if failure of his two-way radio communications constitutes an emergency. To determine if a complete communication failure exists, a pilot should listen to all of the aircraft's operational radio receivers, since Air Traffic Control, Flight Service Stations, and control towers have the capability of transmitting on most NAVAIDs. Each pilot who is experiencing two-way communications failure when operating under IFR rules shall proceed as follows:

VFR Conditions: A pilot should land as soon as practicable (not necessarily as soon as possible) if the flight is conducted in VFR conditions or encounters VFR weather conditions, and notify ATC.

IFR Conditions: If the failure occurs in IFR conditions, each pilot shall continue the flight according to the following procedures (unless, of course, the pilot encounters VFR conditions):

1. *Route*—A pilot should adhere to the route assigned in the last ATC clearance. In the absence of an assigned route, the pilot should continue by the route that ATC has advised may be expected in a further clearance. If ATC has not assigned a further clearance, the pilot should continue by the route filed in the flight plan. In addition, if being radar vectored, the pilot should continue by the direct route from the point of radio failure to the fix, route, or airway specified in the vector clearance.

2. *Altitude*—A pilot should maintain the highest of the following altitudes or flight levels for the route segment being flown:

A. The altitude or flight level assigned in the last ATC clearance received;

B. The minimum altitude (or flight level, if appropriate) for IFR operations; *or*

C. The altitude or flight level the pilot has been advised to expect in a further clearance. (Figure 10–1)

3. *Departing the Holding Fix*—After holding, a pilot should leave the holding fix at the expect-further-clearance time (EFC), or if an expected approach clearance time (EAC) has been received, the departure from the holding fix

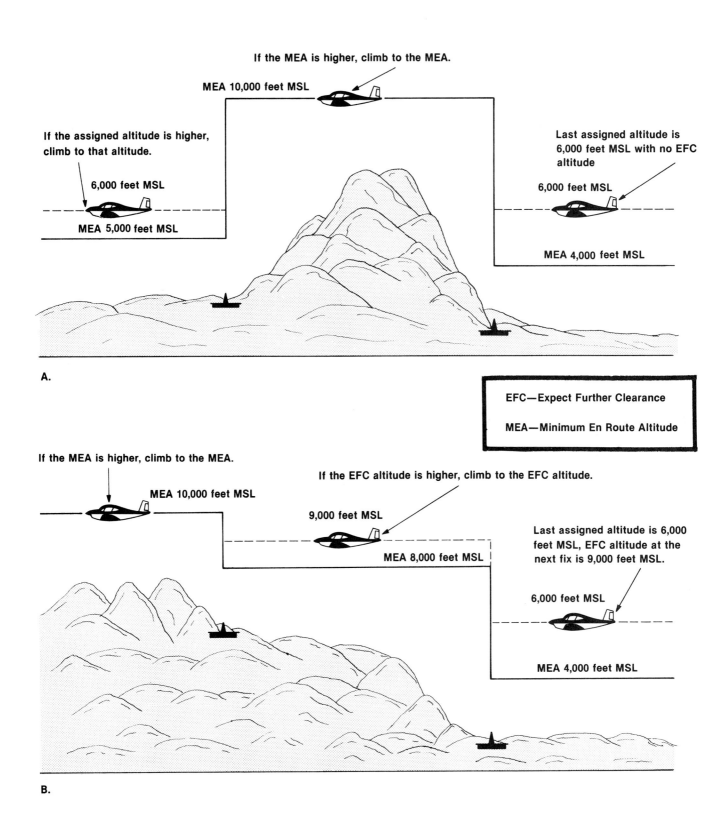

If the MEA is higher, climb to the MEA.

MEA 10,000 feet MSL

If the assigned altitude is higher, climb to that altitude.

6,000 feet MSL

MEA 5,000 feet MSL

Last assigned altitude is 6,000 feet MSL with no EFC altitude

6,000 feet MSL

MEA 4,000 feet MSL

A.

EFC—Expect Further Clearance

MEA—Minimum En Route Altitude

If the MEA is higher, climb to the MEA.

MEA 10,000 feet MSL

If the EFC altitude is higher, climb to the EFC altitude.

9,000 feet MSL

MEA 8,000 feet MSL

Last assigned altitude is 6,000 feet MSL, EFC altitude at the next fix is 9,000 feet MSL.

6,000 feet MSL

MEA 4,000 feet MSL

B.

Figure 10-1 A-C. Examples of Proper Altitudes for Aircraft Experiencing Radio Failure During IFR Conditions

Special Note: All climbs and descents should be initiated over a fix, except when a minimum crossing altitude applies.

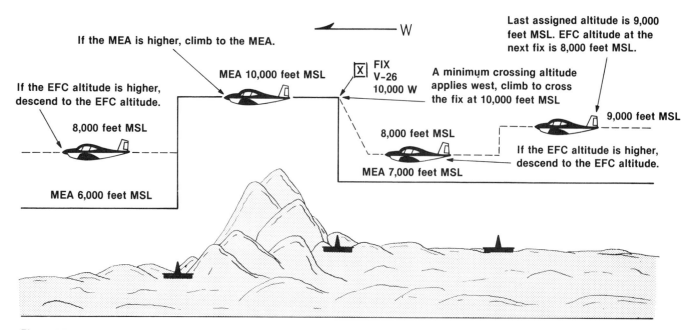

Figure 10-1c

should be timed to arrive over the fix from which the approach begins as close as possible to the expected approach clearance time. [*Note:* The EAC is issued when the aircraft clearance limit *is* designated as the initial, intermediate, or final approach fix for the instrument approach procedure in use. The EFC is issued when an aircraft's clearance limit is a fix that *is not* designated as part of the instrument approach procedure to be expected.] If holding instructions have not been received and the aircraft is ahead of its ETA, the pilot is expected to hold at the fix from which the approach begins. If more than one approach fix is available, it is the pilot's choice because ATC clears all the airspace of other known IFR traffic for 30 minutes.

4. *Approach/Descent*—A pilot should begin descent from the en route altitude or flight level upon reaching the fix from which the approach begins, but not before:

A. The expect approach clearance time (if received), *or*

B. In absence of an expect approach clearance time, the estimated time of arrival as shown on the flight plan as amended with ATC.

If holding were necessary at the facility to be used for the approach at the destination airport, holding descent to the initial approach altitude shall be accomplished in a holding pattern in accordance with the pattern depicted on the approach chart. If no holding pattern is depicted, holding and descent will be accomplished in a holding pattern on the side of the final approach course on which the procedure turn is prescribed.

Radio Failure Transponder Code

10.4 Should a pilot of an aircraft equipped with a coded radar beacon transponder experience a loss of two-way radio capability, the pilot should:

1. Adjust the transponder to reply on Mode A/3, Code 7700 for a period of one minute.

2. After one minute change to Code 7600 and remain on 7600 for a period of 15 minutes or the remainder of the flight, whichever occurs first.

3. Repeat Steps 1 and 2 as practicable. Since some ATC radar facilities do not yet have an automatic alarm for Code 7600, the pilot of the distressed aircraft should first set the transponder to reply on Mode A/3, Code 7700 to increase the probability of early detection of radio failure.

Other Emergency Situations

10.5 Not every emergency situation can be specifically spelled out for every pilot flying every different type of aircraft. Sound judgment and reasoning must prevail during emergency situations. For example, if a single-engine aircraft's generator completely fails during an IFR flight, the appropriate pilot action would be to notify ATC immediately, request an approach at the closest suitable airport, and turn off all electrical equipment not essential to the flight. In this situation, the pilot certainly would not attempt to fly to the destination airport unless, of course, it happened to be the closest suitable airport. Remember, there are few substitutes for good common sense.

Responsibility and Authority of the Pilot in Command

10.6 FAR 91.3 states that the pilot in command of an aircraft is directly responsible for, and is the final authority in, the operation of that aircraft. In an emergency requiring immediate action, the pilot in command may deviate from any general rule or general, visual, or instrument flight rule as provided for in FAR Part 91 to the extent required to meet that emergency. Each pilot in command who deviates from any of these rules *shall at the request of the Administrator* send a written report of that deviation to the Administrator. (Note: In addition, a pilot who deviates from an ATC clearance shall notify ATC of the deviation as soon as possible and obtain an amended clearance if necessary.)

Priority Handling

10.7 A pilot can declare an emergency even though a regulation has not been violated. Any pilot declaring an emergency can be assured of receiving priority handling. FAR 91.75d states that any time priority handling has been provided (especially if it delays other aircraft), the chief of that ATC facility administering the priority handling *may* require the pilot of the distressed aircraft to submit a detailed report within 48 hours.

Operation Under IFR in Controlled Airspace: Malfunction Reports (FAR 91.129)

10.8 The pilot in command of each aircraft operated in controlled airspace under IFR shall report immediately to ATC any of the following malfunctions of equipment occurring in flight:

1. Loss of VOR, TACAN, ADF, or low frequency navigation receiver capability.
2. Complete or partial loss of ILS receiver capability.
3. Impairment of air/ground communications capability.

In each of the required malfunction reports, the pilot in command shall include:

1. Aircraft identification.
2. Equipment affected.
3. Degree to which the capability of the pilot to operate under IFR in the ATC system is impaired.
4. Nature and extent of assistance desired from ATC.

VHF/UHF Direction Finding Steer

10.9 A Direction Finder (DF) is a ground-based radio receiver equipped with a direction-sensing antenna used to determine bearings of radio transmitters. A DF service can be provided on VHF and UHF frequencies by most control towers and Flight Service Stations. Headings are provided to aircraft (equipped with the appropriate transmitting and receiving equipment) by these facilities with DF equipment. These headings, if followed, will lead aircraft to a predetermined point such as the DF station or an airport. DF guidance is given to aircraft in distress or to other aircraft which request the service. Practice DF guidance is provided when controller workload permits. Remember that the accuracy of a VHF/DF steer is subject to line-of-sight limitations as well as fluctuations in the volume of the tone transmitted.

GOOD OPERATING PRACTICES

10.10 The following section defines some rules, practices, and procedures that instrument pilots should be familiar with in order to conduct safe airport operations.

Control Tower Communications Procedures

10.11 In the preceding chapters, the rules specified that pilots are required to maintain two-way radio communication with the control tower while operating within an airport traffic area. However, if an IFR flight plan is closed while en route, ATC requests that a pilot's initial call-up should be completed approximately 15 miles from the airport. This allows the controller to establish the aircraft in a landing sequence. This landing sequence is based upon a direct line from the aircraft's initial position to the runway, and any unexpected maneuvers should be coordinated with the control tower.

Low Approaches

10.12 The low approach is sometimes referred to as a go-around maneuver following an instrument approach, and is normally used when the pilot is executing a series of practice approaches. ATC requests that all low practice approaches should be made straight ahead, with no turns or climbs until the pilot has made a thorough visual check for aircraft in the area.

10.13 In addition, a training maneuver called the Option Approach permits the instructor or examiner, at his option, to make a touch-and-go, low approach, missed approach, stop-and-go, or full stop landing. This procedure can be very beneficial in a training situation and can be used only at those locations with an operational control tower and only after ATC approval.

Landing Procedures

10.14 After landing (unless otherwise instructed by the control tower), a pilot should continue to taxi the aircraft in the landing direction, proceed to the nearest turnoff, and exit the runway without delay. A pilot should *not* turn 180° and taxi back on an active runway without authorization from the control tower. In addition, a pilot who has just landed should *not* change from the tower frequency to the ground control frequency *until* directed to do so by the controller.

Emergency Locator Transmitter (ELT)

10.15 As discussed in chapter 6, ELTs are required for most general aviation aircraft. These ELTs have been developed as a means of locating downed aircraft and their occupants. They are designed to emit a distinctive audio tone for homing purposes on 121.5 MHz and/or 243.0 MHz. The power source for an ELT is capable of providing approximately 48 hours of continuous operation in a wide range of ambient temperatures. Consequently, an ELT tone can expedite search and rescue operations.

10.16 However, caution should be exercised to prevent the inadvertent activation of locator transmitters in the air or while they are being handled on the ground. Aircraft operational testing is authorized on 121.5 MHz as follows:
1. Test should be no longer than three audio sweeps.
2. If the antenna is removable, a dummy load should be substituted during test procedures.
3. Tests shall be conducted only within the time period consisting of the first 5 minutes after every hour. Emergency tests outside of this time must be coordinated with the nearest FSS or control tower. Airborne ELT tests are *not* authorized.

Pre-departure Frequency Management
Procedures for Navigation Receivers

10.17 Prior to an instrument departure, while setting the navigation radios, the pilot should always consider what courses of action might become necessary in the event of an emergency during take-off and/or departure. In case a departure is aborted, it may become necessary to execute a transition to the appropriate local approach facilities in order to return to the airport of departure. Consequently, a minimum of one radio (if possible) should be reserved and properly tuned to the approach facility most likely to be used for an instrument approach procedure.

10.18 The ADF is most often the first radio needed during such an emergency, since the ADF allows the pilot to effect a rapid transition to the compass locator for an ADF or ILS approach. (If an ILS approach procedure is the instrument approach procedure currently in use, it would be advisable to set the number 2 navigation receiver to the ILS facility.) Naturally an ADF or ILS approach procedure may not be provided at many airports, in which case the reserved navigation receiver would most likely be tuned to the local VOR.

CHAPTER 10: QUESTIONS

For answers see Appendix E

1. What codes should be set on the transponder in the event a pilot experiences a complete communications loss?
1. Code 7600.
2. Code 7700 for one minute, then Code 7600.
3. Code 7700.
4. Change every 15 minutes between Codes 7700 and 7600.

2. A pilot declared an emergency, but no regulation was violated. When may ATC request a detailed report?
1. When priority handling has been provided.
2. Only when a regulation is violated.
3. When an accident occurs.
4. Only if the priority handling delays other traffic.

3. A pilot who was originally assigned 4,000 feet MSL discovers that the aircraft has lost all communications capability. The MEA on the next leg is 6,500 feet MSL. The MEA on the following segment (leg) is 3,100 feet MSL. What altitude should be flown on these three segments?
1. 4,000 feet MSL, 6,500 feet MSL, and 6,500 feet MSL.
2. 4,000 feet MSL, 6,500 feet MSL, and 3,100 feet MSL.
3. 4,000 feet MSL, 4,000 feet MSL, and 4,000 feet MSL.
4. 4,000 feet MSL, 6,500 feet MSL, and 4,000 feet MSL.

4. An instrument pilot whose aircraft has experienced total communications failure enters VFR weather conditions. The pilot should:

1. Continue to the destination airport in VFR conditions.
2. Land as soon as possible.
3. Continue to the destination airport under IFR radio failure procedures.
4. Land as soon as practicable, and notify ATC.

5. After applying power on the completion of a practice instrument low approach, a pilot should:

1. Execute a climbing left turn to enter the standard VFR traffic pattern.
2. Execute a 90° climbing left turn above the VFR traffic pattern.
3. Execute a missed approach straight ahead, then visually check for traffic before turning or climbing.
4. Execute a standard missed approach procedure.

6. If an aircraft's generator completely fails while the plane is en route on an IFR flight, what pilot action is necessary?

1. Set Code 7700 into the transponder, turn off all electrical equipment except the transponder, and change course to the closest area of VFR weather conditions.
2. Notify ATC immediately, request an approach at the closest suitable airport, and turn off all electrical equipment not essential to the flight.
3. Turn off all electrical equipment except for one appropriate navigation receiver until execution of the approach at the destination airport.
4. Turn off all electrical equipment except for the transponder and one VOR receiver, set Code 7600 into the transponder, and monitor the VOR receiver for a clearance.

7. If the communications receiver should become inoperative intermittently while operating in controlled airspace under instrument conditions, the appropriate pilot action would be:

1. Report the nature of the malfunction to ATC immediately.
2. Squawk 7600 and continue to the clearance limit.
3. Continue to the clearance limit and file a written report to the administrator within 48 hours.
4. Descend to the MEA and set Code 7700 in the transponder.

8. Assume an aircraft is conducting an IFR operation in controlled airspace and is equipped as follows:

NAV receiver 1 is a VOR receiver.
NAV receiver 2 is a VOR/Localizer/Glide slope receiver.

What action, if any, should a pilot take if the number 1 NAV receiver becomes inoperative?

1. ATC should be advised only if it will be necessary to identify an intersection.
2. The malfunction must be reported immediately to ATC.
3. Proceed "as cleared"; no report to ATC is required.
4. ATC should be advised by written report within 24 hours.

9. What pilot action is necessary when a partial loss of ILS receiver capability occurs while conducting IFR operations in controlled airspace?

1. Report the malfunction to ATC immediately.
2. Request radar vectors to an area where VFR conditions exist.
3. Continue "as cleared" and file a written report, if requested, to the administrator.
4. No action is necessary if the aircraft is equipped with other types of navigation receivers.

10. If emergency authority is used to deviate from provisions of an ATC clearance, the pilot shall:

1. Set the transponder on Code 0000.
2. Land as soon as possible and notify ATC upon touchdown.
3. Notify ATC as soon as possible and obtain an amended clearance.
4. Send a written report to ATC within 48 hours.

11.

Physiological Considerations of Flight

11.1 The human body has been able to adapt to a wide range of hostile conditions—from extreme heat and cold to lack of food and water. Aviation increases the challenge to man's adaptive ability. The combination of high altitude and increasing operational complexity of modern aircraft has caused aviators to more closely examine the medical aspects of flight. This chapter discusses some of the basic medical facts important to all pilots.

MIDDLE EAR DISCOMFORT

11.2 Aerotitis is a condition in which persons have difficulty equalizing the pressures between the middle ear cavity and the surrounding atmosphere. This discomfort is more prevalent among pilots and passengers with head colds or throat inflammation because it hinders the eustachian tube from opening properly. Pressure on the eardrum (while descending) can be relieved by frequent swallowing or yawning. If this procedure fails to relieve pressure in the middle ear, a pilot should close his mouth and exhale steadily while blocking the nasal passages (Valsalva maneuver). In the event that both procedures are unsuccessful, a climb followed by a more gradual descent may have to be executed to relieve the discomfort.

SINUS DISCOMFORT

11.3 Aerosinusitis results from unrelieved expansion or contraction of air in the head sinuses. The sinus cavities are grouped around and connected to the nasal cavity. Any inflammation of the sinus membranes may prevent the adjustment of pressures. A person does not have voluntary control over the sinus openings as he does with the eustachian tube to the middle ear cavity. Consequently, the general remedy for aerosinusitis is to level off or climb until the pressure equalizes, then descend at a *reduced* rate.

DRUGS

11.4 Perhaps the safest and best rule to follow concerning drugs is to consult an aviation medical examiner prior to taking medicine in any form. Many types of medication produce hazardous side effects that impair the judgment and coordination needed while flying. Common over-the-counter drugs for headache, allergy, gastrointestinal upset, and even the common cold may induce such side effects.

ALCOHOL

11.5 Small amounts of alcohol in the blood stream can adversely affect judgment and coordination. Common sense dictates that no crewmember should fly while under the influence of alcohol. (Remember, as previously mentioned in chapter 6, FAR 91.11 requires that no person may act as a crewmember within 8 hours after the consumption of any alcoholic beverage.)

11.6 Altitude has an adverse effect upon a person under the influence of alcohol. Tests indicate that approximately 2 ounces of alcohol consumed at 15,000 feet produce the same adverse effects as 6 ounces of alcohol consumed at sea level.

11.7 *Special Note: Remember, the body metabolizes alcohol at a fixed rate, and no amount of coffee or other medication will alter this rate.*

SCUBA DIVING

11.8 Flying after scuba diving can be dangerous, particularly if a pilot has been diving to depths for any length of time. Excess nitrogen may be absorbed into a pilot's system under the increased pressure of the water. At altitudes below 10,000 feet, bends may be experienced if sufficient time has not elasped prior to takeoff. It is recommended that 24 hours elapse between completion of a deep-water dive and takeoff in an aircraft.

HYPOXIA

11.9 Hypoxia is a deficiency of oxygen in the tissues of the body. This condition normally occurs at higher altitudes due to a decreased partial pressure of oxygen in the lungs. For example, the pressure of oxygen in the lungs at sea level decreases to approximately one half at 18,000 feet MSL. Consequently, the blood carries a smaller supply of oxygen to the body tissues.

11.10 The important feature of hypoxia is that its onset usually goes unnoticed because there is no pain or discomfort. In fact, the inception of hypoxia may be accompanied by a misleading sense of euphoria. Therefore, a pilot should understand the symptoms of hypoxia and be aware of the approximate altitude at which hypoxia can be experienced.

11.11 Some of the common symptoms of hypoxia that a pilot should be aware of are: loss of visual acuity, an increased sense of well being (euphoria), slow reaction time, impaired thinking, unusual fatigue, and a dull headache. Hypoxia's inception is normally slow but progressive, and a wide individual variance occurs with respect to susceptibility.

11.12 Hypoxia can impair night vision at altitudes below 10,000 feet MSL. But, normally, at altitudes above 10,000 feet MSL, the effects of hypoxia rapidly become critical. Heavy smoking, drugs, and alcohol can further reduce a pilot's tolerance of hypoxia.

11.13 There are various mechanical devices designed to prevent hypoxia in flight. The most common are continuous flow, demand, or pressure demand oxygen breathing systems. These mechanical devices all attempt to increase either the percentage or the pressure of oxygen in the inspired air.

HYPERVENTILATION

11.14 Hyperventilation results when a person increases his breathing rate to a level that upsets the balance of oxygen and carbon dioxide in his system. Increased lung ventilation expels carbon dioxide more rapidly than the body produces it. This results in hypocapnia, a deficiency of carbon dioxide in the blood.

11.15 Although the remedy for hyperventilation is a simple one, it is imperative that the symptoms of hyperventilation be properly diagnosed. Why? Because the symptoms of hypoxia and hyperventilation are similar. Understanding exactly what causes hypoxia and hyperventilation is the answer for both prevention and proper diagnosis.

11.16 *Special Note: Since it is natural to overbreathe when an individual experiences physical or psychological stress, hyperventilation is likely to occur when an individual is scared, excited, or tense.*

11.17 After a proper diagnosis of hyperventilation is concluded, the remedy for this disorder is to increase the level of carbon dioxide in the body. This can be accomplished in a number of ways, some of which are:
1. Slowing down the breathing rate.
2. Intermittently holding your breath.

CARBON MONOXIDE

11.18 If carbon monoxide enters the aircraft cabin, it usually enters through the heating system. Generally, this gas will remain undetected because it is colorless, odorless, and tasteless.

11.19 For biochemical reasons, carbon monoxide has a greater ability to combine with the hemoglobin of the blood than does oxygen. In addition, it may take several days to fully recover and clear the body of all carbon monoxide. Opening a window and breathing fresh air, or landing for a short duration, will not appreciably relieve the effects of carbon monoxide.

11.20 Some of the symptoms that indicate carbon monoxide poisoning are: irrational thinking, uneasiness, dizziness, and in the more advanced stages, a possible headache. A pilot suspecting carbon monoxide infiltration should shut off the heaters, open the air ventilators, descend to a lower altitude, and land at the nearest airfield.

VERTIGO

11.21 Instrument pilots may encounter a conflict between the attitude indications of the flight instruments and the false sensations they may experience. This conflict, called vertigo, may cause a pilot to lose spatial orientation, specifically, to lose orientation in relation to the earth's surface. Spatial disorientation may cause violent illness similar to car or sea sickness. Although all pilots are not equally prone to vertigo, it normally presents a greater problem for relatively inexperienced pilots.

11.22 In addition to vision, the two senses an individual uses to maintain his balance are gravitational pull on muscles and joints (kinesthesia) and the movement of fluid in the inner ear (vestibular sense). Vertigo can be induced by flight maneuvers that produce unusual pressures on the muscles and vestibular senses. For example, gravitational pull and centrifugal force may produce virtually the same senses in the muscles and joints. In the same manner, the vestibular sense can also cause a conflict with what the eyes are seeing. Remember that the most accurate sense to use to maintain equilibrium is vision.

11.23 *Special Note: Pilots should disregard all senses but vision to maintain instrument flight. (Believe in your instruments.)*

CHAPTER 11: QUESTIONS

For answers see Appendix E

1. A pilot flying in instrument conditions experiences vertigo. To overcome this sensation, the pilot must:
  1. Fold the head forward and close both eyes.
  2. Make a 60° banked turn in each direction. This will stimulate the other two senses.
  3. Look outside the cockpit and attempt to establish a ground reference.
  4. React to and believe in the instrument indications.

2. No person may act as a crewmember within:
  1. Eight hours after the consumption of any alcoholic beverage.
  2. Ten hours after the consumption of any alcoholic beverage.
  3. Sixteen hours after the consumption of any alcoholic beverage.
  4. Twenty-four hours after the consumption of any alcoholic beverage.

3. One of the major early symptoms of hypoxia is:
  1. A hearing loss.
  2. A decrease in day vision.
  3. Euphoria.
  4. Vertigo.

4. Momentarily opening all the aircraft air vents in flight has what effect on carbon monoxide poisoning?
  1. It will completely clear up all symptoms.
  2. Little effect. It often takes several days to recover from carbon monoxide poisoning.
  3. It will partially clear up the symptoms so the pilot can continue the flight.
  4. It will aggravate the symptoms.

Bibliography

In order to maintain maximum accuracy and consistency with current FAA format, terminology, and testing procedures, certain portions of this text contain government publication excerpts that were directly quoted or were closely followed in format or terminology. Contained within this bibliography are the primary government-produced publications that were used in the compilation of this text.

Airman's Information Manual/Basic Flight Information and ATC Procedures, Department of Transportation, Federal Aviation Administration, (Washington, D.C.: U.S. Government Printing Office, 1979).

Airport/Facility Directory, Department of Commerce, National Oceanic and Atmospheric Administration, National Ocean Survey, Washington, D.C..

Aviation Weather, AC 00-6A, FAA Flight Standards Service and National Weather Service, (Washington, D.C.: U.S. Government Printing Office, Revised 1975).

Aviation Weather Services, AC 00-45A, FAA Flight Standards Service and National Weather Service, (Washington, D.C.: U.S. Government Printing Office, Revised 1977).

Cessna Model 310J Owner's Manual, Cessna Aircraft Company, Wichita, Kansas.

Civil Use of U.S. Government Instrument Approach Procedure Charts, AC 90-1A, Department of Commerce, Environmental Science Services Administration, Coast and Geodetic Survey, (Washington, D.C.: U.S. Government Printing Office, 1968).

Federal Aviation Regulations, Department of Transportation, Federal Aviation Administration, (Washington, D.C.: U.S. Government Printing Office).

Flight Instructor Instrument-Airplane Written Test Guide, AC 61-70, Department of Transportation, Federal Aviation Administration, Flight Standards Service, (Washington, D.C.: U.S. Government Printing Office, 1974).

Flying DME ARCs, AC 90-62, Department of Transportation, Federal Aviation Administration, (Washington, D.C.: U.S. Government Printing Office, 1973).

Hurt, H.H., Jr., *Aerodynamics for Naval Aviators*, NAVAIR 00-80T-80, Issued by The Office of the Chief of Naval Operations Aviation Training Division, (Washington, D.C.: U.S. Government Printing Office, 1965).

IFR and VFR Pilot Exam-O-Grams, Department of Transportation, Federal Aviation Administration, Flight Standards National Field Office, Oklahoma City, Oklahoma.

Instrument Flying, AFM 51-37, Department of the Air Force, Air Training Command, (Washington, D.C.: U.S. Government Printing Office, 1971).

Instrument Flying Handbook, AC 61-27B, Department of Transportation, Federal Aviation Administration, Flight Standards Technical Division, (Washington, D.C.: U.S. Government Printing Office, 1971).

Instrument Rating (Airplane) Written Test Guide, AC 61-8C, Department of Transportation, Federal Aviation Administration, Flight Standards Technical Division, (Washington, D.C.: U.S. Government Printing Office, Revised 1972).

Instrument Rating Written Test Guide, AC 61-8D, Department of Transportation, Federal Aviation Administration, (Washington, D.C.: U.S. Government Printing Office, Revised 1977).

Medical Handbook for Pilots, AC 67-2, Department of Transportation, Federal Aviation Administration (Washington, D.C.: U.S. Government Printing Office).

Pilot's Operating Handbook and FAA Approved Airplane Flight Manual (Baron TH-773), Beech Aircraft Corporation, Wichita, Kansas, 1976.

Pilot's Operating Handbook and FAA Approved Airplane Flight Manual (Bonanza S35), Beech Aircraft Corporation, Wichita, Kansas, Revised 1977.

United States Government Instrument Approach Procedures, Department of Commerce, National Oceanic and Atmospheric Administration, National Ocean Survey, Riverdale, Maryland.

United States Government Operational Profile Descent Procedures, Department of Commerce, National Oceanic and Atmospheric Administration, National Ocean Survey, Riverdale, Maryland.

United States Government Standard Instrument Departures for Civil Aerodomes, Department of Commerce, National Oceanic and Atmospheric Administration, National Ocean Survey, Riverdale, Maryland.

United States Government Standard Terminal Arrival Routes, Department of Commerce, National Atmospheric Administration, National Ocean Survey, Riverdale, Maryland.

United States Standard for Terminal Instrument Procedures, Department of Transportation, Federal Aviation Administration, (Washington D.C.: U.S. Government Printing Office, 1976).

Appendix A:
Clearance Shorthand

SHORTHAND NOMENCLATURE

WORD AND PHRASES

ABOVE	ABV
ADVISE	ADV
AIRPORT	A
AND	&
APPROACH	AP
APPROACH CONTROL	APC
ATC CLEARS	CLS
BOUND	B
EASTBOUND	EB
INBOUND	IB
OUTBOUND	OB
CLEARED AS FILED	CAF
CLIMB (TO)	↗
CONTACT (NAME, FREQUENCY)	DEN 127.2
COURSE	CRS
CROSS	X
CRUISE	↗
DEPARTURE CONTROL	DPC
DESCEND (TO)	↘
DIRECT	DR
EXPECT APPROACH CLEARANCE	EAC
EXPECT FURTHER CLEARANCE	EFC
FLIGHT PLANNED ROUTE	FPR
FURTHER CLEARANCE	FC

HEADING	HDG
HOLD (DIRECTION)	H-E
JET ROUTE (NUMBER)	J-15
MAINTAIN (ALTITUDE)	M150
OUTER COMPASS LOCATOR	LOM
OUTER MARKER	OM
RADAR VECTOR	RV
RADIAL	RAD
REPORT LEAVING	RL
REPORT OVER	RO
REPORT REACHING	RR
SQUAWK (CODE)	SQK 1024
TRACK	TR
TURN LEFT	LT
TURN RIGHT	RT
VICTOR AIRWAY (NUMBER)	V-26

SAMPLE CLEARANCE:

ATC CLEARS (AIRCRAFT IDENTIFICATION) AS FILED, MAINTAIN ONE TWO THOUSAND, SQUAWK ONE ZERO TWO FOUR.

CAF M120 SQK 1024

Appendix B:

International-ICAO Morse Code and Phonetic Alphabet

0	— — — — —	Zero		I	• •	India
1	• — — — —	One		J	• — — —	Juliett
2	• • — — —	Two		K	— • —	Kilo
3	• • • — —	Three		L	• — • •	Lima
4	• • • • —	Four		M	— —	Mike
5	• • • • •	Five		N	— •	November
6	— • • • •	Six		O	— — —	Oscar
7	— — • • •	Seven		P	• — — •	Papa
8	— — — • •	Eight		Q	— — • —	Quebec
9	— — — — •	Nine		R	• — •	Romeo
A	• —	Alpha		S	• • •	Sierra
B	— • • •	Bravo		T	—	Tango
C	— • — •	Charlie		U	• • —	Uniform
D	— • •	Delta		V	• • • —	Victor
E	•	Echo		W	• — —	Whiskey
F	• • — •	Foxtrot		X	— • • —	X-ray
G	— — •	Golf		Y	— • — —	Yankee
H	• • • •	Hotel		Z	— — • •	Zulu

Appendix C:

Conversion Charts

DISTANCE CONVERSION CHART

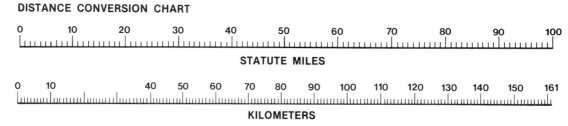

STATUTE MILES

KILOMETERS

NAUTICAL MILES

TO CONVERT DISTANCES: Vertically align a straight edge through the distance to be converted, intersecting the other two scales.

C 1

INCHES OF MERCURY-MILLIBARS-
KILOPASCALS CONVERSION

Inches of Mercury (In. Hg.)	Millibars (MB)	KiloPascals (KPA)
30.30	1026.1	102.61
30.20	1022.7	102.27
30.10	1019.3	101.93
30.00	1015.9	101.59
*29.92	*1013.2	*101.32
29.90	1012.5	101.25
29.80	1009.1	100.91
29.70	1005.7	100.57
29.60	1002.3	100.23

C 2   *Standard Atmospheric Pressure

TEMPERATURE CONVERSION TABLE
CENTIGRADE

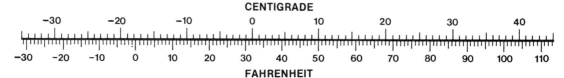

C 3   **FAHRENHEIT**

STANDARD ATMOSPHERE TABLE

ALTITUDE (FEET)	TEMPERATURE (°F)	(°C)	ATMOSPHERIC PRESSURE (INCHES OF MERCURY) (IN. HG.)	(KILOPASCALS) (KPA)
0	59.0	15.000	29.92	101.32
1,000	55.4	13.019	28.86	97.73
2,000	51.9	11.037	27.82	94.21
3,000	48.3	9.056	26.82	90.82
4,000	44.7	7.075	25.84	87.50
5,000	41.2	5.094	24.90	84.32
6,000	37.6	3.113	23.98	81.21
7,000	34.0	1.132	23.09	78.19
8,000	30.5	-.850	22.22	75.25
9,000	26.9	-2.831	21.39	72.43
10,000	23.3	-4.812	20.58	69.69
11,000	19.8	-6.794	19.79	67.02
12,000	16.2	-8.775	19.03	64.44
13,000	12.6	-10.756	18.29	61.94
14,000	9.1	-12.737	17.58	59.53
15,000	5.5	-14.718	16.89	57.20
20,000	-12.3	-24.624	13.75	46.56
25,000	-30.2	-34.530	11.10	37.59
30,000	-48.0	-44.436	8.89	30.10
35,000	-65.8	-54.342	7.04	23.84
40,000	-69.7	-56.500	5.54	18.76
45,000	-69.7	-56.500	4.35	14.73
50,000	-69.7	-56.500	3.42	11.58

C 4

GREENWICH MEAN TIME

Greenwich Mean Time (GMT) was designed to standard-ize navigational procedures across the 24 time zones of the world. GMT or "Zulu" time (Z) is based on the local time on the 0° meridian of longitude or the Prime Meridian at Greenwich, England. Since all aviation operations use GMT, the following table is designed to simplify the conversion procedures from GMT to local time or local time to GMT.

TIME ZONE TO BE CONVERTED TO GMT	GMT CONVERSION FACTOR	
	STANDARD TIME *ADD CONVERSION FACTOR TO LOCAL 24 HOUR CLOCK TIME*	DAYLIGHT SAVINGS TIME *ADD CONVERSION FACTOR TO LOCAL 24 HOUR CLOCK TIME*
PACIFIC	+8	+7
MOUNTAIN	+7	+6
CENTRAL	+6	+5
EASTERN	+5	+4

THE FOLLOWING EXAMPLES ILLUSTRATE THESE RELATIONSHIPS:

CONVERTING LOCAL TIME (STANDARD) TO GMT

Time Zone	Local Time	24 Hour Clock Time	Conversion Factor TO ADD FOR GMT	GMT
Pacific	11:00AM	1100	+8	1900
Mountain	12:00Noon	1200	+7	1900
Central	1:00PM	1300	+6	1900
Eastern	2:00PM	1400	+5	1900

CONVERTING GMT TO LOCAL TIME (STANDARD)

Time Zone	GMT	Conversion Factor TO SUBTRACT FOR LOCAL TIME	24 Hour Clock Time	Local Time
Pacific	0700	-8	2300	11:00PM*
Mountain	0700	-7	2400	12:00Mid*
Central	0700	-6	0100	1:00AM
Eastern	0700	-5	0200	2:00AM

*Note that the date would be one day earlier with respect to the GMT date.

Appendix D:
Check Lists

A pilot preparing for an instrument flight should check the following items *in addition* to the aircraft check list.

Before starting the engine(s), the following checks should be completed:

1. Equipment and printed materials—Appropriate handbooks, charts (*organized*), computer, aircraft documents, and flashlight (for night operations).
2. Pitot head—Check pitot heat operations (switch on pitot heat, check for amperage rise, and feel pitot head) and pitot head for blockage.
3. Static ports—Check for blockage.
4. Deicing and anti-icing equipment—Availability and fluid quantity.
5. Airspeed indicator—Proper reading.
6. Attitude and heading indicators—Uncaged (if applicable).
7. Turn and slip indicator—Needle centered, tube full of fluid and ball centered (assuming the aircraft is stationary on a level ramp).
8. Vertical velocity indicator—Zero indication. If it does not have a zero indication, tap the panel gently. If it stays off the zero reading and is not adjustable, the ground indication must be interpreted as the zero position during flight.
9. Magnetic compass—Full of fluid.
10. Clock—Wind (if appropriate) and set to the correct time.
11. Suction gage—Proper reading.

After starting engine(s) the following checks should be completed:

1. Suction gauge or electrical indicators—Check the source of power for the gyro instuments. The suction developed should be appropriate for the instruments in that particular aircraft. If the gyros are electrically driven, check the generators and inverters for proper operation.
2. Magnetic compass—Check the card for freedom of movement and be sure that the bowl is full of fluid. Determine compass accuracy by comparing the indicated heading against a known heading while the aircraft is stopped or taxiing straight. Remote Indicating Compasses should also be checked against known headings.
3. Heading indicator—Allow 5 minutes after starting engine(s) for the gyro rotor of the vacuum-operated heading indicator to attain normal operating speed. Before taxiing, or while taxiing straight, set the heading indicator to correspond with the magnetic compass heading. Check for proper operation while turning. Before takeoff, recheck the heading indicator. If the magnetic compass and deviation card are accurate, the heading indicator should show the known taxiway or runway direction when the aircraft is aligned with them (within 5°).

Electric gyros should also be set and checked against known headings. Allow 3 minutes for the electric gyro to attain operating speed. A gryrosyn (slaved gyro) compass should be checked for slaving action and its indications compared with those of the magnetic compass.

4. Attitude Indicator—Allow the same times as noted above for gyros to attain normal rotor speed. If the horizon bar erects to the horizontal position and remains at the correct position for the attitude of the aircraft, or if it begins to vibrate after this attitude is reached and then slowly stops vibrating altogether, the instrument is operating properly. If the horizon bar fails to remain in the horizontal position during straight taxiing, or tips in excess of 5° during taxi turns, the instrument is unreliable.

Adjust the miniature aircraft with reference to the horizon bar for the particular aircraft while on the ground. For some tricycle-geared aircraft, a slightly nose-low attitude on the ground will give a level flight attitude at normal cruising speed.

5. Altimeter—With the altimeter set to the current reported altimeter setting, note and record any variation between the known field elevation and the altimeter indication. If the variation is in the order of plus or minus 75 feet (0.075 in Hg.), the accuracy of the altimeter is questionable and the problem should be referred to an appropriately rated repair station for evaluation and possible correction.
6. Turn and slip indicator/turn coordinator—Check the turn needle for right and left deflection and for positive return to the center position. The check can be made by noting the indications during taxi turns. The ball should move freely in the tube and no bubbles should appear in the fluid.
7. VOR receiver accuracy check—Perform a VOR accuracy check (if necessary) at the proper location and make the appropriate logbook entry.
8. Radio equipment check—Turn on all radio equipment that is to be used during the proposed flight and set as desired.
   A. Weather radar—Tuned to the appropriate configuration as necessary.
   B. Transponder—Set in the appropriate code and switch to standby position.
   C. VOR receivers—Using the OBS set the appropriate VOR radials to be used during departure and set to appropriate frequency. If possible, check station identification.
   D. ADF—Tune and identify appropriate station and test operation of needle. (Check to determine if the needle points toward the appropriate LF/MF facility and rotates during a turn.)
   E. Marker beacons—Adjust light intensity (place in dim setting for night operations). Press to test.
   F. DME—Set to appropriate frequency and, if possible, check station identification.
9. Deicing and anti-icing equipment—Check operation.

Appendix E:
Answers to Chapter Questions and Exercises

Chapter 1: Answers

Question	Answer	Reference Paragraph(s)	Reference Figure(s)	Remarks
1	2	1.19		
		1.20		
2	4	1.20		
3	1	1.15		
4	4	1.30		
5	1	1.32		
		1.34 (7)		
6	2	1.34 (5)		
7	4	1.17		
		1.18		
8	2	1.4		
9	4	1.25		The reason a pilot wants to increase left aileron *and* increase right rudder is to *maintain* the same rate of turn.
10	3	1.69		
11	4	1.69		
12	1	1.50		
13	2	1.69		

Chapter 2: Answers

Question	Answer	Reference Paragraph(s)	Reference Figure(s)	Remarks
1	2	1.29		
		2.80		
		2.81		
2	4	2.81		
3	1	2.62		
4	1	2.9		
		2.16		
		2.25		
5	1	2.10	2–5	
		2.13		
6	4	2.12		
		2.13		
7	3	2.18		
8	2	2.74		
9	2	2.61		
10	1	2.14	2–6	
11	3	2.52	2–20	
		2.53		
12	4	2.35		
		2.36		
		2.39		
13	1	2.20		
14	3	2.36	2–18	
15	1	2.75	2–27	
		2.76	2–28	
16	1	2.68	2–25	
		2.69		
17	1	2.34	2–17	
18	2	2.34		
		2.40		
19	1	2.37	2–19	
		2.38		
20	3	2.39		
		2.41		
21	2	2.80		
22	1	2.60		Note: The pointer denotes indicated airspeed while the color-coded operating ranges are in calibrated airspeed.

Question	Answer	Reference Paragraph(s)	Reference Figure(s)	Remarks
23	1	2.70		
24	4	2.64		
25	2	2.62		
26	4	2.49		
27	4	2.76		Note: Assume after the pilot lands at the destination airport and adjusts the altimeter to the correct altimeter setting, the altimeter setting would increase .20 inches or 200 feet. Therefore the altimeter would indicate 1000 feet at touchdown.
28	2	2.22		
29	1	2.78		
30	3		2-29	

Chapter 3: Answers

Question	Answer	Reference Paragraph(s)	Reference Figure(s)	Remarks
1	2	3.99 3.108 3.118 3.122	3-22	
2	3	3.122		
3	4	3.129		
4	3	3.159	3-37	
5	1	3.17		
6	2	3.44 3.46		
7	1	3.24		
8	3		3-20	
9	4	3.136		
10	4	3.150 3.151 3.153		
11	4	3.45		
12	4	3.136		
13	4	3.99 3.101 3.102 3.103 3.108 3.111		
14	1	3.10		
15	1	3.160		
16	3	3.181		
17	2	3.116 3.118		
18	3	3.66		
19	4	3.1		
20	1	3.56		
21	1	3.11		
22	3	3.16 3.17		
23	2	3.71		
24	2		3-20	
25	1		3-20	
26	4	3.134		
27	1	3.1 3.89		
28	3	3.148		
29	1	3.176 3.177 3.179 3.180		

Question	Answer	Reference Paragraph(s)	Reference Figure(s)	Remarks
30	2		3–44	
31	1		3–42	
32	4	3.168	3–42	
33	1	3.1		
34	1	3.170	3–42	
35	3	3.169 3.171		
36	3	3.30		
37	4	3.11 3.54 3.55		
38	4		3–15	
39	2	3.136		
40	1	3.24		
41	4	3.36 3.37 3.41 (3) (4) 3.52 (6) (7)		
42	1	3.7		
43	3	3.45		
44	3	3.89 (2)		
45	1	3.112		
46	4	3.27 (2) 3.29 (2) 3.39		
47	2	3.148		
48	2	3.94		
49	4	3.34		
50	1	3.165		
51	3		3–20	
52	3		3–11	
53	4	3.61 3.62 3.63		
54	4	3.22		
55	3	3.86		
56	4	3.127		
57	2	3.10	3–4	
58	1	3.87		
59	2	3.131	3–28	
60	4	3.57		
61	1	3.108		
62	1	3.125		
63	2		3–27	
64	1	3.99 3.101	3–22 3–23	
65	1	3.20		
66	3	3.71		
67	4	3.164 (2)		
68	3	3.154		
69	4	3.10 (1)		
70	1	3.72		
71	2	3.148		
72	1	3.162 3.163	3–39 3–40	
73	2	3.72		
74	4	3.24		
75	3	3.133		
76	1	3.41 (2) (3) 3.52 (6) 3.54		
77	4	3.160–.164 3.173–.183	3–38 3–43	Remember to compare the radar summary chart to the weather depiction chart since both of these charts are of *reported* weather conditions.

Question	Answer	Reference Paragraph(s)	Reference Figure(s)	Remarks
78	2	3.165–.166	3–41	
79	3	3.185		
80	4	3.4		

Chapter 4: Answers

Question	Answer	Reference Paragraph(s)	Reference Figure(s)	Remarks
1	4	4.80	4–26	
2	1		4–43	
3	1	4.167	4–47	
4	2		4–49	
5	3		4–49	
6	3	4.16 4.17	4–6 4–7	
7	4		4–49	
8	1	4.101 4.109 4.110 4.111		
9	4	4.79	4–26	
10	1		4–49	
11	2	4.63 4.64	4–22	
12	4	4.16 4.17 4.18 4.20 4.23	4–4 4–5 4–6 4–7 4–8 4–9	Perhaps one of the best methods of solving this problem is to mentally picture four quadrants around each VOR station as in Figure 4–7. The 266° and 341° radials should be pictured as the radials that center the CDI and produce a FROM indication on the TO/FROM indicator when the OBS is set to 266° and 341° respectively.
13	4	4.16 4.17 4.23	4–6 4–7	
14	2	4.120 4.122	4–33 4–34	
15	2	4.132		
16	1		4–46	
17	2	4.12		
18	1	4.156		
19	2	4.43 4.46 4.51 4.53 4.55	4–18 4–20	
20	1	4.173		
21	4	4.133		
22	4	4.8 (3) 4.14	4–7	
23	4	4.24 (5–6)	4–9	
24	1	4.153 (3)		
25	2	4.84 (1) (C)	4–28	
26	1	4.109 4.110 4.125 4.127		
27	4	4.63 4.64	4–22	
28	2	4.67 4.68 4.69	4–24	
29	1	4.137		
30	2	4.55	4–21	

Question	Answer	Reference Paragraph(s)	Reference Figure(s)	Remarks
		4.58		
31	2	4.47	4–19	
32	2	4.134		
33	2	4.79	4–26	
34	3	4.153 (7)	4–42	The traffic would be located at a 240° (8x30°) angle with respect to the aircraft's direction of travel (track) or, in other words, 120° (360°–240°) to the left of the aircraft's direction of travel.
35	1	4.16	4–6	
		4.18	4–7	
		4.23		
36	2	4.77		
37	1	4.111		
38	1	4.67	4–24	
		4.68		
		4.69		
39	3	4.128		
40	2	4.173		
41	3	4.163		
42	4		4–43	
43	2	4.163		
44	1	4.164 (2)	4–44	
45	4	4.8 (3)	4–7	
		4.14	4–9	
		4.100	4–30	
		4.121		
		4.131 (1)		
46	4	4.172 (2)		
47	2	4.147	4–39	
		4.148	4–40	
		4.152		
48	1	4.120	4–33	
49	4	4.101	4–30	Remember, it is the localizer *not* the glide slope that includes a voice feature on its frequency.
		4.103		
		4.104		
		4.105		
		4.106		
50	2	4.27	4–10	
		4.28		
51	2	4.96	4–33	
		4.101		
		4.119		
		4:134		
52	4	4.44	4–18	
		4.45		
		4.46		
53	1	4.84	4–28	
54	2	4.8		
55	1	4.72		
56	2	4.165		
57	2		4–49	

Chapter 5: Answers

Question	Answer	Reference Paragraph(s)	Reference Figure(s)	Remarks
1	3	5.17	5–12	
2	1	5.14	5–9	
3	4	5.44		
4	2	5.8	5–18 (A,B,C,D)	
		5.36		

Question	Answer	Reference Paragraph(s)	Reference Figure(s)	Remarks
5	1	5.22 5.23	5–15	
6	4	5.13 5.14 5.15 5.16	5–9 5–10 5–11	Note: An aircraft consuming 26 gal./hr. will use 19.5 gallons in 45 minutes. If the consumption was reduced to 18 gal./hr. the remaining flying time is 65 minutes (19.5 ÷ 18). 65 minutes flying time less 45 minutes reserve leaves 20 minutes flying time.
7	4	5.21		
8	1	5.11 5.36	5–18 (A,B,C,D)	
9	4	5.36 (9)		
10	2	5.45 5.46 5.47 5.48	5–20 5–21	Note: The computer can be used to recheck the answer (5.27).
11	3	5.60 5.61 5.62	5–27	
12	1	5.56	5–24	
13	2	5.23	5–15	
14	3	5.46	5–21	
15	3	5.59	5–26	Note: The solutions for problems using this graph can be arrived at by using the same basic procedures as those practiced when solving problems using the Climb—One Engine Inoperative Graph.
16	1	5.53	5–23	Note: The solutions for problems using this graph can be arrived at by using the same basic procedures as those practiced when solving problems using the Takeoff Distance Over 50-Foot Obstacle Graph.
17	4	5.56	5–24	Note: The solutions for problems using this graph can be arrived at by using the same basic procedures as those practiced when solving problems using the Time-Fuel-Distance to Climb Graph.
18	4	5.53	5–23	

Exercise A

Question	Answer
1	:35
2	430 NM
3	145 MPH
4	182 KTS
5	2:03-1/2
6	35 SM
7	4:00
8	180 MPH
9	8.4 SM

Exercise B

Question	Answer
10	38 gallons
11	13.5 GPH
12	4:10
13	144 PPH
14	60 pounds
15	4:48

Exercise C

Question	Answer
16	5 minutes
17	12 minutes
18	550 FPM
19	500 FPM
20	5 minutes

Exercise D

Question	Answer
21	69 SM
22	460 SM
23	208 NM
24	150 SM
25	3.9 NM
26	126.5 MPH
27	165 KTS
28	134.5 KTS
29	510.5 MPH
30	221.5 KTS

Exercise E

Question	TAS (KTS)	Density Altitude (Ft.)
31	151	500
32	158	12,000
33	200	22,300
34	209	11,800
35	150.5	9,800

Exercise F

Question	MH	WCA	GS(KTS)	TH
36	228°	−7°	107	233°
37	158.5°	−11.5°	172.5	148.5°
38	317°	−10°	192	310°
39	286°	+10°	134	290°
40	223.5°	+12.5°	137	212.5°

Exercise G

Question	Answers Pressure Altitude (Ft.)	Density Altitude (Ft.)
41	0	0
42	3,000	5,300
43	4,800	4,250
44	1,845	4,500
45	–305	Below sea level

Exercise H

Question	Answer
46	2400 feet
47	3950 feet
48	3100 feet
49	3400 feet
50	3450 feet

Exercise I

Question	Answer
51	1300 feet
52	800 feet
53	1450 feet
54	900 feet
55	1150 feet

Exercise J

Question	Time to Climb (Min.)	Fuel to Climb (Gal.)	Distance to Climb (NM)
56	6	4.0	15
57	10	6.0	25
58	14	8.1	36
59	11.5	6.3	29.5
60	9	5.2	23

Exercise K

Question	Answer
61	88 MPH
62	95 MPH

Exercise L

Question	Rate of Climb (FPM)	Climb Gradient (%)
63	325	3.2
64	270	2.6
65	150	1.4

Exercise M

Question	Answer
66	9.7 gal./hr.
67	18.8 gal./hr.

Exercise N

Question	Rate of Climb (FPM)	Climb Gradient (%)
68	1375	14
69	850	9
70	125	1.1

Exercise O

Question	Answer
71	131 minutes
72	119 minutes
73	166.5 minutes
74	89 minutes

Chapter 6: Answers

Question	Answer	Reference Paragraph(s)	Reference Figure(s)	Remarks
1	4	6.16		
2	2	6.8 (c,d)		Paragraph (d) of this regulation should be thoroughly reviewed for night operations when carrying passengers.
3	4	6.3 6.8 (c,d,e)		
4	4	6.8 (a,e)		
5	2	6.32 6.33 (b)		
6	2	4.12 6.24 (b)		
7	2	6.33 (c)		
8	1	6.24 (a,b,c)		
9	4	6.22		
10	3	6.7		
11	1	6.19 (2)		
12	4	6.5 (a,b,c) 6.7	6–1	

Question	Answer	Reference Paragraph(s)	Reference Figure(s)	Remarks
13	1	6.24 (d) 6.25		
14	1	6.24 (a)		
15	3	6.16		
16	1	6.10 6.11		
17	3	6.12		
18	2	6.32		
19	1	5.13 5.14 5.15 6.32		
20	3	6.30 (a)		
21	4	6.16 6.18		
22	4	6.20 (d)		A pilot may take off and assume the 100-foot ascent mark as a zero rate of climb reference.
23	2	6.35 (a,b)		
24	3	6.34 (a,b)	6–6	
25	1	6.5 (b)	6–1	
26	3	4.15 4.16 6.24 (b)	4–5 4–6	
27	4	6.4 6.30		
28	2	6.4		
29	1	6.15 6.22 6.24 6.26		
30	2	6.8 (e)		
31	3	6.2		
32	4	6.26 6.29 (a) 6.30 (a)		
33	1	6.20 (e)		
34	2	6.39	6–7	
35	4	6.33 (c)		
36	4	6.37		
37	3	6.30 (a) (1) 6.37		
38	2	6.30 (a) (1)		
39	4	6.30		

Chapter 7: Answers

Question	Answer	Reference Paragraph(s)	Reference Figure(s)	Remarks
1	1	7.8 7.11 7.12		
2	4		7–4	
3	4	7.40		
4	1	7.40 (5) 7.50 7.51 7.52 7.53		
5	1	7.49		
6	3	3.148 5.36 7.59 7.60 7.61		

Question	Answer	Reference Paragraph(s)	Reference Figure(s)	Remarks
7	3	7.43	7–11	Remember, when an R follows a frequency the FSS only receives and does not transmit on that frequency.
8	3	7.22		
9	1	7.43	7–11	
10	1	7.20	7–8	STAR charts are reviewed in greater detail in paragraph 9.4 and Fig. 9–1.
11	2		7–4	
12	4	7.39 7.40 (3)		
13	2	7.9 7.11	7–5 7–6	
14	4	7.8		
15	4		7–1 (A) 7–1 (D)	
16	1	7.40 (1)	7–9	
17	2	7.22		
18	3	7.22		
19	1	7.51 7.52	7–13 7–14	
20	4	7.40 (2)		
21	2	7.45	7–12	
22	4	7.8 7.11 7.12		Note: Initial FDC NOTAMs are disseminated by teletype transmissions. This transmitted information is received at local Flight Service Stations.
23	2		7–1 (B)	
24	1	7.22		
25	4	7.43	7–11	
26	2		7–1 (A,B,C,D)	
27	3	7.40 (4)		
28	3	7.25		
29	1		7–19	
30	4	7.75		
31	1	7.65		
32	3	7.64 7.76		
33	3	7.43 7.46		
34	2	7.50 7.51	7–13	
35	2	7.44	7–12	
36	1	7.25 7.35 7.37		
37	4	7.61		Note: V–422 changes at TWERP Intersection and proceeds to Chicago Heights VORTAC south of V–8. Note: The only airway to the alternate airport is V–429.
38	1	5.11 5.14 5.40 7.66		
39	3	7.43	7–11	
40	1	7.43	7–11	
41	1	7.69 7.70 7.71		
42	2	7.74 (3)		
43	1	7.40 (1)		
44	4	7.64		
45	1	7.67 7.68		

Question	Answer	Reference Paragraph(s)	Reference Figure(s)	Remarks
46	4	4.11 6.24 (b)	7–2	Note: To determine if an airport has a VOR test facility, the Airport Directory section of the Airport/Facility Directory must be consulted.
47	2	7.18		
48	2	7.22		
49	3	7.44	7–12	
50	2	7.78		
51	3	7.12		Note: There is no specific time that an FDC NOTAM of a temporary nature will remain in effect.
52	3	7.69		
53	1	7.8		Note: FAR 91.5 paragraph 6.2 is also an important consideration when answering this question.
54	4	7.22		
55	3	7.35		
56	1	7.30		
57	1	7.30		Refer to the En Route Low Altitude Chart legend in the appendix.
58	3	7.30		
59	4	7.41 7.42	7–10	
60	3	7.47 7.73		

Chapter 8: Answers

Question	Answer	Reference Paragraph(s)	Reference Figure(s)	Remarks
1	4	8.110 (3)		
2	4	8.110 (6)		
3	3	8.64 (2) 8.100 8.102		
4	1	8.20		
5	1	8.110 (5)		
6	1	8.109		The MEA and MOCA are considered to be minimum IFR altitudes.
7	2	8.85 8.87	8–10	
8	3	8.85 8.87	8–10	
9	2	8.64 (6)		
10	4	8.23 8.24 (4) 8.109 8.112		
11	3	8.80		
12	3	8.5		
13	4	8.30 (3) (4)		
14	3	8.40		
15	1	8.105		
16	4	8.71		
17	2	8.40		
18	1	8.60		
19	1	8.68		
20	1	8.45		
21	2	8.92		
22	1	8.97		
23	3	8.69		
24	2	8.9 (1,2,3)		
25	4	8.106 8.107 8.108	8–12	
26	1	8.113 (2) (3)		
27	2	8.93		
28	3	8.41		
29	4	8.63 (2)		

Question	Answer	Reference Paragraph(s)	Reference Figure(s)	Remarks
		8.64 (1,2,3,4,5)		
30	2	8.49		
31	3	8.7 (1)		
32	4	8.2		
		8.3		
		8.9 (1)		
		8.17		
		8.26		
33	3	8.77		
34	2	8.47	8–1	
35	4		8–1	19 + 15 + 17 + 18 + 93 = 162
36	1		8–1	Remember to study the notes.
37	3		8–1	Note: An aircraft with a ground speed of 120 knots will travel 2 nautical miles per minute. Consequently, for this aircraft, a climb rate of 300 feet per nautical mile equals 600 feet per minute.
38	4	8.64 (2)		
39	2	8.84	8–6	
		8.86	8–7	
40	1		8–11	
41	4	8.82		
42	3	8.106		
43	1	8.109	8–13	
		8.110 (2)		
44	3	8.27		
45	2	8.2		
		8.110 (3)		
46	4	8.98		
47	3	8.44		
48	4	8.41		
		8.42 (2)		

Chapter 9: Answers

Question	Answer	Reference Paragraph(s)	Reference Figure(s)	Remarks
1	3	9.81	9–9	
		9.82		
		9.83		
2	2	9.51		
		9.52		
		9.53		
3	1		9–13	
4	3	9.101	9–14	
		9.102	9–16	
5	2	5.11	9–18	
		5.36		
		5.40		
6	4	9.110 (2)		
7	3	9.104		
8	3	9.74	9–10	Remember to read *all* notes on the approach chart.
			9–11	
9	2	9.1	9–10	Note the LOM is the center point of the sector.
10	4	9.33	9–22	Note ASR services are available at Pueblo.
11	1	9.104		
12	1	9.28		
13	1	9.128		
14	3	9.126		
15	3		9–10	
16	4	9.76	9–10	
			9–11	
17	1		9–13	Review the notes on the approach chart.

Question	Answer	Reference Paragraph(s)	Reference Figure(s)	Remarks
18	3	9.87	9–13	
			9–14	
			9–18	
19	4	9.37		
20	2	9.46		
21	2	9.110 (4)		
22	1		9–10	
			9–11	
23	3	9.116		
24	4	9.73		
25	4	9.74	9–4	
			9–11	
26	3	9.74	9–4	
			9–11	
27	2	9.106	9–5	
			9–18	
28	4	9.94	9–16	
		9.96		
29	4	9.88		
30	2	9.5		
		9.6		
		9.7		
31	2	9.91		
32	1	9.52		
		9.53		
33	4	9.95		
34	4	9.115	9–22	
35	4	9.87	9–15	
		9.98	9–18	
		9.104		
36	1	9.106	9–18	
37	2		9–13	
38	4		9–13	Note that the minimum altitude for glide slope interception is 2,200 feet MSL, and the altitude of the glide slope over the outer marker is 2,156 feet MSL. Therefore, the glide slope will be intercepted prior to reaching the outer marker.
39	4	9.47		
		9.48		
		9.49		
		9.50		
40	2	9.53		
41	1	9.1		
		9.87		
		9.124		
42	2	9.107		
		9.108		
		9.109		
43	3	9.2	9–1	
44	3	9.121		
		9.122		
45	2	9.127		
46	1	9.87	9–18	Note that the NDB is located on the airport and is the MAP.
47	4	9.98		Read the Special Note regarding the Columbia altimeter setting.
		9.102		1360 + 140 = 1500
48	1	9.107	9–19	
		9.108		
49	4	9.53		
		9.54		
50	2	9.2		
		9.3		
51	2	9.35		
52	2	9.49 (1)		

Question	Answer	Reference Paragraph(s)	Reference Figure(s)	Remarks
53	4	9.48		
		9.51		
		9.52		
54	1	9.123		
55	1	9.82 (4)		The approach chart stipulates that a procedure turn is required.
56	1	9.1	9–15	
		9.99	9–16	
57	1	9.1	9–5	
		9.84	9–10	
			9–14	
58	3	5.11	9–16	
		5.36	9–17	
		5.40	9–18	
		9.87		
		9.99		
59	4	9.110 (3)		
60	2	9.120		
		9.121		
		9.122		
61	4	7.49		Some of the information contained in paragraph 7.49 (En Route Low Altitude Chart VOR Changeover Points) can be applied in a similar manner to other types of charts. Note that the VOR changeover point is located where the magnetic course changes from 265° to 270°.
62	1	9.114		
63	3	9.125		

Chapter 10: Answers

Question	Answer	Reference Paragraph(s)	Reference Figure(s)	Remarks
1	2	10.4		
2	1	10.7		ATC *may* request a report even though other aircraft were not delayed.
3	4	10.3 (2)		
4	4	10.3		
5	3	10.12		
6	2	10.5		
7	1	10.8		
8	3	10.8		
9	1	10.8		
10	3	8.16		
		8.17		
		10.6		
		10.7		

Chapter 11: Answers

Question	Answer	Reference Paragraph(s)	Reference Figure(s)	Remarks
1	4	11.21		
		11.22		
		11.23		
2	1	11.5		
3	3	11.10		
4	2	11.1		

Appendix F:
Glossary

METEOROLOGICAL CONTRACTIONS

about	ABT
above	ABV
above clouds	ACLD
above ground level	AGL
above sea level	ASL
absolute (temperature)	A
abundant	ABNDT
accelerate	ACLT
accompany	ACPY
accumulate	ACCUM
across	ACRS
acting	ACTG
active	ACTV
actual wind factor	ALWF
Adirondack	ADRNDCK
ADIS notice	ADNOT
advance	ADVN
advection	ADVCTN
advice	ADV
advisory	ADVY; ADVRY
affect	AFCT
after	AFT
after dark	AFDK
afternoon	AFTN
again	AGN
agree	AGR
ahead	AHD
aircraft	ACFT
Airmen's Meteorological Information	AIRMET
air mass	AMS
AIRMET	WA
airport	ARPT
airway	AWY
Alaskan Standard Time (time groups only)	A
Allegheny	ALGHNY
all quadrants	ALQDS
aloft	ALF
along	ALG
alternate	ALTN
altimeter setting	ALSTG
altimeter setting indicator	ASI
altitude	ALT
altocumulus	AC
altocumulus castellanos	ACCAS
altostratus	AS
American Meteorological Society	AMS
amend	AMD
amendment	AMDT
amount	AMT
analysis	ANLYS
ante meridian	AM
anticyclonic	ACYC
anticipate	ANCPT
Appalachian	APLCN
approach	APCH
approximate	APRX
Arctic (air mass)	A
area forecast	FA
around	ARND

ascend	ASND
Atlantic	ATLC
atmospherics	SFERICS
Aurora Borealis	AURBO
Automatic Meteorological Observing System	AMOS
automatic program unit high speed	APUHS
automatic program unit low speed	APULS
Auxiliary Aviation Weather Facility	AAWF
available	AVBL
average	AVG
aviation	AVN
Aviation Area Forecast Center	FA CENTER
backing	BCKG
balloon	BLN
balloon ceiling (weather reports only)	B
baroclinic; baroclinic prognosis	BACLIN
barometer	BRM
barotropic; barotropic prognosis	BATROP
base of overcast	BOVC
basic meteorological services	BMS
beach	BCH
become	BCM
before	BFR
before dark	BFDK
began, begin	BGN
beginning of precipitation (followed by time in minutes past the hour) (weather reports only)	B
behind	BHND
below	BLO
beneath	BNTH
better	BTR
between	BTN; BTWN
between layers	BL
beyond	BYD
blanket	BLKT
blizzard	BLZD
blowing dust (weather reports only)	BD
blowing sand (weather reports only)	BN
blowing snow (weather reports only)	BS
blowing spray (weather reports only)	BY
border	BDR
boundary	BNDRY
break	BRK
breaks in higher overcast	BRKHIC
breaks in overcast	BINOVC
brief	BRF
broken	BKN
build	BLD
buildup	BLDUP
calm (weather reports only)	C
cancel	CNL; CNCL
Cascades	CASCDS
category	CTGY
ceiling	CIG
center	CNTR
Centigrade	CEN
central	CNTRL
Central Standard Time	CST
Central Standard Time (time groups only)	C
chance	CHC
change	CHG
Chesapeake	CHSPK
circulate	CRLC
circumnavigate	CIRNAV
cirrocumulus	CC

cirrostratus	CS	drizzle	DRZL
cirrus	CI	duration	DURN
clear	CLR	during	DURG
clear air turbulence	CAT	dust (weather reports only)	D
clear and smooth	CLRS		
clear or scattered clouds and visibility greater than ten miles	CAVU	early	ERY
		east	E
cloud	CLD	echo height information not available	RHINO
cloud and visibility OK (no clouds below 5000 ft; vis 6SM or more; no precipitation or thunderstorms)		elevate; elevation	ELEV
		elsewhere	ELSW
	CAVOK	embedded	EMBDD
coast	CST	ending	ENDG
Coastal Zone Management	CZM	ending of precipitation (followed by time in minutes past the hour) (weather reports only)	E
cold (air mass)	K		
cold front	CDFNT	enhanced	ENHNCD
cold front, -al passage	CFP	enhancement	ENHNCMNT
commence	CMNC	entire	ENTR
Common Aviation Weather Subsystem	CAWS	Environmental Meteorological Support Unit	EMSU
complete	CMPLT	equatorial (air mass)	E
condition	COND	especially	SPCLY
confine	CFN	estimated (weather reports only)	E
considerable	CSDRBL	estimate	EST
continental (air mass)	C	evening	EVE
Continental Divide	CONTDVD	except	EXCP; XCP
continue; continuously	CONT	expect	EXPC; XPC
convective	CNVTV	expected operations forecast	EOF
conversion	CNVSN	extend	EXTD
convert	CNVRT	extensive	EXTSV
cover	CVR	extreme	EXTRM
cumulonimbus mamma	CBMAM		
cumulonimbus mammatos (mammatocumulus)	CM	Fahrenheit	FAH
		falling	FLG
cumulus	CU	feet; foot	FT
cumulus fractus	CUFRA	feet per minute	FPM
cyclogenesis	CYCLGN	filed but impracticable to transmit	FIBI
cyclonic	CYC	filling	FILG
		Fleet Weather Central	FWC
damage	DMG	flood stage	FLDST
danger	DGR	flood warnings issued	FLWIS
daybreak	DABRK	flurry	FLRY
daylight	DALGT	fog (weather reports only)	F
decrease	DCR	follow	FLW
deep	DP	forecast	FCST
deepening	DPNG	forecast wind factor	FRWF
definite	DFNT	forenoon	FORNN
degree	DEG	form	FRM
degree Celsius	C	forming	FRMG
delay	DLA	fort	FT
dense	DNS	forward	FWD
depth	DPTH	freeze	FRZ
deteriorate	DTRT	freezing drizzle (weather reports only)	ZL
develop	DVLP	freezing level	FRZLVL
dew point	DWPNT	freezing rain (weather reports only)	ZR
diameter	DIAM	frequent	FQT
difficult	DFCLT	from	FM
diffuse	DFUS	front	FNT
diminish	DMSH	frontal passage	FROPA
direct readout INFRARED	DRIR	frontal surface	FROSFC
dissipate	DSIPT	Frontogenesis	FNTGNS
distant	DSNT	frontolysis	FNTLYS
district	DIST	frost	FRST
ditto	DO	frozen	FRZN
doubtful	DBTF	further, farther	FTHR
downslope	DNSLP		
downdrafts	DWNDFTS	general	GEN
downward vertical velocity	DVV	gradient	GRAD
drift	DRFT	gradual, -ly	GRDL
drizzle (weather reports only)	L		

greater	GTR	intermittent	INTMT
Greenwich Mean Time (time groups only)	Z	inter-mountain region	INTRMTRGN
ground	GND	inversion	INVRN
ground fog	GNDFG	irregular	IREG
ground fog (weather reports only)	GF	isolated	ISOLD
ground fog estimated ___ feet deep	GFDEP		
ground visibility	GV	jet stream	JTSTR
Gulf of Alaska	GLFALSK		
Gulf of Mexico	GLFMEX	killing frost	KFRST
Gulf of St. Lawrence	GLFSTLAWR	knots	KT
gusts	GSTS		
gusty	GSTY	lake	LK
gusts reaching ___ knots (weather reports only)	G	land	LND
		large	LRG
		later	LTR
hail (weather reports only)	A	layer; layers; layered	LYR
hail (small) (weather reports only)	AP	level	LVL
hailstones	HLSTO	lift	LFT
half	HLF	light	LGT
hard freeze	HDFRZ	lightning	LTG; LTNG
haze (weather reports only)	H	lightning cloud-to-cloud	LTGCC
haze layer aloft	HLYR	lightning cloud-to-cloud, cloud-to-ground	LTGCCCG
haze layer estimated ___ feet deep	HDEP	lightning cloud-to-ground	LTGCG
hear; here; hour	HR	lightning cloud-to-water	LTGCW
heavy	HVY	lightning in clouds	LTGIC
height	HGT	likely	LKLY
high	HI	limit	LMT
high clouds visible	HCVIS	Limited Aviation Weather Reporting Station	LAWRS
high level forecast	HIFOR	line	LN
highest temperature	HITMP	little	LTL
highest temperature equaled for all time	HIEAT	little change	LTLCG
highest temperature equaled for the month	HIEFM	little change in temperature	LCTMP
highest temperature equaled so early	HIESE	local, locally	LCL
highest temperature equaled so late	HIESL	long range	LGRNG
highest temperature exceeded for all time	HIXAT	long wave	LGWV
highest temperature exceeded for the month	HIXFM	lower	LWR
highest temperature exceeded so early	HIXSE	lowest temperature	LOTMP
highest temperature exceeded so late	HIXSL	lowest temperature equaled for all time	LOEAT
horizon	HRZN	lowest temperature equaled for the month	LOEFM
however	HWVR	lowest temperature equaled so early	LOESE
Hudson Valley	HDSVLY	lowest temperature equaled so late	LOESL
hundred	HND	lowest temperature exceeded for all time	LOXAT
hurricane	HURCN	lowest temperature exceeded for the month	LOXFM
hurricane report	HUREP	lowest temperature exceeded so early	LOXSE
		lowest temperature exceeded so late	LOXSL
ice crystals (weather reports only)	IC		
ice fog (weather reports only)	IF	mainland	MNLD
ice pellets	IP	mainly	MNLY
icing	ICG	main meteorological office	MMO
icing in clouds	ICGIC	map analysis	MA
icing in clouds and precipitation	ICGICIP	marginal	MRGL
icing in precipitation	ICGIP	marginal visual flight rules	MVFR
immediate	IMDT	maritime (air mass)	M
important	IMPT	maritime	MRTM
improve	IPV	marked	MKD
impulse	IMPL	maximum	MAX
inches	IN	mean sea level	MSL
increase	INCR	measured ceiling	M
indefinite	INDEF	melting level	MLTLVL
indicate	INDC	merging	MEGG
information	INFO	meteorological	MET
inland	INLD	middle	MID
instability	INSTBY	midnight	MIDN
intense	INTS	mile(s)	MI
intensify	INTSFY	millibars	MB
intensity unknown (weather reports only)	U	minimum	MIN
interior	INTR	missing	MISG
intermediate	INTMD	missing (weather reports only)	M

mixed	MXD	partly	PTLY
moderate	MDT	passage; passing	PSG
moderate or greater	MOGR	patches of shallow fog not deeper than two	
Mohawk Valley	MHKVLY	meters	MIFG
moisture	MSTR	patchy	PTCHY
morning	MRNG	peninsula	PEN
mostly	MSTLY	period	PD
mountain	MTN	persist	PRST
move	MOV	pilot balloon observation	PIBAL
		pilot report pertaining to meteorological	
		conditions	PIREP
National Climatic Center	NCC	pilot requests forecast	PIRFC
National Oceanic and Atmospheric		pilot to forecaster service	PFSV
Administration	NOAA	Polar (air mass)	P
National Weather Service	NWS	portion	PTN
National Weather Service Support Facility	WSSF	position	PSN
National Weather Service Support Unit	WSSU	positive vorticity advection	PVA
Naval Weather Service Office	NWSO	possible	PSBL
narrow	NRW	precaution	PRCTN
nautical miles	NMI	precipitation	PCPN
near	NR	precipitation ceiling (weather reports only)	P
negative vorticity advection	NVA	predominant; predominate	PDMT
next	NXT	prepare	PRP
night	NGT	present	PRSNT
nimbostratus	NS	present indications are	PRIND
no change in weather	NCWX	pressure	PRES
non-persistent	NPRS	pressure falling rapidly	PRESFR
no pilot balloon observation, high, gusty,		pressure rising rapidly	PRESRR
surface wind	PIWI	prevail	PVL
no pilot balloon observation, snowing	PISO	priority delayed weather	PDW
no pilot balloon observation, unfavorable sea		probable	PBL
conditions	PISE	prognostic; prognosis, progress	PROG
no RAWIN observation, communications out	RACO		
no RAWIN observation, high and gusty winds	RAWI	quadrant	QUAD
no RAWIN observation, no balloons available	RABA	quasistationary	QSTNRY
no RAWIN observation, no gas available	RAHE		
no RAWIN observation, unfavorable weather	RAWE	radar cloud detection report	CD
no report will be filed next collection unless		radar cloud detection report not available	RCDNA
weather changes significantly; taking PIBAL		radar cloud detection report no echoes	
observations	NORPI	observed	RCDNE
normal	NML	radar cloud detector inoperative due to	
north; northern	N	breakdown until	RCDNO
northeastern	NERN	radar cloud detector inoperative due to	
northwest	NW	maintenance until	RCDOM
no small craft or storm warnings are being		radar operating below prescribed standard	ROBEPS
displayed	NSCSWD	radar weather report	RAREP
number	NMBR	radar weather report equipment inoperative due	
numerous	NMRS	to breakdown	PPINO
		radar weather report equipment inoperative due	
obscure	OBSC	to maintenance	PPIOM
observe; observation	OBS	radar weather report no echoes observed	PPINE
occasional, occasionally	OCNL	radar weather report not available, or	
occlude	OCLD	omitted (for a reason different than those	
occluded front	OCFNT	otherwise stated)	PPINA
occluded frontal passage	OFP	radiosonde analysis and verification unit	RAVU
occlusion	OCLN	radiosonde balloon release	RABAR
occur	OCR	radiosonde balloon wind data	RABAL
offshore	OFSHR	radiosonde observation	RAOB
on shore	ONSHR	radiosonde observation data	RADAT
on top and smooth	OTAS	radiosonde observation icing at _____	RAICG
orographic	ORGPHC	radiosonde observation freezing levels	RAFRZ
other	OTR	radiosonde report already sent in PIBAL	RAPI
otherwise	OTRW	radiosonde not filed	RAFI
outlook	OTLK	ragged	RGD
over	OVR	rain (weather reports only)	R
overcast	OVC	rainfall	RAFL
overrun	OVRN	rain shower (weather reports only)	RW
over mountains	OMTNS	range height indicator not operating on scan	RHINO

rapid	RPD	southeast	SE
reach	RCH	southwest	SW
reconnaissance	RECON	Space Environment Laboratory	SEL
region	RGN	Space Environment Service Center	SESC
Regional Headquarters, U.S. Weather Bureau	WBRH	speed	SPD
relative	RLTV	special	SPL
relative humidity	RH	spread	SPRD
remain	RMN	sprinkle	SPKL
repeat	RPT	squall	SQAL
replace	RPLC	squall (weather reports only)	Q
restrict	RESTR	squall line	SQLN
retard	RTRD	stable	STBL
return	RTRN	stagnation	STAGN
ridge	RDG	standing lenticular altocumulus	ACSL
rising	RSG	standing lenticular cirrocumulus	CCSL
rough	RUF	standing lenticular stratocumulus	SCSL
route	RTE	(station name) clear or scattered clouds and	
runway visibility values	RVV	visibility greater than ten, remainder of	
runway visibility not available	RVVNO	report missing (weather reports only)	DCAVU
runway visibility observer	RVO	station pressure	SP
runway visual range _____	RVR	steady	STDY
runway visual range not available	RVRNO	storm	STM
		stratiform	STFRM
Satellite Operations Control Center	SOCC	stratocumulus	SC
scattered	SCT	stratus	ST
second	SEC	stratus fractus	STFRA
section	SEC; SXN	strong	STG
sector	SCTR	subside	SBSD
Service ''A'' Data Interchange System	ADIS	summary	SMRY
several	SVRL	sunrise	SR; SNRS
severe	SVR	sunset	SS; SNST
severe local storms	SELS	supplementary aviation weather reports	SAWRS
severe weather forecast	WW	Support Service Group	SSG
shallow	SHLW	surface	SFC
shift	SHFT	swelling	SWLG
short	SHRT	Synchronous Meteorological Satellite	SMS
shortly	SHRTLY	synoptic	SYNOP
significant	SGFNT	system	SYS
shower	SHWR		
SIGMET	WS	ten minute mean runway visual range _____	RVRM
significant meteorological information	SIGMET	ten minute mean runway visual range not	
sky clear	SKC	available	RVRMNO
sleet	SLT	temperature	TEMP
sleet showers (weather reports only)	EW	temporary	TMPRY
slight	SLGT	tendency	TNDCY
slope	SLP	terminal	TRML
slow	SLO	terminal forecast	FT
small	SML	terrain	TRRN
small hail (weather reports only)	AP	thereafter	THRFTR
smoke	SMK	thick	THK
smoke (weather reports only)	K	thin	THN
smoke layer aloft	KLYR	thousand	THSD
smoke layer estimated _____ feet deep	KDEP	through	THRU
smoke over city	KOCTY	throughout	THRUT
smooth	SMTH	thunder	THDR
snow	SNW	thunderhead	THD
snow (weather reports only)	S	thundershower	TSHWR
snow depth increase in past hour	SNOINCR	thundersqualls	TSQLS
snowfall	SNWFL	thunderstorm	TSTM
snowflake	SNFLK	thunderstorm (weather reports only)	T
snow grains (weather reports only)	SG	today	TDA
snow pellets (weather reports only)	SP	tomorrow	TMW
snow showers (weather reports only)	SW	tonight	TNGT
Solar-Geophysical Data	SGD	top of overcast	TOVC
solid	SLD	topping	TPG
somewhat	SMWHT	toward	TWD
south; southern	S		
South Plains	SPLNS		

towering	TWRG
towering cumulus	TCU
trace	T
tropical (air mass)	T
tropopause	TROP
trough	TROF
turbulence	TURBC
unknown	UNKN
unlimited	UNL
unofficial	UNOFFL
unrestricted	UNRSTD
unseasonable	UNSBL
unstable	UNSTBL
until	TIL
up and down drafts	UDDF
up drafts	UPDFTS
upper	UPR
Upper Atmosphere Geophysics	UAG
up stream	UPSTRM
upper winds	UWNDS
upper winds observation made by radio methods and without optical aid	RAWIN
upslope	UPSLP
upward vertical velocity	UVV
valley	VLY
variable	VRBL
variable (weather reports only)	V
veer	VR
velocity	VLCTY
vertical motion	VRT MOTN
vicinity	VCNTY
violent	VLNT
visibility	VSBY
visibility decreasing rapidly	VSBYDR
visibility increasing rapidly	VSBYIR
warm	WRM
warm front	WRMFNT
warm front, -al passage	WFP
warm (air mass)	W
warning	WRNG
Wasatch Range	WSTCH
water	WTR
waterspout	WTSPT
wave	WV
weak	WK
weaken	WKN
weather	WEA; WX
weather report will not be filed for transmission	FINO
Weather Service Forecast Office	WSFO
Weather Service Office	WSO
west; western	W
widely	WDLY
widespread	WDSPRD
will	WL
will be issued	WIBIS
wind	WND
wind shift	WSHFT
World Data Centers in Western Europe	WDC-1
World Data Centers throughout Rest of World	WDC-2
worse	WRS

FREQUENTLY USED AERONAUTICAL ABBREVIATIONS

(Other than those previously covered in Meteorological Contractions)

AAS	Airport Advisory Service
A/C	Approach Control
ADCUS	Advise Customs
ADF	Automatic Direction Finder
AID	Airport Information Desk
AIM	Aiman's Information Manual
ALS	Approach light system
apchg	approaching
ARSR	Air Route Surveillance Radar
ARTCC	Air Route Traffic Control Center
ASDE	airport surface detection equipment
ASR	Airport Surveillance Radar
ATC	air traffic control
ATCT	air traffic control tower
ATIS	Automatic Terminal Information Service
BC	back course
bcn	beacon
bcst	broadcast
bldg	building
brg	bearing
CFR	crash fire rescue
CIFFR	common IFR room
clsd	closed
cmsnd	commissioned
cntrln	centerline
Comlo	Compass locator
const	construction
crcg	circling
CS/T	combined station/tower
ctc	contact
CTLZ	Control Zone
dcmsnd	decommissioned
DF	direction finder
DME	UHF standard (TACAN compatible) distance measuring equipment
dsplcd	displaced
DVFR	Defense Visual Flight Rule
emerg	emergency
equip	equipment
FL	Flight Level
FM	fan marker
freq	frequency
FSS	Flight Service Station
GS	glide slope
GWT	gross weight
HIRL	High Intensity Runway Lights
hwy	highway
ICAO	International Civil Aviation Organization
ident	identification
IFR	Instrument Flight Rules
IFSS	International Flight Service Station
ILS	instrument landing system
IMC	instrument meteorological conditions
intl	international

ISMLS	Interim Standard Microwave Landing System		rcv	receive
			rcvg	receiving
J-bar	jet runway barrier		rcvr	receiver
			rdo	radio
kHz	kilohertz		REIL	Runway End Identifier Lights
			req	request
lat	latitude		rqrd	required
lctd	located		rgt	right
LDA	Localizer type directional aid		RRP	Runway Reference Point
lgts	lights		RTS	returned to service
lgtd	lighted		RVRC	Runway Visual Range Center
LMM	compass locator at middle marker ILS		RVRT	Runway Visual Range Touchdown
lndg	landing		RVRR	Runway Visual Range Rollout
loc	localizer		RWY	Runway
LOM	compass locator at outer marker ILS			
long	longitude		SDF	Simplified Directional Facility
LRCO	Limited Remote Communications Outlet		SID	Standard Instrument Departure
			SM	statute mile(s)
MAA	maximum authorized altitude		STAR	Standard Terminal Arrival Route
mag	magnetic		STOL	Short take-off & landing runway
maint	maintain, maintenance		svc	service
MALS	Medium Intensity Approach Light System			
MALSR	Medium Intensity Approach Light System with RAIL		T	true (after a bearing)
			TACAN	UHF navigational facility—omnidirectional course and distance information
MCA	minimum crossing altitude			
MEA	minimum en route IFR altitude		TCA	Terminal Control Area
MHz	megahertz		TCH	Threshold Crossing Height
min	minimum or minute		tfc	traffic
MIRL	Medium Intensity Runway Edge Lights		thr	threshold
MLS	Microwave Landing System		tkof	takeoff
MM	middle marker ILS		tmprly	temporarily
MOCA	minimum obstruction clearance altitude		TPA	Traffic Pattern Altitude
MRA	minimum reception altitude		TRACON	Terminal Radar Approach Control
muni	municipal		TRSA	Terminal Radar Service Area
			tsmt	transmit
NA	not authorized		tsmtg	transmitting
natl	national		tsmtr	transmitter
NAVAID	navigational aid		TWEB	transcribed weather broadcast
NDB	Non-directional Radio Beacon		twr	tower
NM	nautical mile(s)		twy	taxiway
Nr	number			
			UHF	Ultra high frequency
obstn	obstruction		unavbl	unavailable
OM	outer marker ILS		unctld	uncontrolled
oper	operate		unlgtd	unlighted
opn	operation			
OTS	Out of Service		VASI	Visual Approach Slope Indicator
			VFR	visual flight rules
PAR	Precision Approach Radar		VGS	Visual Guidance System
permly	permanently		VHF	Very high frequency
			VMC	Visual meteorological conditions
quad	quadrant		VOR	VHF Omnidirectional Radio Range
			VORTAC	Combined VOR and TACAN System
RAIL	Runway Alignment Indicator Lights		VOT	a VOR Receiver testing facility
RAPCON	radar approach control (USAF)			
RATCF	radar air traffic control facility (USN)		WS	Weather Service
RCAG	Remote Center air/ground		wt	weight
RCLS	Runway Centerline Lights System			
RCO	Remote Communications Outlet		Z	Greenwich Mean Time

Appendix G:
Reference Illustrations

G1 **Airspeed Indicator**

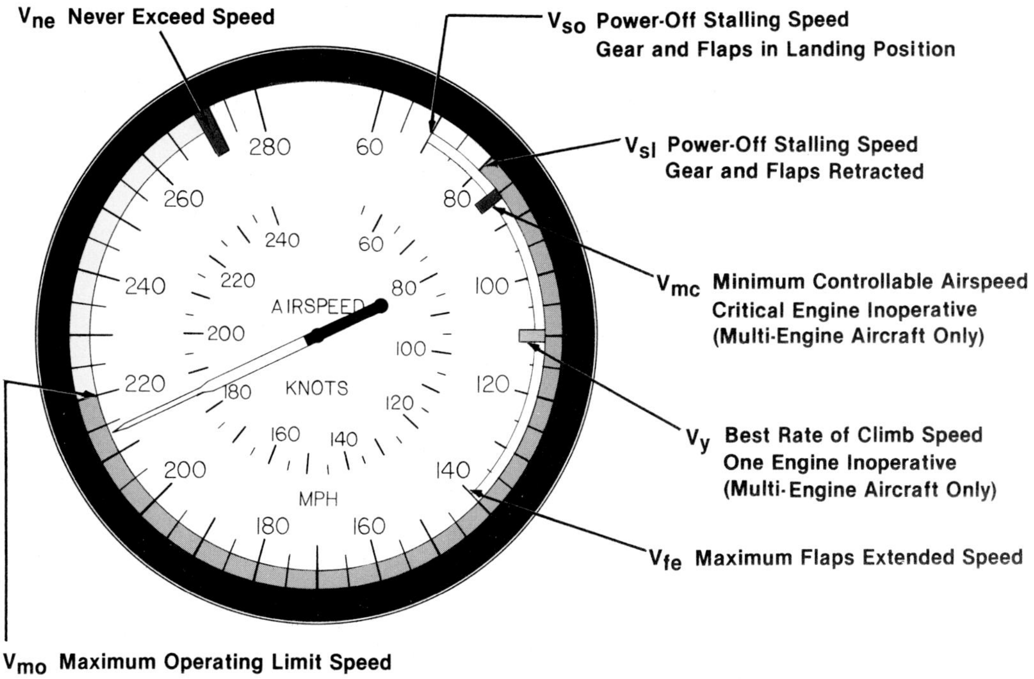

Vne Never Exceed Speed
Vso Power-Off Stalling Speed Gear and Flaps in Landing Position
Vsl Power-Off Stalling Speed Gear and Flaps Retracted
Vmc Minimum Controllable Airspeed Critical Engine Inoperative (Multi-Engine Aircraft Only)
Vy Best Rate of Climb Speed One Engine Inoperative (Multi-Engine Aircraft Only)
Vfe Maximum Flaps Extended Speed
Vmo Maximum Operating Limit Speed
AIRSPEED
KNOTS
MPH

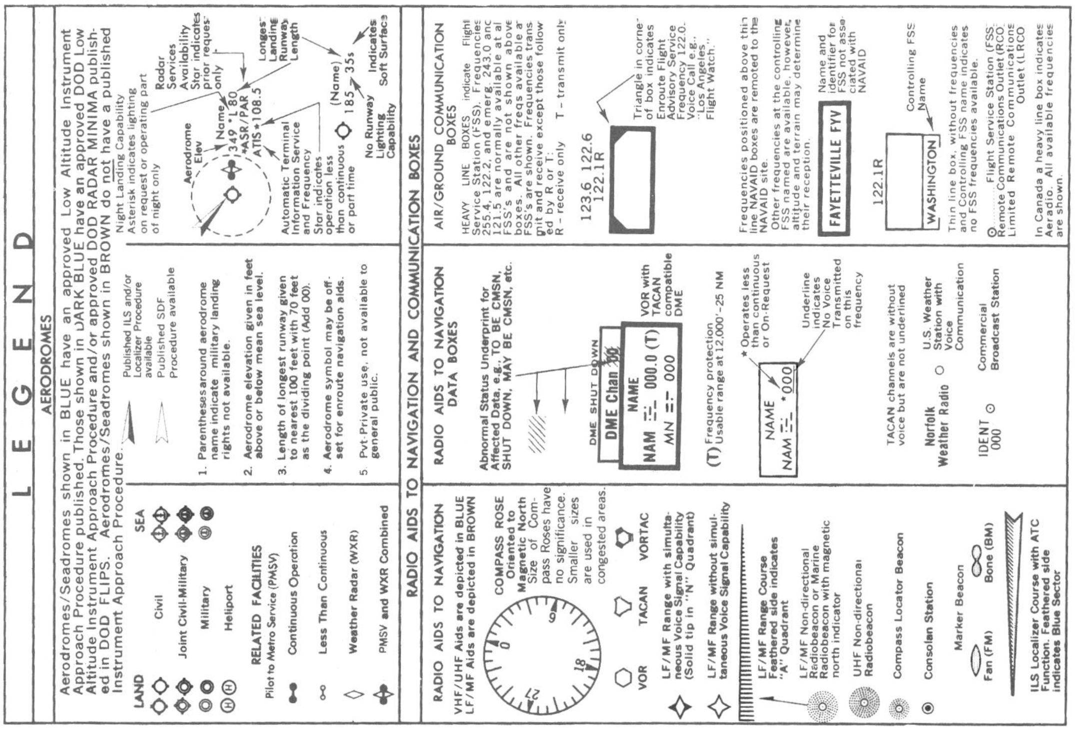

LEGEND
AERODROMES
RADIO AIDS TO NAVIGATION AND COMMUNICATION BOXES

G2 En Route Low Altitude Chart Legend

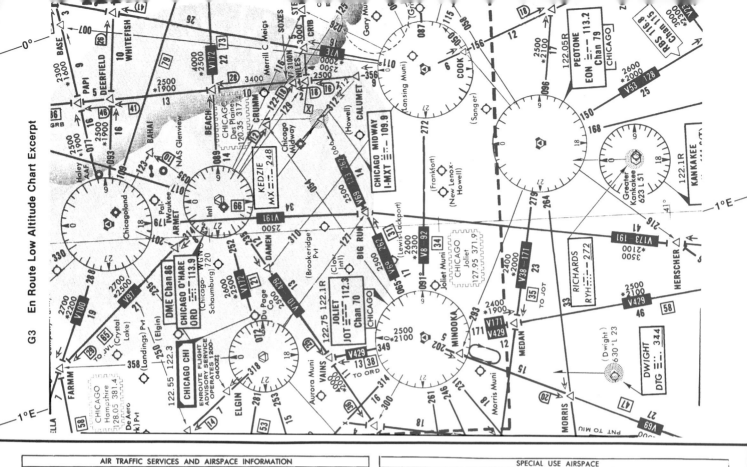

G3   En Route Low Altitude Chart Excerpt

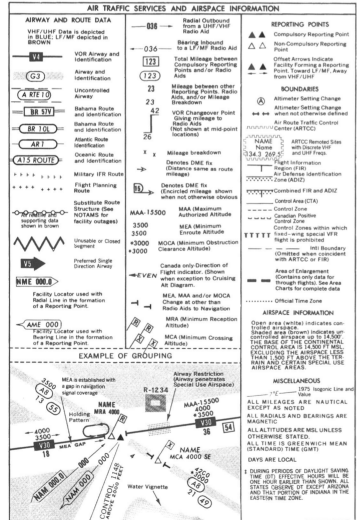

AIR TRAFFIC SERVICES AND AIRSPACE INFORMATION

AIRWAY AND ROUTE DATA

VHF/UHF Data is depicted in BLUE; LF/MF depicted in BROWN

V4	VOR Airway and Identification
G3	Airway and Identification
A RTE 10	Uncontrolled Airway
BR 57V	Bahama Route and Identification
BR 10L	Bahama Route and Identification
AR 1	Atlantic Route Identification
A15 ROUTE	Oceanic Route and Identification
+++++	Military IFR Route
+++++	Flight Planning Route

Substitute Route Structure (See NOTAMS for facility outages)

Air relative and supporting data shown in brown

Unusable or Closed Segment

V5 Preferred Single Direction Airway

NME 000.0

Facility Locator used with Radial Line in the formation of a Reporting Point.

AME 000.0 Facility Locator used with Bearing Line in the formation of a Reporting Point.

EXAMPLE OF GROUPING

036 Radial Outbound from a UHF/VHF Radio Aid

036 Bearing Inbound to a LF/MF Radio Aid

123 Total Mileage between Compulsory Reporting Points and/or Radio Aids

123 Mileage between other Reporting Points. Radio Aids, and/or Mileage Breakdown

23 Mileage between other Reporting Points. Radio Aids, and/or Mileage Breakdown

23 VOR Changeover Point Giving mileage to Radio Aids (Not shown at mid-point locations)

42 / 26

x Mileage breakdown

→ Denotes DME fix (Distance same as route mileage)

15 Denotes DME fix (Encircled mileage shown when not otherwise obvious)

MAA-15500 MAA (Maximum Authorized Altitude)

3500 / 3500 MEA (Minimum Enroute Altitude)

*3000 / *3000 MOCA (Minimum Obstruction Clearance Altitude)

←EVEN Canada only-Direction of Flight indicator. (Shown when exception to Cruising Alt Diagram.)

MEA, MAA and/or MOCA Change at other than Radio Aids to Navigation

MRA (Minimum Reception Altitude)

MCA (Minimum Crossing Altitude)

REPORTING POINTS

▲▲ Compulsory Reporting Point

△△ Non-Compulsory Reporting Point

▲▲ Offset Arrows Indicate Facility Forming a Reporting Point. Toward LF/MF, Away from VHF/UHF

BOUNDARIES

Ⓐ Altimeter Setting Change

↔ Altimeter Setting Change when not otherwise defined

Air Route Traffic Control Center (ARTCC)

NAME / Name / 134.3 269.5 ARTCC Remoted Sites with Discrete VHF and UHF Freqs.

Flight Information Region (FIR)

Air Defense Identification Zone (ADIZ)

Combined FIR and ADIZ

Control Area (CTA)

Control Zone

Canadian Positive Control Zone

TTTTT Control Zones within which fixed-wing special VFR flight is prohibited

Int'l Boundary (Omitted when coincident with ARTCC or FIR)

▬ ▬ Area of Enlargement (Contains only data for through flights). See Area Charts for complete data

······· Official Time Zone

AIRSPACE INFORMATION

Open area (white) indicates controlled airspace.
Shaded area (brown) indicates uncontrolled airspace up to 14,500'. THE BASE OF THE CONTINENTAL CONTROL AREA IS 14,500 FT MSL, EXCLUDING THE AIRSPACE LESS THAN 1,500 FT ABOVE THE TERRAIN AND CERTAIN SPECIAL USE AIRSPACE AREAS.

MISCELLANEOUS

7°E 1975 Isogonic Line and Value

ALL MILEAGES ARE NAUTICAL EXCEPT AS NOTED

ALL RADIALS AND BEARINGS ARE MAGNETIC

ALL ALTITUDES ARE MSL UNLESS OTHERWISE STATED.

ALL TIME IS GREENWICH MEAN (STANDARD) TIME (GMT)

DAYS ARE LOCAL

‡ DURING PERIODS OF DAYLIGHT SAVING TIME (DT) EFFECTIVE HOURS WILL BE ONE HOUR EARLIER THAN SHOWN. ALL STATES OBSERVE DT EXCEPT ARIZONA AND THAT PORTION OF INDIANA IN THE EASTERN TIME ZONE.

SPECIAL USE AIRSPACE

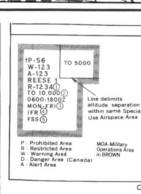

SPECIAL USE AIRSPACE WILL INCLUDE:

① Area Identification: In Canada area ident is preceded by the letters CY (CANADA) followed by a number (PROVINCE).

② Effective Altitude ceilings are shown up to but not including 18,000. When the airspace encompasses all altitudes in the low altitude structure, no altitude will be shown. The word "to" (an altitude) means "to and including" (that altitude).

③ Operating Time: When continuous no time is shown.
Days: Sunrise to Sunset
Nights: Sunset to Sunrise
Hours: Given in GMT, e.g., 0600-1300Z.
Mon-Fri: Indicates area does not exist on Sat. or Sun.
1 Mar-15 June: Indicates area in use only through dates given
By NOTAM: Area activated by NOTAM.
Days are local

④ Weather Conditions during which the area is in operation. When continuous no weather is shown.
VFR: Used only during VFR conditions.
IFR: Used only during IFR conditions.

⑤ Voice Call of controlling Agency for enroute clearance through area. No A/G unless indicated.

† Indicates complete information in tabulation on front panel.

Line delimits altitude separation within same Special Use Airspace Area

P - Prohibited Area
R - Restricted Area
W - Warning Area
D - Danger Area (Canada)
A - Alert Area

MOA-Military Operations Area in BROWN

CRUISING ALTITUDES - U.S.

VFR above 3000' AGL
IFR - Outside controlled airspace
IFR within controlled airspace as assigned by ATC
All courses are magnetic

G2 continued

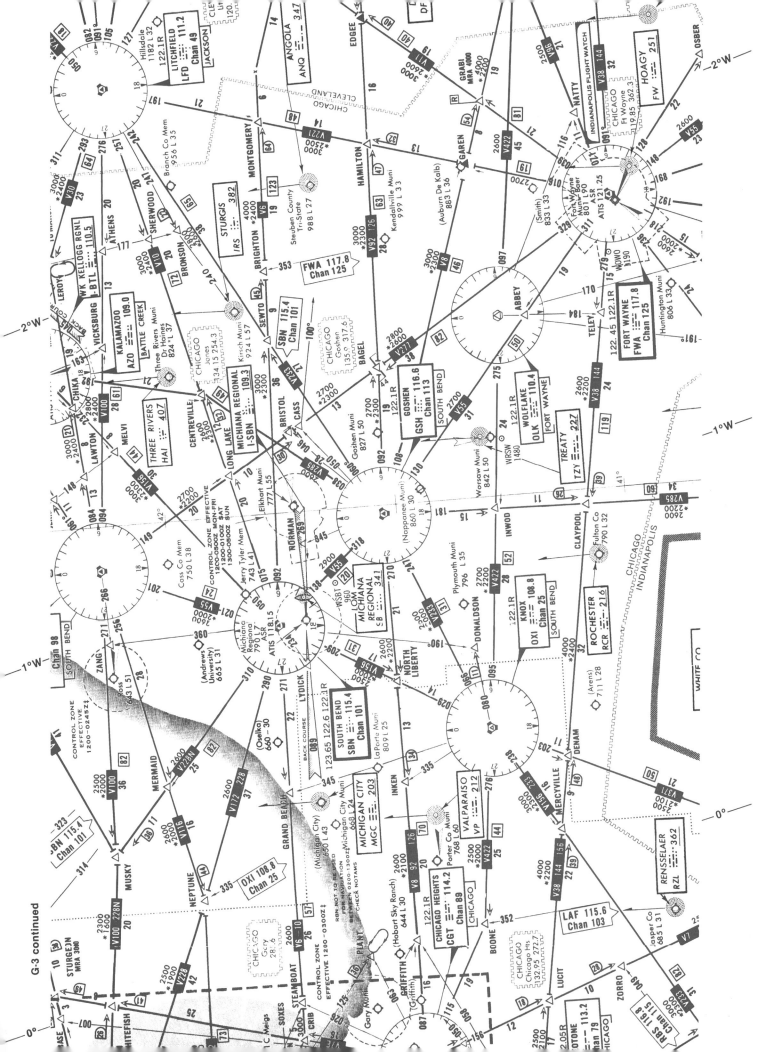

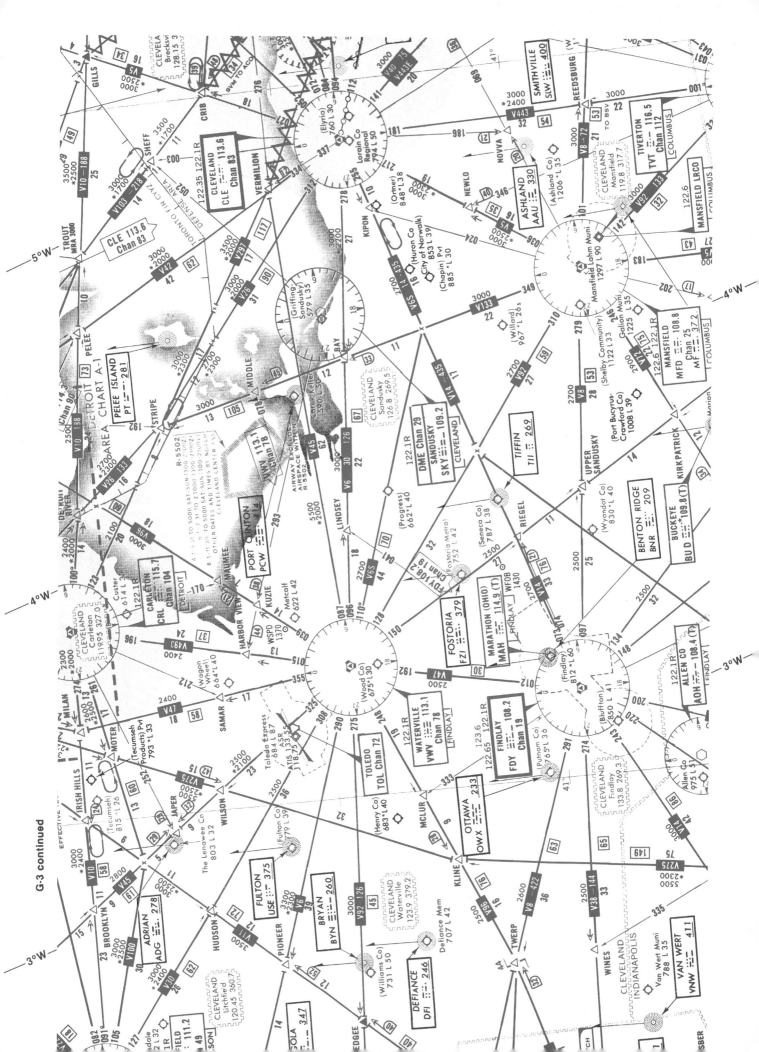

G-3 continued

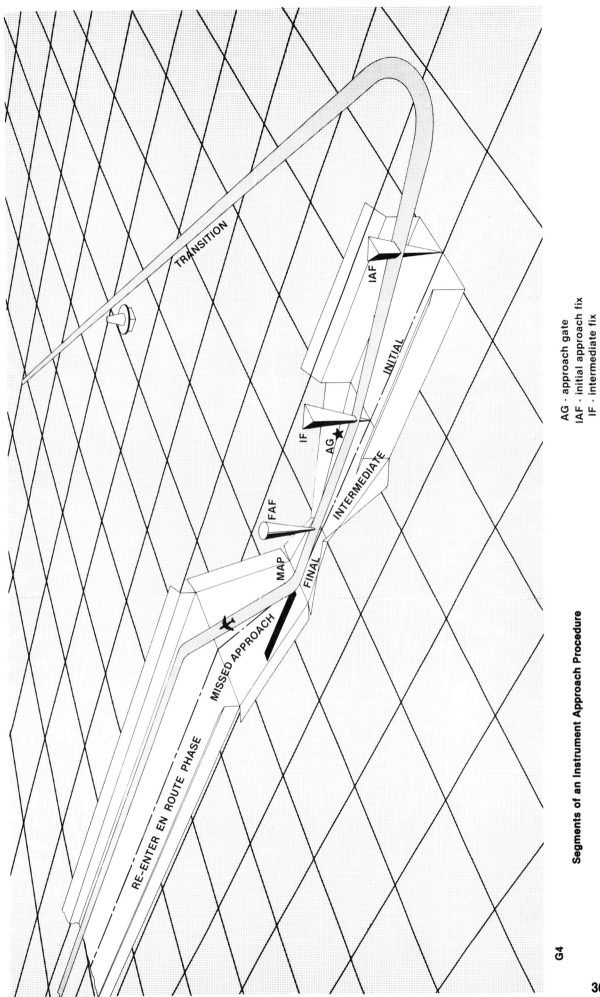

Segments of an Instrument Approach Procedure

AG - approach gate
IAF - initial approach fix
IF - intermediate fix
FAF - final approach fix
MAP - missed approach point

G4

365

Index

Abbreviated IFR departure clearance, 8.6–8.7

Absolute altitude, 2.74

AC (convective outlook), 3.154–3.156

Acceleration error, 2.39–2.41

Accelerate-stop distance graph, 5.49–5.50

ADF (automatic direction finder), 4.33–4.34
  common errors, 4.65
  homing, 4.47–4.49
  magnetic bearing interception, 4.63–4.64
  orientation, 4.42–4.46
  receiver, 4.35–4.36, 4.114
  station passage, 4.49, 4.57
  stations, 4.37–4.41
  time/distance check, 4.59–4.62
  tracking, 4.50–4.58

ADIZ (Air Defense Identification Zone), 7.26

Adiabatic, 3.1

Adiabatic lapse rates, dry and moist, 3.7

Advection fog, 3.88–3.89

Aerodrome sketch, 9.103–9.106

Aerodynamic factors of flight, 1.1–1.73

Aerosinusitis, 11.3

Aerotitus, 11.2

Aft center of gravity, 1.39–1.40, 1.42–1.43, 1.45

Agonic lines, magnetic variation, 2.30

AIM (Airman's Information Manual), 7.4

Airborne check points, 4.11

Aircraft
  approach categories, 9.91
  inspections, 6.15
  lights, 6.21
  maintenance, 6.14
  ratings
    category, 6.3
    class, 6.3
    instrument, 6.3
    type, 6.3
  speed, 8.97–8.98
  stability, 1.44–1.45

Air Defense Identification Zone (ADIZ), 7.26

Air density, 1.7–1.8

Airman's Information Manual (AIM), 7.4

Air mass circulation, 3.12–3.17

Air mass classifications, 3.18

Air mass thunderstorms, 3.46–3.50
  convective, 3.47–3.48
  nocturnal, 3.50
  orographic, 3.49

AIRMET (WA), 3.149–3.150, 3.153

Airplane Flight Manual, 1.46–1.48

Airport/Facility Directory, 7.5–7.6, 9.32

Airport surface detection equipment (ASDE), 4.146

Airport surveillance radar (ASR), 4.146, 9.35–9.36, 9.38, 9.73

Airport traffic areas, 7.27

Air Route Surveillance Radar (ARSR), 4.146

Air Route Traffic Control Centers (ARTCC), 7.6, 7.41–7.42, 8.2, 9.12

Airspace, types of, 7.23–7.38

Airspeed
  airspeed maximums, 8.97
  calculation of TAS, 2.61
  changes in, 2.64
  in a turn, 1.19–1.21
  related to drag, 1.4, 1.9
  related to lift, 1.6, 1.9
  symbols and definitions, 2.58–2.59
  types, 2.60–2.61

Airspeed indicator
  errors in, 2.55–2.57
    compressibility error, 2.56
    density error, 2.57
    position error, 2.55
  function of, 2.54
  operating ranges, 2.62–2.63

Air stability, 3.6–3.11

Air Traffic Control Radar Beacon System (ATCRBS), 4.149

Airway/route course changes, 8.106–8.108

Airworthiness, 6.17

Airworthiness certificates, 6.16, 6.19

Alcohol, 11.5–11.7

Alert area, 7.32

Alternate airport
  IFR weather minimums, 6.33
  landing minimums, 9.111–9.113
  requirements, 6.33

Alternate airways, 7.36

Alternate minimums listing, 9.111

Alternate static source, 2.48–2.51

Altimeter, 2.45, 2.67–2.77, 4.86–4.87, 6.22, 6.28
  errors, 2.71
  settings (en route), 8.80–8.81
  system tests and inspections, 6.22, 6.28

Altitude
  changes with air temperature changes, 2.75–2.77
  designations, IFR, 7.39–7.40
  in communication failure, 10.3
  in flight planning, 7.62–7.65
  types of, 2.74

Altitude changes, en route, 8.99–8.105

Ambiguity indicator, 4.8

Amended clearances, 8.16–8.18

Angle of attack, 1.3, 1.6, 1.10–1.12

Angle of bank, 1.17–1.21

Anticollision lights, 6.21

Anticyclones, 3.15

Approach categories, 9.91

Approach charts, 9.22, 9.56, 9.63–9.115

Approach clearance, 9.15–9.18

Approach control, 9.11–9.15
  radar, 9.14–9.15

Approach, during communications failure, 10.3

Approach gate, 9.1

Approach lighting systems, 4.112–4.113

Approach procedures, 9.19–9.22, 9.56–9.61
  identification, 9.64–9.68
  minimums, 6.33
  procedure turn not required, 9.83

Arc interception, 4.83–4.85

Arcs, 4.81–4.82

Area charts, 9.11

Area forecast (FA), 3.137–3.144

Area navigation (RNAV)
  High Altitude Charts, 7.16
  route system, 4.135–4.139, 7.13, 7.16

Arm, 1.37

ARSR (Air Route Surveillance Radar), 4.146

ARTCC (Air Route Traffic Control Centers), 7.41–7.42, 8.2, 9.12

ARTCC boundaries/symbols, 7.41–7.42

ARTCC communication frequencies, 8.62

Artificial horizon, 2.15

ASDE (Airport Surface Detection Equipment), 4.146

ASR approaches, 4.146, 9.35–9.36, 9.38, 9.73

ATC clearance, 6.37
  deviation from, 10.6

ATC transponder equipment, 6.26, 6.28
  tests and inspections, 6.27

ATCRBS (Air Traffic Control Radar Beacon System), 4.149

ATIS (Automatic Terminal Information Service), 8.29–8.34, 9.13

Attitude indicator, 2.15–2.21
  errors, 2.22
  pre-flight check, 2.19–2.20
  types of, 2.16–2.18

Automatic direction finder (ADF), 4.33–4.34

Automatic gain control, 4.10

Automatic pressure altitude reporting equipment, 6.28

Automatic Terminal Information Service (ATIS), 8.29–8.34, 9.13

Autopilot system, 4.143

Avionics requirements, fixed wing aircraft, 6.31

Back course approach, 9.88

Balanced forces in flight, 1.5, 1.9, 1.11–1.12

Bank instruments, 2.78

Best Rate of Climb and Best Angle of Climb Graph, 5.57

Biennial Flight Review, 6.8

Calibrated airspeed (CAS), 2.60

Calibrated altitude, 2.74

Cancellation of IFR flight plan, 9.126–9.127

Carbon monoxide, 11.18–11.20

Carburetor icing, 3.73–3.81

Category II holding lines, 4.183

CDI (course deviation indicator), 4.8
   aircraft displacement, 4.24
   interpretation, 4.15, 4.18
   movement, 4.19
   sensitivity, 4.14
Ceiling, 3.104–3.107
Center of gravity, (C.G.)
   changing loads-effect on C.G., 1.69–1.73
   computation of, 1.68
   definition of, 1.37
   forward and rearward, 1.38–1.45
   moment envelope, 1.64
   range, C.G., 1.37
   related to stability, 1.42–1.45
Centigrade-Fahrenheit relationship, 3.3, 5.19
Centrifugal force, 1.17, 1.24
Certificates
   airworthiness, 6.16, 6.17, 6.19
   flight instructor, 6.3
   medical, 6.4–6.7
   pilot, 6.3, 6.4, 6.7
Certification, 6.3–6.7
   civil aircraft, 6.16
   pilot, 6.4
C.G. (center of gravity), 1.37, 1.45, 1.64, 1.68–1.73
Changeover point (COP), 7.49
Chord line, 1.3
Circling approaches, 9.93, 9.99, 9.101
Circular flight computer, 5.39–5.40
Civil aircraft
   airworthiness, 6.17
   certification, 6.16, 6.19
   operating limitations, 6.18
Civil radar instrument approach minimums, 9.115
CL (centerline lighting), 4.162
Clearance delivery, 8.9–8.10
Clearance limit, 8.4
Clearances, 8.2–8.28
   abbreviated IFR departure clearance, 8.6–8.7
   amended clearances, 8.16–8.18
   clearance delivery, 8.9–8.10
   clearance receipt, 8.8, 8.10–8.15
   cruise clearance, 8.5
   emergency clearance deviation, 10.6
   readback procedure, 8.25–8.28
   special VFR clearances, 8.23–8.24
   VFR on Top clearances, 8.109–8.112
   VFR restrictions, 8.20–8.22
Clear ice, 3.70–3.71
Climb and descent, changes in balanced forces, 1.11–1.12
Climb-Balked Landing Graph, 5.66
Climb-One Engine Inoperative, 5.59
Clouds, 3.19–3.22
   categories of, 3.19–3.20
   estimating cloud base heights, 3.21–3.22
   types of clouds related to air stability, 3.10
Cold front, 3.25–3.27
Communications failure, 10.3, 10.4
Communications procedures, 8.57–8.73
   control tower, 10.12

en route with ATC, 8.61–8.63
Compass, 2.28–2.43
   construction, 2.31
   errors, 2.33–2.43
   magnetic forces, 2.28–2.29
   reading the compass, 2.32
   remote indicating, 2.27
   use in turns, 2.37
   variation, 2.30
Compass locator, 4.38–4.39, 4.111
Components of lift, 1.13–1.15
Composite flight plan, 7.70–7.72
Compressibility error, 2.56, 5.25–5.26
Computers flight
   circular, 5.39–5.40
   E 6-B, 5.3–5.38
Concentric rings, 9.70
Condensation level, 3.1
Condenser-Discharge Sequenced Flashing Light Systems, 4.158
Conditionally unstable air, 3.9
Contact approach, 9.51–9.55
Continental control area, 7.28
Control areas, 7.29
Control tower communications procedures, 10.12
Controlled airspace, 6.26, 6.37, 7.24–7.36
Controlled firing area, 7.32
Control zone, 7.30
Convective air mass thunderstorms, 3.47–3.48
Convective cloud base height-estimating, 3.22
Convective currents, 3.47–3.48, 3.53–3.55
Convective outlook (AC), 3.154–3.156
Convective SIGMET (WST), 3.151
Convergence, 3.8
COP (changeover point), 7.49
Coriolis force, 3.1, 3.14, 3.16
   as related to pressure gradient force, 3.14, 3.16
   as related to wind speed, 3.14, 3.16
Course changes, 8.106–8.108
Course deviation indicator (CDI), 4.8
Course selector, 4.8
Critical altitude, 5.44
Cross pointer indicator, 4.118–4.123
Cruise clearance, 8.5
Cruise climb power, 5.44
Cyclones, 3.15

Datum reference plane, 1.37
Decision height (DH), 9.1
Density altitude, 2.74, 5.27–5.28, 5.48
Density error, airspeed indicator, 2.57
Departure and en route procedures, 8.1–8.116
Departure communications, 8.58–8.60
Departure navigation, 8.51–8.56
Descent and climb, changes in balanced forces, 1.11–1.12
Descent below MDA or DH, 9.95
Deviation errors, compass, 2.33
Dew point, 3.1
Dew point temperature, 3.1, 3.87
DF (direction finder), 10.10
DH (decision height), 9.1

Direct entry, 8.84–8.87
Directional gyro, 2.23–2.27
Direction finder (DF), 10.10
Direct route flights, 7.73–7.77
   minimum IFR altitudes, 7.76–7.77
Disorientation, 11.21
Displaced threshold lighting, 4.164
Distance conversion, 5.20
Distance measuring equipment (DME), 4.73–4.85, 4.114, 6.20, 9.66–9.68
DME (distance measuring equipment), 4.73–4.85, 4.114, 6.20, 9.66–9.68
   arc interception, 4.83–4.85
   flying DME arcs, 4.81–4.82
   ILS/DME, 4.76
   LOC/DME, 4.76
   slant range error, 4.79–4.80
   station passage, 4.80
   TACAN, 4.74–4.75, 4.77
   VOR/DME, 4.73–4.77
   VORTAC, 4.73–4.75, 4.77
DME fix arrow, 7.40
Drag
   as related to thrust, 1.9
   induced, 1.4
   parasitic, 1.4
Drugs, 6.36, 11.4

E 6-B flight computer, 5.3–5.38
EAC (expect approach clearance), 8.83, 10.3
Echo movement, 3.178–3.179
Echoes, precipitation, 3.173–3.180
Economy cruise power, 5.44
EFC (expect further clearance), 8.83, 10.3
ELT (emergency locator transmitter), 6.23, 10.8–10.9
ELT tests, 10.9
Emergency deviation from rules, 10.6
Emergency frequency, 10.2
Emergency locator transmitter (ELT), 6.23, 10.8–10.9
Emergency procedures, 10.2
Emergency situations, 10.5, 10.1–10.9
Empty weight, 1.37
En route altitude changes, 8.99–8.105
En route facilities ring (plan view), 9.71
En Route Flight Advisory Service (Flight Watch/EFAS), 8.77–8.78
En Route High Altitude Charts, 7.15
En Route Low Altitude Charts, 7.14, 7.17, 7.19–7.53
   ARTCC boundaries/symbols, 7.41–7.42
   changeover points, 7.49
   depiction of airspace, 7.23–7.38
   depiction of reporting points, 7.46–7.48
   IFR altitude designations, 7.39–7.40
   ILS, Localizer, SDF symbols, 7.44–7.45
   intersections, 7.50–7.53
   legend, 7.22
   Radio Aids to Navigation Data Boxes, 7.43
En route weather information, 8.74–8.79
Entry procedures (holding pattern), 8.84–8.88

367

Expect approach clearance (EAC), 10.3
Expect further clearance (EFC), 10.3

FAF (final approach fix), 9.1
Fahrenheit-Centigrade relationship, 3.3,
  5.19
Fan Marker, 4.129
FD (Forecast Winds & Temperatures Aloft
  Chart), 3.184-3.186
FDC NOTAMs, 7.11-7.12
FDI (flight director indicator), 4.143
Federal Airway System, 7.13-7.17
Feeder facilities ring, 9.72
Final approach, 9.1
Final approach fix (FAF), 9.1
Flags, 4.8, 4.124
Flight computer
  circular, 5.39-5.40
  E 6-B computer
    density altitude, 5.27-5.28
    distance conversion, 5.20
    fuel consumption, 5.13-5.16
    rate of climb, 5.17-5.18
    temperature conversion, 5.19
    time-speed-distance, 5.4-5.12
    true airspeed, 5.21-5.26
    wind correction angle and ground
      speed, 5.29-5.38
Flight director indicator (FDI), 4.143
Flight experience, 6.8-6.9
Flight instruction requirements, 6.12
Flight instruments, 2.1-2.81
Flight level, 2.74
Flight log, 6.11
Flight plan, IFR, 6.33, 6.37, 7.1-7.2, 7.67-
  7.72
  activation of, 8.49
  amending, while en route, 8.95
  cancellation of, 9.126-9.127
  no SID, 8.45
Flight planning, 7.1-7.79
  publications, 7.3-7.7
  RNAV, 7.78-7.79
  selecting & flight planning the route,
    7.54-7.66
Flight review, 6.8
Flight time, 6.10
  instrument, 6.11
  pilot in command, 6.11
Flight visibility, 3.125
Flight Watch Service, 8.77-8.78
Fog, 3.88-3.89
Forecast-Report Summary Table, 3.187
Forecast Winds & Temperature Aloft
  Chart (FD), 3.184-3.186
Forward and rearward C.G.'s, 1.38-1.45
Freezing level data, 3.131
Frequency change, 8.67, 8.73
Frontal thunderstorms, 3.44
Frontogenesis, 3.1
Frontolysis, 3.1
Fronts, 3.23-3.32, 3.63
  cold front, 3.25-3.27
  occluded front, 3.31-3.32
  stationary front, 3.30
  warm front, 3.28-3.29
Fuel consumption problems, 5.13-5.16
Fuel flow vs. brake horsepower, 5.60-

5.62
Fuel requirements, IFR flight, 6.32, 7.66

General pilot limitations, 6.13
Glide path, 4.118, 4.122-4.123, 4.131
Glide slope, 4.102-4.107, 4.113, 4.114,
  4.117, 4.172
GMT (Greenwich Mean Time), 3.95,
  Appendix C-5
Go-around maneuver, 10.13
Good operating practices, 10.11-10.16
Government Produced Instrument
  Approach Procedure Charts, 9.22, 9.56,
  9.63-9.115
    aerodrome sketch, 9.103-9.106
    landing minimum section, 9.90-
      9.102
    margin identification, 9.64-9.68
    plan view, 9.69-9.83
    profile view, 9.84-9.89
Graphic Notices and Operational Data
  Publication, 7.7, 9.32
Greenwich Mean Time (GMT), 3.95,
  Appendix C-5
Gross weight, 1.37
Ground control, 8.9-8.10
Ground speed, 5.29-5.40, 9.104
Ground visibility, 3.125
Guidance display, 4.136
Gyroscopic instruments
  common instruments, 2.2
  preflight check, 2.19
  principles, 2.3-2.6

HAA (height above airport), 9.1
Handoff, 8.54
HAT (height above touchdown), 9.1
Heading indicators
  basic gyroscopic indicator, 2.23
  errors in, 2.24
  gyro slaved to magnetic compass,
    2.27
  power sources, 2.25-2.26
  purpose, 2.24
Height above airport (HAA), 9.1
Height above touchdown (HAT), 9.1
Hijack transponder code, 8.41
Holding during radio communications
  failure, 10.3
Holding fix, 8.83
Holding patterns, 8.82-8.94
  dimensions, 8.89-8.90
  entry procedure, 8.84-8.88
  maximum holding speeds, 8.93-8.94
  timing, 8.91-8.92
  turns, 8.88
Homing, ADF, 4.47
Horizon bar, 2.20
Horizontal Situation Indicator (HSI),
  4.143
HSI (Horizontal Situation Indicator),
  4.143
H-VOR, 4.3
Hyperventilation, 11.14-11.17
Hypoxia, 11.9-11.13

Ice pellets, 3.71
Icing, 3.64-3.85, 3.144, 3.172

anti-icing and deicing aids, 3.82-3.85
  induction system icing, 3.73-3.81
  structural icing, 2.48, 2.52, 3.67-3.72
ILS (Instrument Landing System), 4.76,
  4.91-4.94
    errors, 4.131
    identification, 4.101
    receiving equipment, 4.114-4.130
    system components, 4.95-4.113
ILS approach, 9.39-9.41
  ILS approach/procedures that do not
    require a procedure turn, 9.83
(IM) inner marker, 4.127, 4.129
Inclinometer, 2.7, 2.11-2.14
Indicated airspeed (IAS), 2.60
  changes in, 2.64
Indicated altitude, 2.74
Induced drag, 1.4
In-flight weather advisories (WST, WS,
  WA), 3.149-3.156
Initial approach, 9.74-9.77
Inoperative Components or Visual Aids
  Table, 9.107-9.110
In-runway lighting, 4.161
Inspections
  aircraft, 6.15
  altimeter system, 6.22
  preflight gyro, 2.19
  requirements, 6.15
Instrument and equipment requirements
  flight at and above 24,000 feet MSL,
    6.20
  general requirements, 6.20
  IFR, 6.20
  VFR (day), 6.20
  VFR (night), 6.20
Instrument Approach Lighting System,
  4.157-4.158
Instrument Approach Procedure Charts,
  9.22, 9.56, 9.63-9.115
    aerodrome sketch, 9.103-9.106
    landing minimum section, 9.90-
      9.102
    margin identification, 9.64-9.68
    non-precision charts, 9.58
    plan view, 9.69-9.83
    precision charts, 9.59
    profile view, 9.84-9.89
Instrument competency check, 6.8
Instrument flying; aerodynamic factors,
  1.1-1.73
Instrument Landing Systems (ILS), 4.76,
  4.91-4.94
Instrument ratings, 6.3-6.4
Instruments
  bank, 2.78
  pitch, 2.78
  power, 2.78
  recovery from unusual attitudes,
    2.80-2.81
Integrated Automatic Flight Control
  Systems, 4.140-4.144
Intermediate approach, 9.77
International Standard Atmosphere (ISA),
  3.4
Intersections, 7.50-7.53
Isobar, 3.1
  related to air mass circulation, 3.12-

3.16
Isogonic lines, magnetic variation, 2.30
Isotherm, 3.1

Jet airways, 7.13, 7.15
Jet Route System, 7.13, 7.15
Jet streams, 3.1, 3.63

Kinesthesia, 11.22
Kollsman window, 2.70–2.72

Landing clearance, 9.23
Landing minimums, IFR, 9.94–9.95
   publication of, 9.96–9.102
Landing priority, 9.46
Landing procedures
   general, 10.15
   to avoid wake turbulence, 1.34–1.35
Lapse rates, 3.1, 3.4–3.9
   adiabatic, 3.7
   average temperature lapse rate, 3.4
   sounding slope, 3.9
LDA (Localizer Type Directional Aid),
   4.133, 9.65
Lenticular clouds, 3.59
LF/MF transmitter, 4.35
Lift, 1.3–1.15
   components of, 1.13–1.15
   in a climb or descent, 1.11–1.12
   in a turn, 1.13–1.15
   related to air density, 1.7–1.8
   related to airspeed, 1.6
   related to weight, 1.5
Lighting aids, 4.154–4.182
   Condenser-Discharge Sequenced
     Flashing Light Systems, 4.158
   control of lighting systems, 4.175–
     4.182
   displaced threshold lighting, 4.164
   in-runway lighting, 4.161
   instrument approach lighting
     systems, 4.157–4.158
   rotating beacon, 4.155–4.156
   runway edge light systems, 4.159–
     4.160
   Runway End Identifier Lights (REIL),
     4.163
   visual approach slope indicator,
     4.165–4.172
Lightning and precipitation static, 3.40–
   3.42
Lights, aircraft, 6.21
Liquor and drugs, 6.36, 11.4–11.7
Load factor, 1.16–1.18
Loading limitations, 1.50–1.51
LOC (Localizer, 4.76, 4.97–4.100, 4.114,
   4.116, 4.118–4.121, 4.131, 9.65
Localizer (LOC), 4.76, 4.97–4.100, 4.114,
   4.116, 4.118–4.121, 4.131, 9.65
Localizer Type Directional Aid (LDA),
   4.133, 9.65
Locator transmitters, 6.23, 10.8–10.9
Logbooks, 6.11
Loss of radio communications, 10.3
Low Altitude Charts, 7.19–7.20, 7.22–
   7.53
Low approaches, 10.13–10.14
L-VOR, 4.3

MAA (Maximum Authorized Altitude),
   7.40
Magnetic compass, 2.28–2.43
   compass construction, 2.31
   errors in, 2.33–2.43
     acceleration, 2.39–2.41
     causes of error, 2.33
     deviation error, 2.33
     magnetic dip, 2.34
     northerly turn error, 2.35–2.36
     oscillation, 2.42
   magnetic forces, 2.28–2.29
   reading the compass, 2.32
   use in turns, 2.37
   variation, 2.30
Magnetic course, 5.33, 5.36–5.37, 7.59–
   7.60
Magnetic dip, 2.34
Magnetic heading, 5.36–5.37
Magnetic variation, 2.30
Maintenance, aircraft, 6.14
Maintenance of FAA NAVAIDs, 4.134
Malfunction reports, under IFR in con-
   trolled airspace, 10.16
Maneuvering speed (Va), 2.59, 2.63
MAP (missed approach point), 9.35–9.87
Marker beacons, 4.108–4.110, 4.114,
   4.125–4.130
Maximum authorized altitude (MAA),
   7.40
Maximum except take-off power (METO),
   5.44
Maximum gross weight, 1.37
Maximum holding speeds, 8.93–8.94
Maximum landing weight, 1.37
Maximum take-off power, 5.44
MCA (minimum crossing altitude), 7.40,
   8.99
MDA (Minimum Descent Altitude), 9.1,
   9.35–9.36, 9.95
MDA/DH concept, 9.94–9.95
MEA (minimum en route altitude), 7.40
Mechanical convection, 3.8
Medical certificates, 6.4–6.7
MHA (minimum holding altitude), 8.94
Middle ear discomfort, 11.2
Middle marker (MM), 4.10
Military Operations Area (MOA), 7.32,
   7.33
Minimums
   alternate, 9.111
   circling, 9.93
   landings, 9.94–9.102
   straight-in, 9.92, 9.97–9.98, 9.100–
     9.102
Minimum crossing altitude (MCA), 7.40
Minimum descent altitude (MDA), 9.1,
   9.35–9.36
Minimum en route altitude (MEA), 7.40
Minimum holding altitude (MHA), 8.94
Minimum IFR altitudes, 9.18
Minimum obstruction clearance altitude
   (MOCA), 7.40
Minimum reception altitude (MRA), 7.40
Minimum safe altitudes (MSA), 9.1
Minimum vectoring altitude (MVA), 9.1
Missed approach point (MAP), 9.35, 9.87
Missed approach procedures, 9.121–9.124

MM (middle marker), 4.10
MOA (Military Operations Area), 7.32,
   7.33
MOCA (minimum obstruction clearance
   altitude), 7.40
Mode, 4.149
Mode Annunciator Panel, 4.143
Moment, 1.37
Moment envelope, 1.64
Mountain waves, 3.59
MRA (minimum reception altitude), 7.40
MSA (minimum safe altitude), 9.1
MSL (Mean Sea Level), 9.1
MVA (minimum vectoring altitude), 9.1

National Airspace System, 4.2
National Ocean Survey (NOS), 7.5, 9.4,
   9.61
NAVAIDs, 4.1, 4.80, 4.134
NAV/COMM system, 4.7
Nautical miles conversion, 5.20,
   Appendix C-1
NDB (non-directional radio beacon),
   4.37–4.41, 9.65
Nocturnal air mass thunderstorms, 3.50
No-gyro approach, 9.37
Nonconvective SIGMETs (WS), 3.152
Non-directional radio beacon (NDB),
   4.37–4.41, 9.65
Non-precision approach procedure (mini-
   mums), 6.33, 9.86–9.88, 9.110
Non-radar approaches, 9.14
Nonstandard Alternate Minimums Chart,
   9.111
Nonstandard holding pattern, 8.83, 8.85,
   8.87
NoPT (no procedure turn), 9.77, 9.81,
   9.82, 9.83
Northerly turn error, 2.35–2.36
NOS(National Ocean Survey), 7.5, 9.4,
   9.61
NOTAM (Notice to Airmen), 3.130, 7.8–
   7.12, 9.4, 9.110
NOTAMs (D), 7.9
NOTAMs (L), 7.10
Notices to Airmen (NOTAM), 3.130, 7.8–
   7.12, 9.4, 9.110

OAT (outside air temperature), 5.25
OBS (omni bearing selector), 4.8
Occluded front, 3.31–3.32
Off flag, 4.8
Olive Branch Routes, 7.7
OM (outer marker), 4.109
Omnidirectional range, 4.2
Omnirange, 4.2
Operating limitations & marking require-
   ments; civil aircraft, 6.18
Operating speeds, airspeed, 2.58–2.59
Option approach, 10.14
Orographic, 3.1
Orographic air mass thunderstorms, 3.49
Oscillation error, 2.42–2.43
Outer marker (OM), 4.109
Outer marker–middle marker substitutes,
   9.110
Outside air temperature (OAT), 5.25
Oxygen breathing systems, 5.67–5.68

Oxygen deficiency, 11.9–11.13
Oxygen duration, 5.67–5.68
Oxygen requirements, 6.34

PAR (Precision Approach Radar), 4.146, 9.34, 9.38, 9.73
Parachute jump areas, 7.7
Parallel entry, 8.84, 8.86–8.87
Parasitic drag, 1.4
PCA (Positive Control Area), 6.30, 7.31
Performance charts, 5.41–5.43
    accelerate-stop distance, 5.49–5.50
    best rate and angle of climb, 5.57
    climb-balked landing, 5.66
    climb-one engine inoperative, 5.59
    cruise power settings, 5.63–5.65
    density altitude, 5.48
    fuel flow vs. brake horsepower, 5.60–5.62
    oxygen duration, 5.67–5.68
    pressure altitude, 5.45–5.47
    take-off distance over 50-foot obstacle, 5.51–5.53
    terms, 5.44
    time-fuel-distance to climb, 5.54–5.58
Performance terms, 5.44
Phraseology (pilot/controller), 8.66–8.73
Physiological factors, instrument flight
    aerosinusitis, 11.3
    aerotitis, 11.2
    alcohol, 11.5–11.7
    carbon monoxide, 11.18–11.20
    drugs, 11.4
    hyperventilation, 11.14–11.17
    hypoxia, 11.9–11.13
    middle ear discomfort, 11.2
    scuba diving, 11.8
    sinus discomfort, 11.3
    vertigo, 11.21–11.23
Pilot certificates, 6.3, 6.4
Pilot/controller phraseology, 8.66–8.73
Pilot-in-command
    certification, 6.4
    flight time, 6.11
    general limitations, 6.13
    recent flight experience requirements, 6.8
    responsibility and authority of, 10.6
Pilot limitations, 6.13
Pilot logbooks, 6.11
Pilot weather reports (PIREPs), 3.132–3.133
PIREPs (Pilot weather reports), 3.132–3.133
Pitch instruments, 2.78
Pitot static system, 2.44–2.77
    alternate static source, 2.48–2.51
    emergency procedures, 2.51
    instruments that rely on the pitot static system, 2.45
Pitot tube, 2.52–2.53
Portable electronic devices, 6.35
Positive Control Areas (PCA's), 6.30, 7.31
Position error, airspeed indicator, 2.55
Position reports, 7.47, 8.65
Power instruments, 2.78
Precession, 2.5–2.7

Precipitation, 3.1
Precipitation static, 3.42
Precision approach, 9.34, 9.38, 9.73
Precision Approach Charts, 9.59
Precision approach glide slope intercept altitude, 9.85
Precision approach procedure (minimums), 6.33, 9.110
Precision approach radar (PAR), 4.146
Preferred IFR routes, 7.6
Preflight action, 6.2
Preflight inspections, gyro instruments, 2.19
Preflight regulations, 6.1–6.39
Pressure altimeter
    accuracy, 2.70
    errors, 2.71
    function, 2.67
    reading, 2.68–2.69
Pressure altitude, 2.74, 5.21–5.26, 5.45–5.47
Pressure Altitude Chart, 5.45–5.47
Pressure gradient force, 3.12–3.16
Pressure lapse rate, 2.73, 3.4
Pre-taxi clearance delivery, 8.9–8.10
Prevailing visibility, 3.108–3.110
Primary and supporting instruments, 2.78–2.79
Primary radar, 4.147
Principles of the gyroscope, 2.3–2.6
Priority handling, 10.7
Procedure turn, 9.78–9.83
    limitations on, 9.82
    procedure turn not required, 9.83
Profile Descent Charts, 9.8
Profile descent clearances, 9.9
Profile descent procedures, 9.5–9.9
Profile view, 9.84–9.89
"Prog" Charts, 3.165–3.172
Prohibited area, 7.32
Proper sensing, 4.23
Publications, for flight planning, 7.3–7.7

Radar (Radio Detection and Ranging), 4.145–4.153
    limitations of radar, 4.153
    primary & secondary radar, 4.147–4.152
Radar advisories, 9.25, 9.26, 9.32, 9.41–9.45
Radar altimeter, 4.86–4.90
Radar approach control, 9.14–9.15
Radar approaches, 9.33–9.45, 9.48
Radar instrument approach minimums, 9.115
Radar contact, phraseology, 8.69–8.73
Radar handoff, 8.54
Radar monitoring of instrument approaches, 9.42–9.45
Radar monitoring service, 9.40
Radar sequencing and separation, 9.28–9.30, 9.32
Radar Summary Chart, 3.173–3.183
Radar vectoring, 9.73
Radar weather reports (SD) (RAREP), 3.134
Radials, 4.2
Radio Aids to Navigation and Communi-

cation Data Boxes, 7.43
Radio communications failure, 10.3
Radio emergency frequency, 10.2
Radio failure transponder code, 10.4
Radio magnetic indicator (RMI), 4.66–4.72
Random RNAV routes, 7.78–7.79
Rate of climb problems, 5.17–5.18
Rate of turn, 1.19–1.21
Rate of turn instrument, 2.10
Ratings, pilot certificates, 6.3
RCAG sites (Remote Center Air/Ground), 7.42
RCLS (Runway Centerline Lighting Systems), 4.162
Readback procedures (clearances), 8.25–8.28
Recent IFR flight experience, 6.8, 6.9
Regulations
    aircraft lights (FAR 91.73 a,b,d), 6.21
    airworthiness (FAR 91.27, 91.29), 6.16–6.17, 6.19
    altimeter System Tests & Inspections (FAR 91.170 a,c), 6.22
    ATC clearance and flight plan required (FAR 91.115), 6.37
    ATC transponder equipment (FAR 91.24 b,c), 6.26
    ATC transponder tests & inspections (FAR 91.177), 6.27
    certificates and ratings, (FAR 61.5 a,b, 61.3 a,c,e), 6.3–6.4
    Civil Aircraft Certification (FAR 91.27 a,b), 6.16
    data correspondence between automatically reported pressure altitude data and the pilot's altitude reference (FAR 91.36 a,b,c), 6.28
    emergency locator transmitter (FAR 91.52), 6.23
    flight instruction requirements (FAR 91.21 a,b), 6.12
    flight plan, information required (FAR 91.83 b,c), 6.33
    flight time (FAR Part 1.1), 6.10
    fuel requirements for IFR flight (FAR 91.23), 6.32
    general pilot limitations (FAR 61.31 c,d,e), 6.13
    inspections (FAR 91.169), 6.15
    instrument & equipment requirements (FAR 91.33), 6.20
    liquor and drugs (FAR 91.11), 6.36
    logbooks, (FAR 61.51 a,c), 6.11
    maintenance (FAR 91.163 a, 91.165), 6.14
    medical requirements (FAR 61.23), 6.5–6.7
    operating limitation and marking requirements (FAR 91.31 b), 6.18
    pilot certification (FAR 61.3 a,c,e), 6.4
    pilot limitations (FAR 61.31 c,d,e), 6.13
    portable electronic devices (FAR 91.19), 6.35
    positive control areas & route segments (FAR 91.97), 6.30

preflight action (FAR 91.5 a,b), 6.2
recent flight experience (FAR 61.57), 6.8, 6.9
supplemental oxygen, (FAR 91.32), 6.34
terminal control areas (FAR 91.90), 6.29
VFR weather minimums (FAR 91.105, 91.107), 6.38, 6.39
VOR equipment check, IFR (FAR 91.25), 6.24
REIL (runway end identifier lights), 4.163
Relative bearing, 4.43
Relative humidity, 3.86–3.87
Relative wind, 1.2–1.3
Remote center air/ground sites, 7.42
Remote indicating compass, 2.27
Reporting points, 7.46–7.48, 8.63
Reports to ATC or FSS facilities, 8.63–8.65, 9.125
Required reports, 8.63
Restricted airspace, 8.113
Restricted area, 7.32
Reverse sensing, 4.23
Rime ice, 3.69
RMI (Radio Magnetic Indicator), 4.66–4.72
    arc interception, 4.82, 4.84
    VOR accuracy checks, 4.72
RNAV (area navigation), 4.135–4.139
RNAV flight planning, 7.78–7.79
RNAV route system, 7.13, 7.16
Roll clouds, 3.52
Rotating beacon, 4.155–4.156
Route segments, 6.30
Route systems, 7.13–7.17
Routing, during radio communications failure, 10.3
RRL (Runway Remaining Lighting), 4.162
Runway Centerline Lighting System (RCLS), 4.162
Runway Edge Light Systems, 4.159–4.160
Runway End Identifier Lights (REIL), 4.163
Runway Profile Descent Charts, 9.8–9.9
Runway Remaining Lighting (RRL), 4.162
Runway Visibility (RVV), 3.125–3.128
Runway Visual Range (RVR), minimums, 9.110
RVR (Runway Visual Range), 3.125
    minimums, 9.110
    RVR report, 3.126–3.128
    types of RVR, 3.125

Safety pilot, 6.12
SAs (Surface Aviaton Weather Reports), 3.91–3.124
    altimeter setting, 3.122–3.124
    intensity symbols, 3.111–3.113
    location identifier and type of report, 3.95–3.98
    remarks, 3.124
    sea level pressure, 3.115
    sky condition and ceiling, 3.99–3.107
    temperature and dew point, 3.116–3.117
    visibility, 3.108–3.110
    weather and obstructions to vision,

3.111–3.114
    wind direction and speed, 3.118–3.121
SDF (Simplified Directional Facility), 4.132
Secondary Radar, 4.148
Sense Indicator, 4.8
Severe weather watch, 3.155–3.156, 3.181
SID (Standard Instrument Departure), 8.43–8.48
Side-step maneuver, 9.120
SIGMETs, 3.149–3.152
Significant Weather Prognostic Chart, 3.165–3.172
Simplified Directional Facility (SDF), 4.132
Simultaneous ILS approaches, 9.39–9.41
Sinus discomfort, 11.3
Skids, 1.25–1.26
Slaved gyro magnetic compass, 2.27
Slips and skids, 1.22–1.26, 2.12
Sounding, 3.1
Sounding slope, 3.9
Special flight permit, 6.19
Special Notice Area Graphics, 7.7
Special use airspace, 7.32–7.33
Special VFR clearances, 8.23–8.24
Speed, restrictions,
    maximum holding speeds, 8.93
    aircraft speed, 8.97
Squall line thunderstorms, 3.45
Stability (air), 3.1, 3.6–3.11
    cloud types related to, 3.10
    how to measure, 3.7
    situations conducive to, 3.11
    vertical motion of atmosphere, 3.8
Stability and center of gravity, 1.42–1.45
Stage I service, 9.25, 9.32
Stage II service, 9.26, 9.32
Stage III service, 9.28–9.30, 9.32
Stall speed vs. angle of attack, 1.16–1.18
Standard alternate minimums, 6.33, 9.111
Standard atmospheric conditions, 3.3
Standard instrument departures (SIDs), 8.43–8.48
Standard-rate turn, 2.10, 2.13
Standard holding pattern, 8.83, 8.84, 8.86
Standard terminal arrival routes, 8.43, 9.2–9.4
Standard vertical separation, 9.30
Standing waves, 3.59
STARs, 8.43, 9.2–9.4
Static ports, 2.46–2.48
Static pressure, 2.45–2.46, 2.54
Static stability, 1.42–1.45
Stationary front, 3.30
Statute miles conversion, 5.20, Appendix C-1
Steering computer, 4.143
Stepdown fix, 9.86
Straight-in minimums, 9.92, 9.97, 9.98, 9.100–9.102
Sublimation, 3.1
Supplemental oxygen requirements, 6.34
Supplementary components (ILS), 4.96
Supporting instruments, 2.79
Surface Analysis Chart, 3.157–3.159
Surface aviation weather reports (see

SAs), 3.91–3.124
Surface check points, 4.11
Surface friction, 3.16–3.17
Surveillance Approach Radar (ASR), 9.33, 9.35–9.36, 9.38, 9.73

TACAN (tactical air navigation), 4.74–4.75, 4.77
Take-off distance over 50-foot obstacle, 5.51–5.53
Take-off minimums and departure procedures, 9.114
TAS (true airspeed), 2.60–2.61
Taxiway turnoff lights, 4.162
TCAs (terminal control areas), 6.26, 6.29, 7.34
TDZ elevation (touchdown zone elevation), 9.105
TDZ lighting (touchdown zone lighting), 4.161–4.162
Teardrop procedure, 8.84, 8.86–8.87, 9.79
Temperature convergence factor, 3.21–3.22
Temperature inversion, 3.1, 3.11, 3.62
Temperature lapse rate, 3.4
Terminal Area Graphics, 7.7
Terminal Control Areas (TCAs), 6.26, 6.29, 7.34
Terminal Forecast (FT), 3.135–3.136
Terminal procedures, 9.1–9.128
Terminal radar programs (VFR aircraft), 9.24–9.32
Terminal Radar Service Area (TRSA), 9.28–9.32
    TRSA Graphics, 7.7
Thermal convection, 3.8
Thrust, 1.9
Thunderstorms, 3.33–3.57
    air mass thunderstorms, 3.46
    classification, by source of lift, 3.43
    conditions that must be present, 3.34
    convective air mass thunderstorms, 3.47–3.48
    frontal thunderstorms, 3.44
    lightning and precipitation static, 3.40–3.42
    nocturnal air mass thunderstorms, 3.50
    orographic air mass thunderstorms, 3.49
    piloting procedures in and near thunderstorms, 3.51, 3.52
    Pressure changes, 3.39
    size and height, 3.38
    squall line thunderstorms, 3.45
    stages of development, 3.34–3.37
    turbulence, 3.53–3.63
Timed approach, 9.1
Timed approaches from a holding fix, 9.116–9.119
Time-fuel-distance to climb, 5.54–5.58
Time-speed-distance problems, 5.4–5.12
To/From indicator, 4.8
    interpretation, 4.16–4.18
To VFR conditions on Top, 8.111–8.112
Touchdown zone elevation (TDZ), 9.105
Touchdown zone lighting (TDZ), 4.161–4.162

Tracking, 4.50–4.55, 4.58
Traffic advisories, 9.31, 9.128
Transcribed weather broadcasts, 8.75
Transition area, 7.35
Transition fix, 9.16
Transitioning to Area Charts, 9.11
Transponder, 4.149–4.152
    requirements, 6.26
    tests and inspections, 6.27, 6.28
Transponder codes, 8.37, 8.41–8.42, 10.2,
    10.4
Transponder operation procedures, 8.35–
    8.42
Transponder phraseology, 8.40
Tri-Color Visual Approach Slope Indica-
    tor, 4.173–4.174
Tropopause, 3.1
Troposphere, 3.1
TRSA (Terminal Radar Service Area),
    9.28–9.32
TRSA Charts, 9.32
True airspeed (TAS), 2.60–2.61, 5.21–5.26
True altitude, 2.74–2.76
True bearing, 4.43
True course, 5.33
True heading, 5.33, 5.36–5.37
Turbulence, 3.53–3.63
    convective currents, 3.54
    fronts and jet streams, 3.63
    mountain waves, 3.59–3.60
    obstructions to wind flow, 3.58
    wind shear, 3.61
Turn and slip indicator, 2.7–2.14
Turns
    aerodynamic factors in, 1.13–1.26
    airspeed in, 1.19–1.21
    compass turns, 2.37
    radius of turn, 1.19–1.21
    rate of turn, 1.19–1.21, 2.10, 2.13
    related to lift, 1.13–1.15
    skidding turns, 1.25–1.26
    slipping turns, 1.24, 1.26
T-VOR, 4.3

Uncontrolled airspace, 7.25, 7.37–7.38
Unusual attitudes, 1.27
    recovery, instruments used, 2.80–
    2.81
    recovery, nose high, 1.28, 1.30
    recovery, nose low, 1.29–1.30
Upslope wind, 3.1
Useful load, 1.37

Valsalva maneuver, 11.2
Variation, 2.30
VASI (visual approach slope indicator),
    4.165–4.172
VDP (visual descent point), 9.88–9.89
Vector analog computer, 4.136–4.137
Vectors, 8.116
    wind triangle vector, 5.30–5.32
Vertical guidance, 4.139
Vertical motion of the atmosphere, 3.8
Vertical navigation (VNAV), 4.139
Vertical separation, 9.30
Vertical velocity indicator, 2.45, 2.65–
    2.66
Vertigo, 11.21–11.23

Vestibular sense, 11.22
VFR Conditions on Top, 8.109–8.110
VFR flight instruments and equipment,
    6.20
VFR Over the Top, 8.112
VFR radar advisory service, 9.25, 9.32
VFR radar advisory and sequencing, 9.26,
    9.32
VFR radar sequencing and separation,
    9.28–9.30, 9.32
VFR restrictions (clearances), 8.20–8.22
VFR weather minimums, fixed wing air-
    craft, 6.38, 6.39
VHF Omnidirectional Radio Range, 4.2
VHF/UHF direction finding steer, 10.10
Victor airways, 7.13–7.14, 7.33, 7.36
Virga, 3.20
Visibility, types of, 3.125–3.128
Visual approach, 9.45–9.50
Visual approach slope indicator, 4.165–
    4.172
Visual descent point (VDP), 9.88
VOR
    accuracy, 4.9
    calibration, 4.10
    common errors, 4.32
    efficiency, 4.9
    frequencies/class, 4.3
    identification, 4.5
    orientation, 4.15
    position determination, 4.21, 4.22
    receiver, 4.8
    receiver checks, 4.10
    receiving equipment, 4.7
    roughness, 4.9
    signals, 4.7
    stations, 4.2, 4.3
    time/distance checks, 4.26–4.30
    tracking, 4.23–4.24
    track interception, 4.31
VOR/DME, 9.66
VOR equipment check, 6.24
VOR receiver check points, 7.6
VOR route system, 7.13–7.14
VORTAC (VOR-TACAN), 4.73–4.75,
    4.135, 9.68
Vortex avoidance procedures, 1.34–1.35
Vorticies, 1.31–1.35
VOT (VOR test facility), 4.11, 4.12, 4.76,
    6.24

WA (AIRMET), 3.153
Wake turbulence, 1.31–1.35
Wall Planning Charts, 7.18
Warm front, 3.28–3.29
Warning area, 7.32
Warning flags, 4.8, 4.124
Weather broadcasts, 8.74–8.79
Weather reports and forecasts
    area forecasts (FA), 3.137–3.144
    convective outlook (AC), 3.154–3.156
    echo movement, 3.178–3.180
    Forecast-Report Summary Table,
    3.184
    freezing level data, 3.131
    fronts, 3.23–3.32, 3.63
    heights of bases and tops of sky cover
      layers, 3.129

in-flight weather advisories (WST,
    WS, WA), 3.149–3.153
information en route, 8.74–8.79
NOTAMs, 3.130
pilot weather reports, 3.132–3.133
Radar Summary Chart, 3.173–3.183
radar weather reports, 3.134
runway visual range and runway
    visibility, 3.125–3.128
sequence reports, 3.91–3.93
Significant Weather Prognostic Chart,
    3.165–3.172
Surface Analysis Chart, 3.157–3.159
Surface Aviation Weather Reports
    (SAs), 3.91–3.124
Surface Prog Chart, 3.167
terminal forecast, 3.135–3.136
terms, weather-related, 3.1
Weather Depiction Chart,
    3.160–3.164
winds and temperatures aloft (FD),
    3.145–3.148
Weather Depiction Chart, 3.160–3.164
Weather Forecast-Report Summary Table,
    3.184
Weather minimums, fixed wing aircraft,
    6.38, 6.39
Weight
    related to lift, 1.5
    related to angle of attack, 1.10
Weight and balance, 1.36–1.73
    changing loads, effect on C.G.,
      1.69–1.73
    computation of, 1.52–1.73
      computation method, 1.66–1.68
      graph method, 1.64–1.65
      table method, 1.55–1.63
    definitions of terms, 1.37
    effect on flight, 1.36
    parameters, 1.46–1.47
Wind correction angle (WCA), 5.33
Wind correction angle and ground speed
  problems
    circular computer, 5.39–5.40
    E 6-B computer, 5.29–5.38
      magnetic course, 5.33
      true course, 5.33
      true heading, 5.33
      wind correction angle, 5.33
      wind problem errors, 5.38
      wind triangle, 5.30–5.33
Winds and temperatures aloft forecast
  (FD), 3.145–3.148
Wind shear, 3.53, 3.61
Wind speed, related to Coriolis Force,
    3.14
Wind triangle
    terms, 5.33
    vectors, 5.30–5.32
Wing-tip bearing change, 4.26, 4.60
WS (nonconvective SIGMET), 3.152
WST (convective SIGMET), 3.151

Yawing effect, 1.22

Zone of confusion, width, 4.16
Zulu, 3.95, Appendix C-5